PROGRESS IN ARMS CONTROL?

Readings from
SCIENTIFIC AMERICAN

PROGRESS IN ARMS CONTROL?

With Introductions by
Bruce M. Russett
Yale University

Bruce G. Blair
Yale University and The Brookings Institution

W. H. Freeman and Company
San Francisco

Many of the *Scientific American* articles in *Progress in Arms Control?* are available as separate Offprints. For a complete list of articles now available as Offprints, write to W. H. Freeman and Company, 660 Market Street, San Francisco, California 94104.

Copyright © 1969, 1972, 1973, 1974, 1975, 1976, 1977, 1978, 1979 by SCIENTIFIC AMERICAN, INC.

No part of this book may be reproduced by any mechanical, photographic, or electronic process, or in the form of a phonographic recording, nor may it be stored in a retrieval system, transmitted, or otherwise copied for public or private use without written permission from the publisher.

Printed in the United States of America

2 3 4 5 6 7 8 9 DO 0 8 9 8 7 6 5 4 3 2

PREFACE

This book is entitled *Progress in Arms Control?*—with a question mark. On the one hand, nuclear war has been avoided, despite the fears of many people over the past 33 years. Since the 1960s a variety of important agreements have been reached, both between the two superpowers and among a much wider circle of nations, to reduce the threat of war and at least in some degree to curb the arms race. On the other hand, the limited scope of these agreements is increasingly apparent. The threat of nuclear war remains with us. In the face of a new generation of strategic weapons (including cruise missiles, more accurate ICBMs, "neutron bombs," and capabilities for attacking satellites in space) and a seemingly deteriorating international political climate, the threat may actually be growing again. Efforts to control nuclear technology are like running on a treadmill that moves at fluctuating speeds. In some years we seem to progress a little, in another even a fairly fast run results in retrogression. Political creativity and technical expertise are continually strained, with the outcome always in doubt.

In this volume we have compiled some of the excellent articles on arms control and nuclear strategy that have appeared over the years in *Scientific American*. These articles are marked by technological sophistication yet are written in a language that should be readily understandable by readers who lack advanced education in the physical sciences. We have added a commentary to bring some of the previously published material up to date and to provide data on the nuclear strategic balance at the time of editing. As social rather than physical scientists, we have stressed in our commentary the political influences and constraints on arms control efforts. In choosing the selections and writing our commentary, we have focused exclusively on nuclear strategy and arms control. Other issues, such as those concerning conventional weapons and the arms trade or biological and chemical weapons, had to be excluded despite their importance.

In addition to the articles and our commentary, the volume includes major portions of the texts of some international agreements and a bibliography to suggest sources for further reading. There are no footnotes, but material referred to in the text can be found in the bibliography.

We are grateful to Yale University for the many ways in which it facilitates inquiry, and to The Brookings Institution, where Bruce Blair served as Foreign Policy Fellow during 1977–1978. Of course, we alone are responsible for our statements in this volume.

September 1978   Bruce M. Russett
                                                                              Bruce G. Blair

Note on cross-references: References to articles included in this book are noted by the title of the article and the page on which it begins; references to articles that are available as Offprints, but are not included here, are noted by the article's title and Offprint number; references to articles published by SCIENTIFIC AMERICAN, but which are not available as Offprints, are noted by the title of the article and the month and year of its publication.

CONTENTS

I Arms Acquisition and the Threat of Armageddon

		Introduction 2
YORK	1	The Debate over the Hydrogen Bomb 8
YORK	2	The Great Test-Ban Debate 17

II SALT I and Its Background

		Introduction 28
RATHJENS	3	The Dynamics of the Arms Race 33
YORK	4	Military Technology and National Security 44
RATHJENS AND KISTIAKOWSKY	5	The Limitation of Strategic Arms 57
SCOVILLE	6	Missile Submarines and National Security 69
GARWIN	7	Antisubmarine Warfare and National Security 82
GREENWOOD	8	Reconnaissance and Arms Control 94
	9	Selections from ABM Treaty, Interim Agreement, and Related Documents on SALT Phase I 106

III SALT II: Limited Negotiations

		Introduction 114
YORK	10	Multiple-Warhead Missiles 122
CARTER	11	Nuclear Strategy and Nuclear Weapons 132
DRELL AND VON HIPPEL	12	Limited Nuclear War 144
KAPLAN	13	Enhanced-Radiation Weapons 155
SCOVILLE	14	The SALT Negotiations 163
TSIPIS	15	Cruise Missiles 171

IV The Global Politics of Arms Control

		Introduction 182
EPSTEIN	16	The Proliferation of Nuclear Weapons 186
ROSE AND LESTER	17	Nuclear Power, Nuclear Weapons and International Stability 203
MYRDAL	18	The International Control of Disarmament 217
	19	Major Provisions of the Treaty on the Non-Proliferation of Nuclear Weapons 230

Bibliography 231
Index 235

Arms Acquisition
and the Threat
of Armageddon

I | Arms Acquisition and the Threat of Armageddon

INTRODUCTION

It is easy to become inured to the risks that modern arms imply. For 40 years most major countries of the world have either been at war or, during the tensions of the cold war, have faced the prospect of deadly international violence. Only a minority of the world's citizens can recall an extended period in their adult lifetimes when peace seemed relatively secure. At present many people may feel that the threat of war has receded, thanks to the achievement of an apparently stable "balance of terror" between the two nuclear superpowers. But new technological developments and weapons procurements could upset that balance in the 1980s, especially during an intense crisis, when either side may be tempted to launch an attack in order to preempt a possible strike by the other.

Modern arms are fearsome because of their number and their power. They pose three different kinds of dangers, for which different remedies may be appropriate. First, there is simply the enormous economic burden—financial, and more important, in terms of resources squandered. Second, there is the possibility—always subject to some debate but impossible to dismiss—that the continued accumulation of ever more sophisticated weapons, whether by a single power or by several, will increase international tension and therefore the likelihood of a major war. Finally, there is the near certainty that if nuclear war should occur, it would be by far the most destructive one humankind has ever experienced, and very possibly the last one—Armageddon.

The amount that the world spends on military purposes in one year alone now exceeds the value of the entire output of the world in 1900 (measured in constant dollars; that is, not counting the effects of inflation). In 1913, immediately before World War I, roughly 3 to $3\frac{1}{2}$ percent of total world output was devoted to the military; now the proportion is about double, or between 6 and 7 percent of the world output (gross national product of all countries). A recent report of the Stockholm International Peace Research Institute indicates that current world military expenditures equal the value of the gross national product of all Latin American and African countries combined, or total worldwide government expenditures on education, or the total income of the poor countries that account for more than half of the world's population. President Carter, in his October 1977 address to the United Nations, noted that "worldwide military expenditures are now in the neighborhood of $300 billion a year. Last year the nations of the world spent more than 60 times as much equipping each soldier as we did educating each child." The two superpowers, the United States and the Soviet Union, account for by far the largest proportion of this expenditure (roughly 30 percent each). However, the fastest militarizing area of the world is the Third World—especially the Middle East, where, measured in constant dollars, military expenditures have gone up by almost 17 percent annually since 1955. What this means in terms of world opportunities foregone—in terms of misery, ignorance, starvation, and disease left unchanged—cannot be measured precisely, but it can be imagined. While we may have become accustomed to this waste, its magnitude is new and we cannot be indifferent to it.

It would be shameful enough if "mere" waste were the only thing at issue, but there is more. National governments may arm because they are afraid of other nations or because they wish to intimidate them. In either case, fear and tension result. Some analysts insist on the validity of the adage "If you wish peace, prepare for war." A strong defense is supposed to preserve the peace by making it clear that an aggressor will be defeated. Perhaps so. But an equally plausible argument can be made that one nation's arms will be seen as a threat to the security of another, thus stimulating the other nation to increase the number and quality of its own arms. The purposes behind arming may be misunderstood, creating fear and tension where they would not have existed otherwise. Especially in periods of international crisis, these tensions may erupt into a rapid spiral of fear, threat, and the initiation of violence.

This is especially a problem with those modern weapons that give an advantage to the side that strikes first. A persistent worry for American officials has been that

U.S. strategic forces will become vulnerable to attack—that despite their immense destructive potential, such forces might be wiped out in a surprise attack before they could be launched. In a sense this is an old fear, and one of the immediate causes for the outbreak of World War I. Each of the continental powers had mobilization plans such that once a country began to move its forces, they could not be halted without leaving them disorganized and especially vulnerable to attack. Now, however, the power of nuclear weapons has greatly increased the magnitude of danger. Continued changes in technology—greater missile accuracy, the means to find and destroy enemy nuclear submarines before they can launch their missiles, and the possibility of an effective anti-ballistic missile system—mean that the threat of war ebbs and flows with changes in the relative advantage of offense to defense. A combination of enormous destructive power, offensive advantages, and intense international political tension could produce the danger of a war without precedent, a situation that would mock simple adages.

Again, the problem is unique because of the unique power of the destructive forces available. Before World War II, military aircraft had a combat radius of but a few hundred miles and could only carry a ton or so of high-explosive bombs. But now bombers and missiles can reach halfway around the globe, carrying payloads whose explosive power can be nearly 100 million times that of a pre–World War II bomber. The combination of nuclear weapons and modern delivery vehicles is lethal. The intercontinental missile moves from launch to impact in less than 30 minutes, can be very accurate, and is extremely difficult to intercept. The proposed American MX missile would carry ten warheads, each with a destructive force of 350 kilotons and independently targetable to an accuracy of 100 meters (or about 110 yards). With current weapons, both the United States and the Soviet Union could kill at least 75 million people and destroy between 50 and 75 percent of the industrial capacity of the other country. All this is "assured destruction"; that is, it can be inflicted even after a country has already been attacked, using only those strategic forces that survived. It is this combination of nuclear weapons and their delivery, especially the H-bomb and the ICBM, that led Jerome Wiesner and Herbert York, in an earlier *Scientific American* reader on arms control, to declare, "Both sides in the arms race are thus confronted by the dilemma of steadily increasing military power and steadily decreasing national security."

The group of nuclear physicists who built the first American nuclear weapons were well aware that they had created something with the power to transform the nature of warfare, not merely something that added a "normal" increment to war's destructiveness. J. Robert Oppenheimer, on seeing the first blast at Alamogordo, recalled words from the Bhagavad-Gita, "I am become death, destroyer of worlds." Niels Bohr had earlier sent a letter to President Roosevelt and Prime Minister Churchill, warning them of "a weapon of unparalleled power . . . which will completely change all future conditions of warfare," and which, in the absence of international control, promised to become "a perpetual menace to human security." Other scientists also feared a horrendous arms race and called for international agreements. Many of them, shocked by their creation and its possible uses, founded publications and organizations, such as the *Bulletin of the Atomic Scientists* and the Federation of American Scientists, which are still centrally concerned with these issues.

The efforts of these scientists, and those of many others who saw the new dangers, were quickly overwhelmed by the Soviet-American hostility that followed World War II and initiated the cold war. The United States did put forward a proposal, known as the Baruch Plan, in which it offered to surrender the atomic bomb if an international agency was established to control all forms of nuclear energy development. While to most Americans this seemed to be a generous offer, it was not so regarded by the Soviet leaders—and the grounds for disagreement represented issues that have hampered all subsequent arms control talks. The American proposal called for the establishment of an international agency first, which would have the power to control development and to inspect within the territories of all nations. After such an agency was functioning, the United States would give up the atomic bomb. The Soviet Union, however, saw this as a promise to give up the atomic bomb only after the control agency had made it impossible for any other state to acquire the bomb. The Russians (as the weaker power with a potential nuclear capability) wanted to have their own bomb before establishing the agency. Furthermore, as so often since, the Soviet government—suspicious, isolated, and maintaining strict secrecy—would not accept an agency with strong powers of inspection. Thus, no compromise was possible. Many Americans thought their country's "monopoly" of the atomic bomb would hold for 10 or 20 years, and there was therefore no hurry for an agreement with the Russians. The Russian government, however, was making very strenuous research and development efforts in nuclear energy, and it soon became confident in its ability to do what it thought necessary. The American monopoly was ended in August 1949 with the first Russian atomic explosion, announced by President Truman a month later.

With the expansion and intensification of the cold war, followed by the outbreak of the Korean war in June 1950 (which many Americans feared was merely a prelude to more dangerous Soviet attacks elsewhere), hardly any serious efforts were made to negotiate controls or limits on nuclear weapons. Both superpowers added to their atomic stockpiles (the American stockpile being substantially larger, since America started first) and began to acquire long-distance bombers capable of carrying these bombs to the other country's territories. The next big question about nuclear weapons was argued within the governments of the two countries in great secrecy. We know little about Soviet decision making during this period, but the issues discussed by the Russians must have been very similar to those dominating American discussions: Could a "superbomb," or hydrogen bomb, a thousand times more powerful than the atomic bomb be built? If so, what would be the consequences if we built it first? Would it give us a great military advantage? Would the Russians merely produce their own soon after in response to our effort, leaving the world under the horror of a much-expanded destructive capacity with no gain in anyone's security? If we didn't build it, would the Russians go ahead and build their own anyway, leaving us behind and possibly at their mercy?

In the first selection in this volume Herbert F. York, who was a physicist participating in the development of the H-bomb, describes the debate that went on. This discussion contains an implicit image of the arms race as an action-reaction process; much of what one side does is in reaction to (or perhaps in anticipation of) what the other side is expected to do—and vice versa.

During the early cold war years, it was common for Americans to think of the arms race as simply an effort to keep up with or stay ahead of the Russians. That is, Russian action caused continuing American reaction. Thus the arms race supposedly was fueled by Russian political and military advances in Eastern Europe, by Russian failure to disarm substantially after the war, and indeed by Russian development of a tactical military capability to invade Western Europe. Occasionally America might introduce a new weapons system first—like the atomic bomb—but even there the intention was merely thought to be defensive and anticipatory. The new weapon was either to counter an already existing Soviet capability (for example, atomic bombs for strategic delivery to counterbalance Russian tactical capacity for ground war in Europe) or simply to do first what the Russians would surely do anyway (such as developing the H-bomb). Such a view could be summed up as "we can be provoked; they must be deterred."

By the late 1950s, however, this view came to be widely questioned. As we look back, it is clear that the 1940s and 1950s constituted a period of overwhelming American military superiority. Any Soviet advantage in ground forces was more than offset by American strategic superiority. Throughout this period the United States declared that its policy was one of "massive retaliation"; any Soviet attack anywhere would be met "by means and in places of our own choosing." The threat to strike the Soviet Union itself with nuclear weapons was unmistakable. Furthermore, the American capability was there: a force of strategic bombers that was far larger than that of the Russians. American strategic dominance became recognized. Moreover, Americans and Russians—both government representatives and scientists at international "Pugwash" conferences—began to meet to discuss arms control problems. Many Russians sincerely seemed to view their country as peaceloving and intent only on keeping close to the military pace set by the United States. From this a more sophisticated view of the arms race emerged: Each side responded to the arms purchases of the other in a reciprocally stimulated race. Such a view became embodied in common perceptions and in some analytical models of arms dynamics, with mathematical expressions of action and reaction patterns. In Part II we shall see examples of "arms race dynamics" thinking.

While this represents an advance over one-sided "we can be provoked; they must be deterred" kinds of explanations, the action-reaction model ignores the forces within both superpowers that drive each to ever higher arms levels. For these forces the existence of a rival power provides an excuse for arms development, if not the actual reason. Some European scholars have characterized this phenomenon as a form of national *autism*— an analogy to the autistic child, who lives mentally sealed off from the world. The acts of such a child are almost exclusively responses to internal stimuli, and he or she is oblivious to any messages—hostile or benign— from other people.

Here, then, come all the familiar charges about a military-industrial complex of soldiers and sellers who feed each other at the public expenditures trough and about self-serving Russian and American officials who want new weapons and bigger armies simply to maintain a bureaucratic power base.

Some of these explanations put special blame on the American capitalist economy, with military contractors and labor unions seeking personal profit from arms sales. These explanations allege that a capitalist economy has a tendency toward overseas expansion and needs military spending to protect that expansion and to maintain a high level of demand for its products. Other such general explanations, however, note that personal and bureaucratic interests in the Soviet state economy may have much the same effect and so do not blame capitalism per se. An intriguing wrinkle on military-industrial complex arguments concerns the Soviet Union particularly. It is increasingly clear that the most dynamic, efficient part of the Soviet economy is the arms sector. After years of emphasizing military matters, the development of agriculture and consumer goods production has stagnated. In the long run, a transfer of Soviet resources from military to civilian needs might revive civilian production. But in the short run, shifts from the productive military part of the economy to less efficient sectors might well reduce the overall economic growth rate.

Certainly bureaucratic interests do operate in both countries; they are especially likely to resist the shrinkage of their accumulated resources. (Hence the difficulty in reducing the power of any large bureaucratic establishment, even after its initial purpose—whether fighting a war, suppressing crime, or eradicating a particular disease—has been achieved.) This at least partly explains why both the American and Soviet military establishments remained so large and powerful after World War II. Also, certain shocks from outside (the Korean war for the United States, the Cuban missile crisis for Russia) may lead to a military buildup that has its full effect many years later, when weapons systems first ordered just after the shock are finally deployed.

All in all, each of the explanations described above probably carries a part of the truth. The Russians are more than occasionally malign; the two superpowers are trapped in a spiral of unending competition; domestic actors with selfish economic, bureaucratic, and ideological concerns do exist and flourish. However, to sort out these various influences and to decide which is more important in determining particular policies or decisions for arms acquisitions constitute an extraordinarily difficult problem.

Bureaucratic momentum toward continuing weapons purchases may occasionally be broken. Sometimes it occurs as the result of difficult and drawn-out negotiations between the superpowers, as happened most dramatically with the partial test ban in 1963 and the treaty limiting anti-ballistic missile systems in 1972. (Both of these will be discussed later.) Once in a while it may happen as a result of special self-restraint on one side. Between 1955 and 1968, both U.S. and Soviet military expenditures in constant dollars rose almost annually. But then, as a result of popular revulsion to the Vietnam war, American military expenditures, expressed in 1979 dollars, declined every year from 1968 ($161 billion) to 1975 ($112 billion).

Estimates of Soviet expenditures during this period are controversial, since converting rubles to dollars and controlling for Soviet inflation are problematical. Nevertheless, there is general agreement that while American expenditures declined, Soviet spending increased steadily (by 3 to 4 percent annually in real terms), exceeding the American total by 20 to 40 percent since 1974. From 1967 to 1977, Soviet investment in strategic forces was about $2\frac{1}{2}$ times the investment by the United States, and Soviet land and sea forces also grew in number and strength relative to the United States. (The Russians allocate about 20 percent of their forces to China and the Far East.) Data on some of these trends are given in Tables 1.1, 1.2, and 1.3. Thus while American bureaucratic and military-industrial forces were restrained, those on the Soviet side were not.

Simple action-reaction explanations would lead us to expect that once the upward spiral had been arrested on the American side, a downward spiral might ensue and end the arms race. No such thing happened. Responding in large part to the lack of Soviet restraint, American military spending began to rise again, with real increases (1979 dollars) of $5 billion in 1976, $6 billion in 1977, and $1 billion in 1978. The arms race probably cannot be ended without occasional unilateral restraint. But unilateral restraint alone will probably not bring about simple reciprocation. To halt or reverse the arms race, explicit negotiated agreements are also necessary, in which each side's adherence is in some way proven to the other.

A number of important, though limited, agreements have been signed. The first arose from a variety of concerns in the 1950s that still remain. One concern, first emerging in the scientific community and then among the general public, is about the dangers of radioactive fallout from nuclear tests. Information accumulated that such radiation, released into the atmosphere and settling

Table 1.1 Military Expenditures for Major Powers, 1967–1979 (millions of dollars)

Year	United States Total[a]	United States Strategic[b]	United States[a]	U.S.S.R.[c]	West Germany	France	Great Britain	Iran
1967	160,800	13,900	71,700	n.a.	5,400	5,900	5,500	n.a.
1968	161,300	15,300	75,100	n.a.	4,800	6,200	5,600	n.a.
1969	159,500	16,900	77,800	n.a.	5,800	5,700	5,500	n.a.
1970	144,900	13,200	75,600	n.a.	6,200	6,000	5,900	n.a.
1971	131,100	12,800	72,900	n.a.	7,300	6,400	6,700	n.a.
1972	127,100	11,900	76,600	84,400	9,000	7,400	7,900	1,200
1973	121,800	11,100	79,000	90,000	13,300	9,800	9,000	2,100
1974	115,500	9,500	81,800	111,000	13,900	10,000	10,000	5,600
1975	111,600	9,300	86,200	124,000	16,100	14,000	11,100	8,800
1976	116,400	8,800	95,900	127,000	15,200	12,900	10,700	9,500
1977	122,600	10,600	108,300	140,000	16,600	13,700	11,214	7,900
1978	123,700	9,800	116,800	152,000	n.a.	n.a.	n.a.	n.a.
1979 (est.)	126,000	9,600	126,000	164,000	n.a.	n.a.	n.a.	n.a.

NOTE: Figures in first two columns are in constant 1979 dollars. Figures in remaining columns are in current dollars.

[a]Excludes foreign military assistance.

[b]Budgets prior to 1967 (in millions of constant 1979 dollars): 1946 = 18,200; 1951 = $23,500; 1956 = $27,900; 1961 = $31,900; 1963 = $25,500; 1965 = $15,400. Excludes research and development.

[c]Expenditure data are subject to error. These are recent American CIA estimates. Official U.S.S.R. budgets include only a small fraction of items classified as defense in other countries, and conversion of rubles to dollars is imprecise.

SOURCES: International Institute of Strategic Studies (IISS), *The Military Balance, 1977–1978*. London: IISS, 1977, and editions for 1974–75 and 1975–76; Office of the Assistant Secretary of Defense (Comptroller), unpublished computer printouts; Department of Defense, *Annual Report for FY 1979*; U.S. Congress, Joint Economic Committee, Subcommittee on Priorities and Economy in Government, *Allocation of Resources in the Soviet Union and China—1977*, hearings, 95th Cong. 2nd sess. part 1, 23 June 1977.

Table 1.2 Military Manpower for Major Powers, 1967–1977 (figures in thousands)

Year	United States[a]	U.S.S.R.	West Germany	France	Great Britain	China
1967	3,446	3,220	452	500	417	n.a.
1968	3,547	3,220	440	505	405	n.a.
1969	3,454	3,300	465	503	383	n.a.
1970	3,066	3,305	466	506	373	n.a.
1971	2,699	3,375	467	502	365	2,880
1972	2,391	3,375	467	501	363	2,880
1973	2,253	3,425	475	504	362	2,900
1974	2,174	3,525	490	503	355	3,000
1975	2,130	3,575	495	503	345	3,250
1976	2,087	3,650	495	513	344	3,525
1977	2,088	3,675	489	502	339	3,950
1978 (est.)	2,069	n.a.	n.a.	n.a.	n.a.	n.a.

[a]Excludes civilian defense manpower; for example, excludes 1,008,000 Department of Defense civilians for 1978.

SOURCES: International Institute of Strategic Studies (IISS), *The Military Balance, 1977–1978*, London: IISS, 1977, and editions for 1974–1975 and 1975–1976; Office of the Assistant Secretary of Defense (Comptroller), unpublished computer printouts; Department of Defense, *Annual Report for FY 1979*; U.S. Congress, Joint Economic Committee, Subcommittee on Priorities and Economy in Government, *Allocation of Resources in the Soviet Union and China—1977*, hearings, 95th Cong., 2nd sess., part 1, 23 June 1977.

back to earth in subsequent weeks or months, carried substantial risks of cancer and genetic damage to living individuals and to future generations.

It was true that radioactivity originating from weapons tests represented only a fraction of the total radiation experienced by most citizens from the normal background radiation of the earth and from medical X rays. Nevertheless, that fraction was growing and promised to grow further as weapons tests by the superpowers continued and as other states intent on becoming nuclear powers began testing. Precise knowledge of the effects of such additional low-level radiation was lacking and is still subject to much scientific controversy today. However, it became clear that while the risks to any particular individual were low, test-caused radiation would cause tens of thousands of cases of premature

Table 1.3 Strategic Delivery Vehicles for Nuclear Powers, 1963–1978

Country	1963	1964	1965	1966	1967	1968	1969	1970	1971	1972
U.S.A.										
ICBM	424	834	854	904	1,054	1,054	1,054	1,054	1,054	1,054
SLBM	224	416	496	592	656	656	656	656	656	656
Long-range bombers	630	630	630	630	600	545	560	550	505	455
U.S.S.R.										
ICBM	90	190	224	292	570	858	1,028	1,299	1,513	1,527
SLBM	107	107	107	107	107	121	196	304	448	500
Long-range bombers	190	175	160	155	160	155	145	145	145	140
United Kingdom										
ICBM	—	—	—	—	—	—	—	—	0	n.a.
SLBM	—	—	—	—	—	—	—	—	64	n.a.
Bombers	—	—	—	—	—	—	—	—	50	n.a.
France										
ICBM	—	—	—	—	—	—	—	—	9	n.a.
SLBM	—	—	—	—	—	—	—	—	16	n.a.
Bombers	—	—	—	—	—	—	—	—	36	n.a.
China										
ICBM	—	—	—	—	—	—	—	—	20	n.a.
SLBM	—	—	—	—	—	—	—	—	0	n.a.
Bombers	—	—	—	—	—	—	—	—	30	n.a.

SOURCES: International Institute of Strategic Studies (IISS), *The Military Balance, 1977–78*, London: IISS, 1977, and editions for 1976–1977 and 1971–72; Department of Defense, *Annual Report for FY 1979*.

NOTE: For Britain, France, and China, the bombers have only intermediate range, and the figures listed as ICBMs are really IRBMs and MRBMs. Nevertheless, they are usually assigned to strategic forces, and the countries' proximity to the Soviet Union makes them plausible in that role. The British SLBM is the Polaris A3 and has three warheads. French and Chinese missiles are not MIRVed.

deaths and major genetic damage worldwide. Growing information and alarm on this matter were reflected in the monthly column of *Scientific American* entitled "Science and the Citizen," which remains an excellent source of information on arms control issues today. The problem worried not just Americans but also people who lived in countries not possessing nuclear weapons but who nevertheless were subject to fallout.

The second concern was about nuclear proliferation—the likelihood that many additional states, whether to gain political advantage or simply to strengthen their security, would acquire their own nuclear weapons. Britain exploded its first bomb in 1952, and France followed in 1960; it was feared that as many as a score of other nations might follow in fairly quick order. If many more countries had nuclear weapons, the probability might greatly increase that nuclear war would arise somewhere in the world, perhaps spreading globally.

Finally, many thoughtful observers feared continuing Soviet-American cold war hostility and the bilateral accumulation of modern weapons. Such people focused on a test ban as the first major step that might improve the political climate between the superpowers. A test ban would respond to popular fears and show that agreements to slow the arms race were possible.

Out of these concerns came the announcement in 1958 that the United States would cease nuclear testing if the Soviet Union would do likewise. This moratorium was to be continued while formal negotiations between the two powers at Geneva were under way. The Russians agreed, but negotiations went very slowly due to fears among some people on both sides that a test ban would mean foregoing an advantage in developing new weapons. Also, there was great scientific uncertainty over the ability to detect violations of the agreement and much controversy over how much risk such violations would pose. Consistent with their general positions on arms control and disarmament, the Americans insisted on on-site inspection of suspicious events, a demand that the Soviets vigorously resisted. The French conducted their first test in 1960, and in September 1961 Soviet Premier Khruschev announced that his country would resume testing, which it did. Included in the new tests was a very large (about 50 megatons) and dirty bomb.

Negotiations nevertheless continued. Scientists generally agreed that nuclear tests above ground could readily be detected by devices available to both superpowers; the only question concerned relatively small underground tests that might be interpreted as earthquakes and that would not release radiation into the atmosphere. Finally, in December 1962, Premier Khruschev offered to permit three seismic stations on Soviet soil and three on-site inspections per year. President Kennedy welcomed this unusual Soviet concession but said that at least eight to ten inspections would be necessary. Ultimately the Russians withdrew their apparent concession. To break the inspection impasse, the two powers prohibited only atmospheric testing; underground tests could continue. Public fears about radiation fallout would be allayed, some weapons development would be slowed, and a better political atmosphere might result that would encourage other Soviet-American negotiations to proceed. At the same time, by permitting underground tests, both sides could keep their laboratories and scientific establishments intact, develop many new systems, and retain big technological leads over newer nuclear powers and nonnuclear states. This last fact was not lost on other countries. France, China, and India, among others, refused to become parties to the test ban, and many others protested the superpowers' reluctance to give up their advantage. (France ultimately suspended atmospheric testing in 1974 in response to world pressure.)

Thus a unilateral move by the United States (the test ban moratorium) helped to create the conditions for an agreement. But the final step had to be a formal treaty signed and ratified by the two superpowers. And it was final only in a very limited way; the search for a comprehensive test ban still continues in 1978. Other articles in *Scientific American* (and cited in the bibliography) detail some of the further negotiations and considerations, including the seismic detection problem, inspection controversy, and the kinds of weapons development that might be foreclosed by a comprehensive prohibition on testing.

The second selection in Part I is another article by Herbert F. York (former director of research and engi-

1973	1974	1975	1976	1977	1978
1,054	1,054	1,054	1,054	1,054	1,054
656	656	656	656	656	656
442	437	432	387	373	349
1,527	1,575	1,618	1,527	1,477	1,400
628	720	784	845	909	900
140	140	135	135	135	140
n.a.	n.a.	n.a.	0	0	n.a.
n.a.	n.a.	n.a.	64	64	n.a.
n.a.	n.a.	n.a.	50	50	n.a.
n.a.	n.a.	n.a.	18	18	n.a.
n.a.	n.a.	n.a.	48	64	n.a.
n.a.	n.a.	n.a.	50	50	n.a.
n.a.	n.a.	n.a.	65	70	n.a.
n.a.	n.a.	n.a.	0	0	n.a.
n.a.	n.a.	n.a.	65	80	80

neering for the U.S. Defense Department) that discusses some of these test-ban issues. First published in 1972, it considers what information is needed for the development of MIRV (multiple independently-targeted re-entry vehicle) warheads and what might be required for ABM (anti-ballistic missile) systems and other weapons. York concludes that the information required is available from previous tests or could be obtained from laboratory work. No major breakthrough has resulted from continued underground testing or seems likely from future testing, although some valuable information has been obtained. He then argues that a comprehensive test ban should be concluded, principally as a restraint on nuclear proliferation: The world must see the superpowers as calling a definite halt to at least one kind of their own nuclear weapons development. More about this issue is contained later in the volume.

In 1974 President Nixon and General Secretary Brezhnev signed the Threshold Test Ban Treaty prohibiting all tests (including those underground) with an anticipated yield of 150 kilotons. This was followed in 1976 by the Treaty on Underground Nuclear Explosions for Peaceful Purposes, which forbade peaceful nuclear explosions (PNEs) exceeding 150 kilotons. Both sides, by "gentleman's agreement," have complied with these basic obligations. When he took office, however, President Carter called the new treaties a "wholly inadequate step" and refused to ask for Senate ratification. Since 150 kilotons is so high (the Hiroshima bomb was 20 kilotons), the measure would do little to curb the arms race or satisfy nonnuclear powers. Instead, Carter declared that "the time has come to end all explosions of nuclear devices, no matter what their claimed justification—peaceful or military," and he pursued negotiations for a comprehensive test ban.

For years the Soviet government insisted that PNEs should be permitted, especially for big earth-moving projects such as digging new harbors. The American government maintained that such explosions had little practical utility and would merely serve as a loophole to evade a ban on weapons testing. Then in November 1977 Secretary Brezhnev stated that the Soviet Union was prepared to agree to a moratorium on nuclear explosions for peaceful purposes as well as a ban on all nuclear weapons tests "for a definite period." At about the same time, Arms Control and Disarmament Agency Director Paul Warnke suggested, in Congressional testimony, a possibility that the Russians would indeed accept some automated seismic stations on their territory and limited on-site inspection, as first indicated in 1962. These developments are despite the fact that the Soviet government long seemed unwilling to conclude an agreement that did not include China as a signatory; both the Chinese and the French have made it clear that they will not sign a test ban.

With the PNE objection dropped, it looked as though a comprehensive test ban was the offing. One postulated advantage of a comprehensive treaty is the increased uncertainty that both powers might develop about the reliability of their existing nuclear weapons. Tests of new weapons are routinely supplemented by tests of existing ones, simply to be sure that the stockpile would perform adequately in a war. If both sides lost some of this certainty over the years, they might hesitate to launch an attack that could misfire. By this reasoning, deterrence is strengthened by any factor that contributes to a prospective attacker's lack of confidence that everything will work according to plan.

The comprehensive test ban treaty nevertheless encountered some difficulties. One was the familiar fear that very low-yield explosions could not be reliably detected. A new wrinkle, however, concerned the near-pure or pure fusion bomb, also known as the neutron or "enhanced radiation" bomb. Such weapons have been speculated upon for many years; indeed, in August 1961 "Science and the Citizen" referred to this concept, developed by Edward Teller. A neutron bomb would produce a small blast and little heat compared with an ordinary nuclear weapon of similar yield, but much radiation. In effect, it would be a lethal weapon against people, but do relatively little damage to physical structures. As such it could be used defensively in heavily built-up areas, such as Western Europe, preserving most of the cities if not their inhabitants. (An article in Part III of this book discusses this weapon.)

Although a subject of some controversy, in 1978 the United States appeared ready to order production of neutron bombs, primarily for a deterrent in Europe where the balance of forces has been shifting against NATO. Despite the controversy, the neutron bomb has not seemed a major threat to arms race stability or crisis stability—it is far less dangerous, for example, than new high-accuracy missile systems that are capable of destroying hardened missile silos. (See the discussion of MaRV [maneuverable re-entry vehicles] and the proposed MX missile in Part III of this book.) Although the United States has essentially completed development of the neutron bomb, the Russians probably lag behind. The United States would not need to test a new neutron bomb; the Russians would. And the Russians have now warned that they will deploy neutron bombs if the United States does. Thus, a new and unanticipated hurdle to a comprehensive test ban may arise.

The period of American nuclear predominance is gone. Soviet and American strategic forces are roughly equivalent now, if numbers, type, and technological sophistication all are considered. Maintaining this rough equivalence is now a primary concern, and it will not be maintained by some automatic, invisible hand. A shift away from equivalence would again raise the threat of war. So, too, would technological change that favors the attacker and degrades the security of the other side's deterrent force. Problems of nuclear arms control—and the more ambitious goal of disarmament—remain. Avoiding war, lowering tensions, and reducing the waste of the arms race remain as goals to be pursued.

The Debate over the Hydrogen Bomb

by Herbert F. York
October 1975

A recently declassified report sheds light on the original U.S. decision to develop the "Super." The unanimous opposition of the Oppenheimer committee, overruled then, appears now to have been basically correct

In 1948 Czechoslovak Communists carried out a coup in the shadow of the Red Army and replaced the government of that country with one subservient to Moscow. Also in 1948 the Russians unsuccessfully attempted to force the Western allies out of Berlin by blockading all land transport routes to the city. In early 1949 the Communist People's Liberation Army captured Peking and soon afterward established the People's Republic of China. Taken together, these and similar but less dramatic events were generally perceived in the West as resulting in the creation of a monolithic and aggressive alliance stretching the full length of the Eurasian continent, encompassing almost half of the world's people and threatening much of the rest. Then in the fall of 1949 the Russians exploded their first atomic bomb and ended the brief American nuclear monopoly.

At the end of World War II most atomic scientists in the U.S. had estimated that the U.S.S.R. would need four or five years to make a bomb based on the nuclear-fission principle; the time interval from the first American test to the first Russian one turned out to be four years and six weeks. Even so, nearly everyone, including most U.S. Government officials and most members of Congress, reacted to the event as if it were a great surprise. Many of them had either forgotten or had never known the experts' original estimates, and in any case the accomplishment simply did not fit the almost universal view of the U.S.S.R. as a technologically backward nation.

Besides being a great surprise the Russian test explosion was a singularly unpleasant one. The U.S. nuclear monopoly had been seen by many as compensating for the difference between the hordes of conscripts supposedly available to the Communist bloc and the smaller armies available to the Western countries. Coming as it did at a time when virtually all Americans saw the cold war as rapidly going from bad to worse, the Russian test was seen as a challenge that demanded a reply. The immediate challenge being nuclear, a particularly intensive search for an appropriate response was conducted by those responsible for U.S. nuclear policy.

Most of the proposed responses involved substantial but evolutionary changes in the current U.S. nuclear programs: expand the search for additional supplies of fissionable material, step up the production of atomic weapons, adapt such weapons to a broader range of delivery vehicles and end uses, and the like. One proposal was radically different. It called for the fastest possible development of the hydrogen bomb, which was widely referred to at the time as the superbomb (or simply the Super). This weapon, based on the entirely new and as yet untested principle of thermonuclear fusion, was estimated to have the potential of being 1,000 or more times as powerful as the fission bombs that had marked the end of World War II. Work on the theory of the superbomb had already been going on for seven years, but it had never had a very high priority, and so far it had yielded no practical result. A number of scientists and politicians endorsed the proposal, but for years Edward Teller had been its leading advocate. The superbomb proposal led to a brief, intense and highly secret debate.

The opponents of the proposal argued that neither the possession of the new bomb nor the initiation of its development was necessary for maintaining the national security of the U.S., and that under such circumstances it would be morally wrong to initiate the development of such an enormously powerful and destructive weapon. In essence they contended that the world ought to avoid the development and stockpiling of the superbomb if it was at all possible, and that a U.S. decision to forgo it was a necessary precondition for persuading others to do likewise. Furthermore, they concluded that the dynamism and relative status of U.S. nuclear technology were such that the U.S. could safely run the risk that the U.S.S.R. might not practice similar restraint and would instead initiate a secret program of its own.

The advocates of the superbomb maintained that the successful achievement of such a bomb by the Russians was only a matter of time, and so at best our forgoing it would amount to a deliberate decision to become a second-class power, and at worst it would be equivalent to surrender. They added that undertaking the development of the superbomb was morally no different from developing any other weapon.

The secret debate about what the American response ought to be took place within the Government itself. Many organizations were involved, including the National Security Council, the Department of Defense, the Department of State and the Congressional Joint Committee on Atomic Energy, but the initial focus of the debate lay within the Atomic Energy Commission.

The early official reaction of the AEC's Los Alamos Scientific Laboratory to the Russian test was a proposal to step up the pace of the nuclear-weapons program in all areas. Among other measures, Norris E. Bradbury, the director, recommended that the laboratory go on a six-day work week and that they expand the staff, particularly in theoretical physics.

This acceleration was to include not only programs for improving fission weapons by conventional means but also tests of the booster principle. (In this context "booster" refers to a synergistic process in which the explosion of a comparatively large mass of fissionable fuel, say plutonium or uranium 235, causes a comparatively small mass of thermonuclear fuel, say deuterium and tritium, to burn violently. The high-energy neutrons produced in the thermonuclear process then react back on the fission explosion, boosting, or accelerating, it to a higher efficiency than would otherwise be the case.) The booster concept had been known for several years, and even before the Russian test it had been agreed to include a full-scale experimental test of the process in a 1951 nuclear-test series. The AEC's Director of Military Application, General James McCormack, Jr., received these proposals from the Los Alamos laboratory and sought the advice of the AEC's scientific experts on them. Other AEC division heads were similarly studying proposals for expanding the relevant programs within their jurisdiction.

At the same time Teller, then at Los Alamos, Ernest O. Lawrence, Luis W. Alvarez and Wendell M. Latimer at the University of California at Berkeley, Robert LeBaron at the Department of Defense, Senator Brien McMahon, Chairman of the Joint Committee on Atomic Energy, his staff chief William L. Borden and Commissioner Lewis L. Strauss of the AEC had all come to focus on the superbomb as the main element of the answer to the Russian atomic bomb, and they initiated a concerted effort to bring the entire Government around to their point of view as quickly as possible.

As a result of all this concern and activity the AEC called for a special meeting of its General Advisory Committee to be held as soon as possible. This committee was one of the special mechanisms established by the Atomic Energy Act of 1946 for the purpose of managing the postwar development of nuclear energy in the U.S. Its function was to provide the AEC with scientific and technical advice concerning its programs. The members of the committee were all men who had been scientific or technological leaders in major wartime projects. J. Robert Oppenheimer, who was elected chairman of the committee,

FIRST SUPERBOMB TEST in which a large thermonuclear, or fusion, explosion was successfully ignited by a comparatively small fission explosion took place at the Eniwetok Proving Ground in the Marshall Islands on November 1, 1952 (local time). The device, with the code name Mike, released an amount of energy equivalent to that released by the explosion of 10 megatons, or 10 million tons, of TNT. As had been predicted five years earlier by the scientist members of the General Advisory Committee of the Atomic Energy Commission, yield of first superbomb was approximately 1,000 times larger than the yield of the first atomic, or all-fission, bombs.

had been director of the Los Alamos laboratory during the period when the first atomic bomb had been designed and built there. The other members, all scientists, were Oliver E. Buckley, James B. Conant, Lee A. DuBridge, Enrico Fermi, I. I. Rabi, Hartley Rowe, Glenn T. Seaborg and Cyril S. Smith. Many of the members of this committee and later General Advisory committees also served on other high-level standing committees and some key ad hoc committees, and so a rather complex web of interlocking advisory-committee memberships developed. As a result several of these men, including Oppenheimer, had much more influence than the simple sum of their various committee memberships would indicate.

Oppenheimer was not only the formal leader of the General Advisory Committee but also, by virtue of his personality and background, its natural leader. His views were therefore of special importance in setting the tone and determining the content of the committee's reports in this matter, as in most other matters.

Throughout Oppenheimer's service on the committee he generally supported the various programs designed to produce and improve nuclear weapons. At the same time he was deeply troubled by what he had wrought at Los Alamos, and he found the notion of bombs of unlimited power particularly repugnant. Ever since the end of the war he had devoted much of his attention to promoting the international control of atomic energy with the ultimate objective of achieving nuclear disarmament. He and Rabi had in effect been the originators of the plan for nuclear-arms control that later became known as the Baruch Plan. Oppenheimer's inner feelings about nuclear weapons were clearly revealed in an often quoted remark: "In some sort of crude sense which no vulgarity, no humor, no overstatement can quite extinguish, the physicists have known sin, and this is a knowledge which they cannot lose."

The call for the special meeting, in addition to raising the question of a high-priority program to develop the Super, also asked the committee to consider priorities in the broadest sense, including "whether the Commission is now doing things we ought to do to serve the paramount objectives of the common defense and security." As for the Super, the Commission wanted to know "whether the nation would use such a weapon if it could be built and what its military worth would be in relation to fission weapons." The meeting of the Oppenheimer committee was held on October 29 and 30, 1949; all members were present except Seaborg, who was in Europe. The committee in the course of its deliberations heard from many outside experts in various relevant fields, including George F. Kennan, the noted student of Russian affairs, General Omar Bradley, Chairman of the Joint Chiefs of Staff, and the physicists H. A. Bethe and Robert Serber. Toward the end of the two-day meeting the advisers had a long session with the Atomic Energy commissioners and with their intelligence staff. The next day the committee prepared its report.

The General Advisory Committee report consisted of three separate sections that were unanimously agreed on and two addenda giving certain specific minority views. In 1974 the report was almost entirely declassified, with only a very few purely technical details remaining secret.

Part I of the report dealt with all pertinent questions other than those directly involving the Super. The advisory committee in effect reacted favorably to the proposals of the various AEC division directors with regard to the expansion of the facilities for separating uranium isotopes, for producing plutonium and for increasing the supplies of uranium ore. These proposals and the committee's endorsement of them were followed eventually by a substantial increase in the rate of production of fissionable materials.

In Part I the committee also recommended the acceleration of research and development work on fission bombs, particularly for tactical purposes. Under the heading "Tactical Delivery" the report stated: "The General Advisory Committee recommends to the Commission an intensification of efforts to make atomic weapons available for tactical purposes, and to give attention to the problem of integration of bomb and carrier design in this field."

This quoted paragraph deserves special emphasis, since it has often been suggested that Oppenheimer, Conant and some of the others opposed nuclear weapons in general. They did apparently find them all repugnant, and they did try hard to create an international control organization that would ultimately lead to their universal abolition. In the absence of any international arms-limitation agreements with reliable control mechanisms, however, they explicitly recognized the need to possess nuclear weapons, particularly for tactical and defensive purposes, and they regularly promoted programs designed to increase their variety, flexibility, efficiency and numbers. For the next few years, right up to the time Oppenheimer's security clearance was removed, he continued strongly to promote the idea of an expanded arsenal of tactical nuclear weapons. The only type of nuclear weapon the General Advisory Committee opposed—and it did so openly—was the Super.

Part I of the report further recommended that a project be initiated for the purpose of producing "freely absorbable neutrons" to be used for the production of uranium 233, tritium and other potentially useful nuclear materials. Perhaps most important of all in the present context, Part I also stated: "We strongly favor, subject to favorable outcome of the 1951 Eniwetok tests, the booster program." This short phrase makes it abundantly clear that the Oppenheimer committee favored conducting research fundamental to understanding the thermonuclear process, and that its grave reservations were specifically and solely focused on one particular application of the fusion process.

Part II discussed the Super. It outlined what was known about the hydrogen bomb, and it expanded on the unusual difficulties its development presented, but it concluded that the bomb could probably be built. In part it said: "It is notable that there appears to be no experimental approach short of actual test which will substantially add to our conviction that a given model will or will not work. Thus, we are faced with a development which cannot be carried to the point of conviction without the actual construction and demonstration of the essential elements of the weapon in question. A final point that needs to be stressed is that many tests may be required before a workable model has been evolved or before it has been established beyond reasonable doubt that no such model can be evolved. Although we are not able to give a specific probability rating for any given model, *we believe that an imaginative and concerted attack on the problem has a better than even chance of producing the weapon within five years.*"

That last sentence (the italics are added) deserves special emphasis. It has been suggested in the past that the General Advisory Committee in general and Oppenheimer in particular were deceptive in their analysis of the technological prospects of the Super; in other words, that they deliberately painted a falsely gloomy picture of its possibilities in order to reinforce their basically ethical opposition to its development. Given the technological circumstances then prevailing, this statement of the program's prospects could hardly have been more positive.

The report then discussed what might be called the "strategic economics" of the Super as they were then conceived: "A second characteristic of the super bomb is that once the problem of initiation has been solved, there is no limit to the explosive power of the bomb itself except that imposed by requirements of delivery. [In addition there will be] very grave contamination problems which can easily be made more acute, and may possibly be rendered less acute, by surrounding the deuterium with uranium or other material.... It is clearly impossible with the vagueness of design and the uncertainty as to performance as we have them at present to give anything like a cost estimate of the super. If one uses the strict criteria of damage area per dollar, it appears uncertain to us whether the super will be cheaper or more expensive than the fission bombs."

In Part III the committee members got to what to them was the heart of the matter, the question of whether or not the Super should be developed: "Although the members of the Advisory Committee are not unanimous in their proposals as to what should be done with regard to the super bomb, there are certain elements of unanimity among us. We all hope that by one means or another the development of these weapons can be avoided. We are all reluctant to see the United States take the initiative in precipitating this development. We are all agreed that it would be wrong at the present moment to commit ourselves to an all-out effort toward its development.

"We are somewhat divided as to the nature of the commitment not to develop the weapon. The majority feel that this should be an unqualified commitment. Others feel that it should be made conditional on the response of the Soviet government to a proposal to renounce such development. The Committee recommends that enough be declassified about the super bomb so that a public statement of policy can be made at this time."

In the two addenda those members of the committee who were present (that is, all except Seaborg) explained their reasons for their proposed "commitment not to develop the weapon." The first addendum was written by Conant and signed by Rowe, Smith, DuBridge, Buckley and Oppenheimer. In part it said: "We base our recommendation on our belief that the extreme dangers to mankind inherent in the proposal wholly outweigh any military advantage that could come from this development. Let it be clearly realized that this is a super weapon; it is in a totally different category from an atomic bomb. The reason for developing such super bombs would be to have the capacity to devastate a vast area with a single bomb. Its use would involve a decision to slaughter a vast number of civilians. We are alarmed as to the possible global effects of the radioactivity generated by the explosion of a few super bombs of conceivable magnitude. If super bombs will work at all, there is no inherent limit in the destructive power that may be attained with them. Therefore, a super bomb might become a weapon of genocide.

"We believe a super bomb should never be produced. Mankind would be far better off not to have a demonstration of the feasibility of such a weapon until the present climate of world opinion changes.

"In determining not to proceed to develop the super bomb, we see a unique opportunity of providing by example some limitations on the totality of war and thus of limiting the fear and arousing the hopes of mankind."

Contrary to a frequently suggested notion, the members of the Oppenheimer committee were not at all unmindful of the possibility that the U.S.S.R. might develop the Super no matter what the U.S. did. Indeed, they regarded it as entirely possible and explained why it would not be crucial: "To the argument that the Russians may succeed in developing this weapon, we would reply that our undertaking it will not prove a deterrent to them. Should they use the weapon against us, reprisals by our large stock of atomic bombs would be comparably effective to the use of a 'Super.'"

The minority addendum, signed by Fermi and Rabi, expressed even stronger opposition to the Super but loosely coupled an American renunciation with a proposal for a worldwide pledge not to proceed: "It is clear that the use of such a weapon cannot be justified on any ethical ground which gives a human being a certain individuality and dignity even if he happens to be a resident of an enemy country.

"The fact that no limits exist to the destructiveness of this weapon makes its very existence and the knowledge of its construction a danger to humanity as a whole. It is necessarily an evil thing considered in any light.

"For these reasons we believe it important for the President of the United States to tell the American public, and the world, that we think it wrong on fundamental ethical principles to initiate a program of development of such a weapon. At the same time it would be appropriate to invite the nations of the world to join us in a solemn pledge not to proceed in the development of construction of weapons of this category."

As with the majority, Fermi and Rabi also explicitly took up the possibility that the Russians might proceed on their own, or even go back on a pledge not to: "If such a pledge were accepted even without control machinery, it appears highly probable that an advanced state of development leading to a test by another power could be detected by available physical means. Furthermore, we have in our possession, in our stockpile of atomic bombs, the means for adequate 'military' retaliation for the production or use of a 'Super.'"

On December 2 and 3, five weeks after the special meeting, the General Advisory Committee convened for one of its regularly scheduled meetings and carefully reviewed the question of the Super once again. According to Richard G. Hewlett, the AEC's official historian, Oppenheimer reported to the commissioners that no member wished to change the views expressed in the October 30 report.

For a time it appeared that the views of the Oppenheimer committee had a chance of being accepted. David E. Lilienthal, chairman of the AEC, was receptive to the committee's point of view. He similarly favored two parallel responses to the Russian test: (1) increasing the production of fission weapons and developing a greater variety of them, particularly for tactical situations, and (2) officially announcing our intention to refrain from proceeding with the Super while simultaneously reopening and intensifying the search for international control of all kinds of weapons of mass destruction. Lilienthal considered the complete reliance on weapons of mass destruction to be a fundamental weakness in U.S. policy, and he viewed a "crash" program on the hydrogen bomb as foreclosing what might be the last good opportunity to base U.S. foreign policy on "something better than a headlong rush into war with weapons of mass destruction." "We are," he said, "today relying on an asset that is readily depreciating for us, i.e., weapons of mass destruction. [A decision to go ahead with the Super] would tend to confuse and, unwittingly, hide that fact and make it more difficult to find some other course."

As we know now, the advice of the Oppenheimer committee was rejected. Early in 1950 President Truman, acting on the basis of his own political judgment and on the totality of the advice he had received on the matter, issued directives designed to set in motion a major U.S. program to develop the hydrogen bomb.

It is not possible here to give a full description of what happened next, but the following chronological outline of the Russian and American superbomb programs is designed to show how the "race" for the superbomb did in fact come out, and to facilitate making judgments about the General Advisory Committee's advice and about "what might have been."

First of all, it is now known that both countries initiated high-priority programs for the development of a hydrogen bomb at about the same time (late 1949–early 1950), and both had been seriously studying the subject for some years before that.

The first U.S. test series that included experiments designed to investigate thermonuclear explosions took place at Eniwetok in the spring of 1951. Known as Operation Greenhouse, the series included two thermonuclear experiments. One, with the code name Item, was a test of the booster principle. This experiment, it must be emphasized, was planned and programmed before the first Russian atomic-bomb test. The other (which actually took place first) was called George. It was a response to Joe 1, as the first Russian atomic-bomb test was called by the U.S. intelligence establishment. Reduced to its essentials, the purpose of the experiment was to show, as a minimum, that a thermonuclear reaction could under ideal conditions be made to proceed in an experimental device. This experiment came to play a key role in the Super program. As Teller later put it: "We needed a significant test. Without such a test no one of us could have had the confidence to proceed further along speculations, inventions and the difficult choice of the most promising possibility. This test was to play the role of a pilot plant in our development."

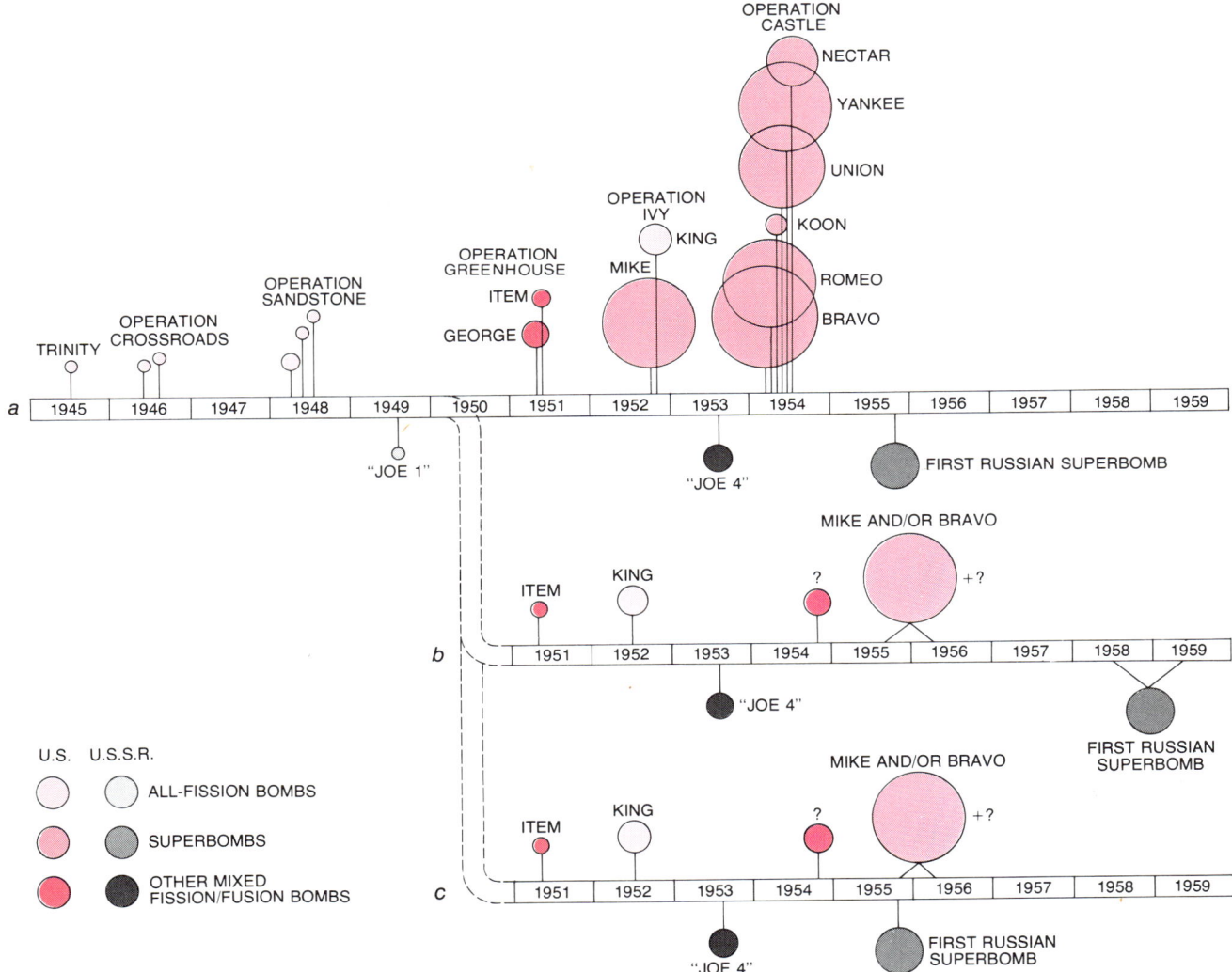

TWO HYPOTHETICAL OUTCOMES are postulated in an effort to evaluate how much risk would have been involved in a U.S. decision not to proceed with the superbomb. They are depicted in this historical chart as branches of the time line representing the actual world (*a*). The first branch is referred to by the author as the "most probable alternative world" (*b*), the second as the "worst plausible alternative world" (*c*). Both branches originate at January, 1950, the date President Truman announced his decision to go ahead with the superbomb. The circles denote nuclear-test explosions; the labels are U.S. code names. Area of each circle is proportional to the region that could be destroyed by that bomb. Bombs of "nominal" size (less than 50 kilotons) have been omitted after 1950.

The George shot served its purpose well. During the final stages of calculations concerned with the expected performance of this device, Teller and Stanislaw Ulam came up with the climactic idea that made it possible to achieve the goal of the superbomb program: they invented a configuration that would make it possible for a small fission explosion to ignite an arbitrarily large fusion explosion.

The first test of a device designed to ignite a large thermonuclear explosion by means of a comparatively small quantity of fissionable material took place at Eniwetok on November 1, 1952 (local time). The device, known as Mike, produced a tremendous explosion, equivalent in its energy release to 10 megatons (10 million tons) of TNT. As had been repeatedly predicted since the early 1940's, the yield was roughly 1,000 times larger than the yield of the first atomic bombs. For certain practical reasons relating to the pioneering nature of the test, this first version of the Teller-Ulam configuration had liquid deuterium as its thermonuclear fuel. (The last point needs special emphasis. The Teller-Ulam invention, contrary to folklore, was not the notion of substituting easy-to-handle lithium deuteride for the hard-to-handle liquid deuterium. That possibility had been recognized several years earlier.)

Also in November, 1952, the U.S. tested a very powerful fission bomb, with the code name King, that had an explosive yield of 500 kilotons, or half a megaton. Its purpose was to provide the U.S. with an extraordinarily powerful bomb by means of a straightforward extension of fission-weapons technology, in case such large bombs should become necessary for any strategic or political reason. Originally proposed by Bethe as a substitute for the Super program, it became instead a backup for it.

The first Russian explosion involving fusion reactions took place on August 12, 1953. Russian descriptions of this test and later ones confirm that it was not a superbomb. It was only some tens of times as big as the standard atomic bombs of the day, about the same size as but probably smaller than King, the largest U.S. fission bomb. It evidently involved one of several possible straightforward configurations for igniting a fairly small amount of thermonuclear material with a comparatively large amount of fissionable material. It was the first device anywhere to use lithium deuteride as a fuel, and presumably it could have been readily converted into a practical weapon if there had been any point in doing so. It seems to have been a development step the U.S. bypassed in its successful search for a configuration that would make it possible to produce an arbitrarily large explosion with a relatively small quantity of fissionable material.

In the spring of 1954 the U.S. successfully exploded six more variants of the superbomb in Operation Castle. Their yields varied widely. The first and most famous of these tests, with the code name Bravo, was exploded on March 1, 1954, at Bikini. Its design, which was initiated before the Mike explosion, also incorporated the Teller-Ulam configuration, but it had the more practical lithium deuteride as its thermonuclear fuel. Bravo's yield was 15 megatons, even more than Mike's, and it was readily adaptable to delivery by aircraft.

On November 23, 1955, the U.S.S.R. exploded a bomb that had a yield of a few megatons. According to a statement made by Secretary Khrushchev, this device involved an "important new achievement" that made it possible by "using a relatively small quantity of fissionable material...to produce an explosion of several megatons." Khrushchev's remark is generally taken as confirmation that the test was the first one in which the Russians incorporated the Teller-Ulam configuration or something like it. It also used lithium deuteride as a fuel and was therefore a true superbomb, comparable to the U.S. Bravo device exploded 20 months earlier, except for its yield, which was still probably only about a fifth the yield of Bravo.

With this chronology in mind, what can one say about what might have happened if the U.S. had followed the advice of Oppenheimer and the rest of the General Advisory Committee, backed by Lilienthal and the majority of the AEC commissioners, and had not initiated a program for the specific purpose of developing the Super in the spring of 1950?

At best the invention of very large, comparatively inexpensive bombs of the Super type would have been forestalled or substantially delayed. Very probably the work on the booster principle, which presumably would still have gone forward, would have led eventually to the ideas underlying the design of very big bombs, but those ideas might well have been delayed until both President Eisenhower and Secretary Khrushchev were in power. Those two leaders were both more seriously interested in arms-limitation agreements than their predecessors had been, and it is at least possible that they might have been able to deal successfully with the superbomb. To be sure, such a favorable result was not very probable (certainly it had much less than an even chance of coming about), but its achievement would have been so beneficial to mankind that at least some small risk was clearly worth running.

To evaluate just how much risk would have been involved let us next examine three other outcomes, which I have labeled the "actual world," the "most probable alternative world" and the "worst plausible alternative world" [*see illustration on page 13*].

In both of the hypothetical alternative worlds I assume that the U.S. would have forgone the development of the Super but that the Russians would have ignored this American restraint and would have proceeded at first just as they did in the actual world. I also assume that the U.S. would have vigorously followed the positive elements of the Oppenheimer committee's advice; thus the booster project and other ideas for improving fission bombs would have been accelerated. The difference between the most probable alternative world and the worst plausible alternative world lies in the timing of the test of the first Russian superbomb. In the worst plausible world I assume that this test would have come on the same date that it did in the actual world. In the most probable alternative world, however, I assume that the test would have been substantially delayed.

In both of the two hypothetical alternative worlds, then, the Russians in August, 1953, would have exploded Joe 4, a large bomb deriving part of its explosive energy from a thermonuclear fuel and yielding a few hundred kilotons. Such a device, however, would have had no real effect on the "balance of terror." In both alternative worlds the U.S. would surely have already tested the 500-kiloton all-fission bomb in November, 1952 (or probably earlier, since the timing of Operation Ivy was determined by the availability of the much more complicated Mike device). Therefore the explosion of Joe 4 would have meant that the U.S.S.R. had caught up with but not surpassed the U.S. insofar as the capability of producing enormous damage in a single explosion was concerned.

Then what would have happened? From that point the Russians might conceivably still have gone on to produce their multimegaton explosion in

November, 1955, but I think it is very probable that they would not have done so until much later. In the actual world they had the powerful stimulus of knowing from our November 1952 test that there was some much better, probably novel way of designing hydrogen bombs so as to produce much larger explosions than the one they demonstrated in their August 1953 experiment. A careful analysis of the radioactive fallout from the Mike explosion may well have provided them with useful information concerning how to go about it. In the hypothetical world where the U.S. would have followed the Oppenheimer-Lilienthal advice that stimulus and information would have been absent. Moreover, a comparison of the way nuclear-weapons technology advanced in the U.S. and the U.S.S.R. during that period makes it seem likely there would have been a much longer delay—probably some years—before they took that big and novel a step without such stimuli and information. Therefore in the most probable alternative world the first Russian superbomb test would have been delayed until well after the first American superbomb test (in other words, delayed until 1957 or 1958), whereas in the worst plausible alternative world it would have occurred just when it did in the actual world: in August, 1955.

What would the U.S. have done in the meantime?

It would have been known immediately that the Russian explosion of August, 1953, was partly thermonuclear and that this test was many times as big as the Russians' previous explosions. If one assumes that following this Russian test the American program in the worst plausible world would have gone along just as it did in the actual world following President Truman's 1950 decision, then the U.S. would have set off the Mike explosion in April, 1956. A simple duplication of those earlier events at this later time, however, would have been unlikely. Any analysis of U.S. reactions to technological advances by the U.S.S.R. shows that the detection of the August 1953 event would have resulted in the initiation of a very large, high-priority American program to produce a bigger and better thermonuclear device. Such a program would undoubtedly have had broader support than the one actually mounted in the spring of 1950. Moreover, the general scientific and technological situation in which a hydrogen-bomb program would have been embedded in 1953 would have been significantly different from the actual one in 1950. For one thing, the kind of theoretical work in progress on the Super before President Truman's decision would have continued and would have provided a solider base from which to launch a crash program. In addition the booster program would presumably have continued along the path already set for it in 1948 (which included a test of the principle in 1951), and therefore in 1953 there would have been available some real experimental information concerning thermonuclear reactions on a smaller scale.

Last but not least, there had been great progress in computer technology between 1950 and 1953. When the real Mike test was being planned, fast electronic computers such as MANIAC and the first UNIVAC either were not quite operating or were in the early stages of their operating career. By a year or so later they were in full running order and much experience had been gained in their utilization, so that they would have been much more effective in connection with any hypothetical post–Joe 4 American crash program. For all these reasons it is plausible to assume that the U.S. would have arrived at something like the Teller-Ulam design for a multimegaton superbomb either in the same length of time or, even more likely, in a somewhat shorter period, say sometime between September, 1955, and April, 1956.

These dates bracket the actual date when the Russians arrived at roughly the same point in the actual world. A few months' difference either way at that stage of the program, however, would not have been meaningful. It takes quite a long time, typically several years, to go from the proof of a prototype to the deployment of a significantly large number of weapons based on it. Differences in production capacity would have played a much more important role than any small advantage in the date of the first experiment, and such differences as then existed surely favored the U.S. Hence even in the worst plausible alternative world the nuclear balance would not have been upset. Moreover, in the most probable alternative world the date the Russians would have arrived at that stage would have been delayed until well after the first large U.S. Mike-like explosion had showed them there was a better way; thus in this most probable case the U.S. would still have enjoyed a substantial lead.

In short, the common notion that has persisted since late 1949 that some sort of disaster would have resulted from following the Oppenheimer-Lilienthal advice is in retrospect almost surely wrong. Moreover, even if by some unlikely quirk of fate the Russians had achieved the Superbomb first, the large stock of fission bombs in the U.S. arsenal, together with the 500-kiloton all-fission bomb for those few cases where it would have been appropriate, would have adequately ensured the national security of the U.S.

This history and the conjectures about possible alternative pasts show that Op-

J. ROBERT OPPENHEIMER AND EDWARD TELLER met at a Washington reception in 1963. Behind the two men is Glenn T. Seaborg, who was then chairman of the AEC. At the left is Oppenheimer's wife. Oppenheimer had just received the Fermi Award of the AEC. Ten years earlier, in the aftermath of the secret debate over whether or not the U.S. should proceed with the development of the hydrogen bomb, he had been banned from all Government work by virtue of the fact that his security clearance had been removed. Teller had been a leading advocate of the development of the hydrogen bomb from the early 1940's. The General Advisory Committee of the AEC, of which Oppenheimer was chairman, had recommended in 1949 that the U.S. not initiate an "all-out" effort to develop the Super.

penheimer, Conant, Fermi, Rabi and the others were right in their advice about the Super, and that they were right for the right reasons. They had correctly assessed the relative technological state of affairs, correctly judged the margin of safety inherent in the situation and correctly projected the ability of the U.S. to catch up rapidly if that should become necessary. The national security of the U.S. did not require the initiation of a high-priority program to develop the Super. It was therefore entirely appropriate to attempt to use the first Russian atomic explosion as a lever for reopening the entire question of nuclear-arms control.

The authors of the report could not, of course, predict the details of the alternative chronologies outlined above, and they did not try to do so, but they could and did correctly assess the general situation and the limits of the probable futures inherent in it. The large rate of production of fissionable material already in effect, the planned expansion in that rate, the resulting immense stock of fission weapons forecast for the early and middle 1950's and the existence of an entirely adequate means for delivering those weapons guaranteed that even the sudden surprise introduction of a few superbombs by the U.S.S.R. could not really upset the balance of power. The situation was reinforced by the projection, which proved to be correct in the King shot, that if need be the power of the World War II fission bombs could be multiplied up to the megaton range simply by more astutely employing the techniques and materials already known and available.

In the course of presenting its general admonition not to proceed with the crash development of the Super, the Oppenheimer committee made certain specific predictions about it. An examination of these predictions shows that they stood the test of time fairly well.

In their discussion of the superbomb the committee members said that "an imaginative and concerted attack on the problem has a better than even chance of producing the weapon within five years." Four years and four months later Bravo, the first practical American thermonuclear weapon, was tested at Bikini. Given the unknowns and uncertainties existing at the time, that is a remarkably accurate prediction. They went on to say that "once the problem of initiation has been solved, there is no upper limit...except that imposed by requirements of delivery." That also seems to be the case. The largest bomb exploded so far (by the Russians in 1961) is said to have been some 58 megatons, four times the size of Bravo, and there is every reason to believe bombs could indeed be made even larger than that.

The report also said that there "appears to be no experimental approach short of an actual test which will add to our conviction that a given model will or will not work" and that "many tests may be required before a workable model has been evolved." History has borne out the first part of the prediction. A quarter of a century had to pass and other inventions had to be made before thermonuclear explosions were produced on a laboratory scale by means of lasers, and even those are probably not closely relevant to the superbomb problem. The second part of the prediction turned out to be less precise. The number of U.S. tests needed to develop and check out a bomb was three: George, Mike and Bravo. The Russians needed only two tests, but they had an invaluable piece of information that was not available to the American workers: the sure knowledge that both small and large thermonuclear explosions were really possible. These numbers were very probably smaller than the "many" the Oppenheimer committee had in mind, but even so they were in each case sufficient to provide the other side with an adequate early warning that thermonuclear work was in progress.

Another interesting and perceptive technological prediction is contained in the report's statement about "very grave contamination problems which can easily be made more acute...by surrounding the deuterium with uranium." The very high levels of radioactive fallout associated with large hydrogen bombs do in fact result from such use of uranium. The very first test of a practical superbomb, Bravo, produced a blanket of fallout that evidently contributed to the death of one innocent bystander (the radioman of the *Fortunate Dragon*, a Japanese fishing ship) and came within a hair's breadth of killing hundreds of Marshall Islanders living on two nearby atolls. The fallout accident in turn provided the initial spark behind the movement to ban nuclear-weapons tests that ultimately led to the Partial Test-Ban Treaty of 1963.

The foregoing account is, I think, enough to show that the Oppenheimer committee's advice was sound, but it may not be enough to show unequivocally that President Truman should have taken this sound advice. The President, unlike the AEC commissioners and their advisers, had to take into account a broader array of information and political ideas than those discussed in detail here. The overall intensity of the cold war was increasing, Mao Tse-tung and Joseph Stalin had proclaimed the Sino-Soviet bloc and many important Republicans were withdrawing or modifying their support of the bipartisan foreign and military policies that had been in effect since the beginning of World War II. As the fall of 1949 wore on and the arguments about the Super began to leak out from behind the curtain of secrecy, those opinions favoring the Super were, in the overall context of the time, both simpler and more widely persuasive than those opposing it. There can be little doubt that Congressional and public opinion was beginning to come down heavily on the side of a strong response to the first Russian atomic-bomb test, and building the Super seemed to many to be just the kind of thing to keep the Russians in their place. President Truman, a professional politician, could therefore have concluded that rejecting the Super and running even a small risk of being second best was politically too difficult an alternative. Moreover, his decision to proceed with the Super, made on January 31, 1950, was based on the advice of the special committee of the National Security Council charged with studying the matter. Those committee members responsible for international relations (Secretary of State Dean Acheson) and national defense (Secretary of Defense Louis A. Johnson) strongly supported going ahead; the only reservations were expressed by the one committee member who was not responsible for those elements of national-security policy, namely Lilienthal, chairman of the AEC.

Nonetheless, it now seems clear to me in retrospect that President Truman should have taken the advice of the Oppenheimer committee; he should have held back on initiating the development of the Super while making another serious try to achieve international control over all nuclear arms, particularly the Super. The benefits that could have flowed from forestalling the Super altogether were incalculable; the chances of succeeding in doing so were small, but so were the risks in trying. It was certainly one of the few opportunities, and as Lilienthal said then, it may have been the last good opportunity to base American foreign policy on something better than reliance on weapons of mass destruction or, as it is now phrased, on the prospect of "mutual assured destruction."

The Great Test-Ban Debate

by Herbert F. York
November 1972

The trend of events in weaponry and in arms control tends to refute arguments presented a decade ago against a limited nuclear-test ban and to indicate that the time may be ripe for a comprehensive test ban

The modest but significant progress toward the control of nuclear weapons that has been made during the past nine years has brought to the fore the question that was raised in the first place: Is the time ripe for a treaty prohibiting all tests of nuclear weapons? Indeed, both the limited-test-ban treaty of 1963 and the nonproliferation treaty of 1968 contain clauses obligating the signatories to seek to achieve a treaty establishing a comprehensive ban. The issue is therefore being debated again [see "National Security and the Nuclear-Test Ban," by J. B. Wiesner and H. F. York, on page 129]. This time, however, it is possible to employ hindsight to sharpen foresight, because most of the arguments being made against a comprehensive test ban now are essentially the same as the ones that were put

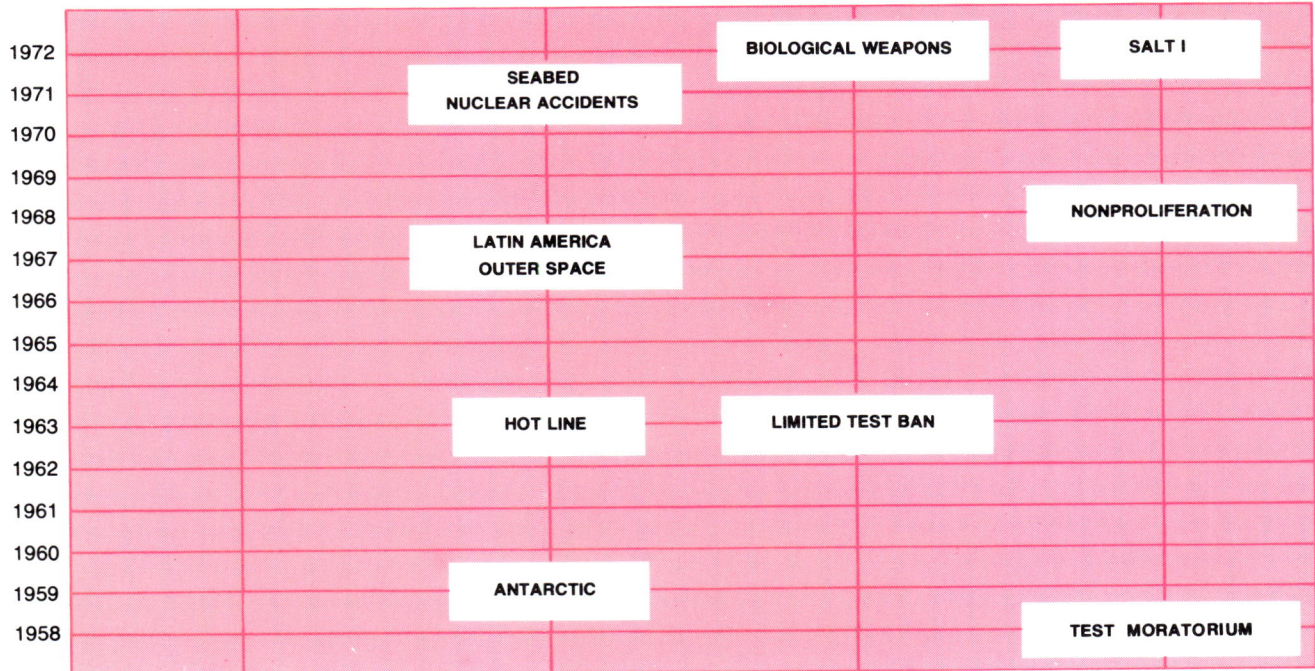

CHRONOLOGY OF ARMS-CONTROL AGREEMENTS adopted since 1958 is traced. The test moratorium lasted only from 1958 to 1961, but the work that went into it and the climate that it created provided the basis for all the other agreements. SALT stands for strategic-arms-limitation talks, which were conducted between the U.S. and the U.S.S.R. for more than two years and culminated in the agreements of last May limiting the deployment of antiballistic-missile systems and freezing strategic offensive missiles.

forward in the long debate preceding the adoption of the limited test ban. An examination of how those arguments look in the light of experience will help to supply a basis for estimating how much weight they should be given in the present debate.

The questions involved are of two general types. One type has to do with the means for monitoring a test ban to ensure that the signatories are complying with the treaty. That subject was recently reviewed in these pages [see "Extending the Nuclear-Test Ban," by Henry R. Myers, the article beginning on page 283]. The other type has to do with the potential effects of a test ban on the national security of the parties to a treaty or any other agreement. I shall limit my discussion to questions of this type.

In the debates of a decade and more ago (from 1957 to 1963, to be more precise) the national-security matters most frequently raised by people who opposed or seriously questioned the test ban came under the following general headings: anti-ballistic-missile (ABM) systems, weapons effects, pure fusion bombs, improvement of the yield-to-weight ratio of nuclear weapons and new knowledge, possibly involving military surprises. Let us review the arguments and the subsequent developments under each heading.

In the early 1960's claims were made by Russian officials that the U.S.S.R. had solved the problem of intercepting and destroying incoming ballistic missiles. Not long afterward U.S. intelligence activity discovered that the Russians were indeed beginning to deploy an ABM system. Moreover, the extensive series of nuclear tests conducted by the Russians during 1961 and 1962 had included explosions at altitudes that would be of interest to designers of an ABM system. The U.S. had also conducted a number of high-altitude tests, leading certain scientists and military officials to assert that this country had enough knowledge to design an ABM system. Secretary of Defense Robert S. McNamara and other high officials did not agree, however, and so no ABM-system deployment was then authorized in this country.

Opponents of a test ban contended that the reason for the difference between the Russian decision to deploy and the U.S. decision not to deploy must be that the Russians knew something we did not know. They suggested that this something had been discovered during the Russian test series. Some opponents went on to speculate that the reason the Russians were now willing to consider a test ban was that they had learned some essential secret and saw the test ban as a way of preventing the U.S. from learning it.

For example, the physicist Edward Teller said: "I think there is a disparity in knowledge, and the disparity of knowledge today means a disparity of power tomorrow.... I believe that, because they have acquired this knowledge, they don't need any more atmospheric tests, and I believe that is why Khrushchev is willing to sign the treaty at present." Senator Strom Thurmond said: "All it will take to put the Soviets in a dominant nuclear position is two

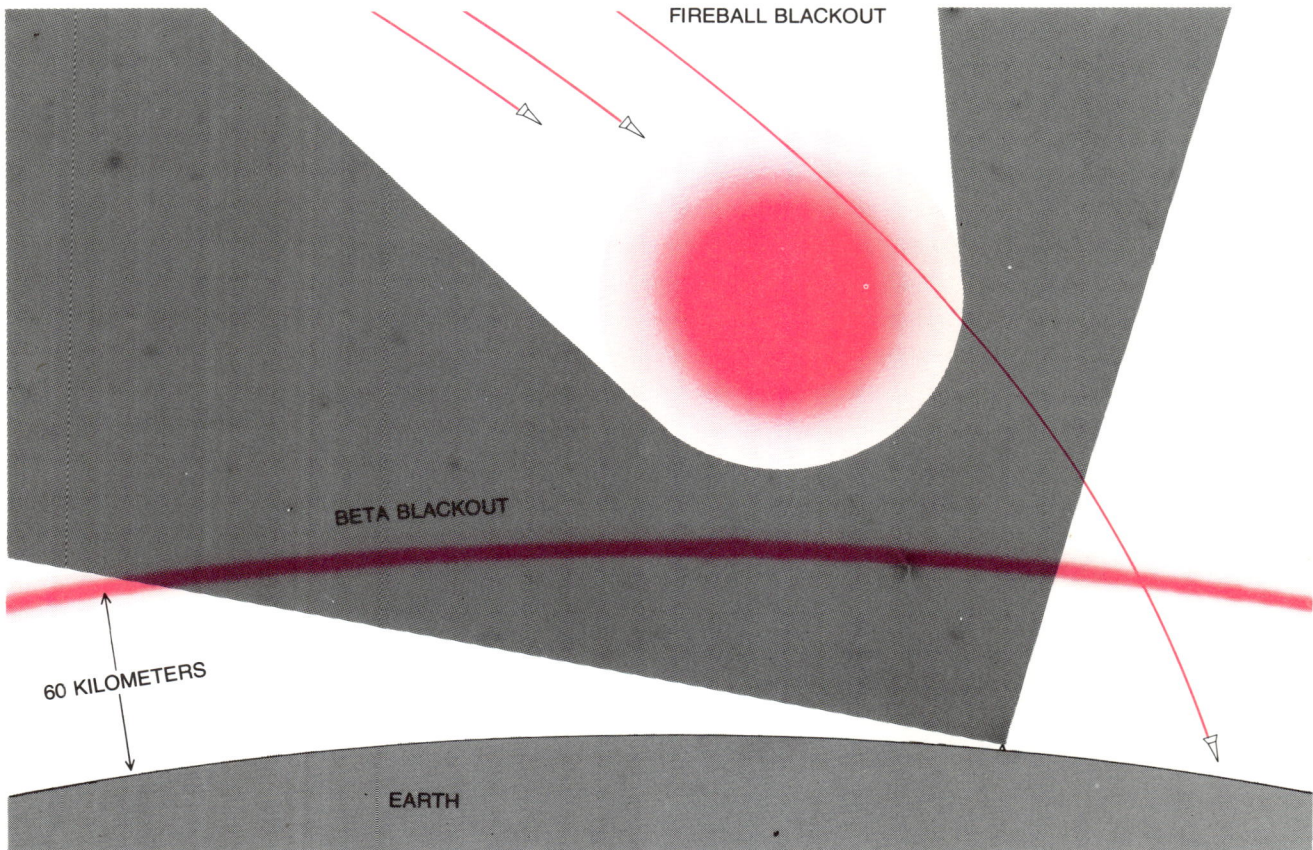

BLACKOUT PHENOMENON was a possibility raised as an argument against the limited test ban. The concern was that a nuclear explosion at high altitude would produce ionized air that would for a time be opaque to the defender's radar. "Fireball blackout" would result when heat from the explosion stripped electrons from air molecules, and "beta blackout" would result from electrons released in the decay of fission products. Continued testing was said to be needed to produce a defensive missile system that could withstand such effects. The difficulty of creating any adequate antimissile system has made the blackout argument peripheral.

things: one, enough time to build up a stockpile of the already perfected Red antimissile missile, which will render our huge arsenal of ICBM's [intercontinental ballistic missiles] useless, and second, ratification of the test-ban treaty that will prevent the United States from high-altitude tests necessary for completion of our own Nike X antimissile-missile program, thereby leaving America defenseless against Red missiles."

When pressed for details, the opponents of the test ban commonly referred to several matters on which, they said, insufficient information existed, at least in the U.S. One matter was the blackout phenomenon, in which a nuclear explosion at high altitude produces a large volume of ionized air that is for a time opaque to radar. There were also allusions to certain long-range "kill" mechanisms that would work against incoming warheads. Here it was argued that tests were needed in order to design defensive warheads that would produce such effects and offensive warheads that would survive the effects.

On the other side of the argument it was contended that the U.S.S.R. had not gained any special advantage due to some private knowledge about high-altitude effects. Harold Brown, who was then Director of Defense Research and Engineering, said: "I feel rather strongly that they [the Russians] are not substantially ahead of us." He added that it was not a defect in nuclear knowledge that had prevented the U.S. from deploying ABM systems but rather that "the U.S. decided not to deploy the Nike Zeus because its effectiveness was inadequate against U.S. penetration aids...and we assume the same would be true of the Soviet penetration-aid capability." The U.S. Joint Chiefs of Staff said that "development of the U.S. [ABM] system does not depend on atmospheric testing and hence this treaty will not significantly influence any imbalance that may exist."

What have subsequent events revealed about these claims and predictions? The Russian ABM program proceeded erratically from the base described in 1963. After several periods of delay that indicated indecision and uncertainty, the Moscow ABM system (now called the Galosh system) was reported early this year to have fewer than 100 ABM vehicles ready for launching. The system was generally judged to be quite inadequate for coping with an attack against it by U.S. missiles. Russian ABM installations that had at one time been reported around Leningrad and Tallinn either were dismantled or turned out to have a different purpose. Nothing that has happened since the test-ban debate has confirmed the notion that the U.S.S.R. knew something the U.S. did not know. Indeed, the Russian decision to deploy the Galosh system seems to have been due to a poor understanding of just how easy it is to penetrate systems of that type and size.

On the U.S. side the development of an ABM system continued through the 1960's at a level of about $500 million per year. The system slowly evolved, as did the political situation both domestically and internationally. Finally, near the end of the Johnson Administration, a decision was made to deploy an ABM

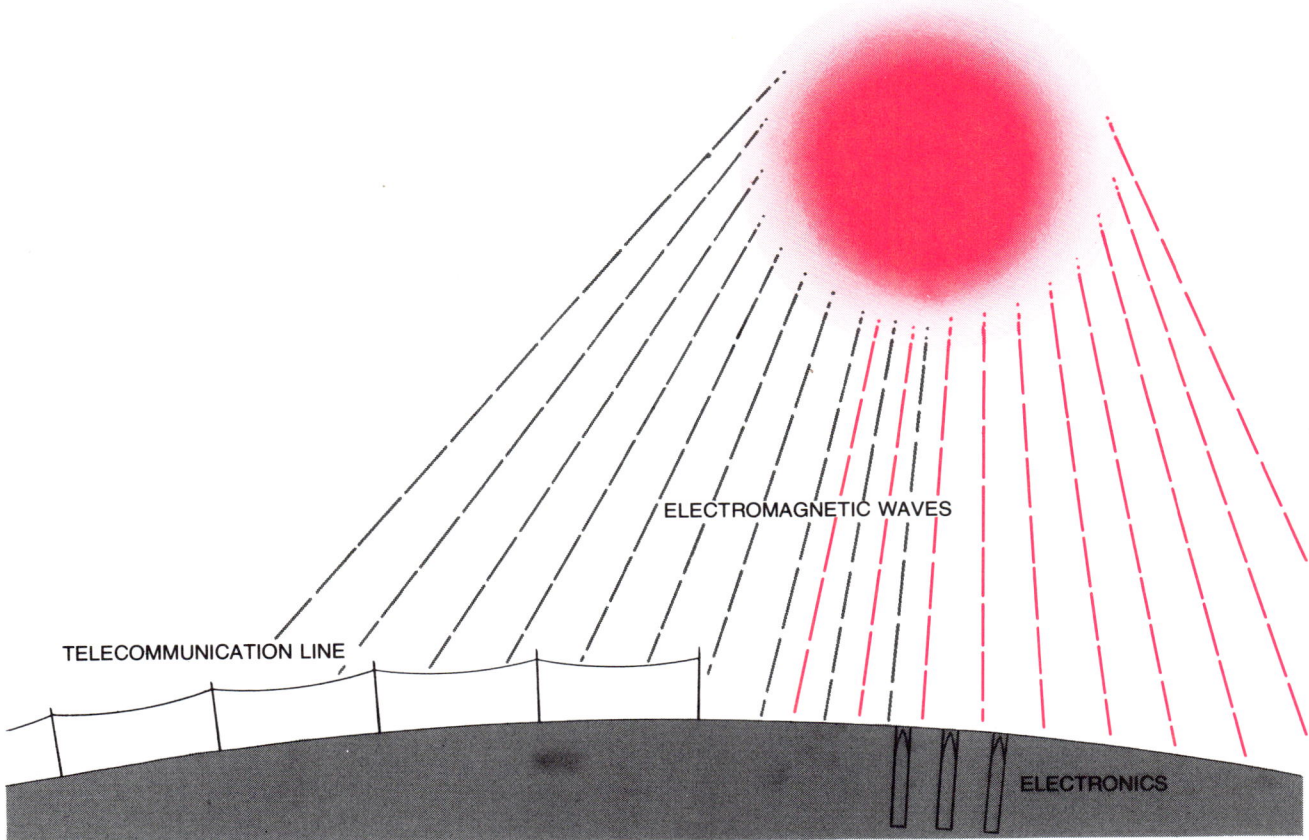

"TREE" AND "EMP" PHENOMENA have been raised as arguments for continued testing. TREE stands for transient radiation effects on electronics, and EMP stands for electromagnetic pulse. They both arise from nuclear explosions. The phenomena can disrupt electrical communications on the ground and can cause electronic equipment on missiles to malfunction. In this "pin-down" tactic the defending nation supposedly could not launch its missiles. The weakness of the argument is that the tactic would be ineffective in view of the large variety of retaliatory weapons that would be available to the defender and the extent of their dispersal.

system called Sentinel around certain cities. The main reason given was that it would provide protection against a prospective Chinese missile force.

After considerable public reaction this decision was rescinded, and a deployment of the same equipment under a new name (Safeguard) was proposed by the Nixon Administration. The Senate accepted the proposal after a long debate about the effectiveness of the system and the problems being met in developing it. In the entire debate developments in nuclear weaponry were never cited as having a crucial role in the various decisions concerning deployment. The serious questions that were raised about the feasibility of the system all had to do with such matters as the computers, the radar and the problems posed by decoys and MIRV's (multiple independently targetable reentry vehicles). When nuclear problems such as blackout were mentioned, it was only peripherally and never as constituting a major problem.

None of this proves that nuclear-weapons development and weapons-effect research are entirely irrelevant to ABM development, but it does indicate that recent research and development in this field have been far from essential. Apparently any lack of perfection in weapons can be overcome in the design of other parts of the system. Moreover, as the ABM program has shifted from Sentinel to Safeguard and now to the site-defense system (sometimes called Hardsite), the emphasis has shifted from interception at great distances and high altitudes to interception near the target at relatively low altitudes, where the phenomena to be dealt with are much better known.

I turn now to weapons effects. During the years when nuclear weapons were tested aboveground, the basic effects—blast, radiation, fallout—that kill, injure and destroy were studied in great detail. These are the weapons effects that matter; the entire concept of deterrence, which all sides cite as the main reason for maintaining nuclear forces, is based wholly on the threat of unacceptable levels of death and destruction through these effects. For decades the phenomenology of these effects has been known with a precision that far exceeds the practical use of the information.

In addition to these basic phenomena one hears of a few other more exotic effects that are of technical interest in connection with certain duels between nuclear weapons. Uncertainties about such effects are sometimes raised as an issue in test-ban debates. Among the effects are "TREE" and "EMP."

TREE stands for transient radiation effects on electronics. It is an old problem that has become relatively more important as more complex devices have been introduced into nuclear-weapons systems. It is also mainly of interest in connection with duels in outer space, where there is nothing to attenuate radiation, which therefore would far outreach other effects such as blast.

EMP stands for electromagnetic pulse. It refers to the fact that a nuclear explosion produces a large electromagnetic field, which in turn can induce large electric currents in conductors at substantial distances. Such currents, if nothing is done about them, can sometimes produce destructive effects in insufficiently protected equipment.

Some of the people who work on nuclear weapons have envisioned an attack in which an enemy explodes a series of warheads high over U.S. missile fields, producing a series of TREE and EMP phenomena (or other long-range effects) timed in such a way that the U.S. could not launch its missiles while the barrage continued. (The tactic is known as "pin-down.")

It is impossible to believe that real political or military leaders would consider such an effort in the face of the variety and dispersion of retaliatory weapons that could be employed. Even so, the claim that further research was

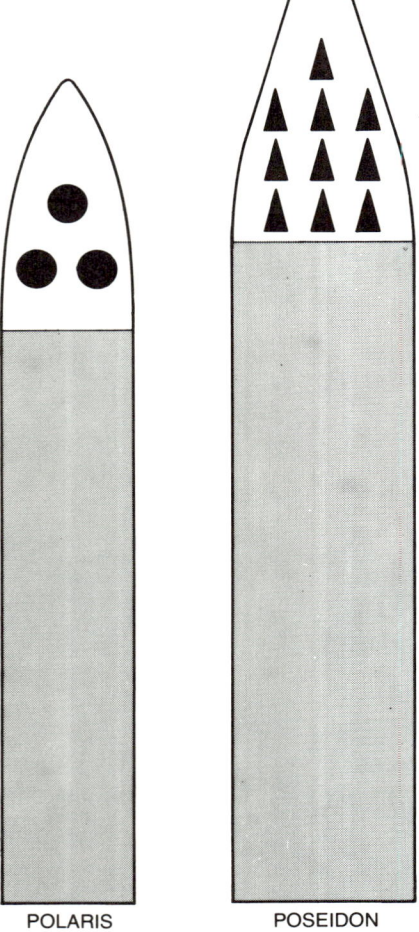

POLARIS AND POSEIDON missiles are compared. The older Polaris has three reentry vehicles that are not independently targetable, whereas the Poseidon has 10 MIRV's (multiple independently targetable reentry vehicles). It has been said that the Poseidon warhead could not have been developed under a comprehensive test ban. The author argues that the Polaris warhead could have well been adapted for the Poseidon missile.

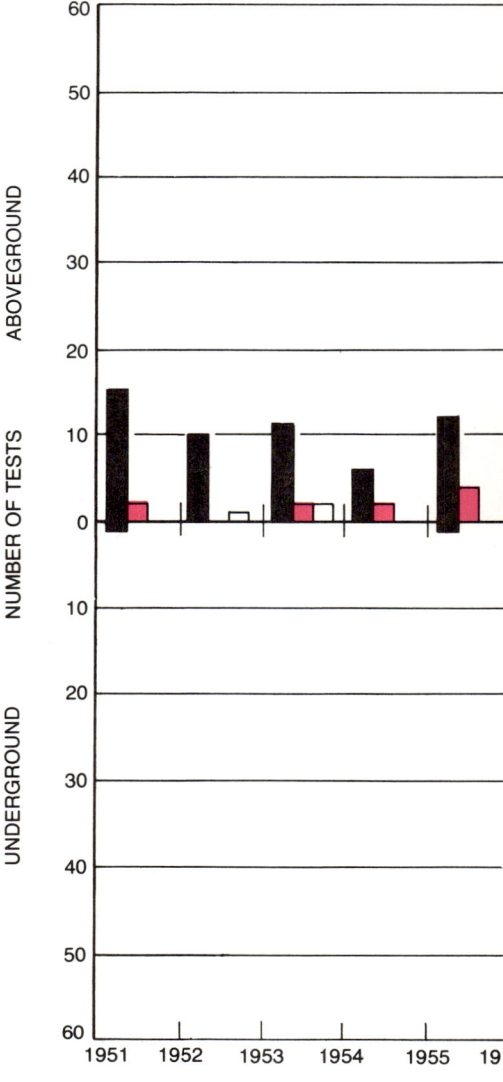

NUCLEAR TESTING by the U.S. (black), the U.S.S.R. (color) and all other nations

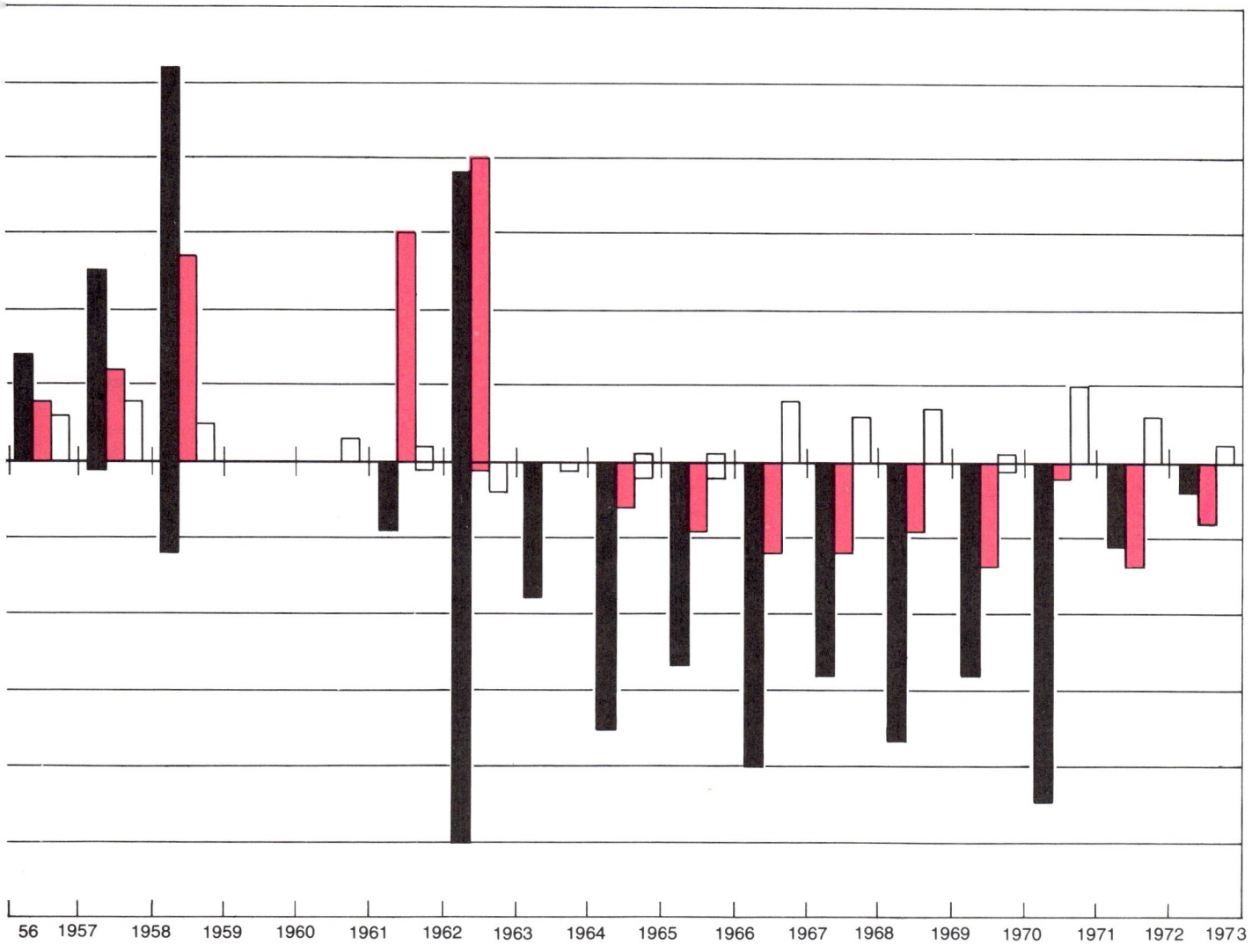

(*open bars*) is charted from 1951 to the fall of 1972. The gap near the center reflects the moratorium on testing nuclear weapons from 1958 to 1961. The figures were obtained from various sources by the Stockholm International Peace Research Institute (SIPRI).

needed on this matter was advanced in the early 1960's as an argument against the test ban. (At the time the argument was largely conducted behind the curtain of secrecy that surrounds much military activity; public discussion of the issue became possible only later.)

All the more exotic effects were observed before the partial test ban went into effect. They were not as thoroughly studied as the basic effects, however, and in addition certain new forms of interaction between these phenomena and specific weapons systems have been found since 1963. At first it was thought that it would be difficult to learn more about the exotic effects in underground explosions, and that possibility was raised as an argument against the partial test ban. Later it turned out that a good deal can be learned about the effects from underground testing and by other means. In 1968 Vice-Admiral Lloyd M. Mustin, director of the Defense Atomic Support Agency, reported to Congress: "We think we have the interaction of threats with these two systems [Minuteman and Polaris] well understood and identified and very carefully developed and sophisticated countermeasures far advanced."

In sum, no really new phenomena produced by the explosion of nuclear weapons has been discovered in about 15 years, and there is no good reason to expect that any will be forthcoming. In those years the U.S. has refined its knowledge of the effects of specific systems and in specific environmental situations. Even at that level of detail we have long since passed the point of diminishing returns. The remaining uncertainties are small compared with the other uncertainties about any nuclear attack: the kind, number, yield and accuracy of the weapons; the targets selected; the timing, the relation to other attacks or to political moves, and so on. These are the uncertainties that will dominate the thinking of any statesman who may one day be considering the use of nuclear weapons. No doubt there is more to be learned about weapons effects, but the matter is largely of interest to specialists, and concern about it should have no bearing on important political questions such as whether or not to ban further nuclear tests.

Pure-fusion bombs and bombs with a high ratio of fusion to fission (also called neutron bombs) were seen in the late 1950's as offering a number of ad-

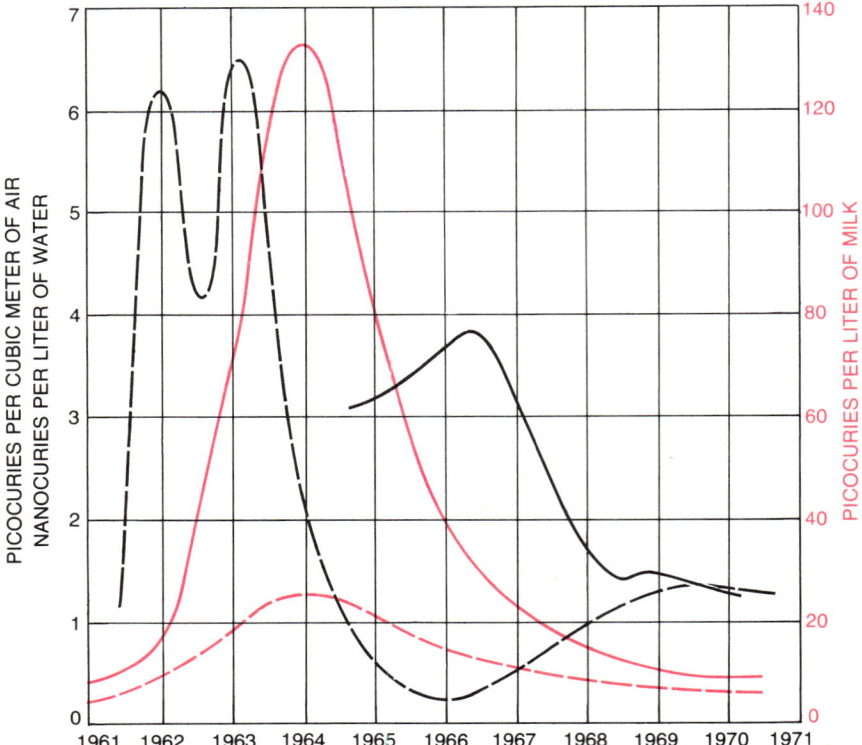

RADIOACTIVE FALLOUT has declined since nuclear testing by the U.S. and the U.S.S.R. has been done underground as a result of the limited test ban. The chart, based on data from the U.S. Environmental Protection Agency, shows gross beta radiation in the air (*broken black curve*), tritium in water (*solid black curve*), strontium 90 in milk (*broken colored curve*) and cesium 137 in milk (*solid colored curve*). Some of the radioactivity is natural.

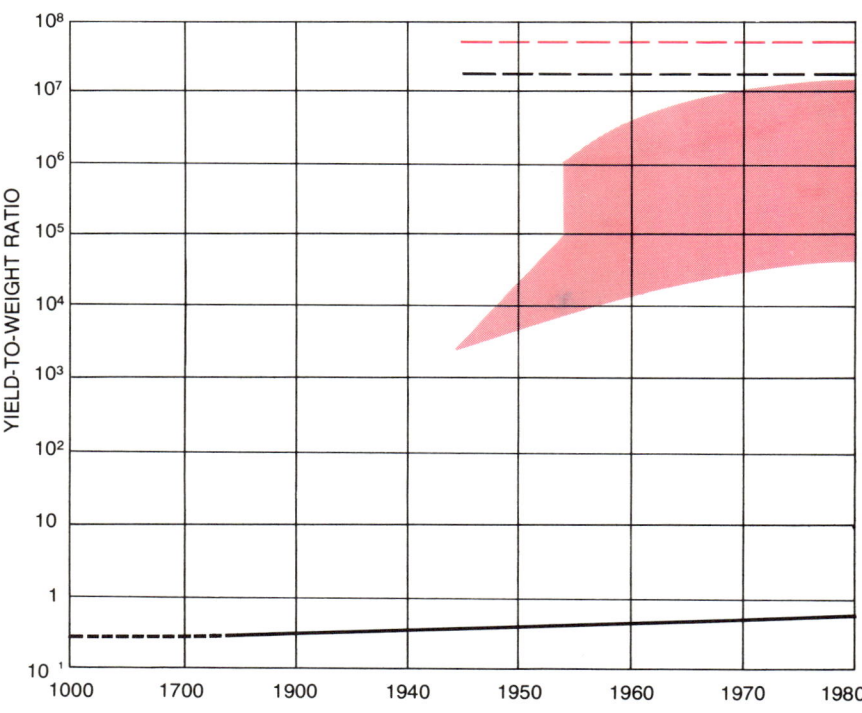

RATIO of yield to weight of nuclear weapons (*colored band*) and conventional weapons (*black line*) is charted. Lower part of nuclear-weapon band represents fission bombs; upper part, thermonuclear bombs. Broken lines represent theoretical maximum for fusion (*color*) and fission (*black*). The slowness of the rise in recent years is due in part to emphasis on other matters such as dimensions and decreasing vulnerability to nearby explosions.

vantages, and the need to develop them was therefore raised as an argument against a test ban. Teller, for example, was reported to have said to a Republican committee on nuclear testing in 1963: "We have started the development of clean and cheap nuclear explosives. We need more tests to complete this development. Clean and cheap nuclear explosives are needed for battlefield use, for peaceful applications and for missile defense." John A. Wheeler of Princeton University was reported as telling the same group: "As a physicist and specialist on nuclear fission I see a decisive loss to national security from a test ban. It will prevent us from developing a technology of pure hydrogen devices free of fission fallout.... The new technology will have important peacetime applications in mining and earth-moving and will revolutionize ground warfare. ... It is unconscionable to renounce for the free world a revolutionary device which others will then make without our knowledge."

On the other side, William C. Foster, director of the U.S. Arms Control and Disarmament Agency, said that the expert advice he had received was that pure-fusion weapons would not be of great advantage. The reason, he said, was that "they would constitute primarily a cheaper substitute for the explosive components in our already large stockpile of nuclear weapons."

How did matters turn out? The pure-fusion bomb remains undeveloped, and responsible people no longer talk much about it as being the basis of a new revolution in weaponry. When officials of the Department of Defense and the Atomic Energy Commission present arguments for continued testing now, they do not rate the need for fission-free bombs any higher than the need for other and more orthodox modifications and improvements.

A pure-fusion explosion may yet be achieved as a result of all the effort that has been expended. It would be a technological accomplishment, but the likelihood that it would have any large military or political value seems small. The basic fact is that the nuclear capability of the major nuclear powers is already supersaturated in the sense that it can produce more varieties of death, destruction and horror than anyone can seriously contemplate seeking to inflict.

It was also stated during the debate preceding the test ban of 1963 that further improvement in the yield-to-weight ratio of nuclear weapons was in prospect and that certain other improvements and modifications were both possible and necessary. Among them were decreased vulnerability to nearby nuclear explosions and increased safety of weapons. Substantial progress has indeed been made along these lines since 1963. The important question, however, is: How important and how relevant has the progress been?

The Poseidon missile provides a basis for discussion. It is more advanced than its predecessor, the Polaris A-3, in many ways. It is bigger, it can carry a larger payload a longer distance and it has improved accuracy. Moreover, its payload is of the MIRV type: each missile launches a "bus," which has on board a large number of reentry missiles, each of which can be accurately and independently targeted. None of these advances depended on nuclear tests.

M. Carl Walske, Jr., assistant to the Secretary of Defense for Atomic Energy, recently stated that the warhead for the Poseidon MIRV was developed after the limited test ban went into effect, and he argued that if the ban had been comprehensive, nothing like the present Poseidon MIRV could have been developed. I believe his statement is highly misleading. If a pre-1963 warhead such as the one for the Polaris A-3 had been adapted for the Poseidon, the Poseidon MIRV would have had either lower multiplicity (fewer independent missiles) or a shorter range, but it could have had a higher total yield.

Presumably the new Poseidon warhead has been further modified so as to reduce its vulnerability to attempts to intercept it. These modifications apparently resulted in a reduction of the yield-to-weight ratio. In any case such modifications were superfluous, since the basic multiple-warhead feature is in itself the most effective means for penetrating anti-ballistic-missile defenses of the kind that now exist. It does so simply by overwhelming the defense with larger numbers. The only requirement is that the individual warheads be hardened enough and separated enough so that one interceptor must be launched for each reentry vehicle. An A-3 warhead on a MIRV bus of the Poseidon type would easily satisfy this requirement.

Defense penetrability beyond what could be achieved in 1963 is needed only against an ABM defense consisting of very large numbers of relatively sophisticated interceptors. No such defense now exists—nor, I believe, is there any serious prospect of one in the foreseeable future. To say the least, deployment of the post-1963 Poseidon warhead is premature.

It is small wonder that the concern over surprises and new knowledge persists. One need only recall the early years of nuclear development to realize that surprises and new knowledge abounded at that time. The phenomenon of nuclear fission was discovered in 1938. The first nuclear-test device was exploded only seven years later, which was also the first (and so far the only) time that nuclear bombs were employed in warfare. In terms of energy output those bombs

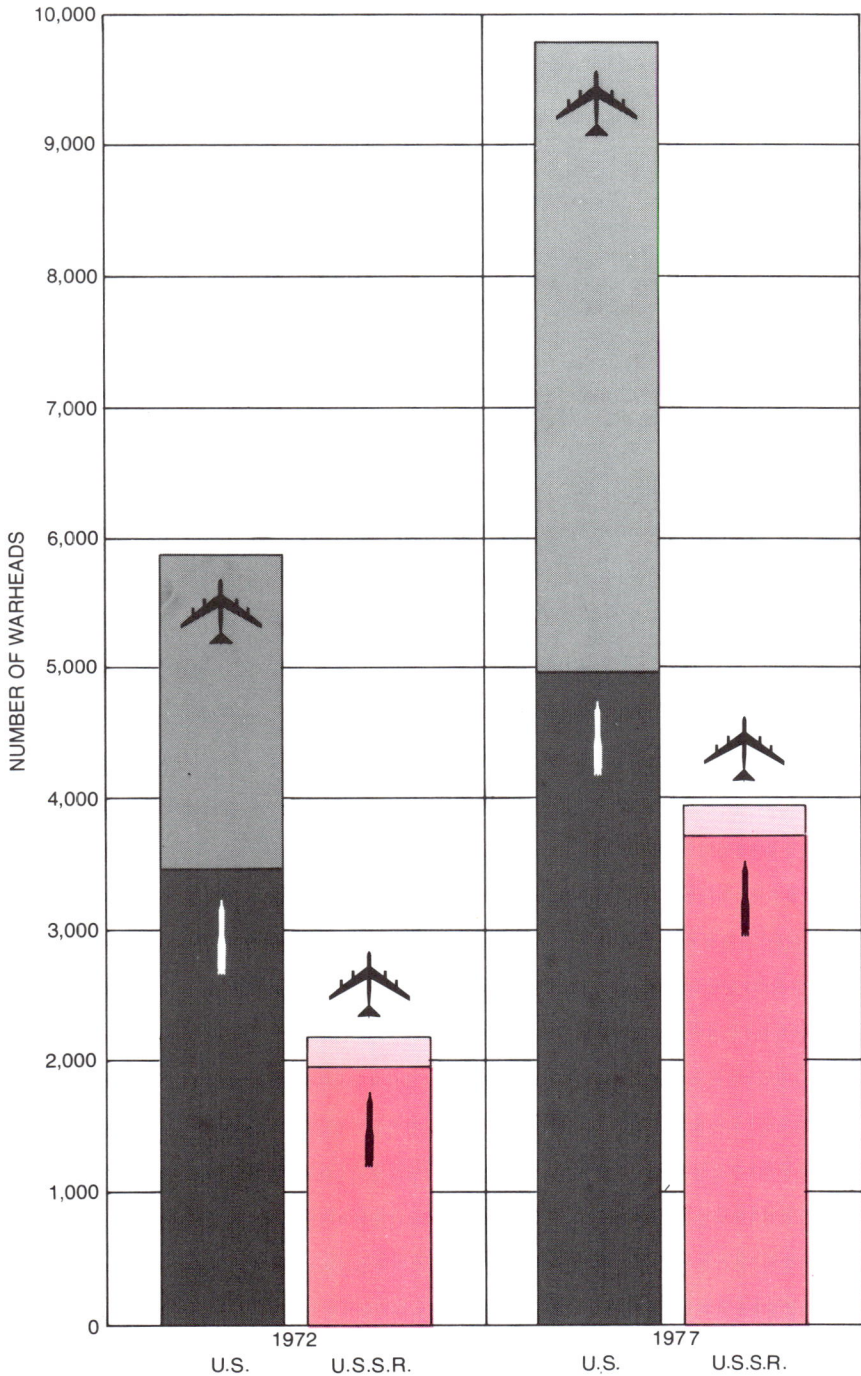

BALANCE OF POWER between the U.S. and the U.S.S.R. is charted in terms of nuclear warheads in 1972 and 1977, the end of the period for which the SALT I agreements are to remain in effect. The missile symbol represents missile-launched warheads and the airplane symbol represents bomber-launched missiles. The chart is based on data from the U.S. Arms Control and Disarmament Agency, which points out that the U.S. has more but smaller missiles than the U.S.S.R. and that the megatonnage represented is approximately equal.

were 1,000 times larger than the biggest chemical bombs.

Seven years later the first thermonuclear device was exploded. It was 1,000 times as large in output of energy as the first atomic bombs. Both of these huge technological steps can be characterized as breakthroughs, and they had major political and military consequences. No such huge gains in yield were made thereafter, but during the next seven years fundamentally important factors such as yield-to-weight ratio continued to improve radically. By 1960 the yield-to-weight ratio of fission bombs was two orders of magnitude (100 times) larger than it had been at the beginning. Means also had been found for both reducing the size and increasing the yield-to-weight ratio of thermonuclear weapons, again by order-of-magnitude amounts.

As a result of such developments many people came to believe politically significant technological breakthroughs had become the norm for nuclear technology. One thus finds many leaders in the field emphasizing the likelihood and importance of further technological surprises and arguing that no bars should be raised against obtaining new knowledge. In 1963, questioning the limited-test-ban treaty, John S. Foster, Jr., then director of the Lawrence Radiation Laboratory (he is now director of defense research and engineering in the Department of Defense), said: "We are involved in a field of technology that is not fully understood, nor its applications, and hence new experiments frequently bring surprises." Teller said a ban would "prohibit future science" and was "directed against knowledge." In 1961 Representative Chet Holifield, then chairman of the Joint Committee on Atomic Energy, expressed concern about "the ultimate general effect on weapons technology of a continuing test ban," which would "inevitably stifle developments undreamed of at the present time." He added: "Concepts are now being considered by our scientists which could be as revolutionary as the H-bomb [was] in 1949." General Curtis E. LeMay, as Chief of Staff of the U.S. Air Force in 1963, said: "We are just at the beginning of our investigations into the nuclear-weapons field."

On the other side, proponents of a test ban expressed doubt about the importance of specific potential breakthroughs and saw as unlikely the possibility that any such development would upset the balance of power. William Foster of the disarmament agency, supporting the limited test ban, suggested that nuclear science was maturing. "The point of diminishing returns in improving weight-yield ratios is fast approaching," he said.

At the time of the debate on the partial test ban the issue of surprises and new knowledge was still difficult to resolve. On the one hand there was the record of a remarkable series of discoveries, technological advances and politically significant applications. On the other hand no further breakthroughs were then in sight, with the possible exception of the pure-fusion bomb, and of that many experts said it would be technologically novel but without great political or military significance.

Now, however, it seems to me that this issue has been resolved. Nuclear weapons have been further refined, and there is greater understanding of the details of certain effects, but no new knowledge or surprises remotely similar in kind or importance to those of the first two nuclear decades have been reported or claimed. Moreover, the nuclear arsenal is so large and varied that the significance of new inventions is small in any case. Compared with the danger of further proliferation of nuclear weapons, the danger that the U.S. will be overwhelmed by an unsuspected breakthrough seems vanishingly small.

Let us turn now to the arguments that were made in 1963 and earlier in support of the limited test ban. Five principal points were made and can be set forth here in quotations of participants: (1) "A nuclear test ban treaty would constitute a significant step in the

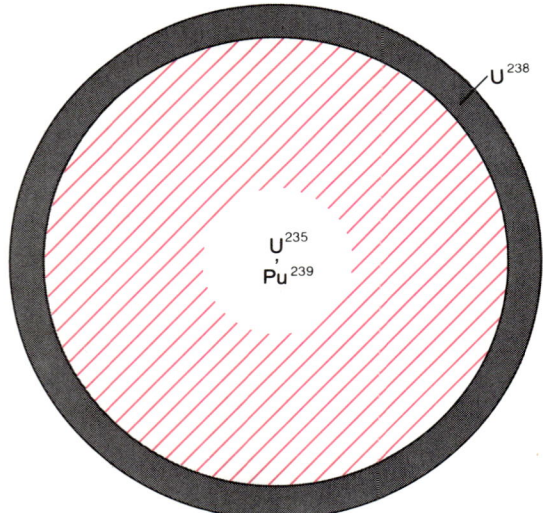 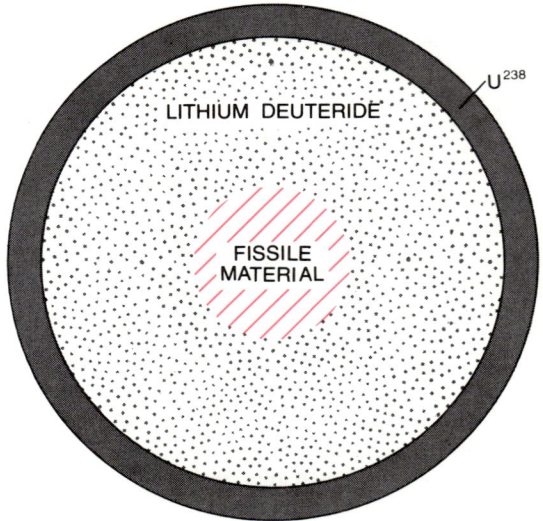

NUCLEAR WEAPONS are depicted schematically. At left a fission bomb is shown just as the nuclear explosion starts. A supercritical mass of fissile material has been rapidly assembled by means of high explosive, which is not shown, and a chain reaction is initiated by a neutron from a source near the mass. The uranium 238 reflects some neutrons and provides some additional inertia but does not otherwise participate importantly in the reaction. The drawing of a thermonuclear bomb (right) explains its known properties, although no detailed design has ever been made public. Fissile material in the central core explodes, producing much heat and many neutrons. The neutrons convert some of the lithium 6 surrounding the core to tritium, and the heat causes thermonuclear deuterium-deuterium and deuterium-tritium reactions to take place in the lithium deuteride. These reactions in turn produce neutrons having enough energy to cause the surrounding uranium 238 to fission, thus releasing still more energy and additional quantities of neutrons.

direction of slackening the arms race" (Dean Rusk). (2) It would preserve for a "longer period our present nuclear advantage" (William Foster). (3) "The treaty will curb the pollution of the atmosphere" (President Kennedy). (4) It would create a political climate in which "new opportunities for further steps toward turning the arms race downward might well be more within the realm of possibility than at present" (Rusk). (5) "A nuclear test ban would constitute a significant first step in achieving control over the further spread of nuclear weapons" (Foster).

Each of the statements also amounted to a prediction. Let us see how the predictions stand up in 1972. The limited test ban probably did slow down the arms race between the U.S. and the U.S.S.R., but it cannot be considered to have been outstandingly successful in this respect. It probably has severely limited the further development of very large thermonuclear weapons, but the rate of nuclear testing has continued at about the same level—although the tests are now underground.

Similarly, the treaty does not appear to have done much to preserve the "nuclear advantage" of the U.S. Since the treaty was signed, the U.S.S.R. has achieved rough parity with the U.S. in strategic weapons. In any event, the degree of "overkill" in the nuclear capability of both countries is such that further technological advances would make little political or military difference.

The treaty has been quite effective in curbing radioactive pollution of the atmosphere. Although France and China have continued to conduct nuclear tests in the atmosphere, the tests are far less frequent than was the case when the U.S. and the U.S.S.R. were conducting them. Moreover, without the treaty there would be no hope of persuading those nations and other potential nuclear powers to accept similar restraints. Meanwhile, in the absence of a comprehensive test ban such hazards as underground contamination, earthquakes and leakage of radioactive substances into the atmosphere remain possible.

The record of the treaty in creating an environment that made further moves toward arms control possible is excellent. The treaty has been followed by agreements to prohibit nuclear weapons in space (1967), make Latin America a non-nuclear zone (1967), bar further proliferation of nuclear weapons (1968), rule out the seabed for the emplacement of nuclear weapons (1971) and prohibit the use of biological weapons (1972). One might also cite the "hot line" agreements of 1963 and 1971 and the recent strategic-arms-limitation talks (SALT) that resulted in agreement by the U.S. and the U.S.S.R. to put ceilings on their offensive and defensive missiles.

One should also recognize, however, that many of the treaties are peripheral to the main problem and in effect prohibit actions that no nation particularly wanted to undertake anyway. The British disarmament expert Philip J. Noel-Baker, reviewing the results of the 1959 treaty that demilitarized Antarctica, commented that "while disarming Antarctica, we put 7,000 nuclear weapons in Europe; we should have disarmed Europe and put those weapons in Antarctica." Nonetheless, all the agreements are steps in the right direction, and collectively they add up to something significant. Moreover, they help to make arms-control and disarmament measures seem more feasible.

Probably the most important result of the limited test ban has been its contribution to inhibiting the further proliferation of nuclear weapons. Since the treaty was signed, only China has begun testing nuclear weapons, and the Chinese program to develop nuclear weapons had been set in motion long before 1963. The cause was greatly aided by the nonproliferation treaty, which now has some 70 signatories in addition to the original adherents (the U.S., the United Kingdom and the U.S.S.R.). It also seems evident that the treaty has deterred nonsigners from testing.

Indeed, the most important reason for moving now toward a comprehensive ban on testing nuclear weapons is that it would strengthen and reinforce the nonproliferation treaty. The present situation contains elements of hypocrisy and unfairness, since the two major nuclear powers are trying to persuade other nations that nuclear weapons are unnecessary while at the same time both are conducting test programs.

To sum up, a decade of hindsight on the debates preceding the limited-test-ban treaty of 1963 suggests the following main conclusions:

1. The predictions of major surprises and ominous developments were wrong. There has been no "third revolution" in nuclear weapons. The atmospheric tests before 1963 and the underground tests since then have not produced a solution to the problem of developing an ABM system that would be likely to have more than limited success.

2. On the other hand, the passage of

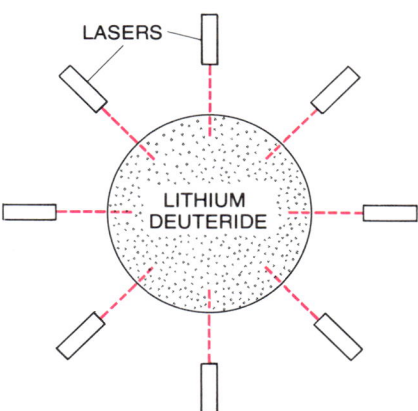

PURE-FUSION BOMB, which has yet to be developed, would entail heating the fusion material without the use of a fission explosion. Lasers could perhaps produce the necessary initial conditions, but the technology seems to be formidable. Achieving such a bomb would be a technological feat, but it seems probable that the achievement would not have any great political or military value beyond the present nuclear bombs.

time has confirmed the more moderate claims that there was substantial progress to be made in improving the yield-to-weight ratio, hardening weapons against interception, making better fits to new delivery systems and so on. The questions to be asked, however, are how progress in these areas has affected the nuclear balance and whether such technical progress is politically significant. The answers seem to be that, if anything, continued testing has further degraded whatever nuclear advantage the U.S. still had in 1963 and that the political significance of nuclear weapons is derived from the huge numbers of such weapons rather than from their technical sophistication.

3. The limited test ban has not done much to slow the main arms race between the two superpowers. The reason is the limited nature of the agreement. A comprehensive ban in 1963 probably would have done much more.

4. On the other hand, the limited ban has accomplished several of the most important objectives that were were set for it. In ascending order of importance they are cleaner air, the establishment of a political climate conducive to much additional progress in arms control and disarmament and the distinct slowing of the spread of nuclear weapons.

On balance, therefore, the limited test ban can be described as a success. Clearly, however, it needs to be extended to prohibit underground testing. A comprehensive treaty may now be within grasp; we must reach for it while we can.

SALT I and Its Background

II

II SALT I and Its Background

INTRODUCTION

The 1959 National Intelligence Estimate (NIE) contained a dismal prediction: The U.S.S.R. would deploy between 350 and 640 intercontinental ballistic missiles (ICBMs) by the middle of 1963. In the wake of Sputnik, Soviet superiority in long-range missiles appeared imminent. It was a threat that incited the United States to expand and accelerate its own strategic program. From 1959 through 1963, the United States allocated $146 billion (constant 1979 dollars) for strategic forces.

But the forecasters erred. By mid-1963, the Soviets had built fewer than 100 missile launchers, and their overall strategic force compared unfavorably with America's force of manned bombers (650) and its burgeoning arsenal of operational Atlas, Titan, and Minuteman ICBMs (200) and Polaris missiles in submarines (144). Over the next several years, the United States widened its numerical lead in strategic missile launchers. At enormous expense, the U.S.S.R. caught up by the end of the decade. This episode illustrates how uncertainty about an adversary's intentions and capabilities can stimulate a senseless arms spiral. In a climate of antagonism and distrust, ambiguity begets "worse case" fears, which in turn cause overreactions and arms race instability. George W. Rathjens discusses action-reaction cycles in the article entitled "The Dynamics of the Arms Race." He identifies two related forms of instability—crisis instability and arms race instability—and he considers the impact of anti-ballistic missiles (ABMs) and multiple independently-targeted re-entry vehicles (MIRVs) on each form. The essay presents the orthodox view of the arms race as well as the orthodox arms control solution.

It has become evident that uncertainty about threats to national security is not followed automatically by a standard response. For instance, in the late 1950s U.S. intelligence experts predicted a missile gap that did not materialize; but in the 1960s they consistently underestimated the magnitude of the Soviet strategic buildup. Although the development of MIRVs may well have been an overreaction to ABM construction around Moscow, as Rathjens contends, the U.S. reaction took another form as well: overtures to the U.S.S.R. to begin formal arms negotiations.

When word of Soviet ABM construction reached President Johnson in 1966, he immediately signaled to the Soviets his desire to ban ABMs. Progress toward formal talks was slow. During preliminary, informal meetings between the two governments, the United States pressed for a settlement of the ABM problem, while Soviet representatives argued that defensive systems were not proper subjects for negotiation. The Russians were concerned about strategic offensive systems, such as bombers and missiles.

Finally in August 1968, after a long and heated debate within the Kremlin had cooled and after President Johnson had announced plans to deploy a "thin" ABM system known as Sentinel, Moscow and Washington set a date to inaugurate SALT. But the long-awaited diplomatic triumph was short-lived—the Soviet Union invaded Czechoslovakia the very next day. The invasion ruled out Johnson's visit to Moscow, which had been scheduled for September, and it delayed SALT for another year.

President Nixon was elected in November 1968, and SALT finally began in November 1969 at Helsinki. Gerard C. Smith, whom President Nixon appointed to direct the Arms Control and Disarmament Agency, headed the U.S. delegation. Other members of the delegation included Paul Nitze, who has become a prominent critic of SALT, and Harold Brown, who is presently Secretary of Defense. Vladimir Semenov, a deputy foreign minister, chaired the U.S.S.R. delegation. (He still holds the position.)

In 1969 any use of strategic nuclear weapons by either side against the other would have been suicidal for attacked and attacker alike. Both Smith and Semenov realized this. They knew that both governments had amassed a large inventory of strategic nuclear weapons—1,300 warheads for the U.S.S.R. and 4,000 for the United States; that both sides possessed sophisticated means for delivering these weapons; and that defenses were so ineffective and weapons survivability so assured that neither side could gain by attacking the other side first. Probably the most significant fact was that by the beginning of SALT, nuclear weapons and their delivery systems could be used rapidly and for a variety of purposes.

During the 1950s and 1960s nuclear weapons and delivery systems were often maintained at separate locations. States of readiness were relatively low. For example, ICBMs in Russia evidently stood empty throughout the Cuban missile crisis. Their warheads reportedly were kept in storage bunkers as far as 50 miles away. According to a special NIE prepared during the Cuban missile crisis of 1962, Soviet missiles emplaced in Cuba required up to eight hours to fire after a decision to launch. At the time, Soviet deterrence relied heavily on cruise missile submarines, but firing the missiles required the submarine to surface and prepare the launching apparatus.

During the pre-SALT years, both governments were working out organizational arrangements for exercising operational command over strategic forces. The development of coherent organizational arrangements lagged far behind the physical deployment of an enormous amount of raw power.

By 1969 the situation had changed dramatically. Command control had matured. States of readiness were high (a Minuteman missile could be launched in seconds). The time element of nuclear war diminished from weeks or days to hours or minutes. Each side could promptly destroy the industrial capacity and most of the civilian population of the adversary. This deterrent, called assured destruction, was the dominant feature of U.S. declaratory doctrine. Both delegations realized the existence of the capability for mutual assured destruction.

The development and deployment of early warning systems as well as refinements in command control made a variety of options available, for instance, a doctrine of "launch-on-warning." The second article, written by Herbert F. York and entitled "Military Technology and National Security," devotes special attention to the human and institutional dimensions of nuclear warfare and to the dangers of launch-on-warning.

Most assessments of weapons programs focus on the technical details of the system hardware; they lack an adequate appreciation of such factors as human skills and motivation, the difficulties of processing information in organizations, human error in control systems, and so forth. York evaluates ABM from both perspectives. He argues that the prominent technical solution to U.S. ICBM vulnerability—namely, the deployment of an ABM system—relies heavily on an unquantifiable and quite unpredictable human element.

An alternative method of ICBM protection is the posture of launch-on-warning. York discusses the procedure and its risks. Although not taken very seriously by most sophisticated analysts, interest in the launch-on-warning procedure was renewed about 1977. A serious threat to U.S. land-based missiles began to be projected. Many analysts believed that this threat could materialize within three to eight years, depending on the rate of Soviet SS-18 and SS-19 MIRV deployments. The idea of hedging by launch-on-warning seemed more practical than it did when York's article appeared in 1969. In 1971 the United States deployed its first early warning satellite in a high-altitude, "stationary" orbit over the Soviet Union. Warning of ICBM attack can be received in about 30 minutes, compared with 12 to 15 minutes for ground-based systems. By 1976, the United States had deployed two similar satellites over the Western Hemisphere in order to detect submarine missile attacks. Launch-on-warning also may seem attractive because it can be implemented cheaply without massive new weapons acquisitions. But it would bring great risks as well.

A high state of operational readiness coupled with an intrinsically imperfect system for warning and command control is a potentially dangerous combination. In a crisis, the risks of accidental war are compounded. The SALT delegations agreed that any nuclear incident, whether accidental, unauthorized, or deliberate, would carry an extremely high risk of escalation to all-out nuclear war. Reducing this risk had high priority at SALT.

Preliminary discussion parallel to the main SALT negotiations led to the formation of two special working groups. One group focused on arrangements for Soviet-American consultation in the event of a nuclear incident. The other worked to improve the so-called Hot Line, which is the direct communications link between Moscow and Washington. The original Hot Line agreement was signed in 1963, just before the Limited Test Ban Treaty. The efforts of the working groups to supplement this agreement ended successfully with two new agreements signed in Washington in September 1971. The "Agreement on Measures To Reduce the Risk of Outbreak of Nuclear War between the U.S.A. and the U.S.S.R." consists of three main pledges:

1. A pledge to take measures that each country considers necessary to safeguard against accidental or unauthorized use of nuclear weapons.

2. A pledge to notify each other immediately should a risk of nuclear war arise from detection by early warning systems of unidentified objects or from accidental, unauthorized, or other unexplained incidents involving a possible detonation of a nuclear weapon.

3. A pledge to give advance notification of planned missile launches beyond the territory of the launching party and in the direction of the other party.

The 1971 agreement to improve the Hot Line provided for the establishment of multiple-terminal satellite communications between Washington and Moscow. The U.S. Intelsat system and the U.S.S.R. Molniya II system were to replace the original Hot Line circuits, which consisted of a wire telegraph routed Washington-London-Copenhagen-Stockholm-Helsinki-Moscow and a radio telegraph routed Washington-Tangier-Moscow. The new satellite system went into regular service in January 1978.

While the working groups dealt with problems of accidental war and crisis management, the main SALT negotiations focused on ABM and strategic offensive arms. The third article in this part directly addresses these principal subjects of negotiation. Entitled "The Limitation of Strategic Arms," the article was written by George Rathjens and George Kistiakowsky (once President Eisenhower's assistant for science and technology) just as SALT was beginning.

The authors considered MIRV to be "the watershed issue for SALT." If MIRV deployment could not be checked, then the utility of an ABM ban would be greatly diminished, the strategic balance would be changed materially, and an escalation of the arms race could be expected. This article foreshadows the decline of fixed land-based ICBMs as a secure retaliatory force. We shall see this issue again in the next section (on the SALT II negotiations), because unfortunately SALT I did not limit MIRV deployment. The United States began to deploy MIRVs in 1970, while SALT was in progress. The Soviet Union achieved an initial MIRV capability in 1975.

Indeed, it became clear early on that SALT would not substantially restrict strategic offensive weapons. An initial disagreement over the definition of *strategic* blocked progress. The Soviet delegates sought to include any weapons capable of reaching the territory of the other side. U.S. bombers stationed on aircraft carriers or based in Europe, so-called forward-based systems, fit this specification. The U.S. representatives objected, holding that intercontinental offensive weapons were the proper subjects of negotiation.

Efforts to break the deadlock failed, and the Soviets then sought to confine the negotiations to ABM systems. The United States again objected, insisting that this approach was inconsistent with the goals of SALT. Both sides ultimately agreed to concentrate on an ABM treaty but at the same time to negotiate certain limitations on intercontinental offensive systems. Both sides further agreed to emphasize offensive forces during the second round of SALT. Disagreement over the inclusion of forward-based systems nevertheless remained a major stumbling block.

The Interim Agreement on Offensive Arms (printed at the end of this section) froze the number of missile launchers at the number existing or under construction as of 26 May 1972. The agreement established ceilings of 1,054 landbased ICBMs for the United States and 1,618 for the Soviet Union. It permitted the United States 710 submarine-launched ballistic missiles (SLBMs). This figure was 54 more than the actual number deployed on 26 May 1972, but the United States could reach the allowed ceiling only by replacing its 54 older Titan ICBM launchers. Likewise, the U.S.S.R. was allowed a maximum of 950 SLBM launchers, which was 210 more than the number then deployed. Additional SLBM launchers were permitted only if the Soviets replaced older ICBM or SLBM launchers. The United States has retained its Titan force. The Soviets have retired many older ICBMs and SLBM launchers.

Proponents of SALT defended the higher Soviet ceilings on the grounds that the United States held substantial advantages in technology and numbers of warheads. Critics advocated numerical parity, a position reflected in the Jackson amendment to the Senate resolution approving the Interim Agreement. The amendment "urges and requests the President to seek a future treaty that, inter alia, would not limit the United States to levels of intercontinental strategic forces inferior to the limits provided for the Soviet Union." The reference to intercontinental systems effectively rules out any U.S. compromise on the issue of forward-based nuclear forces.

The Interim Agreement did not cover strategic bombers, but the omission of MIRV limitations proved far more significant. The article by Rathjens and Kistiakowsky anticipated the root problems of wide-scale MIRV deployments. Their analysis remains timely and valid, as evidenced by the growing concern about the impending vulnerability of fixed land-based missiles. Today as never before, MIRV programs threaten to upset strategic stability.

Because ICBMs are becoming vulnerable, the U.S. deterrent depends heavily on missile submarines. The Polaris fleet of 10 submarines deployed in the Pacific and the 31 Poseidons deployed in the Atlantic are practically immune to attack. Furthermore, the submarine force maintains a high degree of readiness and carries a huge nuclear arsenal. Missile submarines take advantage of forward bases outside U.S. territory (Guam, Scotland, and Spain) in order to reduce the time needed to reach launch stations. About 55 percent of the submarine force is maintained on launch-ready alert, compared with about 15 percent of the Soviet fleet, which deploys mainly from the Soviet port of Murmansk. Owing to higher alert rates and a MIRV lead, today approximately 2,446 U.S. versus 140 Soviet SLBM warheads are at sea and are thus protected against sudden attacks on naval ports.

The arsenal of U.S. submarine warheads is three times as large as the inventory of U.S. ICBM warheads, and it exceeds the number in the entire strategic force of the Soviet Union. The Poseidon and Polaris inventory stands at about 4,500 warheads, and the smallest warhead yields twice as much destructive energy as the bombs dropped on Hiroshima and Nagasaki. But what makes the submarine so vital today is not the enormous destructive power on alert at sea but the ability to patrol undetected. The long- and short-term survivability of submarines is secure, as it was in 1972 when Herbert Scoville, Jr., wrote "Missile Submarines and National Security." The article is the fourth selection in this part.

Scoville summarizes the history of the ballistic missile submarine program since its inception, outlines the deterrent role of the system, discusses its future, and evaluates the need for a planned longer-range missile and a new missile submarine. He recommends against the ULMS project (now called the Trident program); however, the program is proceeding as proposed. The first Trident missile, with a range of 4,000 nautical miles (n.m.) compared to a 2,400-n.m. range for current missiles, is to be backfitted into Poseidon submarines and will become operational by 1980. The first Trident missile submarine will be delivered in the same or following year.

The invulnerability of the submarine leads Scoville to conclude that "the Navy will increasingly be the principal military guardian of our national security." On balance, this assessment seems valid. However, serious problems remain in the area of command, control, and communications. MIRV deployments are rapidly increasing the number of Soviet warheads and concomitantly expanding the number of potential U.S. targets. There is a strong likelihood that a growing number of weapons are targeted against command, control, and communications assets. Reliable communication between ballistic missile submarines and the national command authorities—the President or his designated successor, and the Secretary of Defense—is becoming less certain every day.

Scoville describes communications systems that have since been disapproved—for example, Sanguine ELF—or that have become more vulnerable to jamming or physical attack—for example, fixed and airborne VLF stations. SSBNs do not enjoy many of the benefits of satellite communications that bombers and ICBMs do, since satellites use radio frequencies that do not penetrate seawater. Also, the missile submarine is the only strategic weapon that is not equipped with a safeguard system known as "permissive action link" (PAL). Unlike PAL-configured bombers and ICBMs, the missile submarine is physically capable of launching nuclear weapons without higher authority. In sum, the missile submarine possesses weaknesses that probably will moderate the trend toward heavier reliance on it.

Richard L. Garwin surveys the technology of antisubmarine warfare (ASW) in the fifth article, entitled "Antisubmarine Warfare and National Security." He wrote the article just after the Moscow signing of the ABM treaty and the interim agreement. Although Garwin determines that ASW does not at present threaten either side's submarine deterrent, he argues that limitations on ASW methods could help preserve and enhance this stability.

The article breaks new ground. In the first place, it examines a technology that is normally cloaked in secrecy. But more importantly, it introduces the idea of controlling operational military *activities*. Garwin suggests such arms control possibilities as prohibitions against active tracking of missile submarines, the creation of sanctuary areas for submarines, and providing, during a conventional war, safe-conduct routes through mine fields for each other's ballistic missile submarines. The purpose of such measures is not just to preserve each side's submarine deterrent. Garwin believes that they would help eliminate groundless fears of ASW threats, reduce unintentional attrition of missile submarines in the course of conventional conflict, and forestall any escalation to all-out war. (Ranking naval officers have testified before Congress that in a warfighting situation the Navy "would not be in a position of differentiating their attack submarines from their SSBNs," and that "in a conventional war all submarines are submarines. They are all fair game.")

Garwin's general recommendations are very compatible with the Accident Measures Agreement and the incidents-at-sea agreement signed in 1971. The former agreement pledged each party "to act in such a manner as to reduce the possibility of its actions being misinterpreted by the other Party." Garwin's perspective is also clearly related to that of York, who reminded us that the initiation and conduct of war are fundamentally human events subject to human fears, failures, and foibles. The argument for controlling ASW methods in order to reduce the chances of misinterpretation and escalation is both novel and persuasive.

But so far, the scope of SALT has been much narrower. It has not encompassed restrictions on operational activities. SALT I (1969–1972) concentrated on limiting hardware, and except for the ABM Treaty, controls on hardware were quantitative rather than qualitative.

The main achievement of SALT I was the ABM Treaty, given at the end of this section. Although failure to control MIRV somewhat devalued its military significance, the treaty certainly advanced the cause of arms control and contributed to strategic stability. The ABM Treaty calls for quantitative and qualitative controls; the exact worth of these controls is incalculable, since no one knows how far or how successfully the rivals would have pushed ABM technology if given a free hand to do so. Certain ABM systems are banned completely. It prohibits development, testing, or deployment of sea-based, air-based, space-based, or mobile land-based ABM systems or components. And it blocks entry into such esoteric fields as laser techniques. The Treaty imposes precise limits on the ABM systems that may be deployed.

Article V of the Interim Agreement and Article XII of the ABM Treaty contain provisions pertaining to verification. The parties explicitly recognize the legitimacy of "national technical means of verification," pledge not to interfere with such means, and agree not to use deliberate concealment measures to impede verification.

Satellite reconnaissance is the primary "national technical means of verification." The sixth article, entitled "Reconnaissance and Arms Control," examines satellites and other means used to verify compliance with the SALT I accords. Ted Greenwood, the author of the article, finds that the United States can verify Russian observance of the ABM Treaty and Interim Agreement with high confidence, and vice versa.

Satellites and other means are well suited for verifying quantitative limitations on fixed land-based missiles but are less capable of verifying certain qualitative limitations, such as MIRV configuration. For example, it is practically impossible to distinguish between a Soviet SS-18 ICBM armed with a single warhead and one armed with multiple warheads. Similarly, it has been argued that the U.S.S.R. could not ascertain the exact configuration of every U.S. Minuteman ICBM.

But verification capabilities do not fall into neat categories, such as being strong on quantitative but weak on qualitative dimensions. The ABM Treaty calls for qualitative restrictions that are verifiable. Greenwood determines that a ban on MIRV testing could be verified and compliance with Garwin's recommended constraints on operational activities, such as submarine tracking, could be monitored. Certain other qualitative limitations may be verified with lower confidence. The range of U.S. cruise missiles or of Soviet Backfire bombers poses special problems. The prospects for verifying certain quantitative controls are also uncertain. For example, it will be hard to count numbers of cruise missiles and mobile land-based ICBMs, such as the Soviet SS-16. The United States may deploy either Minuteman ICBMs or the new MX ICBM as part of a "multiple-aim-point system" (MAP). The MAP system is based on the "shell-and-pea" concept. ICBMs would be randomly assigned to silos, which would greatly outnumber the number of ICBMs. MAP may require the building of some 10,000 silos for 1,000 or less missiles. While a deceptive basing mode such as MAP is designed to enhance ICBM survivability, its design could preclude Soviet verification by technical means alone. New, cooperative arrangements will probably be required to verify compliance with SALT II agreements. One of the major problems of verifying mobile missiles and many other weapons is that they can be moved at night or under the cover of clouds. Surveillance is still quite limited under these conditions. New infrared and radar sensors that could remove existing deficiencies may be deployed over the next ten years.

No scheme of verification can divine past, present, or future intentions nor can monitoring programs provide all of the information needed to assess actual strategic capabilities. Nevertheless, a consensus exists that SALT I helped establish rough parity of capabilities. The ceilings were approximately equal, and mutual assured destruction was preserved. The ABM Treaty ruled out the deployment of a nationwide system of defense against nuclear attack. Regardless of which side struck first, the other side could strike back with enormous destructive power. Even if all bombers and ICBMs were destroyed, without ABM defenses the aggressor could not blunt retaliation by submarine forces.

Hence many experts believe SALT I reflected a shared understanding that nuclear war cannot be won. Among the other common understandings implicit in SALT I, Herbert York identifies the following: (1) the deployment of defensive weapons can accelerate the arms race just as much as the deployment of offensive weapons; (2) defense of the nation against a massive nuclear attack is impossible; and (3) too much secrecy can unnecessarily stimulate the arms race, and therefore certain forms of intelligence gathering are necessary and legitimate.

Other experts disagree with these inferences. Recent advances in detection and tracking radar, electronic miniaturization, infrared sensors, and other components have convinced some analysts of the feasibility of ballistic missiles defense (BMD), and even perhaps of nationwide defense against missile attack. The legitimation of overhead satellite reconnaissance is regarded by some as a mixed blessing. Along with the benefits of improved intelligence and verification comes the ability to locate and target the opponent's deterrent. Some observers cite the war-fighting, war-winning theme of Soviet military doctrine as evidence that mutual assured destruction is a uniquely Western concept and that superiority rather than parity is the principal goal of the Soviet Union. A different argument holds that the United States pays lip service to the idea of assured destruction while basing actual strategic war plans on damage limitation doctrine and counterforce strategy—attacking military rather than urban-industrial targets. The issue of counterforce strategy will appear again in the next part.

Despite secure retaliatory forces, each side continues to explore new and better ABM defenses and ASW methods (in recent years Soviet "Yankee-class" submarines have become very vulnerable), to maintain and augment arsenals that vastly exceed what is needed for assured destruction alone, and to fear the other side's counterforce potential. The codification of mutual assured destruction—even if both sides understood and endorsed the concept—did not shackle the arms competition.

The first phase of SALT ended on 26 May 1972, when President Nixon and General Secretary Brezhnev signed the ABM Treaty and the Interim Agreement. The preamble to the ABM Treaty declared each side's intentions to end the nuclear arms race at the earliest possible date and to reduce strategic arms. No reductions were achieved. During the two and a half years of talks, the United States added about 2,000 nuclear warheads to its strategic arsenal, and U.S.S.R. added about 1,000 to its. The trend continues on the Soviet side, and may soon resume on the American.

The U.S. Senate ratified the treaty and agreement on 30 September 1972. The ABM Treaty has unlimited duration. The Interim Agreement expired in October 1977, but by mutual agreement the two governments extended it until a new agreement is reached.

The Dynamics of The Arms Race

by George W. Rathjens
April 1969

Recent decisions by the U.S. and the U.S.S.R. threaten to upset the stability of the present strategic military balance. The net result may be simply to decrease the security of both countries

The world stands at a critical juncture in the history of the strategic arms race. Within the past two years both the U.S. and the U.S.S.R. have decided to deploy new generations of offensive and defensive nuclear weapons systems. These developments, stimulated in part by the emergence of China as a nuclear power, threaten to upset the qualitatively stable "balance of terror" that has prevailed between the two superpowers during most of the 1960's. The new weapons programs portend for the 1970's a decade of greatly increased military budgets, with all the concomitant social and political costs these entail for both countries. Moreover, it appears virtually certain that at the end of all this effort and all this spending neither nation will have significantly advanced its own security. On the contrary, it seems likely that another upward spiral in the arms race would simply make a nuclear exchange more probable, more damaging or both.

As an alternative to this prospect, the expectation of serious arms-limitation talks between the U.S. and the U.S.S.R. holds forth the possibility of at least preventing an acceleration of the arms race. In the circumstances it seems worthwhile to inquire into the nature of the forces that impel an arms race. In doing so we may determine how best to damp this newest cycle of military competition, either by mutual agreement or by unilateral restraint, before it is beyond control.

There are a number of new weapons systems under development in both the U.S. and the U.S.S.R., but the possibilities that are likely to be at the center of discussion not only in the forthcoming negotiations but also in the current Congressional debate are the anti-ballistic-missile (ABM) concept and the multiple-independently-targeted-reentry-vehicle (MIRV) concept. These systems, one defensive and the other offensive, can usefully be discussed together because of the way they interact. In fact, the intrinsic dynamics of the arms race can be effectively illustrated by concentrating on these two developments.

It is now 18 months since former Secretary of Defense McNamara announced the decision of the Johnson Administration to proceed with the deployment of the Sentinel system: a "thin" ABM system originally described as being intended to cope with a hypothetical Chinese missile attack during the 1970's. The technology of the Sentinel system and some of the means a determined adversary might employ to defeat it were discussed in some detail a year ago in this magazine [see "Anti-Ballistic-Missile Systems," by Richard L. Garwin and Hans A. Bethe, the article beginning on page 164]. At this point I should like to review some of the background of the ABM problem.

Before the Sentinel decision most of the interest in a ballistic-missile defense for the U.S. was focused on the Nike-X program. This concept involved the use of two kinds of interceptor to protect the population and industry of the country against a hypothetical Russian missile attack. Interception would first be attempted outside the earth's atmosphere with Spartans, long-range missiles with nuclear warheads in the megaton range. The effectiveness of the defense, however, would depend primarily on the use of Sprints, short-range missiles with kiloton-yield warheads designed to intercept incoming missiles after they have reentered the atmosphere. The system also envisaged suitable radars and computers to control the engagement.

The Spartans could in principle defend large areas; indeed, about a dozen sites could defend the entire country. A defense based solely on them could be rendered ineffective, however, by fairly simple countermeasures, in particular by large numbers of lightweight decoys (which would be indistinguishable to a radar from an actual reentry vehicle containing a warhead) or by measures that would make the radar ineffective, for example the use of nuclear explosions, electronic jammers or light, widely dispersed metal "chaff."

The effectiveness of a Sprint defense would be less degraded by such countermeasures. Light decoys could be distinguished from actual reentry vehicles because they would be disproportionately slowed by the atmosphere and possibly because their wake in the atmosphere would be different. Radar blackout would also be much less of a problem. Because of their short range, however, Sprints could defend only those targets in their immediate vicinity. Thus an adversary could choose to attack some cities with enough weapons to overwhelm the defense while leaving others untargeted. Heavy radioactive fallout could also be produced over large parts of the country by an adversary's delivering large-yield weapons outside the areas covered by Sprint defenses. A nationwide defense of the Sprint type would therefore require a nationwide fallout-shelter program.

Although combining Sprints and Spartans in a single system, as was proposed for the Nike-X system, would complicate an adversary's penetration problem, in a competition with a determined and resourceful adversary the advantage in an offense-defense duel would still lie with the offense. As a result, in spite of strong advocacy by the Army and support from the other branches of the military and from members of Congress, the decision to deploy the Nike-X system was never made.

At the heart of the debate about whether or not to deploy the Nike-X system was the question of what the Russian reaction to such a decision would be. It was generally conceded that the system might well save large numbers of lives in the event of war, if the U.S.S.R. were simply to employ the forces projected in the available intelligence estimates. On that basis proponents argued in favor of deployment in spite of the high costs, variously estimated as being from $13 billion to $50 billion. Such deployment was opposed, particularly by Secretary McNamara, because of the belief that the U.S.S.R. could and would improve its offensive capabilities in order to negate whatever effectiveness the system might have had. Indeed, because the deployment of a U.S. ABM system would introduce large uncertainties into the calculus of the strategic balance, there were occasional expressions of concern that the U.S.S.R. might overreact. Hence the damage inflicted on us in the event of war might even be greater than it would be if the Nike-X system were not deployed.

The Sentinel system announced in 1967 would have far less capability than

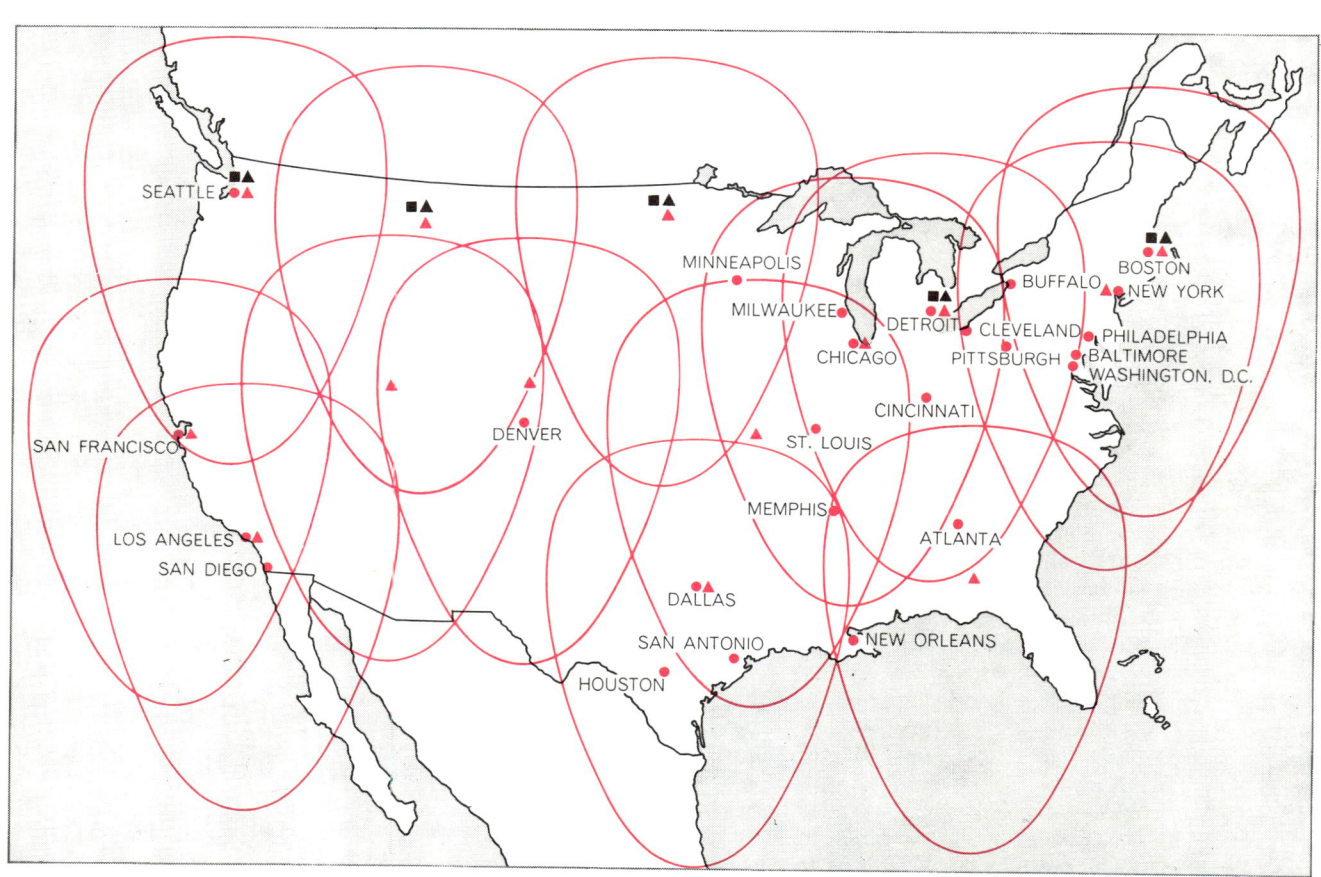

▲ SPARTAN SITE

▲ SPRINT SITE

■ PAR SITE

● 25 LARGEST CITIES

SENTINEL SYSTEM, a "thin" anti-ballistic-missile (ABM) system described by the Johnson Administration as being intended to defend the U.S. against a hypothetical Chinese missile attack in the 1970's, is depicted on this map in its original form. The main defense would be provided by Spartan missiles, long-range ABM missiles with nuclear warheads in the megaton range, designed to intercept incoming missiles outside the earth's atmosphere. The Spartans would be deployed at about 14 locations in order to provide a "thin" or "light" area defense of the whole country. The range of each "farm" of Spartans is indicated by the egg-shaped area around it; for missiles attacking over the northern horizon, the intercept range of the Spartan is elongated somewhat to the south. The Sentinel system would also include some Sprint missiles, short-range ABM missiles with much smaller warheads, designed to intercept incoming missiles after they have reentered the atmosphere. The Sprints were originally to be deployed to defend only the five or six perimeter acquisition radars, or PAR's, which were to be deployed across the northern part of the country. In President Nixon's proposed modification of the Sentinel scheme Spartans, Sprints and PAR sites would be deployed in a somewhat different array to provide additional protection for our land-based retaliatory forces against a hypothetical surprise attack by the Russians.

the Nike-X system. It would include some Sprint missiles to defend key radars (five or six perimeter acquisition radars, or PAR's, to be deployed across the northern part of the country), but the main defense would be provided by Spartan missiles located to provide a "thin" or "light" defense for the entire country [see illustration on opposite page]. Spokesmen for the Johnson Administration argued that such a deployment would be almost completely effective in dealing with a possible Chinese missile attack during the 1970's, but that it would be so ineffective against a possible Russian attack that the U.S.S.R. would not feel obliged to improve its strategic offensive forces as a response to the decision. Both arguments were seriously questioned.

Garwin and Bethe, for example, contended that even the first-generation Chinese missiles might well be equipped with penetration aids that would defeat the Sentinel system. Other experts pointed out that the system, like the Nike-X system, could never be tested adequately short of actual war, and that in view of its complexity there would be a high probability of a catastrophic failure.

The contention that the U.S.S.R. would not react to the Sentinel decision seemed at least as questionable as the assertions of great effectiveness against the Chinese. Whatever the initial capability of the Sentinel system, it seemed clear that the Sentinel decision would at least shorten the lead time for the deployment of a system of the Nike-X type. Moreover, the fact that Sentinel was strongly and publicly supported as a first step toward an "anti-Soviet" system could hardly escape the attention of Russian decision-makers.

Since the announcement of the Sentinel decision, and particularly since the change in the Administration, the arguments in favor of the decision have become confused. It has been variously suggested by Administration spokesmen that the primary purpose would be (1) to defend the American population and industry against a possible Chinese attack, (2) to provide at least some protection for population and industry against a possible Russian attack, (3) to defend Minuteman missile sites against a possible Russian attack and (4) to serve as a bargaining counter in strategic-arms-limitation talks with the U.S.S.R. It might be noted that no one in recent months has seriously suggested that a Russian reaction to the decision is unlikely. In fact, all but the first

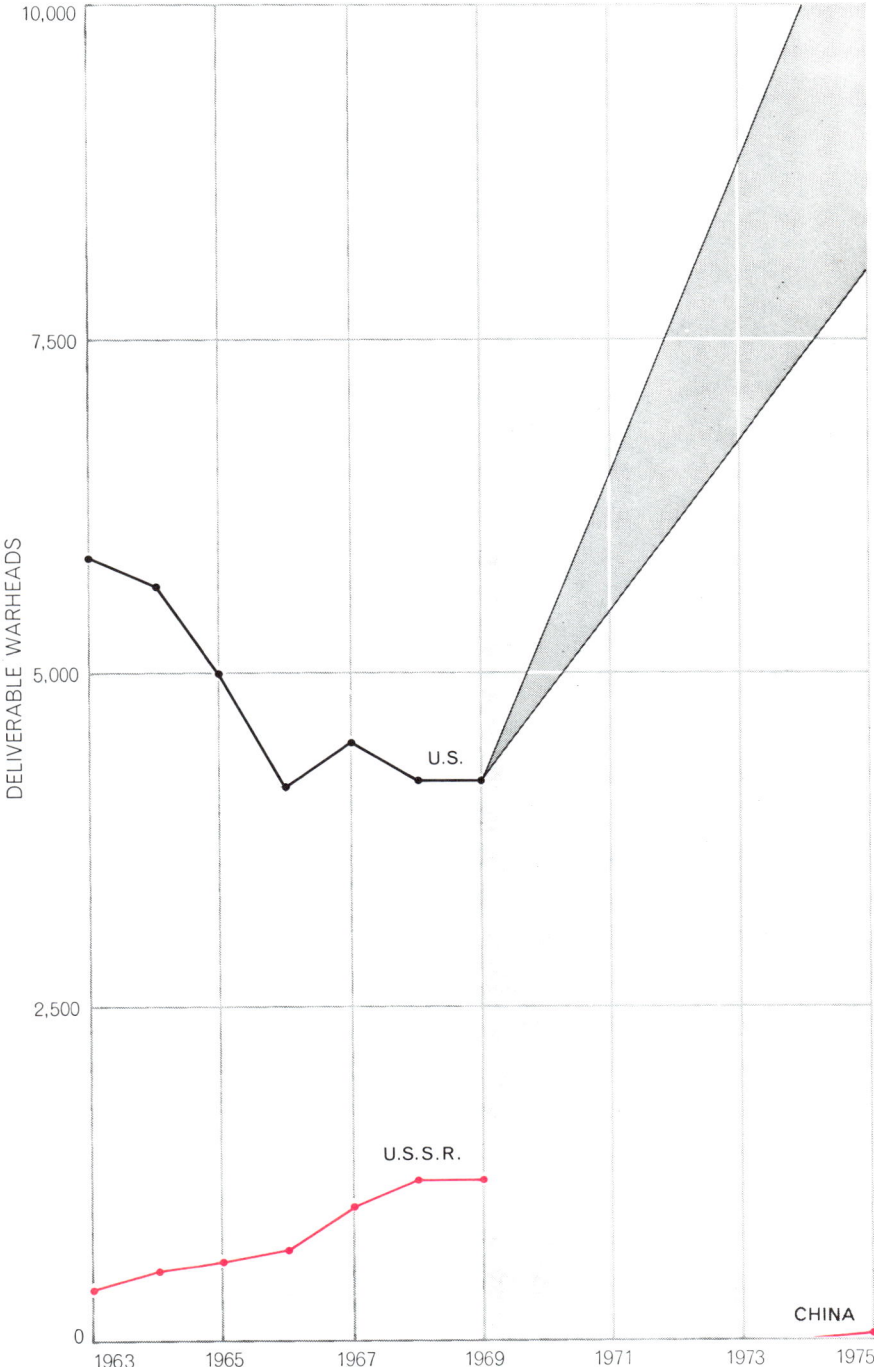

STRATEGIC OFFENSIVE FORCES of the U.S., the U.S.S.R. and China are compared here in terms of the number of megaton-range nuclear warheads the U.S. could deliver against either of the two other powers as of a given date, and vice versa. The U.S. missile force grew rapidly during the 1960's, offsetting a partial phasing-out of intercontinental bombers. The Russian bomber force, meanwhile, has remained at a constant level, while their missile force has grown steadily and shows no sign of leveling off. Thus at present the U.S. maintains a superiority over the U.S.S.R. of about four to one in numbers of deliverable warheads. The hypothetical Chinese strategic force was recently estimated by Secretary of Defense Laird to be 20 to 30 deliverable warheads by the mid-1970's. The effect of the present U.S. program to equip its Minuteman III and its Poseidon missiles with multiple independently targeted reentry vehicles (MIRV's) would be to increase greatly the number of U.S. deliverable warheads by 1975 (dark gray area). It is not known what compensating actions, if any, will be taken by the other powers in response to this development. It has been estimated by former Secretary of Defense McNamara that 400 one-megaton warheads would suffice to destroy 75 percent of the industry and 33 percent of the population of the U.S.S.R.

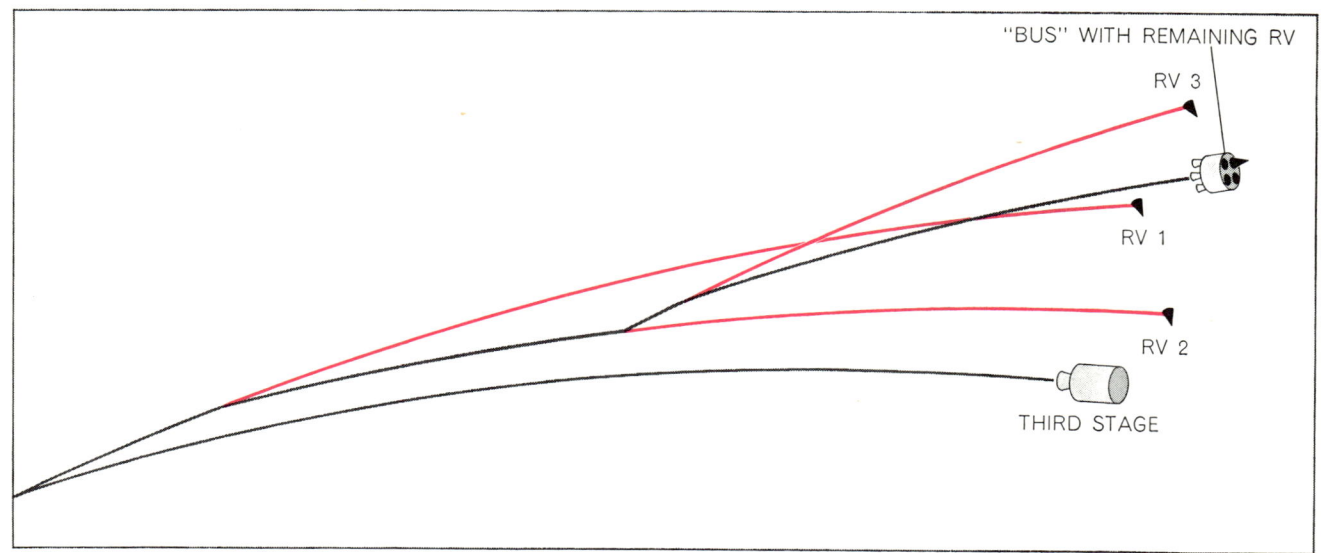

MIRV CONCEPT on which the current U.S. Minuteman III and Poseidon programs are based is illustrated by the idealized drawings on these two pages. Each offensive missile will carry aloft a "bus," containing a number of individual reentry vehicles, or RV's (in this example four are shown). A single guidance and propulsion system will control the orientation and velocity of the bus, from which the reentry vehicles will be released sequentially (*left*). After each release there will be a further adjustment in the velocity

of the arguments cited above imply the likelihood of a Russian response.

President Nixon's reaffirmation, albeit with some modification, of the Sentinel decision was presumably made on the basis of his judgment that the first and third of the aforementioned arguments justify the costs of such a system, not only the direct dollar cost but also the cost in terms of the impact on Russian decision-making and any other costs that may be imputed to the system. Whether or not his decision is correct depends strongly on how serious the possibility of a Russian reaction is. Before dealing further with that question it will be useful to bring MIRV's into the picture.

The problem of simulating an actual warhead reentry vehicle is a comparatively easy one, provided that the attacker need not be concerned with differences in the interaction of decoys and warheads with the atmosphere during reentry. If one wishes to build decoys and warheads that will be indistinguishable down to low altitudes, however, the problem is a formidable one, particularly if one demands high confidence in the indistinguishability of the two types of object. Improved radar resolution and increased traffic-handling and data-processing capability make the problem of effective decoy design increasingly difficult. The development of interceptors capable of high acceleration will also complicate the offense's problem. With such interceptors the decision to engage reentering objects can be deferred until they are well down into the atmosphere; the longer the defense can wait, the more stringent are the demands of decoy simulation on the offense.

As the problem becomes more difficult, the ratio of decoy weight to warhead weight increases. There comes a point at which, if one wants really high confidence of penetration, one might just as well use several warheads on each missile rather than a single warhead and several decoys, each of which may be as heavy, or nearly as heavy, as a warhead. Hence multiple warheads are in a sense the ultimate in high-confidence penetration aids (assuming that one relies on exhaustion or saturation of defense capabilities as the preferred tactic for defeating the defense). To be effective, however, multiple warheads must be sufficiently separated so that a single interceptor burst will not destroy more than one incoming warhead. Moreover, the utility of multiple warheads for destroying targets, particularly small ones that would not justify attack by more than one or two small warheads, will be greatly enhanced if they can be individually guided.

In principle each reentry vehicle could have its own "post-boost" guidance and propulsion system. That, however, is not the concept of the MIRV's in our Poseidon and Minuteman III missile systems, which are now under development. Rather, a single guidance and propulsion system will control the orientation and velocity of a "bus" from which reentry vehicles will be released sequentially [*see illustration on these two pages*]. After each release there will be a further adjustment in the velocity and direction of the bus. Thus each reentry vehicle can be directed to a separate target. The targets can be rather widely separated, the actual separation depending on how much energy (and therefore weight) one is willing to expend in the post-boost maneuvers of the bus. It is an ingenious—and demanding—concept.

Two rationales have been advanced for the decision to proceed with the U.S. MIRV programs. One is that with MIRV's the U.S. can have a high confidence of being able to penetrate an adversary's ABM defenses. The apparent deployment of a limited Russian ABM system in the vicinity of Moscow and U.S. concern about a possibly more widespread Russian ABM-system deployment have been important considerations in the decision to go ahead with the U.S. MIRV programs.

The second rationale is that a MIRV system enables one to strike more targets with a given number of boosters than would be the case if one were using one warhead per missile. This rationale has been important for two reasons.

First, it enabled spokesmen for the Johnson Administration to argue against expanding the size of our strategic missile force during a period when Russian forces were growing rapidly. They were able to contend in the face of political opposition on both flanks that, whereas

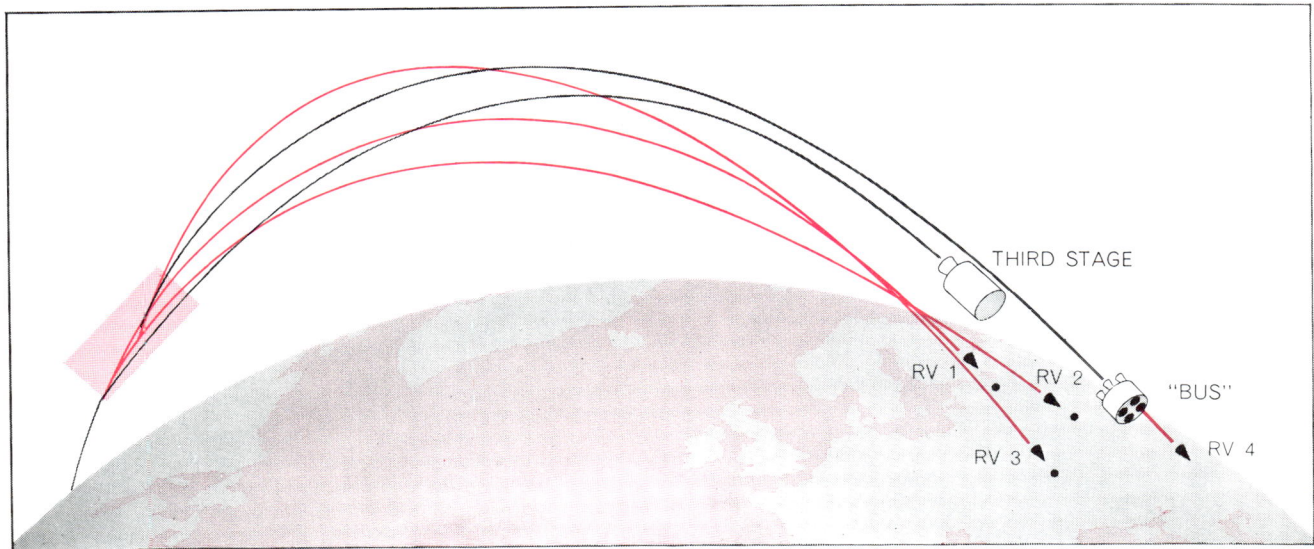

and the direction of the bus. Thus each reentry vehicle can be directed to a separate target (*right*). The actual separation of the targets depends on how much energy (and therefore weight) one is willing to expend in the post-boost maneuvers of the bus. Besides being a potentially attractive means of penetrating an adversary's ABM defenses, MIRV's could conceivably be effective some day as a "counterforce" weapon, that is, a system capable of destroying the adversary's strategic offensive forces in a preemptive attack.

we did not contemplate expanding the number of our offensive missiles, the number of warheads we could deliver would increase rapidly.

Second, it raised the prospect of a missile force that could be used as a very effective "counterforce" weapon. This means that with MIRV's a limited number of missiles might be capable of destroying a larger intercontinental-ballistic-missile (ICBM) force in a preemptive attack. To achieve this performance, however, particularly against hardened offensive missile sites, would require a substantial improvement in accuracy and a high post-boost reliability—no mean feats with a device as complicated as the MIRV bus.

What bearing will the deployment of the ABM and the MIRV systems have on the future of the arms race? In attempting to answer this difficult question it is instructive to consider the extent to which the choices of each of the superpowers regarding strategic weapons have been influenced by the other's decisions.

The actual role of this action-reaction phenomenon is a matter of considerable debate in American defense circles. Indeed, the differences in views on this question account for most of the dispute of the past few years regarding the objectives to be served by strategic forces and their desired size and qualities. Thus whether the U.S. should be content with an adequate retaliatory, or "assured destruction," capability or go further and try to build a capability that would permit us to reduce damage to ourselves in the event of war must clearly depend on a judgment on whether Russian defense decisions could be influenced significantly by our decisions. Those who have felt that Russian defense planning would be responsive to our actions have held that for the most part any attempt by us to develop such "damage-limiting" capabilities with respect to the U.S.S.R. would be an effort doomed to failure. The U.S.S.R. would simply improve its offensive capabilities to offset the effects of any measures we might take. This was the basis for the rejection by the American leadership of the requests by the Army for large-scale ABM-system deployment and for the rejection of requests by the Air Force for much larger ICBM forces.

Although there is considerable evidence to support the claim that the action-reaction phenomenon does apply to defense decision-making, to explain all the major decisions of the superpowers in terms of an action-reaction hypothesis is an obvious oversimplification. The American MIRV deployment has been rationalized as a logical response to a possible Russian ABM-system deployment, but there were also other motivations that were important: the desire to keep our total missile force constant while increasing the number of warheads we could deploy, the long-term possibility of MIRV's giving us an effective counterforce capability, and finally the simple desire to bring to fruition an interesting and elegant technological concept.

Nevertheless, the action-reaction phenomenon, with the reaction often premature and/or exaggerated, has clearly been a major stimulant of the strategic arms race. Examples from the past can be cited to support this point: (1) the American reaction, indeed overreaction, to uncertainty at the time of the "missile gap," which played a central role in the 1960 Presidential election but was soon afterward shown by improved intelligence to be, if anything, in favor of the U.S.; (2) the Russian decision to deploy the "Tallinn" air-defense system, possibly made in the mistaken expectation that the U.S. would go ahead with the deployment of B-70 bombers or SR-71 strike-reconnaissance aircraft; (3) the U.S. response to the Tallinn system (which until recently was thought to be an ABM system) and to the possible extension of the Moscow ABM system into a countrywide system. It was in order to have high assurance of its ability to get through these possible Russian ABM defenses that the U.S. embarked on the development of various penetration aids and even of new missiles: Minuteman III and Poseidon.

These examples have in common the fact that if doubt exists about the capabilities or intentions of an adversary, prudence normally requires that one respond not on the basis of what one expects but on a considerably more pessimistic projection. The U.S. generally

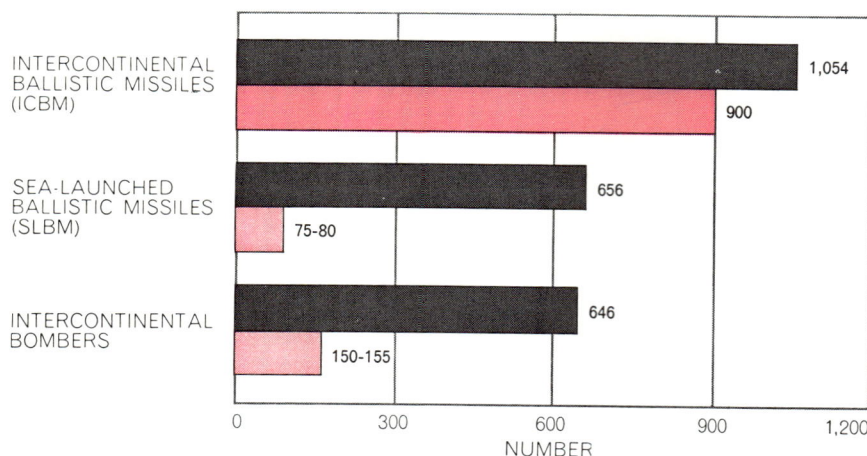

INVENTORY of the intercontinental delivery vehicles possessed by the U.S. (*gray*) and the U.S.S.R. (*color*) as of October, 1968, shows that in this category also the U.S. continues to hold a clear superiority over the U.S.S.R. This measure is not entirely satisfactory, however, in that it does not take into account qualitative differences in the various systems, the expected interactions during a nuclear exchange or the match of the weapons with the targets. When such factors are taken into account, the differences between the U.S. and the U.S.S.R. are not significant. In his final "posture" statement for fiscal 1969, for example, former Secretary McNamara estimated that, barring drastic changes in the strategic balance, in an all-out nuclear exchange in the mid-1970's each country could inflict a minimum of 120 million fatalities on the other—regardless of which country struck first.

bases its plans—and makes much of the fact—on what has become known as the "greater-than-expected threat." In so doing, the Americans (and presumably the Russians) have often overreacted. The extent of the overreaction is directly dependent on the degree of uncertainty about any adversary's intentions and capabilities.

The problem is compounded by lead-time requirements for response. According to the Johnson Administration, the decisions to go ahead with Minuteman III, Poseidon and Sentinel had to be made when they were because of the possibility that in the mid-1970's the Russians might have a reasonably effective ABM system and the Chinese an ICBM capability. The Russians had to make a decision to develop the Tallinn system (if the decision was made because of the B-70 program) long before we ourselves knew whether or not we would deploy an operational B-70 force.

Once the decisions to respond to ambiguous indications of adversary activity were made it often proved impossible to modify the response, even when new intelligence became available. For example, between the time the Sentinel decision was announced and the first Congressional debate on the appropriation took place during the summer of 1968, evidence became available that the Chinese threat was not developing as rapidly as had been feared. Yet in spite of this information those in Congress who attempted at that time to defer the appropriation for Sentinel failed. Similarly, at this writing, as the Poseidon and Minuteman III programs begin to gain momentum, it seems much less likely than it did at the time of their conception that the U.S.S.R. will deploy the kind of ABM system that was the Johnson Administration's main rationale for these programs. On the Russian side, the Tallinn deployment continued long after it became clear that no operational B-70 force would ever be built.

Of the kinds of weapons development that can stimulate overresponse on the part of one's adversary, it is hard to imagine one more troublesome than ABM defenses. In addition to uncertainty about adversary intentions and the need (because of lead-time requirements) for early response to what the adversary might do, there is the added fact that the uncertainties about how well an ABM system might perform are far larger than they are for strategic offensive systems. The conservative defense planner will design his ABM system on the assumption that it may not work as well as he hopes, that is, he will overdesign it to take into account as fully as he can all imaginable modes of failure and enemy offensive threats. The offensive planner, on the other hand, will assume that the defense might perform much better than he expects and will overdesign his response. Thus there is overreaction on both sides. These uncertainties result in a divergent process: an arms race with no apparent limits other than economic ones, each round being more expensive than the last. Moreover, because of overreaction on the part of the offense there may be an increase in the ability of each side to inflict damage on the other.

All one needs to make this possibility a reality is a triggering mechanism. The Russian ABM program, by stimulating the Minuteman III and Poseidon programs, may have served that purpose. The Chinese nuclear program may also have triggered an action-reaction chain, of which the Sentinel response is the second link [*see illustration on page 42*].

It can be assumed that there will be considerable pressure and effort to make Sentinel highly effective against a "greater than expected" Chinese threat. Such a system will undoubtedly have some capability against Russian ICBM's. Russian decision-makers, who must assume that Sentinel might perform better than they expect, will at least have to consider this possibility as they plan their offensive capabilities. More important, they will have to respond on the assumption that the Sentinel decision may foreshadow a decision to build an anti-Russian ABM system. Hence it is probably not a question of whether the U.S.S.R. will respond to Sentinel but rather of whether the U.S.S.R. will limit its response to one that does not require a U.S. counterresponse, and of whether it is too late to stop the Sentinel deployment.

It is apparent that reduction in uncertainty about adversary intentions and capabilities is a *sine qua non* to curtailing the strategic arms race. There are a number of ways to accomplish this (in addition to the gathering of intelligence, which obviously makes a great contribution).

First, there is unilateral disclosure. In the case of the U.S. there has been a conscious effort to inform both the American public and the Russian leadership of the rationale for many American decisions regarding strategic systems and, to the extent consistent with security, of U.S. capabilities. This has been done particularly through the release by the Secretary of Defense of an annual "posture" statement, a practice that, it is hoped, will be continued by the U.S. and will be emulated someday by the U.S.S.R. This would be in the interest of both countries. Because there has been no corresponding effort by the Russians the U.S. probably overreacts to Russian decisions more than the U.S.S.R. does to American decisions. (At least it is easier to trace a causal relationship between Russian decisions and U.S. reactions than it is between U.S. decisions and Russian reactions.)

Second, negotiations to curtail the arms race (even if abortive) or any other dialogue may be very useful if such efforts result in a reduction of uncertainty about the policies, capabilities or intentions of the parties.

Third, some weapons systems may be less productive of uncertainty than others that might be chosen instead. For example, it is likely to be less difficult to measure the size of a force of submarine-launched or fixed missiles than it is to measure the size of a mobile land force. Similarly, it would be easier to persuade an adversary that a small missile carried only a single warhead than would be the case with a large vehicle. Such considerations must be borne in mind in evaluating alternative weapons systems.

In short, although uncertainty about adversary capabilities and intentions may not always be bad (in some instances the existence of uncertainty has contributed to deterrence), the U.S. and the U.S.S.R. would seem well advised to make great efforts to avoid giving each other cause for overreacting to decisions because of inadequate understanding of their meaning.

The importance of somehow breaking the action-reaction chains that seem to drive the arms race is obvious when one considers the enormous resources involved that could otherwise be used to meet pressing social needs. In addition, there is particular importance in doing so at present because the concurrent deployment of MIRV's and ABM systems is likely to have drastic destabilizing consequences. It is conceivable that one of the superpowers with an ABM system might develop MIRV's to the point where it could use them to destroy the bulk of its adversary's ICBM force in a preemptive attack. Its air and ABM defenses would then have to deal with a much degraded retaliatory blow, consisting of the sea-launched forces and any ICBM's and aircraft that might have survived the preemptive attack. The problems of defense in such a contingency would remain formidable. They would be significantly less difficult, however, than if the adversary's ICBM force had not been seriously depleted. In fact, the defense problem would be relatively simple if a large fraction of the adversary's retaliatory capability were, as is true for the U.S. and to a far greater degree for the U.S.S.R., in its land-based ICBM's, most of which would presumably have been destroyed.

It may seem unlikely that either superpower would initiate such a preemptive attack, in view of the great uncertainties in effectiveness (particularly with respect to defenses) and the disastrous consequences if even a comparatively small fraction of the adversary's retaliatory force should get through. With both MIRV's and an ABM system, however, such a preemptive attack would not seem as unlikely as it does now. It might not appear irrational to some, for example, if an uncontrollable nuclear exchange seemed almost certain, and if by striking first one could limit damage to a significantly lower level than if the adversary were to strike the first blow. In short, if one or both of the two superpowers had such capabilities, the world would be a much more unstable place than it is now.

Obviously neither superpower would permit its adversary to develop such capabilities without responding, if it could, by strengthening its retaliatory forces. The response problem becomes more

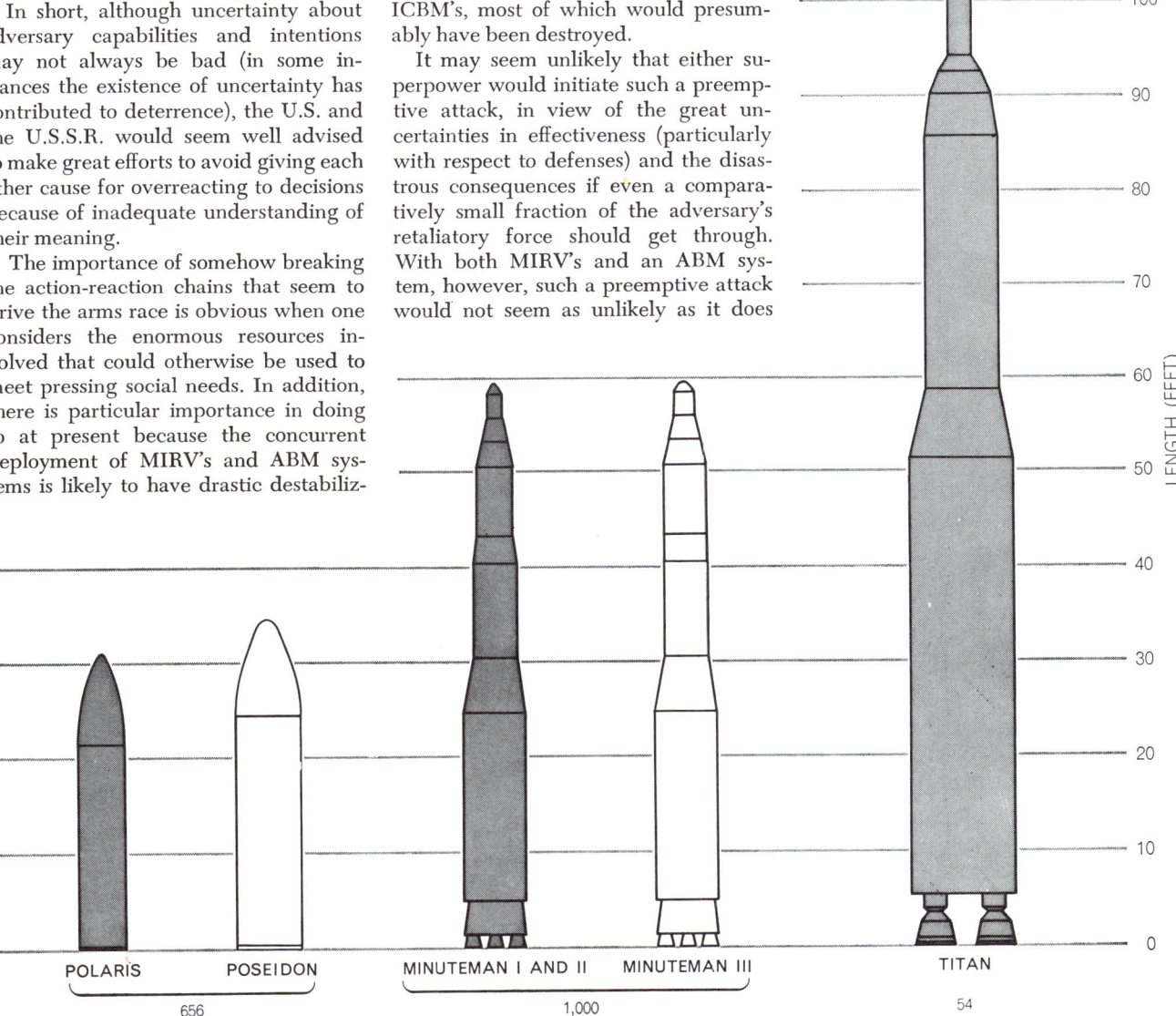

U.S. OFFENSIVE MISSILES currently deployed or under development are drawn here to scale. The sea-based Polaris and Poseidon and the land-based Minutemen are capable of carrying warheads with a total explosive yield of about one megaton each. The land-based Titan II can carry a warhead of more than five megatons. Poseidon and Minuteman III, which are under development, are designed to carry MIRV warheads. The total number of missiles scheduled for deployment in each category is indicated at the bottom.

difficult, however, if the adversary develops both MIRV's and an ABM system than if only one is developed.

Against a MIRV threat alone there are such obvious responses as defense of ICBM sites or greater reliance on sea-launched or other mobile systems. Such responses are likely to be acceptable because, whereas the costs of highly invulnerable systems are large (perhaps several times larger than the costs of simple undefended ICBM's), only relatively small numbers of such secure retaliatory weapons would be required to provide an adequate "assured destruction" capability. Indeed, a force the size of the present Polaris submarine fleet would seem to be more than adequate. The response to an ABM system alone might also be kept within acceptable limits because the expenditures required to offset the effects of defense are likely to be small compared with the costs of the defense.

If it is necessary to acquire retaliatory capabilities that are comparatively invulnerable to MIRV attack in numbers sufficient to saturate or exhaust ABM defenses, however, the total cost could be very great. In fact, if one continued to rely heavily on exhaustion of defenses as the preferred technique for penetration, the offense might no longer have a significant cost-effectiveness advantage over the defense. Thus the concurrent development of MIRV's and ABM systems raises the specter of a more precarious balance of terror a few years hence, a rapidly escalating arms race in the attempt to prevent the instabilities from getting out of hand, or quite possibly both.

With this background about the roles of uncertainty and the action-reaction phenomenon in stimulating the arms race, one can draw some general conclusions about the functions and qualities of future strategic forces. We must first recognize that two kinds of instability must be considered: crisis instability (the possibility that when war seems imminent, one side or the other will be motivated to attack preemptively in the hope of limiting damage to itself) and arms-race instability (the possibility that the development or deployment decisions of one country, or even the possibility of such decisions, may trigger new development or deployment decisions by another country).

The first kind of instability is illustrated in the chart on the opposite page, which is based on former Secretary McNamara's posture statement for fiscal 1967. This shows that—assuming two possible expanded Russian threats, various damage-limiting efforts by the U.S. and failure of the U.S.S.R. to react to extensive U.S. damage-limiting efforts by improving its retaliatory capability—American fatalities in 1975 would be only about a third as great in the event of a U.S. first strike as they would be in the case of a Russian first strike. (In the present situation the advantage of the attacker is negligible.) Obviously if war seemed imminent, with the strategic balances assumed in this example, there would be tremendous pressure on the U.S. to strike first. There would be corresponding pressure on the U.S.S.R. to do likewise if a Russian first strike could result not only in a much higher level of damage to the U.S. but also in a diminution in damage to the U.S.S.R. The incentives would be mutually reinforcing.

To minimize the chance of a failure of deterrence in a time of crisis, it seems important for both the U.S. and the U.S.S.R. to develop strategic postures such that preemptive attack would have as small an effect as possible on the anticipated outcome of a thermonuclear exchange. Actually, of course, it is extremely unlikely that the Russians would passively watch the U.S. develop the extensive damage-limiting postures assumed in the foregoing example. Instead they would probably react by modifying their posture so that the advantage to the U.S. of attacking preemptively would be less than is indicated in the chart. Thus the example can also be used to illustrate the second kind of instability.

To the extent that one accepts the action-reaction view of the arms race, one is forced to conclude that virtually anything we might attempt in order to reduce damage to ourselves in the event of war is likely to provoke an escalation in the race. Moreover, many of the choices we might make with damage-limitation in mind are likely to make preemptive attack more attractive and war therefore more probable. The concurrent development of MIRV's and ABM systems is a particularly good example of this.

One is struck by the fact that there is an inherent inconsonance in the objectives spelled out in our basic military policy, namely "to deter aggression at any level and, should deterrence fail, to terminate hostilities in concert with our allies under conditions of relative advantage while limiting damage to the U.S. and allied interests." Hard choices must be made between attempting to minimize the chance of war's occurring in a time of crisis and attempting to minimize the consequences if it does occur.

The decisions made by U.S. planners in recent years with respect to new weapons development and deployment reflect a somewhat inconsistent philosophy on this point. The U.S. has generally avoided actions whose primary rationale was to limit damage that the U.S.S.R. might inflict on it, actions to which the Russians would probably respond. Accordingly the U.S. has not deployed an anti-Russian ABM system and has given air defense a low priority.

On the other hand, where there were reasons other than a desire to improve American damage-limiting capability with respect to the U.S.S.R., the U.S. has proceeded with programs in spite of their probably escalating effect on the arms race or their effect on first-strike incentives. This was true in the case of the MIRV's and Sentinel.

The U.S. will face more such decisions. For example, it may appear necessary to change the U.S. strategic offensive posture in order to make American forces less vulnerable to possible Russian MIRV attack. The nature of these decisions will depend on the importance attached to the action-reaction phenomenon and to the effect of improved counterforce capabilities on the probability of war. Emphasis on these two factors

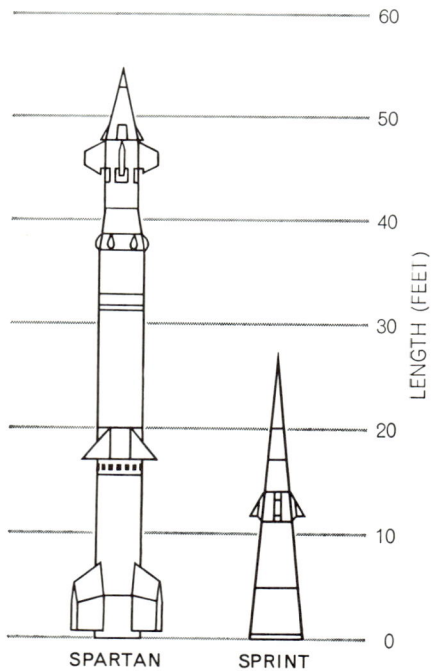

U.S. DEFENSIVE MISSILES currently being deployed as part of the modified Sentinel system are drawn here to scale. The Spartan and Sprint carry warheads in the megaton range and kiloton range respectively.

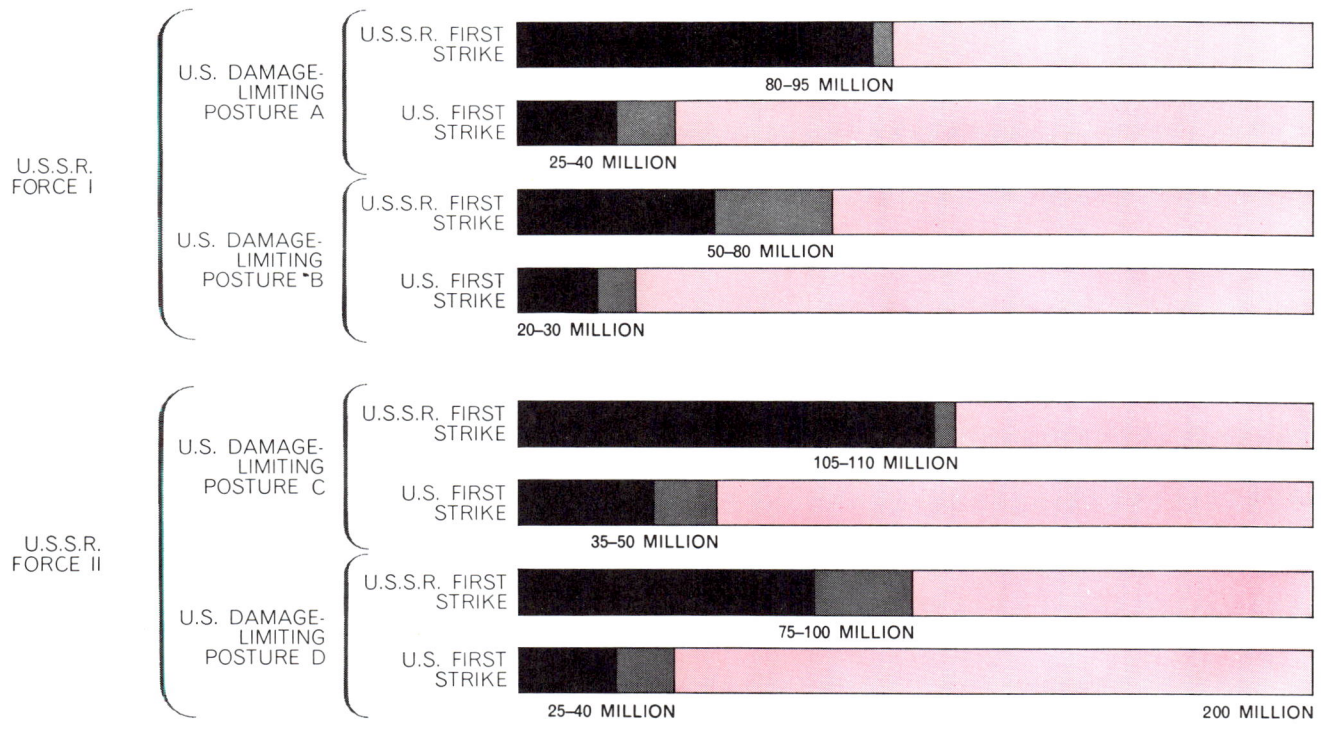

U.S. FATALITIES in a variety of hypothetical nuclear exchanges in the mid-1970's are rounded off to the nearest five million in this bar chart. U.S.S.R. force *I* is basically an extrapolation of current Russian forces reflecting some future growth in both offensive and defensive capability; force *II* assumes a major Russian response to our deployment of an ABM system. Two of the four U.S. damage-limiting programs, postures *A* and *B*, are tailored against U.S.S.R. force *I*; the other two, postures *C* and *D*, are tailored against U.S.S.R. force *II*. The chart illustrates the basic incompatibility between a policy of attempting to minimize the consequences of nuclear war and a policy of attempting to minimize the probability of nuclear war. If war seemed imminent, with the strategic balances as hypothesized in this chart, there would be tremendous pressure on both sides to strike first, and as a result of this added incentive the chances of escalation would be enhanced. The chart is based on information contained in former Secretary McNamara's posture statement for fiscal 1967.

implies discounting options that would increase U.S. counterforce capability against Russian strategic forces, which in turn might provoke an expansion of Russian offensive forces. Options requiring long lead times would also be discounted, since decisions regarding them might have to be made while there was still uncertainty about whether the U.S.S.R. was developing MIRV's.

Should more weight be given in the future to developing damage-limiting capabilities? Or should more weight be given to minimizing the probability of a thermonuclear exchange and curtailing the strategic arms race? It is hard to see how one can have it both ways.

In spite of some changes in technology, there is little to indicate that the U.S. could get very far with damage-limiting efforts, considering the determination of the Russians and the options available to them for denying the attainment of such U.S. capabilities. The emergence of new nuclear powers, the rapid pace of technological advance and the other important demands on American resources suggest that a clear first priority should be assigned to moderating the action-reaction cycle. Moving toward greater emphasis on damage-limitation would seem justified only if the U.S. can persuade itself that the Russians will not react to American moves as the U.S. would to theirs, and if means can be chosen that will not increase the probability of war.

No treatment of the dynamics of the strategic arms race would be complete without some discussion of the possibility of ending it, or at least curtailing it, through negotiations. Both the urgency and the opportunity are great, but the latter may be waning. This opportunity is in part a consequence of the present military balance, as well as of somewhat changed views in both the U.S. and the U.S.S.R. about strategic capabilities and objectives.

With the rapid growth in its strategic offensive forces during the past few years, the U.S.S.R. can at long last enter negotiations without conceding inferiority or (which is worse from the Russian point of view) exposing itself to the possibility of being frozen in such a position. Moreover, the U.S.S.R. may at long last be prepared to accept the prevailing American view about the action-reaction phenomenon, and about the intrinsic advantage of the offense and the futility of defense. The apparent decision of the Russians not to proceed with a nation-wide ABM system at present, and their professed willingness to enter into negotiations to control both offensive and defensive systems, may be evidence of this convergence of viewpoints.

On the American side there is at long last a quite general, if not yet universal, acceptance of the concept of nuclear "sufficiency": the idea that beyond a certain point increased nuclear force cannot be translated into useful political power. Acceptance of this concept is an almost necessary condition to termination of the arms race.

In considering negotiations with the U.S.S.R. on the strategic arms problem, the first factor to be kept in mind is the objectives to be sought. It would be a mistake to expect too much or to aspire to too little. One obvious aim is to re-

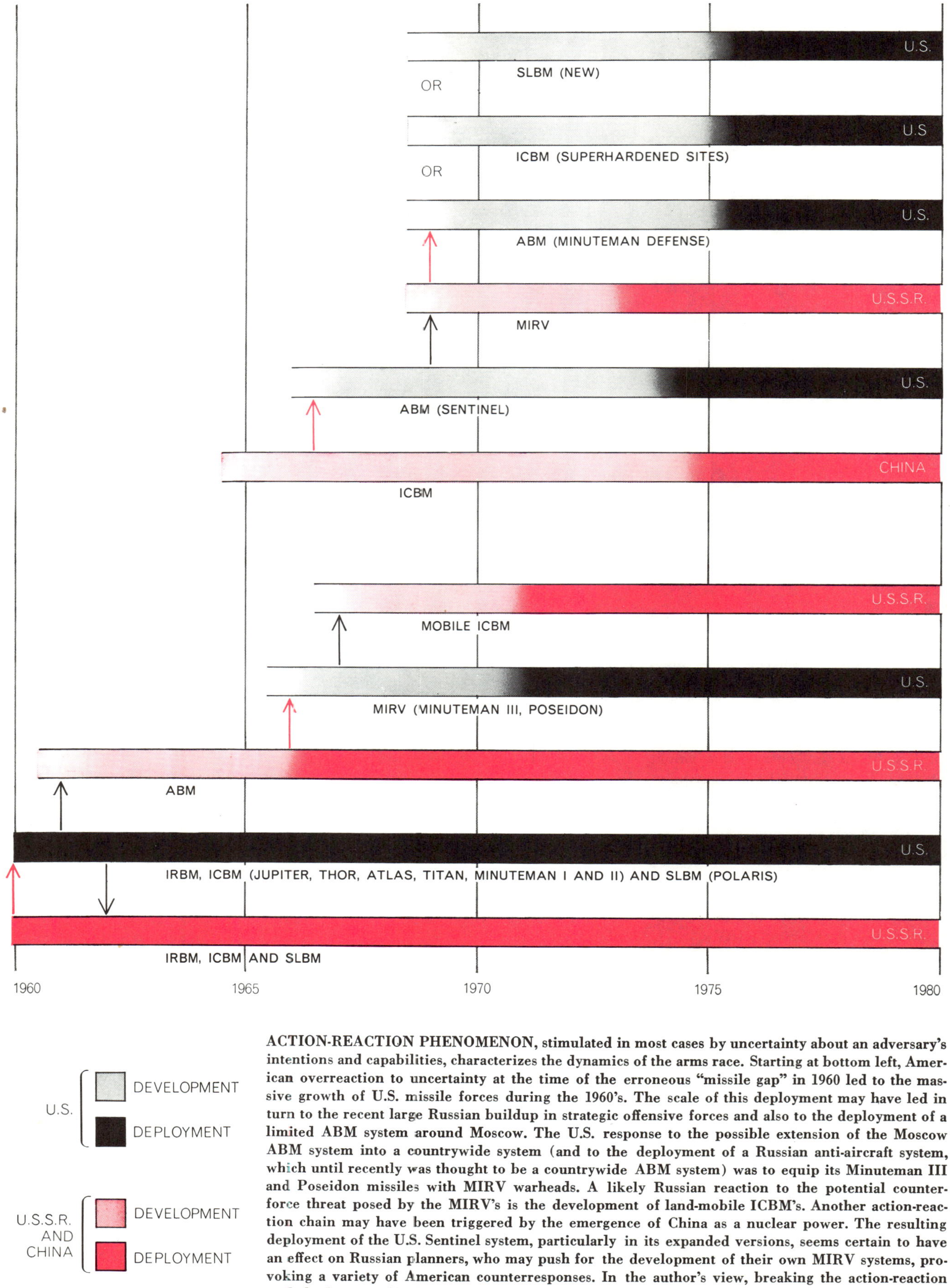

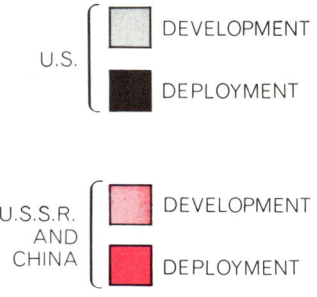

ACTION-REACTION PHENOMENON, stimulated in most cases by uncertainty about an adversary's intentions and capabilities, characterizes the dynamics of the arms race. Starting at bottom left, American overreaction to uncertainty at the time of the erroneous "missile gap" in 1960 led to the massive growth of U.S. missile forces during the 1960's. The scale of this deployment may have led in turn to the recent large Russian buildup in strategic offensive forces and also to the deployment of a limited ABM system around Moscow. The U.S. response to the possible extension of the Moscow ABM system into a countrywide system (and to the deployment of a Russian anti-aircraft system, which until recently was thought to be a countrywide ABM system) was to equip its Minuteman III and Poseidon missiles with MIRV warheads. A likely Russian reaction to the potential counterforce threat posed by the MIRV's is the development of land-mobile ICBM's. Another action-reaction chain may have been triggered by the emergence of China as a nuclear power. The resulting deployment of the U.S. Sentinel system, particularly in its expanded versions, seems certain to have an effect on Russian planners, who may push for the development of their own MIRV systems, provoking a variety of American counterresponses. In the author's view, breaking the action-reaction cycle by limiting ABM defenses should be given first priority in any forthcoming arms-control talks.

duce strategic armaments in order to lessen significantly the damage that would be sustained by the U.S. (and the U.S.S.R.) in the event of a nuclear exchange. Regrettably this goal is not likely to be realized in the near future. In the first place, any initial understandings will probably not involve reductions in strategic forces. Even if they did, the reductions would be limited. One cannot expect potential damage levels to be lowered by more than a few percent, even with fairly substantial cuts in strategic forces, because the capabilities of the superpowers are already so great.

Other objectives have been considered: reducing the incentives to strike preemptively in time of crisis, reducing the probability of accident or miscalculation, and increasing the time available for decision-making in the hope that the increased opportunity for communication might prevent a nuclear exchange from running its full course. Last but not least, one might also hope to change the international political climate so as to lessen tension, to reduce the incentive for powers that currently do not have nuclear weapons to acquire them and to increase the possibility for agreement by the superpowers on other meaningful arms-control measures.

It is reasonable to expect that successful negotiations might to some degree achieve all these objectives except the first: the reduction of potential damage. To focus on any one objective, or combination of objectives, however, is to obscure the immediate problem. In spite of the restraint of the U.S. in its choices regarding strategic weapons development and deployment during the first two-thirds of this decade, it now appears that in the absence of some understanding between the U.S. and the U.S.S.R. the action-reaction sequence that impels the arms race will not be broken. Therefore the immediate objective of any negotiations must be simply to bring that sequence to a halt, or to moderate its pace so that there will be a better chance of ending the arms race than is offered by continuing the policies of the past two decades.

In retrospect, controlling or reversing the growth of strategic capabilities could have been accomplished more easily a few years ago, when the possibility of ABM-system deployment seemed to be the main factor that would trigger another round in the arms race. Now the prospect of ABM systems is more troublesome because of technological advances. In addition, there are the two other stimuli already discussed: the possibility of effective counterforce capabilities as a result of the development of MIRV's, and the possibility that the Chinese nuclear capability may serve as a catalyst to the Russian-American action-reaction phenomenon.

Obviously, short of destroying China by nuclear attack, there is little the U.S. can do about Chinese capabilities except to make sure that it does not give them more weight in its thinking than they deserve. This leaves the option of trying to break the ABM-MIRV chain by focusing on the control of MIRV's or ABM defenses.

Whereas one might hope to limit both, if a choice must be made the focus should clearly be on the control of ABM defenses. Verification of compliance would be relatively simple and could probably be accomplished without intrusive inspection. In addition, the incentive to acquire MIRV's for penetrating defenses would be eliminated, although the incentive to acquire them for counterforce purposes would remain.

The problems of verifying compliance with an agreement to control MIRV's would be much more difficult. Moreover, if an ABM system were deployed, there would be great pressure to abrogate or violate any agreement prohibiting MIRV deployment because MIRV's offer high assurance for penetrating defenses. Although reversing the MIRV decision would be difficult, reversing the Sentinel one would present less of a problem.

To be attractive to the U.S.S.R. any proposal to limit defenses would almost certainly have to be coupled with an agreement to limit, if not reduce, inventories of deployed strategic offensive forces. In principle this should not be difficult, since it need not involve serious verification problems.

Complicating any attempt to reach an understanding with the U.S.S.R. on the strategic balance, however, is the fact that the American and Russian positions are not symmetrical. The U.S. has allies and bases around the periphery of the U.S.S.R., whereas the latter has neither near the U.S., unless one counts Cuba. It is clear that a Pandora's box of complications could be opened by any attempt in the context of negotiations on the strategic balance to deal with the threat to America's allies posed by short-range Russian delivery systems, and with the potential threat to the U.S.S.R. of systems in Europe that could reach the U.S.S.R. even though they are primarily tactical in nature. One may hope that initial understandings will not have to include specific agreements on such thorny issues as foreign bases and dual-purpose systems.

Virtually all the above is based on the premise that for the foreseeable future each side will probably insist on maintaining substantial deterrent capabilities. For some time to come there will unfortunately be little basis for expecting negotiations with the U.S.S.R. to result in a strategic balance with each side relying on a few dozen weapons as a deterrent. The difficulties and importance of verification of compliance at such low levels, the problem of China, the existence of large numbers of tactical nuclear weapons on both sides and the general political climate all militate against this. At the other extreme, negotiations would almost necessarily fail if either party based its negotiating position on the expectation that it might achieve a significant damage-limiting capability with respect to the other.

Thus the range of possible agreement is quite narrow. There is a basis for hope, if both sides can accept the fact that for some time the most they can expect to achieve is a strategic balance at quite high, but less rapidly escalating, force levels, and if both recognize that breaking the action-reaction cycle should be given first priority in any negotiations, and also in unilateral decisions.

There will be risks in negotiating arms limitation. These must be weighed not against the risks that might characterize the peaceful world in which everyone would like to live, or even against the risks of the present. Rather, the risks implicit in any agreement must be weighed against the risks and costs that in the absence of agreement one will probably have to confront in the 1970's.

Whether the superpowers strive to curtail the strategic arms race through mutual agreement or through a combination of unilateral restraint and improved dialogue, they should not do so in the mistaken belief that the bases for the Russian-American confrontation of the past two decades will soon be eliminated. Many of the sources of tension have their origins deep in the social structures and political institutions of the two countries. Resolution of these differences will not be accomplished overnight. Restraining the arms race, however, may shorten the time required for resolution of the more basic conflicts between the two superpowers, it may increase the chances of survival during that period, and it may enable the U.S.S.R. and the U.S. to work more effectively on the other large problems that confront the two societies.

4 Military Technology and National Security

by Herbert F. York
August 1969

The ABM debate is analyzed in the context of a larger dilemma: the futility of searching for technological solutions to what is essentially a political problem

The recent public hearings in the Senate and the House of Representatives on anti-ballistic-missile (ABM) systems have provided an unprecedented opportunity to expose to the people of this country and the world the inner workings of one of the dominant features of our time: the strategic arms race. Testimony has been given by a wide range of witnesses concerning the development and deployment of all kinds of offensive and defensive nuclear weapons; particular attention has been paid to the interaction between decisions in these matters and the dynamics of the arms race as a whole.

In my view the ABM issue is only a detail in a much larger problem: the feasibility of a purely technological approach to national security. What makes the ABM debate so important is that for the first time it has been possible to discuss a major aspect of this larger problem entirely in public. The reason for this is that nearly all the relevant facts about the proposed ABM systems either are already declassified or can easily be deduced from logical concepts that have never been classified. Thus it has been possible to consider in a particular case such questions as the following:

1. To what extent is the increasing complexity of modern weapons systems and the need for instant response causing strategic decision-making authority to pass from high political levels to low military-command levels, and from human beings to machines?

2. To what extent is the factor of secrecy combined with complexity leading to a steadily increasing dominance of military-oriented technicians in some vital areas of decision-making?

3. To what extent do increasing numbers of weapons and increasing complexity—in and of themselves—complicate and accelerate the arms race?

My own conclusion is that the ABM issue constitutes a particularly clear example of the futility of searching for technical solutions to what is essentially a political problem, namely the problem of national security. In support of this conclusion I propose in this article to review the recent history of the strategic arms race, to evaluate what the recent hearings and other public discussions have revealed about its present status and future prospects, and then to suggest what might be done now to deal with the problem of national security in a more rational manner.

The strategic arms race in its present form is a comparatively recent phenomenon. It began in the early 1950's, when it became evident that the state of the art in nuclear weaponry, rocket propulsion and missile guidance and control had reached the point in the U.S. where a strategically useful intercontinental ballistic missile (ICBM) could be built. At about the same time the fact that a major long-range-missile development program was in progress in the U.S.S.R. was confirmed. As a result of the confluence of these two events the tremendous U.S. long-range-missile program, which dominated the technological scene for more than a decade, was undertaken. The Air Force's Thor, Atlas and Titan programs and the Army's Jupiter program were started almost simultaneously; the Navy's Polaris program and the Air Force's Minuteman program were phased in just a few years later.

More or less at the same time the Army, which had had the responsibility for ground-based air defense (including the Nike Ajax and Nike Hercules surface-to-air missiles, or SAM's), began to study the problem of how to intercept ICBM's, and soon afterward initiated the Nike Zeus program. This program was a straightforward attempt to use existing technology in the design of a nuclear-armed rocket for the purpose of intercepting an uncomplicated incoming warhead. The Air Force proposed more exotic solutions to the missile-defense problem, but these were subsequently absorbed into the Defender Program of the Department of Defense's Advanced Research Projects Agency (ARPA). The Defender Program included the study of designs more advanced than Nike Zeus, and it also incorporated a program of down-range measurements designed to find out what did in fact go on during the terminal phases of missile flight.

By 1960 indications that the Russians were taking the ABM prospect seriously, in addition to progress in our own Nike Zeus program, stimulated our offensive-missile designers into seriously studying the problem of how to penetrate missile defenses. Very quickly a host of "penetration aid" concepts came to light: light and heavy decoys, including balloons, tank fragments and objects resembling children's jacks; electronic countermeasures, including radar-reflecting clouds of the small wires called chaff; radar blackout by means of high-altitude nuclear explosions; tactics, such as barrage, local exhaustion and "rollback" of the defense, and, most important insofar as the then unforeseen consequences were concerned, the notion of putting more than one warhead on one launch vehicle. At first this notion simply involved a "shotgun" technique, good only against

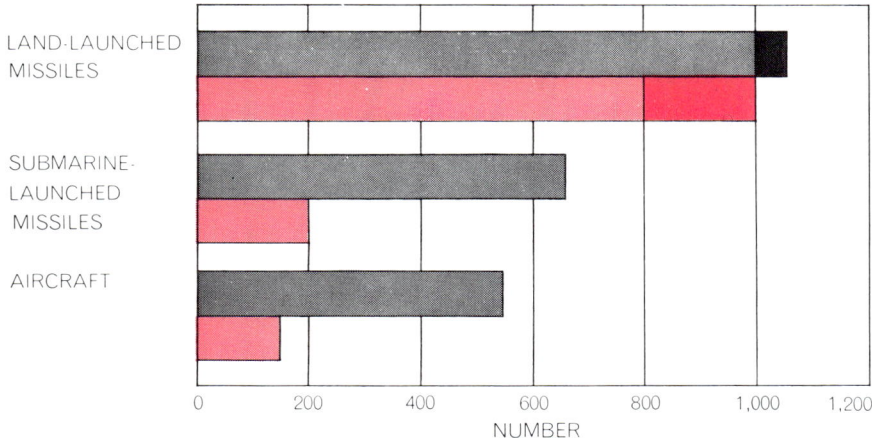

PRESENT STATUS of the deployment of strategic offensive forces by the U.S. (*gray*) and the U.S.S.R. (*color*) shows that the two superpowers are about even in numbers of intercontinental ballistic missiles (ICBM's), and that the U.S. is ahead in both long-range aircraft and submarine-launched ballistic missiles (SLBM's) of the Polaris type. The U.S. ICBM's consist almost entirely of Minutemen (*light gray*), which carry a nuclear warhead with an explosive yield in the megaton range; there currently remain only 54 of the larger Titans (*dark gray*) in our strategic forces. The smaller Russian missiles (*light color*) are mostly SS-11's, which are roughly equivalent in size to our Minutemen. The larger Russian missiles (*dark color*) are SS-9's, which are comparable in size to our Titans. The figures used are from a speech given by Secretary of Defense Melvin R. Laird on March 25.

large-area targets (cities), but it soon developed into what we now call MIRV's (multiple independently targeted reentry vehicles), which can in principle (and soon in practice) be used against smaller, harder targets such as missile silos, radars and command centers.

This avalanche of concepts forced the ABM designers to go back to the drawing board, and as a result the Nike-X concept was born in 1962. The Nike-X designers attempted to make use of more sophisticated and up-to-date technology in the design of a system that they hoped might be able to cope with a large, sophisticated attack. All through the mid-1960's a vigorous battle of defensive concepts and designs versus offensive concepts and designs took place. This battle was waged partly on the Pacific Missile Range but mostly on paper and in committee meetings. It took place generally in secret, although parts of it have been discussed in earlier chapters in this book [see "National Security and the Nuclear-Test Ban," by Jerome B. Wiesner and Herbert F. York, on page 129, "Anti-Ballistic-Missile Systems," by Richard L. Garwin and Hans A. Bethe, on page 164, and "The Dynamics of the Arms Race," by George W. Rathjens, on page 177].

This intellectual battle culminated in a meeting that took place in the White House in January, 1967. In addition to President Johnson, Secretary of Defense Robert S. McNamara and the Joint Chiefs of Staff there were present all past and current Special Assistants to the President for Science and Technology (James R. Killian, Jr., George B. Kistiakowsky, Jerome B. Wiesner and Donald F. Hornig) and all past and current Directors of Defense Research and Engineering (Harold Brown, John S. Foster, Jr., and myself). We were asked that simple kind of question which must be answered after all the complicated ifs, ands and buts have been discussed: "Will it work?" The answer was no, and there was no dissent from that answer. The context, of course, was the Russian threat as it was then interpreted and forecast, and the current and projected state of our own ABM technology.

Later that year Secretary McNamara gave his famous San Francisco speech in which he reiterated his belief that we could not build an ABM system capable of protecting us from destruction in the event of a Russian attack. For the first time, however, he stated that he did believe we could build an ABM system able to cope with a hypothetical Chinese missile attack, which by definition would be "light" and uncomplicated. In recommending that we go ahead with a program to build what came to be known as the Sentinel system, he said that "there are *marginal* grounds for concluding that a light deployment of U.S. ABM's against this possibility is prudent." A few sentences later, however, he warned: "The danger in deploying this relatively light and reliable Chinese-oriented ABM system is going to be that pressures will develop to expand it into a heavy Soviet-oriented ABM system." The record makes it clear that he was quite right in this prediction.

Meanwhile the U.S.S.R. was going ahead with its own ABM program. The Russian program proceeded by fits and starts, and our understanding of it was, as might be supposed in such a situation, even more erratic. It is now generally agreed that the only ABM system the Russians have deployed is an area defense around Moscow much like our old Nike Zeus system. It appears to have virtually no capability against our offense, and it has been, as we shall see below, extremely counterproductive insofar as its goal of defending Moscow is concerned.

Development and deployment of offensive-weapons systems on both sides progressed rapidly during the 1960's, but rather than discuss these historically I shall go directly to the picture that the Administration has given of the present status and future projection of such forces.

Data recently presented by the Department of Defense show that the U.S. and the U.S.S.R. are about even in numbers of intercontinental missiles, and that the U.S. is ahead in both long-range aircraft and submarines of the Polaris type [*see illustration on this page*]. The small Russian missiles are mostly what we call SS-11's, which were described in the hearings as being roughly the equivalent of our Minutemen. The large Russian missile is what we call the SS-9. Deputy Secretary of Defense David Packard characterized its capability as one 20-megaton warhead or three five-megaton warheads. Our own missiles are almost entirely the smaller Minutemen. There currently remain only 54 of the larger Titans in our strategic forces. Not covered in the table are "extras" such as the U.S.S.R.'s FOBS (fractional orbital bombardment system) and IRBM's (intermediate-range ballistic missiles), nor the U.S.'s bombardment aircraft deployed on carriers and overseas bases in Europe and elsewhere. There are, of course, many important details that do not come out clearly in such a simple tabular presentation; these include payload capacity, warhead yield, number of warheads per missile and, often the most important, warhead accuracy.

In the area of defensive systems designed to cope with the offensive systems outlined above, both the U.S. and the

U.S.S.R. have defenses against bombers that would probably be adequate against a prolonged attack using chemical explosives (where 10 percent attrition is enough) and almost certainly inadequate against a nuclear attack (where 10 percent penetration is enough). In addition the U.S.S.R. has its ineffective ABM deployment around Moscow, usually estimated as consisting of fewer than 100 antimissile missiles.

What all these complicated details add up to can be expressed in a single word: parity. This is clearly not numerical equality in the number of warheads or in the number of megatons or in the total "throw weight"; in fact, given different design approaches on the two sides, simultaneous equality in these three figures is entirely impossible. It is, rather, parity with respect to strategic objectives; that is, in each case these forces are easily sufficient for deterrence and entirely insufficient for a successful preemptive strike. In the jargon of strategic studies either side would retain, after a massive "first strike" by the other, a sufficiently large "assured destruction capability" against the other in order to deter such a first strike from being made.

There is much argument about exactly what it takes in the way of "assured destruction capability" in order to deter, but even the most conservative strategic planners conclude that the threat of only a few hundred warheads exploding over population and industrial centers would be sufficient for the purpose. The large growing disparity between the number of warheads needed for the purpose and the number actually possessed by each side is what leads to the concept of "overkill." If present trends continue, in the future all or most missiles will be MIRVed, and so this overkill will be increased by perhaps another order of magnitude.

Here let me note that it is sometimes

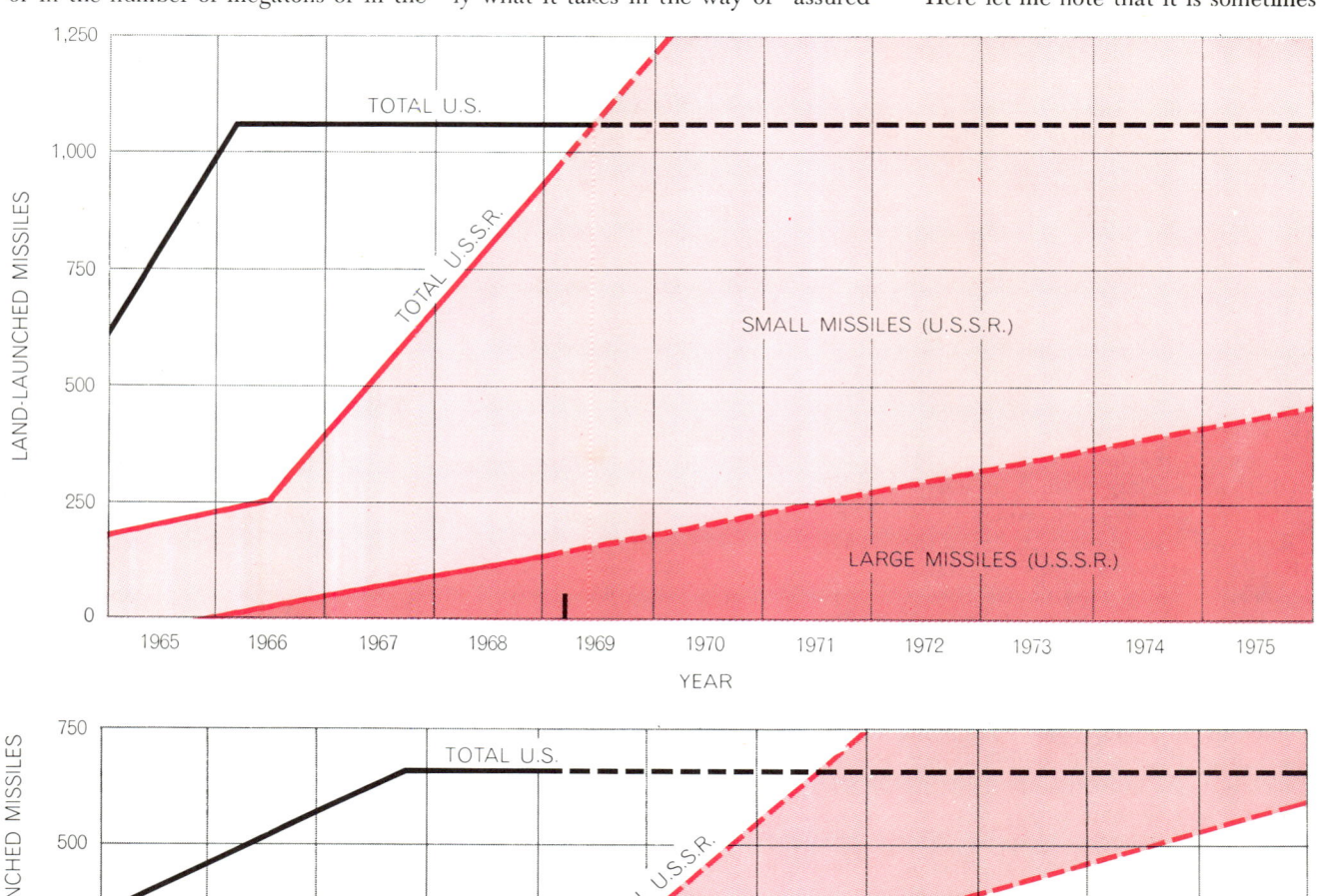

EXTRAPOLATED TRENDS in the deployment of strategic offensive missiles by the U.S. and the U.S.S.R. are indicated by the broken lines in this pair of charts, which are based on a presentation by Deputy Secretary of Defense David Packard to the Senate Foreign Relations Committee on March 26. The chart at top shows the numbers of deployed ICBM's for both sides during the period 1965–1975. The Russian total is broken down into "small" missiles (the one-megaton SS-11's) and "large" missiles (the multimegaton SS-9's). The chart at bottom shows the deployed SLBM's during the same period. The extrapolations suggest that the Russians will be even with us in ICBM's quite soon and will catch up in SLBM's sometime between 1971 and 1977. One important factor omitted from the charts is the imminent deployment by both sides of MIRV's (multiple independently targetable reentry vehicles).

argued that there is a disparity in the present situation because Russian missile warheads are said to be bigger than U.S. warheads, both in weight and megatonnage; similarly, it is argued that MIRVing does not increase overkill because total yield is reduced in going from single to multiple warheads. This argument is based on the false notion that the individual MIRV warheads of the future will be "small" when measured against the purpose assigned to them. Against large, "soft" targets such as cities bombs *very much* smaller than those that could be used as components of MIRV's are (and in the case of Hiroshima were proved to be) entirely adequate for destroying the heart of a city and killing hundreds of thousands of people. Furthermore, in the case of small, "hard" targets such as missile silos, command posts and other military installations, having explosions bigger than those for which the "kill," or crater, radius slightly exceeds "circular error probable" (CEP) adds little to the probability of destroying such targets. Crater radius depends roughly on the cube root of the explosive power; consequently, if during the period when technology allows us to go from one to 10 warheads per missile it also allows us to improve accuracy by a little more than twofold, the "kill" per warhead will remain nearly the same in most cases, whereas the number of warheads increases tenfold.

In any case, it is fair to say that in spite of a number of such arguments about details, nearly everyone who testified at the ABM hearings agreed that the present situation is one in which each side possesses forces adequate to deter the other. In short, we now have parity in the only sense that ultimately counts.

Several forecasts have been made of what the strategic-weapons situation will be in the mid-1970's. In most respects here again there is quite general agreement. Part of the presentation by Deputy Secretary Packard to the Senate Foreign Relations Committee on March 26 were two graphs showing the trends in numbers of deployed offensive missiles beginning in 1965 and extending to 1975 [*see illustrations on page 46*]. There is no serious debate about the basic features of these graphs. It is agreed by all that in the recent past the U.S. has been far ahead of the U.S.S.R. in all areas, and that the Russians began a rapid deployment program a few years ago that will bring them even with us in ICBM's quite soon and that, if extended

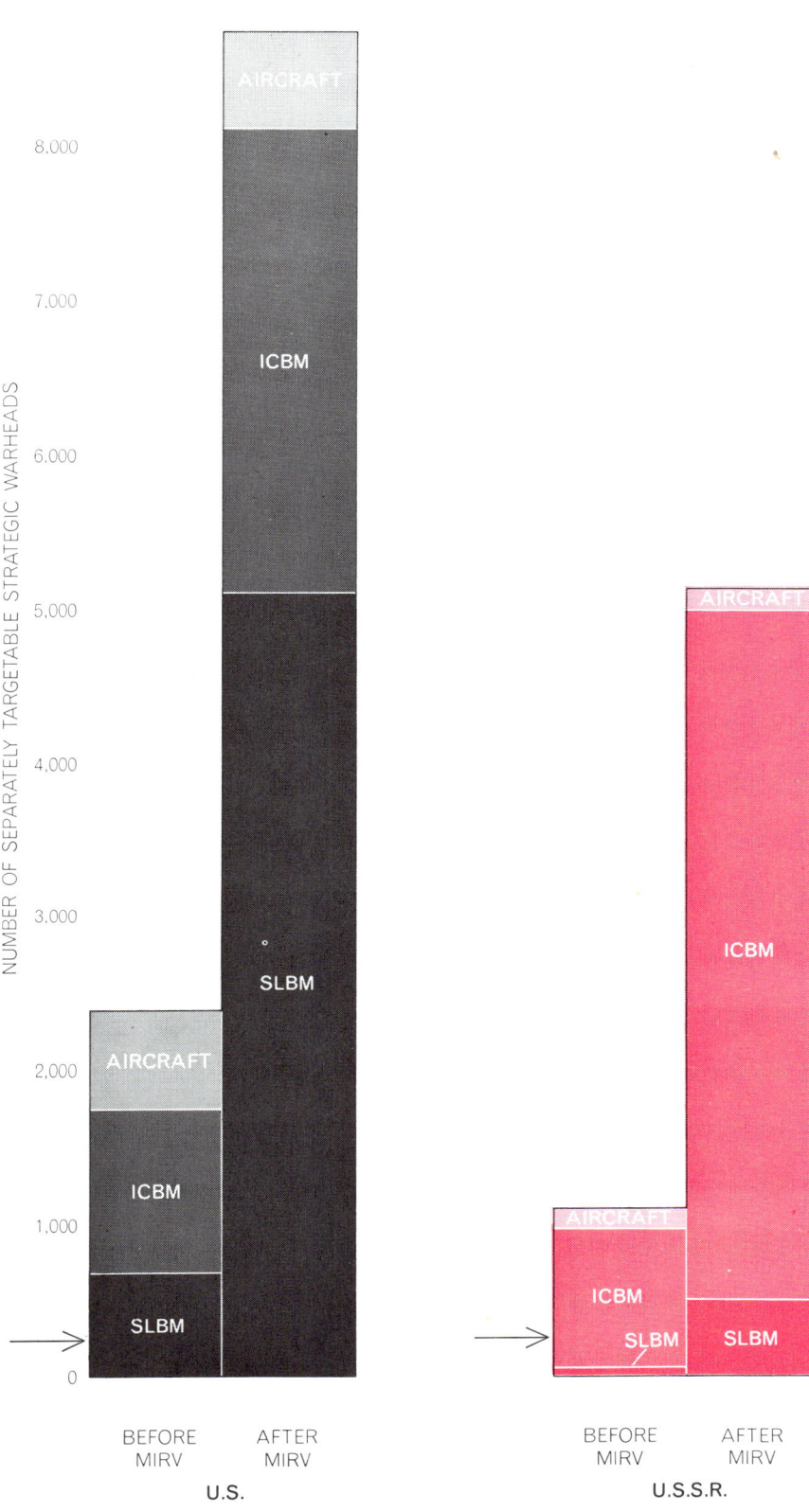

IMPACT OF MIRV on the strategic balance is emphasized in this chart, which is based on one prepared by the staff of the Senate Foreign Relations Committee and presented by Senator Albert Gore of Tennessee on March 26. The chart depicts the strategic balance in terms of separately targetable strategic warheads before and after MIRVing, which is expected to take place in the next five years. The two black arrows near the bottom indicate the number of warheads that could devastate the 50 largest cities on each side.

ahead without any slowdown, would bring them even in submarine-launched ballistic missiles (SLBM's) sometime between 1971 and 1977.

One important factor that the Department of Defense omitted from its graphs is MIRV. Deployment plans for MIRV's have not been released by either the U.S. or the U.S.S.R., although various rough projections were made at the hearings about numbers of warheads per vehicle (three to 10), about accuracies (figures around half a mile were often mentioned, and it was implied that U.S. accuracies were better than Russian ones) and about development status (the U.S. was said to be ahead in developments in this field). A pair of charts emphasizing the impact of MIRV was prepared by the staff of the Senate Foreign Relations Committee [see illustration on page 47].

One could argue with both of these sets of charts. For example, one might wonder why the Senate charts show so few warheads on the Russian Polaris-type submarine and why they show only three MIRV's on U.S. Minutemen; on the other hand, one might wonder whether the Department of Defense's projected buildup of the Russian Polaris fleet could be that fast, or whether one should count the older Russian missile submarines. Nonetheless, the general picture presented cannot be far wrong. Moreover, the central arguments pursued throughout the ABM hearings (in both the Senate Foreign Relations Committee hearings in March and the Senate Armed Services Committee hearings in April) were not primarily concerned with these numerical matters. Rather, they were concerned with (1) Secretary of Defense Melvin R. Laird's interpretation of these numbers insofar as Russian *intentions* were concerned, (2) the validity of the Safeguard ABM system as a response to the purported strategic problems of the 1970's and (3) the arms-race implications of Safeguard.

As for the matter of intentions, those favoring the ABM concept generally held that the only "rational" explanation of the Russians' recent SS-9 buildup, coupled with their multiple-warhead development program and the Moscow ABM system, was that they were aiming for a first-strike capability. One must admit that almost anything is conceivable as far as intentions are concerned, but there certainly are simpler, and it seems to me much more likely, explanations. The simplest of all is contained in Deputy Secretary Packard's chart. The most surprising feature of this chart is the fact that the Russians were evidently satisfied with being such a poor second for such a long time. This is made more puzzling by the fact that all during this period U.S. defense officials found it necessary to boast about how far ahead we were in order to be able to resist internal pressures for still greater expansion of our offensive forces.

Another possible reason, and one that I believe added to the other in the minds of the Russian planners, was that their strategists concluded in the mid-1960's that, whatever the top officials here might say, certain elements would eventually succeed in getting a large-scale ABM system built, and that penetration-aid devices, including multiple warheads, would be needed to meet the challenge. Whether or not they were correct in this latter hypothetical analysis is still uncertain at this writing. Let us, however, pass on from this question of someone else's intentions and consider whether or not the proposed Safeguard ABM system is a valid, rational and necessary response to the Russian deployments and developments outlined above.

To many of those who have recently written favorably about ABM defenses or who have testified in their favor before the Congressional committees, Safeguard is supported mainly as a prototype of something else: a "thick" defense of the U.S. against a massive Russian missile attack. This is clearly not at all the rationale for the Safeguard decision as presented by President Nixon in his press conference of March 14, nor is it implied as more than a dividend in the defense secretaries' testimony. The President said that he wanted a system that would protect a *part* of our Minuteman force in order to increase the credibility of our deterrent, and that he had overruled moving in the direction of a massive city defense because "even starting with a thin system and then going to a heavy system tends to be more provocative in terms of making credible a first-strike capability against the Soviet Union. I want no provocation which might deter arms talks." The top civilian defense officials give this same rationale, although they put a little more emphasis on the "prototype" and "growth potential" aspects of the system. For simplicity and clarity I shall focus on the Administration's proposal, as stated in open session by responsible officials.

From a technical point of view and as far as components are concerned, President Nixon's Safeguard system of today is very little different from President Johnson's Sentinel system [see illustrations on page 51]. There are only minor changes in the location of certain components (away from cities), and elements have been added to some of the radars so that they can now observe submarine-launched missiles coming from directions other than directly from the U.S.S.R. and China. As before, the system consists of a long-range interceptor carrying a large nuclear weapon (Spartan), a fast short-range interceptor carrying a small nuclear weapon (Sprint), two types of radar (perimeter acquisition radar, or PAR, and missile-site radar, or MSR), a computer for directing the battle, and a command and control system for integrating Safeguard with the national command. I shall not describe the equipment in detail at this point but pass on directly to what I believe can be concluded from the hearings and other public sources about each of the following four major questions: (1) Assuming that Safeguard could protect Minuteman, is it needed to protect our deterrent? (2) Assuming that Safeguard "works," can it in fact safeguard Minuteman? (3) Will it work? (4) Anyway, what harm can it do?

First: Assuming that Safeguard could protect Minuteman, is it needed to protect our deterrent?

Perhaps the clearest explanation of why the answer to this first question is "no" was given by Wolfgang K. H. Panofsky before the Senate Armed Services Committee on April 22. He described how the deterrent consists of three main components: Polaris submarines, bombers and land-based ICBM's. Each of these components alone is capable of delivering far more warheads than is actually needed for deterrence, and each is currently defended against surprise destruction in a quite different way. ICBM's are in hard silos and are numerous. Polarises are hidden in the seas. Bombers can be placed on various levels of alert and can be dispersed.

Since the warning time in the case of an ICBM attack is generally taken as being about 30 minutes, the people who believe the deterrent may be in serious danger usually imagine that the bombers are attacked by missile submarines, and therefore have only a 15-minute warning. This is important because a 30-minute warning gives the bombers ample time to get off the ground. In that case, however, an attack on all three components cannot be made simultaneously; that is, if the attacking weapons are launched simultaneously, they

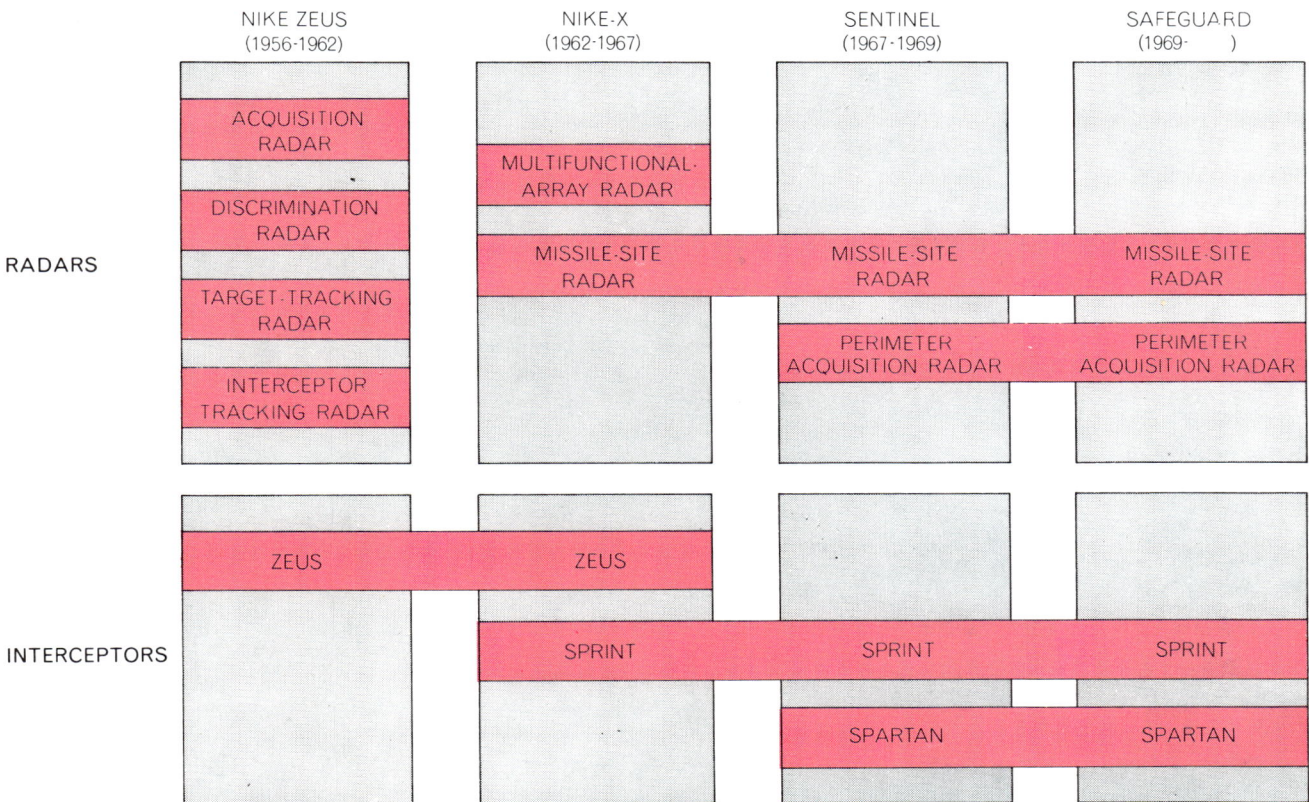

EVOLUTION OF U.S. ABM SYSTEMS is represented in this illustration, which is adapted from a chart introduced by Daniel J. Fink in his testimony before the Senate Foreign Relations Committee on March 6. In general the radar components of the successive designs have progressed from slow, mechanically steered, single-function radars to fast, electronically steered, multifunction radars. The slow Zeus ABM missile has been superseded by the short-range Sprint (for terminal defense) and the long-range Spartan (for area defense). The components of the Safeguard system are the same as those that were originally intended for the earlier Sentinel system.

cannot arrive simultaneously, and vice versa.

Thus it is incredible that all three of our deterrent systems could become vulnerable in the same time period, and it is doubly incredible that we could not know that this would happen without sufficient notice so that we could do something about it. There is, therefore, no basis for a frantic reaction to the hypothetical Russian threat to Minuteman. Still, it is sensible and prudent to begin thinking about the problem, and so we turn to the other questions. We must consider these questions in the technological framework of the mid-1970's, and we shall do this now in the way defense officials currently seem to favor: by assuming that this is the best of all possible technological worlds, that everything works as intended and that direct extrapolations of current capabilities are valid.

Second: Assuming that Safeguard "works," can it in fact safeguard Minuteman?

One good approach to this problem is the one used by George W. Rathjens in his testimony before the Senate Armed Services Committee on April 23. His analysis took as a basis of calculation the implication in Secretary Laird's testimony that the Minuteman force may become seriously imperiled in the mid-1970's. Rathjens then estimated how many SS-9's would have to be deployed at that time in order to achieve this result. From this number, and the estimate of the current number of SS-9's deployed, he got a rate of deployment. He also had to make an assumption about how many Sprints and Spartans would be deployed at that time, and his estimates were based on the first phase of Safeguard deployment. These last numbers have not been released, but a range of reasonable values can be guessed from the cost estimates given. Assuming that the SS-9's would have four or five MIRV warheads each by that time, Rathjens found that by prolonging the SS-9 production program by a few months the Russians would be able to cope with Safeguard by simply exhausting it and would still have enough **warheads left to imperil Minuteman, if that is indeed their intention** [see illustration on page 56].

The length of this short safe period does depend on the numbers used in the calculations, and they of course can be disputed to a degree. Thus if one assumes that it takes fewer Russian warheads to imperil Minuteman (it can't be less than one for one!), then the assumed deployment rate is lower and the safe period is lengthened; on the other hand, if one notes that the missile-site radars in our system are much softer than even today's silos, then the first attacking warheads, fired directly at the radars, can be smaller and less accurate, so that a higher degree of MIRVing can be used for attacking these radars and a shorter safe period results. To go further, it was suggested that the accuracy/yield combination of the more numerous SS-11's might be sufficient for attacking the missile-site radars, and therefore, if the Russians were to elect such an option, there would be no safe period at all. In short, the most that Safeguard can do is either delay somewhat the date when Minuteman would be imperiled or cause the attacker to build up his forces at a somewhat higher rate if indeed imperiling Minuteman by a fixed date is his purpose.

In the more general case this problem

SPRINT ABM MISSILE was photographed during a test flight at the White Sands Missile Range in New Mexico. The photograph, which was released by the U.S. Army's Nike-X Project Office in March, 1966, shows the second stage of the missile heated to incandescence by friction with the atmosphere. Because of the extremely high speed of the Sprint, the missile's skin in places reaches temperatures hotter than inside its rocket motor. The bulges are created by the guidance fins at the rear of the second stage.

is often discussed in budgetary terms, and the "cost-exchange ratio" between offense and defense is computed for a wide variety of specific types of weapon. Such calculations give a wide variety of results, and there is much argument about them. However, even using current offense designs (that is, without MIRV), such calculations usually strongly favor the offense. This exchange ratio varies almost linearly with the degree of MIRVing of the offensive missiles, and therefore it seems to me that in the ideal technological future we have taken as our context this exchange ratio will still more strongly favor the offense.

Third: Will it work? By this question I mean: Will operational units be able to intercept enemy warheads accompanied by enemy penetration aids in an atmosphere of total astonishment and uncertainty? I do not mean: Will test equipment and test crews intercept U.S. warheads accompanied by U.S. penetration aids in a contrived atmosphere? A positive answer to the latter question is a necessary condition for obtaining a positive answer to the former, but it is by no stretch of the imagination a sufficient condition.

This basic question has been attacked from two quite different angles: by examining historical analogies and by examining the technical elements of the problem in detail. I shall touch on both here. Design-oriented people who consider this a purely technical question emphasize the second approach. I believe the question is by no means a purely technical question, and I suggest that the historical-analogy approach is more promising, albeit much more difficult to use correctly.

False analogies are common in this argument. We find that some say: "You can't tell me that if we can put a man on the moon we can't build an ABM." Others say: "That's what Oppenheimer told us about the hydrogen bomb." These two statements contain the same basic error. They are examples of successes in a contest between technology and nature, whereas the ABM issue involves a contest between two technologies: offensive weapons and penetration aids versus defensive weapons and discrimination techniques. These analogies would be more pertinent if, in the first case, someone were to jerk the moon away just before the astronauts landed, or if, in the second case, nature were to keep changing the nuclear-reaction probabilities all during the development of the hydrogen bomb and once again after it was deployed.

Proper historical analogies should involve modern high-technology defense systems that have actually been installed and used in combat. If one examines the record of such systems, one finds that they do often produce some attrition of the offense, but not nearly enough to be of use against a nuclear attack. The most up-to-date example is provided by the Russian SAM's and other air-defense equipment deployed in North Vietnam. This system "works" after a fashion because both the equipment designers and the operating crews have had plenty of opportunities to practice against real U.S. targets equipped with real U.S. countermeasures and employing real U.S. tactics.

The best example of a U.S. system is somewhat older, but I believe it is still relevant. It is the SAGE system, a complex air-defense system designed in the early 1950's. All the components worked on the test range, but by 1960 we came to realize, even without combat testing, that SAGE could not really cope with the offense that was then coming into being. We thereupon greatly curtailed and modified our plans, although we did continue with some parts of the system. To quote from the recent report on the ABM decision prepared by Wiesner, Abram Chayes and others: "Still, after fifteen years, and the expenditure of more than $20 billion, it is generally conceded that we do not have a significant capability to defend ourselves against a well-planned air attack. The Soviet Union, after even greater effort, has probably not done much better."

So much for analogies; let us turn to the Safeguard system itself. Doubts about its being able to work were raised during the public hearings on a variety of grounds, some of which are as follows:

First, and perhaps foremost, there is the remarkable fact that the new Safeguard system and the old Sentinel system use virtually the same hardware deployed in a very similar manner, and yet they have entirely different primary purposes. Sentinel had as its purpose defending large soft targets against the so-called Chinese threat. The Chinese threat by definition involved virtually no sophisticated penetration aids and no possibilities of exhausting the defense; thus were "solved" two of the most difficult problems that had eliminated Nike Zeus and Nike-X.

Safeguard has as its primary purpose defending a part of the Minuteman force against a Russian attack. It is not credible that a Russian attack against the part of the Minuteman force so defended would be other than massive and sophisticated, so that we are virtually right back to trying to do what in 1967 we said we could not do, and we are trying to do it with no real change in the missiles or the radars. It is true that defending hard points is to a degree easier than defending cities because interception can be accomplished later and at lower altitudes, thus giving discrimination techniques more time to work. Moreover, only those objects headed for specific small areas must be intercepted. These factors do make the problem somewhat easier, but they do not ensure its solution, and plenty of room for doubt remains.

Second, there is the contest between penetration aids and discrimination techniques. This was discussed at length by Richard L. Garwin and Hans A. Bethe in the article beginning on page 164 and mentioned also in varying degrees of detail by many of those who testified recently concerning the ABM issue. The Russian physicist Andrei D. Sakharov, in his essay "Thoughts on Progress, Coexistence and Intellectual Freedom," put the issue this way: "Improvements in the resistance of warheads to shock waves and the radiation effects of neutron and X-ray exposure, the possibility of mass use of relatively light and inexpensive decoys that are virtually indistinguishable from warheads and exhaust the capabilities of an antimissile defense system, a perfection of tactics of massed and concentrated attacks, in time and space, that overstrain the defense detection centers, the use of orbital and fractional-orbital attacks, the use of active and passive jamming and other methods not disclosed in the press—all of this has created technical and economic obstacles to an effective missile defense that, at the present time, are virtually insurmountable."

I would add only MIRV to Sakharov's list. Pitted against this plethora of penetration aids are various observational methods designed to discriminate the real warheads. Some of the penetration devices obviously work only at high altitudes, but even these make it necessary for the final "sorting" to be delayed, and thus they still contribute to making the defense problem harder. Other devices can continue to confuse the defense even down to low altitudes. Some of the problems the offense presents to the defense can no doubt be solved (and have been solved) when considered separately and in isolation. That is, they can be

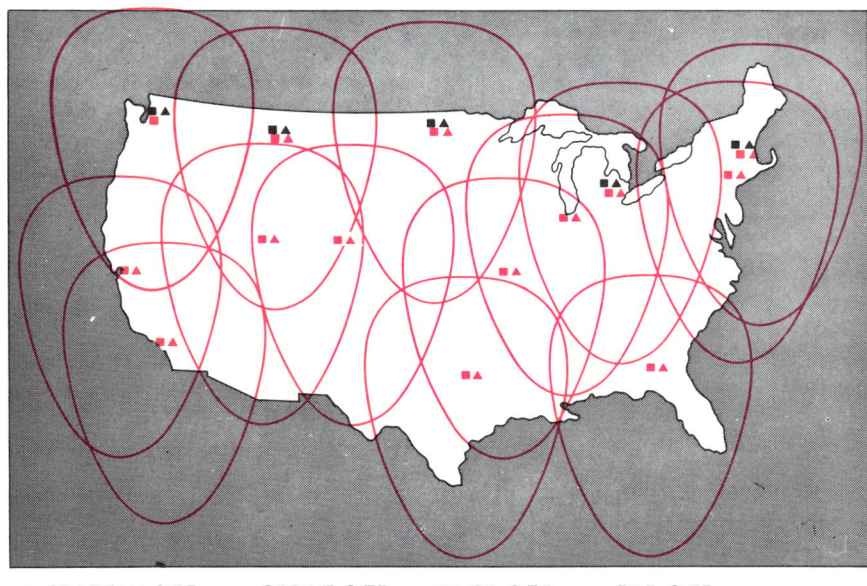

SENTINEL SYSTEM was described by the Johnson Administration as a "thin" ABM system designed to defend the U.S. against a hypothetical Chinese missile attack in the 1970's. The main defense was to be provided by long-range Spartan missiles. The Spartans would be deployed at about 14 locations in order to provide an area defense of the whole country. The range of each "farm" of Spartans is indicated by the egg-shaped area around it; for missiles attacking over the northern horizon the intercept range of the Spartan is elongated somewhat to the south. The Sentinel system would also include some short-range Sprint missiles, which were originally to be deployed to defend the five or six perimeter acquisition radars, or PAR's, which were to be deployed at five sites located across the northern part of the country. Missile-site radars, or MSR's, were to be deployed at every ABM site.

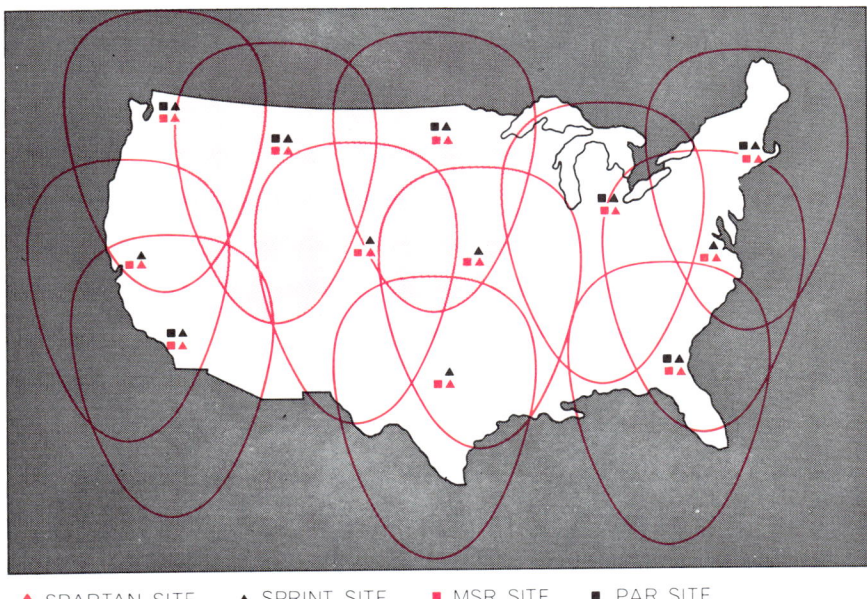

SAFEGUARD SYSTEM, President Nixon's proposed modification of the Sentinel scheme, uses essentially the same components in a slightly different array to accomplish an entirely different primary purpose: the defense of a part of our Minuteman force against a hypothetical surprise attack by the Russians. Phase I of Safeguard covers the construction of ABM sites at two Minuteman "fields": one near Malmstrom Air Force Base in Montana and the other near Grand Forks Air Force Base in North Dakota (*colored areas*). The completed system would have a total of 12 sites, each with Sprint and Spartan coverage, located somewhat farther away from the cities. In addition two new PAR sites would be included in order to observe submarine-launched missiles coming from directions other than due north.

solved for a time, until the offense designers react. One must have serious reservations, however, whether these problems can ever be solved for any long period in the complex combinations that even a modestly sophisticated attacker can present. Further, such a contest *could* result in a catastrophic failure of the system in which all or nearly all interceptions fail.

Third, there is the unquantifiable difference between the test range and the real world. The extraordinary efforts of the Air Force to test operationally deployed Minutemen show that it too regards this as an important problem. Moreover, the tests to date do seem to have revealed important weaknesses in the deployed forces. The problem has many aspects: the possible differences between test equipment and deployed equipment; the certain differences between the offensive warheads and penetration aids supplied by us as test targets and the corresponding equipment and tactics the defense must ultimately be prepared to face; the differences between the installation crews at a test site and at a deployment site; the differences in attitudes and motivation between a test crew and an operational crew (even if it is composed of the same men); the differences between men and equipment that have recently been made ready and whom everyone is watching and men and equipment that have been standing ready for years during which nothing happened; the differences between the emotional atmosphere where everyone knows it is not "for real" and the emotional atmosphere where no one can believe what he has just been told. It may be that all that enormously complex equipment will be ready to work the very first time it must "for real," and it may be that all those thousands of human beings have performed all their interlocking assignments correctly, but I have very substantial doubts about it.

Fourth, there is the closely related "hair-trigger/stiff-trigger" contradiction. Any active defense system such as Safeguard must sit in readiness for two or four or eight years and then fire at precisely the correct second following a warning time of only minutes. Furthermore, the precision needed for the firing time is so fine that machines must be used to choose the exact instant of firing no matter how the decision to fire is made. In the case of offensive missiles the situation is different in an essential way: Although maintaining readiness throughout a long, indefinite period is necessary, the moment of firing is not so precisely controlled in general and hence human decision-makers, including even those at high levels, may readily be permitted to play a part in the decision-making process. Thus if we wish to be certain that the defense will respond under conditions of surprise, the trigger of the ABM system, unlike the triggers of the ICBM's and Polarises, must be continuously sensitive and ready—in short, a hair trigger—for indefinitely long periods of time.

On the other hand, it is obvious that we cannot afford to have an ABM missile fire by mistake or in response to a false alarm. Indeed, the Army went to some pains to assure residents of areas near proposed Sentinel sites that it was imposing requirements to ensure against the accidental launching of the missile and the subsequent detonation of the nuclear warhead it carries. Moreover, Army officials have assured the public that no ABM missiles would ever be launched without the specific approval of "very high authorities."

These two requirements—a hair trigger so that the system can cope with a surprise attack and a stiff trigger so that it will never go off accidentally or without proper authorization—are, I believe, contradictory requirements. In saying this I am not expressing doubt about the stated intentions of the present Army leaders, and I strongly endorse the restrictions implied in their statements. I am saying, however, that if the system cannot be fired without approval of "the highest authorities," then the probability of its being fired under conditions of surprise is less than it would be otherwise. This probability depends to a degree on the highly classified technical details of the Command and Control System, but in the last analysis it depends more on the fact that "the highest authority" is a human being and therefore subject to all the failures and foibles pertaining thereto.

This brings us to our fourth principal question: Anyway, what harm can it

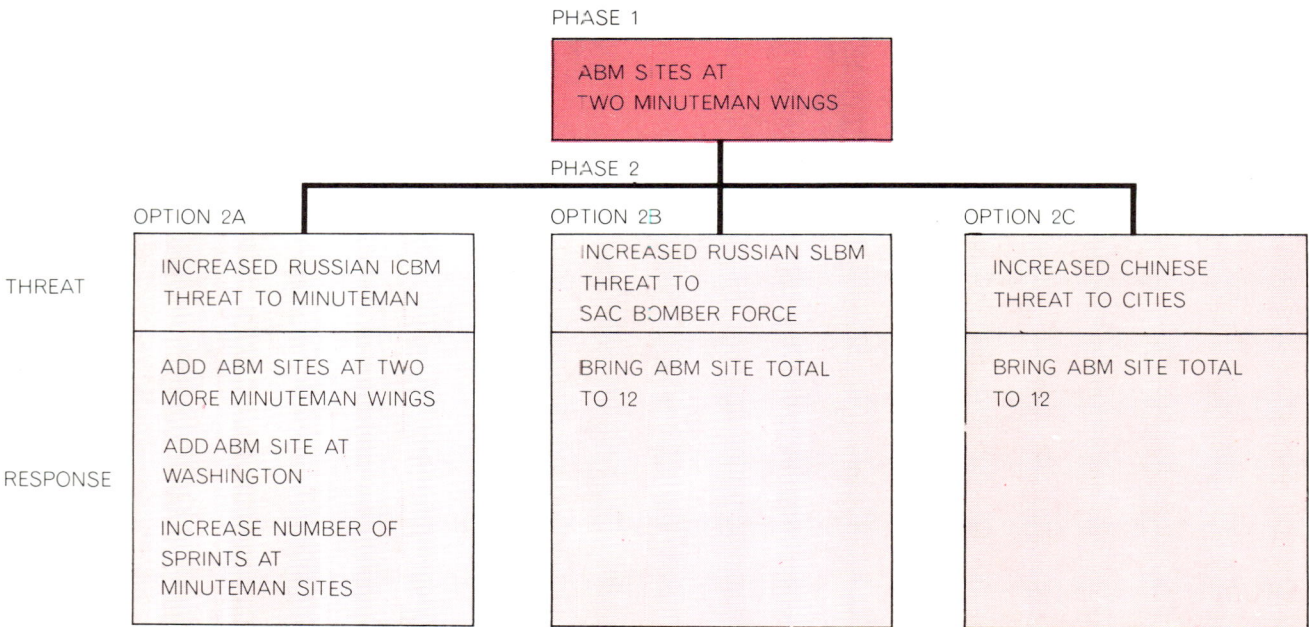

SAFEGUARD PHASE II provides for three different optional responses to various potential threats in the 1970's. A possible further addition would be sites in Alaska and Hawaii. This chart is also adapted from Deputy Secretary Packard's testimony on March 26.

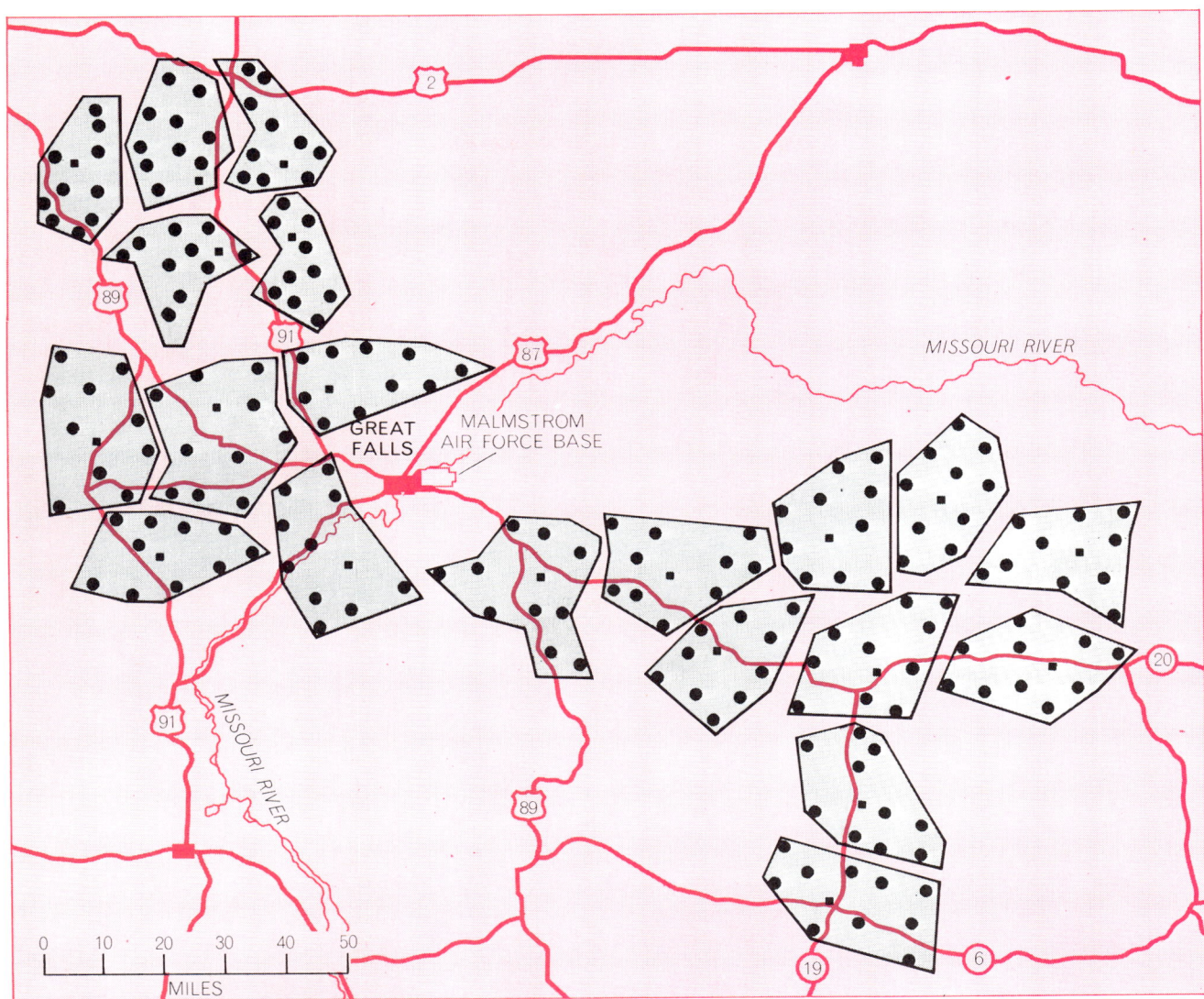

■ CONTROL CENTER   ● MINUTEMAN SILO

MINUTEMAN MISSILE BASE in the vicinity of Malmstrom Air Force Base is shown on this map, which is based on information released by the Department of the Air Force. The Minuteman missiles are grouped in 20 flights of 10 missiles each for a total of 200 missiles. Every flight has its own control center, each of which is capable of launching an entire squadron of 50 missiles.

do?

We have just found that the total deterrent is very probably not in peril, that the Safeguard system probably cannot safeguard Minuteman even if it "works," that there is, to say the least, considerable uncertainty whether or not it will "work." Nonetheless, if there were no harm in it, we might be prudent and follow the basic motto of the arms race: "Let us err on the side of military safety." There seem to be many answers to the question of what harm building an ABM system would do. First of all, such a system would cost large sums of money needed for nondefense purposes. Second, it would divert money and attention from what may be better military solutions to the strategic problems posed by the Administration. Third, it would intensify the arms race. All these considerations were discussed at the hearings; I shall comment here only on the third, the arms-race implications of the ABM decision.

It is often said that an ABM system is not an accelerating element in the arms race because it is intrinsically defensive. For example, during the hearings Senator Henry M. Jackson of Washington, surely one of the best-informed senators in this field, said essentially that, and he quoted Premier Kosygin as having said the same thing. I believe such a notion is in error and is based on what we may call "the fallacy of the last move." I believe that in the real world of constant change in both the technology and the deployed numbers of all kinds of strategic-weapons systems, ABM systems are accelerating elements in the arms race. In support of this view let us recall one of the features of the history recited at the start of this article.

At the beginning of this decade we began to hear about a possible Russian ABM system, and we became concerned about its potential effects on our ICBM and Polaris systems. In response the MIRV concept was invented. Today there are additional justifications for MIRV besides penetration, but that is how it started. Now, the possibility of a Russian MIRV is used as one of the main arguments in support of the Safeguard system. Thus we have come one full turn around the arms-race spiral. No one in 1960 and 1961 thought through the potential destabilizing effects of multiple warheads, and certainly no one predicted, or even could have predicted, that the inexorable logic of the arms race would carry us directly from Russian talk in 1960 about defending Moscow against missiles to a requirement for hard-point defense of offensive-missile sites in the U.S. in 1969.

By the same token I am sure the Russians did not foresee the large increase in deployed U.S. warheads that will ultimately result from their ABM deployment and that made it so counterproductive. Similarly, no one today can describe in detail the chain reaction the Safeguard deployment would lead to, but it is easy to see the seeds of a future acceleration of the arms race in the Nixon Administration's Safeguard proposal. Soon after Safeguard is started (let us assume for now that it will be) Russian offense planners are going to look at it and say something such as: "It may not work, but we must be prudent and assume it will." They may then plan further deployments, or more complex penetration systems, or maybe they will go to more dangerous systems such as bombs in orbit. A little later, when some of our optimistic statements about how "it will do the job it is supposed to do" have become part of history, our strategic planners are going to look at Safeguard and say something such as: "Maybe it will work as they said, but we must be prudent and assume it will not and besides, *now* look at what the Russians are doing."

This approach to strategic thinking, known in the trade as "worst-case analysis," leads to a completely hopeless situation in which there is no possibility of achieving a state of affairs that both sides would consider as constituting parity. Unless the arms race is stopped by political action outside the two defense establishments, I feel reasonably sure there will be another "crash program" response analogous to what we had in the days of the "missile gap"—a situation some would like to see repeated.

I also mentioned in my own testimony at the ABM hearings that "we may further expect deployment of these ABM systems to lead to the persistent query 'But how do you know it *really* works?' and thus to increase the pressures against the current limited nuclear-test ban as well as to work against amplifying it." I mentioned this then, and I mention it again now, in the hope that it will become a self-defeating prediction. It is also important to note that the response of our own defense establishment to the Russian ABM deployment, which I have outlined above, was not the result of our being "provoked," and I emphasize this because we hear so much discussion about what is a "provocative" move and what is not. Rather, our response was motivated by a deep-seated belief that the only appropriate response to any new technical development on the other side is further technical complexity of our own. The arms race is not so much a series of political provocations followed by hot emotional reactions as it is a series of technical challenges followed by cool, calculated responses in the form of ever more costly, more complex and more fully automatic devices. I believe this endless, seemingly uncontrollable process was one of the principal factors President Eisenhower had in mind when he made his other (usually forgotten) warning: "We must be alert to the... danger that public policy could itself become the captive of a scientific-technological elite." He placed this other warning, also from his farewell address, on the same level as the much more familiar comment about the military-industrial complex.

Several alternative approaches to Safeguard for protecting Minuteman have been discussed recently. These include superhardening, proliferation, a "shell game" in which there are more silos than missiles, and land-mobile missiles. Although I was personally hopeful before the hearings that at least one of these approaches would maintain its invulnerability, a review of the recent debates leaves me now with the pessimistic view that none of them holds much promise beyond the next 10 years.

Silo-hardening most probably does work now, in the sense that the combination of SS-11 accuracy and yield and Minuteman silo-hardening works out in such a way that one incoming warhead (and hence one SS-11 missile) has less than a 50-50 chance of destroying a Minuteman. If one considers the technological trends in hardening, yield per unit weight, MIRVing and accuracy, however, it does seem convincing that this is a game in which the offense eventually will win. Albert Wohlstetter, testifying in favor of the Safeguard system before the Senate Armed Services Committee, quoted a paper he wrote with Fred Hoffman in 1954 (long before any ICBM's were actually in place anywhere) predicting that the ability of silo-hardening to protect offensive missiles would run out by the end of the 1960's. That was a remarkably prescient study and is wrong only in numerical detail.

If we take the same rosy view of technology that was taken in almost all the pro-ABM arguments, then hardening will not work for more than another five years. My own view of the technological future is clearly much less rosy, but I do believe that the situation in which hardening is no longer the answer could come by, say, 1980 or, more appropriately, 1984.

Proliferation of Minuteman would have worked in the absence of MIRV. Now, however, it would seem that the ability to MIRV, which no doubt can eventually be carried much further than the fewfold MIRV we see for the immediate future, clearly makes proliferation a losing game as well as the dan-

FIRST SALVO LAUNCH of Minuteman ICBM's was made at Vandenberg Air Force Base in California on February 24, 1966. Photograph was released by U.S. Air Force.

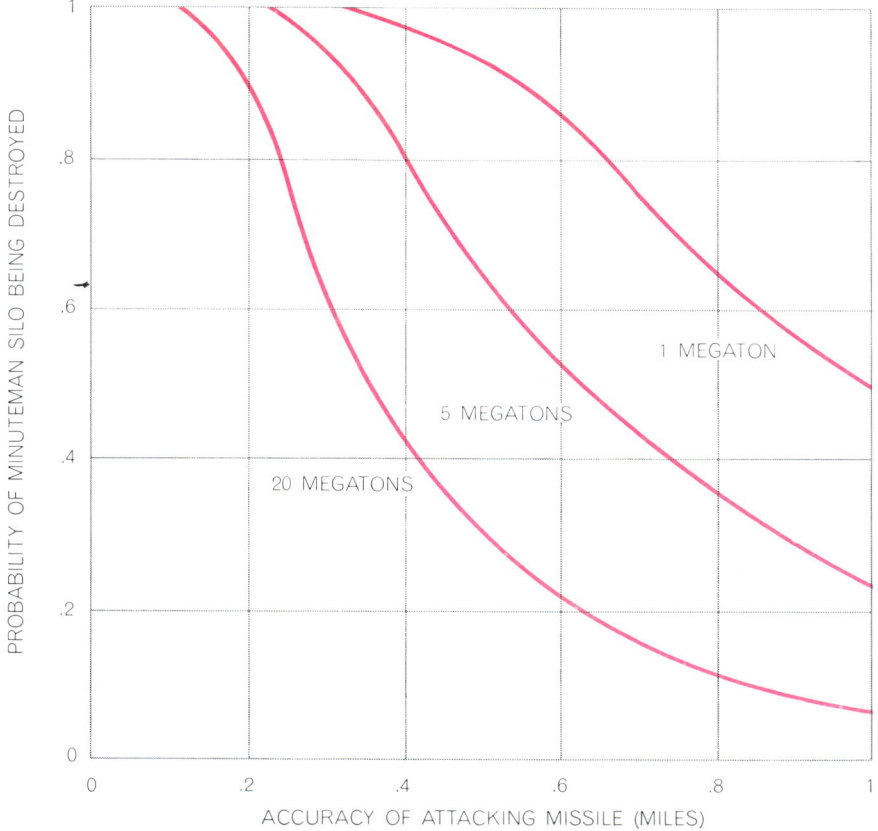

VULNERABILITY OF MINUTEMAN is revealed in this graph, which relates probability of destruction of a hardened Minuteman silo to accuracy for three different sizes of attacking warhead. This graph was interpreted by Deputy Secretary Packard as demonstrating the seriousness of the threat to Minuteman posed by the large Russian SS-9 missile, which he said is capable of carrying either one 20-megaton warhead or three five-megaton warheads.

gerous one it always was.

The "shell game" has not in my view been analyzed in satisfactory detail, but it would appear to have a serious destabilizing effect on the arms race. Schemes have been suggested for verifying that a certain fraction of the missile holes are in fact empty, but one can foresee a growing and persistent belief on each side that the "other missiles" must be hidden somewhere.

Road-mobile and rail-mobile versions of Minuteman have been seriously studied for well over a decade. These ideas have always foundered on two basic difficulties: (1) Such systems are inherently soft and hence can be attacked by large warheads without precise knowledge of where they are, and (2) railroads and highways all pass through population centers, and large political and social problems seem unavoidable.

Where does all this leave us insofar as finding a technical solution for protecting Minuteman is concerned? One and only one technically viable solution seems to have emerged for the long run: Launch on warning. Such an idea has been considered seriously by some politicians, some technical men and some military officers. Launch on warning could either be managed entirely by automatic devices, or the command and control system could be such as to require authorization to launch by some very high human authority.

In the case of the first alternative, people who think about such things envision a system consisting of probably two types of detection device that could, in principle, determine that a massive launch had been made and then somewhat later determine that such a launch consisted of multiple warheads aimed at our missile-silo fields. This information would be processed by a computer, which would then launch the Minutemen so that the incoming missiles would find only empty holes; consequently the Minutemen would be able to carry out their mission of revenge. Thus the steady advance of arms technology may not be leading us to the ultimate weapon but rather to the ultimate absurdity: a completely automatic system for deciding whether or not doomsday has arrived.

To me such an approach to the problem is politically and morally unacceptable, and if it really is the only approach, then clearly we have been considering the wrong problem. Instead of asking how Minuteman can be protected, we should be asking what the alternatives to Minuteman are. Evidently most other people also find such an idea unacceptable. As I mentioned above, the Army has found it necessary to reassure people repeatedly that ABM missiles would not be launched without approval by "the highest authorities," even though this is clearly a far less serious matter in the case of the ABM missiles than in the case of Minuteman.

The alternative is to require that a human decision-maker, at the level of "the highest authorities," be introduced into the decision-making loop. But is this really satisfactory? We would be asking that a human being make, in just a few minutes, a decision to utterly destroy another country. (After all, there would be no point in firing at *their* empty silos.) If, for any reason whatever, he was responding to a false alarm, or to some kind of smaller, perhaps "accidental," attack, he would be ensuring that a massive deliberate attack on us would take place moments later. Considering the shortness of the time, the complexity of the information and the awesomeness of the moment, the President would himself have to be properly preprogrammed in order to make such a decision.

Those who argue that the Command and Control System is perfect or perfectable forget that human beings are not. If forced to choose, I would prefer a preprogrammed President to a computer when it came to deciding whether or not doomsday had arrived, but again I feel that this solution too is really unacceptable, and that once again, in attempting to defend Minuteman, we are simply dealing with the wrong problem. For the present it would seem the Polarises and the bombers are not, as systems, subject to the same objections, since there are now enough other approaches to the problem of ensuring their invulnerability to sudden massive destruction.

In my view, all the above once again confirms the utter futility of attempting to achieve national security through military technology alone. We must look elsewhere. Fortunately an opportunity does seem to be in the offing. There appears to be real promise that serious strategic-arms-limitation talks will begin soon. The time is propitious. There is in the land a fairly widespread doubt about the strictly military approach to security problems, and even military-minded politicians are genuinely interested in exploring other possibilities. The essay by Academician Sakharov, as well as the statements of Russian officials, indicate genuine interest on the other side. The time is propitious in another sense: both sides will be discussing the matter from a position of parity. Moreover, this parity seems reasonably stable and likely to endure for several years.

Later, however, major deployments of sophisticated ABM systems and, even more important, widespread conversion of present single-warhead systems to MIRV will be strongly destabilizing and will at least give the impression that parity is about to be upset. If so, the motto of the arms race, "Let us err on the side of military safety," will come to dominate the scene on both sides and the present opportunity will be lost. Therefore in the short run we must do everything possible to ensure that the talks not only start but also succeed. Although the ABM decision may not forestall the talks, it would seem that success will be more likely if we avoid starting things that history has shown are difficult to stop once they are started.

Such things surely include deployment of ABM missiles and MIRV's. There have been successes in stopping programs while they were in the development phase, but seldom has anything been stopped after deployment had started. The idea of a freeze on deployment of new weapons systems at this time and for these reasons is fairly widespread already, but achieving it will require concerted action by those believing strongly in the validity and necessity of arms limitations as a means of increasing national security. Thus the principal result of the recent national debate over the ABM issue has been to make it clear that Safeguard will safeguard nothing, and that the right step for the immediate future is doing whatever is necessary (such as freezing present deployments and developments) to ensure the success of the coming strategic-arms-limitation talks.

In addition, the ABM debate has served to highlight more serious issues (for example the implications of MIRV for the arms race) and to raise serious questions about other weapons systems. For instance, I suggest that we have also found that silo-based missiles will become obsolete. The only sure method for defense of Minuteman beyond, say, the mid-1970's seems to be the unacceptable launch on warning. As long as we must have a strategic deterrent, we must find one that does not force us to turn the final decision over to either a computer or a preprogrammed President. Minuteman was conceived in the 1950's and served its purpose as a deterrent through the 1960's, but it appears that in the 1970's its threat to us will exceed its value, and that it and other silo-based missiles will have to go. The deterrent must have alternatives other than "go/no-go," and for the 1970's at least it would now appear that other strategic weapons (Polaris/Poseidon and bombers) could provide them. I expect, however, that as the continuing national debate subjects the whole matter of strategic arms to further public scrutiny we shall learn that these other alternatives also have dangerous flaws, and we shall see confirmed the idea that there is no technical solution to the dilemma of the steady decrease in our national security that has for more than 20 years accompanied the steady increase in our military power.

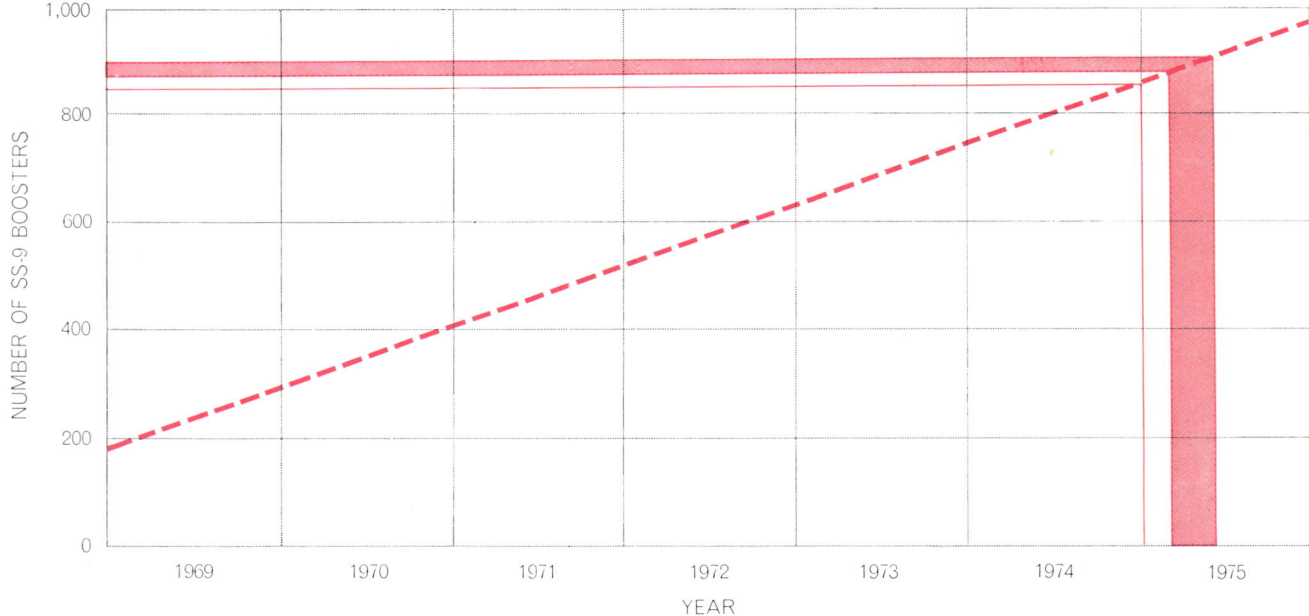

SAFEGUARD COULD BE NULLIFIED within a few months after its Phase I deployment, according to this graph, which is based on calculations presented by George W. Rathjens in his testimony before the Senate Armed Services Committee on April 23. His analysis took as a basis of calculation the implication in Secretary Laird's testimony that the Minuteman force may become seriously imperiled in the mid-1970's. Assuming that the Russian SS-9's would have four or five MIRV warheads each by that time, Rathjens then estimated that approximately 850 SS-9's would have to be deployed in order to achieve this result. From this number, and the estimate of the current number of SS-9's deployed (about 200), he got a rate of deployment (about 100 per year). Making certain assumptions about the numbers and effectiveness of the Spartan and Sprint ABM missiles that would be deployed at that time, Rathjens found that by prolonging the SS-9 production program by two to five months the Russians would be able to cope with Safeguard by simply exhausting it and would still have enough warheads to imperil Minuteman. Recently different numerical assumptions have been made, but they do not change the general conclusion that the proposed Safeguard system is much too thin to safeguard Minuteman.

The Limitation of Strategic Arms

by G. W. Rathjens and G. B. Kistiakowsky
January 1970

The long-term prospects for the strategic-arms-limitation talks would be greatly enhanced by an early agreement to ban further tests of multiple independently targeted reentry vehicles (MIRV's)

The preliminary phase of the strategic-arms-limitation talks ("SALT") between the U.S. and the U.S.S.R. was conducted in a convivial atmosphere and with a refreshing lack of familiar rhetoric. The road ahead for the negotiations nonetheless remains a steep and slippery one. The fact that the talks were delayed for as long as they were by both sides is not an encouraging sign. The initial unwillingness of the Russian leadership to negotiate because of the American involvement in Vietnam and the subsequent unwillingness of the American leadership to negotiate because of the Russian intervention in Czechoslovakia both reflect a failure to perceive the extraordinary and possibly fleeting nature of the opportunity presented at this particular juncture in the arms race and a failure to recognize that the strategic-arms confrontation can and should be largely decoupled from other sources of conflict between the two superpowers. More recent delays, first by the U.S. and then by the U.S.S.R., reinforce the view that on both sides there has been a fundamental failure in the ordering of priorities—a failure to recognize that the dangers to national security associated with arms-control agreements can be far less than those inherent in the ongoing arms race.

As the substantive phase of the arms talks is about to begin, it is still not obvious that policy-making circles of the two superpowers have consonant views about such basic questions as what objectives strategic forces serve, what relative roles offensive and defensive strategic forces play and what the desired effects of limitations on such forces are. If it should develop that there is no agreement on these points, it may not be possible to negotiate any meaningful limitation on strategic forces.

This article is written in the hope that by stimulating discussion of these questions the differences between the two powers may become more clearly understood and in time narrowed. Even if the talks fail to produce significant agreement, a better grasp of the issues involved will be in the ultimate interest of everyone.

A number of recent developments make the prospects for successful negotiations seem to be more favorable now than they might have been some years ago. Advances in the strategic reconnaissance capabilities of the superpowers (chiefly in the area of surveillance by artificial satellites) are steadily reducing the need for intrusive inspection to establish the degree of compliance with possible future agreements. Thus the thorny issue of verification may be less of a barrier to agreed arms limitation than it has been in the past. In addition the rapid growth of Russian offensive-missile forces has effectively erased a disparity with the U.S. that existed in the past, thereby making an arms-limitation agreement a more realistic possibility. Finally, there is the growing popular realization—at least in the U.S. and presumably also in the U.S.S.R.—that each side already has an enormous "overkill" capacity with respect to the other, and that further escalation in strategic-force levels would entail tremendous costs and new dangers at a time when both countries are confronted with a host of other pressing demands on their resources.

Although these developments would seem to favor successful negotiations, they are possibly outweighed by developments on the other side of the ledger. The most troublesome items are two emerging technical capabilities: multiple independently targeted reentry vehicles (MIRV's) and anti-ballistic-missile (ABM) defenses. It is frequently argued that the development and deployment of either (or particularly both) of these systems by one superpower could lead to a situation in which a decision to attempt a preemptive attack against the other's strategic forces might be considered rational. Indeed, some strategic planners contend that the threat is so great that offsetting actions must be started even before it is clear whether or not the adversary intends to acquire either a MIRV or an ABM capability. It is our belief that such arguments are largely fallacious and are made without real appreciation of the fact that a thermonuclear war between the superpowers, considering the vulnerability of the two societies, is a totally irrational policy choice. No combination of tactics and

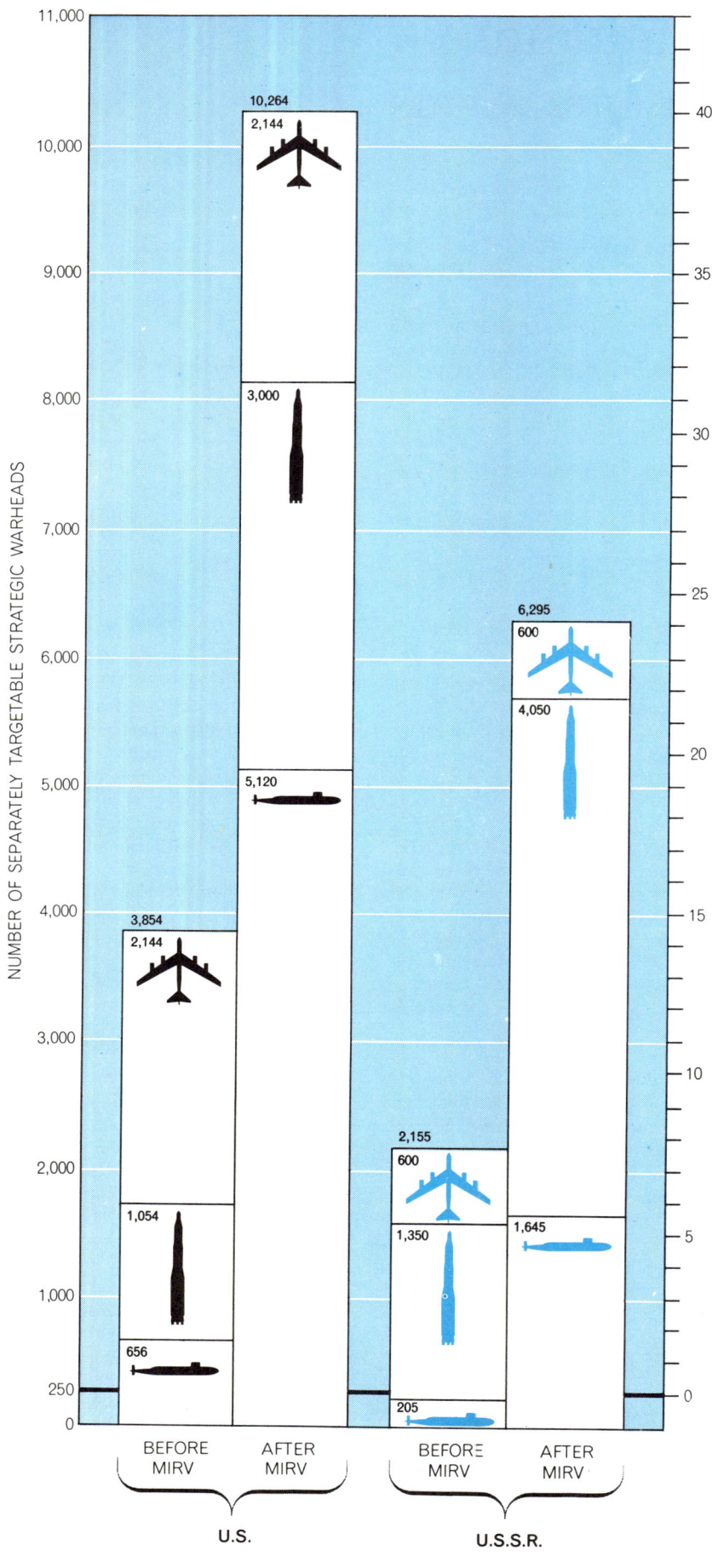

weapons, offensive and defensive, could provide either power with sufficient assurance that at least a small fraction of its adversary's weapons would not be successfully delivered, thus inflicting in retaliation damage that would be clearly unacceptable.

We are confronted here, however, with a paradox that will haunt the rest of this discussion. Unilateral decisions regarding the development and procurement of strategic-weapons systems, and hence planning for arms-control negotiations, have been and will continue to be greatly influenced by a fundamentally simpleminded, although often exceedingly refined, form of military analysis. This approach, sometimes characterized as "worst-case analysis," invariably ascribes to one's adversary not only capabilities that one would not count on for one's own forces but also imputes to him a willingness to take risks that would seem insane if imputed to one's own political leadership. Thus the U.S. will react to Russian MIRV and ABM programs, and vice versa, whether or not national security demands it. Even if the reaction is totally irrational, it nonetheless becomes as much a part of reality as if the decision were genuinely required to preserve a stable strategic balance. We reluctantly accept the fact that in both the U.S. and the U.S.S.R. policy will be influenced excessively by those military planners and their civilian allies who persist in behaving as if a thermonuclear war could be "won," and in asserting that responsible political leaders on the other side may initiate it on that assumption.

The development of a strategic nuclear capability by lesser powers, particularly China, seems also destined to complicate efforts to curtail the strategic-

STRATEGIC BALANCE between the U.S. and the U.S.S.R. is shown at left in terms of the numbers of separately targetable strategic nuclear warheads already deployed and the numbers projected for 1975 if present plans to deploy multiple independently targeted reentry vehicles (MIRV's) go into effect. The symbols indicate the means of delivery; the numbers give the actual total of deliverable warheads in each category. The scale at right suggests the enormous "overkill" capacity possessed by each side in either circumstance; it is calibrated in units of 250—a highly conservative estimate of the number of nuclear warheads required to devastate the 50 largest cities on each side. The chart includes only strategic (that is, intercontinental) nuclear warheads, not tactical or intermediate-range nuclear weapons.

arms race between the superpowers. Here there are essentially two problems. First, what was said earlier about the unacceptability of nuclear war between the superpowers may be less applicable to conflicts between emerging nuclear powers, because their political leadership will be less knowledgeable about the effects of nuclear warfare and because the nuclear stockpiles involved will, at least initially, not be large enough to ensure the destruction of entire societies. Thus, with proliferation, the probability of thermonuclear war is likely to increase, and the superpowers will have a real basis for concern about their becoming involved. Second, a phenomenon not unlike the much discussed action-reaction effects of ABM defenses and MIRV's is likely to come into play. Nuclear proliferation may complicate Russian-American efforts to curtail the strategic-arms race even more than the objective facts warrant, as each superpower overreacts not only to the development of new centers of nuclear power but also to the other's reaction to them.

In fact, the rising threat of nuclear proliferation is already increasing the pressure in the U.S. (and probably in the U.S.S.R.) to develop defenses that might be effective at least for a few years against emergent nuclear powers. The enthusiasts talk about neutralizing completely the effects of such developments; the realists propose measures aimed at reducing the damage that might be inflicted in the unlikely event of a nuclear attack by a smaller power. Unfortunately the capabilities that might prove effective, for instance an ABM system adequate to cope with first-generation Chinese missiles, would probably lead the other superpower to expand or qualitatively improve its strategic forces.

The other major considerations that will have a bearing on the prospects for SALT are domestic. As the failure of American policy in Southeast Asia and its implications become apparent, it seems likely that there will be a sharp reaction in an important segment of American society, with the polarization of attitudes proceeding even further than it has in the past year or two. It will be a difficult time for arms-control negotiations. Indeed, the strategic-arms-limitation talks are likely to be a divisive factor in the same way that the recent debate on the Safeguard ABM system was.

The situation in the U.S.S.R., although less clear, seems no more promising. The controversy between China and the U.S.S.R. might lead one to expect that accommodation and cooperation with the West would be increasingly attractive to the Russian leadership. But that controversy, like the recent Russian difficulties in eastern Europe, is also likely to be a factor in reinforcing the trend toward orthodoxy and conservatism within the U.S.S.R., which is hardly a favorable augury for an arms-control agreement.

Thus for SALT to be successful will require not only that the two governments be sincere in approaching the talks but also that they be prepared to display leadership and steadfastness of purpose in dealing with domestic opposition. On both sides there will have to be a rejection of many of the premises on which military policy has been at least partially based for two decades, for example the importance of "superiority" in strategic strength, the concept of "winning" a thermonuclear war, and the view that one can build meaningful defenses against a thermonuclear attack. The leadership in each nation will be confronted with arguments about the great risks inherent in various kinds of agreement—barely feasible (or at least not provably unfeasible) developments that might be taken advantage of by an adversary. Such arguments will undoubtedly resemble those to which the Kennedy Administration had to respond, when in connection with the nuclear-test-ban treaty it was asserted that the U.S.S.R. might conduct nuclear tests behind the moon or behind the sun to our great disadvantage. If agreement is to be reached, such arguments will have to be judged for what they are: nightmares of people who have focused so narrowly on such problems that they simply lack the perspective for weighing the risks of agreement against the risks implicit in continuing the arms race without any agreed constraints.

In the case of the U.S. the President will have a special problem and a formidable challenge, perhaps the greatest faced by any American leader since President Wilson's effort at the end of World War I to gain acceptance for his views regarding the Treaty of Versailles and the League of Nations. Although most Americans, including probably a majority of those who supported President Nixon in his campaign for the Presidency, would support him in his efforts to reach an arms-control agreement, almost certainly the conservative wing of the President's political supporters will counsel him to exercise extreme caution in approaching SALT. In so doing this latter group will give unwarranted weight to the technical and military risks that might be involved in any agreement under consideration. It is equally certain that the military will attempt to influence him with similar arguments, both through its direct channels and through its Congressional allies.

It is inconceivable that any meaningful agreement can be reached if the views of these groups should prevail. They need not, of course. Exercising broader judgment, the President can reject such advice and, as suggested above, draw on very substantial nationwide support for an agreement. Should he choose to do so, he will be in a better position to make his decision politically acceptable than would have been the case for any of his recent predecessors, or for that matter for his opponent in the last election. There is almost certainly a sizable segment of the American body politic that could accept a decision by President Nixon to conclude a very far-reaching agreement as a result of SALT that would not accept a similar position were it offered by, say, a liberal Democratic president.

President Nixon's prospects for such an achievement will be enhanced if the SALT negotiators make substantial progress in the next few months. With momentum established as a result of some limited agreement, and with the prospects of broader agreements before them, both the American and the Russian leadership might well make the judgment that it would be worthwhile to expend the political capital that might be required to effect broader agreements. If, on the other hand, the talks bog down in procedural discussions or in defense of obviously non-negotiable positions, the political leadership in both the U.S. and the U.S.S.R. will be in a weakened position in dealing with those who are most skeptical and fearful of an agreement. Thus the importance of early limited agreement in connection with SALT cannot be overestimated.

In what areas might such limited agreement be immediately feasible? In order to answer this question we must first examine some of the technical realities of the present strategic balance. We believe that for the foreseeable future technological considerations will continue to make nuclear offensive forces dominant over nuclear defensive forces. In other words, we assert that, as has been the case since the initial deployment of thermonuclear weapons, it will be easier to destroy a technologically advanced society than to defend one. What can and should be done both in structuring strategic forces in the absence of agreement and in agreeing to limitations is critically dependent on whether or not this judgment is correct. There is some dispute about its correctness in the U.S. For example, some assert that with recent developments in ABM technology it may be possible to offset the effects of an incremental expenditure on offensive capabilities by a similar or even lesser expenditure on defenses. Nonetheless, we share the prevailing view that defense of population, at least against a determined adversary with comparable resources, is essentially hopeless.

To facilitate discussion we shall now define two terms that have come to be applied to strategic forces and to their uses. By "damage limitation" we mean the prevention of damage to industry and population in a nuclear war or the reduction of such damage to below the levels that might be expected without the use of certain damage-limiting measures or systems. Antiaircraft or ABM defenses of cities would be categorized as being damage-limiting systems. The use of civil defense measures such as population shelters or evacuation of threatened cities would be regarded as damage-limiting measures. So would be attempts to limit the adversary's ability to inflict damage by preemptively attacking any component of his offensive strategic forces. By "assured destruction" we mean the destruction with high confidence of the adversary's society. Measures to achieve such destruction, or systems that might be used for the purpose, would be characterized as assured-destruction measures or systems. They include the use of offensive missiles and bombers against civilian targets, as distinguished from strictly military targets.

With these definitions we recast our earlier statement about the relative roles of offensive and defensive strategic weapons to assert: *In the superpower confrontation any attempt to build significant damage-limiting capabilities can be offset by changes in the adversary's assured-destruction capabilities.* To take a specific example, attempts to limit and reduce the damage to American society by deploying ABM defenses (including appropriate civil defense measures) can be offset by qualitative and quantitative improvements in the adversary's offensive capabilities at a cost to him certainly no greater than the cost of the damage-limiting measures taken. What is more, we believe that by and large such responses will occur, in spite of the fact that realistic security considerations do not necessarily require a response. Even a very large-scale and technically sophisticated American ABM system could not be counted on to prevent totally unacceptable destruction in the U.S. by a Russian attack—even by an attack launched in retaliation after the Russian forces had already been preemptively struck. Such an American ABM system would in no way make our strategic forces more useful as political instruments, and hence no Russian response would really be required to preserve the effectiveness of the U.S.S.R.'s assured-destruction forces. Because of fear, conservatism and uncertainty, however, it seems a foregone conclusion that a fully compensating buildup in Russian strength would follow.

There may, of course, be circumstances in which damage-limiting efforts will be effective. Each of the superpowers would temporarily be able to maintain a strategic posture that might greatly limit the damage to it in a conflict with a lesser nuclear power such as China. This will be particularly true if a preemptive, or "counterforce," attack against the lesser power's strategic nuclear forces is not excluded.

Moreover, if a nuclear exchange between the two superpowers should ever occur, parts of the strategic forces in being at that time probably would be used for active defense or in attacks on the strategic forces of the opponent. Thus they would be used in a damage-limiting role. Their effect would not be great, however, simply because the overkill capacity of each superpower's assured-destruction capabilities is so enormous. Both superpowers almost certainly now have the ability to destroy at least half of the adversary's population and three-quarters of his industrial capacity in spite of any damage-limiting measures that might be undertaken by the other. This situation has come about as a result of two factors. A strategic doctrine has developed, at least in the U.S., that has called for the maintenance of a very great assured-destruction capability under all conceivable circumstances. The doctrine has been one that could be easily implemented simply because thermonuclear weapons and strategic delivery systems are cheap in terms of the damage they can inflict on civilian targets.

This tremendous buildup of offensive forces means that the effectiveness of the last weapons used in destroying another society (in fact, the effectiveness of something like the last 90 percent of all weapons used) would be relatively small, since those already expended would have left so little to destroy. The amount of life and property saved by damage-limiting efforts would be dwarfed by the amount destroyed by weapons whose delivery could not be prevented.

We believe this situation will not change significantly in the near future. Any realistic approach to limitations on strategic armaments in the near future must almost certainly be in the context of the maintenance of very great assured-destruction capabilities. Agreements that would embody quite different strategic balances might result if any of several changes were to occur: technological breakthroughs that would lead to the dominance of the defense over the offense, the development of a high degree of trust between the U.S. and the U.S.S.R., the willingness of both nations to accept intrusive inspection, or an increased appreciation that strategic forces designed to inflict much lower damage levels would also serve effectively as a deterrent. We do not see any of these changes as short-term possibilities.

Because the assured-destruction, or damage-inflicting, capabilities of the two superpowers are so large and so varied, the present strategic balance is remarkably insensitive to either qualitative or quantitative changes in strategic forces. Even major changes in force levels, including the neutralization of entire systems (for example all bomber aircraft), would not be likely to have major effects on the damage levels one would expect each of the superpowers to suffer in a nuclear war. Worldwide radioactive fallout might be reduced significantly, but as far as the superpowers are concerned, cross-targeting with other systems would ensure that all major population and industrial centers would continue to be in jeopardy. When considered in the framework of the virtually certain collapse of an entire society, changes of a few percent in fatalities, which is all one might expect with foreseeable changes in strategic-force levels, are not likely to affect political decisions. Although it may have been correct some years ago to characterize the balance of terror as a "delicate" one, it is not so today, nor is it likely to be so in the foreseeable future. It will not be easily upset. Opponents of the Safeguard ABM decision have argued with some effect (although obviously not with complete success) that the U.S. deterrent was most unlikely to be in jeopardy at any time in the near future simply because of its diversity and because of the improbability of the U.S.S.R.'s being able to develop damage-limiting capabilities and tactics that would effectively neutralize all the deterrent's components.

We have argued so far that one general premise on whose acceptance a successful SALT outcome depends is

RELATIVE DESTRUCTIVENESS of several currently deployed thermonuclear weapons is illustrated here in relation to the damage caused by the nuclear bomb that was exploded over Hiroshima on August 5, 1945. The colored circles superposed on the map denote each weapon's "lethal area": the area within which the number of survivors equals the number of fatalities outside the circle. For a perfectly uniform population distribution the lethal area times the population density gives the total number of people killed in the explosion. At present most of the strategic warheads deployed by the U.S. and the U.S.S.R. are in the megaton range or larger. Even after MIRVing all the strategic warheads on both sides will exceed the estimated 15-kiloton explosive yield of the Hiroshima bomb.

that the offense will continue to dominate the defense for the foreseeable future. A second technical generalization that may be equally important is: *The uncertainty about the effectiveness of damage-limiting capabilities will be considerably greater than about assured-destruction capabilities*. This statement can be supported by a number of arguments. First, the characteristics of the target against which assured-destruction capabilities would be used (population and industry) will be known with some precision and will change only slowly with time. On the other hand, the characteristics of the systems (and the environment) against which damage-limiting capabilities must operate (adversary's warheads, delivery vehicles and launch facilities) will be generally less well known and more susceptible to rapid variation, both in quality and in number, at the option of the adversary. Second, some of the damage-limiting systems (such as ABM defenses, antiaircraft defenses and under some circumstances antisubmarine warfare, or ASW, systems) must function at the time chosen by the adversary for his offensive, whereas for assured destruction there is a much bigger "time window" during which performance will be acceptable. The effectiveness of submarine-launched missiles in destroying cities will not depend much on the instant of launch. Third, damage limitation generally will involve the use of more intimately coupled systems (for example the radars, computers and missiles of an ABM system), inviting the possibility of "catastrophic" technical failures. All these factors tend to make the advance estimates of the effectiveness of assured-destruction systems far more reliable than estimates of damage-limiting systems.

The inherent uncertainty in effectiveness that characterizes the performance of damage-limiting systems has been of profound importance in the Russian-American strategic-arms race. Each side has reacted to the development, or even the possible development, by the other of damage-limiting capabilities by greatly strengthening its offensive forces—to the point of overreaction because of the conservative assumption that the adversary's damage-limiting forces will be far more effective than they are in fact likely to be. For example, the uncertainty about the possible deployment and effectiveness of a large-scale Russian ABM defense has provided the primary rationale for the U.S. decision to introduce MIRV's into both land-based and sea-based missile forces, the net effect being a severalfold increase in the number of warheads these forces will be able to deliver. Barring unforeseeable technical developments, we must expect that the great uncertainty that characterizes the performance of damage-limiting systems will continue, and we must base our approach to SALT on that assumption.

If one accepts the judgments we have made about the relative effectiveness of defense and offense, about the insensitivity of assured-destruction capability to changes in force levels and about the uncertainty that characterizes damage-limiting efforts, one is led to some possibly useful generalizations about the forthcoming substantive phase of SALT.

First, the level of damage that each of the superpowers can inflict on the other is not likely to be altered significantly in the near future. Measures that might possibly be agreed on could change the level of damage that each side could inflict on the other by at most

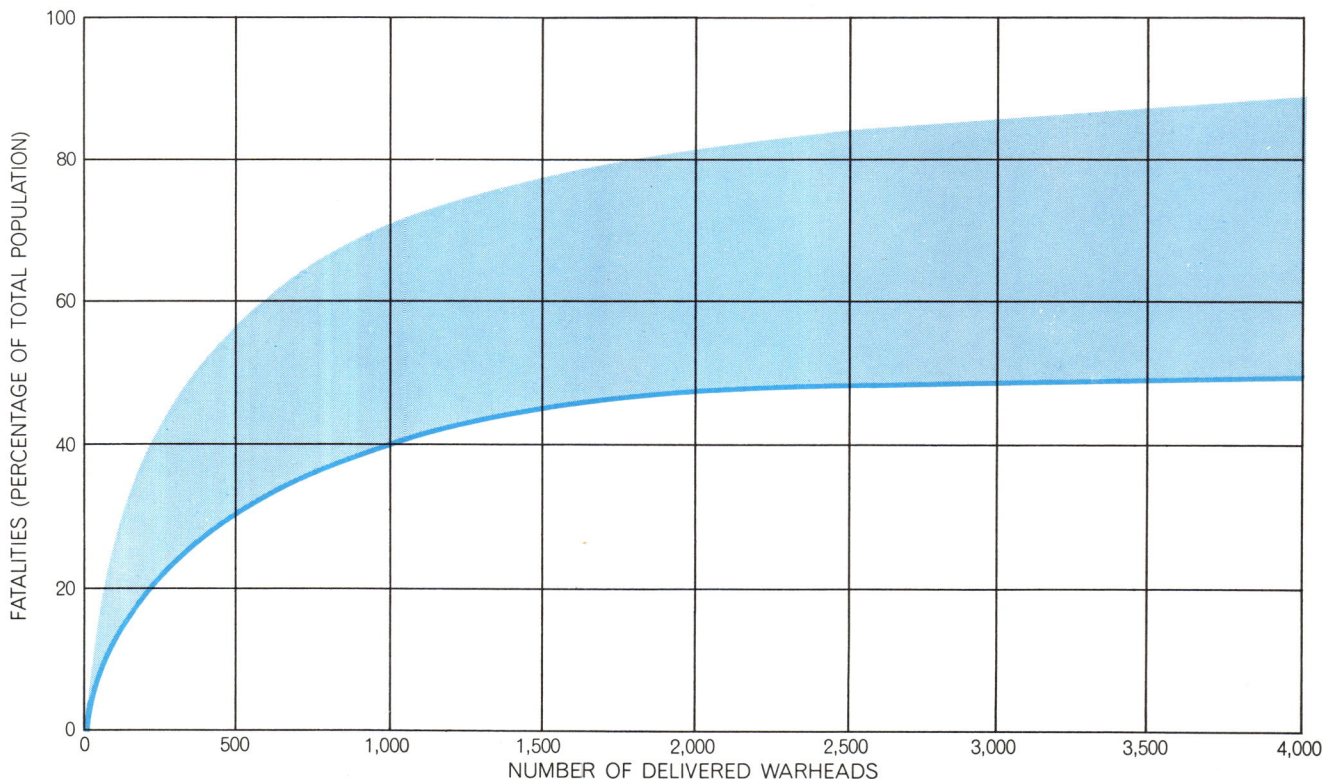

FUTILITY of seeking to mitigate the consequences of a full-scale nuclear exchange between the two superpowers by negotiating modest reductions in strategic-force levels or by resorting to moderately effective "damage-limiting" measures is illustrated in this graph, in which the expected fatalities in the U.S.S.R. are plotted as a function of the number of U.S. megaton-range warheads delivered. The solid curve indicates the immediate, easily calculable fatalities; the shading represents the fact that the total fatalities would probably be much larger. In either case, because of the very large number of deployed weapons, the effects of small changes in the total of delivered weapons would be negligible. The expected effects of a Russian attack against the U.S. would be similar.

a few percent. Therefore the problem of the reduction in damage in the event of war should probably be given low priority as a short-term negotiation objective. More realistic objectives of the negotiations could be to lower the level of tension between the superpowers and so reduce the probability of nuclear war.

but they were!

Second, apart from possible worldwide fallout effects and domestic political considerations, neither side need be much concerned about the possibility of modest, or even substantial, expansions in the strategic offensive forces of the other side, nor about precise limitations on those forces, as long as the other side does not have a damage-limiting capability. Because of the large overkill capacities discussed above, even large increases in strategic forces will have little military effect.

Third, measures to constrain the introduction or improvement of damage-limiting systems, particularly those whose performance is expected to be highly uncertain, merit high priority. The introduction or improvement of damage-limiting capabilities by either side is likely to result, as we have noted, in an excessive reaction by the other. Because of the insensitivity of the strategic balance to modest changes in force levels, a move toward the development of a narrowly circumscribed damage-limiting capability by one side could in principle be tolerated without undue concern by the other. Such a move might be perceived, however, as an indicator of the adversary's intent to develop an across-the-board damage-limiting capability. (Witness Secretary of Defense Laird's public reaction to a possible Soviet SS-9 MIRV capability.) This, coupled with the fact that a development of damage-limiting capabilities can be offset rather quickly and cheaply, virtually ensures a reaction. The overall effect of such an action-reaction cycle on the ability of each side to inflict damage on the other is likely to be small, but the expenditures of both sides on strategic armaments are likely to be much increased, as will be the tensions between them.

Fourth, owing to the large uncertainty that characterizes the effectiveness of damage-limiting systems and tactics, the two superpowers will face a very troublesome dilemma if, on the one hand, they try to develop effective damage-limiting capabilities with respect to emerging nuclear powers and, on the other, they attempt to limit the strategic-arms race between themselves. With a few exceptions, such as a deployment of Russian intermediate-range ballistic missiles (IRBM's) in Siberia, the measures that could have long-term effectiveness against a third country's nuclear strength would appear to the other superpower to foreshadow an erosion in its own assured-destruction, or deterrent, capability. This creates an authentic problem of conflicting desires. We would hope that in efforts to deal with this problem the usefulness of damage-limiting capabilities with respect to the lesser nuclear powers would not be overrated. Although such damage-limiting capabilities probably would be effective in reducing damage in the event that a lesser power attempted a nuclear attack against one of the superpowers, we question whether either superpower would ever be willing to take action against a lesser power on the assumption that damage-limiting efforts would be 100 percent effective, that is, on the assumption that "damage denial" with respect to a lesser power could be achieved. Considering one's inability to have high confidence in the effectiveness of damage-limiting measures, and considering the effects of even a single thermonuclear weapon on a large American or Russian city, we doubt that efforts to develop damage-limiting capabilities with respect to the smaller powers would materially increase the options the superpowers would have available for dealing with these powers.

With this background in mind one would be in a good position to evaluate the relative desirability of limiting various strategic systems if each were unambiguously useful only for damage limitation or assured destruction. Unfortunately many existing or prospective strategic systems may play several roles, a factor that greatly complicates the problem.

Of all the ambiguous developments now under way none is more troublesome than MIRV. The development of a MIRV capability may facilitate the maintenance of an assured-destruction capability by providing high assurance that ABM defenses of industry and population can be penetrated. Given sufficient accuracy, reliability and yield, however, MIRV's may also make it possible for a small number of missiles to destroy a larger number of fixed offensive facilities, even if they are "hardened" against the effects of nuclear weapons.

Although the effectiveness of a given missile force in a damage-limiting pre-emptive attack against an adversary's intercontinental ballistic missile (ICBM) force might be much increased through the use of such MIRV's, it does not necessarily follow that the deployment of the MIRV's would make such a strike more likely. As we have noted, in the context of a confrontation between superpowers such an attack would surely be irrational, no matter how severe the crisis, simply because no responsible political leader could ever have high confidence in the effectiveness of the attack and in the effectiveness of the other damage-limiting measures that would be required to keep the damage from a retaliatory response down to acceptable levels. Although MIRV's are not likely to have much actual effect on the willingness or ability of nations to use strategic nuclear forces to attain political objectives, we must accept the fact that arms policies will, to a substantial degree, be based on the assumption that they might be so used.

Beyond that, there is the problem of the impact of MIRV's on events if a crisis should ever escalate to the point where limited numbers of nuclear weapons will have been employed by the superpowers against each other. At some point in the process of escalation it is likely that one or both powers would initiate counterforce attacks against the other's remaining offensive forces. Such an attack would probably come earlier if one or both sides had counterforce-effective MIRV's than if neither did.

Because of what we regard as unwarranted, but nevertheless real, concern about MIRV's being used in a pre-emptive counterforce attack, and because of more legitimate concern that once a thermonuclear exchange has begun MIRV's may make further escalation more likely, MIRV development may well have a critical impact on the outcome of SALT, and for that matter on the force levels of the two sides independent of the talks. It is generally, although not universally, accepted that the tests of MIRV's have not yet gone far enough for one to have confidence that their reliability and accuracy would be sufficient to assure their effectiveness in a counterforce role against hardened ICBM's. On the other hand, the MIRV principle is now demonstrated, and the expectation is common that with perhaps the second generation of such systems, if not with the first, MIRV's will be effective as counterforce weapons.

If no constraints are put on the development of MIRV's, it is likely that each superpower will go ahead with such development and (in the case of the U.S. at least) an early deployment program. This will be regarded as particularly urgent if ABM deployment continues, or even if there continues to be evidence of significant research and development that might later lead to ABM deployment. Assuming that MIRV programs do continue, each superpower will perceive in the other's deployment a possible threat to its fixed-base ICBM's and will react to counter that threat. The U.S. has already begun to do so in deciding to go ahead with an active ABM defense of Minuteman sites: the Safeguard program. Acceleration in the U.S.S.R.'s missile-launching submarine program and a possible mobile-ICBM program are plausible reactions to the U.S. MIRV programs.

We anticipate that in the absence of agreements the technological race will go much further. It seems likely that the arguments to "do something" about the vulnerability of fixed ICBM's will increase in tempo and will carry the day in both the U.S. and the U.S.S.R. Superhardening alone will be perceived to be a losing game, considering how easily any moves in that direction could be offset by further improvements in missile accuracy. A defense of the Safeguard type will probably also be judged to be a losing proposition. A very heavy defense with components specifically optimized for the defense of hardened ICBM's might be one response. There is likely to be even further reliance on mobile systems: missile-launching submarines, new strategic bombers and, in the case of the U.S.S.R., probably mobile ICBM's. It is conceivable that fixed ICBM's may be given up altogether, although the arguments we have advanced against the acceptability of attacking them preemptively would still be valid.

It is also likely in the absence of agreements that one or the other of the superpowers will deploy ABM systems that will provide more extensive and effective defense of population and industry than either the present Russian defenses around Moscow or the projected Phase II of Safeguard. Defense against a Chinese missile capability may be the rationale, but it is to be expected that the other superpower will respond to any such deployment both by emulation and by increasing its strategic offensive capabilities.

Whereas the strategic-forces budget of the U.S. now amounts to about $9 billion per year (excluding some rather large items for nuclear warheads, research and development, command and control, communications and intelligence activities), outlays for strategic systems could well double by the mid-1970's. Continuing large expenditures on strategic systems are probably also to be expected in the U.S.S.R.

As we have stated, there appears to be no basis for expecting SALT to lead to significant reductions in the assured-destruction capabilities of the superpowers. Therefore other objectives must command our attention. The most important objective is of course to reduce the probability that a thermonuclear exchange will ever take place.

The major factors affecting that probability are likely not to be simply technical but to be largely political. They involve the degree of tension that will exist between the superpowers based on international political considerations, on domestic politics in each country and in an important sense on the strategic-arms race itself. We believe that in contrast to some previous eras, when the motivations for continuing arms races were largely political and economic conflicts, the strategic-arms race now has a life of

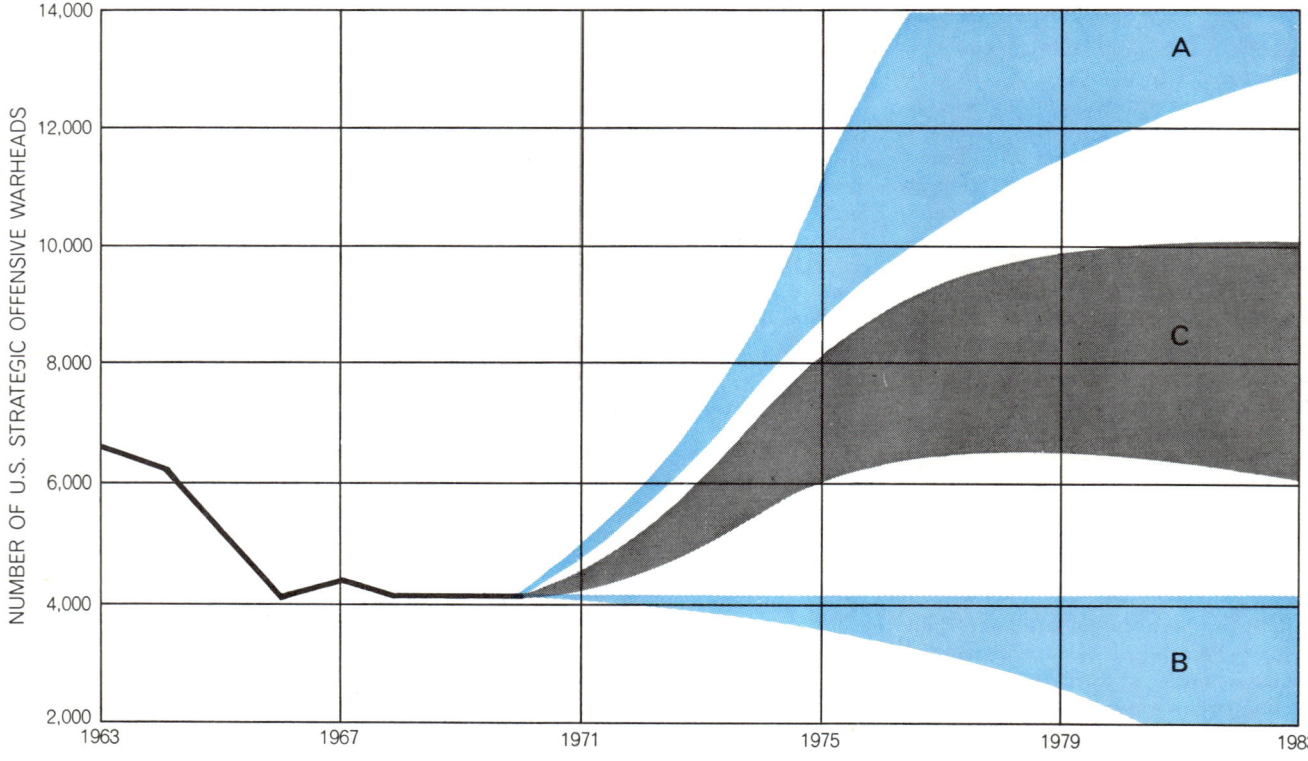

PROJECTED EFFECTS associated with three possible outcomes of the strategic-arms-limitation talks are expressed in the graphs on these two pages in terms of the number of U.S. strategic offensive warheads (*left*) and the U.S. budget for strategic forces (*right*). With no agreement (*A*) the number of weapons and the strategic-forces budget are likely to grow with no obvious limit. A SALT agreement that included a prohibition on the development and deployment of MIRV's (*B*) could lead to stability in strategic forces and a reduction in the budget to a level required to maintain them. With an agreement that did not constrain MIRV's (*C*) there would certainly be an increase in the strategic-forces budget for a few years as the composition of these forces changed, probably accompanied by the replacement of some fixed-base offensive missiles by mobile systems (either land-based or sea-based) or possibly by

its own. For instance, the strategic-weapons programs of each superpower are more dependent on the programs of the other than on the levels of tension between the two countries. If this race can be attenuated, it would have a number of effects that would result in a diminution of tensions and hence in a reduction in the risk of war. That is perhaps the major reason for the urgency of a serious SALT effort. Keeping budgets for strategic forces at low levels is desirable in its own right in that significant resources, both financial and intellectual, will be freed for more constructive purposes. More important, in the U.S. lower military budgets will diminish the role of what President Eisenhower termed the military-industrial complex: those who have a propensity for, and in some cases obviously a vested interest in, the acquisition of more armaments and in exciting and maintaining an often unwarranted attitude of alarm and suspicion regarding an adversary's intentions. Lower military budgets in the U.S.S.R. would almost certainly have a similar desirable effect.

A poorly designed agreement could of course prove to be a vehicle for increasing suspicion and tension. Venturing into the realm of unprovable value judgments, however, we assert that it is not beyond the wit of man to design agreements that would result in there being less objective cause for concern than if the strategic-arms race continues unabated. In general, it would seem that any understanding that slowed the rate of development and change of strategic systems would have an effect in the right direction.

Beyond affecting the probability of a nuclear exchange's beginning, one would like to see strategic forces structured so that there would be at least some possibility that, if an exchange started, it would not have to run its course. A necessary but of course not sufficient condition for this is that there be no particular advantage to be gained from precipitate launch of more nuclear weapons after a few have been dispatched. By this criterion vulnerable ICBM's would seem to be the quintessence of undesirability. If both sides have them, each will recognize that if they are withheld, they may be destroyed.

Whether or not MIRV development and deployment will be controlled may not be a question for the SALT negotiators to consider, because of the inability of one side or the other to decide in a timely fashion the position it wishes to take on the issue. The rate of MIRV development is so rapid that the question may thus be settled before the substantive phase of the talks is well advanced. If such development is still in doubt, however, either because the talks get to such substantive issues very quickly or because of a moratorium on MIRV testing, MIRV limitation should be an issue of the highest priority.

The arguments for preventing deployment of MIRV's advanced enough to be effective counterforce weapons are persuasive. They have been made at great length elsewhere (for example in public hearings before committees of the Senate and the House of Representatives). We simply summarize here by pointing out that if MIRV deployment is prevented, it may be possible to freeze the strategic balance at something approximating its present level. Most of the incentive to defend hardened ICBM's or to replace them with mobile systems will

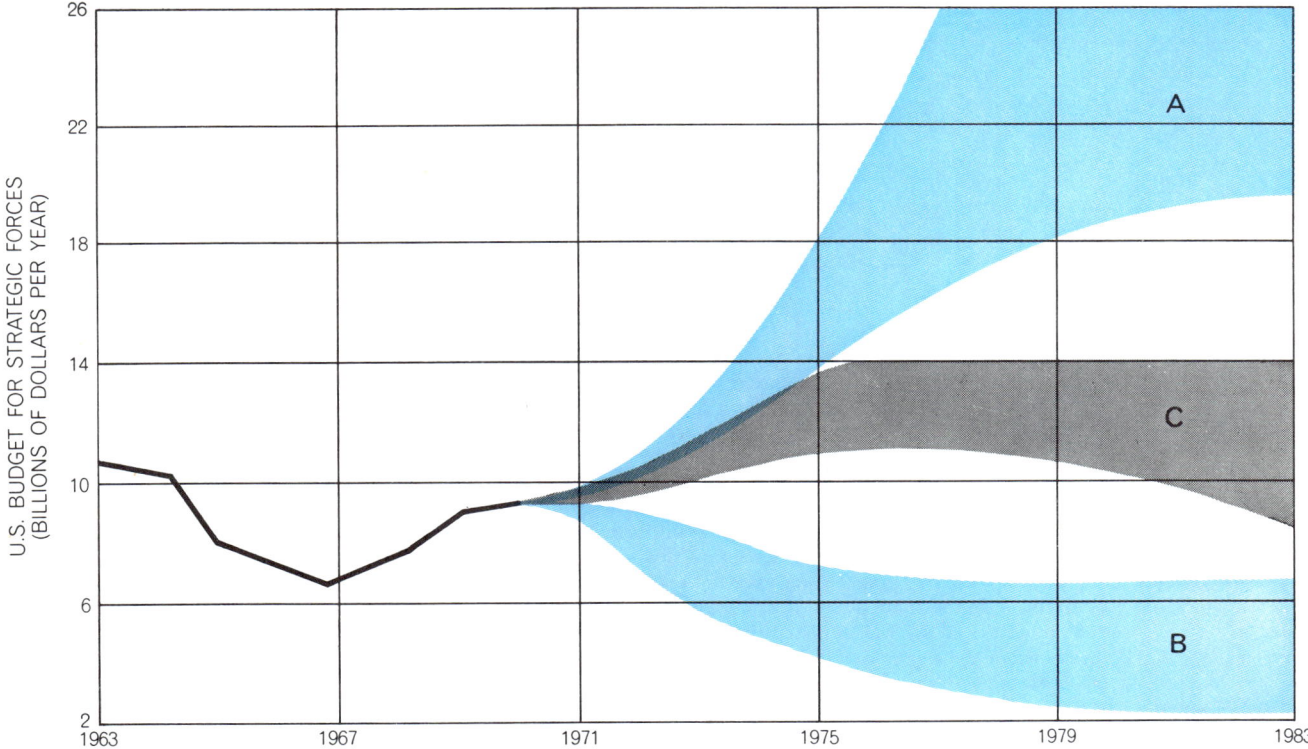

"superhardening" and heavy specialized ABM defense of missile sites. Assuming under case C that a large-scale ABM defense of population is prohibited, there would be little military rationale for either side to acquire large additional numbers of offensive warheads. Nonetheless, the numbers might increase significantly with the implementation of present plans to deploy MIRV's. Future Russian strategic-forces levels would probably display similar trends, but budget projections would differ somewhat. The Russian budget for strategic weapons is possibly at an unprecedentedly high level now, considering the present rapid rate of growth in their strategic systems. Thus in case B the drop in the strategic-forces budget for the U.S.S.R. might be sharper than for the U.S., and in the two other cases there would be a less pronounced increase. Estimates are in constant-value 1969 dollars.

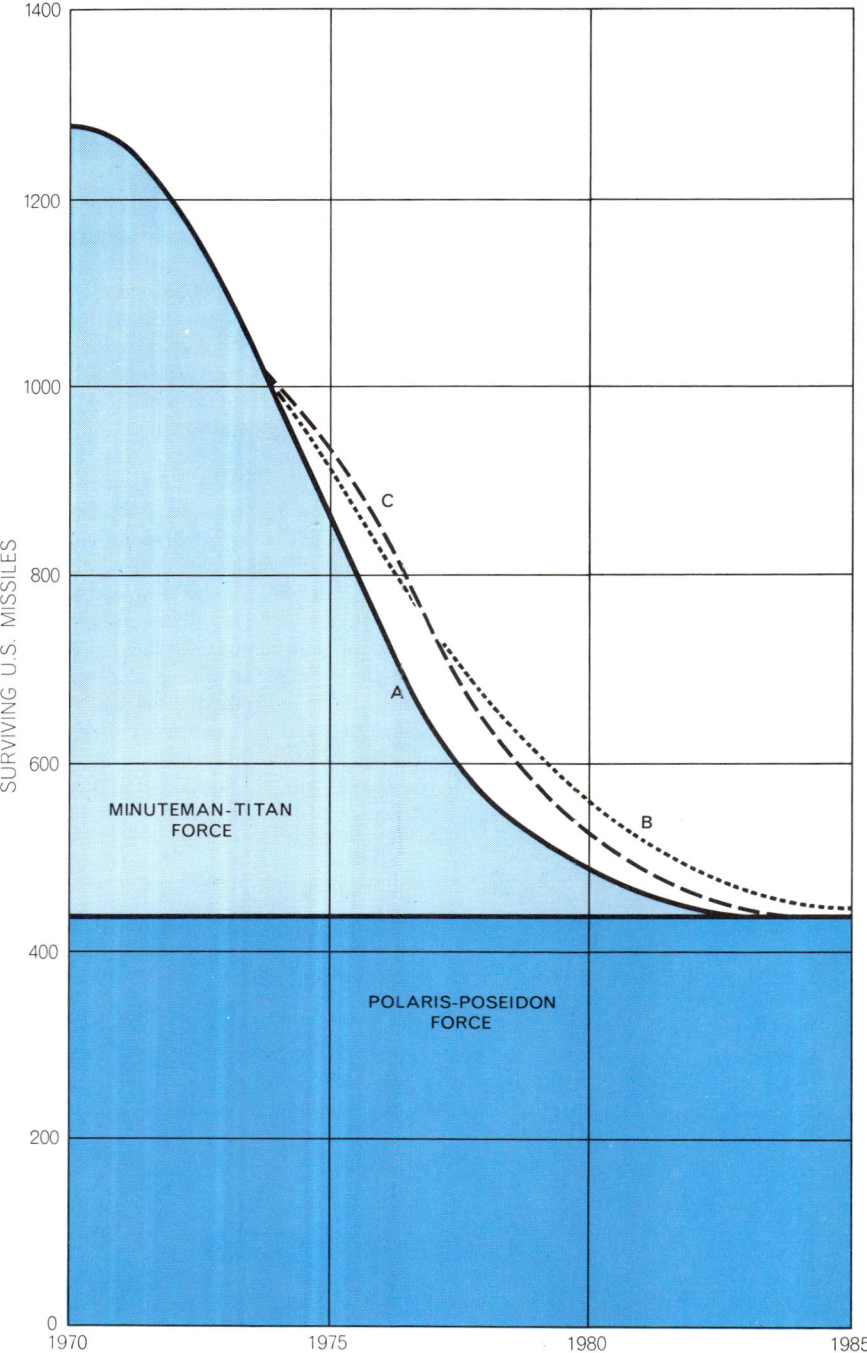

DIMINISHING UTILITY of fixed-base intercontinental ballistic missiles (ICBM's) as a component of the U.S. "assured-destruction" forces would result from further development and deployment of MIRV's, even in the event of a SALT agreement that freezes the number of missiles on both sides. In preparing this graph it was assumed that in a preemptive, or counterforce, strike against the U.S. the U.S.S.R. would target its SS-9 missile force (estimated to be frozen at 280 missiles) at the U.S. Minuteman-Titan force. The numbers of surviving U.S. ICBM's are based on the assumption that each SS-9 will carry one 25-megaton warhead in 1970, three five-megaton warheads in 1975, nine 500-kiloton warheads in 1980 and 25 50-kiloton warheads in 1985; delivery accuracies are assumed to improve by a factor of two every five years. Curve A assumes that no additional measures are taken to protect the already "hardened" U.S. ICBM force. Curve B assumes that the blast resistance of the ICBM sites is improved by "superhardening" so that by 1972 they can withstand three times the overpressure sustainable in 1970. Curve C assumes full operational capability (and a generous estimate of performance) of the Safeguard ABM system by 1978. It is apparent that neither superhardening nor active defense (unless many times more effective than Safeguard) is likely to extend the period of invulnerability for U.S. ICBM's by very much. (The number of surviving submarine-launched missiles is based on the assumption that a third of the Polaris-Poseidon force is destroyed in port by the Russian preemptive attack.)

have been reduced, if not eliminated.

The arguments for continuing MIRV testing and then deployment because MIRV's may someday be required to penetrate an adversary's ABM defenses are not convincing. There is little doubt that currently designed U.S. MIRV's could be deployed on a time scale short compared with that required for deployment of any significant Russian ABM defenses. Accordingly there is no need for any MIRV deployment pending firm evidence that the U.S.S.R. is beginning the construction of such defenses. And there is no need for further research and development tests unless a counterforce capability is intended. For similar reasons the U.S.S.R. should also abstain from further multiple-warhead tests and deployment, which it can do at no great risk to its security.

Essential to the survival of an agreement not to test MIRV's would be a prohibition of large-scale ABM deployment. If ABM systems were deployed, the pressures to deploy MIRV's and to test them frequently in order to maintain confidence in their reliability would be overwhelming. Furthermore, there would undoubtedly be great domestic pressures to develop and test more sophisticated penetration aids. Under such circumstances neither side could have any confidence that the other was not developing counterforce-effective MIRV's. An ABM freeze would be a logically required companion measure to any agreement prohibiting MIRV's.

Assuming that ABM deployment and MIRV testing are both frozen, the other important component of a strategic-arms-limitation agreement would be an understanding to maintain something like parity in ICBM-force levels by freezing these levels or preferably reducing them, and if necessary permitting replacement of fixed-base ICBM's by mobile systems whose levels could be verified by unilateral means. In the absence of such a measure there would be the possibility of one side's gaining such a superiority in missile strength that, with improved accuracies and even without MIRV's, would enable it to knock out a large fraction of its adversary's forces by delivering a counterforce attack against them. The reasons for concern about such a possibility have been identified above: the probability of arms-race escalation and the reduction in whatever small chance there may be of a nuclear exchange's being terminated short of running its suicidal course.

If the development of MIRV's that are perceived by the adversary to have counterforce capability cannot be prevented (and we are pessimistic about preventing it), the relative importance of some of the measures discussed above will be changed materially. A prohibition on large-scale ABM deployment would still be desirable, but it would be less important; it would not in this case prevent the MIRV genie from escaping the bottle. Moreover, continuing development and deployment of MIRV's would make a large-scale ABM defense unattractive simply on cost-effectiveness grounds.

A provision permitting the replacement of fixed ICBM's by mobile systems would seem virtually unavoidable because of concern about the vulnerability of the ICBM's to counterforce attack. Indeed, in the interest of stabilizing arms at low levels, and to minimize concern about damage-limiting strikes, agreements could probably include measures that would enhance the viability of mobile systems. An area of agreement that would seem to merit most serious consideration would be prohibition on certain improvements in antisubmarine-warfare capabilities. Actually the possibility of breakthroughs in antisubmarine warfare is extremely remote. It is probable that through noise reduction, extension of missile range and other techniques the gap between ASW capability and the capability of the missile-launching submarine to escape detection and destruction will widen rather than narrow. Yet it seems likely from recent debate in the U.S. that the present American leadership, and presumably the leadership of the U.S.S.R. as well, would be reluctant to rely solely on a missile-launching submarine force for deterrence, given the possibility of further ASW development by its adversary. Constraints on ASW such as a limitation on the number of hunter-killer submarines would increase the acceptability to both sides of relying more heavily on missile-launching submarines for deterrence.

Similar arguments might be made for limitations on or curtailment of air defense. Such moves would seem less realistic on three counts. First, compliance with limitations on air-defense capabilities could probably not be verified with unilateral procedures as well as could limitations on ASW systems, or for that matter on ABM systems. Intelligence on short-range antiaircraft systems is likely to be poorer than on hunter-killer submarines, specialized ASW aircraft or large-sized components of ABM systems. Second, the overlap between tactical and strategic antiaircraft capabilities is considerable, and neither superpower is likely to be willing to greatly reduce tactical antiaircraft capabilities in the context of SALT. ASW capabilities (except for destroyers) would, on the other hand, have little role other than attack against an adversary's missile-launching submarines. This is far truer now than it was a few years ago because the realization is more widespread that a major war involving large antishipping campaigns is extremely unlikely. Third, neither the U.S. nor the U.S.S.R. is likely to have enough confidence in bombers to rely much on them in a missile age even if air defenses are constrained, whereas both superpowers obviously are prepared to rely heavily on submarine-launched missiles.

Finally, if counterforce-effective MIRV's were a reality, and if as a consequence both sides were to place reliance very largely on mobile systems, additional offensive weapons on one side could not be used effectively to limit the other side's ability to retaliate. Considering this fact and the fact that since strategic-force levels are already at least an order of magnitude larger than is rationally required for deterrence, there would be little incentive for either side to acquire additional offensive capabilities. Also in this situation it would hardly matter if either side were to introduce new assured-destruction systems such as, for example, small mobile ICBM's that could not be easily counted.

Even this incomplete discussion shows that the strategic balance between the superpowers is likely to be very different depending on whether or not MIRV development and ABM deployment are allowed to continue. Both possibilities will have a serious impact on future strategic postures, but with respect to ABM deployment nothing much is going to happen overnight. Dealing with the issue of MIRV development, although perhaps no more important, is far more urgent. That is why it is the watershed issue for SALT. If counterforce-effective MIRV's (and large-scale ABM deployment) can be stopped, the present strategic balance of force levels may endure for some time. If such MIRV's are deployed, the balance will unavoidably change in qualitative ways. How large an escalation in the arms race will result will depend on whether agreement to constrain or cut back other strategic systems could still be negotiated.

We have attempted here to present an objective analysis of the prospects for various agreements to limit strategic armaments. In so doing we are aware that many of our readers will be dismayed that our discussion has been in the context of each superpower's preserving the capability of destroying the other. This has been so not because we ourselves favor the continuing retention of huge stocks of thermonuclear weapons but because we have tried to be realistic. The distrust that exists between the U.S. and the U.S.S.R. will induce both to preserve the capability of destroying the other; such a capability, as we have noted, is unfortunately easier to attain than an effective defense of one's own society, whether or not there are agreements on strategic armaments. Both superpowers will preserve this capability because they see it as the only effective deterrent to the war that neither wants or could win.

The most that can reasonably be expected of the forthcoming talks is a move toward a strategic balance where (1) uncertainties about the adversary are reduced and with them some of the tensions; (2) each side can inflict a level of damage on the other sufficient to destroy its society but neither feels a need to maintain a great overkill capability as a hedge against possible damage-limiting efforts by the other; (3) there will be an improved chance that a thermonuclear exchange, should one begin, would be terminated short of running its course, and (4) the levels of expenditure on strategic armaments are lower, so that larger fractions of the resources available to each society can be used for more constructive endeavors.

We believe that the realization of these objectives would be a tremendous accomplishment and one that is possible without the solution of the deep-seated political problems of the Russian-American confrontation. To go further will require dealing with those problems. We do not believe, however, that the superpowers can afford to delay attacking the strategic-arms race while trying to solve political differences. Regrettably the situation with respect to technical developments (MIRV's, ABM defenses and nuclear proliferation), and quite possibly with respect to domestic politics as well, will probably make strategic-arms-limitation negotiations less likely to be successful several years hence than now. Time is of the essence, and we write with a feeling of urgency. Although our tone is pessimistic, we do not despair. We are convinced that latent public support for an agreement could be exploited by effective political leadership on both sides to reverse the trends we have lived with for two decades.

Missile Submarines and National Security

by Herbert Scoville, Jr.
June 1972

Land-based missiles are giving way to submarine missiles as a secure deterrent to a nuclear first strike. The question now is whether or not the U.S. should spend perhaps $40 billion on a new missile fleet

In recent years, as the nuclear-weapons arsenals of both the U.S. and the U.S.S.R. have continued to grow, the concept of deterrence has become almost universally accepted as the key to maintaining national security and preventing the outbreak of a nuclear war. "Winning" a nuclear exchange is no longer regarded as a rational strategic objective; in such an exchange everyone, participant and nonparticipant alike, would be a loser. In keeping with the deterrence principle President Nixon affirmed in his State of the World Message of February 9 that "our forces must be maintained at a level sufficient to make it clear that even an all-out surprise attack on the U.S. by the U.S.S.R. would not cripple our capability to retaliate." For the Russians to feel secure they must have a similar capability; only then would a stable strategic balance exist.

The primary attribute required of any deterrent force is the ability to survive a "counterforce," or preemptive, attack. Ballistic-missile submarines are almost ideally suited to satisfying this requirement. Although they are expensive compared with other strategic weapons (more than $100 million per submarine exclusive of the missiles), their mobility and invisibility make them virtually immune to destruction in a surprise attack. In contrast, land-based intercontinental ballistic missiles (ICBM's) can readily be located with the aid of surveillance satellites, so that they must be regarded as "targetable" in the event of an enemy first strike. Attempts to "harden" such fixed missile-launchers (that is, to increase their resistance to the effects of nuclear explosions) are in the long run doomed to futility, since in the absence of qualitative arms-control agreements improvements in offensive missiles, particularly improvements in accuracy, will inevitably make fixed missile-launchers vulnerable and hence reduce confidence in their deterrence value.

The advent of multiple independently targetable reentry vehicles (MIRV's),

	SUBMARINES	MISSILES	WARHEADS		MAXIMUM TARGETS	
			BEFORE MIRV	AFTER MIRV	BEFORE MIRV	AFTER MIRV
U.S.	41	656	1,712	5,440	656	5,120
U.S.S.R.	26 (42)	416 (672)	416 (672)		416 (672)	

MISSILE-SUBMARINE FORCES of the U.S. and the U.S.S.R. are compared in this table. The submarines of both fleets are designed to carry 16 ballistic missiles each. The U.S. is currently in the process of converting 31 of its total of 41 deployed Polaris submarines to carry Poseidon missiles, each of which is capable of carrying up to 14 multiple independently targetable reentry vehicles (MIRV's); on the average each Poseidon will be able to deliver 10 nuclear warheads on 10 separate targets or at intervals on the same target. (The remaining payload can be devoted to various "penetration aids" intended to foil a potential enemy anti-ballistic-missile, or ABM, system.) Before the MIRV program began the bulk of the U.S. missile-submarine fleet was armed with Polaris A-3 missiles, which feature a multiple reentry vehicle (MRV) capable of carrying three warheads; these warheads are not, however, widely separable and are aimable only in shotgun fashion at a single target. After MIRVing is complete the remaining 10 ships in the Polaris fleet will continue to be armed with A-3 missiles. The Russian missile-submarine fleet consists at present of 26 ships deployed and about 16 more under construction, but this program could continue. (Known future submarine and missile totals are given in parentheses.) Since its missiles carry only one warhead each, however, the number of warheads it can launch is no greater than the total number of its missiles. Moreover, in a crisis military strategists in the U.S.S.R. must add to the U.S. totals the missile-submarine forces of France and Great Britain, each of which may eventually consist of four submarines and 64 missiles.

which are currently being deployed on a large scale by the U.S., creates a situation in which the "exchange ratio" strongly favors the attacker. Thus a single missile with, say, six warheads can potentially destroy six enemy ICBM's if they are caught in their silos. Moreover, strategic bombers are extremely vulnerable while they are on the ground and would therefore be very susceptible to annihilation in a surprise missile attack. Attempts to avoid this weakness by maintaining aircraft on continuous airborne alert have proved to be expensive and potentially dangerous. Even the current 15-minute ground alert is not completely satisfactory, since adequate warning would be more difficult to obtain if fractional-orbital-bombardment systems (FOBS) or depressed-trajectory missiles launched from submarines were used to attack the bombers.

Hence given the present state of military technology and reasonable anticipated advances, the primary element in the strategic-deterrent forces of both the U.S. and the U.S.S.R. will continue to be the ballistic-missile submarine. All other strategic systems will remain secondary. Moreover, it seems likely that any agreement that may emerge in the near future from the strategic-arms-limitation talks (SALT) will further enhance the relative importance of the missile-submarine forces. Since the chances that MIRV's will be limited by a SALT agreement are extremely low, ICBM's will become increasingly vulnerable. The more likely limitations on anti-ballistic-missile (ABM) systems, on the other hand, would guarantee the retaliatory capability of even a comparatively small number of submarine-launched ballistic missiles (SLBM's). The expected failure to limit antiaircraft defenses and to restrain qualitative improvements in offensive-missile systems would further decrease the value of strategic bombers. Although there will probably not soon be restrictions on antisubmarine-warfare (ASW) measures, the technology in this area is so far behind that it could not possibly threaten the submarine deterrent, if it can threaten it at all, until far in the future. In sum, the Navy will increasingly be the principal military guardian of our national security.

What characteristics must an SLBM force have in order to fulfill its function as a deterrent against the initiation of nuclear warfare by the U.S.S.R.? (Since China is so far behind both the U.S. and the U.S.S.R. in this respect, the same forces would be more than adequate to deter China as well.) First of all, the submarines should be designed to operate in, and fire their missiles from, large enough ocean areas in a variety of directions around the U.S.S.R. so as to decrease their vulnerability to ASW detection and tracking and to facilitate the penetration of any ABM system. The closer these areas are to ports in the U.S., the less will be the time lost in moving to and from operational stations and the less will be the need for overseas bases. Higher submarine speeds will also reduce this travel time and increase the ability to break contact with a trailing ASW submarine or surface vessel. The gains here may be marginal, particularly since tracking vessels will probably be faster than any missile submarine. The faster a submarine moves through the water, however, the more noise it will produce, and in countering ASW measures quietness may be much more important than speed. The reduction of submarine noise is the most critical element in preventing detection and continuous covert tracking, both of which must rely on passive acoustic sensors.

If an ABM defense is a realistic possibility, then the submarine missiles must have enough payload capacity to allow the use of multiple warheads and other penetration aids. The entire submarine force should be large enough so that the destruction of a few submarines by a concerted enemy attack, by slow attrition or perhaps by a series of accidents does not seriously degrade its overall capability. If continuous tracking by antisubmarine submarines or other ASW

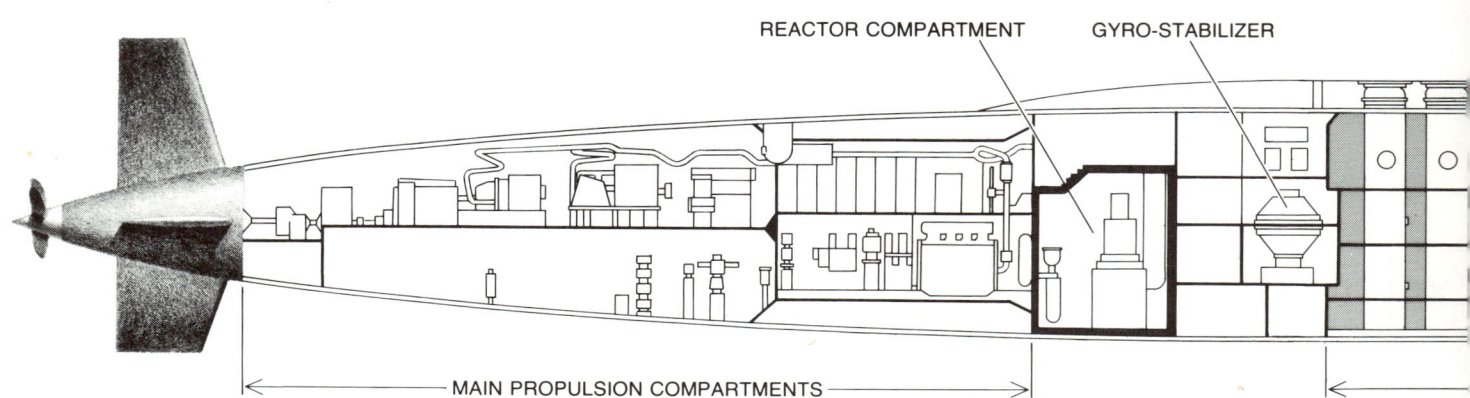

TYPICAL POLARIS SUBMARINE, in this case an advanced model belonging to the Lafayette, or 616, class is shown schematically in the cutaway drawings on these two pages. The nuclear-powered submarine has a length of 425 feet, a beam of 33 feet and a submerged displacement of 8,250 tons. In addition to its 16 ballistic-missile silos it is equipped with four bow torpedo tubes. Each of its

vessels ever becomes a realistic operation on a large scale, then the more vessels there are in the missile-submarine fleet, the harder it will be for this tactic to be successful in destroying the entire force. Ballistic-missile submarines cannot be used to attack other submarines and are no threat to the SLBM deterrent of the other side.

In addition to an adequate number of submarines, missiles and warheads, it is essential to have secure and reliable communications between these vessels and their command authorities. It is not enough to send the submarines to sea with sealed orders. Controls to prevent inadvertent or unauthorized firing are an absolute necessity, and reliable methods for ordering retaliation in the event of a surprise attack are required. These communications must be jam-proof; the potential attacker cannot be allowed to hope that a communications failure might prevent a retaliatory strike.

The submarines must also be able to navigate accurately, so that after they have moved through the oceans into their operational areas they will always be in a position to fire their missiles at predetermined targets. High navigational accuracy is not as great a requirement for a retaliatory strike against cities as it would be if the submarines were to be used in a counterforce role for destroying such "hard" targets as enemy missile sites. In fact, if one side wishes to use missile submarines only as deterrent weapons, then it is important that the accuracy-yield combination of the system not be so great as to give the other side concern that the submarines have a first-strike capability against land-based ICBM's; otherwise the position of mutual stable deterrence will be eroded.

With these general principles in mind, let us examine how the U.S. missile-submarine forces have developed over the years. The U.S. launched the first nuclear-powered submarine, the *Nautilus*, in 1955, but it was not until the late 1950's that development of long-range missiles had proceeded to the point that these could be installed in such submarines. The first ballistic-missile submarine, the *George Washington*, became operational in November, 1960. It was armed with 16 solid-fuel Polaris A-1 missiles, which could be fired at a rate of about one per minute. The range of this missile was about 1,200 nautical miles and the warhead yield about one megaton. The submarines were designed to fire their missiles while submerged, using compressed gases to expel the missile; the rocket engine is then ignited after the missile has cleared the surface. By 1963, 12 more Polaris submarines were operational.

Meanwhile the development of more advanced missiles continued. The next-generation missile, the A-2, had a range of about 1,500 nautical miles. The first test of the A-3 missile, with a range of 2,500 nautical miles and a "triplet" reentry vehicle, was conducted from a submerged submarine in the fall of 1963. The triplet reentry vehicles, which could carry three individual nuclear warheads each, did not have independent guidance; the three warheads were intended to reenter the atmosphere in a shotgun pattern with the target at the center. Since such warheads cannot be aimed at separate targets, they do not alter the exchange ratio and do not provide any first-strike advantage. Their advent was therefore not in itself regarded as destabilizing.

In the early 1960's there was considerable debate over the appropriate size of the Polaris fleet. The Navy originally sought 48 ships, and the final decision was to build 41. One factor limiting the number of submarines is the problem of manpower recruitment. Nuclear-submarine duty, which involves 60-day underwater cruises, calls for a certain type of person who is not easy to find and who must be highly trained. Normally each vessel has two crews of about 140 men who go on alternate patrols.

By the end of 1966 all 41 Polaris submarines were operational; eight carried A-2 missiles and 33 were eventually

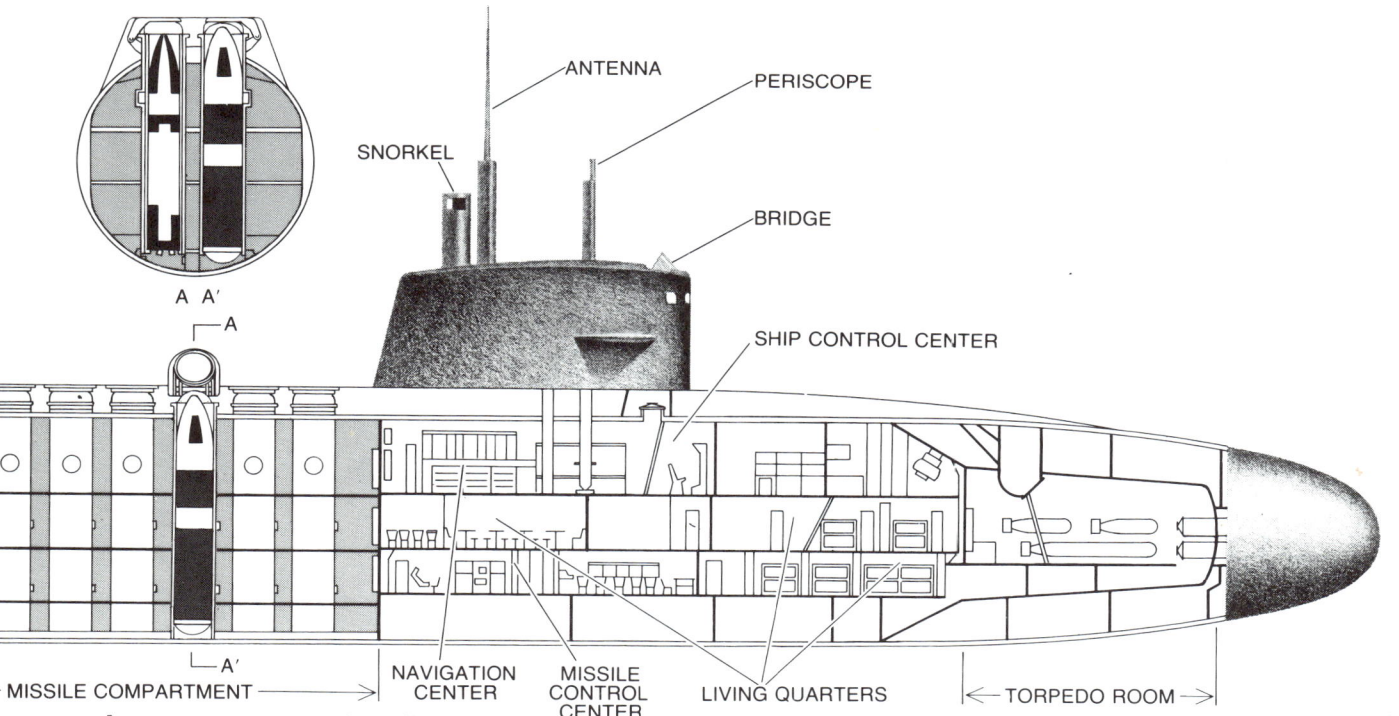

alternate crews consists of 14 officers and 126 enlisted men. The transverse section (*AA'*) shows the relative sizes of the Polaris A-3 missile (*left*) and the Poseidon C-3 missile (*right*). All the 31 missile submarines in this class will be converted to the Poseidon MIRV system by 1976. The Russian Y-class submarines, although not as advanced, are believed to be roughly similar in design.

fitted out with *A-3*'s. Thus the force carried a total of 1,712 warheads, but since the triplet warheads cannot be aimed separately, 656 was the maximum number of separate targets that could be hit. Of course, not all of these submarines can be kept at operational stations at all times. In general a submarine spends 60 days at sea and 30 days in port for maintenance. In addition the submarine might take five or more days to move from the U.S. to its launch point and the same period to return. If a submarine wished to avoid detection by moving quietly and therefore slowly, the travel time would be even greater. Thus the number of submarines at launch stations at any one time could be reduced to some 20 to 25 ships. The situation is improved by using forward bases (on Guam, at Holy Loch in Scotland and at Rota in Spain), which reduces the time needed to reach launch stations from five or six days to one or two days.

With a range of 2,500 nautical miles, a submarine-launched missile can hit Moscow from most of the North Atlantic (inside an arc extending from the tip of Greenland to North Africa), from the Mediterranean and even from some parts of the Indian Ocean, a total sea area of about six million square miles [*see illustration below*]. The sea area from which a submarine-launched missile could hit important targets other than Moscow, say targets only 200 miles inside the U.S.S.R., is even larger [*see illustration on opposite page*]. One high-ranking Navy officer reported in 1964 that a Polaris submarine equipped with the *A-3* missile could operate in 15 million square miles of ocean area while

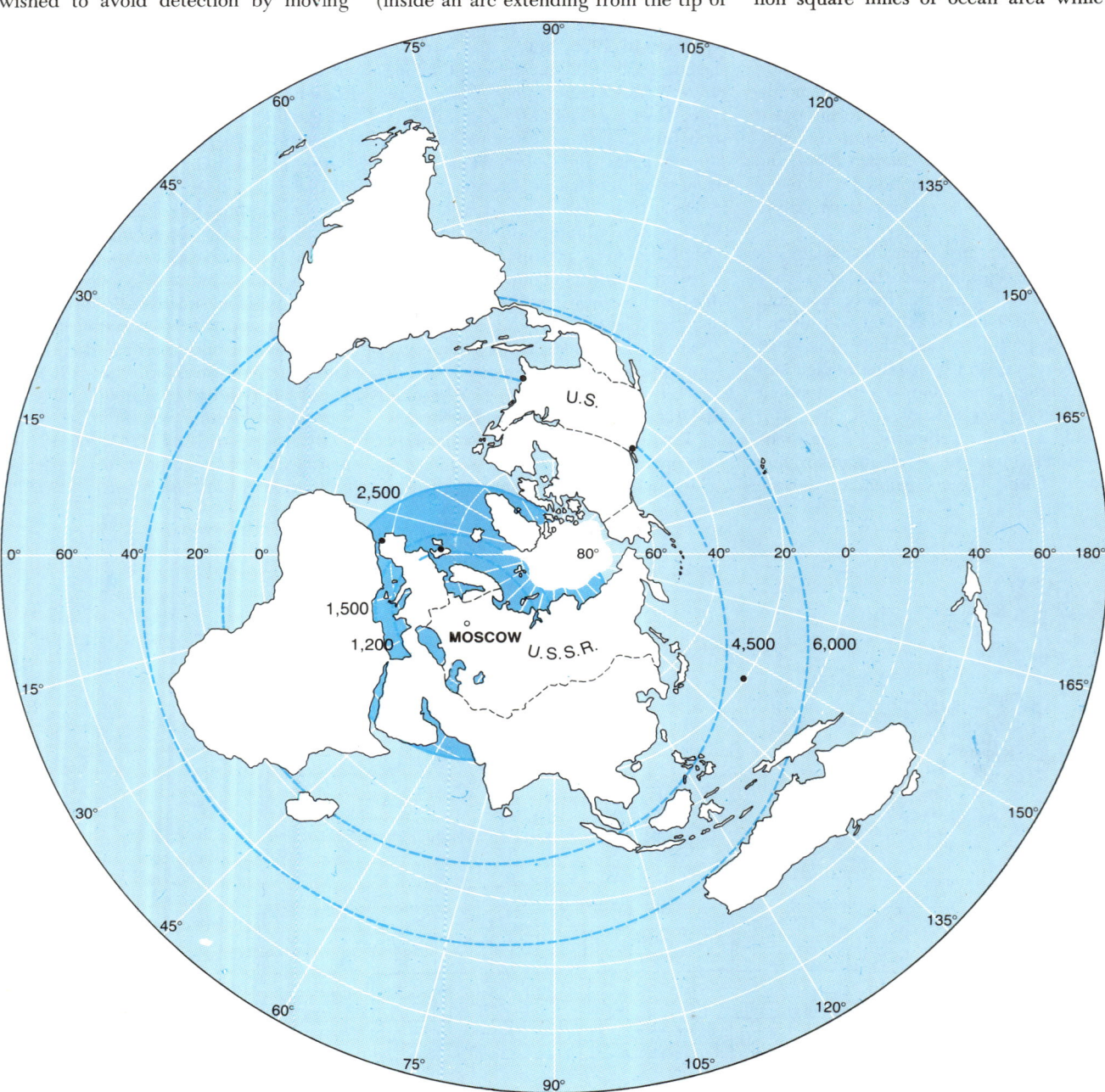

RANGE OF U.S. SUBMARINE MISSILES defines the operational sea areas from which submarine-launched ballistic missiles (SLBM's) could hit strategically important targets in the U.S.S.R. In the map at left the target is assumed to be Moscow; in the map at right the targets are assumed to include population centers and industrial complexes within 200 miles of the border of the U.S.S.R. (*gray areas*). The contours in the map at left are actually circles; their somewhat misshapen appearance is caused by the polar projection used in plotting the map. The contours in the map at right are concentric with the border of the U.S.S.R. The solid colored

covering its targets in the U.S.S.R. No land target anywhere in the world is inaccessible from attack by the A-3 missile.

Although mobility provides a submarine with the tremendous advantage of improving its survivability, it creates a new problem: the determination of its location at the moment when the missile is to be launched toward its target several thousand miles away. Unless the missile is provided with some means of determining its position during flight or with a terminal-homing capability, the accuracy at the impact point can never be better than the uncertainty in the launch point. To determine the launch position calls for accurate submarine navigation, which is made more difficult by the requirement that in order to avoid disclosing its presence the submarine should not surface to determine its location. The attitude of the ship with respect to the vertical and true north at the time of the launch is also needed. When the missile force is being used for deterrent purposes, an accuracy greater than a few thousand feet is not needed; it is only necessary to be able to hit a large urban complex. Today this order of accuracy in locating the position and attitude of a submarine can be readily achieved. The U.S. has made tremendous advances in the development of inertial-navigation systems in recent years, and reasonably accurate position fixes can be obtained even after the submarine has been submerged at sea for many days.

The inertial-navigation system in a Polaris submarine is a complex system of gyroscopes, accelerometers and com-

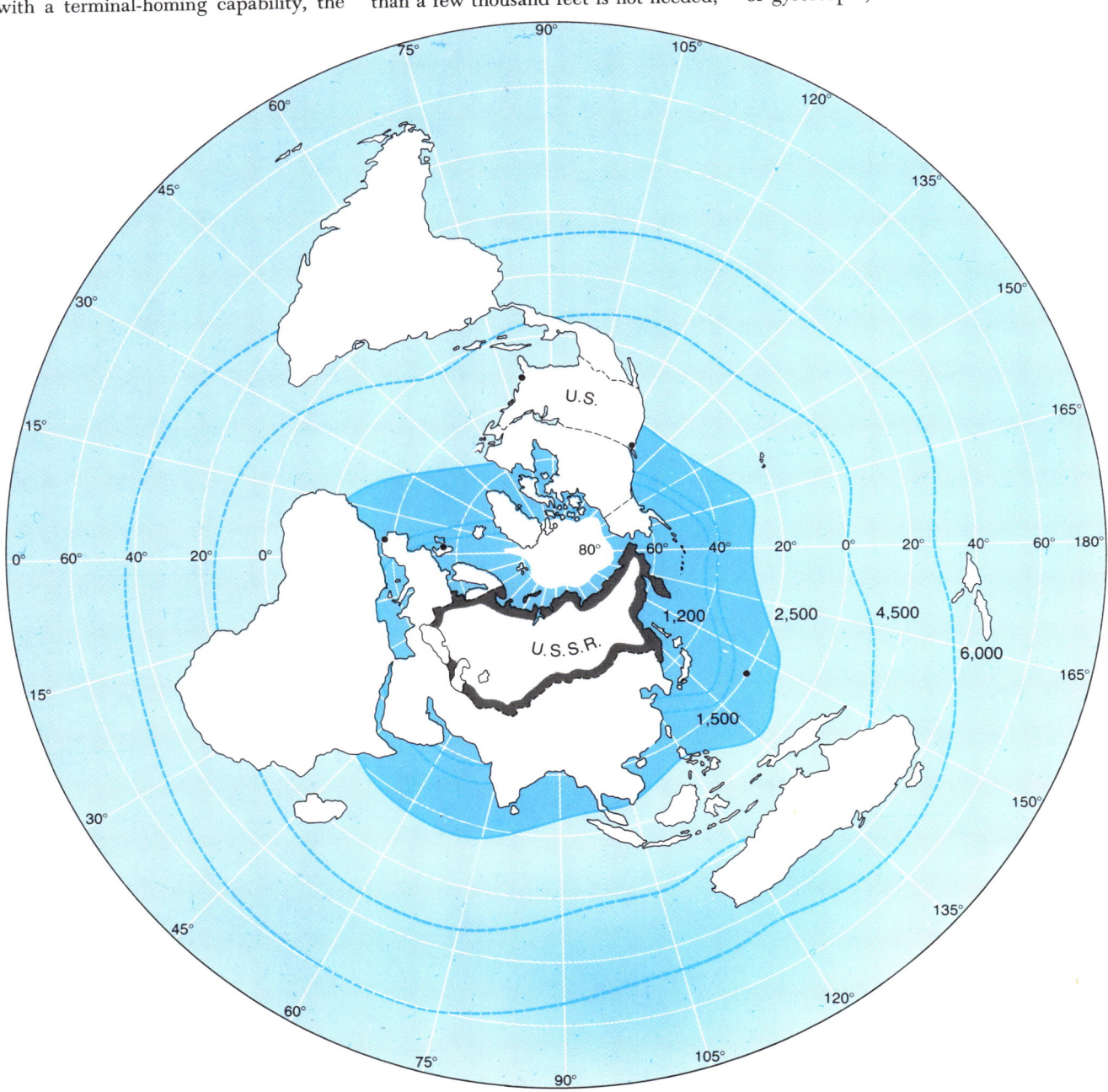

contour in each map shows the range of the Polaris A-3 and the nominal range of the Poseidon C-3 missiles (2,500 nautical miles). The two inner broken colored contours in each case show the ranges of the older Polaris A-1 and A-2 missiles (1,200 and 1,500 nautical miles respectively). The two outer broken colored contours show the estimated ranges of the Navy's proposed undersea long-range missile system, which envisions two new generations of missiles, the ULMS 1, with a range of 4,500 nautical miles, and the ULMS 2, with a range of 6,000 nautical miles. Black dots denote home ports and forward bases of the U.S. missile-submarine fleet.

puters that relate the movement and the speed of the ship in all directions with respect to true north. If an initial position is known, then this system will provide continuous data on the ship's position. For an absolutely stationary submarine, or one whose motion can be corrected for, inertial sensors can determine without external data the vertical, the true north, the latitude and all velocity components by inertially sensing the earth's gravitational and rotational vectors, but there is no way of determining the longitude by inertial means. Submarines that have been voyaging at sea for protracted periods and whose inertial-navigation errors may have become unacceptably large can, by trailing an antenna while they are still submerged, get a radio "position fix" from navigation satellites or land-based transmitters. It may also be possible to locate a submarine by reference to accurately known geographical landmarks on the ocean bottom such as seamounts. In sum, the present technology has advanced to the point where the location and attitude of the submarine could in principle no longer be the critical factor in obtaining missile accuracies down to less than an eighth of a mile.

A deterrent force must also be able to receive communications from national command centers. Direct command and control originating with the President and with many verification checks is vital to prevent unauthorized launching; it is also essential that command authorities be able to communicate in times of crisis with the submarine captains without fear of interference by the other side. Otherwise communication would

RANGE OF RUSSIAN SUBMARINE MISSILES is estimated in these two maps in order to show the operational sea areas from which their SLBM's could hit targets anywhere in the U.S. (*left*) and targets within 200 miles of the U.S. border (*right*). Alaska and Hawaii are excluded from consideration. Again the solid colored contour in each map shows the present range of the Russian Y-class missiles (1,300 nautical miles). The inner broken colored contour in each case shows the range of the previous generation of Russian SLBM's (700 nautical miles). The outer broken colored contour in each case shows the range of a new Russian missile that

be the Achilles' heel of the submarine deterrent. There are a number of means of communicating with a submarine, at least one way from shore to ship, that do not require the submarine to surface. Very-low-frequency (VLF) radio waves can penetrate a short distance into the water, so that a receiving antenna does not need to be exposed at the surface. Moreover, the submarine can operate at a considerable depth, since it can trail an antenna as much as several hundred feet above its deck. The U.S. has a number of land-based VLF transmitters at various locations around the world for communication with Polaris submarines, and more recently an airborne VLF system has been devised in order to eliminate the possibility that the fixed land-based stations would be destroyed in a surprise attack.

The use of satellites for relaying messages to submarines provides an alternative means of communication. Recently much research has been devoted to extremely-low-frequency (ELF) waves, which can penetrate even deeper into the water. The Navy project named Sanguine proposed to set up a vast antenna for this purpose in Wisconsin. The data rate of such a system would be quite low, but it would be adequate for command-communication purposes. The project has run into difficulties with local residents because of the large antenna currents and the potential hazard to living things. For communication from a submarine to the command center the problem is more difficult; it calls at the very least for trailing an antenna close to the surface and must in any case be avoided in order to prevent disclosure of

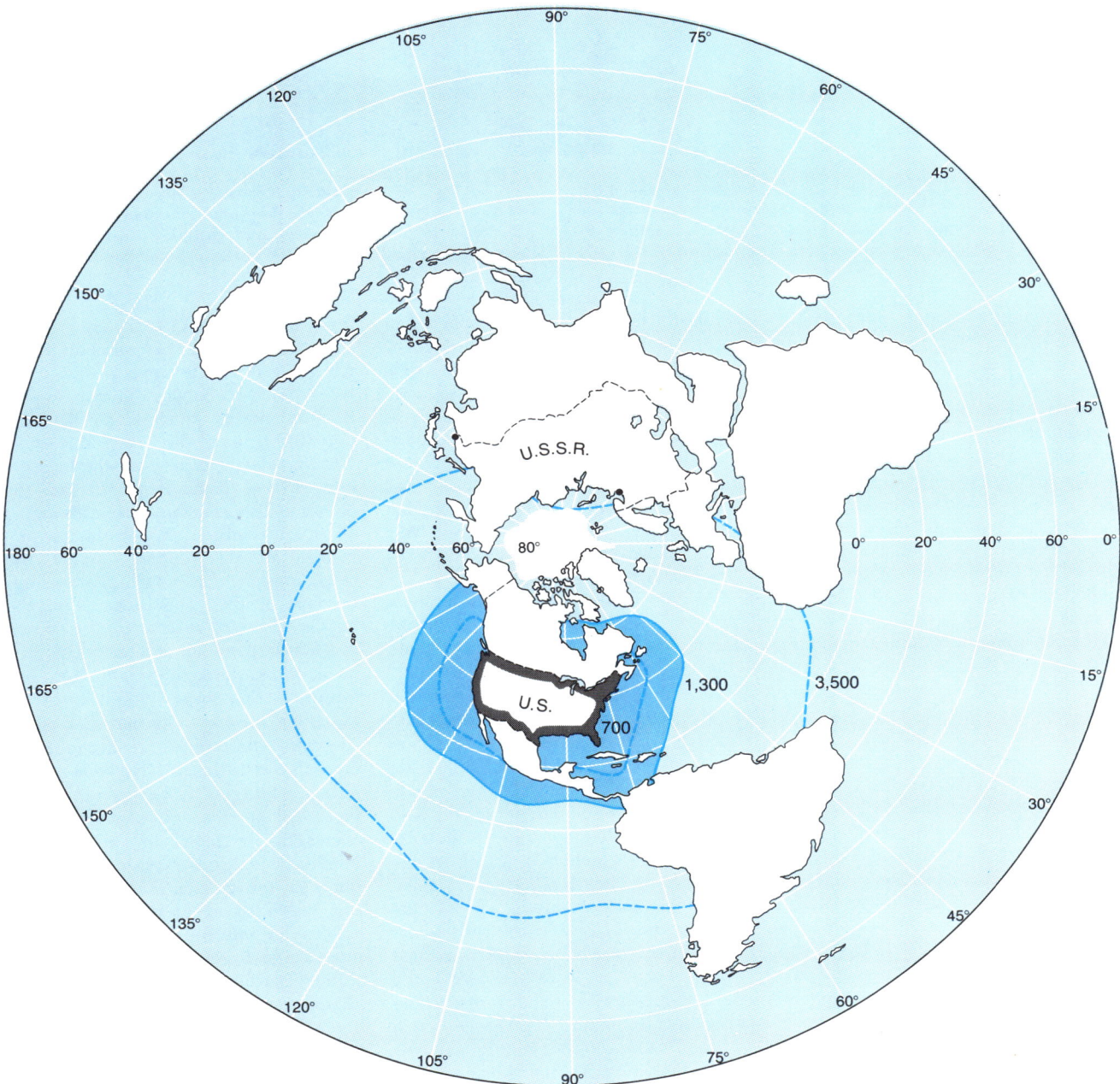

has recently been tested; this missile, however, is believed by U.S. strategic planners to be too long to fit readily in the present Y-class missile submarines. The black dots indicate the shipyards of the Russian missile-submarine fleet; the U.S.S.R. has no forward bases for its missile submarines. In general the greater distance from the Russian missile-submarine fleet's home ports to their operational launching areas, combined with their lack of forward bases, means that their submarines waste more time in getting "on station." Hence the U.S.S.R. requires more missile submarines than the U.S. to maintain the same deterrent force operational at any one time.

U.S. MISSILE SUBMARINE, the U.S.S. *Lafayette*, namesake of the advanced 616 class of Polaris vessels, was photographed while she cruised in the Atlantic Ocean during her builder's sea trials in April, 1963. The *Lafayette* was built in the shipyards of the Electric Boat Division of the General Dynamics Corporation in Groton, Conn. As originally deployed, this submarine was armed with 16 solid-fueled Polaris *A-2* missiles; it is scheduled to be converted to Poseidon *C-3* missiles with MIRV warheads sometime before 1976.

the submarine's location to listening enemy radios. Fortunately such communication is not essential to the viability of the submarine deterrent force.

By the end of 1966 the U.S. submarine-missile force together with its support systems was by itself more than adequate to deter any nuclear attack on the U.S. It had more than enough missiles and warheads to devastate the U.S.S.R. even when only a fraction of the submarines were on station. It could operate in ocean areas on all sides of the U.S.S.R., and the Russian ASW capability was quite rudimentary, with virtually no ability to "draw down" the size of the U.S. fleet. At that time the Russians had no ABM system deployed.

Military technology did not, however, stand still. The need to operate in restricted sea areas close to the northern coast of Europe and the Mediterranean in order to reach Moscow and other interior Russian cities created fears that someday ASW measures might become a threat. More important, concern that the U.S.S.R. might deploy a large ABM system capable of coping with our missile-submarine force was becoming more acute every day. The Russians were in the process of deploying an ABM defense around Moscow, using a large interceptor missile estimated to have a single-warhead yield large enough to destroy all three warheads of the Polaris *A-3*. In addition they were deploying radars and defensive missiles in the "Tallinn system" widely throughout the U.S.S.R. Some "worst case" analyses of U.S. planners, particularly during the early phases when factual information was limited, postulated that these facilities were for ABM defense. Later, as more data became available, the predictions were scaled down to the effect that the Tallinn system was an antiaircraft defense that could perhaps be upgraded to provide an ABM capability. (Now even this upgrading is not considered practicable by most experts.)

As a result research and development proceeded on a next-generation missile for the Polaris submarine that would give increased future assurance of penetrating any ABM defense and would at the same time give the submarines enough flexibility to operate at greater distances from the U.S.S.R. To increase either the payload or the range significantly called for a larger missile, and the resulting Poseidon missile required enlarging the launching tubes in the Polaris submarines, a costly and time-consuming task requiring 13 or more months. Since many of the submarines were due for overhaul in any case, however, the two shipyard activities could be combined with a minimum loss in operational readiness for the fleet as a whole. The cost of converting a Polaris submarine to carry the advanced Poseidon missiles is on the average $29 million, with another $38 million for normal submarine overhaul and replacement of the nuclear fuel.

The new Poseidon missile is about twice as heavy as the Polaris *A-3* and has a payload about four times as great. Although its nominal range of about 2,500 nautical miles is the same as that of the *A-3*, a trade-off between range and payload is always possible, so that the potential range of the Poseidon is somewhat greater. The new missile incorporates MIRV technology, that is, the ability to disperse many warheads aimed at separate targets. The technique developed for this purpose employs the "bus" approach, in which shortly after burnout of the propulsion stages the missile's final stage (the bus) is aimed at a first target point and releases a warhead, which then follows a ballistic trajectory to that target while the bus is redirected toward a second aim point. The same procedure can be repeated until all the warheads have been sent to individual targets. If a single target is to be attacked, then MIRV technology allows the warheads to approach the target at widely spaced intervals and on different trajectories so that no more than one warhead can be destroyed by a single ABM interceptor. The Poseidon is reported to be capable of carrying 14 warheads, each with a yield of about 50 kilotons, several times the yield of the bomb that destroyed Hiroshima. Warheads can be traded off for either ABM penetration aids or increased range. The nominal complement is usually taken as being 10 MIRV warheads. Department of Defense officials have repeatedly stated that these warheads do not have the accuracy-yield combination to provide a first-strike capability against hardened silos (a "circular-error probability" of about an eighth of a mile or better would be needed with that yield), but the Russians might still be concerned on this score.

As with the Polaris A-3, a Poseidon missile with a range of 2,500 nautical miles can launch warheads at Moscow not only from large areas of the North Atlantic and the Mediterranean but also from some parts of the Indian Ocean, a total area of about six million square miles. Targets within 200 miles of the border of the U.S.S.R. can be reached from some 15 million square miles. These large ocean areas present great problems for any possible future ASW system. To deploy detection and tracking systems throughout these waters is a prodigious, if not impossible, task. Furthermore, on short notice these areas might be somewhat enlarged if it ever became critical by reducing the Poseidon payload, either by eliminating penetration aids or by cutting down the number of warheads in each missile.

The first Poseidon missile was tested in August, 1968, and the development of the entire Poseidon system was completed two years later. The first Polaris submarine went to sea with Poseidon missiles in March of last year. At present about 10 submarines have been converted. The program calls for modifying 31 submarines to carry these new missiles, leaving 10 to be equipped with the older A-3's. When the program is completed in 1976, the U.S. submarine force will be able to launch 5,440 warheads at 5,120 separate targets. It should be possible to keep considerably more than half of these submarines on station at all times, and in times of crisis the operational readiness can be stepped up if necessary. This is an awesome force, capable of overwhelming even a massive ABM defense system. There is, of course, no evidence that the Russians have any intention of building a large ABM system with nationwide coverage, and it is highly likely that such a system will be precluded in the first stage of a strategic-arms-limitation treaty.

Even one missile submarine can launch 160 warheads at separate industrial centers in the U.S.S.R., an attack that the Russians could not afford even if the U.S. had been annihilated. This means that any ASW system would have to be able to eliminate almost instantaneously every single submarine, a herculean task. Today it is difficult, if not impossible, to destroy even a single submarine that follows skilled evasion tactics. Yet if ABM defenses were forbidden by treaty, an ASW system that has still to be devised would be the only threat to the submarine deterrent. That is one reason why an ABM agreement at SALT would by itself be such an important gain to the security of both the U.S. and the U.S.S.R.

The U.S.S.R. has always lagged considerably behind the U.S. in the development of nuclear submarines and SLBM's. The first Russian nuclear submarine was built about four years after the *Nautilus,* and Admiral Hyman G. Rickover, the director of the U.S. nuclear-submarine program from the beginning, has made it clear he believes the Russian submarines are technically inferior to the U.S. ships. The first Russian ballistic-missile submarines were diesel-powered and therefore had limited endurance and cruising range. Their first nuclear-powered missile submarine carried only three missiles with a 300-nautical-mile range, which in later models was extended to about 700 nautical miles.

By the late 1960's it must have been obvious to military planners in the U.S.S.R. that their land-based ICBM's would become increasingly vulnerable to the U.S. MIRV's, which were then under development and which had been publicly justified as providing an improved counterforce capability. The Russian deterrent needed shoring up with a more effective SLBM force, whose value had been demonstrated by the U.S. In 1966 the U.S.S.R. launched its first Y-class submarine, which carries 16 missiles with a reported range of 1,300 miles. This class of vessels was similar to the Polaris submarines, which the U.S. had put into operation seven years earlier. All the Russian SLBM's deployed so far have had storable liquid fuels,

RUSSIAN MISSILE SUBMARINE, a representative Y-class vessel, is remarkably similar in appearance and general dimensions to the earlier U.S. Polaris designs. The ship carries 16 liquid-fuel missiles with a reported range of about 1,300 nautical miles. Each missile is armed with a single nuclear warhead with a yield of about one megaton. This photograph was released by the U.S. Navy in 1970.

whereas all the U.S. missiles have had solid fuels. The Russians apparently decided to continue with the Y-class design and began building submarines at a rapid pace, initially at the rate of six to eight per year and currently at nine per year. Two shipyards are engaged in this work, one at Severodvinsk on the Arctic Sea and one in Siberia on the Pacific. At present the Russians have about 26 Y-class submarines operational and another 16 under construction.

Although the Russians have tested a new missile with a range of about 3,500 miles, John Stuart Foster, Jr., chief research scientist for the Department of Defense, recently reported that this missile was so long that he did not believe the Y-class submarine could be modified to launch it. The Russians have never even tested multiple warheads on their submarine missiles, let alone MIRV's. Their missiles are each armed with a single warhead with a yield of about one megaton. These missiles have no capability for attacking our ICBM silos, but it has been postulated that they might be employed to attack our bombers on the ground and our command and control centers, using a depressed trajectory to achieve the necessary surprise. The missiles have not, however, been tested in this mode, and this approach would, in any case, entail a reduction in their already limited range.

The U.S.S.R. will have a slightly larger ballistic-missile submarine fleet than the U.S. when it completes those vessels now under construction (42 to 41). Even then, however, the capabilities of the Russian fleet will be far inferior to those of the U.S. Polaris fleet. President Nixon in his 1972 State of the World Message said that "our missiles have longer range and are being equipped with multiple independently targetable warheads. Moreover, our new submarines are now superior in quality." The shorter range of the Russian missiles requires that their submarines operate fairly close to the U.S. coast in order to be able to strike inland U.S. targets; this makes the Russian submarines potentially more vulnerable to a U.S. ASW system [see illustration on page 74]. On the other hand, the population centers and industrial complexes on the east and west coasts of the U.S. can be reached from much larger ocean areas, and these targets would be quite satisfactory if the SLBM's were to be used for deterrent purposes [see illustration on page 75]. The restricted range would be a serious factor only if the SLBM's were to be used against our bomber bases or missiles in the interior of the U.S.

There are other reasons why the parity between the U.S. and the U.S.S.R. in operational submarines cannot be evaluated on numerical grounds alone. Since bases in the U.S.S.R. are farther from the operational launching areas and since the Russians have no locations available for forward bases, more time is wasted getting submarines on station and it takes more submarines to maintain the same deterrent force operational at any one time. It would take Russian submarines a minimum of six days in the Atlantic and eight days in the Pacific to reach the nearest launch stations, so that the transit time to and from home ports, in many cases a quarter to a third of the duration of the patrol, seriously degrades the operational readiness of the Russian fleet. This disadvantage can be only partly alleviated by using submarine tenders for maintenance and crew exchange at sea. Moreover, in any East-West comparison the small British and French missile-submarine fleets, each of which may eventually consist of four submarines and 64 missiles, must be added to the U.S. total. Thus, whereas the Russians now have an adequate missile-submarine deterrent, their fleet is markedly inferior to that of the U.S. and its allies and provides no threat to the U.S. deterrent.

As the first phase of SALT is drawing to an end, then, it is becoming universally recognized that ballistic-missile

ARRANGEMENT OF MISSILE SILOS in a Lafayette-class Polaris submarine is revealed by the open silo doors in this view. The submarine, the U.S.S. *Sam Rayburn*, was photographed at Newport News, Va., at about the time of her commissioning in December, 1964.

CONVERSION of the Polaris submarine U.S.S. *James Madison* to accommodate the new, larger Poseidon missile was undertaken in February, 1969, and was completed in June, 1970. This photograph shows the *Madison*, the first of 31 such missile submarines to be converted, being test-fitted for the new Poseidon missile system at the Groton shipyards of the General Dynamics Electric Boat Division.

submarines are the essential foundation of a secure and stable strategic balance. Under these circumstances it is only natural to investigate ways to still further improve submarine missile systems. The U.S. has had a research and development program in this area for several years, so that the developments at the frontiers of technology could be incorporated in the successor to the Polaris-Poseidon system. The particular system proposed by the Navy for this role has been called ULMS, for undersea long-range missile system.

One obvious way to improve the present submarine missile would be to extend its range, making possible the launching of missiles from larger ocean areas in all directions around the U.S.S.R. Increasing the missile's payload would allow the incorporation of more warheads per missile or additional ABM-penetration aids. Payload can, of course, always be traded off for range. A longer-range missile would reduce the time required to move from U.S. ports to launching areas and thereby reduce the need for overseas basing in order to maintain the submarines on station for a larger fraction of their cruising time. With a range of 4,500 nautical miles a missile could reach Moscow shortly after the submarine leaves the U.S., whereas with a range of 2,500 nautical miles at least three days' travel would be required. Thus for a 60-day cruise lengthening the missile range by 2,000 miles could increase the period of operational effectiveness by about 10 percent if forward bases were abandoned.

More advanced guidance systems employing terminal control (the ability to change the path of the warhead during reentry) are being developed to avoid interception by ABM systems or to improve accuracy. Higher accuracy obtained by this means or others is not required if missiles are to be used as deterrent weapons. Indeed, it might be construed by the other side as an attempt to attain a counterforce capability for a first strike. Although it is more difficult to acquire such a capability with a submarine missile system than with an ICBM because of the inherent limitations on the payload and the nuclear explosive yield and because of navigational complications, there are no scientific barriers to its achievement. The greatest technical restriction on the use of SLBM's for a counterforce first strike may lie in command and control. It may be feasible to preprogram and command the initial launchings, but there will inevitably be failures. The difficulties of directing subsequent firings to destroy the silos missed the first time appear to be virtually insurmountable.

The submarine itself can be improved

by making it quieter as it moves through the water, thereby rendering detection and tracking by passive acoustic techniques more difficult. Although increasing the speed of the submarine will make it somewhat harder for enemy ASW ships to follow it, the higher speed will also raise the level of noise produced by the submarine. In any case it is probably a losing proposition for a missile submarine to try to outrun an ASW vessel, which can always be designed to move faster. High speed will enable the submarine to reach its launch area more rapidly and thus reduce the time it spends in a nonoperational condition, but again the potential gains are not large, and they may be outweighed by the disadvantages. If all other factors are equal, it will require a bigger power plant and larger submarine, both of which will increase cost and detectability. Increasing the depth at which a submarine can operate is not particularly significant, at least for the depths that are likely to be achieved in the next generation of submarines; submarines can be detected acoustically and destroyed by nuclear depth charges or homing torpedoes at any reasonable depth.

If space for more and larger missiles is needed to increase the destructive capacity and the ABM-penetrability of any single submarine, then larger submarines with bigger power plants will be required. The larger the submarines, however, the fewer the ships that will be available for the same investment. Therefore if funds are limited (and they always are), this means a smaller fleet, which is more vulnerable to being wiped out in a simultaneous surprise attack. Thus there are many trade-offs in system design, and the final decision on a successor to the Polaris-Poseidon system should be based only on the nature of the specific threat.

In 1971 $104.8 million was appropriated for the advanced development of ULMS. Although this expenditure still left options open, it was a major step on the path toward procuring a specific new submarine system. This year the Department of Defense is seeking $977 million for ULMS. If that amount is authorized, the U.S. will be irrevocably committed to a large and very expensive new shipbuilding program. Unclassified details of the proposed ULMS program are still scarce, but it appears that the submarine in the system would be quite large (more than twice the size of the Polaris ships) and that it would be capable of launching 20 to 24 large missiles equipped with MIRV's. It is proposed to have a higher maximum speed and to incorporate the latest available silencing techniques, although these two objectives are competitive.

The ULMS program has been divided into two parts. The first stage (ULMS 1) would involve a new missile with a range of about 4,500 nautical miles capable of being deployed in the present Polaris submarines as well as in any new vessel. The second stage (ULMS 2) would include the development of the new submarine and a still more advanced missile with a range of about 6,000 miles that would be too big to be

FIRST SUCCESSFUL TEST LAUNCH of a Poseidon missile from a submerged submarine was carried out in October, 1970. The missile was launched from the *James Madison*. The Poseidon missile, like the earlier Polaris models, is expelled from its silo by compressed gas; its rocket engine is then ignited after the missile has cleared the surface of the water.

substituted for the Poseidon in the existing Polaris ships. A maneuvering reentry vehicle (MARV) is also being developed for the new ULMS missiles. According to one estimate, the total cost of a program for 30 such ULMS vessels would be $39.6 billion [*see illustration at right*].

So far no convincing case has been made for the need to proceed with a replacement for the Polaris-Poseidon system and for making a commitment to a new large, high-speed submarine. Russian construction of SLBM's is no justification for ULMS; the Russian missile submarines do not in any way threaten the Polaris deterrent. Numerical superiority in launchers is meaningless; all authorities agree that the U.S. is far ahead qualitatively and can deliver from submarines about 5,000 warheads to fewer than 700 for the U.S.S.R. Even if we foolishly choose to race the Russians in the number of SLBM's, ULMS is certainly not the way to do it; each ULMS system will probably cost five or more times per missile launched than the Russian Y-class system.

The Poseidon with 10 or more MIRV's on each missile has a far greater capability than is needed to overwhelm any Russian ABM system that can be foreseen at present. Admiral Thomas H. Moorer, chairman of the Joint Chiefs of Staff, testified in February that "the Moscow ABM system even with improved radars and more and better interceptors could still be saturated by a very small part of our total missile force. In any event, the programmed Minuteman III and Poseidon forces, with their large number of reentry vehicles, provide a hedge against a future large-scale Soviet ABM deployment." Since such a large-scale ABM deployment will almost certainly be precluded by a first-stage SALT agreement, there is nothing in the ABM area that would require replacement of the Poseidon; in fact, even the Poseidon MIRV's will not be needed if a SALT ABM treaty is realized.

Therefore it is necessary to examine antisubmarine warfare to determine if there is anything that would currently justify the major ULMS step. Without going into a detailed analysis of possible ASW measures and countermeasures, suffice it to say that no evidence has yet been presented that the Russian ASW program could present a threat to the Polaris deterrent in the next decade. [See "Antisubmarine Warfare and National Security," by Richard L. Garwin, the article beginning on page 248]. Admiral Levering Smith, director of the

RESEARCH, DEVELOPMENT, TEST AND EVALUATION	MILLIONS OF DOLLARS
SUBMARINE	$800
MANEUVERING REENTRY VEHICLE (MARV)	$600
ULMS 1 MISSILE	$2,100
ULMS 2 MISSILE	$1,500
PROCUREMENT	
SUBMARINES (30 AT AVERAGE COST OF $400 MILLION EACH)	$12,000
ULMS 1 MISSILES (ENOUGH FOR 500 LAUNCHERS AT AVERAGE COST OF $8 MILLION EACH)	$4,000
ULMS 2 MISSILES (ENOUGH FOR 600 LAUNCHERS AT AVERAGE COST OF $11 MILLION EACH)	$6,600
SUPPORT	
ULMS REFIT FACILITIES (ONE PER 15 SHIPS AT COST OF $1,800 MILLION FOR FIRST, $1,200 MILLION FOR SECOND)	$3,000
OPERATION AND MAINTENANCE (FOR 30 SHIPS AT AVERAGE COST OF $30 MILLION PER YEAR FOR 10 YEARS)	$9,000
TOTAL	$39,600

ESTIMATE OF TOTAL COST of the Navy's proposed ULMS program was prepared by Members of Congress for Peace through Law. The first stage of the ULMS program (ULMS 1) would involve a new missile with a range of about 4,500 nautical miles capable of being deployed in the present Polaris submarines as well as in any new vessels. The second stage (ULMS 2) would include the development of a new, larger submarine and a still more advanced missile with a range of about 6,000 miles. A special maneuvering reentry vehicle (MARV) is being developed for these new, larger missiles. The entry under research, development, test and evaluation for the submarine includes the cost of all nonmissile subsystems and integration work. The procurement estimates assume that the new program would eventually involve 30 new submarines. The support estimates assume a need for two special refit facilities for the ULMS ships and include crew-related costs for 10 years. The cost of the ULMS 1 missile program by itself is estimated to come to about $6.7 billion.

Navy's Strategic Systems Project, testified in 1969 that even the new generation of Russian ASW submarines will not be able to follow our Polaris submarines, and that the U.S.S.R. has no specific new ASW methods that would make the Polaris fleet vulnerable to attack. That is still true today. The U.S. has spent tens of billions of dollars on ASW efforts over the past 20 years and still does not have any system that could even begin to approach the kind of capability that would be needed to eliminate 20 to 30 missile submarines almost simultaneously. The Russians are far behind the U.S. in this area, and they have the serious geographical disadvantages of remoteness from and unavailability of land areas contiguous to the oceans in which their ASW systems would have to operate. Since the nature of the potential ASW threat to the Polaris-Poseidon system cannot even be foreseen at this point, ULMS, if built now, may be designed to cope with the wrong threat. The most obvious improvement to Polaris-Poseidon would be to increase the range of the missile in order to enlarge the ocean areas from which missiles could be launched. The deployment of such a new long-range missile might cost nearly seven billion dollars, however, and in any case, as the maps on pages 6 and 7 show, the Poseidon system already has a tremendous operational flexibility and is not threatened in its present launch areas.

Thus there are strong arguments for keeping both the ULMS missile and the ULMS submarine options in the research and early development stage. This would allow the exploration of all approaches, including smaller, slower but quieter submarines, and would avoid the making of a premature commitment to a large, expensive submarine and missile program. We must not fall into the trap of buying new military hardware just because we have made technological advances; there is no quicker way to price ourselves out of the security market. The submarine missile force is the backbone of our deterrent; its present strength and invulnerability obviate the need for its replacement for at least a decade.

7 Antisubmarine Warfare and National Security

by Richard L. Garwin
July 1972

The missile-submarine deterrents of the U.S. and the U.S.S.R. are not threatened by current antisubmarine technology. It is argued that this state of affairs should be maintained by the two powers

The treaty and executive agreement recently signed by the U.S. and the U.S.S.R., the culmination of three years of the strategic-arms-limitation talks (SALT), formally recognize that the two countries accept the military and political value of mutual deterrence as a means of forestalling an all-out nuclear war. The accords remove one potential threat to the effectiveness of strategic offensive missiles, on which deterrence rests, by prohibiting the U.S. and the U.S.S.R. from constructing nationwide anti-ballistic-missile (ABM) defenses. By ensuring the effectiveness of our offensive missiles, the ABM treaty greatly enhances our future security. The SALT accords, however, do not prohibit either country from qualitatively improving its offensive missile forces, for example by equipping missiles with multiple independently targeted reentry vehicles (MIRV's) or by improving the accuracy or explosive yield of missile warheads, perhaps to the point where the offensive missiles have a high probability of being able to destroy land-based missiles in their silos (if they were to remain there until they were hit). The U.S. could in fact replace Minuteman with a larger missile in the same silo, thereby multiplying the "throw weight" of the Minuteman force by a factor of three or four. As a result of this possibility each country will be concerned to maintain the invulnerability of its submarine-based strategic missiles, which are essentially immune to attack from land-based weapons [see "Missile Submarines and National Security," by Herbert Scoville, Jr., the article beginning on page 235].

A potential threat to the submarine-based deterrent already exists in the antisubmarine-warfare (ASW) forces that both the U.S. and the U.S.S.R. possess. Fortunately, in the present state of the art, the technology of antisubmarine warfare is even less effective in a disabling strike against ballistic-missile-launching submarines than it is against nuclear-powered submarines designed to attack surface ships. Nevertheless, given the importance of the submarine-based deterrent, it is not too early to examine the feasibility of arms-control limitations on possible methods of antisubmarine warfare that might eventually threaten the survivability of missile-launching submarines.

In this article I shall distinguish between antisubmarine-warfare techniques whose utility is tactical (the protection of surface shipping) and techniques that would be specifically useful against submarines carrying strategic offensive missiles. I hope to show that one could limit antisubmarine-warfare methods that would threaten the submarine-based deterrent without impairing one's ability to protect surface shipping from submarine attack. The precedent set by the prohibition of nationwide ABM systems shows that both the U.S. and the U.S.S.R. have a strong interest in preserving a controllable, survivable force of submarine-launched ballistic missiles (SLBM's). Even if a conventional war were to break out between the two powers, one could hope to continue to deter mutual nuclear annihilation by arranging for the SLBM forces of the two countries to survive. To that end one might now consider a possible SALT II agreement to provide safe passage for missile-launching submarines along designated routes to the open ocean. This is only one example of what might be in the interest of both the U.S. and the U.S.S.R.

Mutual acceptance of invulnerability for ballistic-missile submarines of the U.S. and the U.S.S.R. does not extend, however, to all possible roles for those submarines. For instance, a deterrent role for the ballistic-missile submarine does not require that all boats be in firing position near the surface and able to coordinate their fire within seconds. Nor does it require that they all be able to survive for several months after the outbreak of a major war without suffering any losses, deliberate or inadvertent, through antisubmarine warfare. The principle of deterrence would seem to be adequately served if ballistic-missile submarines on station could survive a full first-strike onslaught for a few hours in order to fire their weapons and if submarines not on station but in sanctuary or in the broad ocean reaches had a good probability of surviving a prudent trip of five or 10 days to firing position.

If war should break out between the U.S. and the U.S.S.R. and if nuclear weapons were used only at sea, the major consequence would be the destruction of each country's relatively few capital surface ships. Submarines, by and large, would survive. Although one cannot exclude the use of nuclear weapons against missile-carrying submarines, they do not change the conclusions. I shall argue the compatibility of an invulnerable submarine-based deterrent force with the active conduct of a tactical, nonnuclear and antisubmarine war.

Antisubmarine warfare involves at least four activities that proceed in logical sequence: intelligence, detection, localization and destruction. An optional tracking stage of hours or days can be imagined between localization and destruction. If the antisubmarine weapon is an antisubmarine mine, of course, no tracking is involved and the other activities are collapsed in time (although potentially intelligence can be fed into the mine from outside in advance or at arbitrary intervals).

Intelligence includes such information as the number of enemy submarines of each class, for example attack submarine (SS), nuclear-powered attack submarine (SSN), ballistic-missile-launching submarine (SSB), nuclear-powered ballistic-missile-launching submarine (SSBN) or cruise-missile-launching submarine (SSG or SSGN). Other kinds of information include number and range of missiles, number and type of torpedoes, speed and endurance, noise level, and sonar and radar capability. In addition to this intelligence on force levels and technical characteristics there is tactical intelligence, dealing broadly with the number of enemy submarines out of port, the number in each ocean basin, operating tactics, special vulnerabilities and so on. Tactical intelligence shades into detection and localization when a submarine can be limited to a certain area.

Over the years various methods have been employed for detecting submarines, including the detection of periscopes by radar, radio-frequency direc-

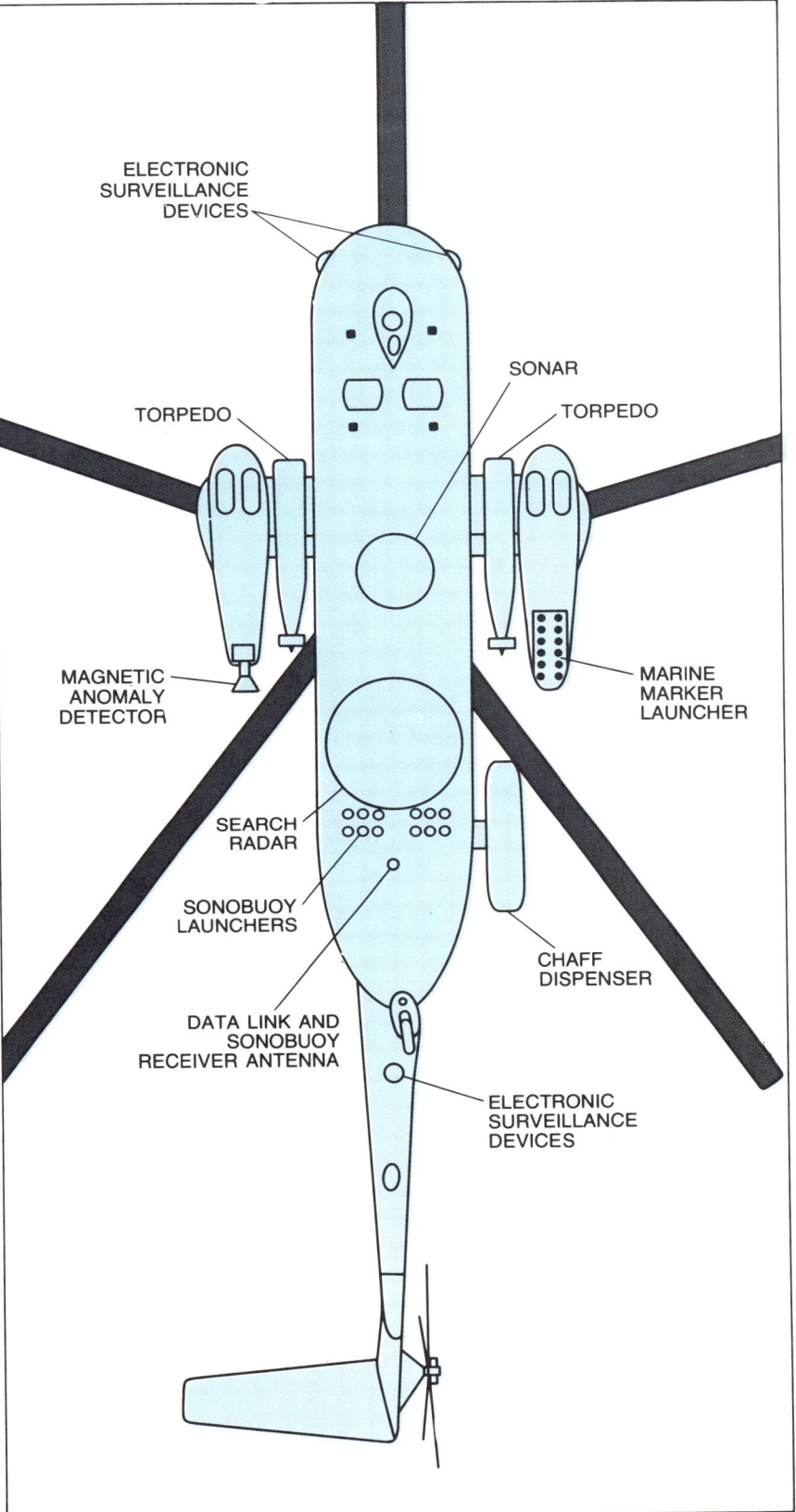

ADVANCED ANTISUBMARINE HELICOPTER, designated the SH-3H, is viewed from below in this schematic diagram. The helicopter is equipped with five different submarine-detection systems and is armed with a pair of lightweight 12-inch Mark 46 active acoustic homing torpedoes. The first eight SH-3H helicopters, built by the Sikorsky Aircraft Division of United Aircraft Corporation, are scheduled to be delivered to the U.S. Navy in mid-1972.

tion finding and visual sighting from aircraft. Although all play a role in tactical antisubmarine operations, the only currently effective way to locate a submerged submarine from any distance is by the use of acoustic methods, which can be either passive or active. Passive techniques include dispersed or concentrated arrays of fixed hydrophones, sonobuoy fields and hydrophones mounted either on surface vessels (usually destroyers) or on other submarines. Active techniques all require some kind of sonar gear: a sound generator combined with a hydrophone to receive reflected sound waves. Sonar systems can be mounted on submarines, surface ships or on devices towed at various depths from ships or helicopters. In addition sonar gear can be deployed in fixed underwater systems.

Passive techniques rely simply on the detection of noise generated by a submarine. When a submarine is running at high speed, the principal sound energy detectable at long range is radiated primarily by the propeller and by water flowing around the hull of the ship. At low speeds the major source of submarine noise is sound generated by installed machinery of various kinds, particularly rotating machinery that is unbalanced. Even a very noisy submarine, however, radiates less than one watt of acoustic power. One can therefore imagine the problem of detecting this tiny signal at long range in the presence of noise from waves and wind, undersea life and hundreds—even thousands—of surface vessels.

The propagation of sound in the ocean is extremely complex. Since the velocity of sound under water varies with temperature, pressure and salinity, it also varies with depth, position and season. These variations in sound velocity under some conditions bend underwater sound waves as much as 15 degrees, so that there is no guarantee that noise radiated from a submarine will consistently reach even the most sensitive passive listening post. On the other hand, sound waves are guided for thousands of miles with surprisingly little loss if they happen to be generated in the deep sound channel, a plane of minimum sound velocity lying at a depth of some 4,000 to 6,000 feet. A sound signal can travel 3,000 miles in the deep sound channel and still retain 1 percent of the intensity it had after traveling only 30 miles (suffering only cylindrical spreading loss). The existence of the deep sound channel is of no direct help in submarine detection, however, because existing submarines cannot safely descend to that depth and would be unwise to do so even if they could. When a near-surface hydrophone is moved away from a near-surface submarine sound source, the received signal often drops rapidly beyond a few kilometers and then rises to a high level again in successive "convergence zones" at multiples of about 50 kilometers (the distance required for a sound wave initially horizontal to be refracted through and beyond the deep sound channel and to return again to the surface).

Detecting a submarine in the immense background of ocean noise requires discrimination or processing gain. The desired source is known to be a point within a few hundred meters of the surface. Moreover, the source can be assumed to have a stationary spectrum in which there are usually strong line components. For decades large cadres of competent technicians have been working on the problems of extracting the submarine's "signal" from the noise in which it is immersed; the result has been a large variety of systems emphasizing different choices of available parameters, guided by operational considerations, analysis or tradition.

Basically the signal received from a source at a given assumed point can be enhanced with respect to noise or other point sources by adding in a coherent way the signals received at hydrophones located in different places. In a fixed dispersed array hundreds or thousands of hydrophones could be distributed throughout an entire ocean basin. The signals detected by the various instruments could be fed into a large computer provided with a program that assumes that a submarine, located somewhere in the detection area, successively occupies many possible points; for each point the program could introduce an appropriate time delay in the electrical output from each hydrophone. The computer could then add delayed electrical signals and ask whether the resulting integrated signal resembles the sound from a submarine or is simply just noise.

In a fixed concentrated array the hydrophones might be spread in a line no more than a few hundred meters long. Here the computer tests the result of integrating the various signals after inserting time delays allowing for the sound source to lie in some n number of distinguishable directions in a 360-degree arc. With processing equipment of sufficient size and power one can arrange for the beams from n directions to be formed simultaneously rather than sequentially, thereby ensuring that no signal is lost. Both dispersed and concentrated fixed arrays can incorporate hydrophones at various depths; by introducing vertical directivity the signal from distant sources is enhanced and locally generated surface noise is reduced.

Sonobuoy fields are most expeditiously sown from and monitored by aircraft. The U.S. has both shore-based aircraft (the P-3C) and sea-based aircraft (the S-2 and soon the S-3) equipped to drop sonobuoys weighing a few kilograms from either low or high altitude. A hydrophone, dangling from each sonobuoy at a substantial depth, picks up pressure signals that are then relayed by radio to the aircraft. In principle the signals could be added coherently, as are the signals from fixed arrays, but this would be difficult with sonobuoy fields since the buoys have considerable freedom of movement. The alternative is to monitor the field by listening to one sonobuoy after another to determine whether or not a submarine is in the vicinity. Processing gain can still be obtained from a single hydrophone by making a time or frequency analysis of the sound signal. An aircraft will have a search rate of so many thousand square kilometers per hour, limited not so much by its flight speed as by its ability to monitor each sonobuoy effectively.

The most highly regarded vessel for passive acoustic detection of submarines is another submarine, since it is far quieter than a surface ship. Moreover, a hunter-killer submarine is large enough to carry an array of hydrophones to produce a narrow listening beam for long-range detection. Depending on the sound-velocity profile and the noise level of the hunted and the hunter, the effective range for passive detection can vary from less than a kilometer to 100 kilometers or more. Factors affecting range include the reflection of sound waves from the ocean surface and ocean bottom and the signal-processing capability of the hunter submarine. As might be expected, passive acoustic measures become less effective as submarine designers learn to build quieter vessels and submarine commanders learn how to minimize the radiation of noise. In any event a submarine lying "dead" in the water cannot be detected by passive techniques. As a result the U.S. and the U.S.S.R. both rely heavily on active acoustic-detection, or sonar, systems.

Although sonar gear is installed routinely on both surface vessels and submarines, one of the potentially most effective antisubmarine measures makes

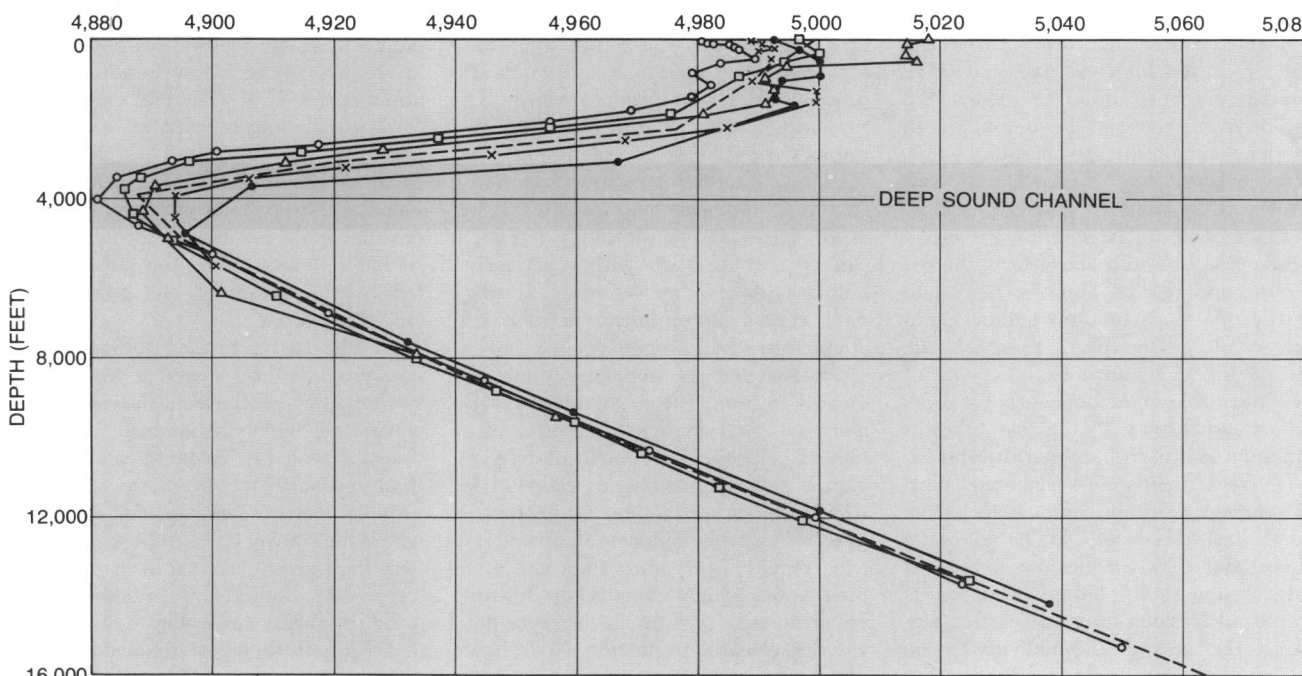

VELOCITY OF SOUND IN THE OCEAN varies with temperature, pressure and salinity, and hence also with depth, as can be seen from this record of a series of measurements made at several locations in the North Atlantic Ocean. As a consequence of the complex nature of underwater acoustic conditions there is no guarantee that noise radiated from a submarine will consistently reach even the most sensitive acoustic-detection device. Sound waves generated in the deep sound channel, a plane of minimum sound velocity lying at a depth of approximately 4,000 feet in this part of the Atlantic (*dark colored band*), can be guided for thousands of miles with little loss, but this is of no direct help in submarine detection, since existing submarines cannot operate at that depth.

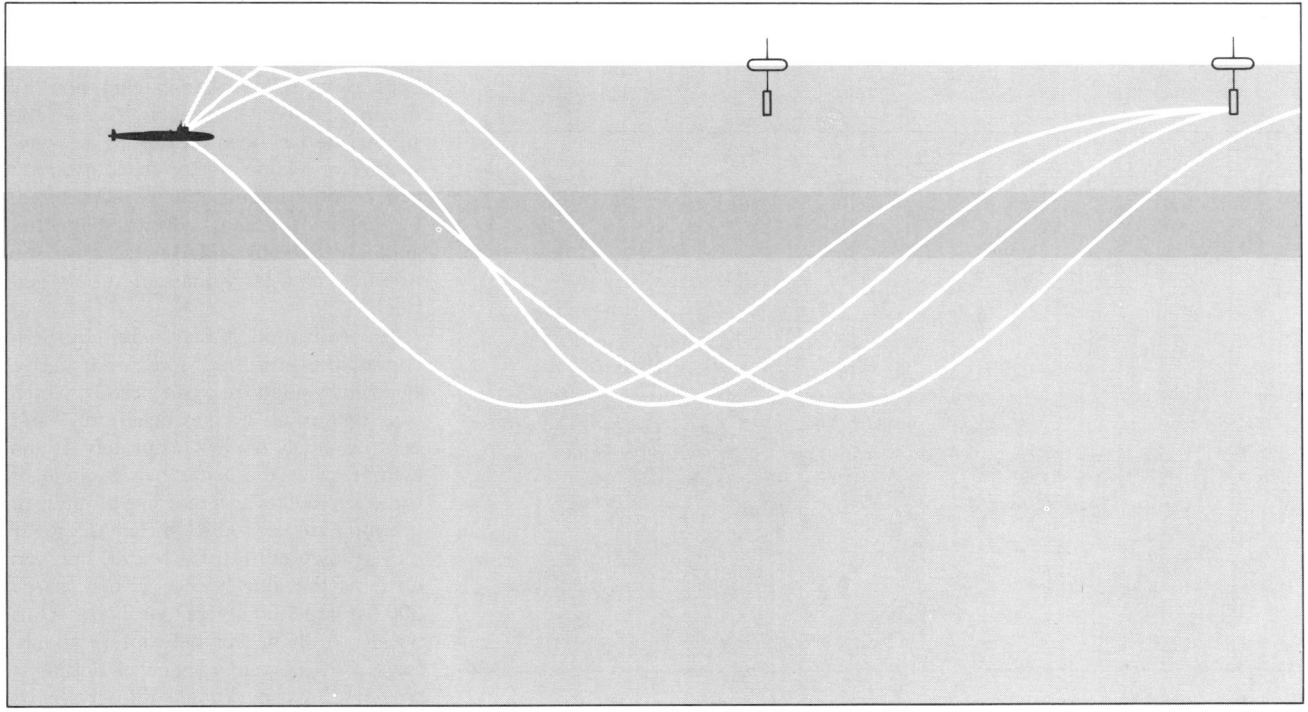

"CONVERGENCE ZONES" are observed when a near-surface acoustic detector is moved away from a near-surface submarine sound source. The received signal often drops rapidly beyond a few kilometers and then rises to a high level again at multiples of about 50 kilometers. The successive intervals that mark the convergence zones correspond to the distance required for a sound wave initially horizontal to be refracted through and beyond the deep sound channel and to return again to the surface of the ocean.

use of helicopters operating from carriers, destroyers or other sea platforms. The sonar devices are lowered from the helicopter by winch and can descend to depths of several hundred meters. An explosive charge can be detonated to produce an omnidirectional sound wave, or magnetostrictive or piezoelectric systems can be used to generate narrow beams of sound. The sound-wave probe is reflected from the sea surface, the sea bottom and marine animals, large and small, as well as from any submarine in the vicinity. The reflected signals are picked up and transmitted by way of the hoist cable to the helicopter for processing and display. To achieve efficient radiation and useful angular discrimination from helicopter-suspended platforms one uses sound frequencies in the range between one and 10 kilohertz (1,000 and 10,000 cycles per second) as compared with the subkilohertz waves employed for long-range detection. Signals in the range of 100 kilohertz to one megahertz attenuate so rapidly and become so scattered that they are not useful for submarine detection at long range.

In principle active sonars can detect moving objects more readily than stationary objects, because the Doppler shift in the sonar echo can be used to enhance the signal. On the other hand, even when the acoustic energy is confined to an ocean layer including the submarine, active sonars suffer a two-way loss: the power illuminating the target falls off directly with the distance, which means that the return signal decreases as the square of the distance. In other words, for equivalent received signals an active sonar must illuminate the target with at least as much energy as the target is radiating by itself (assuming that it is radiating and not just lying dead in the water), although detection can be accomplished with weaker signals because the precise form of the signal is known and often chosen to be best adapted to signal processing.

The purpose of active sonar is not necessarily to sweep the oceans clear of submarines; such systems are often employed to provide a submarine-free region a few kilometers in diameter in which merchant or military ships can be free from attack. When submarines had only unguided torpedoes to attack shipping, active sonars mounted on destroyers or suspended from helicopters provided reasonable protection. Now, however, submarines carry acoustic homing torpedoes with a range of 10 kilometers or more. And the cruise missiles carried by many Russian submarines have an effective range of hundreds of kilometers, which means that active sonar cannot provide a point defense against such submarines.

In the past decade much work has been done on active sonar systems anchored to the ocean bottom in an effort to provide detection of submarines at ranges of hundreds of kilometers. These fixed-active systems, as they are called, emit a narrowly focused beam of sound at frequencies of a few hundred hertz and a power level of several megawatts. Such installations not only are expensive but also have the drawback of broadcasting their location, which makes them vulnerable to countermeasures. The opposition need not even destroy the installation; by sampling the pulses emitted by the system it can contrive to "spoof" or jam it.

An alternative to the fixed-active sonar system is the semiactive, or bistatic, system, in which the transmitters and receivers are widely separated. Such systems are probably harder to spoof or jam than ordinary active sonars and they provide more leeway in the depth at which the transmitter can be located. At very high power levels a deep transmitter is less limited by cavitation: the rapid expansion and collapse of bubbles that arise from gases dissolved in the water.

After a submarine has been detected in a certain target area, say an area 50 kilometers square, the next step is to pinpoint its position. Localization can be done from the air, from the surface or from below the surface. If an aircraft such as a P-3 or an S-2 is employed, it can drop directional sonobuoys that are capable of indicating the bearing from the sonobuoy to the submarine. The aircraft then follows along this line by dropping more sonobuoys. When the submarine has been located to an accuracy of one kilometer or so, its position can be determined still more precisely by low-level passes with a magnetic-anomaly detector (MAD) to sense the presence of a large mass of submerged steel.

If localization is conducted by helicopter, the preferred detector is active sonar suspended from the aircraft, which can determine range accurately and bearing somewhat less accurately. If one assumes that the sonar has a range of three kilometers and that five minutes of listening are needed each time the sonar unit is lowered into the water, one can estimate that one helicopter can search 300 square kilometers per hour. Thus within an hour six helicopters should have a 50 percent chance of finding a single submarine known initially to be in a square area 50 kilometers on a side.

If the search is conducted by surface ships, active sonar is used in essentially the same way as by helicopters except that a surface ship does not have nearly

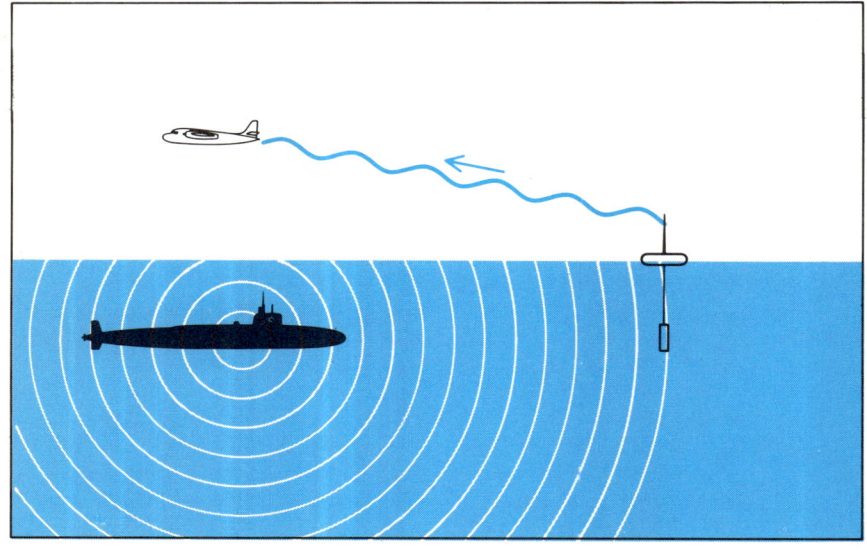

PASSIVE ACOUSTIC DETECTION of a submerged submarine relies on picking up the noise radiated by the submarine itself. In this case the passive acoustic detector is a hydrophone dangling from a buoy at a substantial depth; signals detected by the hydrophone are relayed by radio to the aircraft for analysis. Hydrophones of this type and size can be sown by aircraft in either dispersed or concentrated arrays. Larger hydrophones can also be mounted on the hulls of surface vessels (usually destroyers) or on other submarines.

the speed advantage over a submarine that a helicopter has. This disadvantage is partly compensated for by the surface ship's ability to carry a sonar of much higher power and effectiveness than the equipment a helicopter can carry.

Underwater search by one or more hunter-killer submarines is perhaps the slowest but not necessarily the least effective way of localizing a submarine. A hunter-killer submarine has an optimum search speed of between five and 15 knots. For a given sonar range the area searched increases linearly with speed, but the self-noise generated as speed increases reduces the effective sonar range. Hence the optimum search speed is a compromise.

In antisubmarine-warfare exercises an "enemy" submarine that with much effort has been detected and localized is often tracked for hours or even days. The tracking skill thus developed in peacetime, however, has little applicability in wartime. Under wartime conditions an enemy submarine would ordinarily be sunk as soon as it was localized. As for tracking the other side's ballistic-missile submarines 24 hours a day in peacetime, the simultaneous tracking of 30 to 50 modern submarines is so difficult that its feasibility seems doubtful. Even if the job could be done, it is the thesis of this article that continuous tracking is distinctly undesirable if one concedes that the nuclear deterrent is valuable and should be preserved.

Let us see nonetheless what continuous tracking involves. Antisubmarine warfare is the primary mission of the U.S. fleet of nuclear-powered hunter-killer submarines, numbering some 57 vessels. Their chief sensor is low-frequency passive sonar. Depending on the state of the sea, they are probably able to detect a moving Russian submarine at distances ranging from a few kilometers to perhaps 20 or 30 kilometers under more favorable conditions. An effort to carry out passive acoustic tracking reliably at a range of 10 kilometers or more in the face of changing sea conditions, normal variations in sound velocity, sea noise and the evasive measures readily available to the quarry seems doomed, however, to failure. If such tracking could be accomplished at all, several hunter-killer submarines would probably have to be assigned to each hunted submarine. Moreover, if the necessity should arise, the destruction of an enemy submarine at a range of 10 kilometers or more before it could fire its missiles might call for a weapon

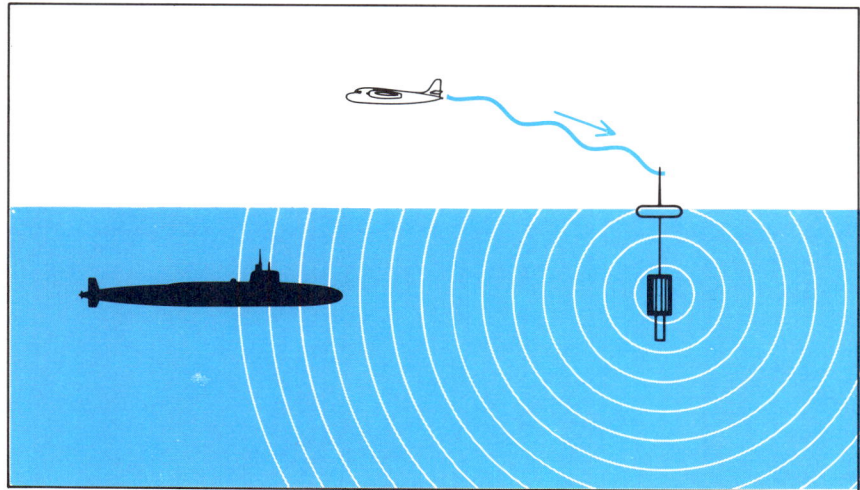
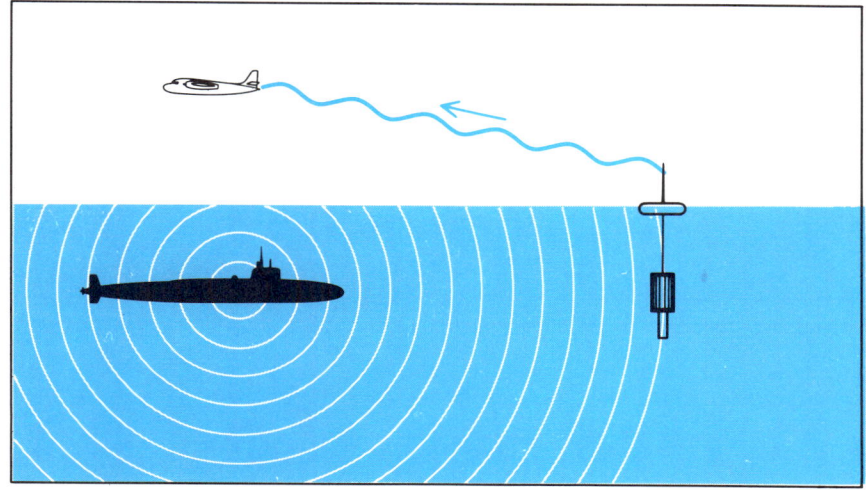

ACTIVE ACOUSTIC DETECTION of a submerged submarine requires a sound generator combined with a hydrophone to receive reflected sound waves. "Sonar" systems of this type suffer a two-way loss: in a near-surface sound channel the power illuminating the target (*top*) falls off directly with the distance, which means that the return signal (*bottom*) decreases as the square of the distance. Deep or bottom-mounted sonars suffer spherical spreading of the sound energy; hence the illuminating power falls off as the square of the distance, and the total energy received at the sonar falls off as the fourth power. Besides being deployed in aircraft-sown sonobuoy fields, sonar systems can be mounted on other submarines, surface ships or on devices towed at various depths from ships or helicopters.

faster than the standard torpedo. For these and other reasons, including the possibility of acoustic countermeasures, my own view is that effective covert tracking is not a plausible disarming threat to the submarine-based deterrent forces of either the U.S. or the U.S.S.R.

Active sonar tracking from submarines, surface vessels or aircraft is another story. Given the mission to maintain at all times the ability to destroy the enemy fleet of ballistic-missile submarines before it could launch its weapons, one would immediately think of active trailing from extremely short range, say a few hundred meters. At that distance a sonar operating at a frequency of 100 to 1,000 kilohertz would be compact and low-powered and could provide a clear pictorial representation of the target. For example, a 1,000 kilohertz (one megahertz) sonar would provide a resolution of 30 centimeters on a target 200 meters away. Mounted on a specialized trailing vehicle (submerged, on the surface or airborne), such a sonar could provide a detailed picture of its quarry every few seconds. The tracker could therefore sail in formation with the quarry without fear of collision.

This is not the place to describe the command-and-control arrangements that would enable the small specialized tracking ship to destroy its quarry on

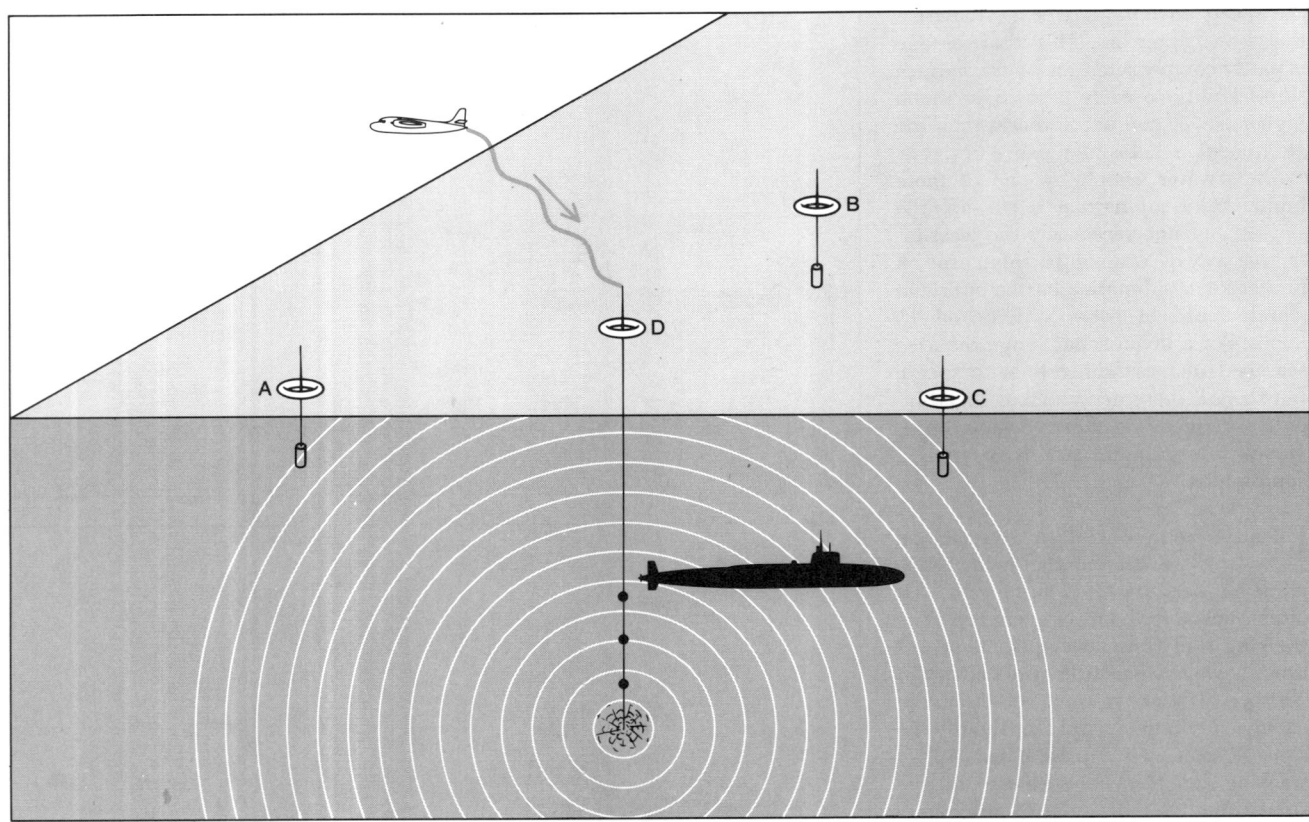
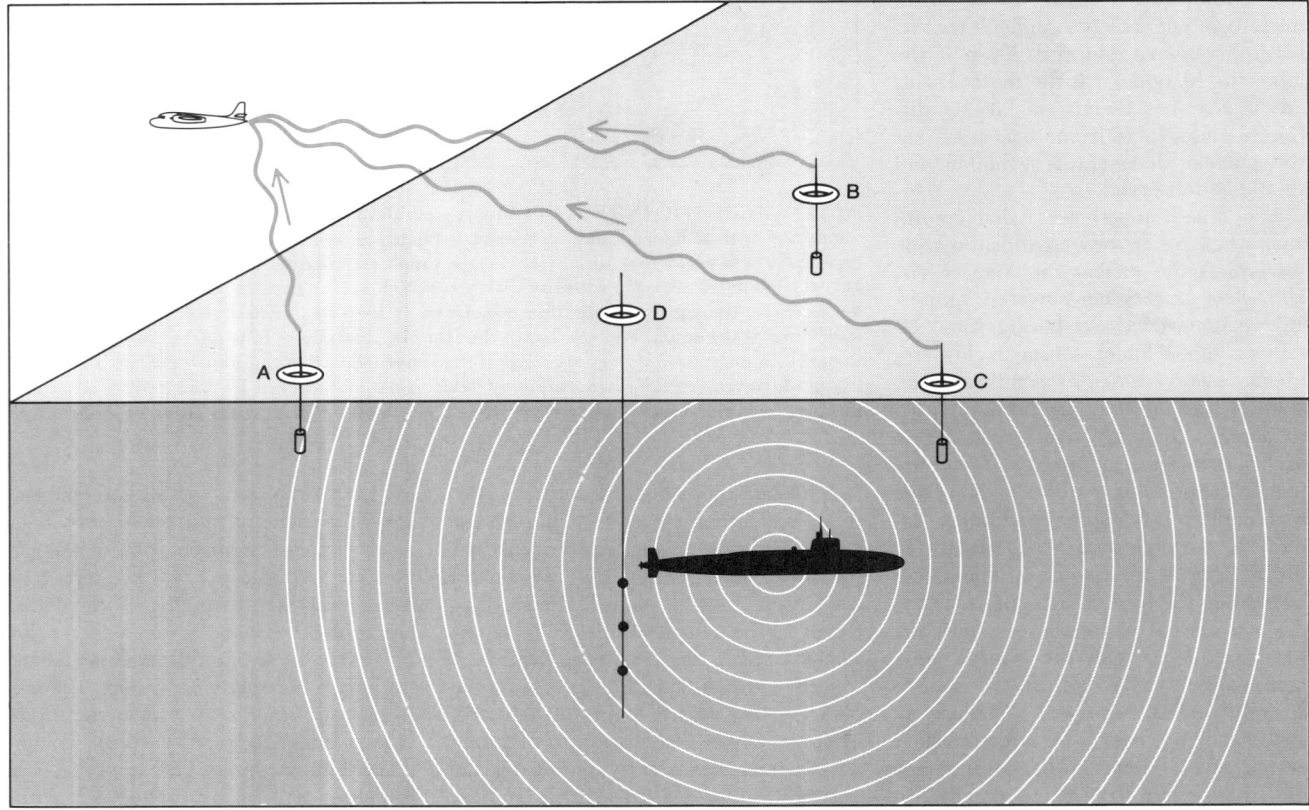

SEMIACTIVE ACOUSTIC DETECTION involves systems in which the transmitters and the receivers are widely separated. In the idealized system portrayed in the pair of diagrams on this page an ASW aircraft has sown a field of passive hydrophones in the vicinity of a submerged submarine. A string of explosive charges is suspended from a similar aircraft-delivered buoy to a depth of several hundred meters. The charges are detonated singly on command to produce a series of omnidirectional sound waves (*top*). The reflected signals, or echoes, are picked up by the hydrophones and transmitted to the aircraft for processing and display (*bottom*).

command or that would lead to the destruction of both ships if the quarry should attempt to use force against the tracker. The important fact is that the characteristics of such a close-in tracking ship (be it a submarine, a surface vessel or an aircraft) are quite different from those of any craft deployed in large numbers today. The craft would need to have endurance and good seakeeping qualities; it would have no need for more than a few torpedoes or other destructive weapons, and none for a large crew or great flexibility of operation.

The chief difficulty in this type of active tracking seems to lie not in maintaining tracking but in ensuring that a tracker is assigned to every ballistic-missile-launching submarine that leaves the home port and crosses a detection barrier of some kind. Obviously the other side will seek to avoid detection by employing various stratagems, perhaps by sending its missile submarines across the barrier in clumps or by mixing them with non-missile-submarine decoys. The many possibilities need not concern us here. As I have argued above, tracking (particularly active tracking) has little application to tactical antisubmarine warfare, but if done successfully and without opposition, it could jeopardize the survivability of the ballistic-missile-submarine forces of the U.S. and the U.S.S.R.

The U.S. Navy has two principal weapons for destroying enemy submarines: the lightweight 12-inch Mark 46 active acoustic homing torpedo and the full-size 21-inch Mark 48 active-passive acoustic homing torpedo (which is just coming into service). The 12-inch torpedo is essentially the only effective antisubmarine weapon available to aircraft and helicopters. It can also be launched from the deck of a ship or delivered by a drone helicopter. A rocket-boosted version has more range and can get to its target faster than the standard Mark 46. The Mark 48 is a long-range torpedo with a large warhead; when it is launched by a hunter-killer submarine, it can be guided electrically by means of a control wire. Like any other weapon, a homing torpedo will not be perfectly reliable in actual combat, and it may be vulnerable to countermeasures.

Specialists in antisubmarine warfare have long been attracted to more effective antisubmarine mines. Such mines could be planted defensively to protect harbors or to cordon off a landing area for an expeditionary force. They could also be used to keep enemy submarines

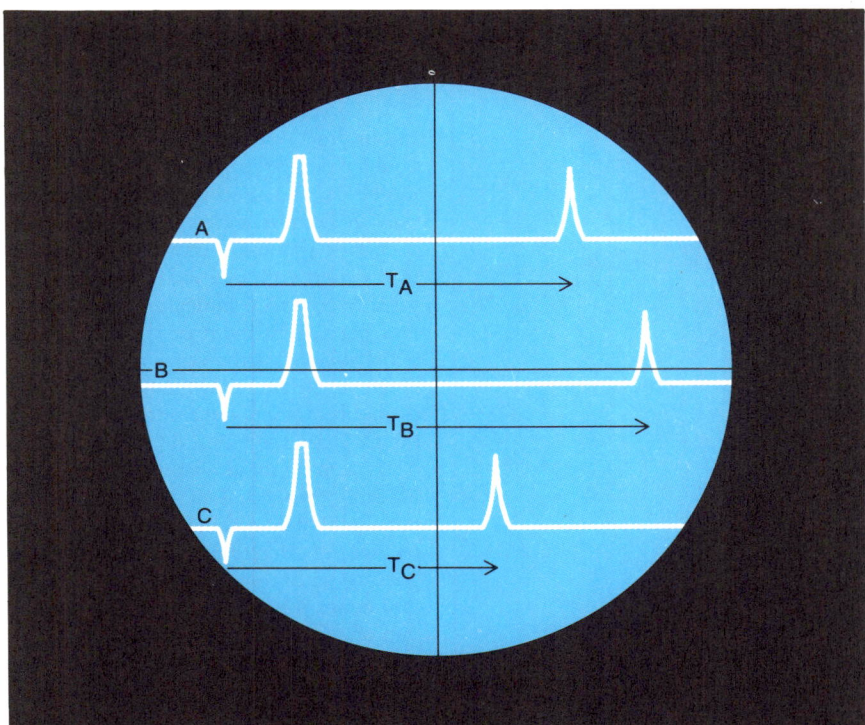

RECEIVED SIGNALS from the semiactive detection system shown in the illustration on the opposite page are processed on board the monitoring aircraft and displayed on a cathode ray tube. The times at which the signals are received from the various hydrophones are then used by an operator to plot the location of the submarine (*see illustration at bottom*).

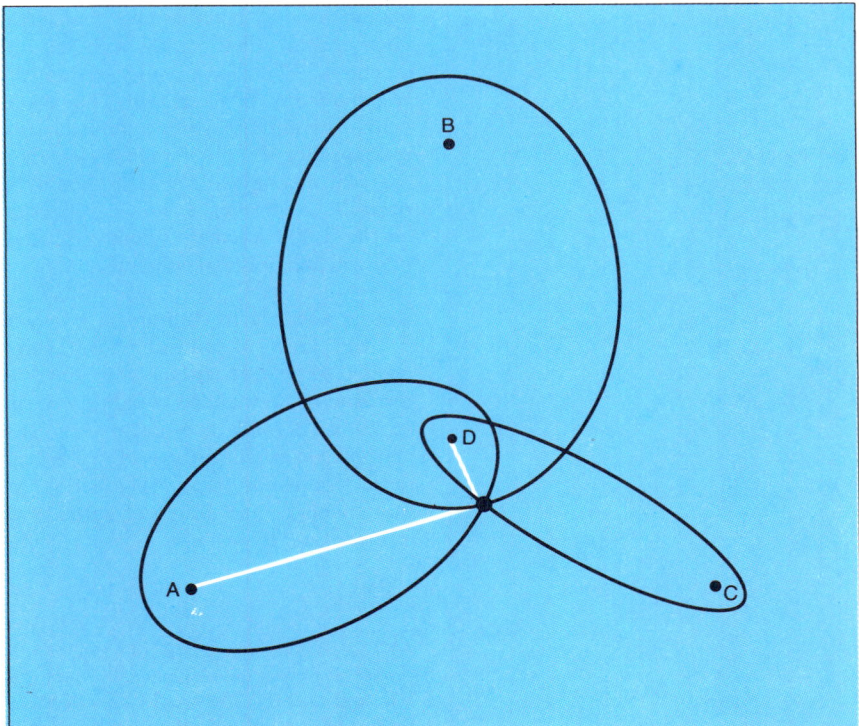

SUBMARINE IS LOCATED on the basis of the times at which the hydrophones picked up the signals reflected from the submarine. The observed time interval T_A between the explosion at D and the reception of the echo at sonobuoy A defines an ellipse with foci at A and D. (The sum of the distances from any point on an ellipse to the two foci is constant.) The information from each hydrophone is used to draw an ellipse on which the submarine is situated. The intersection of the three ellipses indicates the exact location of the quarry.

from leaving their home ports, to create a barrier across straits or even to limit travel in the open ocean.

Since ordinary mines have a limited radius of effectiveness (submarines could pass above or below them), such mines can be used against submarines only in shallow water. There have been recurrent proposals, however, for a mine that would either drive itself downward when a trip wire indicated a submarine was passing below it or drive itself upward when a submarine was detected above it. Mines with this capability are probably under development in both the U.S. and the U.S.S.R.

If such a mine were based on the Mark 46 torpedo, it should cost well under $100,000 and have a 50 percent chance of destroying any submarine passing within one kilometer of it. Thus 500 mines would be enough to cover the gap of 1,000 kilometers between Greenland and the British Isles. Actually the mines would not be sown cheek by jowl in a thin line; they could better be deployed in a minefield 100 kilometers deep with a density of one mine per two kilometers of front so that 500 mines would still suffice.

The mines would allow surface ships to pass without harm, and the commanders of friendly submarines could traverse the minefield safely with the aid of charts. The mines could be remotely activated and deactivated. They could be laid by aircraft, surface ships or submarines. For about $50 million (less than the cost of one destroyer) it should be possible to provide a robust, effective barrier 1,000 kilometers long with low physical and political vulnerability.

Let us now try to distinguish between the kind of antisubmarine force needed to protect surface shipping and the kind of specialized capability needed to find, track and destroy on signal ballistic-missile submarines. Because these two needs impose conflicting requirements on the design of antisubmarine-warfare forces it is not surprising

ANTISUBMARINE MINE of a type that is probably under development in both the U.S. and the U.S.S.R. would have a much greater radius of effectiveness than ordinary mines. The hypothetical device shown incorporates an acoustic homing torpedo, which is designed to drive itself upward when a submarine is detected above it. Such a mine would cost well under $100,000 and have a 50 percent chance of destroying any submarine passing within one kilometer of it.

that the U.S. Navy sometimes takes a self-contradictory position when it tries to argue on the one hand the invulnerability of its Polaris-Poseidon submarine fleet and on the other the effectiveness of its antisubmarine forces. I shall argue that one can develop antisubmarine measures sufficient to protect surface shipping during an actual conflict without developing an antisubmarine capability of such a nature that it jeopardizes the other side's submarine-based nuclear deterrent.

Unlike major cities or even aircraft carriers, merchant ships are plentiful and of modest value; they are substantially less costly and easier to replace than nuclear-powered attack submarines. A merchant ship delivered in 1972 with a speed of 22 knots and a deadweight of 29,000 tons costs about $23 million. A U.S. nuclear submarine costs more than $150 million. The average crew size of nuclear submarines also substantially exceeds that of modern merchant ships. The U.S. has some 100 attack submarines; the U.S.S.R. has about 300 oceangoing submarines of all types. During World War II Germany lost about 700 submarines and sank 2,600 merchant ships, accounting for 13 million tons of shipping in the North Atlantic. Therefore in round numbers Germany lost one submarine for every 17,000 tons of Allied shipping sent to the bottom. If in another war U.S. antisubmarine forces were able to destroy one enemy nuclear-powered attack submarine for every 10 merchant ships sunk, we should probably regard the exchange ratio as being in our favor. In such a war of attrition the nonnuclear-powered submarine could be the greater threat.

A well-protected convoy remains a principal means for protecting surface vessels. With the various antisubmarine measures described above it should be possible to achieve a kill ratio of one enemy submarine for every 10 merchantmen sunk. Although this ratio might be acceptable for ordinary military and civilian cargoes, it would not be satisfactory if the surface vessels carried troops or critical materiel required at a specific time by troops being ferried by air.

Protection for such vessels is ordinarily imagined to be provided by destroyer-escort vehicles with extra-powerful sonars that provide a moving screen extending well beyond torpedo range and within which enemy submarines would have a high probability of being located and destroyed. In my own opinion the best way to create such a screen would be to improve the capability of antisub-

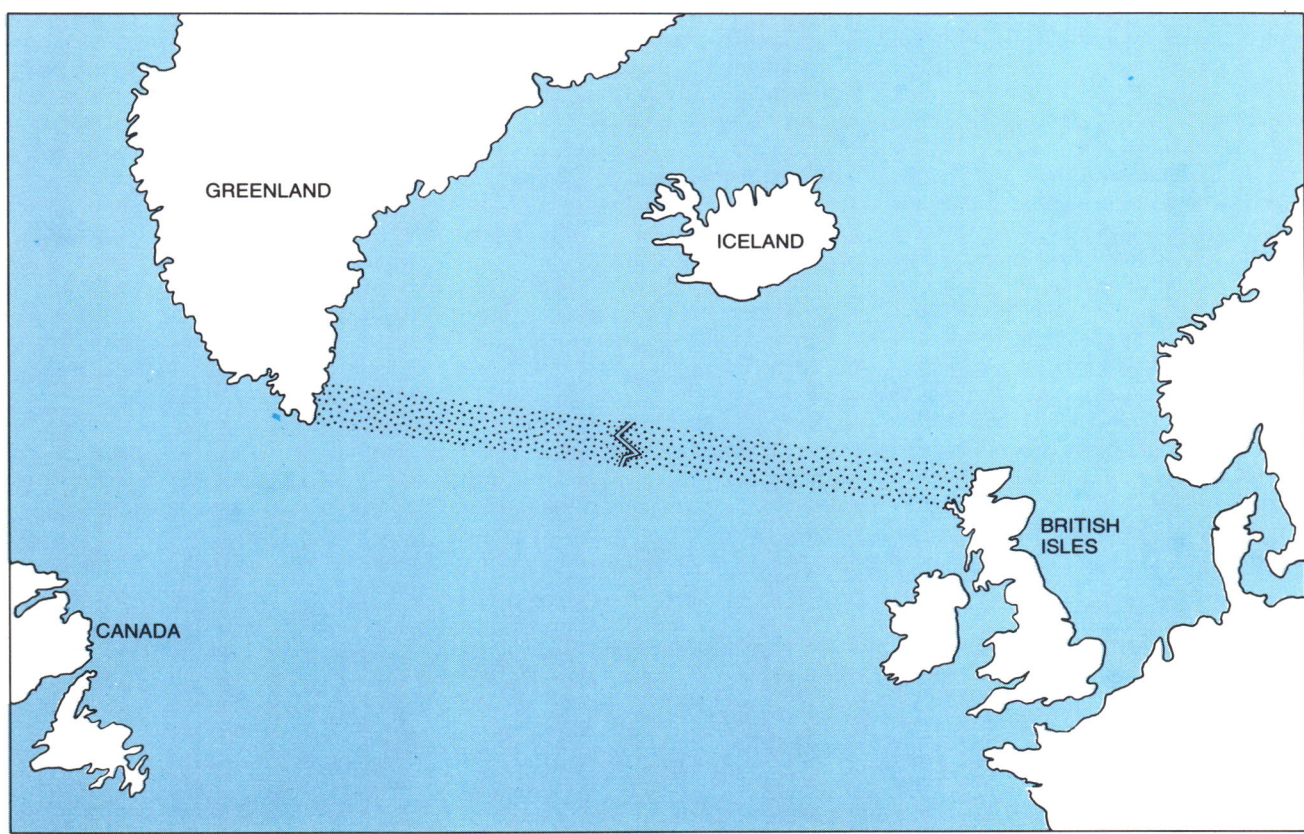

ANTISUBMARINE MINEFIELD based on the use of mines such as the one shown on the opposite page could be laid to create a barrier across the 1,000-kilometer strait between Greenland and the British Isles. For a minefield 100 kilometers deep with a density of one mine per two kilometers of front 500 mines would be needed. The mines would allow surface ships to pass without harm, and friendly submarines could traverse the minefield safely along mine-free lanes with the aid of charts. The mines could be remotely activated and deactivated. The production cost of such an ASW measure (about $50 million) would be less than the cost of one destroyer.

marine helicopters by placing the analysis and data-processing equipment for each helicopter in a van on the deck of a ship rather than in the helicopter itself. With the room saved each helicopter could be provided with several active sonars, which could be deployed by a single helicopter in leapfrog fashion, with the control and signal analysis transmitted by radio between ship and sonars. In this way it should be possible to increase the effectiveness of antisubmarine helicopters by a factor of five, while reducing the crew from four to no more than two persons. Although such improved helicopters can provide a potent local defense, a ballistic-missile-launching submarine could easily move out of range when it detected the approach of such a convoy.

Because a convoy has certain inherent vulnerabilities, such as inviting attack by straight-running torpedoes or by cruise missiles launched from a considerable distance, it is sometimes preferable to allow fast merchant ships to sail independently at maximum speed. The threat to such ships from torpedo attack might be reduced to negligible proportions if each ship carried some retaliatory homing torpedoes that would be launched automatically from the deck of the ship if the ship were struck by a torpedo. This tactic could deter torpedo attack (without defending against it) in just the same way that the strategic offensive force reliably deters a first strike.

The defense of aircraft carriers presents a special problem. An aircraft carrier can scarcely be hidden. Its screws can be heard all the way across an ocean; it is highly visible on radar and can be detected by other means. For these reasons carriers are built to resist damage; as many as a dozen torpedoes are said to be needed to sink one. A close-in defense against torpedo-launching submarines can be provided by the same helicopter-sonar screen already described for the protection of convoys. As some additional protection against cruise missiles launched from a distance of hundreds of kilometers carriers are already equipped with rapid-firing automatic weapons that provide a last-ditch defense. These defenses against cruise missiles could be further improved. One should probably consider installing active antitorpedo defenses directly on the carrier's hull. None of these measures for the defense of aircraft carriers poses any threat to the ballistic-missile submarine.

In any readily foreseeable war between the U.S. and the U.S.S.R. a major part of the conflict at sea will be asymmetrical: an essential mission of the U.S. Navy will be to keep the sea lanes open and an essential mission of the Russian navy will be to close them. Only in preserving the security of their submarine-based ballistic-missile forces are the missions of the two navies symmetrical. By emphasizing the antisubmarine measures discussed here, the U.S. can carry out its two missions; it should be able to protect surface shipping and nullify the Russian attack-submarine force without creating a credible threat to Russia's submarine-based nuclear deterrent. It is this freedom to pursue their individual and opposing interests, while not jeopardizing their common interest in an invulnerable sea-based deterrent, that could lead to arms-control agreements to provide enhanced and equal security for the SLBM deterrent forces.

As we have seen, neither country as yet has the means for negating that deterrent. Even if the U.S. were to improve its tactical antisubmarine techniques to the level I have described, they could not be regarded as a threat to Russia's ballistic-missile submarines. For example, antisubmarine measures that would require, say, 10 days to destroy half of the enemy's ballistic-missile submarines in the open ocean cannot be said to threaten the deterrent. If such measures required only 10 minutes, they would be a real threat.

Moving cordons of antisubmarine vehicles around convoys or aircraft carriers, designed to protect at most 1,000 square kilometers of ocean at a time, can be easily avoided by ballistic-missile-carrying submarines and hence present no threat to them. By the same token the statistical defense of individual merchant ships, triggered only by a torpedo explosion, is no threat.

Would the emplacement of advanced mine barriers be regarded as a threat? A barrier 1,000 kilometers long extending from Greenland to the British Isles could undoubtedly take a substantial toll of deterrent-force submarines that tried to cross it after hostilities began. We are assuming here that the conflict is originally nonnuclear and that both sides want to preserve their submarine-based deterrent to keep it that way. Even if the U.S. did not deliberately cooperate in helping deterrent-force submarines through the minefield, at least half should survive the one-way trip needed to reach firing position. The SLBM force could be stationed behind the minefield without suffering attrition; its deterrent power would not be impaired by the losses suffered on a one-way trip through a barrier if the order were given to move to firing position and launch. On the other hand, the minefield would take a prohibitive toll of antishipping submarines, which must make many trips in and out of their home port.

The question sometimes raised is: How should the U.S. respond if the Polaris-Poseidon fleet should suffer attrition during peacetime under circumstances that seemed suspicious? My personal view is that neither the U.S. nor

ASW AIRCRAFT CARRIER, the U.S.S. *Intrepid*, is capable of launching both ASW aircraft and ASW helicopters. The U.S. has four such carriers, the U.S.S.R. none. The photograph was made during an inspection cruise in the Atlantic Ocean in February, 1971.

the U.S.S.R. has any incentive to covertly reduce the size of the other's deterrent fleet. Furthermore, it is difficult to guarantee that such a covert action is not exposed. Finally, each side has equal vulnerability in its submarine-deterrent fleet.

A more difficult problem is to know how to conduct active, conventional ocean war, including tactical antisubmarine warfare, without an accompanying and unintended attrition of the opponent's submarine-based nuclear deterrent. Let us turn to that problem.

The first step in reducing unintentional attrition would be formal recognition that it is in the mutual interest of the two countries to preserve the submarine-based deterrent not only in peacetime but also indefinitely during a conflict to forestall the escalation to all-out nuclear war. One can imagine many possible arms-control agreements that would then contribute to the continued invulnerability of the submarine-based deterrent.

Such an agreement might have two goals. First, it might prohibit either side from building or deploying a force that is technically capable of destroying the other side's submarine deterrent in a matter of minutes, hours or even a few days. The second goal, which might be more difficult to achieve, would be a set of measures that would reduce or perhaps eliminate the attrition of missile-launching submarines during a conventional war without restricting vigorous warfare to protect (or attack) surface shipping.

The first goal—the peacetime one— might be aided by prohibitions against the active tracking of missile submarines and by the creation of sanctuary areas. There are so many possible technical ways to discourage active tracking unilaterally that it is by no means assured that one side, invest what it will, could follow nearly all its opponent's submarines. It would nonetheless be valuable to reach an early agreement to eliminate fear of this threat, which seems to have no utility other than to threaten the survival of the strategic deterrent. Moreover, such an agreement seems readily verifiable. It should not be difficult for a submarine that is being tracked to recognize that it has (or has not) at all times a companion at a distance of a few hundred to a few thousand meters.

Additional protection for the submarine deterrent force in peacetime could be achieved by creating wide-ocean sanctuaries in which ballistic-missile submarines of one side or the other would be free to patrol, immune from surveillance of any kind. Clearly the sanctuaries must be large compared with the range of antisubmarine detection and attack devices, yet they must not be so large that they interfere with merchant shipping or with the transit routes of naval vessels, including deterrent-force submarines. Problems may arise in connection with third parties but these do not appear insoluble.

To limit the attrition of deterrent-force submarines during a conventional war, the U.S. and the U.S.S.R. might agree to provide safe-conduct routes through minefields or other barriers for each other's ballistic-missile submarines. The problem here is to distinguish between strategic missile submarines entitled to safe passage and attack submarines, which would still be fair game. The simplest solution would be to provide safe passage to any submarine that was effectively running on the surface and could thus be inspected.

Because surfaced submarines are not very good at traversing heavy seas, a submarine could be allowed to travel submerged provided that it towed a buoy emitting a distinctive radio signal. The signal could be monitored by surface ships, aircraft or even by satellites, and the position of such submarines could thus be known precisely and instantaneously. Buoy-towing submarines would be allowed to pass without harassment (although subject to surfacing on call) through clearly marked lanes in barriers; all other submarines would be subject to attack. The number of safe-conduct trips per month could be only enough to permit normal rotation of submarines in the deterrent force.

These three schemes only suggest the scope of possibilities for a SALT II agreement that would enhance the survivability of submarines designed specially for carrying long-range ballistic missiles. I should emphasize that in my opinion such submarines are probably adequately survivable in the absence of a new agreement. An important function of the agreement, however, would be to allay exaggerated fears that our Polaris-Poseidon fleet might suddenly be neutralized by a dramatic advance in the effectiveness of antisubmarine warfare. As a nonnegligible by-product of such an agreement both the U.S. and the U.S.S.R. would be enabled to reallocate either within or outside the military sphere much of the money that is likely to be spent in attempting to endanger the deterrent, if no agreement is forthcoming.

NEWEST ASW AIRCRAFT, the S-3A, was photographed during a test flight earlier this year. The jet-powered aircraft is scheduled to join the U.S. ASW forces in 1974, replacing the propeller-driven S-2. The carrier-based S-3A will carry a digital computer to enable its four-man crew to better analyze underwater sounds and other data. It will be armed with a variety of weapons: acoustic homing torpedoes, mines, depth charges, rockets and missiles.

8 Reconnaissance and Arms Control

by Ted Greenwood
February 1973

Reconnaissance satellites are the chief means relied on by the U.S. and the U.S.S.R. to verify each other's compliance with the SALT I accords. What bearing will they and related systems have on SALT II?

The two major arms-control agreements signed last May in Moscow as a result of the first round of the strategic-arms-limitation talks (SALT I) between the U.S. and the U.S.S.R. both incorporate sections designed to deal with the problem of verification. For example, Article XII of the treaty on the limitation of anti-ballistic-missile (ABM) systems states: "1. For the purpose of providing assurance of compliance with the provisions of this Treaty, each Party shall use national technical means of verification at its disposal.... 2. Each Party undertakes not to interfere with the national technical means of verification of the other Party.... 3. Each Party undertakes not to use deliberate concealment measures which impede verification by national technical means of compliance with the provisions of this Treaty...." Article V of the SALT I interim agreement "on certain measures with respect to the limitation of strategic offensive arms" uses virtually identical language to make the same three points.

What are the "national technical means of verification" mentioned in these documents? How are these systems now being used by each side to unilaterally monitor the other side's compliance or noncompliance with the SALT I accords? What bearing does this mutual capability have on further arms-control agreements, in particular on those that might emerge from the current SALT II negotiations?

In attempting to answer such questions this article will of necessity focus primarily on the subject of observation satellites, since the main restrictions imposed by both of the SALT I agreements can be, and undoubtedly are being, monitored largely by means of sensors carried on board such orbiting photoreconnaissance systems. The primary SALT I restrictions limit each side's ABM missile launchers to 200 at two widely separated sites, impose numerical ceilings on both land-based intercontinental ballistic missiles (ICBM's) and submarine-launched ballistic missiles (SLBM's), regulate the replacement of old ICBM's and SLBM's with new SLBM's and prohibit the exchange of old ICBM's or light ICBM's for heavy ICBM's.

In addition the ABM treaty bans the testing of new types of ABM systems or of other systems or components "in an ABM mode." The monitoring of activities of this type involves not only observation satellites but also other methods specifically suited for the surveillance of missile launchings. Hence systems such as advanced land-based radars, early-warning satellites and shipboard tracking sensors are the second major concern of this article. Such systems are of particular importance to any discussion of the prospect that SALT II will result in meaningful qualitative restrictions of strategic offensive missiles.

In spite of the official secrecy that almost completely hides from public view the observation-satellite programs of both the U.S. and the U.S.S.R., it is possible to make some general observations about the theoretical capabilities of such systems and about their actual performance. For example, it is known that because of the fundamental electromagnetic properties of the earth's atmosphere, satellite-borne sensors are restricted to three spectral "windows": the visible-light wavelengths, a broad infrared band centered on a wavelength of eight microns and certain radar wavelengths. Over the years, as larger booster rockets have made it possible to put heavier instrument packages into orbit, there has been an increase in the number of different sensors and in their resolution and film capacity. At the same time the associated communications systems have also become more sophisticated and their data-transmission rate has increased.

The most useful measure of the quality of an airplane or satellite photoreconnaissance system is ground resolution, a value that is equivalent to the smallest object that can be distinguished on the ground with good contrast. For a camera pointing vertically downward the expression for ground resolution, G, is given by the equation $G = A/300\,FR$, where A is the altitude of the airplane or the satellite in feet, F is the focal length of the camera in feet, R is the joint resolution of the film and optics in lines per millimeter and 300 is a numerical constant characteristic of the units used for the other quantities.

To cite a recent example of space photography, the panoramic camera built by the Itek Corporation for the last three Apollo missions to the moon had a focal length of two feet and photographed the lunar surface from an altitude of approximately 60 miles. The resulting photographs had a ground resolution of about three feet [see illustration, pages 232 and 233]. These numbers, inserted in the equation given above, suggest an optical resolution for the system of better than 180 lines per millimeter.

By way of comparison, it has been reported unofficially that the high-resolution cameras used in the newest generation of observation satellites have a focal length of more than eight feet. Taking eight feet as the focal length and 180 lines per millimeter as the optical resolution, one can calculate that the ground resolution of such a system from a nominal altitude of, say, 100 miles would be 1.2 feet. Actually there is reason to believe that the resolution of the most advanced systems now in service may be even better; as early as 1960 experts in the field were talking about prospective U.S. Air Force cameras with focal lengths on the order of 20 feet. Furthermore, films with a resolution considerably better than 180 lines per millimeter are currently available. A compromise must be made, however, between film resolution and film speed, and rather fast film is needed for satellite photography.

Another factor that must be taken into consideration is the aperture of the camera's optics. Diffraction effects place an upper limit on the optical resolution of any lens system (a limit never attainable in practice). The limit is given by the ratio $.82d/\lambda F$, where d is the aperture in feet and λ is the wavelength in millimeters of the radiation to which the system is sensitive. For a camera with a focal length of eight feet an aperture of one foot would result in a diffraction-limited resolution of 180 lines per millimeter, assuming that one is working with visible light at a wavelength of .55 micrometer.

In practice a much larger aperture would be employed in order to ensure that the optical system is not limited by diffraction. Therefore a camera with a focal length of eight feet and an aperture of three feet would (assuming that it uses film with a resolution of 180 lines per millimeter) provide a ground resolution of 1.6 feet from an altitude of 100 miles. With the same film a camera having a focal length of 20 feet and an aperture of five feet would yield a ground resolution of .7 foot. To achieve a ground resolution of .5 foot the same camera would require film with a resolution of about 330 lines per millimeter.

These simple calculations are based on the assumption that the overall resolution of the system is poorer than the poorest contributing factor, which may be either the diffraction-limited resolution of the optics or the line resolution of the film. Moreover, the results do not take into account various operational degradations, nor do they involve the intrinsic limitation on ground resolution presented by the scattering of light in the atmosphere. The latter limitation amounts to a few inches for an altitude of 100 miles. Nonetheless, it seems clear that the latest U.S. photoreconnaissance satellites are close to achieving resolutions that are limited only by atmospheric effects.

Ground resolution is not the only relevant measure of picture quality. It characterizes an image only at the threshold of what can be barely distinguished. The color and light contrast of the objects being photographed strongly affect their distinguishability. The angle of the sun and the intrinsic reflectivity of an object are also important, since these factors influence the object's apparent brightness. In general the task of identifying an object in a photograph is always more difficult than simply locating it. On the other hand, extended objects such as roads or rail lines can often be distinguished even though their dimensions

RUSSIAN MULTIPLE-WARHEAD TEST was photographed from a U.S. Air Force plane in the vicinity of the projected impact point somewhere in the Pacific Ocean. The three separate reentry vehicles, which were launched by a single SS-9 missile from the Russian missile-testing center at Tyuratam, east of the Aral Sea, are equipped with protective head shields that glow as the vehicles reenter the atmosphere. As a result the vehicles (which for tests of this type bear dummy nuclear warheads) are visible as bright dots in the photograph. The three fainter streaks at lower left were made by fragments of the booster rocket burning up on reentry into the atmosphere. U.S. radars routinely monitor Russian missile tests near both ends of their trajectory, after which specially equipped aircraft and vessels are dispatched to make such photographs. This picture was released by the Department of Defense in 1971.

96   II | SALT I AND ITS BACKGROUND

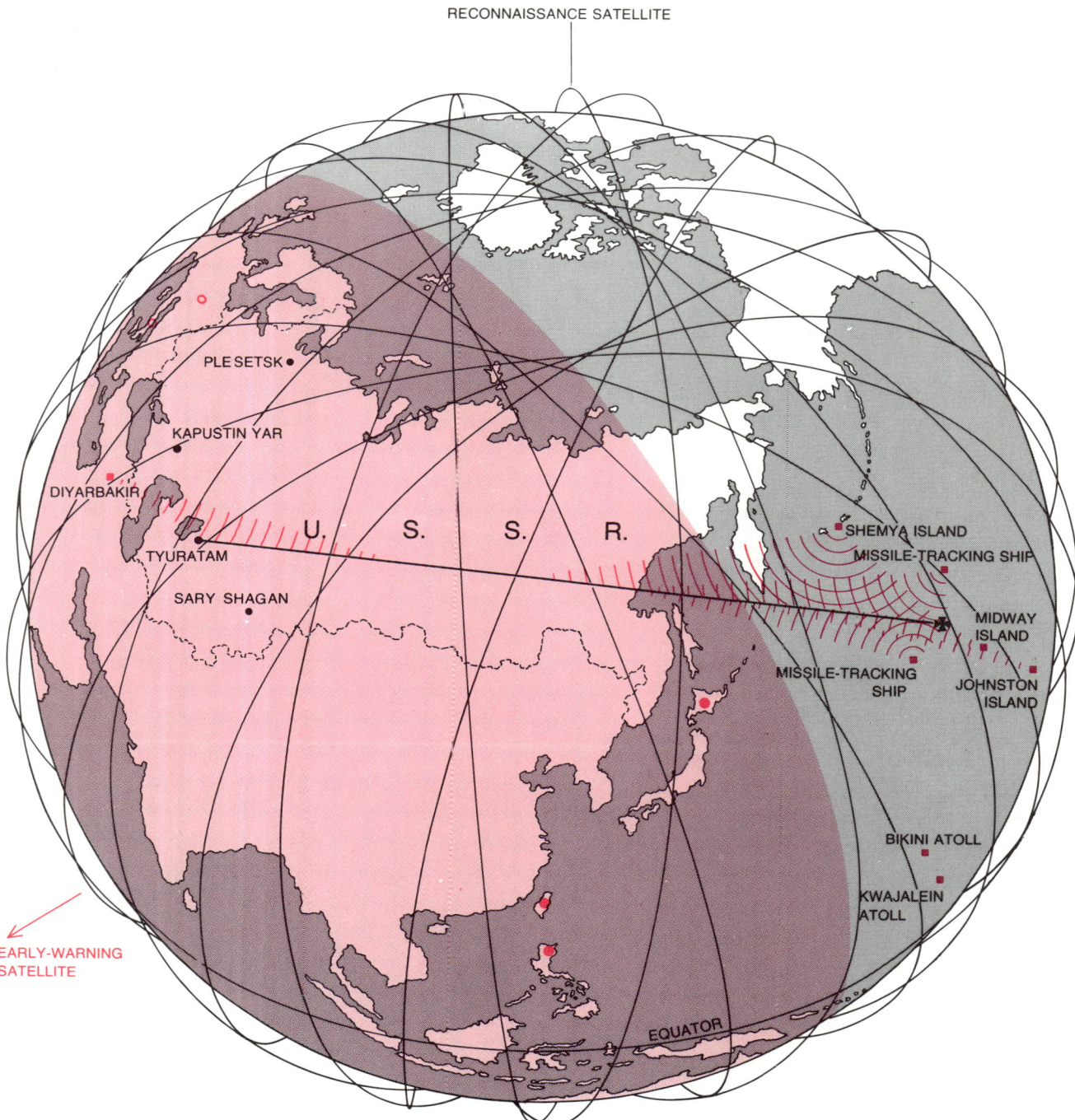

RECONNAISSANCE AND SURVEILLANCE SYSTEMS currently used by the U.S. to verify Russian compliance with the terms of the SALT I agreements are represented schematically in this illustration. U.S. photoreconnaissance satellites are typically launched (from Vandenberg Air Force Base in California) into a near-polar elliptical orbit with an orbital period of approximately 90 minutes and a perigee (lowest point) on the order of 100 miles. The latest, fourth-generation U.S. observation satellite, unofficially called Big Bird, combines the separate functions of area-surveillance photography and close-look photography and hence is required to stay aloft for a much longer period than earlier close-look satellites; orbital times to date have averaged about seven weeks. The orbit of such a satellite remains essentially fixed in space while the earth rotates, with the result that to an earth-based observer the satellite appears to move westward on each successive orbit. Hence most of the earth's surface passes under the orbital path of the satellite. U.S. early-warning satellites, in contrast, are typically launched into near-equatorial, near-synchronous "parking" orbits at altitudes of about 22,300 miles. Two such satellites, launched into identical "figure eight" orbits at the same fixed longitude over the Indian Ocean but lagging each other by 12 hours, can provide continuous infrared coverage of most of the U.S.S.R. and all of China (*light colored area*). The value of early-warning satellites from the point of view of arms control is that they are also capable of monitoring missile tests. The black dots indicate the locations of the major Russian missile-testing launch centers; the black line shows a typical trajectory for a Russian long-range missile test. Also shown are two types of U.S. radar used to monitor Russian missile tests: over-the-horizon transmitters (*colored dots*) and receivers (*open colored circles*), and conventional, or line-of-sight, radars (*colored squares*).

may be far below the calculated ground resolution.

Two different techniques are currently employed by the U.S. to retrieve photoreconnaissance information from space. The first is to return the film itself for processing on the ground. This method preserves all the information that is recorded on the film and is therefore employed for very-high-resolution photographs. The exposed film is ejected from the satellite and is returned to the earth in a special reentry package, which is caught in midair by specially equipped aircraft as it floats by parachute through the latter part of its descent [see illustration on page 100].

For lower-resolution pictures the film can be developed on the satellite and scanned by a television camera or a laser system. This information is temporarily stored and then transmitted to the earth when the satellite passes over one of several ground and shipboard stations around the world. Clearly in order to transmit all the necessary information during the short time in which the satellite is in view of these stations a communications system with a high data-transmission rate is needed.

Once a film pack is returned to the earth it must be developed to maximum advantage and then interpreted. The transmitted pictures must also be recreated and then interpreted. With a ground resolution measured in inches or feet and with a film resolution measured in the hundreds of lines per millimeter, it is clear that by the time enlargements of the photographs are made many man-hours must be expended to interpret them. Indeed, photographic interpretation must be a very large enterprise today both in the U.S. and in the U.S.S.R. It is also no wonder that systems are used to make photographs at less than maximum resolution in order to identify interesting targets for further photography at higher resolution.

In addition to visible-light cameras infrared sensors are used in reconnaissance satellites. Since all bodies at terrestrial temperatures radiate energy that is predominantly in the infrared part of the spectrum, infrared photography is not dependent on the sun for illumination. It is therefore useful for night applications or in polar regions. (Low-light systems have been developed and may also be in service for these purposes.) Perhaps the greatest significance of infrared sensors is their ability to detect things (such as missile silos) that are underground or may be camouflaged. As long as the ground immediately around the object is at a different temperature or has emission characteristics different from those of the surrounding terrain, an underground silo will stand out in an infrared picture. For this reason multispectral photography, a technique for making pictures simultaneously at several wavelengths, is increasingly employed in observation satellites. Although longer-wavelength infrared photography would require much larger optics to achieve resolutions comparable to those attainable with visible-light systems, such high resolution is probably not needed to accomplish the tasks assigned to the infrared sensors.

One of the major obstacles for satellite reconnaissance is, of course, cloud cover. Certain locations, for example the location of Moscow, are rarely free of clouds. The coordination of observation-satellite launchings with information received from weather satellites can overcome this problem to some extent. Moreover, observation satellites currently in service probably have the capability of changing their orbit to take advantage of breaks in the cloud cover.

Observation satellites contribute to the verification of the SALT agreements in a variety of ways. By photographing missile test sites they help to identify new missile systems, to detect changes in operational procedure that may suggest a change in hardware and to monitor testing programs. They can watch industrial facilities, including shipyards for the construction of submarines and plants for the assembly of missiles. Intermittent information on critical aspects of transportation networks can be obtained. The progress of construction of missile silos, ABM radars or ABM launcher sites can be monitored. Wide-area surveys can be made to determine if any activity is underway that violates the agreements.

Although the possibility of artificial earth satellites and their potential for military reconnaissance were recognized immediately after World War II, not until the mid-1950's was the future availability of rocket boosters assured and a satellite program actually initiated. On March 16, 1955, under the sponsorship of the Central Intelligence Agency, the U.S. Air Force issued a formal operational requirement for a strategic satellite system. After a year-long competition the Air Force selected the Lockheed Aircraft Corporation to develop a self-powered satellite vehicle, later named the Agena. This vehicle (along with several later models) was for many years the workhorse of the U.S. observation-satellite program.

The U.S. did not wait for the availability of satellites, however, before beginning a strategic-reconnaissance program. By 1956 U-2 reconnaissance aircraft were making their first flights over the U.S.S.R. Their photographic information supplemented the radar data on Russian missile tests, provided the basis for the gradual downgrading of estimates of the size of the Russian bomber force and eventually convinced most informed observers that the Russian ICBM buildup was proceeding at a much slower pace than had been anticipated. In spite of the considerable usefulness of the U-2 flights, the aircraft had two weaknesses as a sensor platform. First, the limited range of the plane, the endurance of the pilot and the provocative nature of the mission imposed a severe limitation on the area of the U.S.S.R. that could be photographed. As a result of this limitation the lack of U-2 evidence for large numbers of deployed Russian ICBM's was not conclusive proof that only a few existed. Not until reconnaissance satellites had provided much greater coverage of the landmass of the U.S.S.R. could the U.S. intelligence community be certain that missiles had not been deployed and remained undetected. The second weakness of the airplane was its vulnerability. Eventually the Russians developed an antiaircraft missile that could hit the U-2 at 70,000 feet. When Francis Gary Powers was shot down in May, 1960, the U-2 overflights ended, except for certain minor incursions. Satellites, on the other hand, were known to be invulnerable, and would remain so for the then foreseeable future.

Among the many technical problems that had to be solved in order to develop an operational reconnaissance satellite were the stabilization and orientation of the spacecraft, the design and production of light cameras with a long focal length and a large aperture, and the recovery of the data. The possibility of using a television camera was considered very early but was rejected because the desired resolution was not attainable with available technology. In 1957 the decision was made to pursue two parallel approaches: first, direct recovery of a film package; and second, on-board developing and scanning of film followed by radio transmission to ground stations. Techniques for direct recovery were developed using Discoverer satellites as test vehicles. The first successful reentry package was recovered from *Discoverer*

13 on August 11, 1960. Either this package or the one recovered from *Discoverer 14* the following week probably yielded the first satellite photographs of the U.S.S.R. That was just three months after the last U-2 overflight of the U.S.S.R. The first successful radio-transmission observation satellite was *Samos II*, which was put in a polar orbit varying in altitude between 300 and 350 miles on January 31, 1961; this spacecraft carried between 300 and 400 pounds of instruments.

These early successes almost certainly were responsible for the final laying to rest of the myth of the "missile gap." On February 6, 1961, Secretary of Defense Robert S. McNamara told reporters at an informal, off-the-record briefing that a study had yielded no evidence of such a gap. A White House spokesman denied the report, saying that the studies were not yet complete. Intelligence sources, however, soon began to reduce their estimates of the number of Russian missiles. By September, 1961, after the successful recovery of additional Discoverer capsules and with time to analyze the *Samos II* data, the number of deployed Russian ICBM's was reportedly put at 14.

The descendants of the early Samos satellites have been comparatively small radio-transmission observation satellites whose sensors and orbital characteristics are chosen to maximize their degree of coverage. They stay in orbit for three to four weeks. Although their perigee (lowest orbital point) is about 100 miles above the earth's surface, the ellipticity of their orbit greatly reduces their atmospheric drag, thereby increasing their lifetime. With an inclination of 80 to 92 degrees with respect to the Equator, they provide virtually full coverage of the U.S.S.R. and complete coverage of China. These "area surveillance" satellites provide low-resolution coverage of wide regions, and the radio transmission of data makes possible the rapid recovery of intelligence information. Particular areas of interest are identified on the basis of this information and higher-resolution pictures are later made by another satellite with a recoverable film capsule. By early 1962 the size and weight of the camera system had been reduced sufficiently to allow the area-surveillance satellites to be launched by the Thor/Agena booster rather than by the more powerful Atlas/Agena booster used earlier.

The use of the Thrust-Augmented-Thor/Agena D, beginning in May, 1963, indicates that a new generation of satellites was then introduced. The greater throw weight of this booster rocket enabled the satellite to carry a larger camera and more of a consumable payload (including film), resulting in an increase in useful lifetime. These satellites were launched at roughly one-month intervals beginning in the middle of 1963. Until the end of 1965, however, two or more area-surveillance satellites were frequently in orbit at the same time, and occasional delays in the regular launch schedule can be identified. This suggests that problems of reliability necessitated the replacement of satellites that had failed before the completion of their mission and also that problems had sometimes occurred at ground level. Since 1966 one of these satellites has been in orbit for almost half the days of

AREA-SURVEILLANCE SYSTEM similar to the system used in the early U.S. Samos reconnaissance satellites is represented here by a schematic diagram of the interior mechanism of a Lunar Orbiter, the spacecraft used to make a photographic survey of the surface of the moon preparatory to selecting the Apollo landing sites. In both systems the film is exposed and developed by the optical and film-processing elements of the camera subsystem; the developed photographs are then scanned by a television camera, converting the picture into electrical signals for radio transmission back to earth. Cameras for both Lunar Orbiter and Samos were built by the Eastman Kodak Company; film scanners for both spacecraft were built by CBS Laboratories, a division of the Columbia Broadcasting System.

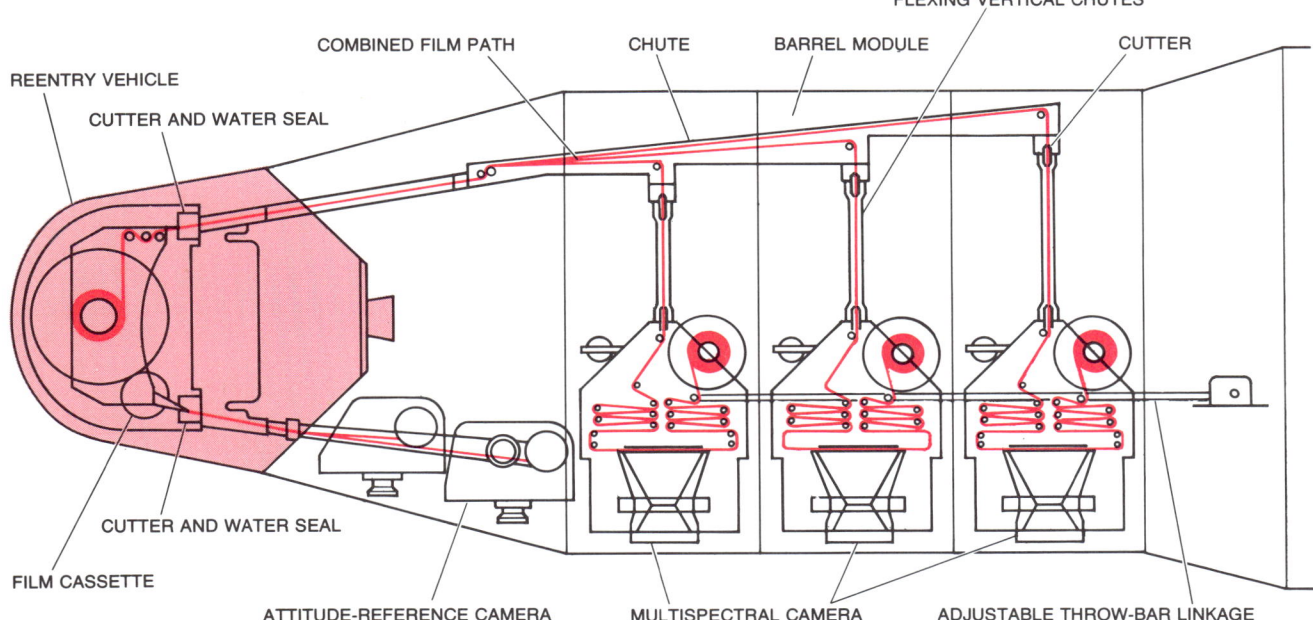

CLOSE-LOOK SYSTEM similar to the system used in the U.S. second-generation Discoverer reconnaissance satellites is represented here by a schematic diagram of the interior mechanism of a proposed nonmilitary satellite. The scheme shown was submitted by the General Electric Company to the National Aeronautics and Space Administration in 1969 for possible use in NASA's earth-resources survey program. In both systems exposed film is fed from several cameras into a recoverable capsule, which is ejected from the satellite and returned to earth for processing. Since this method preserves all the information on the film, it is preferable for high-resolution photography. The recoverable-film system for the Discoverer reconnaissance satellites was produced by General Electric.

the year, and there has been hardly any overlap. One can therefore probably fix the beginning of 1966 as the date of a fully operational status for the area-surveillance satellites.

The first test launch employing the even more powerful Long-Tank-Thrust-Augmented-Thor/Agena was in August, 1966, and that booster was introduced into regular service in May, 1967. The use of this booster also marks the arrival of a heavier, third-generation satellite. It was probably equipped with a camera of longer focal length, a larger film supply, an infrared optical system and a new transmission system with an increased data rate.

The task of these satellites has been to survey wide areas with sensors of moderate resolution and to reveal targets that merit a closer look at higher resolution. In order to provide that closer look, a different type of satellite is used.

The descendants of the Discoverer recoverable-capsule satellites are the close-look satellites. They are heavier than the area-surveillance satellites, reflecting the fact that they carry a camera with a longer focal length and a wider aperture. They are also in a lower orbit, with a perigee of typically about 80 miles, in order to maximize resolution. With this more powerful telescopic system interesting targets identified by an earlier area-surveillance satellite can be rephotographed and examined more closely. To minimize information losses introduced by electronic data storage and transmission, the close-look satellites send their film packs back to the earth in a reentry capsule for midair recovery by aircraft.

The first launching of a close-look satellite appears to have been on April 26, 1962, when a Thor/Agena booster put into orbit a satellite carrying a recovery capsule designated *E-6*. Three days later the capsule and its film were recovered. Judging from the frequency of launchings, this program seems to have achieved operational status by the middle of 1963. With their shorter lifetime in orbit, the close-look satellites had less stringent reliability requirements than the area-surveillance models and were therefore able to reach full operational status more quickly. By 1964 the Atlas/Agena had been introduced as the program's booster, ensuring that heavier satellites with improved capabilities could be placed in orbit. These second-generation high-resolution satellites were launched about once a month and remained in orbit for three to five days before sending their film package back to the earth.

The Titan 3B began to be used for test launches in July, 1966, and came into regular service in August, 1967. With the introduction of this still larger booster the lifetime of the close-look satellites began to increase until by 1968 they remained in orbit for a period averaging some two weeks. This clearly shows that a third-generation satellite had been introduced with a much greater film capacity and the ability to raise its orbit in order to avoid early burnup. It has been suggested that the new satellite could alter its orbit to take advantage of breaks in cloud cover; moreover, it seems likely that several new types of sensor were included in the satellites. Infrared sensors and multispectral photography appear to be the most likely candidates because of their ability to discover and penetrate camouflage and, in the case of the infrared sensors, to operate in the dark. An accurate mapping camera for the purpose of pinpointing the location of strategic targets in the U.S.S.R. may also have been included.

In the past 18 months or so an entirely new fourth generation of observation satellites has been introduced and is now reaching operational status. This satellite, unofficially called Big Bird, weighs more than 20,000 pounds, which makes it much heavier than any previous observation satellite. The spacecraft itself is a modified Agena rocket 10 feet in diameter and 50 feet long. It is launched by the powerful Titan 3D booster.

The extra weight and size of this sys-

MIDAIR RECOVERY of a film capsule from a Discoverer-type reconnaissance satellite is accomplished by means of specially equipped aircraft as the capsule floats by parachute through the latter part of its descent. This photograph, released by the Air Force in 1961, shows a C-119 transport aircraft "as it approaches a Discoverer capsule...somewhere over the Pacific Ocean." At present larger C-130 aircraft are used routinely to recover the much heavier film capsules dropped by the latest-model close-look reconnaissance satellites.

tem result from joining the separate functions of area-surveillance and close-look photography into the one satellite. Big Bird is reported to carry an area-surveillance camera made by the Eastman Kodak Company and an on-board film processor and scanner. The resulting data are reportedly transmitted by means of a new 20-foot unfurlable antenna, which would represent an increase in capacity by a factor of 16 over the older five-foot antennas. In the past, several months would go by before a close-look satellite could be launched to rephotograph an area of interest identified by a low-resolution photograph and its film pack could be recovered. Now, however, Big Bird can be directed to turn on its high-resolution camera (made by the Perkin-Elmer Corporation) during a subsequent pass. Film from this camera, said to have a resolution of less than one foot from an altitude of 100 miles, is returned in one of several recovery capsules. The delay time should now be cut to several weeks.

This dual capability requires that Big Bird remain aloft for a much longer period than earlier close-look satellites. In order to accomplish this result the satellite is placed in a higher and more elliptical orbit. The orbital characteristics of the first Big Bird, launched on June 15, 1971, were a perigee of 111 miles and an apogee of 180 miles. To compensate for this higher altitude and to improve resolution both the focal length and the aperture of the high-power camera had to be increased over those of earlier models. To further increase the satellite's lifetime it has been equipped with an on-board rocket to raise its orbit and prevent early burnup. The times in orbit for the first three satellites were respectively 52 days, 40 days and 68 days. The fourth launching was on October 10, 1972.

Certainly since 1962, and probably earlier, the U.S. has had detailed information on the number and location of Russian strategic missiles. In 1967 President Johnson told a meeting of educators in Tennessee that satellite reconnaissance was worth 10 times the money the U.S. had spent in space. "I know how many missiles the enemy has," Johnson said. He suggested that this knowledge had prevented the country from harboring fears that otherwise might have arisen. From the late 1960's to the present the Department of Defense has regularly published information on the level of Russian ICBM, SLBM and ABM deployment. Both Congress and the public have come to expect such information as part of the Department's budget justification, and in recent years both the Administration and its critics have used the published figures to support their own arguments.

The major task assigned by SALT I to these now protected "national technical means of verification" is to monitor the quantitative limits imposed on the number of ABM launchers, large radars, ICBM's and SLBM's. This is the arms-control task for which observation satellites are best suited. From satellite photographs intelligence analysts are able to monitor silo construction and the transport of missiles to their deployment sites. With multispectral and infrared photography they can detect or penetrate camouflage and monitor nighttime activity. Submarine shipyards are observed on a routine basis to monitor new construction. Similarly, ABM launchers and radar deployments can be observed. There seems to be no doubt that these aspects of the SALT I agreements can be verified by satellite reconnaissance with a high degree of confidence, as long as the Russians live up to their pledge "not to use deliberate concealment measures which impede verification by national technical means."

The more important question, however, is whether or not the Russians could find ways clandestinely to circumvent the restrictions and thereby achieve a military or political advantage over the U.S. Although the actual deployment of prohibited weaponry secretly seems quite impossible, could the Russians simply manufacture additional missiles or radars and then abrogate the treaty at a time of their own choosing and deploy them on a time scale too short for a U.S. response? A full discussion of this problem would have to include an assessment of the internal pressures that might lead the U.S.S.R. to such actions, the possible international political repercussions and an analysis of what the Russians would have to do that would make any difference either militarily or politically.

Although such considerations lie outside this discussion, one can still go part of the way toward dealing with the problem. The continuous monitoring of Russian transportation networks, power-generation plants and manufacturing facilities by observation satellites would make it unlikely that the U.S. could not detect such clandestine activity in time to react in some way. The decrease in delay time provided by Big Bird between the first indication of suspicious activity in an area-surveillance photograph and further photography with a high-resolution camera will certainly reduce the uncertainties involved. Although photography cannot penetrate buildings, infrared and multispectral techniques can often reveal a great deal about activities inside, particularly since activities of special interest may be indicated by changes in standard operating procedures.

Cloud cover remains an impediment to observational activities, but with longer orbital lifetimes and the capability of changing orbit the newer satellites are less constrained than their predecessors. For the clarification of ambiguities both the unilateral techniques of electronic and communications intelligence and the bilateral apparatus of the Standing Consultative Commission (also set up by the SALT I agreements) may be useful. To summarize, the very size and complexity of construction and industrial activity required to build and deploy modern strategic weapons, combined with the breadth of coverage, resolution and multispectral aspects of observation satellites, guarantee that the agreements of SALT I can be verified unilaterally with high confidence. The cost of hardware and manpower for photointerpretation, however, will remain high.

If a future agreement were to impose qualitative restrictions on strategic systems, the U.S. would have to rely on other verification techniques to augment the observation satellites. The usefulness in this regard of systems that monitor missile tests will be considered below. Observation satellites would also, however, have a role to play in monitoring such agreements. Any qualitative improvement in missile weaponry, whether it is new guidance systems, multiple warheads, improved ABM radar, new SLBM's or advanced ICBM's, must be reflected in changes from former manufacturing and testing procedures and equipment. Any new hardware must be delivered to an operational site and

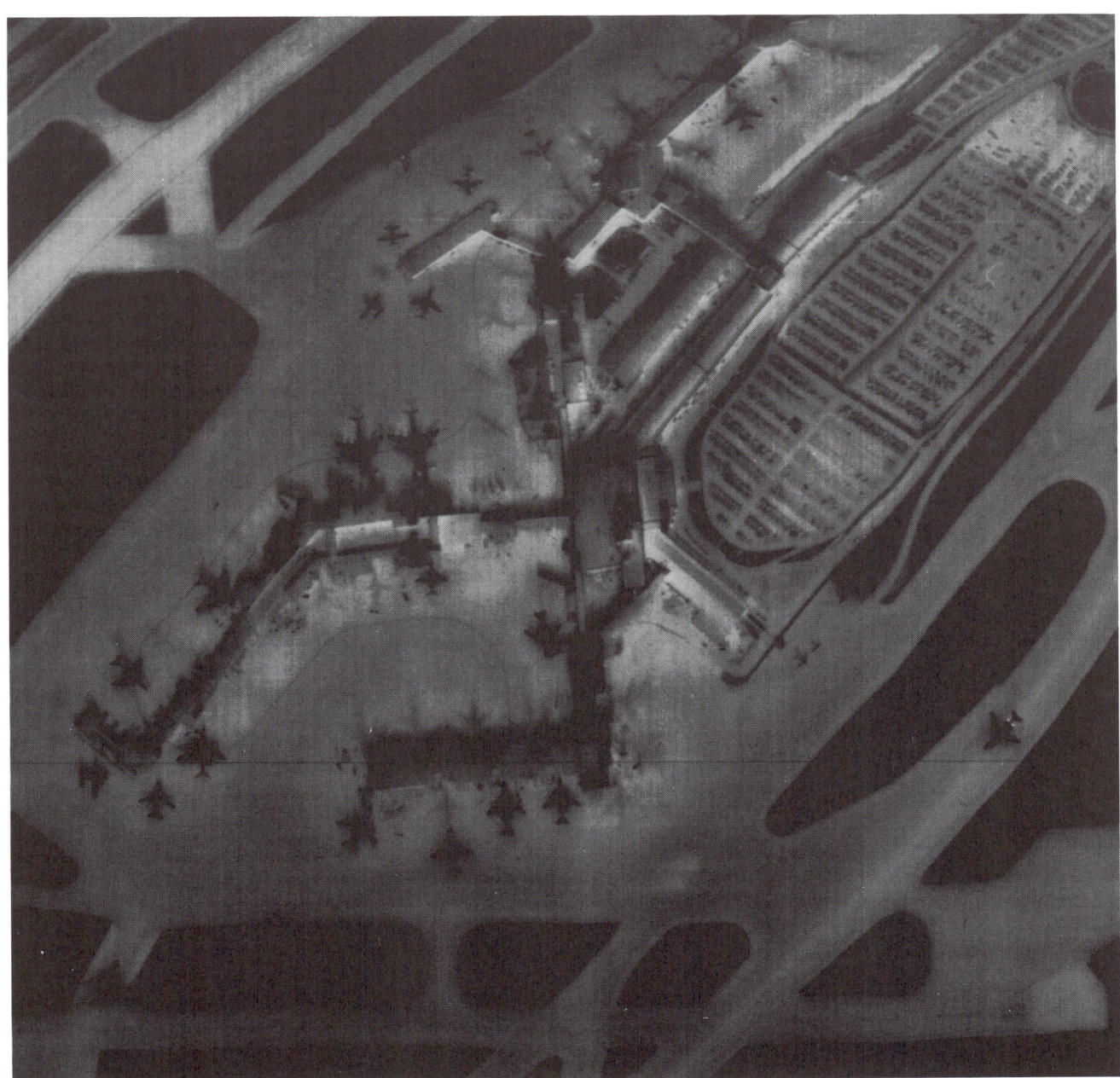

INFRARED PHOTOGRAPH of an airport in Texas was made from an aircraft flying at an altitude of 2,000 feet. Since infrared photography is not dependent on the sun for illumination, it is used in reconnaissance satellites for night applications or in polar regions. The ability of infrared sensors to detect the heat from missile exhausts is suggested by the bright images of the jet exhausts from the aircraft on the runway at lower right. This unusual unclassified photograph was supplied by Texas Instruments Incorporated.

MULTISPECTRAL PHOTOGRAPHY, a technique for making pictures simultaneously at several wavelengths, is increasingly employed in reconnaissance satellites. The four sample photographs shown on these two pages were made by a multispectral scanner on board NASA's Earth Resources Technology Satellite; the line-scanning device employed in this case uses an oscillating mirror to simultaneously record the terrain passing under the spacecraft in four spectral bands: .5 to .6 micrometer (a), .6 to .7 micrometer (b), .7 to .8 micrometer (c) and .8 micrometer to 1.1 micrometers (d). The electronic signals produced by this television system are

installed. These activities can be monitored by satellites.

The surveillance systems that would be useful in the verification of an agreement imposing qualitative restrictions on ballistic missiles include certain land-based line-of-sight radars, over-the-horizon radars, satellite systems and particularly shipboard sensors for terminal observations. As early as the summer of 1955 a U.S. radar at Samsun in Turkey was tracking missile tests from the Russian launch site at Kapustin Yar, northwest of the Caspian Sea. As a result of this monitoring the launching of *Sputnik I* in October, 1957, and the Russian ICBM tests of the same year came as no surprise to the U.S. intelligence community and Government officials with access to such data. They were well aware of the Russian capabilities in this area. By late 1963 or early 1964 a longer-range radar had been installed in Diyarbakir in Turkey, bringing into view missiles launched from the newer Russian test center at Tyuratam, east of the Aral Sea.

Several fixed land-based radars are also available to observe Russian tests near the end of their flights. One of these has been operational on Shemya Island, far out in the Aleutian chain, since at least 1959. This radar can track and provide data on the Russian reentry vehicles that impact either in the test area on Kamchatka Peninsula or in the North Pacific area northwest of the Midway Islands. For the longer-range tests that end in the Pacific southwest of Johnston Island several radars that have been installed for other purposes at the Midway Islands, Bikini Atoll, Kwajalein Atoll and Johnston Island can be employed.

Unlike conventional radar, over-the-horizon, or OTH, radar is not restricted in its range by the curvature of the earth. By reflection from the ionosphere OTH radar can penetrate to great distances, making possible the detection of missiles soon after they are launched. The currently deployed "forward scatter" OTH radar detects the disturbances in the ionosphere caused by the ionized jet of gas emanating from a rocket's motor. Since each type of missile disturbs the ionosphere somewhat differently, a detected missile can be identified by its characteristic OTH signature. In the currently operational system three transmitters are deployed in Taiwan, Japan and the Philippines. These transmitters are matched with corresponding receivers in Italy, Germany and another European country. Although the system was originally intended as an early-warning system for a massive missile attack, it has detected a high percentage of the known single events since 1968. All long-range missiles fired from test sites in the U.S.S.R. are detectable.

Parallel to the observation-satellite developments of the late 1950's and early 1960's there was an expensive and unsuccessful program to develop a satellite early-warning system. For years this program was plagued by unreliabilities in its hardware and by the inability of its infrared sensors to distinguish between rocket-exhaust plumes and sunlight reflected from high clouds. By 1963 an interim capability had been achieved, but not until recently did a high-confidence system exist. The first two operational vehicles of the satellite early-warning network were launched on May 5, 1971, and were placed in near-synchronous orbits over the Indian Ocean at about 65 degrees east longitude. Their orbits have a 10-degree inclination to provide more northern coverage than a truly synchronous orbit would allow. A slight ellipticity of orbit increases the time they spend over the Northern Hemisphere. Two satellites are required to provide continuous coverage. Although the primary mission of these satellites and others deployed at different longitudes is to provide early warning of an ICBM attack, they are of interest here because they also provide a capability to monitor Russian missile tests.

Both the OTH radars and the early-warning satellites can be used to help verify the testing restrictions included in

c  d

then transmitted back to the earth, where they are converted to black-and-white images. The latter in turn can be used to make color composites by registering the images sequentially on color film through the appropriate filters. These particular photographs are shown here only to help illustrate the multispectral technique; their ground resolution (roughly 200 feet from an altitude of 569 miles) in no way compares with the ground resolution obtainable with the current generation of close-look reconnaissance satellites (roughly one foot from an altitude of 100 miles). The region viewed in the photographs includes Vandenberg Air Force Base (*arrow*).

the SALT I ABM treaty. Beyond that they can be used in conjunction with land-based line-of-sight radars to indicate when and where missile tests are taking place and to provide some information about the type of test. These systems would therefore be used to monitor any agreement that imposed numerical or geographical restrictions on missile-testing. As long as a missile test is within view of a line-of-sight radar its point of ballistic impact can be determined. Some characteristics of the reentry vehicle, such as its size and shape, can also be determined from radar observation. The precision of such determinations would depend on the detailed characteristics of both the radar and the reentry vehicle.

The most useful observations for monitoring long-range missile tests are those made from ships and aircraft in the region of impact of the reentry vehicle. From terminal radar and photographic observations detailed information about the reentry system can be derived. If one compares the calculated impact point with the observed impact point and knows the local weather conditions at the point of impact, one can make estimates of the mode of reentry through the atmosphere. For example, one can estimate whether the reentry vehicle has been designed to glide past its ballistic-impact point or to fall short of it.

From the close-range radar pictures of the reentry vehicle and its observed speed of passage through the atmosphere, estimates can be made of its weight and ballistic coefficient (a constant that represents the efficiency of the reentry vehicle in overcoming air resistance). If a powered terminal maneuver is attempted, observing radar and infrared sensors should be able to detect it. Multiple-warhead tests can be easily detected near the impact site, if they are not detected earlier by other techniques.

With all this information readily available to observers near the impact area, it is not surprising that such observations have been made for many years. Since 1961 U.S. ships have monitored Russian missile shots into the Pacific. These observations not only have allowed the intelligence community to keep abreast of qualitative improvements in Russian missile technology but also have provided data on the radar "signatures" of Russian missiles, supplying an important input for the design of ABM radars. The sophistication of current capabilities was demonstrated on April 23, 1970, when a set of photographs of a Russian multiple-warhead test was released to the press by the Department of Defense. It was reported that after shipboard radar had detected the incoming reentry vehicles, aircraft and vessels were dispatched to make the photographs.

The verification of any qualitative restrictions on ICBM's that might emerge from SALT II would rely chiefly on these land-based line-of-sight radars, OTH systems, early-warning satellites and shipboard sensors. An examination of their possibilities and limitations is important to any realistic assessment of what may be possible and desirable in SALT II.

One approach that has been suggested in order to inhibit qualitative improvements in offensive missiles is to restrict the number of missile tests that each side is allowed each year. It is argued that if the restricted number were small enough, the competition between the testing of existing hardware and the development of new hardware would eliminate most or all new developments. Putting aside the questions of uncertainties and asymmetries to which such a limitation might give rise, one can say with high confidence that the limitation itself could be verified. Counting missile firings is just what the early-warning satellites, OTH radar and fixed land-based radars do best. If the purpose of such an agreement is to restrain qualitative improvements, however, a useful extension would be to insist that all sanctioned tests be conducted along designated flight corridors and at preannounced times. Such an extension would

RECENT EXAMPLE of high-resolution space photography is provided by this photograph of a strip of the lunar surface made from the *Apollo 15* command ship after the lunar landing module containing the two Apollo astronauts had already landed on the moon. A panoramic camera with a focal length of two feet, built by the Itek Corporation, was used to photograph the lunar surface from a

facilitate the task of ensuring that qualitative improvements have not been made in spite of the numerical limitations.

Where qualitative restrictions themselves are concerned the verification problem becomes much more difficult. The far-reaching development restrictions built into the ABM treaty, however, may be cause for encouragement. In general a prohibition against new types of boosters, front-end configurations or reentry vehicles could probably be verified with high confidence, particularly if it were imposed on top of the previously suggested restrictions. Since the various identifying signatures of current systems are either well known or will become so with time, any new hardware would be distinguishable by an unrecognized signature. Such an across-the-board standstill might be very useful and perhaps even feasible if both the U.S. and the U.S.S.R. could reconcile themselves to accepting certain technical asymmetries.

Other less restrictive prohibitions can also be considered. For example, since terminal maneuvering can probably be detected, either directly with infrared and radar sensors or indirectly by comparing the calculated and the observed trajectories, such maneuvering might be prohibitable. A prohibition of this type would automatically rule out terminal guidance, which would serve no purpose without corrective terminal maneuvering.

Another possibility, although it would be more difficult to verify, would be to restrict improvements in accuracy. Although an observer can tell where a reentry vehicle lands and probably can tell whether the vehicle went through deliberate terminal maneuvers or exploited an aerodynamic shape in order to arrive at its target, he cannot tell from his own observations alone where it was supposed to land. Therefore information on missile accuracy must come from second-order inference. One way to estimate the accuracy of the guidance systems, but not the reentry techniques, is to monitor the apparent accuracy of the inertial guidance on space missions. Presumably the technology available for space shots is also available for ICBM's. The U.S. has a very capable worldwide network of radars in the Space Detection and Tracking System, and these systems can be used for making such inferences. Nonetheless, trying to limit accuracy by constraining inertial-guidance systems does not seem to be a fruitful approach. Instead, prohibitions against giving reentry vehicles terminal-maneuvering capabilities and high ballistic coefficients might be used to indirectly inhibit improvements in accuracy.

Another concern for the SALT II agenda is multiple-warhead tests. The presence of several warheads can be detected by terminal radar, shipboard radar and possibly by other systems. Could a multiple-warhead system be tested with only one warhead at a time, however, thereby avoiding detection? The full answer must depend on both the detailed structure of the hardware and the confidence required in such a system. A partial answer can be formulated by recognizing that in a world characterized by mutual deterrence the major concern of each side is that the opponent not achieve a capability that can be used for a preemptive, counterforce attack. It seems unlikely that such a capability could be developed and brought to a status of high reliability without a large number of full-system tests. There is a problem, however, in translating the likelihood that the U.S.S.R. could not create such a high-confidence system while it was constrained by an arms-control treaty into a certainty on the part of the U.S. that such a system has not been developed.

In this connection the distinction between MRV's (multiple reentry vehicles) and MIRV's (multiple independently targetable reentry vehicles) may be quite inconsequential, depending on the nature of the systems. For a small separation of the reentry vehicles, systems with either mechanical separation or independent guidance could be conceived. To distinguish one such system from another would be difficult and of little value. For a wide separation, however, independent guidance would be required in order to prevent a degradation of accuracy. Presumably a system that can produce wide separation could also be programmed for small separation and could perhaps be tested without being recognized for what it was. In general it seems very difficult to impose verifiable restrictions on multiple-warhead systems except by a total prohibition or a freezing of present systems.

This article has been concerned with national technical means of verification because these are the techniques mentioned in and protected under the SALT I accords. The conclusion should not be drawn, however, that such technical means of verification are the only means available. Other national (or unilateral, as opposed to on-site, or cooperative) verification techniques include economic analysis, diplomacy, content analysis of documents and speeches, interviewing travelers and participants in scientific meetings, and espionage. Although the utility of these information sources cannot be denied, they do have the disadvantage of relying on inference. Reconnaissance and surveillance, on the other hand, are dependent primarily on the physical properties of electromagnetic sensors and therefore provide less ambiguous information and broader coverage than other techniques.

This discussion cannot even claim to have exhausted the national technical means of verification. Specifically omitted because of the lack of sufficient unrestricted information have been the ships, the aircraft, the satellites and the

height of about 60 miles. The reproduction of the complete strip photograph shown here is approximately a third of the size of the original film. The original has a ground resolution of about three feet, suggesting an optical resolution for the system of better than 180 lines per millimeter of film. The *Apollo 15* landing site is within the small white square at lower center (*see illustration at bottom*).

land-based receivers used for electronic and communications intelligence. The information gathered by these devices, such as radar transmission frequencies and the nature of Russian and Chinese communications networks, may be of greater relevance to military planning than to the verification of the SALT agreements. To the extent that communications can be intercepted and decoded, however, the intelligence community may be able to go beyond its assessment of technical capabilities to clues about political intention.

The major conclusion that can be drawn from the analysis presented here is that the U.S. can, with its observation satellites and missile-test-surveillance systems, verify Russian observance of the SALT I ABM treaty and interim agreement with high confidence. Although the focus of this article has been exclusively on the U.S. capability, the Russians have comparable observation-satellite systems that they also can rely on to verify U.S. compliance. The mutual benefits of verifying each other's activities by national technical means have now been formally recognized in the noninterference and nonconcealment stipulations of the current agreements.

The conclusion of verifiability is not dependent, however, on Russian cooperation in nonconcealment. Although it is much easier to monitor a cooperative target nation, the possibility of cheating on an arms-control agreement must not be ruled out. In fact, the purpose of reconnaissance systems is precisely to detect or deter such cheating.

The next major arms-control negotiations, SALT II, are now under way. There is a widespread hope that in this round of talks the interim SALT I agreement can be transformed into permanent numerical limitations on offensive systems. The verification of such an agreement presents the same issues as SALT I has and could also be accomplished with high confidence by observation satellites and missile-surveillance systems. Even a prohibition of land-mobile systems could probably be verified, although a nonzero numerical limitation might be very difficult to monitor because of the intermittent nature of satellite reconnaissance.

The hope has also been expressed that SALT II may be able to restrain the qualitative arms race in offensive missiles. In this connection there may be a rather attractive package of verifiable restrictions, including a blanket prohibition against the testing of new ICBM boosters and new reentry systems. Since each type of booster or reentry system has a set of unique signatures, the introduction of new hardware could be detected. Such a prohibition would best be accompanied by a numerical limit on the number of tests allowed each year and by a requirement that all allowed tests be both preannounced and along prearranged flight corridors. The first limitation would reduce the opportunities for cheating and increase the incentives for compliance, since the testing of new hardware could only be done if the opportunity to test existing hardware were given up. The second restriction would make the task of verifying the prohibition against new hardware easier. Both restrictions could themselves be verified, since with current surveillance systems no unauthorized test could be conducted clandestinely.

BLOWUP of the *Apollo 15* landing site made from the panoramic strip shown at the top of these two pages clearly reveals the lunar landing module (*dead center*). The resolution of this reproduction, made from third-generation negatives, is considerably poorer, of course, than that of the original, in which the individual experiments set out by the astronauts can be distinguished. In other photographs made with this system the tracks of the "lunar rover" used by the astronauts are also visible. Even so, the intrinsic optical resolution of the system is still much poorer than that of the most advanced satellite-reconnaissance cameras, which are probably close to achieving resolutions that are limited only by atmospheric effects.

Selections from ABM Treaty, Interim Agreement, and Related Documents on SALT Phase I

Major Provisions of the Treaty between the United States of America and the Union of Soviet Socialist Republics on the Limitation of Anti-Ballistic Missile Systems*

ARTICLE I

1. Each Party undertakes to limit anti-ballistic missile (ABM) systems and to adopt other measures in accordance with the provisions of this Treaty.

2. Each Party undertakes not to deploy ABM systems for a defense of the territory of its country and not to provide a base for such a defense, and not to deploy ABM systems for defense of an individual region except as provided for in Article III of this Treaty.

ARTICLE II

1. For the purposes of this Treaty an ABM system is a system to counter strategic ballistic missiles or their elements in flight trajectory, currently consisting of:
   (a) ABM interceptor missiles, which are interceptor missiles constructed and deployed for an ABM role, or of a type tested in an ABM mode;
   (b) ABM launchers, which are launchers constructed and deployed for launching ABM interceptor missiles: and
   (c) ABM radars, which are radars constructed and deployed for an ABM role, or of a type tested in an ABM mode.

2. The ABM system components listed in paragraph 1 of this Article include those which are:
   (a) operational;
   (b) under construction;
   (c) undergoing testing;
   (d) undergoing overhaul, repair or conversion; or
   (e) mothballed.

ARTICLE III

Each Party undertakes not to deploy ABM systems or their components except that:
(a) within one ABM system deployment area having a radius of one hundred and fifty kilometers and centered on the Party's national capital, a Party may deploy: (1) no more than one hundred ABM launchers and no more than one hundred ABM interceptor missiles at launch sites, and (2) ABM radars within no more than six ABM radar complexes, the area of each complex being circular and have a diameter of no more than three kilometers; and
(b) within one ABM system deployment area having a radius of one hundred and fifty kilometers and containing ICBM silo launchers, a Party may deploy: (1) no more than one hundred ABM launchers and no more than one hundred ABM interceptor missiles at launch sites, (2) two large phased-array ABM radars comparable in potential to corresponding ABM radars operational or under construction on the date of signature of the Treaty in an ABM system deployment area containing ICBM silo launchers, and (3) no more than eighteen ABM radars each having a potential less than the potential of the smaller of the above-mentioned two large phased-array ABM radars.

ARTICLE IV

The limitations provided for in Article III shall not apply to ABM systems or their components used for development or testing, and located within current or additionally agreed test ranges. Each Party may have no more than a total of fifteen ABM launchers at test ranges.

ARTICLE V

1. Each Party undertakes not to develop, test, or deploy ABM systems or components which are sea-based, air-based, space-based, or mobile land-based.

2. Each Party undertakes not to develop, test, or deploy ABM launchers for launching more than one ABM interceptor missile at a time from each launcher, nor to modify deployed launchers to provide them with such a capability, nor to develop, test, or deploy automatic or semi-automatic or other similar systems for rapid reload or ABM launchers.

ARTICLE VI

To enhance assurance of the effectiveness of the limitations on ABM systems and their components provided by this Treaty, each Party undertakes:
(a) not to give missiles, launchers, or radars, other than ABM interceptor missiles, ABM launchers, or ABM radars, capabilities to counter strategic ballistic missiles or their elements in flight trajectory, and not to test them in an ABM mode; and
(b) not to deploy in the future radars for early warning of strategic ballistic missile attack except at locations along the periphery of its national territory and oriented outward.

---

*Selections from text of treaty done at Moscow on 26 May 1972. Not published in *Scientific American*.

Article VII

Subject to the provisions of this Treaty, modernization and replacement of ABM systems or their components may be carried out.

Article VIII

ABM systems or their components in excess of the numbers or outside the areas specified in this Treaty, as well as ABM systems or their components prohibited by this Treaty, shall be destroyed or dismantled under agreed procedures within the shortest possible agreed period of time.

Article IX

To assure the viability and effectiveness of this Treaty, each Party undertakes not to transfer to other States, and not to deploy outside its national territory, ABM systems or their components limited by this Treaty.

Article XII

1. For the purpose of providing assurance of compliance with the provisions of this Treaty, each Party shall use national technical means of verification at its disposal in a manner consistent with generally recognized principles of international law.

2. Each Party undertakes not to interfere with the national technical means of verification of the other Party operating in accordance with paragraph 1 of this Article.

3. Each Party undertakes not to use deliberate concealment measures which impede verification by national technical means of compliance with the provisions of this Treaty. This obligation shall not require changes in current construction, assembly, conversion, or overhaul practices.

Article XIII

1. To promote the objectives and implementation of the provisions of this Treaty, the Parties shall establish promptly a Standing Consultative Commission, within the framework of which they will:

(a) consider questions concerning compliance with the obligations assumed and related situations which may be considered ambiguous;

(b) provide on a voluntary basis such information as either Party considers necessary to assure confidence in compliance with the obligations assumed;

(c) consider questions involving unintended interference with national technical means of verification;

(d) consider possible changes in the strategic situation which have a bearing on the provisions of this Treaty;

(e) agree upon procedures and dates for destruction or dismantling of ABM systems or their components in cases provided for by the provisions of this Treaty;

(f) consider, as appropriate, possible proposals for further increasing the viability of this Treaty, including proposals for amendments in accordance with the provisions of this Treaty;

(g) consider, as appropriate, proposals for further measures aimed at limiting strategic arms.

2. The Parties through consultation shall establish, and may amend as appropriate, Regulations for the Standing Consultative Commission Governing procedures, composition and other relevant matters.

Article XV

1. This Treaty shall be of unlimited duration.

2. Each Party shall, in exercising its national sovereignty, have the right to withdraw from this Treaty if it decides that extraordinary events related to the subject matter of this Treaty have jeopardized its supreme interests. It shall give notice of its decision to the other Party six months prior to withdrawal from the Treaty. Such notice shall include a statement of the extraordinary events the notifying Party regards as having jeopardized its supreme interests.

Major Provisions of the Interim Agreement between the United States of America and the Union of Soviet Socialist Republics on Certain Measures with Respect to the Limitation of Strategic Offensive Arms*

Article I

The Parties undertake not to start construction of additional fixed land-based intercontinental ballistic missile (ICBM) launchers after July 1, 1972.

Article II

The Parties undertake not to convert land-based launchers for light ICBMs, or for ICBMs of older types deployed prior to 1964, into land-based launchers for heavy ICBMs of types deployed after that time.

Article III

The Parties undertake to limit submarine-launched ballistic missile (SLBM) launchers and modern ballistic missile submarines to the numbers operational and under construction on the date of signature of this Interim Agreement, and in addition to launchers and submarine constructed under procedures established by the Parties, replacements for an equal number of ICBM launchers of older types deployed prior to 1964 or for launchers on older submarines.

Article IV

Subject to the provisions of this Interim Agreement, modernization and replacement of strategic offensive ballistic missiles and launchers covered by this Interim Agreement may be undertaken.

Article V

1. For the purpose of providing assurance of compliance with the provisions of this Interim Agreement, each Party shall use national technical means of verification at its disposal in a manner consistent with generally recognized principles of international law.

2. Each Party undertakes not to interfere with the national technical means of verification of the other Party operating in accordance with paragraph 1 of this Article.

3. Each Party undertakes not to use deliberate concealment measures which impede verification by national technical means of compliance with the provisions of this Interim Agreement. This obligation shall not require changes in current construction, assembly, conversion, or overhaul practices.

---

*Selections from text of interim agreement done at Moscow on 26 May 1972. Not published in *Scientific American*.

Article VIII

1. This Interim Agreement shall enter into force upon exchange of written notices of acceptance by each Party, which exchange shall take place simultaneously with the exchange of instruments of ratification of the Treaty on the Limitation of Anti-Ballistic Missile Systems.

2. This Interim Agreement shall remain in force for a period of five years unless replaced earlier by an agreement on more complete measures limiting strategic offensive arms. It is the objective of the Parties to conduct active follow-on negotiations with the aim of concluding such an agreement as soon as possible.

3. Each Party shall, in exercising its national sovereignty, have the right to withdraw from this Interim Agreement if it decides that extraordinary events related to the subject matter of this Interim Agreement have jeopardized its supreme interests. It shall give notice of its decision to the other Party six months prior to withdrawal from this Interim Agreement. Such notice shall include a statement of the extraordinary events the notifying Party regards as having jeopardized its supreme interests.

Protocol to the Interim Agreement

The United States of America and the Union of Soviet Socialist Republics, hereinafter referred to as the Parties.

Having agreed on certain limitations relating to submarine-launched ballistic missile launchers and modern ballistic submarines and to replacement procedures, in the Interim Agreement,

Have agreed as follows:

The Parties understand that, under Article III of the Interim Agreement, for the period during which that Agreement remains in force:

The U.S. may have no more than 710 ballistic missile launchers on submarines (SLBMs) and no more than 44 modern ballistic missile submarines. The Soviet Union may have no more than 950 ballistic missile launchers on submarines and no more than 62 modern ballistic missile submarines.

Additional ballistic missile launchers on submarines up to the above mentioned levels, in the U.S.—over 656 mentioned ballistic missile launchers on nuclear-powered submarines, and in the U.S.S.R.—over 740 ballistic missile launchers on nuclear-powered submarines, operational and under construction, may become operational as replacements for equal numbers of ballistic missile launchers of older types deployed prior to 1964 or of ballistic missile launchers on older submarines.

The deployment of modern SLBMs on any submarine, regardless of type, will be counted against the total level of SLBMs permitted for the U.S. and the U.S.S.R.

Agreed Interpretations and Unilateral Statements

1. Agreed Interpretations

(a) *Initialed Statements.*—The texts of the statements set out below were agreed upon and initialed by the Heads of the Delegations on May 26, 1972.

ABM TREATY

[A]

The Parties understand that, in addition to the ABM radars which may be deployed in accordance with subparagraph (a) of Article III of the Treaty, those non-phased-array ABM radars operational on the date of signature of the Treaty within the ABM system deployment area for defense of the national capital may be retained.

[B]

The Parties understand that the potential (the product of mean emitted power in watts and antenna area in square meters) of the smaller of the two large phased-array ABM radars referred to in subparagraph (b) of Article III of the Treaty is considered for purposes of the Treaty to be three million.

[C]

The Parties understand that the center of the ABM system deployment area centered on the national capital and the center of the ABM system deployment area containing JCBM silo launchers for each Party shall be separated by no less than thirteen hundred kilometers.

[D]

The Parties agree not to deploy phased-array radars having a potential (the product of mean emitted power in watts and antenna area in square meters) exceeding three million, except as provided for in Articles III, IV and VI of the Treaty, or except for the purposes of tracking objects in outer space or for use as national technical means of verification.

[E]

In order to insure fulfillment of the obligation not to deploy ABM systems and their components except as provided in Article III of the Treaty, the Parties agree that in the event ABM systems based on other physical principles and including components capable of substituting for ABM interceptor missiles, ABM launchers, or ABM radars are created in the future, specific limitations on such systems and their components would be subject to discussion in accordance with Article XIV of the Treaty.

[F]

The Parties understand that Article V of the Treaty includes obligations not to develop, test or deploy ABM interceptor missiles for the delivery by each ABM interceptor missile of more than one independently guided warhead.

[G]

The Parties understand that Article IX of the Treaty includes the obligation of the US and the USSR not to provide to other States technical descriptions or blueprints specially worked out for the construction of ABM systems and their components limited by the Treaty.

INTERIM AGREEMENT

[H]

The Parties understand that land-based ICBM launchers referred to in the Interim Agreement are understood to be launchers for strategic ballistic missiles capable of ranges in excess of the shortest distance between the northeastern border of the continental U.S. and the northwestern border of the continental USSR.

[I]

The Parties understand that fixed land-based ICBM launchers under active construction as of the date of signature of the Interim Agreement may be completed.

[J]

The Parties understand that in the process of modernization and replacement the dimensions of land-based ICBM silo launchers will not be significantly increased.

[K]

The Parties understand that dismantling or destruction of ICBM launchers of older types deployed prior to 1964 and ballistic missile launchers on older submarines being replaced by new SLBM launchers on modern submarines will be initiated at the time of the beginning of sea trials of a replacement submarine, and will be completed in the shortest possible agreed period of time. Such dismantling or destruction and timely notification thereof, will be accomplished under procedures to be agreed in the Standing Consultative Commission.

[L]

The Parties understand that during the period of the Interim Agreement there shall be no significant increase in the number of ICBM or SLBM test and training launchers, or in the number of such launchers for modern land-based heavy ICBMs. The Parties further understand that construction or conversion of ICBM launchers at test ranges shall be undertaken only for purposes of testing and training.

(b) *Common Understandings.*—Common understanding of the Parties on the following matters was reached during the negotiations:

A. INCREASE IN ICBM SILO DIMENSIONS

Ambassador Smith made the following statement on May 26, 1972:

The Parties agree that the term "significantly increased" means that an increase will not be greater than 10–15 percent of the present dimensions of land-based ICBM silo launchers.

Minister Semenov replied that this statement corresponded to the Soviet understanding.

B. LOCATION OF ICBM DEFENSES

The U.S. Delegation made the following statement on May 26, 1972:

Article III of the ABM Treaty provides for each side one ABM system deployment area centered on its national capital and one ABM system deployment area containing ICBM silo launchers. The two sides have registered agreement on the following statement: "The Parties understand that the center of the ABM system deployment area centered on the national capital and the center of the ABM system deployment area containing ICBM silo launchers for each Party shall be separated by no less than thirteen hundred kilometers." In this connection, the U.S. side notes that its ABM system deployment area for defense of ICBM silo launchers, located west of the Mississippi River, will be centered in the Grand Forks ICBM silo launcher deployment area. (See Initialed Statement [C].)

C. ABM TEST RANGES

The U.S. Delegation made the following statement on April 26, 1972:

Article IV of the ABM Treaty provides that "the limitations provided for in Article III shall not apply to ABM systems or their components used for development or testing, and located within current or additionally agreed test ranges." We believe it would be useful to assure that there is no misunderstanding as to current ABM test ranges. It is our understanding that ABM test ranges encompass the area within which ABM components are located for test purposes. The current U.S. ABM test ranges are at White Sands, New Mexico, and at Kwajalein Atoll, and the current Soviet ABM test range is near Sary Shagan in Kazakhstan. We consider that non-phased array radars of types used for range safety or instrumentation purposes may be located outside of ABM test ranges. We interpret the reference in Article IV to "additionally agreed test ranges" to mean that ABM components will not be located at any other test ranges without prior agreement between our Governments that will be such additional ABM test ranges.

On May 5, 1972, the Soviet Delegation stated that there was a common understanding on what ABM test ranges were, that the use of the types of non-ABM radars for range safety or instrumentation was not limited under the Treaty, that the reference in Article IV to "additionally agreed" test ranges was sufficiently clear, and that national means permitted identifying current test ranges.

D. MOBILE ABM SYSTEMS

On January 28, 1972, the U.S. Delegation made the following statement:

Article V (1) of the Joint Draft Text of the ABM Treaty includes an undertaking not to develop, test, or deploy mobile land-based ABM systems and their components. On May 5, 1971, the U.S. side indicated that, in its view, a prohibition on deployment of mobile ABM systems and components would rule out the deployment of ABM launchers and radars which were not permanent fixed types. At that time, we asked for the Soviet view of this interpretation. Does the Soviet side agree with the U.S. side's interpretation put forward on May 5, 1971?

On April 13, 1972, the Soviet Delegation said there is a general common understanding on this matter.

E. STANDING CONSULTATIVE COMMISSION

Ambassador Smith made the following statement on May 22, 1972:

The United States proposes that the sides agree that, with regard to initial implementation of the ABM Treaty's Article XIII on the Standing Consultative Commission (SCC) and of the consultation Articles to the Interim Agreement on offensive arms and the Accidents Agreement,* agreement establishing the SCC will be worked out early in the follow-on SALT negotiations; until that is completed, the following arrangements will prevail: when SALT is in session, any consultation desired by either side under these Articles can be carried out by the two SALT Delegations; when SALT is not in session, *ad hoc*

---

*See Article 7 of Agreement to Reduce the Risk of Outbreak of Nuclear War Between the United States of America and the Union of Soviet Socialist Republics, signed Sept. 30, 1971.

arrangements for any desired consultations under these Articles may be made through diplomatic channels.

Minister Semenov replied that, on an *ad referendum* basis, he could agree that the U.S. statement corresponded to the Soviet understanding.

F. STANDSTILL

On May 6, 1972, Minister Semenov made the following statement:

In an effort to accommodate the wishes of the U.S. side, the Soviet Delegation is prepared to proceed on the basis that the two sides will in fact observe the obligations of both the Interim Agreement and ABM Treaty beginning from the date of signature of these two documents.

In reply, the U.S. Delegation made the following statement on May 20, 1972:

The U.S. agrees in principle with the Soviet statement made on May 6 concerning observance of obligations beginning from date of signature but we would like to make clear our understanding that this means that, pending ratification and acceptance, neither side would take any action prohibited by the agreements after they had entered into force. This understanding would continue to apply in the absence of notification by either signatory of its intention not to proceed with ratification or approval.

The Soviet Delegation indicated agreement with the U.S. statement.

2. UNILATERAL STATEMENTS

(*a*) The following noteworthy unilateral statements were made during the negotiations by the United States Delegation:

A. WITHDRAWAL FROM THE ABM TREATY

On May 9, 1972, Ambassador Smith made the following statement:

The U.S. Delegation has stressed the importance the U.S. Government attaches to achieving agreement on more complete limitations on strategic offensive arms, following agreement on an ABM treaty and on an Interim Agreement on certain measures with respect to the limitation of strategic offensive arms. The U.S. Delegation believes that an objective of the follow-on negotiations should be to constrain and reduce on a long-term basis threats to the survivability of our respective strategic retaliatory forces. The USSR Delegation has also indicated that the objectives of SALT would remain unfulfilled without the achievement of an agreement providing for more complete limitations on strategic offensive arms. Both sides recognize that initial agreements would be steps toward the achievement of more complete limitations on strategic arms. If an agreement providing for more complete strategic offensive arms limitations were not achieved within five years, U.S. supreme interests could be jeopardized. Should that occur, it would constitute a basis for withdrawal from the ABM Treaty. The U.S. does not wish to see such a situation occur, nor do we believe that the USSR does. It is because we wish to prevent such a situation that we emphasize the importance the U.S. Government attaches to achievement of more complete limitations on strategic offensive arms. The U.S. Executive will inform the Congress, in connection with Congressional consideration of the ABM Treaty and the Interim Agreement, of this statement of the U.S. position.

B. LAND-MOBILE ICBM LAUNCHERS

The U.S. Delegation made the following statement on May 20, 1972:

In connection with the important subject of land-mobile ICBM launchers, in the interest of concluding the Interim Agreement the U.S. Delegation now withdraws its proposal that Article I or an agreed statement explicitly prohibit the deployment of mobile land-based ICBM launchers. I have been instructed to inform you that, while agreeing to defer the question of limitation of operational land-mobile ICBM launchers to the subsequent negotiations on more complete limitations on strategic offensive arms, the U.S. would consider the deployment of operational land-mobile ICBM launchers during the period of the Interim Agreement as inconsistent with the objectives of that Agreement.

C. COVERED FACILITIES

The U.S. Delegation made the following statement on May 20, 1972:

I wish to emphasize the importance that the United States attaches to the provisions of Article V, including in particular their application to fitting out or berthing submarines.

D. "HEAVY" ICBM'S

The U.S. Delegation made the following statement on May 26, 1972:

The U.S. Delegation regrets that the Soviet Delegation has not been willing to agree on a common definition of a heavy missile. Under these circumstances, the U.S. Delegation believes it necessary to state the following: The United States would consider any ICBM having a volume significantly greater than that of the largest light ICBM now operational on either side to be a heavy ICBM. The U.S. proceeds on the premise that the Soviet side will give due account to this consideration.

E. TESTED IN ABM MODE

On April 7, 1972, the U.S. Delegation made the following statement:

Article II of the Joint Text Draft uses the term "tested in an ABM mode," in defining ABM components, and Article VI includes certain obligations concerning such testing. We believe that the sides should have a common understanding of this phrase. First, we would note that the testing provisions of the ABM Treaty are intended to apply to testing which occurs after the date of signature of the Treaty, and not to any testing which may have occurred in the past. Next, we would amplify the remarks we have made on this subject during the previous Helsinki phase by setting forth the objectives which govern the U.S. view on the subject, namely, while prohibiting testing of non-ABM components for ABM purposes: not to prevent testing of ABM components, and not to prevent testing of non-ABM components for non-ABM purposes. To clarify our interpretation of "tested in an ABM mode," we note that we would consider a launcher, missile or radar to be "tested in an ABM mode" if, for example, any of the following events occur: (1) a launcher is used to launch an ABM interceptor missile, (2) an interceptor missile is flight tested against a target vehicle which has a flight trajectory with characteristics of a strategic ballistic missile flight trajectory, or is flight tested in conjunction with the test of an ABM interceptor missile or an ABM radar at the same test range, or is flight tested to an altitude inconsistent with interception of targets against which air defenses are deployed, (3) a radar makes measurements on a cooperative target vehicle of the kind referred to in item (2) above during the reentry portion of its trajectory or makes measurements in conjunction with the test of an ABM radar at the same test range. Radars used for purposes such as range safety or instrumentation would be exempt from application of these criteria.

F. NO-TRANSFER ARTICLE OF ABM TREATY

On April 18, 1972, the U.S. Delegation made the following statement:

> In regard to this Article [IX], I have a brief and I believe self-explanatory statement to make. The U.S. side wishes to make clear that the provisions of this Article do not set a precedent for whatever provision may be considered for a Treaty on Limiting Strategic Offensive Arms. The question of transfer of strategic offensive arms is a far more complex issue, which may require a different solution.

G. NO INCREASE IN DEFENSE OF EARLY WARNING RADARS

On July 28, 1970, the U.S. Delegation made the following statement:

> Since Hen House radars [Soviet ballistic missile early warning radars] can detect and track ballistic missile warheads at great distances, they have a significant ABM potential. Accordingly, the U.S. would regard any increase in the defenses of such radars by surface-to-air missiles as inconsistent with an agreement.

(b) The following noteworthy unilateral statement was made by the Delegation of the U.S.S.R. and is shown here with the U.S. reply:

On May 17, 1972, Minister Semenov made the following unilateral "Statement of the Soviet Side":

> Taking into account that modern ballistic missile submarines are presently in the possession of not only the U.S., but also of its NATO allies, the Soviet Union agrees that for the period of effectiveness of the Interim 'Freeze' Agreement the U.S. and its NATO allies have up to 50 such submarines with a total of up to 800 ballistic missile launchers thereon (including 41 U.S. submarines with 656 ballistic missile launchers). However, if during the period of effectiveness of the Agreement U.S. allies in NATO should increase the number of their modern submarines to exceed the numbers of submarines they would have operational or under construction on the date of signature of the Agreement, the Soviet Union will have the right to a corresponding increase in the number of its submarines. In the opinion of the Soviet side, the solution of the question of modern ballistic missile submarines provided for in the Interim Agreement only partially compensates for the strategic imbalance in the deployment of the nuclear-powered missile submarines of the USSR and the U.S. Therefore, the Soviet side believes that this whole question of liquidating the American missile submarine bases outside the U.S., will be appropriately resolved in the course of follow-on negotiations.

On May 24, Ambassador Smith made the following reply to Minister Semenov:

> The United States side has studied the "statement made by the Soviet side" of May 17 concerning compensation for submarine basing and SLBM submarines belonging to third countries. The United States does not accept the validity of the considerations in that statement.

III

SALT II: Limited Negotiations

III

SALT II:
Limited Negotiations

INTRODUCTION

When formal negotiations resumed at Geneva on 21 November 1972, the military situation seemed conducive to arms restraint. Both the United States and the Soviet Union possessed secure retaliatory forces, and no developments that might endanger either side's assured destruction capability were imminent. The threat of a disarming first strike was—and still remains—nonexistent. Moreover, even in the extreme hypothetical case of a disarming first strike, not only the attacked nation but also the aggressor could expect to suffer from the disastrous aftereffects of nuclear war. A report based on a National Academy of Sciences study concludes:

> It now appears that a massive attack with many large scale nuclear detonations could cause such widespread and long-lasting environmental damage that the aggressor country might suffer serious physiological, economic, and environmental effects even without a nuclear response by the country attacked.

Large reductions in the numbers of bombers and missile launchers and stringent constraints on MIRV deployments were possible without jeopardizing mutual assured destruction. The United States had accumulated thousands of 1-megaton-equivalent weapons, even though only 200 such weapons, according to official Department of Defense estimates, would promptly destroy about 20 percent of the Soviet population and over 70 percent of its industrial capacity. It is estimated that only 140 one-megaton-equivalent weapons would do comparable damage to the United States. (These estimates exclude fatalities from fallout as well as worldwide, long-term human and environmental effects.) Furthermore, SALT I prohibitions against the establishment of nationwide ABM defenses had apparently removed the main incentive for deploying MIRVs—ABM penetration. In light of the ABM Treaty, and because the counterforce potential of MIRVs threatened both arms race and crisis stability, further deployment seemed contrary to the security interests of both sides.

A stable strategic balance presented a unique opportunity to reduce nuclear stockpiles and to impose constraints on the qualitative improvement of the strategic forces. Accordingly, at a summit meeting in Washington in 1973, the two sides agreed to seek both quantitative and qualitative limitations during the second round of negotiations. But despite the seemingly hospitable climate for achieving progress at SALT, some five years elapsed without substantive breakthroughs in the negotiations. At the time of this writing, some major differences had been resolved. Others were still unresolved, and a SALT II agreement appeared months away. This delay is cause for disappointment, as is the awesome strategic buildup that took place during this six-year period.

The 1972 Interim Agreement set a precedent for strategic offensive arms reductions, but it also provided a framework for an intensified arms race. While SALT II negotiations foundered, both the United States and the Soviet Union continued to modernize their strategic forces and to stockpile nuclear weapons. From 1972 through 1977, each side's arsenal nearly doubled in size. The U.S. inventory grew from 5,700 weapons to over 9,000, while Soviet deployments increased from 2,200 weapons to just under 4,000. The United States now has 3,600 one-megaton-equivalent weapons, which represents ten times the destructive power required to devastate the Soviet Union. The Soviets have 5,870 one-megaton-equivalent weapons. In his fiscal year (FY) 1979 *Annual Report*, Secretary of Defense Harold Brown asserted that the United States must have the capability to destroy a minimum of 200 major Soviet cities, which contain 34 percent of the Soviet population (70 million people) and 62 percent of the industrial capacity. Between 300 and 400 one-megaton-equivalent weapons would probably accomplish this objective.

After SALT I the Soviets completed their developmental testing of MIRVs, and in 1975 they began to deploy them on fourth-generation, silo-based ICBMs. The latest-generation ICBMs—the SS-16, SS-17, SS-18, and SS-19—are more powerful and accurate than their predecessors. The SS-16 has probably been deployed in fixed silos and may have been recently deployed in a mobile mode. A fifth generation of ICBMs is about to enter the flight-testing stage. In accuracy and reliability, this generation promises to be the equal of existing U.S. ICBMs. From 1972 to 1978, Soviets also doubled the range of their SLBMs; christened a new "Delta-class" ballistic missile submarine (SSBN) and developed a new SSBN called the Typhoon; flight-tested their first MIRVed SLBM; deployed a modern tactical bomber, the Backfire, having a minor strategic capability; and deployed within range of China a new intermediate-range ballistic missile (IRBM), the SS-20, which may soon be deployed in European Russia and which, with minor modifications, could be converted to an ICBM. Although the Soviets also upgraded their strategic bomber defenses, recent studies conclude that through the late 1980s they could not deploy significant air defenses against penetrating bombers.

U.S. modernization also emphasized qualitative improvements. In 1977 the United States completed its MIRV program, just as the Soviets were entering the early stages of MIRV deployment. The United States modified 550 Minuteman ICBMs and 496 Poseidon SLBMs to carry MIRV warheads. Other qualitative efforts concentrated on developmental programs. The Trident submarine and the Trident ballistic missile, which Scoville examined in an article in Part II, will achieve operational status by 1981. The satellite global positioning system, a constellation of 24 navigation satellites that will transform Trident missiles into highly accurate and deadly counterforce weapons, advanced rapidly toward deployment in the early 1980s. The United States moved toward full-scale development of the bigger and more accurate MX mobile ICBM, which would replace Minuteman, and developed the B-1 bomber. The MK-12A warhead with a 400-kiloton yield was developed to replace 900 of the 1,650 MIRVs carried by Minuteman. Along with guidance improvements for all 1,650 MIRVs, the increased yield of the MK-12A over current MIRV yield (170 kilotons) will significantly increase the hard-target-kill capabilities of the early 1980s Minuteman force. According to the *FY 1979 Arms Control Impact Statement*, these improvements could enable the Minuteman force to destroy over half of the Soviet ICBM force.

Also, in 1972 the United States initiated a program for developing long-range cruise missiles that could be nuclear tipped and launched from a variety of carrier platforms. Under consideration as platforms were jumbo jets, strategic bombers, naval ships, and submarines. The promise of highly accurate (0.01 n.m.) air-launched cruise missiles (ALCMs) for penetrating air defenses and destroying even hardened targets like missile silos led President Carter to cancel the B-1 bomber program in favor of a "stand-off" bomber force. Stand-off bombers will be designed to fire ALCMs from distances that extend beyond the range of Soviet air defenses; the cruise missile then flies on a low-altitude course that in theory would defeat any defensive system that the Russians could devise.

Thus, although the 1972 Interim Agreement succeeded in imposing quantitative ceilings on strategic offensive weapons, the arms momentum did not abate. The high ceilings of SALT I simply diverted the momentum into unrestricted areas—a problem that Rathjens and others call the "displacement effect."

As a result, each side may be developing the ability to mount a successful first strike against the other's land-based missiles, though not against submarine-launched missiles. The problem is compounded by improvements in missile accuracies and the increased number of missiles that have been MIRVed. Analysts often rate the "lethality" of a nuclear warhead against a point target using a measure K, which is the yield of the warhead in megatons to the two-thirds power divided by the square of the CEP (miss distance in nautical miles). (A nautical mile is about 1.15 statute miles, or 1.8 kilometers.)

Because improvements in accuracy increase K much more than do greater weapon yields, the highly accurate American warheads, even though usually smaller than Soviet ones, have had greater lethality. Still greater accuracies will make U.S. missiles a major threat to the survival of Soviet land-based forces. On the other hand, as the Soviet Union increases its number of MIRVs and improves their accuracy, it may be able to destroy most of the American land-based Minutemen. Table 3.1 shows the situation in 1975 and 1978, a period of rapid improvements in Russian missiles. By itself, the table portrays nothing more than a trend of parallel technological change for each missile force. To measure force effectiveness, data bases for the target systems must be introduced, and the vulnerability of the hardened targets must be computed. Despite the increases in total lethality over the past few years, the land-based missiles on both sides remain relatively secure. This situation may soon change. The thought of both sides having first-strike capabilities raises great fears for the stability of deterrence in times of crisis, if either side depended primarily on land-based forces for deterrence. *But so long as the sea-based forces are large and secure*—a questionable assumption in the case of the Soviet submarine force—*and so long as neither side is pursuing a major counterforce strategy with war-winning illusions, the vulnerability of land-based ICBMs need not upset crisis stability.*

To some extent the formal negotiating process itself exacerbates the problem referred to as displacement. Several drawbacks of formal negotiations warrant attention.

The Slow Tempo of Negotiations. The negotiating process is slow, and it is becoming increasingly laborious and time consuming. On the American side, much of the delay stems from domestic criticism of negotiating positions, from political upheavals such as "Watergate," and from presidential campaigns and administration changes. On the Soviet side, the Soviet SALT delegation lacks any real negotiating authority and must obtain instructions from Moscow on practically every detail, however minute.

More and more time and energy are devoted to the unfinished agenda of the previous round of SALT. Differences set aside during or created by SALT I were reasserted quickly at SALT II. For example, the Soviets sought to carry over to SALT II the numerical ceilings established by SALT I, insisted that U.S. forward-based weapons be counted against SALT II limits, and demanded that ceilings on Soviet deployments be raised automatically if the British or French increased their force of ballistic missile submarines. These lingering problems slowed progress at SALT II and have yet to be resolved permanently. Although the Soviets have compromised at Geneva on each of these divisive issues, they will surely reassert them when and if the third round of talks—SALT III—convenes.

The issues grow progressively more complex. The protection of silo-based ICBMs presented an especially difficult problem. At first the United States sought to reduce Soviet missile "throw-weight"—missile payload consisting of guidance systems, re-entry vehicles, explosives, etc.—by cutting back the number of their "heaviest" missiles. The United States regarded heavy missiles, which could be armed with many high-yield and increasingly accurate MIRVs, as a potential threat to the U.S. Minuteman force and therefore offered to cut the U.S. force of B-52 strategic bombers in exchange for Soviet throw-weight concessions.

The Soviets rejected this proposal as well as a later U.S. contention that Soviet throw-weight superiority should be offset by U.S. superiority in the number of permissible MIRV launchers. Two years and two summits—the Washington summit of 1973 and the Moscow summit of 1974—failed to produce a compromise. Instead, the two sides produced in late 1974 the Vladivostok Accords, which imposed a ceiling—2,400 strategic delivery vehicles, of which 1,320 could be MIRV launchers—that was so high as to be meaningless from the standpoint of ICBM protection. After Vladivostok, SALT II faltered as the result of U.S. resistance to limitations on its cruise missiles and Soviet resistance to controls on its Backfire bomber. In addition, the two sides could not agree to a counting rule for verification of MIRVed ballistic missiles. Satellite photography could not distinguish silos containing the single-warhead version of a particular type of missile from those containing the MIRVed version. The United States sought, and recently obtained, a rule that would count against MIRV ceilings all launchers for any type of missile that had been tested in a MIRV configuration. All SS-18 silos, for example, are to be counted against the MIRV ceiling,

Table 3.1 Strategic Missile Forces Deployed by the United States and the U.S.S.R., 1975 and 1978

Missile	Explosive yield of warhead (Mt)		CEP of reentry vehicle (naut. mi.)		Lethality per reentry vehicle (K)		No. of reentry vehicles per missile		Total no. of missiles		Total Lethality of missile force ($K \times N$)	
	1975	1978	1975	1978	1975	1978	1975	1978	1975	1978	1975	1978
					United States							
ICBMs												
Minuteman III	0.17	0.17	0.2	0.15	5	13.7	3	3	550	550	8,250	22,605
Minuteman II	1	1.1	0.3	0.3	11	11.8	1	1	450	450	4,950	5,310
Titan	5	7.4	0.5	0.35	12	31	1	1	54	54	648	1,674
SLBMs												
Poseidon	0.05	0.04	0.3	0.25	1.5	1.9	10	8	496	496	7,440	7,539
Polaris	0.2	0.2	0.5	0.5	1.4	1.4	3	3	160	160	672	672
TOTAL											21,960	37,800
					U.S.S.R.							
ICBMs												
SS-9	20	25	1.0	0.5	7	34.1	1	1	288	183	2,016	6,240
SS-11, SS-13	1	0.5–1.5	1.0	0.55–1.5	1	0.8–2.1	1	1–3	970	778	970	2,187[a]
	—	0.8	—	0.35	—	7.0	—	4	0	70	0	1,960
SS-18/mod. 1	—	25	—	0.3	—	94.8	—	1	0	40	0	3,792
SS-7, SS-8	5	—	1.5	—	1.3	—	1	—	209	—	270	0
SS-18/mod. 2	—	2	—	0.25	—	25.4	—	8–10	0	55	0	12,573
SS-18/mod. 3	—	15	—	0.25	—	97.1	—	1	0	30	0	2,913
SS-19/mod. 1	—	0.6	—	0.3	—	7.9	—	6	0	230	0	10,902
SLBMs												
SS-N-6	1	1.5	1.5	0.55	1	4.3	1	1	528	384	528	1,651
SS-N-8	1	2.0	1.5	0.5	1	6.4	1	1	80	344	80	2,202
SS-N-17	—	2.0	—	0.3	—	17.6	—	1	0	70	0	1,232
SS-N-18	—	0.2	—	0.3	—	3.8	—	3	0	60	0	684
TOTAL											3,864	46,336

NOTE: Estimates for 1975 and 1978 differ in some cases because of different data sources rather than because of missile improvements.
[a]Sum of 48 SS-13s (1 meg., 1.1 CEP, 1 RV) + 490 SS-11/mod. 1s (1.5 meg., 1.25 CEP, 1 RV) + 240 SS-11/mod. 3s (0.5 meg., 0.55 CEP, 3 RVs).
SOURCES: 1975 estimates from "The Accuracy of Strategic Missiles" by Kosta Tsipis. Copyright © 1975 by Scientific American, Inc. All rights reserved. 1978 estimates based on data provided by Robert P. Berman and data from "Beyond SALT II: A Projection of Strategic Force Levels and Costs of U.S. and U.S.S.R.," by John C. Baker and Robert P. Berman, unpublished working paper prepared for the Conference on Economic Consequences of Arms Control Agreements, Harvard University, April 1978.

Table 3.2 Long-Range and Medium-Range Nuclear Delivery Vehicles, (excluding ICBM/SLBM), 1977

Ballistic missiles	United States				U.S.S.R.			
	Type	Range (mi.)	Speed (mach)	No. deployed	Type	Range (mi.)	Speed (mach)	No. deployed
M/IRBM	—	—	—	—	SS-4	1,200	—	500
					SS-5	2,300	—	100
					SS-20	3,000	—	20
Long-range bombers	B-52D	11,500	0.95	80	TU-95 Bear	8,000	0.78	100
	B-52G-H	12,500	0.95	269	Mya-4 Bison	6,000	0.87	35
Medium range bombers	Fb-111A	3,800	2.5	68	TU-16 Badger	4,000	0.80	740
					Backfire B	3,500–6,000	2.5	65
Land-based strike	A11 (Europe-based only)	—	—	350	A11	—	—	1,000
Carrier-based strike	A11	—	—	200	—	—	—	—

even though some will contain the single-warhead version of the SS-18.

At the same time, weapons technology raced forward. In 1975 the Soviets began to convert their heavy missile—the SS-9—from a single-warhead to a multiple-warhead configuration—the SS-18. Some SS-9s were converted to single-warhead SS-18s. The Soviets also initiated a modernization program that would convert the SS-11—a light and unMIRVed missile comparable to the American Minuteman II ICBM—to a heavy and MIRVed weapon system known as the SS-19.

As Soviet flight-testing steadily improved the accuracy of the SS-18 and the SS-19, it became apparent that the displacement effect had outpaced the negotiations, nullifying the results of the 1972 Interim Agreement and the 1974 Vladivostok Accords. A sweeping proposal was required to reverse or even moderate the growing threat to each side's land-based force of ballistic missiles. Such an initiative was made after the election of President Carter and the appointment of Paul Warnke as chief U.S. SALT negotiator. Carter's so-called comprehensive SALT proposal called for relatively stringent limits on the number of land-based MIRV launchers and heavy missiles, an annual quota on the number of ballistic missile flight tests, and a ban on mobile ICBMs and strategic cruise missiles.

But even this landmark proposal, which the Russians rebuffed on the grounds that it would give the United States a unilateral military advantage, could not assure the survivability of silo-based ICBMs. Pentagon officials indicated that a ceiling of 550 MIRVed ICBMs—the level suggested in the Carter plan—would not preclude ICBM vulnerability in the early to mid 1980s. It is now believed that missile accuracy and reliability rather than throw-weight or MIRV numbers are the critical factors in developing a near disarming counterforce capability against silo-based missiles. Once again the displacement effect would nullify the results of even a comprehensive agreement, in this case one that addressed yesterday's threat—MIRVs and throw-weight. Secretary Brown, in his FY 1979 *Annual Report*, said, "It is doubtful that this situation can be reversed by a negotiated accord."

Some basic data on comparative strengths and characteristics of Soviet and U.S. nuclear delivery vehicles are given in Tables 3.2 and 3.3.

Table 3.3 U.S.-Soviet Strategic Balance, 1978

	United States		U.S.S.R.	
	Deliverable warheads[a]	Equivalent megatonnage[b]	Deliverable warheads[a]	Equivalent megatonnage[b]
ICBM	2,154	1,192	3,633	4,474
SLBM	4,448	628	932	1,037
Long-range bombers	2,536	1,784	210	357
TOTAL	9,138	3,604	4,775	5,870

NOTE: These are estimates of static strategic capability derived from Tables 3.1 and 3.2. These measurements are useful in comparing force size but provide limited information about force effectiveness. More elaborate indices can be used to portray effectiveness, but this requires the enumeration of factors not shown here, such as accuracy and defensive capability (see Figure 3.1).

[a]This measures the number of targets that each side can attack. Only separately targetable delivery vehicles are included in missile totals. Bomber totals assume both stand-off missile and gravity bomb deployment.

[b]Equivalent megatonnage measures damage to unprotected area targets. Assuming that a warhead falls within the boundary of the target area, the equivalent megatonnage of a specific weapon is expressed as the two-thirds power of its explosive yield, or $Y^{2/3}$.

SOURCES: International Institute for Strategic Studies (IISS), *The Military Balance, 1977–1978*, London: IISS, 1977, pp. 77–81; J. Baker and R. Berman "Beyond SALT II: A Projection of Strategic Force Levels and Costs of the U.S. and U.S.S.R.," paper prepared for the Conference on Economic Consequences of Arms Control Agreements, Harvard University, April 1978; Library of Congress, *Major U.S. Foreign and Defense Policy Issues*, Washington, D.C.: Government Printing Office, 1977.

Dysfunctions in the Negotiating Process. Ironically, the negotiating process itself can stimulate the arms race. The principle of strategic parity, which both sides appear to endorse, has been defined as "symmetry" (in part because the Jackson amendment to the SALT I agreement dictates such a guideline). The drawback to setting symmetrical limits, whether quantitative or qualitative, is that it is much easier to set equal high ceilings than equal low ceilings. The principle of symmetry tends to drive deployments up rather than down, as it has done in the case of the high ceilings on strategic delivery vehicles and MIRV launchers agreed to at Vladivostok. Soviet MIRV levels will come up the American level, even though Soviet accuracy refinements will then create a new threat to the United States.

The negotiating process helps sustain the arms race in another way: it creates incentives to procure weapons for "bargaining chips." Since the late 1960s, the bargaining chip rationale has been used to support most of the major strategic weapons programs in the United States. Many observers believe this stimulus caused the deployment of some weapons systems—for instance, ABM—that would not have been procured otherwise. This rationale is also a stimulus for the initiation of certain weapons programs—for instance, the cruise missile.

Such programs tend to become less negotiable as they move into advanced stages of development. Over time, they strengthen their bases of support in numerous political and bureaucratic interests; as support solidifies, the weapons are portrayed as essential to national security and become nonnegotiable.

A related rationale is known as "bargaining from a position of strength." Here, the weapon is usually nonnegotiable; its procurement is seen as a means of intimidating the other side into granting concessions. The U.S. MIRV program is often cited as an example of this type of bargaining lever. The MaRV guidance system may be the next such instrument.

The Political and Bureaucratic Imperative. The price of domestic support for a negotiating stance or a final agreement is often paid in the form of concessions to critics. Various factions receive assurances that favored weapons programs will be supported by the administration in exchange for SALT support. Promises of this kind, such as those made to gain support for the Limited Test Ban Treaty and SALT I, help sustain the arms competition and complicate future negotiations. The MX, multiple-aim-point basing, and improved bomber defenses may be the price of SALT II ratification.

SALT: The Symbol and the Institution. A common view of SALT is that it is more a symbol of détente and a means of keeping détente alive than a means of controlling the arms race. Accordingly, the results of SALT are often cosmetic, glossing over substantive disagreements on the most vital issues. For instance, the 1974 Moscow summit produced a protocol that further restricted ABM deployment, but it did not break any deadlocks in the SALT II negotiations. The United States and the Soviet Union agreed not to construct the second ABM complex allowed by the 1972 ABM treaty—a symbolic gesture having utterly no military significance.

A few analysts criticize the institutionalization of SALT, charging that the various domestic agencies that govern SALT activities have assumed the well-known characteristics of large bureaucracies. Certain practices and procedures have grown rigid and less relevant to the most serious security problems facing each side.

The combination of these shortcomings—the inability to prevent arms technology from eluding, outpacing, and nullifying arms agreements; the inclination to build up to symmetry, to create bargaining chips, and to underwrite certain weapons programs in exchange for political support; the dominance of form over substance; and institutional inflexibility—has led to a sharp decline in faith in the value of strategic arms talks.

These failings have led the United States to seek unilateral solutions to security problems such as ICBM vulnerability. Unfortunately, the prominent solutions under consideration do not bode well either for the future of SALT or for reducing the risk of nuclear war. The main alternatives for protecting ICBMs include: (1) ABM defense of the silo-based force, an approach that would require abrogation or amendment of the 1972 ABM Treaty, (2) an expensive, multiple-aim-point system for MX missiles, which would create verification roadblocks while dramatically increasing U.S. counterforce capability against Soviet land-based forces, and (3) launch-on-warning strategy for a vulnerable missile force, the dangers of which are all too obvious.

Our inability to control the scope and intensity of the arms race cannot be blamed solely on the failings of the negotiating process. That the arms race persists, even when conditions seem to favor restraint, suggests that our knowledge of its causes and mechanisms is incomplete. The six articles in this section lend further insight into a complex and poorly understood phenomenon. Two dominant themes in the articles are the following: (1) a clear picture of the arms race relies on an understanding of the organizational, political, and bureaucratic context in which weapons acquisitions occur; and (2) counterforce rather than assured destruction provides the main stimulus and rationale for arms procurement today.

In the first article, entitled "Multiple-Warhead Missiles," Herbert F. York traces the development of the MIRV program from its inception to its deployment. He finds that MIRV evolved from many independent and seemingly unrelated goals and decisions, and he concludes that this diffuseness made MIRV deployment practically inevitable. York argues that even without the stimulus of ABM deployments around Moscow, the MIRV program would probably have been devised and probably at about the same time. Certainly it was *deployed* without the stimulus of substantial Soviet ABM deployments. As noted previously, the 1972 ABM Treaty placed stringent limitations on ABM deployment.

York rejects simple explanations of the arms race, such as action-reaction dynamics. He stresses the contextual factors—organizational, political, and bureaucratic—

which underlie weapons acquisitions like MIRV. Some programs—the ABM and the B-70 and B-1 strategic bombers—can be terminated despite strong support because they are expensive, addressed to an obvious and single purpose, and dependent on a centralized decision-making process. Other programs such as MIRV seem immune. They acquire momentum because the decisions to research, develop, or deploy them are diffuse and incremental, because they are relatively inexpensive, and because they are multipurpose systems that can be promoted by expedient and changing rationales. The cruise missile, MX, and terminal guidance MaRV systems may be more like MIRV than like the bombers in this respect.

One rationale for improving strategic forces is counterforce strategy. The second article, written by Barry Carter and entitled "Nuclear Strategy and Nuclear Weapons," presents a critique of the counterforce strategy, which former Secretary of Defense James Schlesinger revived in 1974. Carter points out that the main reason offered for improving counterforce capabilities against Soviet military targets—including hardened missile silos—is that the United States must match Soviet counterforce improvements. Counterforce matching has been a key element of policy throughout the 1970s. Beginning with Nixon's doctrine of strategic "sufficiency," counterforce equivalence assumed an importance equal to assured destruction. President Carter's strategic doctrine—"essential equivalence"—stresses counterforce as well. *Counterforce matching has emerged as the single most powerful stimulant of the strategic arms race.*

As a form of action-reaction, counterforce matching presents a familiar security dilemma: Both sides seem compelled by it, even though the result may be a mutual, disarming first-strike capability. Defense Secretary Brown recently said, "The United States has no desire for or plans to develop a first strike, disarming capability against the Soviet Union. Accordingly, we shall not seek such a capability provided that the Soviets show similar restraint toward the United States."

But even if the Russians and Americans show restraint, the fact remains that incremental counterforce improvements are constantly made because of improved computers and computer software, better rocket fuels, more accurate measurement of the gravitational fields surrounding launch and target points, and so forth. In addition, there are the quantum jumps in counterforce capability made possible by such innovations as terminal guidance maneuverable re-entry vehicles (MaRVs). Carter discusses this invention and its strategic implications.

If current trends persist, even the submarine force will acquire the capability to knock out hardened missile silos and command centers. The overall trend is clear—and ominous. Strategic forces on both sides are acquiring the characteristics of "damage-limiting" weapons designed for optimal use in a preemptive attack.

Counterforce matching as an acquisitions policy rests on the premise that U.S. strategic forces should not be *perceived* as inferior in performance to Soviet forces. Counterforce strategy as a wartime policy rests on the premise that such a war could be fought and possibly won without catastrophic destruction and without escalating to all-out war. In the words of former Secretary of Defense James Schlesinger, "the likelihood of limited nuclear attacks cannot be challenged on the assumption that massive civilian fatalities and injuries would result."

In the third article, entitled "Limited Nuclear War," Sidney Drell and Frank von Hippel attempt to answer the question "Would the casualties really be few?" After evaluating scenarios postulated by the Department of Defense, the authors reach several related conclusions that challenge Schlesinger's argument:

1. Soviet counterforce strikes causing relatively few casualties would be militarily insignificant.
2. Militarily significant strikes would cause civilian casualties so devastating that the idea of a limited counterforce war loses all meaning.
3. After even the most devastating counterforce attack that could be reasonably postulated, the United States could still strike back with enormous destructive power. Therefore, counterforce strategy would appear to be ineffective and self-defeating from the Soviet point of view.

American strategic forces currently possess some capability for flexible response and city avoidance. In the event of a limited Soviet attack on the United States, it *might* therefore be possible to limit the war for a short time, during which urgent negotiations could proceed. The idea of avoiding massive, deliberate attacks on population centers is attractive on humanitarian and moral grounds. Yet the *ability* to do so, in terms of highly sophisticated communications, command, and control facilities, is very much in doubt. The lack of these facilities makes one question the wisdom of any attempt to carry on a major counterforce war against strategic missile silos or to initiate first use of nuclear weapons under any circumstances. In the article entitled "Enhanced Radiation Weapons," Fred M. Kaplan voices similar concerns and reservations in the context of tactical nuclear warfare. Kaplan examines the so-called neutron bomb, which he characterizes as "the latest development in the U.S. military's search for a 'cleaner,' more usable nuclear weapon." Kaplan presents the case against its deployment. The neutron bomb, urged by many as a means for defending Western Europe against a massive Soviet conventional attack, was a major strategic and political issue in 1978.

The main purpose of President Carter's "comprehensive" SALT proposal was to slow down the counterforce arms race and to protect ICBMs. Herbert Scoville, Jr., examines the Carter proposal in the fifth article of this section, "The SALT Negotiations." Although the Soviets rejected the plan, Scoville finds it useful for illustrating the major current issues in arms control. He discusses the counterforce issues that have complicated the negotiations, especially the difficulty of controlling qualitative advances in technology.

After the Soviets turned down the Carter plan, along with a proposal that would have confirmed the Vladivostok ceilings and deferred for future consideration U.S. cruise missiles and Soviet Backfire bombers, talks resumed within a new three-part framework. The new framework consists of a treaty, a protocol, and a statement of principles for SALT III. Table 3.4 shows the tentative details contained within the new framework at the time of this writing.

Controls on the Soviet Backfire bomber may be agreed to, but perhaps outside the contractual forms of the package. The Soviets indicated willingness to declare intentions not to employ the bomber in an intercontinental role, not to deploy it in ways that might threaten the United States, and not to increase its production rate above the current level. The United States reportedly asked for specific guarantees to restrict its basing and refueling capability.

The Russians balked at the statement of principles proposed by the United States, objecting to fixed numerical targets and reasserting the principle that U.S. and allied forward-based nuclear weapons be counted against future ceilings. Among the elements of the protocol, limitations on "new types of ballistic missiles" had yet to be worked out, and controls on cruise missiles remained in dispute. The Russians sought to limit long-range cruise missiles to aircraft platforms and to deny cruise missile technology to allies of the United States.

Cruise missile technology is revolutionary. Kosta Tsipis examines the technology in his article "Cruise Missiles." There is little to add to the analysis, except to point out that cruise missile verification presents a more difficult problem than Tsipis indicates. He suggests that it is possible, using national technical means of verification, to distinguish tactical from strategic cruise missiles; but it is not now possible because the U.S. Navy has decided to use a turbofan engine instead of a turbojet for the tactical version. Since both short- and long-range versions will have the same type of engine, they will not be distinguishable by their emissions. Furthermore, the use of long-wave infrared sensors on early warning satellites to monitor cruise missile flight tests is not technologically feasible at present. The sensor technology is a decade or so away, and the Soviet Union probably could not deploy the sensors before the end of the century. Finally, it should be noted that a cruise missile built for long range can be quite adequately tested at short range. In fact, for many test purposes, a full-scale wind tunnel demonstration is better than actual flight demonstration at full range. For these and many other reasons, the verifiability of most controls on cruise missiles is extremely limited.

Even if the delegations settle the remaining unresolved issues, the SALT II agreement will be far from ideal. Mainly, it does not contain sufficiently stringent limitations on counterforce weapons and technologies. Many critics fear that the agreement will sanction Soviet war-fighting superiority. As Carter, Drell and von Hippel, and Kaplan have argued in their articles, however, the validity of limited war scenarios is questionable. *Any* use of nuclear weapons carries an extremely high risk of retaliation and escalation and thus is likely to be self-defeating. While stringent controls on counterforce weaponry is to be expected of SALT, expecting the codification of counterforce equivalence is asking too much. The specification of such codification presents an intractable problem inasmuch as modern nuclear forces are composed of quite different geographical, technological, institutional, and human constraints. Counterforce equivalence is usually expressed either in terms of *perceived* or *mathematical* equality. The former defies specification, much less general agreement. The latter is an unrealistic abstraction, compounded of number, size, accuracy, reliability, etc., which usually succeeds only in misinforming and complicating the problem.

The proponents of SALT II contended that the package under negotiation would enhance national security in several ways:

1. Although the Soviets protected their freedom to improve their forces, they also made significant concessions. They dropped their insistence that American forward-based systems be limited by SALT II, even though these weapons are a direct threat to Soviet territory. The Soviets agreed to (1) some constraint on the Backfire, even though it appears designed for theater and naval missions; (2) U.S. deployment of ALCMs, even though Soviet technology lags far behind and Soviet verification is problematic; and (3) a reduction in the total number of their strategic delivery vehicles without requiring any reduction in the total number of our strategic delivery vehicles. For the first time since SALT began, some 300 fewer Soviet strategic launch vehicles would be available for attacking the United States. The Soviets also agreed to a MIRV counting rule that in effect will lower the MIRV ceiling for the Soviets but not for the United States.

2. The sublimit (820) on MIRVed ICBMs would force the Soviets to deploy a fair proportion of MIRVs at sea. Many analysts view this as a favorable shift toward a more balanced, survivable, and stable force.

3. Although the SALT II ceilings are high, the accords would remove much of the uncertainty that leads to faulty estimates of future Soviet capabilities.

4. Depending on final details of the protocol, the agreement would delay the deployment of Soviet mobile missiles as well as the development of fifth-generation Soviet ICBMs.

5. The package may enhance America's bargaining leverage after the protocol expires. The weapon that most concerns the Soviet Union is the cruise missile, which is controlled only for the duration of the three-year protocol. The weapons that most concern the United States are MIRVed ICBMs, which are controlled for the duration of the eight-year agreement.

6. Failure to sign or ratify SALT II could (a) terminate a useful strategic arms dialogue, (b) stimulate the spread of nuclear weapons to other countries, (c) destroy the chances of success in arms control efforts, such as chemical weapons control, a comprehensive test ban, and mutual and balanced force reductions in Europe, (d) render impossible the control of dangerous new technologies, such as antisatellite weapons and lasers,

Table 3.4 The Anticipated SALT II Package

Part I. The Treaty (valid through 1985)	
1. Ceiling on total launcher numbers (includes ICBMs, SLBMs, and long-range bombers; excludes the Soviet Backfire)	
At ratification	2,400
By 1982	2,250
2. Limits on MIRVed missiles plus bombers armed with cruise missiles	
Total	1,320
Subceiling on MIRVed missiles	1,200
Subceiling on MIRVed ICBMs	820
3. Total number of modern large ballistic missiles	308
4. Rapid reload systems (combination of "cold-launch" missile sites plus spare missiles) to be banned.	

Part II. The Protocol (valid through 1980)

1. Ban on deployment of mobile ICBM launchers and on the flight testing of ICBMs from such launchers.
2. Ban on the flight testing and deployment of cruise missiles with ranges exceeding 2,500 kilometers (1,550 statute miles) and on the deployment of cruise missiles with ranges exceeding 600 kilometers (370 statute miles) on sea- or land-based launchers.
3. Limitations on the flight testing and deployment of new types of ballistic missiles.

Part III: Statement of Principles (U.S. proposal)

1. Reducing the aggregate number of launchers to between 1,800 and 2,000.
2. Reducing the subceiling on MIRVed missiles to between 1,000 and 1,100.
3. A lower subceiling on MIRVed ICBMs.
4. A lower limit on the number of modern large ballistic missiles.
5. Further restrictions on the development, testing, and deployment of new ICBMs and SLBMs.
6. Restrictions on the flight testing of ICBMs and SLBMs.
7. Further restrictions on strategic defensive systems, including air defense and civil defense.
8. Steps to strengthen verification.

(e) lead to the abrogation of existing agreements such as the ABM treaty, (f) seriously strain Soviet-American relations, and (g) unleash the most furious arms race to date.

Many observers, ourselves included, sometimes fall victim to a very narrow perspective on SALT. We tend to focus on the limited benefits of SALT—economic, political, and military—rather than the substantial costs that would accrue without it. For example, should SALT II and III succeed, the amount of direct dollar savings would probably be small. Without these agreements, however, U.S. strategic force expenditures would rise substantially. According to a recent study, if SALT II is ratified but SALT III negotiations break down, U.S. strategic force expenditures between 1985 and 1995 could increase as much as $4 billion annually. Major investment costs of strategic defensive systems could add an extra $3.5 billion annually. Baker and Berman summarize the economic implications of SALT:

> It appears that while a SALT II agreement will not result in large direct savings it may have a significant indirect impact on strategic force expenditures by creating a context for defense decisionmaking which reduces the uncertainties and the need to plan as much for the worst case. The effective removal of the threat of a large-scale Soviet ABM system and some type of ceilings on Soviet offensive weapon deployments have reduced the risks that the defense planner must live with. Consequently, many major strategic weapon programs have now become questions of "either/or" rather than "both." An example of this in the past could include the "B-1 or ALCM" decision

of last year and in the future, a "MX ICBM or Trident II SLBM" decision. Without SALT, all of the systems would probably be deployed.

After SALT II, assuming it is signed and ratified, President Carter may have a unique opportunity to make further progress in limiting strategic weapons. Developments in world affairs may impel the Soviets to make further accommodations with the United States. East-West relations in Europe are stable at present. The major actors on the European scene have, as a result of Germany's *Ostpolitik*, accepted the division of Germany and of Europe. The Sino-Soviet conflict and the Soviet deployment of a large defensive force on the Chinese border have enhanced the Soviet interest in stability with the West. Soviet-American cooperation in the Middle East has begun. Finally, the Soviets face the probability of reduced economic growth and an energy shortage over the next decade; they may seek long-term credits from the West, including the United States, especially to develop oil and gas reserves. Internal economic pressures to slow the growth of defense expenditures and to maintain a stable relationship with the United States will build.

If Soviet-American relations improve and if President Carter and General Secretary Brezhnev provide direction and purpose to the relationship—commensurate with the supreme importance of preventing nuclear war—then significant arms reductions may be possible. The easy part of SALT—the still high ceilings of SALT II—is over. The hard part—significant reductions—lies ahead.

10 Multiple-Warhead Missiles

by Herbert F. York
November 1973

MIRV's increase the number of strategic nuclear weapons and now threaten the stability of the nuclear balance of power. Their history shows why they present special problems of arms control

From 1945 to 1970 the number of nuclear warheads in the U.S. strategic arsenal went from zero to about 4,000. From 1970 to mid-1975 the number will increase to almost 10,000. This increase, about half of which has already been achieved, is made possible by a single development in military technology: the multiple independently targeted reentry vehicle (MIRV).

The MIRV system enables a single rocket to launch several warheads, which can be aimed at separate targets or made to approach the same target on different trajectories. Two of its characteristics may have important consequences for military strategy. First, MIRV's are better able to penetrate an anti-ballistic-missile (ABM) system than missiles with a single warhead. Second, because MIRV warheads are numerous and can be guided with great accuracy, MIRV's could lead to an effective "counterforce" weapon, one capable of destroying a very large part of an adversary's retaliatory forces if used in a surprise attack. Counterforce weapons are usually considered the most disruptive to the strategic balance, because they threaten the deterrent on which national security is presumed to depend. A measure of how threatening MIRV's can seem was provided in August, when the U.S. Department of Defense announced that the U.S.S.R. had made its first successful test of a MIRV missile. The Secretary of Defense, James R. Schlesinger, cited the flight test as evidence that the Russians "are seeking a strategic advantage."

In actuality it is highly unlikely that MIRV's could affect the ultimate outcome of a nuclear war between the U.S. and the U.S.S.R. It seems clear that each has ample power to destroy the society of the other, with or without multiple-warhead missiles and whether or not a surprise attack destroys the opposing force. By generating fears of the other side's intentions, however, MIRV's could affect the likelihood that a nuclear war will occur. Thus in the peculiar logic of the nuclear arms race the possession of a potent weapon may diminish national security rather than enhance it. In this context I shall discuss what the MIRV system is and how it works, what its antecedents were in the U.S. arms program and why the decision to build it was made. Finally I shall examine why efforts to stop its development and deployment failed.

Few details of the operation of multiple-warhead missiles have been made public. The dimensions and mass of the individual warheads, for example, have not been revealed, nor has the maximum separation of targets been stated. A general, nonnumerical explanation of the MIRV system can nevertheless be given. It is based on statements made by officials of the Department of Defense, on testimony given before Congressional committees and on data published by nongovernment organizations such as the Stockholm International Peace Research Institute (SIPRI). In addition certain characteristics of the MIRV missile can be inferred from the operation of related devices known to have preceded MIRV's in the weapons and space programs. With this information it is possible to describe a hypothetical flight of a MIRV missile (*see illustration on pages 124 and 125*).

For this purpose let the missile be a land-based intercontinental ballistic missile (ICBM) carrying three independently aimed warheads. (Minuteman III is such a missile.) In the initial stages of flight the main rocket motors put the missile on a trajectory calculated to terminate near the first of the three selected targets. When the fuel of the last of the main rocket stages is exhausted, the final stage containing the warheads and their associated apparatus separates from the rocket and coasts on toward apogee, the point of greatest altitude. The apogee for ICBM's is typically about 800 miles.

Once the stage containing the warheads has separated from the larger stages, propulsion and guidance are provided by the post-boost control system (PBCS), the most important component of the MIRV system [*see illustration on next page*]. The final stage, consisting of the warheads and the PBCS, is often called the "bus"; it carries the warheads as passengers to be discharged at intervals. The bus has an inertial guidance system and small rockets that can modify its velocity and attitude.

After a brief period of coasting the bus refines its trajectory until it is aimed as precisely as possible at the first target. It then gently ejects one of the warheads. In satellite programs that were precursors of MIRV this ejection was accomplished with small springs in compression; the MIRV system could have a similar mechanism.

When the first warhead has been released, the bus alters its course in preparation for releasing the second. It can do this in several ways. First, the bus can increase its speed in the direction of its original orbit, causing the second warhead to impact "downrange," or farther away than the first. A decrease in speed, brought about by firing the rocket in a direction opposite to the direction of motion, will cause the warhead to land "uprange," or closer to the launching site. Another mode of deflection is perpendicular to the plane of the original trajectory. Impulses in this direction will aim the warhead at targets in an arc on each side of the initial target. Finally, by giving the bus an impulse in the plane of the original trajectory but roughly perpendicular to its direction, the second warhead can be aimed at the same target as the first. The second will approach from a higher or lower angle, however, and its arrival will be delayed by as much as several minutes. Ordinarily there would be movement on all three axes.

When the second weapon has been released, the bus is reoriented once again, this time on a new trajectory terminating at the third target. If more than three warheads are incorporated in the bus, the process is repeated until all have been launched at their targets. Several kinds of decoys and other "penetration aids" might also be released with some or all of the warheads.

Numerous engineering compromises are necessary in the design of the bus. The maximum separation between the targets, for example, depends primarily on the total impulse available from the bus propulsion system and therefore on the payload weight allotted to it. MIRV's now in use by the Navy and the Air Force can evidently reach targets separated by distances on the order of a few hundred miles, or a few percent of the total range of the missiles.

A more obvious compromise is that between the number of warheads and their aggregate explosive power, or "yield." Some yield is always lost in the transition from single to multiple warheads. Even in multiple-warhead missiles that do not provide separate guidance for each reentry vehicle much weight, and therefore yield, must be sacrificed to extra heat-shielding for reentry into the atmosphere and to the diseconomies of smaller scale.

For true MIRV's the ratio is even less favorable, because the weight of the post-boost control system as well as that of the shielding must be subtracted from the payload available for the weapons themselves. The engineering is also more complicated, because the missile-maker has more options: he can choose to emphasize wider separation of targets, higher multiplicity of warheads, greater overall range, more penetration aids or higher yield. Presumably, optimum compromises have been found for all these choices; they depend on the nature of the target being attacked and on the defenses to be overcome.

The Department of Defense has not disclosed the yield of the warheads carried by the U.S. missiles now equipped with MIRV's. Estimates have been made, however, that for the purposes of this discussion are sufficiently reliable. (The figures given here are those published by SIPRI.)

Even if the precise yield of a warhead were known, it would be difficult to calculate the amount sacrificed in converting to multiple warheads, since in each case MIRV's were introduced in new missiles that had never carried single warheads. The Navy's Poseidon, for example, is a larger missile than the Polaris it is replacing, and it has twice the payload. Nevertheless, it is estimated to have a smaller yield. The last Polaris to carry a single warhead is reported to have had a yield of about one megaton. The Poseidon is usually said to carry 10 warheads of 50 kilotons each, for a total yield of about half a megaton.

A better indication of the compromises required may be given by the Minuteman III, an Air Force ICBM. The single-warhead versions of Minuteman had yields estimated at from one megaton to two megatons; Minuteman III is said to have three independently aimed warheads of 200 kilotons each, suggesting again that the aggregate yield is one-half or less.

It is important to note that a reduction in total yield does not necessarily imply a reduction in destructive effect. Megatonnage and "throw weight" are not reliable indicators of the destructive capability of nuclear weapons. A better measure is the circular area within which a given warhead will cause some specified degree of damage; this in turn is a function of the "blast overpressure." For overpressures high enough to be effective against military targets the radius of destruction increases roughly as the cube root of the explosive yield; the area of destruction, therefore, increases as the two-thirds power of the yield. For example, if a one-kiloton device could destroy a particular target within an area of one square mile, then to produce

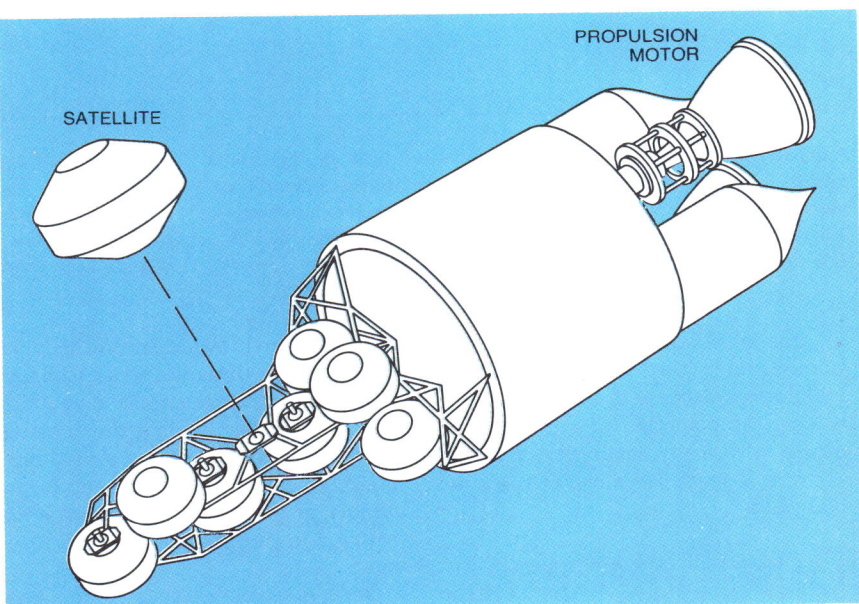

TRANSTAGE, a post-boost control system used with the Titan III booster rocket, is shown carrying defense communication satellites, which it was used to launch beginning in 1966. The satellites are mounted in a tubular frame and are ejected by small springs. The Transtage was the immediate predecessor of the MIRV system used in the Minuteman III ICBM and has been said to incorporate all the essential technology of a MIRV warhead.

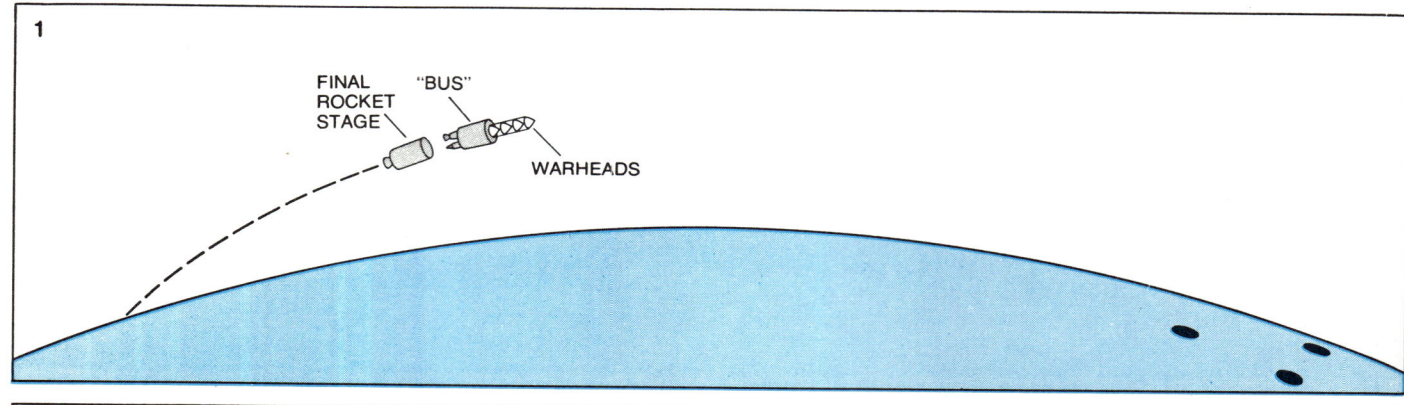

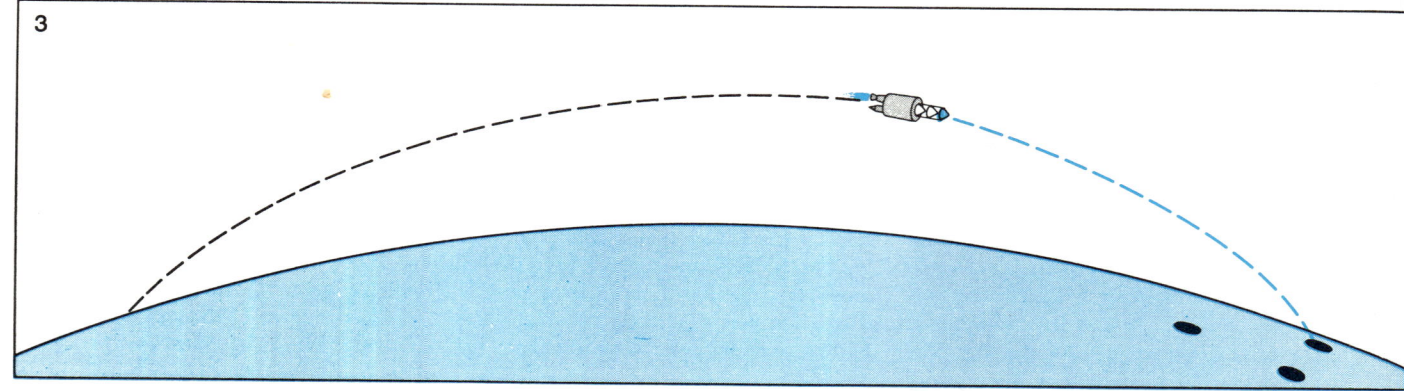

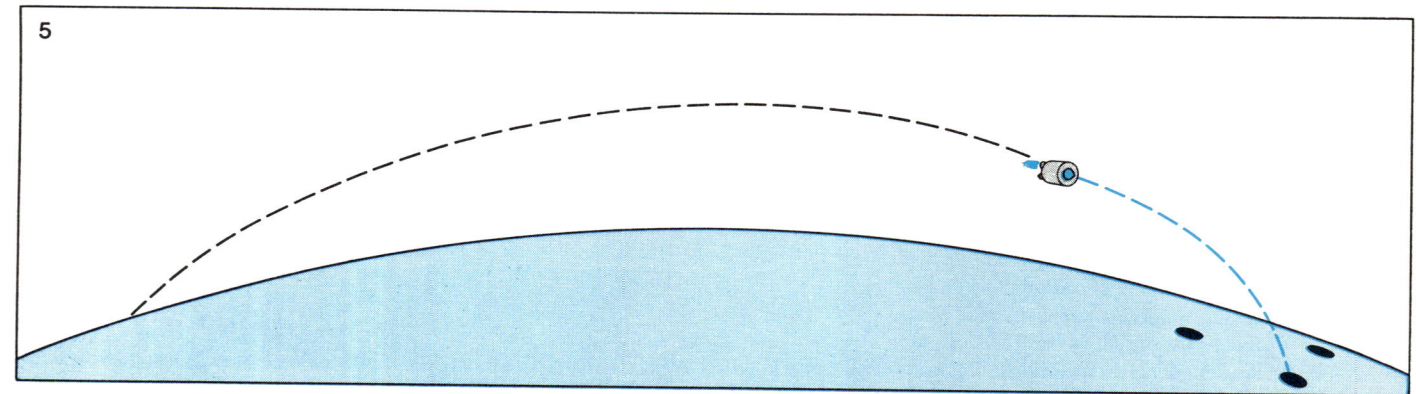

POST-BOOST CONTROL SYSTEM, or "bus," is at the heart of MIRV; its operation is illustrated schematically in these drawings, which show a hypothetical flight of a bus carrying four warheads. When the last of the main rocket stages is exhausted (*1*), the bus, with the warheads attached, separates from it. After coasting briefly the bus adjusts its trajectory until it is aimed as accurately as possible at the first of the selected targets. The first of the warheads is then gently ejected (*2*) and will continue to follow the ballistic trajectory to the target. After firing its rocket motor to add an increment of speed the bus ejects another warhead (*3*), which will

an area of destruction of two square miles would require a warhead of about 2.8 kilotons. Because of this exponential relation the potential for destruction is greater with many small weapons than it is with a single large one of the same total yield.

The history of how multiple-warhead missiles came to be developed in the 1960's and how they came to be deployed in the early 1970's provides an interesting lesson in the structure and operation of the military and military research organizations. The technology necessary for MIRV's evolved from research directed toward several independent and quite disparate goals. Ideas and personnel were exchanged among the various programs, so that the course of development became not a thread but a fabric. It could have been cut in any number of places without seriously impeding the progress of the MIRV system.

Once the technology was developed MIRV assumed a momentum of its own; the chances of halting it were by then slim. In addition a number of quite different arguments were presented in favor of deployment, and apparently any one of several might have been sufficient to gain the necessary Congressional and Department of Defense approval. Many of the development decisions could have been countermanded on several occasions and the result would have been about the same: MIRV's on U.S. missiles at the beginning of the 1970's.

A convenient moment at which to begin an examination of the history of MIRV's is the launching of the first Russian artificial satellite in October, 1957. About a month after the satellite went into orbit, and at least partly in response to the launch, William M. Holaday, director of guided missiles in the Office of the Secretary of Defense, established

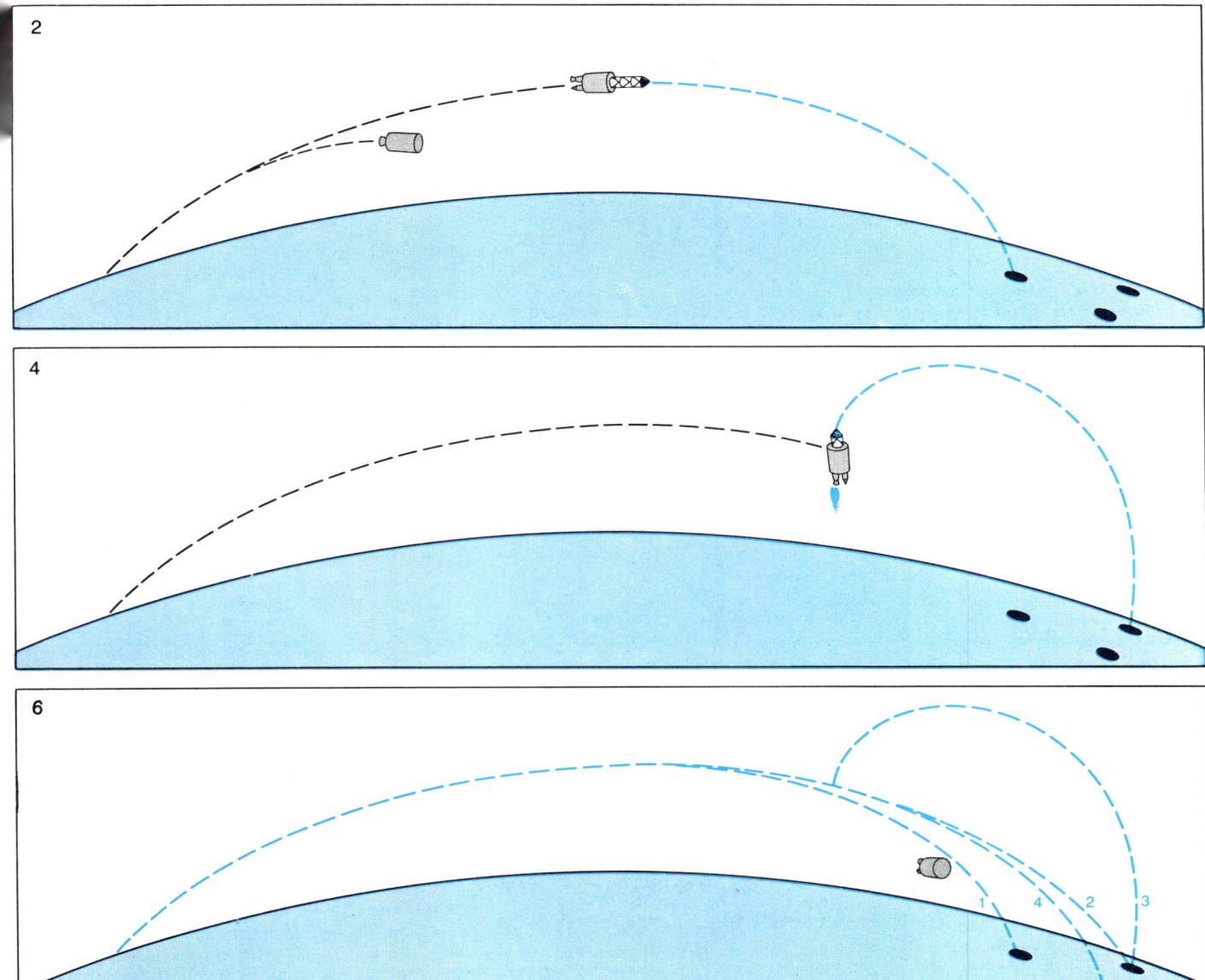

strike a target farther downrange. The bus next increases its velocity in a direction roughly perpendicular to the direction of the trajectory (4), placing the third warhead on a path that will lead it to the same target as the second but will delay its arrival by as much as several minutes. The last warhead is released after the bus has executed a final maneuver, adding a velocity increment in the plane that in this illustration is perpendicular to the page (5). Many other combinations of these movements are possible. Finally, the bus disintegrates on reentering the atmosphere and the warheads reach their assigned targets (6), although not simultaneously.

the Reentry Body Identification Group, with representatives from several agencies of the Department of Defense, from industry, from academic research departments and from such consulting firms as the Rand Corporation. The committee was formed to determine whether or not the designers of offensive ballistic missiles should consider seriously the possibility that defensive missiles might be built by the opposition. In early 1958 the committee reported that missile defense should be given consideration; it also described, however, a number of countermeasures available to the offense.

All but one of the countermeasures proposed by the Reentry Body Identification Group were intended to confuse the radars of the defenders. They included decoys, objects that to radar would resemble a warhead; booster fragments, pieces of the rocket-motor fuel tanks used as decoys but available at no weight penalty; chaff, small lengths of wire dispersed in space to act as a radar reflector; a reduced radar cross section for the warhead, and radar blackouts produced by exploding thermonuclear devices in the upper atmosphere. The remaining proposal, and the most important for this discussion, was the use of multiple warheads. Rather than confuse the defense, multiple warheads simply exhaust it. These countermeasures and others are what are collectively called penetration aids.

Decoys, even cheap and light ones, can approximate the characteristics of a warhead as long as both the decoys and the real weapons are in space, where all objects, regardless of mass and shape, follow ballistic trajectories. Once the decoys enter the atmosphere, however, they are slowed by air resistance to a greater extent than the heavier warheads, and the difference in velocity becomes progressively greater as the reentry bodies reach denser regions of

III | SALT II: LIMITED NEGOTIATIONS

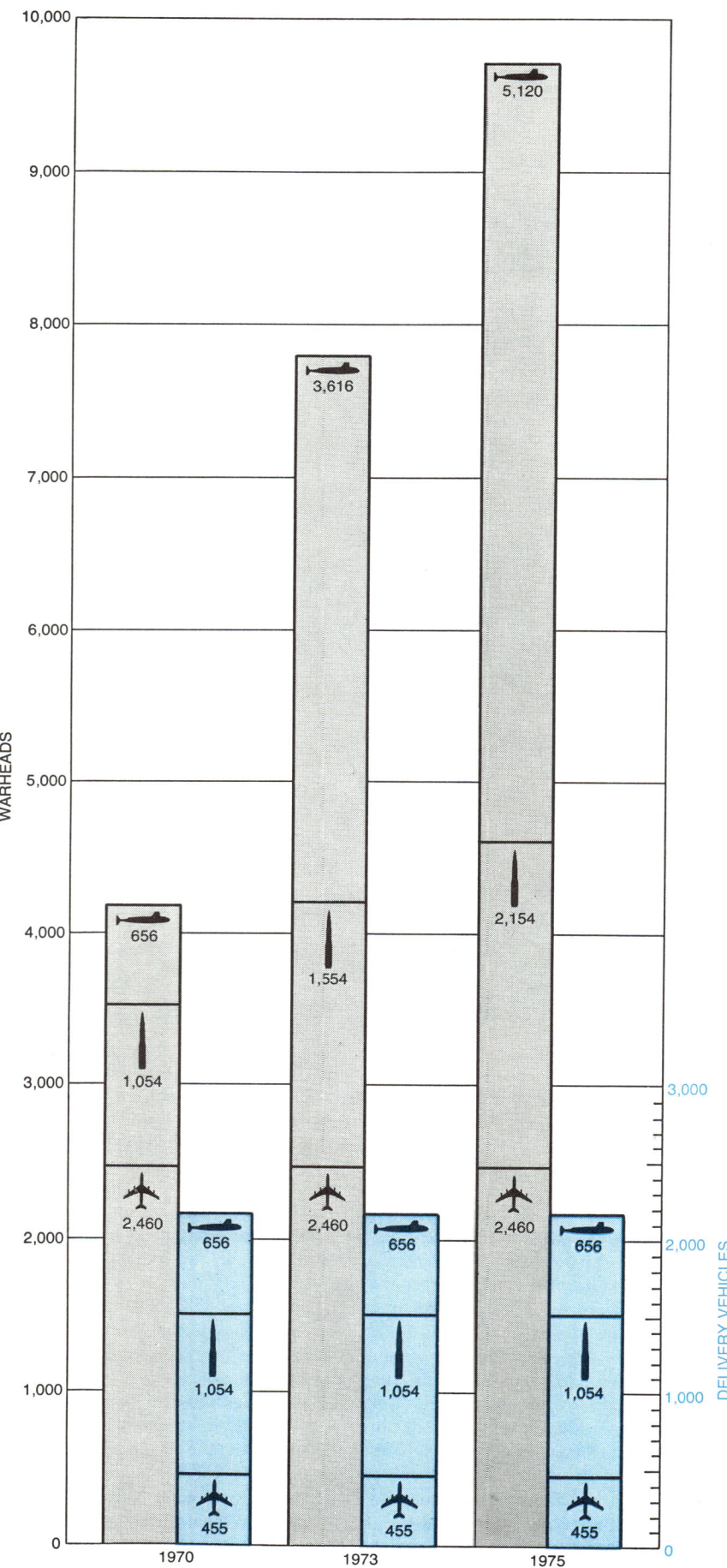

the atmosphere. Booster fragments, chaff and such light decoys as balloons covered with metal foil will disintegrate and burn up in the upper atmosphere. Thus the differential effects of the atmosphere on the reentry bodies enable the defense to discriminate between decoys and weapons (if it is willing to wait until well after they have entered the atmosphere) and to allocate defensive missiles only to the real weapons.

The solution for the offense is to use heavier decoys that will mimic the flight characteristics of real warheads to lower altitudes. As the weight of the decoys approaches that of the warhead itself, however, it becomes more efficient simply to use several warheads.

This was in fact the strategy adopted for the Polaris A-3, the last of the submarine-launched ballistic missiles (SLBM's) in the Polaris series. The A-3 is a multiple-reentry-vehicle (MRV) system with three warheads. The cluster is launched as a unit, on a trajectory chosen to guide it as accurately as possible to the single target. When the rocket has burned out, the three weapons are separated and given small additional impulses. They continue on separate but close trajectories and impact in a triangular pattern, presumably centered on the target. The missile might be compared in principle to a shotgun.

The dimensions of the triangle formed by the impact points of the warheads have never been made public, but the military situation as it was perceived in the late 1950's set obvious limits. The separation had to be more than a few tenths of a mile or all three warheads could have been destroyed by the explosion of a single antimissile missile. On the other hand, they could be no farther

NUMBER OF WARHEADS in the U.S. strategic force will increase almost two and a half times in the first half of the 1970's, even though the number of delivery vehicles (bombers, ICBM's and SLBM's, indicated in the graphs by symbols) will remain constant. The statistics are those published by the Stockholm International Peace Research Institute. The graph marked 1970 represents the force level before any MIRV's were installed; 1973 bars are for early in that year; figures for 1975 show the number of warheads when all Poseidon and Minuteman III MIRV's now planned are deployed. In these charts it is assumed that the Minuteman III carries three warheads and the Poseidon 10 warheads. MRV's are considered single warheads since each MRV assembly could be directed to only one target. The figures given for weapons carried by bombers are approximate and can change quickly.

apart than a few miles or the dimensions of the pattern would have exceeded the size of most cities in the U.S.S.R. The yield of each warhead is estimated to have been about 200 kilotons.

The first Polaris A-3's were deployed in 1964. Even before they joined the strategic-weapons force it was recognized that the MRV warhead would not be able to cope with improved ABM systems. By 1962 or 1963 progress in U.S. defensive missiles and the knowledge that Russian defenses were also being improved made it clear that the separation of warheads in the A-3 MRV was much too small to thwart any but a primitive ABM. Moreover, it was seen that the solution could not be found by increasing the horizontal spread of the impact points; to do so would make the pattern larger than most targets. Another solution was soon found: the MIRV.

The launching of the first Russian satellite and the launching of the first Russian ICBM (which had preceded the satellite by two months) stimulated in the U.S. an outburst of ideas about how to make and use satellites and missiles. The use of penetration aids, as we have seen, was one of the results of this process. Another was the concept of launching more than one satellite with a single rocket.

The earliest proposal of multiple satellite launchings of which I am aware was directed to defense against missile attack. This was the ballistic antimissile boost interceptor (BAMBI). The objective was to intercept an enemy's missiles during the first few minutes of flight, while the booster motors were still operating. Missiles were thought to be particularly vulnerable during this period because simply puncturing their propellant tanks could make them fall thousands of miles short of their target.

Two versions of BAMBI were proposed; both would have placed large numbers of satellites in orbits from which missiles could be detected and destroyed in the early stages of flight. One version, the random-barrage system, would have used many thousands of small satellites, launched by, say, hundreds of boosters. The other, called space patrol air defense (SPAD), would have deployed the small "killer" satellites in a "mother ship" equipped with central guidance and detection devices. On command the mother ship would have oriented itself and determined when, at what rate and in what direction to launch its subsatellites.

Neither of these systems was built, but they were studied on paper by the Advanced Research Projects Agency (ARPA) of the Department of Defense with help from the Rand Corporation. During the early years of ARPA (it was founded in 1958) there was an active interchange of technical personnel between the agency and industry and between the various companies most heavily involved in missile and space technology. As a result many of those who helped to fashion these early proposals were later members of the organizations that designed real multiple-warhead devices.

A quite unrelated development whose basic technology was later adapted to MIRV's was the Able-Star, a second-stage vehicle designed to be used with the Thor booster. It was the first spacecraft where the main propulsion rocket could be shut off and later restarted. The Able-Star used hypergolic propellants (substances that ignite on contact) and incorporated restart, guidance and control devices, a programmer and an accelerometer—all necessary to the operation of MIRV's.

The Able-Star was first tested in space in April of 1960. Two months later it was used in the first multiple satellite launch, in which a Transit II-A satellite and a Naval Research Laboratory solar radiation satellite were placed in near-circular orbits 500 miles above the earth. Once the Able-Star achieved the proper orbit the satellites were detached and separated by a compressed spring, giving the smaller satellite an additional velocity of 1.5 feet per second.

In a subsequent launch the Able-Star was used to place three satellites in similar orbits, although the procedure was only partly successful. In 1963 the Atlas-Agena rocket was used in a more difficult maneuver: placing a pair of satellites in very different orbits. Later versions of the Agena second stage, like the Able-Star, could be stopped and restarted during flight. The satellites, called Vela, were used to monitor compliance with the Limited Test-Ban Treaty of 1963. They were placed 180 degrees apart in orbits from 62,000 to 72,000 miles high.

The immediate technological ancestor of the Air Force version of MIRV was Transtage, a highly flexible post-boost control system. It was crucial in the development of the components and techniques used in MIRV's, yet it was devised for reasons unrelated to the effort to improve missiles and missile warheads.

Transtage was used with Titan III, which in the early 1960's was the largest of the U.S. booster rockets. Transtage had a propulsion system capable of coasting and restarting, like the Able-Star and the Agena, but it carried a larger payload and was capable of more complex and more extensive maneuvers. It was conceived without a specific mission in mind, and it was first used to launch a series of defense communication satellites called IDCSP (for initial defense communication satellite program).

The special requirements of defense communication demanded that the satellites be many and that their orbits be quite high. On June 16, 1966, a Titan III-C and Transtage placed eight 100-pound satellites in eight different equatorial orbits, all at an altitude of about 21,000 miles.

The operation of Transtage was comparable in almost all respects to that of the MIRV bus. Using its ability to coast and restart, it first achieved a near-circular orbit at the proper altitude with a period of 1,334.2 minutes. It gently nudged off one of the subsatellites with compressed springs. Then, with four vernier motors of 50 pounds' thrust (whose main purpose was controlling pitch and yaw), it added a small increment of velocity and ejected a second satellite.

This one would orbit at essentially the same altitude, but with a period of 1,334.7 minutes. The maneuver was repeated for each satellite, until the last was dropped off three minutes after the first in an orbit with a period of 1,347.6 minutes.

Three more groups of IDCSP satellites were launched, using the same technique, at intervals of about six months. The importance of the program in the development of MIRV's was indicated in 1968 by John S. Foster, Jr., the director of Defense Research and Engineering. Asked during his testimony before a Senate subcommittee why he was so confident the Minuteman III and Poseidon MIRV's would work, he cited the successful operation of Transtage as proof that all the essential engineering problems had been solved.

Another way to pursue the relation between these projects and the later MIRV missiles is through the contractors who produced them. For example, Agena was designed by the Lockheed Missiles and Space Company (a subsidiary of the Lockheed Aircraft Corporation), which later designed the Poseidon missile. Similarly, systems engineering for the Titan III and Transtage was done by the Aerospace Corporation, which later did the concept engineering for the

Minuteman III MIRV. Another company involved in the MIRV program for Minuteman was the Space Technology Laboratory of the Thompson Ramo Wooldridge Corporation, which had earlier participated in the Able-Star and Vela satellite programs. In the Air Force itself the Space and Missile Systems Office, which supervised the Transtage program, was soon to begin development of the Minuteman MIRV.

In addition to all these programs, bits and pieces of MIRV technology were invented or reinvented independently in the course of unrelated endeavors. One of them was a study by the Rand Corporation of what advantage the U.S.S.R. might gain from its relatively large missiles. Among other conclusions of the report was the possibility that such missiles might be used to deliver multiple warheads; a MIRV-like device was hypothesized as the means for doing so. Another was a study of orbital offensive weapons, conducted for the Air Force by seven competing firms. In an orbital bombardment system nuclear weapons would be placed in permanent orbit and brought down on their targets from space on receipt of coded instructions. Some of the proposals involved what was essentially a one-passenger bus. The system was never developed, but if it had been, the technology of MIRV's might well have been derived from it.

Another program that could have been used as a point of departure for MIRV was the sequential-payload-delivery system (SPD), used to deliver unarmed warheads from California to Kwajelein Atoll in the Pacific, where they served as test targets in the ABM program. The justification for this system was economic: it is cheaper to attack several targets with a single rocket than to use a separate rocket for each target. The design and construction of the sequential-payload-delivery system was supervised by the Aerospace Corporation, which had been responsible for Transtage.

Almost all the mechanisms and techniques used in MIRV's could also have been derived from the civilian National Aeronautics and Space Administration manned space program, particularly the systems used in lunar exploration. I have described here, however, only those programs that were addressed to some military purpose.

By the mid-1960's it was clear to military planners that a MIRV missile could be built. Even before then, in 1962 and 1963, two independent arguments had been put forward in support of deployment.

One was embodied in the "counterforce" speech given by Secretary of Defense Robert S. McNamara in Ann Arbor, Mich., in 1962. The notion of counterforce did not begin with McNamara; it was a part of military strategy before nuclear weapons were invented. It holds that one should plan to attack an adversary's weaponry, the "counterforce targets," rather than his cities and industries, the "countervalue targets." It is the strategy usually adopted by those who favor expanded deployment of weapons, and it is necessarily the strategy of those who contemplate making a preemptive surprise attack.

McNamara subsequently modified his position on counterforce, but the speech nevertheless stimulated the proposal of MIRV's as a means of increasing the number of targets that could be attacked. Indeed, there can be no doubt that in a counterforce strategy MIRV is a powerful weapon. In a preemptive at-

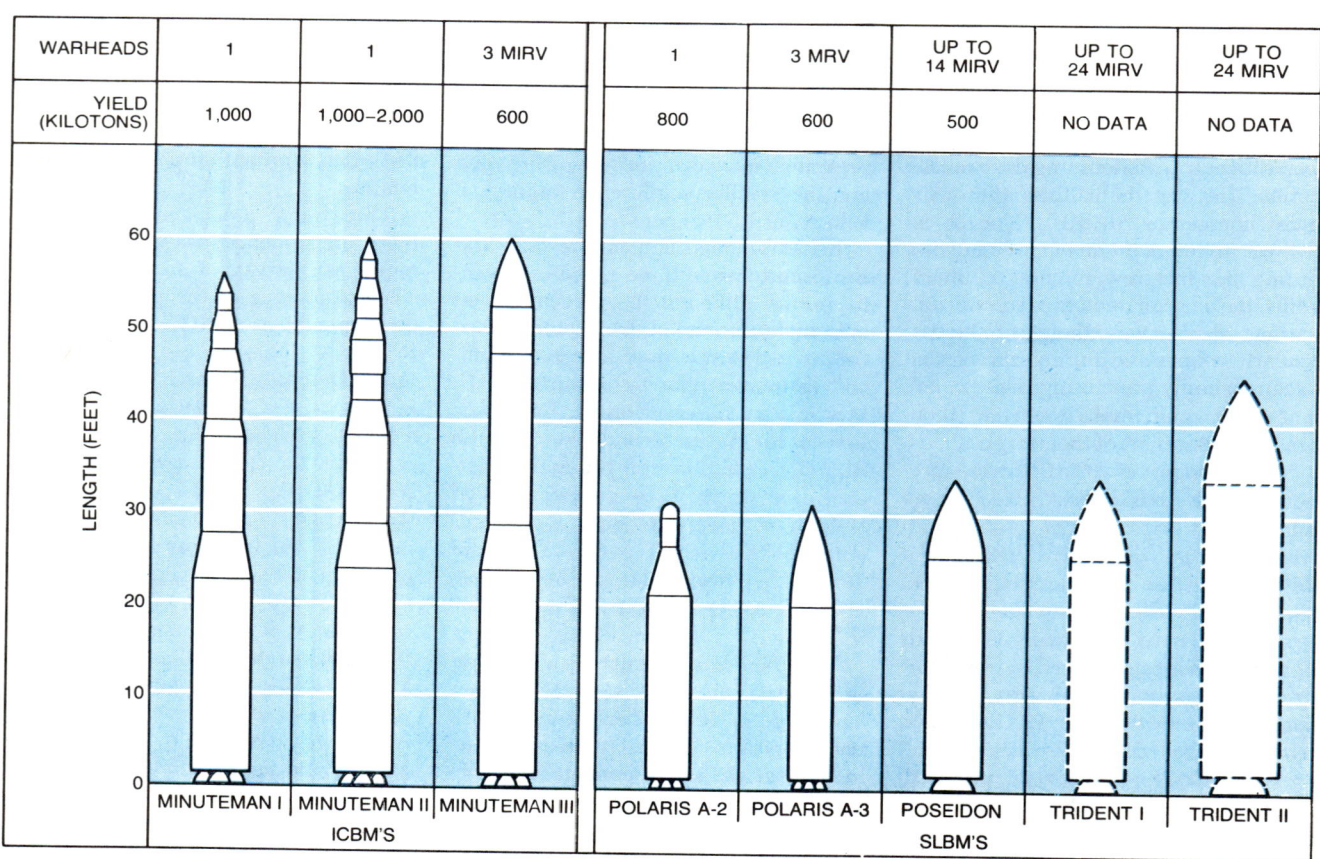

MIRV'S ARE DEPLOYED on two of the six U.S. missiles that are now operational, the Air Force Minuteman III and the Navy Poseidon. Although both have larger payloads than the missiles that preceded them, the total yield of their warheads is less. The Trident I, which could carry as many as 24 warheads, is expected to be introduced by 1978; the Trident II is planned for the mid-1980's.

tack almost perfect system reliability is essential, since the failure to destroy even only a few of the enemy's missiles would result in great harm to the aggressor. Because the reliability of individual missiles is not likely to even approach 100 percent, the first-strike force must be substantially larger than the force being attacked. Even if the adversary offers no defense, several warheads must be allotted to each of his missile silos. If missiles with single warheads are used, the military and economic advantage is clearly with the defender.

MRV's offer no advantage over single warheads; they merely scatter weapons over the target area and give no assurance of hitting a small, specific site. MIRV's, however, substantially improve the chances of the offense. With three or more warheads per missile, designed so that each can be assigned a separate target, a nation could attack an opponent's fixed-base forces without first enlarging its own arsenal. By aiming many weapons at each silo it could greatly increase the probability that all the missiles would be destroyed.

MIRV's also satisfy another major requirement of a first-strike force: high accuracy. If a missile is to be destroyed inside a hardened silo (a buried tube armored with steel and concrete), a warhead must be exploded at quite close range, perhaps even within the "cratering radius" of the weapon. Because the radius of destruction against a hardened target increases very slowly with increasing yield it is generally considered more profitable to improve accuracy than to increase explosive power.

The customary measure of accuracy is the "circular error probable," a circle centered on the target with a radius such that half of the warheads aimed at the target will fall outside the perimeter. To be useful as a counterforce weapon a warhead should have a radius of destruction against its particular target somewhat larger than the circular error probable. For example, if a given warhead has a circular error probable of one mile and a radius of destruction against a given silo of half a mile, far fewer than half of the warheads could be expected to destroy the missiles they are aimed at. To achieve 50 percent reliability the yield could be increased eightfold; the same result could be obtained by a twofold improvement in accuracy.

The second argument favoring the deployment of MIRV emphasized its ability to penetrate missile defenses. Russian nuclear tests at high-altitude in 1961 and 1962 and Premier Khrushchev's famous boast that "You can say our rocket hits a fly in outer space" led many U.S. planners to ascribe to the Russian ABM performance at least as good as that which could in theory be achieved by the U.S. system. In particular it was concluded that a single large antimissile missile could simultaneously destroy all three warheads of the Polaris A-3.

For the Navy there were at least two additional motives for building MIRV's. First, the Polaris A-3 development program was nearing the end, and it was almost automatically assumed that there would be a new generation of sea-launched missiles. Second, improvements in submarine navigation for the first time made high accuracy possible in SLBM's. (In order to launch a missile with a specified accuracy the submarine must know its own position and orientation to at least that degree of accuracy.)

The new missile was at first designated the B-3, but the name was later changed to Poseidon. From the beginning it was evident that it would be a more powerful rocket than the A-3. The increase in power was obtained largely by making the rocket bigger.

At the outset it was not at all clear that MIRV's would be used in the Poseidon. The desire to compete with the Air Force in the counterforce role led some on the Navy staff to favor a large, accurate, single warhead, whereas others, including Harold Brown, who was then the director of Defense Research and Engineering, sought continued emphasis on MRV's as a means of ABM penetration.

The Navy Special Projects Office soon proposed a compromise, a device that was never built but that served as a link between MRV and MIRV. In this concept a bus would have delivered several warheads to a single target but on trajectories that had different apogees. Each warhead would be aimed at the target as accurately as guidance technology would allow; they would arrive at different times, however, and would be spaced as much as 100 miles apart. They would have the same capacity for exhausting a newer, more sophisticated ABM as the Polaris MRV had against a crude ABM. Such a delivery system requires a bus capable of making modest changes in its velocity in the plane of the trajectory and roughly perpendicular to its direction. To transform this proposed bus into one suitable for MIRV's it is necessary only to provide a means of adding small increments of velocity in the other two directions.

Continuing progress in missile guidance and anticipation of even more improvement soon led the Special Projects Office to propose the high-multiplicity MIRV deployed today. The Poseidon is almost twice as heavy as the Polaris A-3 and carries about twice the payload. Its nominal range is about the same, 2,500 miles, but this could be increased by sacrificing payload. It is reported to be capable of carrying as many as 14 warheads, but in most analyses it is usually considered to carry 10. The warheads are estimated to have a yield of 50 kilotons each.

The first boatload of Poseidon missiles was deployed at sea in April, 1971, aboard the missile submarine *James Madison*. Converting from Polaris to Poseidon requires the installation of new launching tubes to accommodate the greater length and girth of the new missile. At least 17 boats have been converted so far, and eventually 31 of the nation's 41 missile submarines will carry Poseidons. Thus if each missile does indeed carry 10 warheads, the number of independently targeted reentry vehicles in the nation's sea-launched fleet will increase from 656 to 5,120.

Although the Poseidon will not be fully deployed for another two years, its successor is already being planned. It is the Trident, a still larger missile that in its final version will have a range of 6,000 miles. Each missile will be armed with as many as 24 independently aimed warheads. The Navy intends initially to build 10 Trident submarines, carrying 24 missiles each.

In the Air Force the argument over single v. multiple warheads persisted into the mid-1960's. Concerned, like the Navy, over progress in missile defenses and over the Russian high-altitude test series, the Air Force began to consider MIRV's as a means of improving penetration. At the same time a steady increase in the perceived number of military targets in the U.S.S.R. stimulated interest in the use of multiple warheads to improve force effectiveness.

On the other hand, the Air Force had for some time been committed to large, single warheads protected against interception by decoys, chaff and other penetration aids. At one point the factional dispute reached the missile-industry press when a contract for the Minuteman III warhead was delayed following the intercession of the director of Defense Research and Engineering.

Early in the debate two versions of MIRV were considered. One employed a bus virtually identical with the Transtage already under development. In the alternative system a rocket booster would have launched a cluster of small, single-stage missiles, each incorporating a propulsion and guidance system. After the cluster as a whole was placed on a trajectory leading to the area of the targets the individual missiles would adjust their velocities separately to impact on their particular targets. The extra weight and extra cost of the individual guidance and control systems made this proposal less attractive than the bus, and its development was never authorized.

The bus type of post-boost control system was selected for Minuteman III in 1964; the first flight of 10 missiles was turned over to the Strategic Air Command in June of 1970 at Minot Air Force Base in North Dakota. Minuteman III carries three warheads, usually said to have a yield of about 200 kilotons each.

The decision to deploy MIRV's was made all but inevitable by the decision to develop them. Weapons systems, once proved feasible, assume a momentum of their own, under the rationale of "If it can be done, it must be done, because if we don't, they will."

Even so, the deployment of MIRV's was debated after the development decisions were made, and the matter was not settled until the missiles were in place in 1970 and 1971. As we have seen, the arguments usually cited in favor of MIRV deployment are improved penetration of missile defenses and an increase in the number of targets that could be attacked. The penetration of an anti-ballistic-missile system was stressed by those who perceived a tradition of defensive measures in Russian history and who therefore believed that the U.S.S.R. would construct such a system. The proliferation of potential targets was emphasized by those who advocated a counterforce mission for U.S. nuclear weapons.

Secretary McNamara had other, primarily political motives for the deployment of MIRV's. Multiple warheads, he contended, offered a less costly way than the addition of more missiles to expand the strategic force and maintain at least some counterforce capability against growing Russian forces. Thus the potential powers of MIRV's were invoked in the arguments of McNamara and his staff against strategic-force expansion.

McNamara also mentioned MIRV's in arguing against deployment of missile defenses. He doubted that the proposed anti-ballistic-missile network would work and believed it might bring on a new cycle in the arms race. He opposed its deployment in the U.S. and tried to persuade Premier Kosygin (at the conference in Glassboro, N.J.) that the U.S.S.R. also should forgo antimissile systems. A U.S. commitment to deploy MIRV's was among his arguments, since MIRV's represent a relatively inexpensive means of overcoming any conceivable antimissile system. Thus, from the point of view of McNamara and some of his immediate associates in the Office of the Secretary of Defense, the deployment of MIRV's could benefit the cause of arms control.

Indeed, the limitation of ABM systems achieved as part of the agreements made in the strategic-arms-limitation talks (SALT I) of 1972 might in part be attributed to the existence of MIRV's. It could be argued that the U.S. and the U.S.S.R. were willing to renounce extensive antimissile systems because MIRV's

STIMULI TO DEVELOPMENT
- FIRST RUSSIAN SATELLITE AND ICBM
- LIMITATIONS OF DECOYS
- RUSSIAN HIGH-ALTITUDE NUCLEAR TESTS
- COUNTERFORCE CAPABILITY
- RUSSIAN ABM AND MRV VULNERABILITY

PRECURSOR DEVICES AND PROGRAMS
- ABLE-STAR
- AGENA
- TRANSTAGE
- SEQUENTIAL PAYLOAD DELIVERY
- MRV
- NASA

PARTICIPANTS IN DEVELOPMENT
- REENTRY BODY IDENTIFICATION GROUP
- ADVANCED RESEARCH PROJECTS AGENCY
- AIR FORCE SPACE AND MISSILE SYSTEMS OFFICE
- NAVY SPECIAL PROJECTS OFFICE
- DIRECTOR OF DEFENSE RESEARCH AND ENGINEERING
- AEROSPACE CORPORATION
- SPACE TECHNOLOGY LABORATORY
- INDUSTRIAL AND CONSULTANT COMPANIES
- ADVISORY COMMITTEES TO ALL OF THE ABOVE

JUSTIFICATIONS FOR DEPLOYMENT
- ABM PENETRATION
- PROLIFERATION OF TARGETS
- COUNTERFORCE STRATEGY
- LIMITATIONS OF FORCE EXPANSION
- DISCOURAGEMENT OF ABM

MULTIFARIOUS PATHS OF DEVELOPMENT, culminating in MIRV warheads, are suggested by a chart showing some of the motives for development, the projects and devices that preceded the weapons, the organizations that participated and the justifications proposed for deployment. The elimination of any one, or even several, of these programs would not have halted MIRV, since develop-

ensured the futility of building them. MIRV's are themselves excluded from the regulation of the SALT I agreements. They are considered a "qualitative" refinement in weaponry and therefore are not subject to restriction. They are expected to be a major topic in the second round of the talks (SALT II), scheduled to conclude by the end of 1974.

If McNamara believed that the deployment of MIRV's could slow the arms race, officials of the U.S. Arms Control and Disarmament Agency saw it differently. As early as 1964 Herbert Scoville, Jr., and George W. Rathjens noted ways in which the deployment of MIRV's could upset the "balance of terror." In particular, they predicted that an adversary could construe the deployment of MIRV's as possible preparations for making a preemptive strike. If a MIRV force is capable of destroying an adversary's ICBM's, that is, if it is an effective and reliable counterforce weapon, it could be considered a threat to the nation's deterrent and to that extent would be provocative. Of course, even a perfect MIRV force could not make a first strike a rational policy, since sea-launched missiles and perhaps bombers would still be able to retaliate, but MIRV's do contribute some increment of instability. For example, in a crisis where nuclear war seemed imminent MIRV's might be perceived as giving an advantage to the aggressor and therefore could encourage a first strike.

Whether or not MIRV's are now sufficiently accurate and reliable to serve as counterforce weapons, they are considered menacing by those responsible for military planning. The MIRV missiles tested in August by the U.S.S.R., for example, were described by Secretary of Defense Schlesinger as leading the U.S.S.R. to "a clear advantage in counterforce capability." Under the SALT I agreement the U.S.S.R. is allowed about 25 percent more offensive missiles than the U.S.; with the deployment of MIRV's, Schlesinger suggested, this superiority in launchers and throw weight could be "married" to equality in technological sophistication.

During most of the period in which MIRV's were under development the program was kept secret and the controversies it entrained were unknown to the public and to many members of Congress. It did not become a political issue until late in 1967, when public debate over deployment began. In the 1968 Presidential campaign Senator Eugene McCarthy echoed the view of the Arms Control and Disarmament Agency, noting that "the introduction of sophisticated anti-ballistic-missile systems and new missiles equipped with multiple warheads threatens to make the situation unstable. With the deployment of such weapons systems, each side will become concerned as to whether in the event of a preemptive attack it will be able to inflict sufficient damage in retaliation—if not, its deterrent will not be credible. The arms race will thus be impelled to a new intensity. In crises, there could be an incentive to launch a first strike."

Later Senator Edward W. Brooke introduced a resolution calling for the suspension of testing of multiple-warhead missiles. Some other senators and a number of other people supported the resolution, but the effort was in vain. The first deployment of MIRV's took place while the issue was being debated.

The MIRV program had many roots and branches. Decisions were made by many people, some only loosely connected with one another, over the course of more than a decade. Of all the stimuli that led to the development of MIRV the most important was the perceived need to penetrate ABM systems whose theoretical capabilities were slowly but steadily improving. Even without the stimulus of ABM, however, MIRV's would probably have been devised, and probably at about the same time. All their essential technology was developed in unrelated programs and for unrelated reasons: Able-Star, Agena, Transtage, sequential payload delivery. During the early phases of development the progress of MIRV was determined largely by the decisions of technologists who were attempting to solve problems presented by nature or responding to their perception of the technological challenges of the Russian missile and space programs.

Once proved feasible, MIRV's were also proved necessary, at least to the satisfaction of those who made the decision to deploy them. That decision was compelled by three factors: (1) the participants in and sponsors of the development program urged application of the new weapon; (2) MIRV's promised to thwart any ABM system the U.S.S.R. might construct and at the same time served as an argument against the deployment of missile defenses by either nation; (3) MIRV offered a relatively inexpensive way to increase the number of Russian targets that could be attacked, and thus ended debate over strategic-force expansion.

Opposed to these arguments were the predictions of the Arms Control and Disarmament Agency that deployment of MIRV's would be perceived as seriously disturbing the strategic balance and in crises would make the most dangerous policy the most profitable one. The first of these predictions has already turned out to be right. The number of people holding such views was negligible, however, and their voices were not powerful. Plans to deploy proceeded while the arguments went on.

In the development of multiple warheads there is a lesson for those who would reduce the world's armaments. Some programs, such as the B-70 bomber and ABM, are expensive, are addressed to a clearly evident and single purpose and depend on what might be called a unitary decision-making process. In principle they can be stopped by direct confrontation. Other programs, however, and MIRV is an example, evolve from many independent and seemingly unrelated goals and decisions. They are too diffuse, too protean, too difficult to define and delimit to be stopped by confrontation. They can be slowed or stopped only by slowing or stopping the arms race as a whole.

---

ment could have taken alternative pathways. Similarly, had some arguments for deployment been refuted, others would have served.

11 Nuclear Strategy and Nuclear Weapons

by Barry Carter
May 1974

The "improved counterforce capability" proposed by the Administration is viewed as not only unnecessary and potentially costly but also likely to undercut the SALT negotiations and increase the risk of nuclear war

"Should a President, in the event of a nuclear attack, be left with the single option of ordering the mass destruction of enemy civilians, in the face of the certainty that it would be followed by the mass slaughter of Americans? Should the concept of assured destruction be narrowly defined and should it be the only measure of our ability to deter the variety of threats we may face?"

The questions asked in the preceding quotation, taken from President Nixon's first foreign-policy report in 1970, have been cited repeatedly in the past few months by Administration spokesmen in an effort to explain and justify some significant changes that are being made in U.S. policy regarding its strategic military forces. The new strategy, spelled out most clearly in Secretary of Defense James R. Schlesinger's annual report for the fiscal year 1975, released in March, seeks "to provide the President with a wider set of much more selective targeting options," and hence greater "flexibility," in choosing an appropriate response to "any kind of nuclear attack."

As the opening quotation illustrates, much of the official rhetoric concerning this new development in U.S. strategic policy has been more misleading than illuminating. To criticize the "assured destruction" doctrine of the past decade or so as planning only for massive retaliation against Russian cities ignores the fact (belatedly acknowledged by Schlesinger) that U.S. strategic forces have for years had the capability, both in weapons and in planning, for a "flexible response." More important, the broad hypothetical issues invoked by such public statements have tended to obscure the more immediate real issues presented by this Administration's recent actions.

The real issues are serious ones. The primary operational question at present is whether or not the U.S. should develop missiles with an improved capability for attacking "hardened" targets in the U.S.S.R. The main rationale offered for developing such an improved "counterforce" capability (so called because it is aimed at an opponent's military forces) is that it is "impermissible" for the U.S. not to "match" certain Russian counterforce developments. There is also the suggestion that these missiles would minimize "unintended collateral damage."

The preceding question in turn raises the subtler issue of how the active promotion of such programs for improved counterforce capabilities affects the stability of the strategic nuclear deterrent and hence the likelihood that there will be a nuclear war. Before one can address these two issues one must understand why public debate should properly focus on such questions and not (at this time anyway) on the kind of questions posed in President Nixon's 1970 remarks.

In the late 1950's and early 1960's U.S. strategic policy went through a series of transformations. By 1962 American military planners recognized that the U.S. would have many more missiles than the U.S.S.R. could have for several years and in fact many more missiles than were required to devastate every major city in the U.S.S.R. A counterforce strategy therefore held out the attractive option of limiting damage to U.S. cities by destroying a substantial part of the Russian strategic forces. In language that sounds remarkably familiar today, Secretary of Defense Robert S. McNamara said in a speech in Ann Arbor, Mich.: "The United States has come to the conclusion that, to the extent feasible, basic military strategy in a possible general nuclear war should be approached in much the same way that more conventional military operations have been regarded in the past. That is to say, principal military objectives, in the event of a nuclear war stemming from a major attack on the alliance, should be the destruction of the enemy's military forces, not of his civilian population."

The Russians, however, continued to deploy land-based intercontinental ballistic missiles (ICBM's) and submarine-launched ballistic missiles (SLBM's). As a result, even if the U.S. sought to limit damage to itself by the partial destruction of the Russian strategic forces, there would still be more than enough Russian forces left to kill tens of millions of Americans. Recognizing this fact, McNamara increasingly emphasized by the mid-1960's the concept of "assured destruction," which he said in 1968 meant the "ability, even after absorbing a well-coordinated surprise first strike, to inflict unacceptable damage on the attacker." This criterion he defined explicitly: "In the case of the Soviet Union, I would judge that a capability on our part to destroy, say, one-fifth to one-fourth of her population and one-half of her industrial capacity would serve as an effective deterrent."

Few concepts have been as maligned or misunderstood as that of assured destruction. Critics label it genocide or use the acronym of "mutual assured destruction" to call it MAD. In fact, the concept seems well designed to serve two purposes. First, by planning the size of U.S. forces on the basis of the "worst case" scenario of an all-out Russian surprise attack, it ensures that the U.S. possesses the ultimate threat: to be able to wipe out the U.S.S.R. or any attacker in retaliation. Second, since the destruction criterion is reasonably precise, the concept provides a useful basis for limiting strategic-weapons procurement and for evaluating arms-control proposals.

While retaining the assured-destruction concept, McNamara and his successor, Clark Clifford, supervised the development of the wide array of weapons that constitutes today's U.S. strategic arsenal. Both the numbers and the characteristics of many of these weapons were consistent with the assured-destruction concept, partly because the U.S. possesses a "triad" of strategic offensive forces and partly because of the hedge against the "highest expected threat." The triad approach seeks to maintain a major retaliatory capability in each component of our strategic offensive forces: ICBM's, SLBM's and long-range bombers. Justified on the grounds that each component presents a different problem for an attacker, difficult and costly problems for his defense and a hedge against unexpected failures in one or both of the other components, the net result of the triad approach is to provide in the aggregate a high degree of confidence that the assured-destruction mission could be carried out.

The hedge against the highest expected threat, as projected in the National Intelligence Estimates, meant that weapons would be developed and sometimes procured as a cushion against Russian developments that, although not considered likely, were possible. The predictable result was that the U.S. came to possess much more powerful forces than were shown by subsequent events to be required for assured destruction. For example, one of the main justifications offered for developing multiple independently targeted reentry vehicles (MIRV's) was to hedge against a greater-than-expected Russian deployment of an anti-ballistic-missile (ABM) system, on the theory that increasing the number of incoming warheads would enable the U.S. offense to penetrate the Russian defense more easily.

Of course, some of the development and procurement decisions also reflected inevitable political and bureaucratic pressures. For example, faced with pressures from the military and from Congress, McNamara apparently thought he could not ask for fewer than 1,000 Minuteman ICBM's.

Finally, the proponents of the assured-destruction concept in the latter half of the 1960's quietly subscribed to secondary strategic objectives, in particular the desire to retain some ability to respond flexibly in the case of an actual attack. If the U.S. were subjected to a "limited" nuclear attack—possibly with a small number of missiles or because of an accidental launch—most thought the President should have a range of options from which to choose. This factor helps to explain why, for example, the Minuteman II warhead, which was first deployed in 1966, could be programmed for up to eight alternative targets, and why there was flexibility in the actual targeting plans.

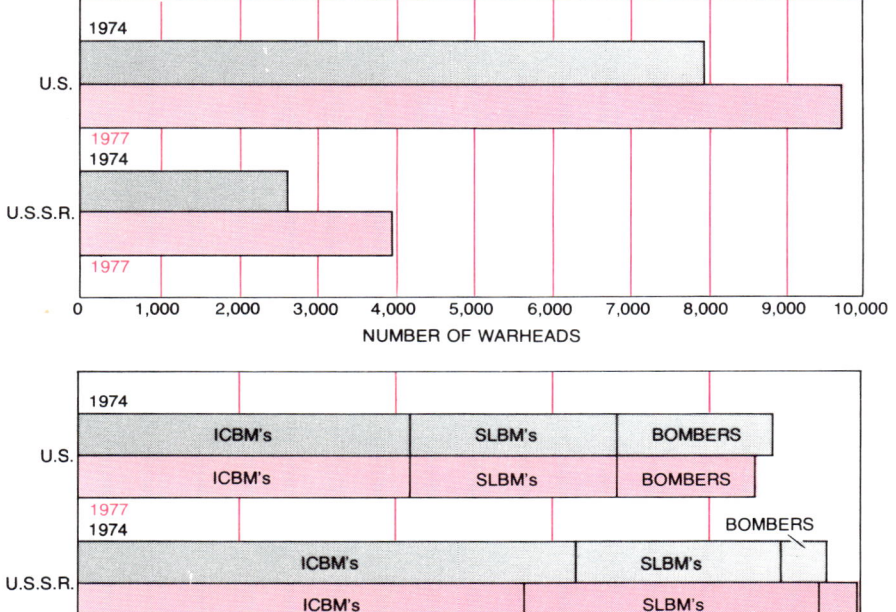

STRATEGIC NUCLEAR ARSENALS of the U.S. and the U.S.S.R. are compared here in terms of two key indicators: the number of individually targetable nuclear warheads, including bombs (*top*) and the number of delivery vehicles (*bottom*). Each pair of bars represents the total operational strategic forces projected for both sides as of mid-1974 (*gray*) and 1977 (*color*), based on data provided by the U.S. Government. The delivery-vehicle bars are broken down into segments representing land-based intercontinental ballistic missiles (ICBM's), submarine-launched ballistic missiles (SLBM's) and long-range bombers. As the bars show, the U.S. is at present either ahead of or in rough parity with the U.S.S.R. in these two categories and is expected to remain so for at least the next few years. This purely numerical representation of the military balance between the two superpowers does not, of course, take into account such important factors as qualitative differences in weapons technology, the larger size of the Russian ICBM's or the thousands of U.S. "tactical" nuclear weapons in Europe, Asia and aboard forward-based ships. More important, regardless of the exact numerical relation of the two arsenals, each side now has, and for the foreseeable future will continue to have, a secure retaliatory capability, that is, more than enough strategic forces to absorb even an all-out nuclear attack by the other side and still be able to retaliate by carrying out a wide variety of limited nuclear attacks or by inflicting an unacceptable level of "assured destruction" on the population and industry of the attacker.

As a result the U.S. ended up with strategic-war capabilities considerably greater than the assured-destruction concept required. That this situation was rarely acknowledged publicly was a serious mistake, the results of which we are now reaping in public misunderstanding of the policies of the past and, more important, in the sometimes surprising ignorance about the present capabilities of the U.S. strategic forces. The simple fact, which cannot be stressed too strongly, is that the U.S. strategic forces are now capable of carrying out a large array of alternative missions, far in excess of assured destruction.

To begin with, assured destruction does not require many forces. Assuming zero or low Russian ABM levels (a reasonable assumption given the 1972 Moscow Treaty limiting ABM systems), the delivered warheads of 220 Minuteman III ICBM's could kill about 21 percent of the Russian population from immediate effects alone and destroy about 72 percent of the Russian industrial capacity. The delivered warheads from 170 Poseidon missiles (which is fewer than the total carried by 12 submarines) could cause a similar level of damage [see illustration on page 136]. Projections of bomber survivability vary greatly, but most experts would estimate that enough B-52's could reach their targets to satisfy easily the traditional assured-destruction criterion.

The total of U.S. strategic forces is, of course, much larger. There are at present 1,054 ICBM's, of which 1,000 are Minuteman missiles and 54 are the older, larger Titans. Of the Minuteman missiles 550 have been or are in the process of being converted to the Minuteman III, which can carry up to three warheads. These MIRV's are estimated to have an accuracy of 1,500 feet or less (expressed in terms of "circular error probable," which means that 50 percent of the warheads are expected to fall within a radius of 1,500 feet of the target). The explosive power, or yield, of each warhead is equivalent to between 170 and 200 kilotons of TNT, or at least 11 times the size of the 15-kiloton bomb dropped on Hiroshima. Rapid retargeting of the Minuteman III will be possible soon with the advent of new computer-software systems, such as the Command Data Buffer system. (All estimates of the numbers and characteristics of U.S. forces used in this article are taken from the statements of U.S. officials, from publications of the International Institute of Strategic Studies and from other reliable publications.)

In addition the U.S. arsenal includes 656 SLBM's, 496 of which are scheduled to become Poseidon missiles. The Poseidon can carry up to 14 MIRV's, but it is usually deployed with 10. Although accuracy might be reduced by uncertainties about the submarine's location, it still is probably less than 3,000 feet. Moreover, even though each warhead is smaller than Minuteman's, there are many more of them and each is still about three times the size of the Hiroshima bomb. Like the Minuteman III warheads, the Poseidon warheads can be retargeted quickly.

Bombers are often viewed as the stepchild of the U.S. strategic triad. The approximately 400 B-52's and 65 FB 111's are unaccountably ignored in many comparative tables of American and Russian strategic forces, notably in President Nixon's first three foreign-policy reports. This is surprising given the fact that an estimated 40 percent of the U.S. budget for strategic offensive forces is spent on bombers. Moreover, from the standpoint of nuclear strikes the per-sortie attrition rate of about 3 percent suffered by the B-52's in their attacks on heavily defended Hanoi demonstrated high survivability. Indeed, most places in the U.S.S.R. would not be as heavily defended as Hanoi, the B-52's would not be making the more vulnerable high-altitude attacks they made there and the bombers would use nuclear warheads to silence air-defense batteries. Each B-52 carries between four and 24 nuclear weapons, the load being a variable mix of gravity bombs and air-to-surface missiles. The bombs can be in the megaton range (that is, equal to 1,000 kilotons) and can be delivered with very high accuracy.

(This accounting of the U.S. strategic

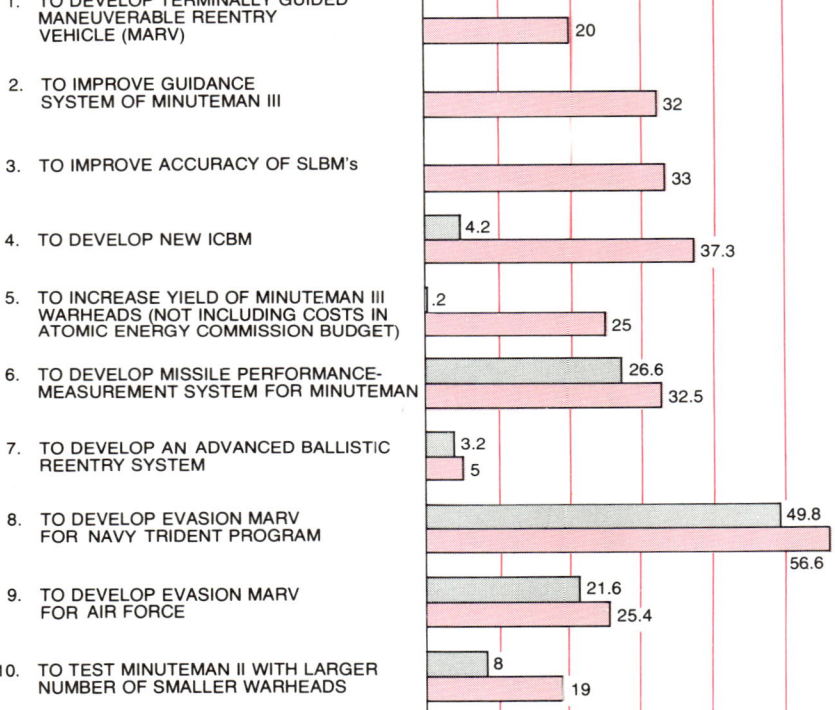

SELECTED ITEMS from the record military-budget request for fiscal year 1975, submitted recently to Congress by the Department of Defense, reveal a sharp across-the-board increase in the amount of money projected to initiate or expand programs that would increase U.S. "counterforce" capability against military targets in the U.S.S.R. (Colored bars are for the fiscal year 1975, gray bars for fiscal year 1974.) Items 1 through 6 refer to programs that will directly affect U.S. counterforce capability by improving the accuracy of land-based and sea-based missiles and by increasing the explosive yield of nuclear warheads. Items 7 through 11 refer to programs that involve indirectly related improvements in missile guidance, warhead multiplicity and warhead yield. Because this list was compiled from several different sources, there is some possibility that programs were double-counted or overlooked.

forces does not include the extensive U.S. "tactical" nuclear forces, many of which could attack targets in the U.S.S.R. In addition to the more than 7,000 tactical nuclear weapons in Europe, many such weapons are deployed in Asia and on forward-deployed ships in the Atlantic and the Pacific.)

In short, the U.S. already has a considerable potential for "limited" strategic strikes. Exactly how much capability depends on the critical assumption of who strikes first and how, as well as on one's assumptions about the nature of the Russian threat. In any case three important factors should be remembered about potential targets in the U.S.S.R.:

1. There are many nonmilitary, industrial targets outside urban centers that would require only one or two nuclear warheads each; such targets include manufacturing plants, power plants and the two construction yards for missile submarines.

2. Except for "hardened" targets, most military targets could be destroyed by only one or two warheads each; such targets include air-defense sites, military airfields, major army bases and submarine bases.

3. Even for hard targets such as missile silos, nuclear-weapons storage facilities and command posts, the use of small numbers of warheads will create a high probability of destruction. For instance, three Minuteman III warheads delivered against three Russian missile silos with a "hardness" about the same as that of the U.S. silos when they were first built would have approximately an 80 percent chance of destroying one silo, whereas seven Minuteman III warheads would have a similar 80 percent probability of knocking out one silo three times as hard. Presumably many Russian missile silos have a hardness in this range.

As a result, even with existing missiles a limited strike by the U.S. that employed 100 missiles or fewer could do substantial damage to the U.S.S.R. and could knock out some Russian ICBM's.

In calculating the sufficiency of our strategic forces, one should not forget the Chinese. For any conceivable "crisis scenario" the total expenditure of U.S. warheads against China could easily come from the present surplus exceeding the weapons needed for the assured-destruction mission against the U.S.S.R. Not only could the U.S. destroy most of the nascent Chinese nuclear forces, but also it has been estimated that a few warheads detonated over 50 Chinese urban centers would destroy half of the urban population (more than 50 million people), more than half of the industrial capacity and most of the key governmental, technical and managerial personnel. Indeed, against fixed targets such as cities the U.S. could use its B-52's, which could return to their bases for other missions.

Not only does the U.S. have this multifaceted capability but also its nuclear strategy has always included plans for attacks other than massive ones on Russian cities. This conclusion is logically inescapable when one realizes that the U.S. has had thousands of strategic warheads since the mid-1960's, has about 7,500 now and is expected to have almost 10,000 by 1977. There are only about 200 major cities in the U.S.S.R. Either the U.S. has aimed a superfluously large number of warheads at each major city or it has planned for other targets all along. Any doubts on this score were resolved by Secretary Schlesinger's statement in March that "our war plans have always included military targets."

President Nixon has made it very clear from the early days of his Administration that he wanted changes in U.S. strategic policy. Neither he nor any other high official, including Secretary Schlesinger, has ever rejected the assured-destruction concept. Rather they have defined assured destruction narrowly to mean only massive retaliation against cities and have said that more options are needed. To date the Nixon Administration has really presented two different sets of what "more" is needed. First there were the "sufficiency criteria," which were publicized in the period from 1970 to 1972. This past year has seen the emergence of a new set of criteria.

The sufficiency criteria, which President Nixon first hinted at in 1970, were spelled out by Secretary of Defense Melvin R. Laird in 1971. They are:

1. "Maintaining an adequate second-strike capability to deter an all-out surprise attack on our strategic forces."
2. "Providing no incentive for the Soviet Union to strike the United States first in a crisis."
3. "Preventing the Soviet Union from gaining the ability to cause considerably greater urban/industrial destruction than the United States could inflict on the Soviets in a nuclear war."
4. "Defending against damage from small attacks or accidental launches."

These four criteria have been explained further, including the fact that the deterrence is for the benefit of U.S. allies as well as the U.S.

The publication of the sufficiency criteria at least moved the public debate off the misleading view that U.S. policies and forces only envisioned massive retaliation against cities, but beyond that there is little new in the criteria. This is partly because they were never clearly explained; accordingly they remained more Delphic than definitive.

The first criterion is simply a basic statement of the assured-destruction concept. The third is a result of the assured-destruction assumption at meaningful levels of destruction; beyond the ability of either side to inflict 75 million fatalities and between 50 and 75 percent industrial damage—levels that would finish either country as a viable society—relative differences in the ability to inflict urban or industrial damage seem insignificant. Besides, much higher levels of destruction can only be achieved with considerable difficulty, since either country soon reaches a point of rapidly diminishing returns in terms of urban or industrial destruction per additional warhead.

The fourth criterion was clearly justification for the Safeguard ABM system. Without getting into the debate over such issues as whether or not the advantage of damage limitation against small attacks or accidental launches outweighs the disadvantage of the Russians' misinterpreting the purposes of any ABM deployment, suffice it to say that the Administration as early as May, 1971, was committed to insignificant ABM levels in the ongoing Strategic Arms Limitation Talks (SALT). The fourth criterion thus became "inoperative."

That leaves the second criterion. It clearly enunciates a desirable objective in strategic policy: to avoid strategic forces or actions that would be destabilizing in a crisis. Although this objective was not explicit before, it was inherent in the assured-destruction objective of providing highly survivable forces that would thereby reduce the incentive for a first strike. The second sufficiency criterion fails to delineate what more, if anything, was needed.

The criteria are silent about the kinds of option other than assured destruction that the President was so concerned about. Moreover, should the U.S. react to protect its allies (still undefined) in the same way that it would to protect its own territory? And what are U.S. strategic objectives with regard to China? In short, except for the flirtation with the ABM possibility, the sufficiency criteria only hinted at new strategic policies rather than establishing them.

Instead of trying to amend the sufficiency criteria, the Administration decided about a year ago simply to scrap them and to start anew in redefining strategic policies. This time Secretary Schlesinger has been the principal spokesman. After some of his press conferences late in 1973 and early in 1974 led to confusion among journalists and other observers as to what the new policies encompassed, the appearance of Schlesinger's annual report in March clarified the issues considerably. At one place in that report the "Principal Features of the Proposed Posture" (a posture Schlesinger clearly likes to refer to as "essential equivalence") are listed:

1. "a capability sufficiently large, diversified, and survivable so that it will provide us at all times with high confidence of riding out even a massive surprise attack and of penetrating enemy defenses, and with the ability to withhold an assured destruction reserve for an extended period of time."

2. "sufficient warning to ensure the survival of our heavy bombers together with the bomb alarm systems and command-control capabilities required by our National Command Authorities to direct the employment of the strategic forces in a controlled, selective, and restrained fashion."

3. "the forces to execute a wide range of options in response to potential actions by an enemy, including a capability for precise attacks on both soft and hard targets, while at the same time minimizing unintended collateral damage."

4. "the avoidance of any combination of forces that could be taken as an effort to acquire the ability to execute a first-strike disarming attack against the USSR."

5. "an offensive capability of such size and composition that all will perceive it as in overall balance with the strategic forces of any potential opponent."

6. "offensive and defensive capabilities and programs that conform with the provisions of current arms control agreements and at the same time facilitate the conclusion of more permanent treaties to control and, if possible, reduce the main nuclear arsenals."

These factors plus the accompanying text in the report provide the best available insight into the proposed new policies. The first factor, combined with the second's requirement of bomber survivability, constitutes essentially a restatement of the assured-destruction concept. It needs no further elaboration here except to note that assured destruction does not require immediate response; indeed, the emphasis on a "second strike" capability and on the survivability of U.S. forces reflects the goal of having time in which to consider what the appropriate response should be.

Skipping briefly to the fourth, fifth and sixth factors, they raise a host of diverse issues—touching on all offensive and defensive strategic programs. There is not sufficient space to treat them comprehensively here; instead the focus will be on their impact on the Administration's concepts of strategic flexibility and limited nuclear war.

The third factor and the balance of the second address the questions of flexibility and limited strategic war directly. The underlying questions can best be summarized as follows: (1) Should the U.S. have a number of response options? (2) Should the U.S. develop missiles with improved counterforce capabilities? (3) Should the U.S. actively promote the idea of improving counterforce capabilities for fighting, if necessary, a limited nuclear war? Since the first question is essentially noncontroversial, the remaining two define the immediate issues.

Schlesinger reports that most of the targeting options in the past have involved "relatively massive responses." He wants to provide the President with a "wider set of much more selective targeting options." There is general agreement among strategic analysts that the U.S. should have a variety of response options other than massive retaliation against cities. These options could be useful, for example, in deterring a limited strategic attack. As Paul C. Warnke, a former Assistant Secretary of Defense, has put it: "There can...be little objection to the concept that our targeting plans should be sufficiently flexible to provide the President with a variety of options in the event of a nuclear attack." Warnke believes "we might be better positioned to deter a less than all-out Soviet attack if we have the refinement of command and control to push only one or a few buttons rather than the entire console...to respond with less than our Sunday punch."

This broad consensus includes those options that draw on the capabilities of present forces and those already well along in development. As we have seen,

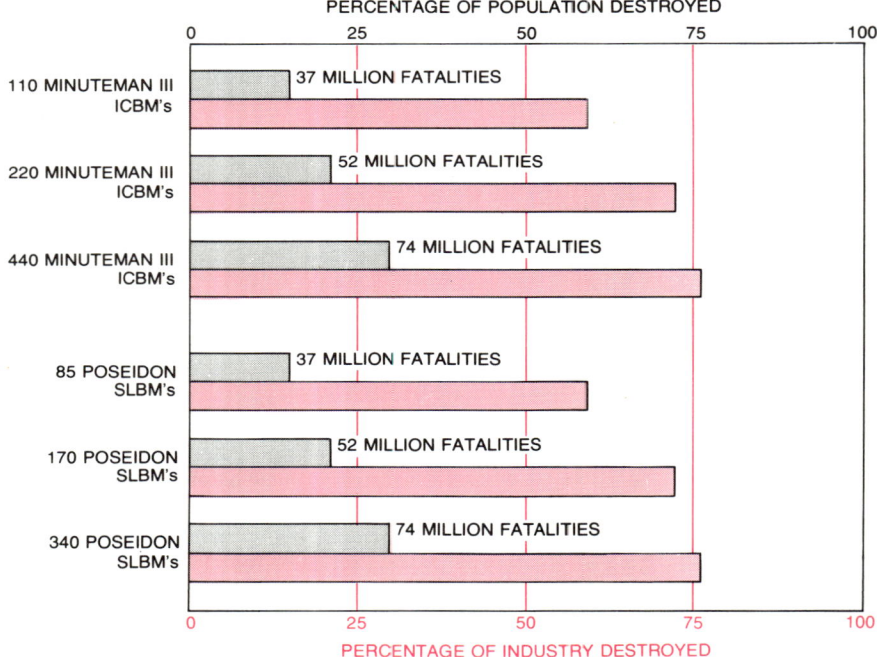

COMPARATIVELY SMALL FRACTIONS of the strategic offensive forces of the U.S. can still destroy much of the population and industry of the U.S.S.R. The figures used to make this bar chart are derived from a table released in 1968 by Secretary of Defense Robert S. McNamara. That table was expressed in terms of alternative numbers of "one-megaton equivalent" warheads; this adaptation uses conservative assumptions to calculate the megaton equivalents of the multiple-warhead Minuteman III and Poseidon missiles. For example, only 10 warheads were assumed to be deployed on each Poseidon instead of the possible 14. The chart is based on the further assumption that the warheads are delivered; since missile reliability is not perfect, a few more missiles would have to be given the order to launch in each case to have the indicated number of warheads reach their targets.

our present forces already have the accuracy-yield combinations to be used effectively to destroy almost anything except hard targets. Even against such hard targets as ICBM silos these forces could destroy large numbers of targets, but they would not do it "efficiently."

Schlesinger makes it clear, however, that he wants more than flexibility, that he wants counterforce options that require new or improved weapons. The incremental options are ones "minimizing unintended collateral damage" and providing a hard-target kill capability that "matches" that of the Russians. To be able to achieve these options Schlesinger seeks programs to develop missiles with improved counterforce capabilities.

The proposed defense budget for the fiscal year 1975 includes a number of such programs. The programs appear to fall into two categories.

First, there are the short-term programs, the ones that involve relatively minor changes and for which initial deployment might easily begin by the late 1970's. The major programs in this category include procurement of more Minuteman III missiles; refinement of the existing guidance system of the Minuteman III to increase accuracy (probably from 1,500 feet down to 700 feet or less); a higher-yield warhead for the Minuteman III identical in configuration with the existing warhead, and a general program to improve and measure the accuracy of SLBM's. The proposed budget also includes funds to flight-test a Minuteman III with a larger number of smaller reentry vehicles. Whether this program will increase counterforce capabilities or not depends on the accuracy and yield of the new warheads.

Second, there are two major long-term programs. Both will require considerable development time, and initial deployment would seem unlikely before 1980. Advanced development will be initiated for a terminally guided "maneuverable reentry vehicle" (MARV) for possible "retrofit" into both ICBM's and SLBM's. Although a MARV warhead has been programmed for some time for the advanced Trident I SLBM, it is not to be terminally guided, being designed for evasion of ABM interceptors rather than for improved accuracy. A new terminally guided MARV, however, will presumably have an accuracy of a few hundred feet. This would give even warheads the size of the Poseidon's a very effective hard-target kill capability.

Further research and development is needed to decide exactly how the new MARV will work. By definition, after the MARV has separated from the "bus," or postboost vehicle, that holds all a missile's warheads, it can maneuver almost up to impact in order to correct its flight path. The corrections could be accomplished in two ways. The most likely development is the homing MARV, what some call the true MARV [see illustration on page 140]. A sensor in the warhead would acquire an image or images of the target or of prominent terrain features nearby (or perhaps would simply acquire an "altitude profile" of the terrain along its flight path). An on-board matching device would match this information with a map stored in its memory. The warhead's flight path would then be corrected either by gas jets or by aerodynamic vanes.

An alternative approach is to use an inertial guidance system in the warhead as well as in the bus. Since the reentry vehicle often separates from the bus early in its flight, an on-board guidance system would allow much later changes in trajectory. The information on position would come, however, from the system's gyroscopes, from stars or even from satellites and not from the target area itself. As a result this approach in theory would probably not be as accurate as the homing approach.

The second long-term program is the development of an entirely new ICBM for the 1980's. This missile, which may even be an air-mobile missile, would include a new guidance system (presumably a terminally guided MARV), which Schlesinger says would give it "a very good capability against hard targets."

How reasonable or necessary is it to develop missiles with improved counterforce capabilities in order to minimize collateral damage or to match the Russians' hard-target kill capability?

It is particularly difficult to understand how these missiles will minimize collateral damage. The warheads Secretary Schlesinger is proposing will probably have at least the yield of the present Minuteman III and Poseidon warheads. Such warheads would cause extensive damage over a wide area. For example, a "small" 100-kiloton bomb exploding in the air over a target would cause substantial fatalities and damage from immediate effects alone over a circle with a radius of 2.5 miles. Since the possible improvement in accuracy for the Minuteman, for example, is at most about 1,000 feet even in the long run, the number of civilian fatalities will hardly be reduced significantly if a warhead at least three to 11 times the size of the Hiroshima bomb lands a few hundred feet closer to the intended target.

A substantially smaller warhead that still provides an improved hard-target kill capability is unlikely to be ready for deployment until the 1980's, since a very accurate terminally guided MARV is needed to allow a significant "trade-off" between lower yield and higher accuracy. Furthermore, the value of much smaller warheads in saving lives must be put in perspective.

First, the way to minimize fatalities, if nuclear weapons must be used, is careful target selection, in other words aiming at targets distant from urban centers. Air-defense sites or air bases in the Arctic and isolated army posts or industrial sites are good examples. For a very limited exchange the differences in fatality levels from an attack on such targets with warheads of, say, 50 kilotons as against five kilotons would not be significant.

Second, if there is a large-scale nuclear exchange, then there simply is no way of keeping civilian damage at a low level. The effects not only of immediate blast but also of radioactivity would kill millions.

Third, in an actual nuclear exchange the successful continuation of a U.S. policy aimed at minimizing civilian casualties depends in large part on what the Russians do, and the Russians have never seemed much attracted to this objective. Their strategic warheads have always been large. Even though they necessarily reduced the size of individual warheads on their ICBM's in order to deploy MIRV's on them, some if not all of the warheads are still in the megaton range.

Schlesinger's main justification for the new counterforce programs is that the U.S. needs an "efficient" hard-target capability to match that of the U.S.S.R. This seems a questionable refinement of the broader theme of "essential equivalence." Schlesinger has on occasion defined essential equivalence to suggest overall balance. For example, he recently testified: "We do not have to have a match for everything in their arsenal. They do not have to have a match for everything in our arsenal."

Whether or not such an overall balance exists today and for the foreseeable future is a question that deserves public debate; a good case can be made for the affirmative. Most important, both the U.S. and the U.S.S.R. have a high-confidence ability to carry out a wide variety of retaliatory options. In terms of static indicators the Russians do have more missiles and greater missile "throw weight." The U.S., however, has more bombers, more warheads (now and for the rest of the decade) and about equal overall throw weight (if bombers are included in the calculations). In terms of qualitative factors U.S. missile submarines are much quieter and hence harder to find than the Russian ones, and U.S. bombers are more modern. Finally, to maintain or even enhance some of its capabilities, the U.S. already has a number of strategic programs well along: the conversion of older missiles to larger Minuteman III and Poseidon missiles, the B-1 bomber and the Trident submarine with its advanced missiles.

Schlesinger, however, avoids the complex question of whether the general U.S.-U.S.S.R. strategic picture is one of overall balance—of essential equivalence. Rather, he selectively focuses on relative counterforce capabilities against ICBM silos. Selective vision is not exactly a new tactic in military analysis. The "missile gap" of 1960 is a classic case; the heated debate over the number of U.S. ICBM's compared with the number of Russian ICBM's ignored the massive U.S. bomber force. Schlesinger's selective vision is even blurred within its own field. Although the Russians are clearly developing new missiles and MIRV's, they apparently have not pursued the accuracy aspect of a counterforce strategy with much zeal. As General George S. Brown, the chief of staff of the Air Force, recently remarked about the new Russian programs, "MIRVing alone won't [take out the Minuteman force]. Accuracy is the other

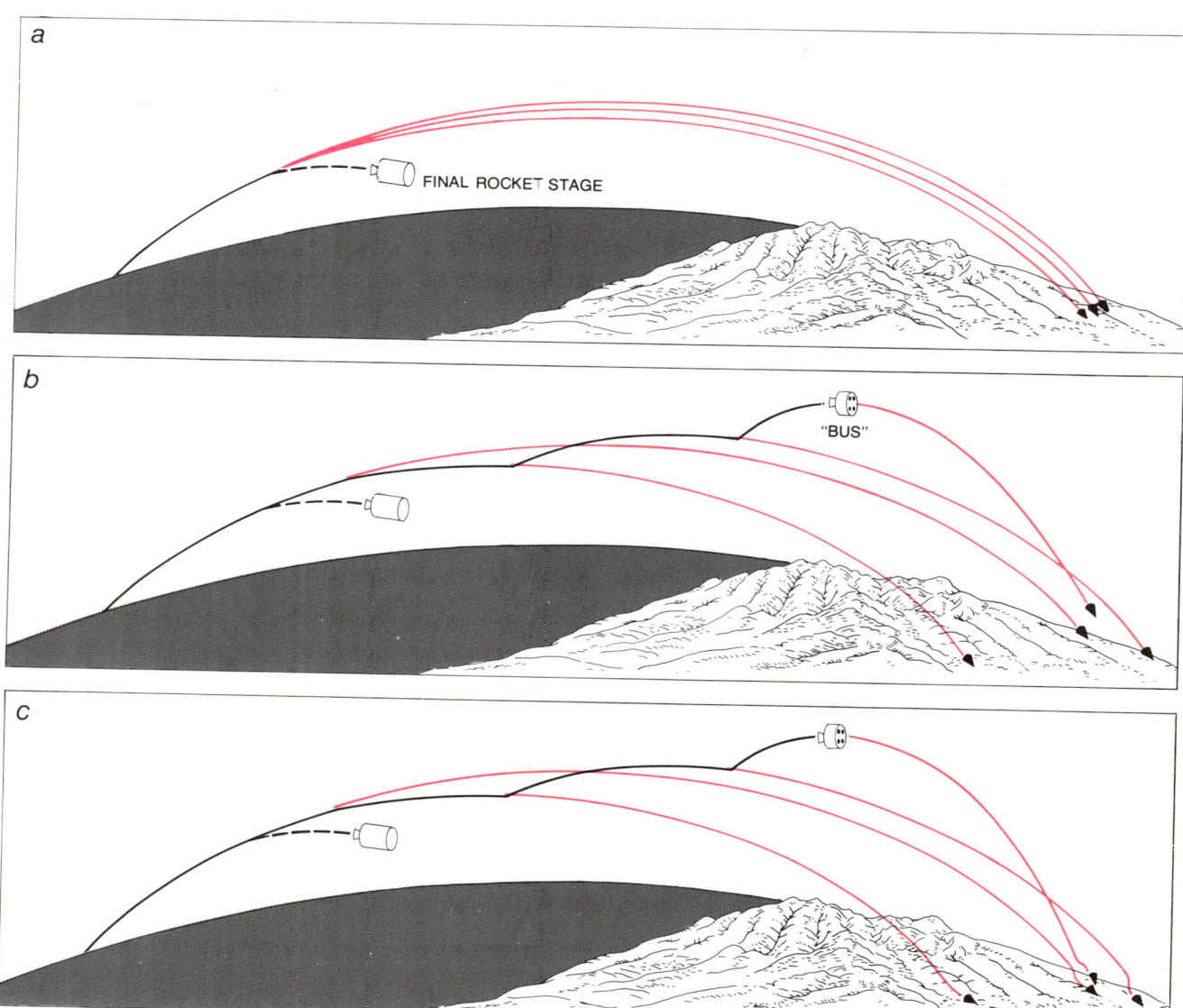

MULTIPLE-WARHEAD MISSILES come in several varieties. The U.S. Polaris A3 missile was equipped with multiple reentry vehicles, or MRV's; it released its warheads simultaneously at a comparatively early stage in the missile's flight; the separate warheads then continued, unpowered and unguided, along the missile's initial ballistic trajectory, falling in a tight pattern (a). The more advanced Minuteman III and Poseidon missiles, now being deployed by the U.S., are equipped with MIRV's (b). These warheads are carried on a "bus," which is capable of changing its direction in flight; after each such change the bus can release another warhead, which then continues, again unpowered and unguided, along that ballistic trajectory. The warheads can fall on widely separated targets. (The Russians started testing MIRV's on some of their missiles last summer, and it is estimated by the U.S. Department of Defense that they could begin deploying them in 1975.) The U.S. now proposes to develop maneuverable reentry vehicles, or MARV's, with terminal guidance (c). Each of these warheads will be capable of greater accuracy (see illustration on page 140).

key element and we haven't seen evidence of accuracy improvement in their work which we would expect to see."

Is there some reason why the U.S. and the U.S.S.R. should have essential equivalence in the capability to destroy missile silos? The arguments against this course of action seem persuasive. There is no benefit in terms of traditional strategic analysis in being able to kill efficiently very large numbers of the other side's silos. As we have established, the U.S. can already destroy some silos, although at a cost of a few U.S. missiles each. Inefficient, limited destruction of silos should suffice for the war scenarios that some envision, in which the U.S. feels it necessary to destroy silos as a way of showing its "resolve." Killing many more silos would not minimize damage to the U.S.; everyone agrees that the U.S. cannot expect to destroy a large enough fraction of the silos or other strategic offensive forces of the U.S.S.R. to limit damage to this country in any meaningful way.

Finally, a critical assumption underlying the preceding discussion is that the silos will have missiles in them when they are destroyed. In fact, the flight time of a Minuteman missile to the Russian missile fields is about 30 minutes. If the Russians were to deploy early-warning satellites, they could detect almost instantaneously the launch of U.S. missiles, which means that the U.S.S.R. could probably have the option of launching many, if not all, of its missiles before the U.S. warheads arrived. Using U.S. warheads against empty silos in empty fields seems a particularly questionable policy.

The full cost of these new programs is unclear. Much depends on the size of the deployments and the extensiveness of the modifications. A useful benchmark is the Minuteman III program; the conversion of 550 older Minuteman missiles into Minuteman III's will cost between $5 billion and $6 billion. Although the costs of some of the new counterforce programs might be comparatively small, the total cost of all the new programs would greatly exceed the Minuteman III costs.

Added to the questions about the analytical reason for the new counterforce programs and the inevitable costs must be the distinct possibility that these programs will be destabilizing and will make arms limitations more difficult to negotiate.

Assuming a crisis situation, a substantial U.S. counterforce capability against Russian ICBM's is more likely to create an incentive for the U.S.S.R. to adopt a hair-trigger, launch-on-warning posture; the Russian leadership would fear that the U.S. might attack first in an attempt to limit damage to itself. These fears would make it even more likely for the U.S.S.R. to attack first in a crisis in order to destroy some of the U.S. ICBM's that had become more tempting targets as a result of the new U.S. counterforce programs.

Schlesinger deplores this instability (as in his fourth feature, cited above, of the new posture), but he and other high officials say that the new U.S. programs are not extensive enough to create such Russian fears. The conceivable accuracy and yield improvements on 1,000 Minuteman missiles, however, even without the terminally guided MARV, could give the U.S. the capability, on paper at least, of destroying between 80 and 90 percent of the Russian ICBM force. The deployment of the MARV or the use of improved SLBM's against the Russian missiles would push that percentage even higher.

The Russian leadership, moreover, might be more conservative than the U.S. leadership in assessing Russian strengths and weaknesses. This conservatism would be based at least partly on the fact that, unlike the balanced reliance in the U.S. on all three elements of the strategic triad, in the U.S.S.R. ICBM's are the primary component of the strategic offensive forces. The U.S.S.R. is allowed up to 1,618 ICBM's under the SALT I Interim Agreement (compared with 1,054 for the U.S.), and the Russians are actively developing four new ICBM's. Moreover, these missiles are under the command of the Strategic Rocket Forces, which since it was created in about 1960 has been one of the most important branches, if not the most important one, of the Russian military. Unlike the U.S. Air Force, which has responsibility not only for ICBM's but also for bombers and many tactical forces, the primary responsibility of the Strategic Rocket Forces is the Russian ICBM force; consequently this organization has every incentive to enhance its role in strategic planning. The Long Range Aviation command, which has responsibility for the Russian bombers, has never had the bureaucratic strength of the Strategic Rocket Forces, and the Russian navy has responsibility for a number of other forces besides missile submarines.

The strategic-planning emphases of the U.S. and the U.S.S.R. differ particularly on the subject of bombers. At present the U.S. has more than 450 intercontinental bombers, about a fourth of which are kept on "ready alert" at a large number of air bases (so that they can avoid being destroyed even in case of surprise attack). The Russians have about 140 long-range bombers. These are qualitatively inferior even to the B-36 bombers deployed by the U.S. in the 1950's, are not kept at as high readiness and are located at just a few air bases. Although a new Russian bomber (named the Backfire by the Pentagon) is just beginning production, it seems primarily intended for targets on the periphery of the U.S.S.R. In any case it is not certain how many Backfires will be built, and the plane appears to lack the critical range and low-altitude capabilities of the B-52's.

As for SLBM's, the U.S.S.R. is building new missile submarines and is allowed more boats and SLBM's than the U.S. under the terms of the SALT agreements. In contrast to the active U.S. MIRV programs for both ICBM's and SLBM's and the new Russian MIRV programs for ICBM's, however, the Russians have not begun testing multiple warheads on their new SLBM. The U.S.S.R., moreover, usually keeps only five or six missile submarines on patrol at any one time, compared with 40 percent of the 41 U.S. boats. In sum, the U.S.S.R. does not seem to give missile submarines the same priority in strategic planning as the U.S.

Schlesinger essentially hinges his denial that first-strike fears by the U.S.S.R. would be enhanced by the planned U.S. improvement in its capabilities against ICBM's on the relative invulnerability of the Russian missile submarines. Compared with the U.S. missile submarines, however, the Russian boats are noisier—an important qualitative disadvantage—and must operate in ocean areas where it is easier for the U.S. to locate and detect them. In addition the U.S. has under way a large, aggressive antisubmarine-warfare program for tactical and strategic uses. It has been reliably estimated that U.S. expenditures in the fiscal year 1972 for antisubmarine warfare were $2.5 billion and that by 1974 they would rise to more than $4 billion. The Russian leaders might well fear, at some future crisis point, that the U.S. had developed a significant antisubmarine-warfare capability, making Schlesinger's suggested ultimate reliance on their missile submarines less than completely reassuring.

One "crisis scenario" that is often concocted to show the danger of the growing Russian counterforce capability against Minuteman and to justify developing improved U.S. counterforce capabilities is an attack or threat of attack by the U.S.S.R. against U.S. ICBM's. The scenario envisions the following chain of events: (1) a real or threatened Russian attack against Minuteman: (2) a realization by the U.S. leadership that it is left or will be left with no more than a capacity to attack Russian cities: (3) major concessions or even surrender by the U.S.

This scenario has an obviously fantastic quality. Even if the internal logic of the scenario were accepted, it still does not justify improving U.S. counterforce capabilities. It does not matter whether the U.S. missiles destroyed are highly accurate or not. What matters is what other U.S. forces can do if these missiles are destroyed. Indeed, as we have seen, by presenting an increased threat to the U.S.S.R., U.S. development of highly accurate missiles might actually make the Russians more likely to attack, thus making the scenario less implausible.

More important, the underlying logic of the scenario is simply wrong, as should be evident to both the U.S. and the Russian leadership. First, the Russians would have to consider that Minuteman might be launched against Russian targets in the 30-minute warning time between the launch of the Russian ICBM's and their arrival at the Minuteman silos. Second, even if a surprised or reasonably cautious U.S. leadership did not launch on warning, a few Minutemen would survive even the most careful attack. Also surviving would be at least the bombers on alert and most if not all of the U.S. missile submarines in the water. (If the attack occurred after an initial crisis period, more bombers than usual would be on alert and more submarines would be in the water.) These combined forces would provide the U.S. with the capacity to carry out a number of limited strikes while still retaining an assured-destruction hedge.

Finally, some U.S. retaliation would seem very likely to the Russian leadership since tens of millions of Americans would be killed in any "Minuteman only" attack. In attacks against silos the bombs are set to explode as close to the ground as possible, thereby picking up much dirt and debris. The fallout from the explosion of thousands of megatons of nuclear weapons over the Minuteman fields would be tremendous, and winds would carry the lethal contamination over many major U.S. cities [see illustration on page 142]. Such calculations of fallout do not even include the possibility of a few Russian warheads going off course and directly hitting populated areas, nor the collateral damage by Russian attacks against other targets, such as bomber bases, many of which are near cities [see illustration on page 143].

Even not assuming a crisis, the consequence of these new U.S. counterforce developments might be to push the U.S.S.R. toward accelerating or expanding existing programs, or starting new ones. The arms race is not as mechanically "action-reaction" as some have suggested, but a substantial new U.S. capability against the primary strategic offensive force of the U.S.S.R. will surely fuel justifications within the Russian bureaucracy for some kind of reaction. This should be particularly true when U.S. antisubmarine-warfare programs, noted above, are also considered.

If the U.S. counterforce programs are allowed to continue beyond the rhetoric of announcing them, these programs would operate to undercut any progress at SALT. Of course, if announcing these programs is just a short-term ploy designed to strengthen the U.S. bargaining position for the impending SALT II

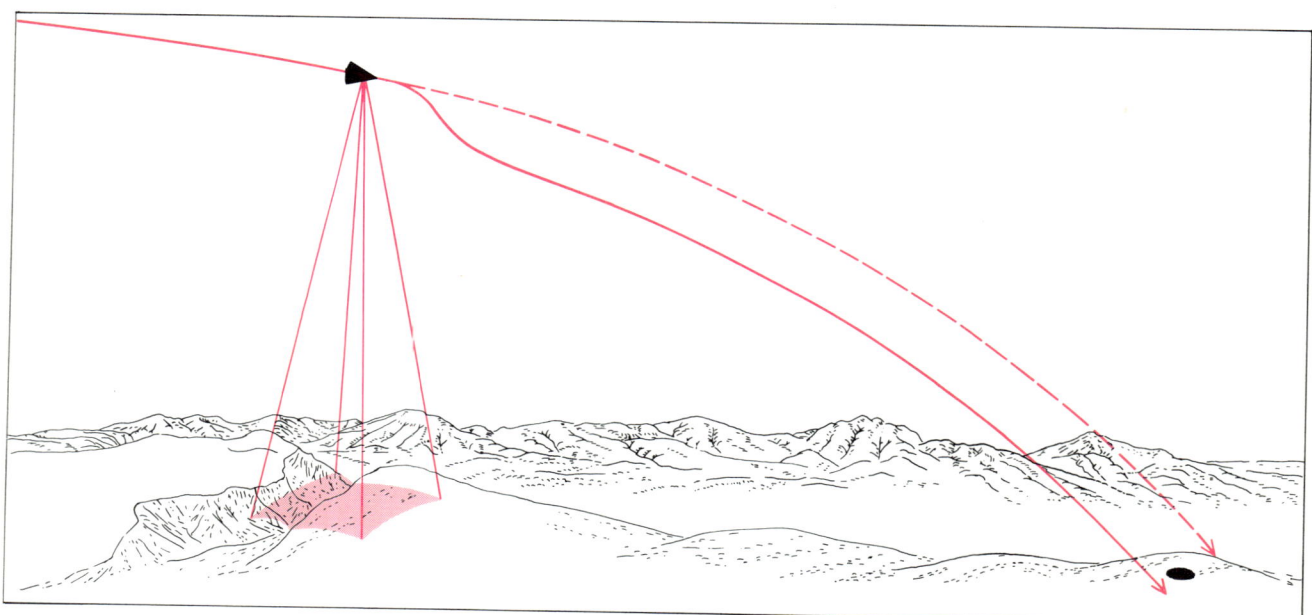

MOST LIKELY CANDIDATE for the proposed terminally guided MARV is the "homing" MARV, depicted in this idealized drawing. (The homing MARV is sometimes referred to as a "true" MARV to distinguish it from another type of terminally guided MARV that would rely on a comparatively straightforward, on-board inertial-guidance system.) The homing MARV would operate by means of an on-board sensor capable of acquiring an image or images of the target area or of some nearby, prominent terrain feature. (Alternatively, the sensor could operate by obtaining an "altitude profile" of the terrain features along its flight path.) It is still unclear what kind of sensor will be used; radar and optical systems are considered among the leading possibilities. Once the target or other feature has been acquired the warhead would be maneuvered under the control of an on-board computer on the basis of feedback information from the sensor. The actual terminal maneuvering could be accomplished by means of gas jets or aerodynamic vanes.

agreements, then little real harm will result. There is no evidence, however, that top Administration officials intend to turn these programs off quickly. And even if there are such intentions, new weapons programs tend to gain a momentum of their own once they are announced. High-level officials become publicly committed to rationales for them, rationales that include more than the systems' just being "bargaining chips." Bureaucracies are created with a vested interest in the continuation and expansion of these programs. Moreover, improvements in accuracy and yield would be particularly difficult to limit explicitly in SALT, making it harder to rationalize publicly any subsequent termination of the program.

Accuracy improvements are generally accepted as being among the most difficult weapons characteristics to limit in an arms-control agreement, because of problems of both definition and verification. Drafting a workable, direct limit on accuracy seems impossible, since the counterforce potential of a warhead depends on the accuracy-yield combination. Moreover, a simple numerical limit on accuracy would not be verifiable. A photograph of a silo or even the missile gives little clue to the kind of small but important differences in accuracy that are being considered here. Closer examination through on-site inspection, even if such inspection could be negotiated, would be insufficient. On-site inspection could indicate whether the warhead was a terminally guided MARV, but this would not establish any particular accuracy. Moreover, on-site inspection includes a heroic assumption that the latest warheads are on the missile and not stored nearby in an area excluded from the on-site inspection provisions.

Surveillance of Russian missile-testing may give some indication of accuracy. The indication, however, is indirect and not conclusive. Test data tell one about the ballistic coefficient (or pointedness) of the warhead, its reentry speed and similar information, all of which helps in estimating accuracy. An outside observer, however, can never be sure what the actual target is. Similarly, course corrections by the warhead would indicate a maneuvering capability but not necessarily terminal guidance or particularly high accuracies.

An indirect way to limit or impede accuracy improvements through SALT would be by placing a strict limit on the number of missile tests. This would make it more difficult to develop advanced guidance techniques and to test them often enough so that the military would have confidence in them. The low limits necessary seem nonnegotiable, however, since they represent a direct challenge to all new strategic programs. Even without accuracy improvements the Pentagon will want to do extensive research and development and operational testing of the new Trident missile and further operational testing of the Minuteman and Poseidon missiles. Similarly, the Russians will want to flight-test extensively their four new ICBM's and their new SLBM as well as their existing arsenal of missiles.

Limits in SALT on the yield of warheads might be more possible, but they would be of uncertain significance. The two sides could limit yield by an agreement that warheads not be larger than a given yield or a given weight. The effect of any such limitation could be circumvented, however, by increasing the number of warheads and by increasing their accuracy. Moreover, it would be difficult to verify the exact yield of a warhead. Even elaborate on-site inspection would not ensure that "advanced" warheads were not hidden nearby. Surveillance of flight tests only gives an estimate of the size of the warhead, and yield per pound of warhead can be varied by warhead design and the richness of the nuclear "fuel" used.

In short, the practical difficulties of fashioning limitations in SALT on the type of counterforce improvements now planned by the U.S. make such limitations unlikely and will instead presumably create strong pressures in the U.S.S.R. to expand old programs or to start new ones that either match or compensate for the U.S. programs. This in turn can only work against other limitations on strategic arms.

Allied concerns about the credibility of the U.S. deterrent are another reason offered for developing missiles with improved counterforce capabilities. Occasionally a specific scenario—a Russian attack in central Europe—is given as a justification for such improvements. Neither the scenario nor the more general invocation of allied claims is persuasive.

The European scenario supposedly demonstrates that the U.S. needs the ability to respond with nuclear weapons in order to show its resolve and to destroy some of the attacking Russian forces. There are, however, already sizable U.S. forces in Europe that could accomplish both of those objectives. Even if the U.S. decided to employ strategic weapons, existing U.S. forces could carry out a wide variety of selective attacks.

As for the broader claims of allied concerns, Morton Halperin, an authority on nuclear strategy, has remarked: "The credibility of the U.S. deterrent to an Ally is primarily a result of the overall U.S.-Ally relationship, which includes economic and political considerations as well as military. To the extent that Allied leaders evaluate U.S. military capabilities, they look especially to the U.S. conventional and nuclear forces in that particular theater of operations. Fine distinctions in the U.S.-Soviet strategic balance or in U.S. strategic policy are unimportant to Allied leaders. Among those Allied analysts who care, opinion is probably split between those who favor the U.S. possessing an efficient silo-kill capability and those who do not."

Among the European strategic analysts who oppose such deployments is Ian Smart, formerly assistant director of the London-based International Institute of Strategic Studies. Smart writes: "Producing and deploying much more accurate strategic missiles...is to be regretted and even feared since...it can only reduce the stability of the strategic balance in any period of acute tension." At least part of this European concern can be attributed to the fact that, in a strategic exchange, the industrialized European countries are very likely targets—if only because of the U.S. forces deployed in or near those countries.

Finally, even assuming that the allies (or even the American people) accord considerable political significance to fine distinctions in the "strategic balance," Schlesinger's proposed counterforce improvements are not very helpful politics. The supposedly important distinctions are usually visible ones such as the number of delivery vehicles, the number of warheads or the throw weight. Schlesinger's accuracy and yield improvements do not affect these indicators, except possibly in the counterproductive way of reducing the number of warheads in order to allow larger ones.

On balance, then, there seem to be strong arguments against developing missiles with improved counterforce capabilities. Collateral damage can best be minimized by shifting targets, not improving accuracies by a few hundred feet. The ability to destroy efficiently large numbers of missile silos in order to "match the Russians" seems not only unnecessary and expensive but also destabilizing. SALT might well be undercut, and the supposed concerns of our allies about the U.S. deterrent are not answered by such programs.

As one gets caught up in considering nuclear-war scenarios and nuclear-weapons capabilities there is a dangerous tendency to forget that the primary objective of nuclear strategy is to avoid nuclear wars, not to fight them.

Given the destructive power of nuclear weapons and the world's lack of experience in using them, crossing the "nuclear threshold" would be a profoundly destabilizing event. It is a delusion to believe one country could employ nuclear weapons, even on a limited scale, and have a high degree of confidence that the response by another nuclear power would be predictable and proportionate. The particular first use might be estimated by the opposing country's observers to be greater than it actually was, or the use might have created more damage than expected (for example through greater-than-expected fallout). The opposing country might not have readily available weapons of the same yield or similar targeting options and decide to escalate. The political reaction in the opposing country might lead to escalation. In short, the possible causes for matters getting out of hand are endless.

To make deterrence work, a country must carefully consider its public attitude toward nuclear war and cautiously select its retaliatory options. This does not mean that the U.S. should have only the single strategic option of massive retaliation against cities. This country already has ample capabilities for lesser options, and it seems appropriate to have the flexibility, at a minimum, for possible responses to accidental or limited launches.

The Nixon Administration, however, is going beyond this. It is seeking the additional capability to attack efficiently large numbers of Russian missile silos. Not only might this counterforce option be destabilizing in itself but also the Administration's promotion of the option and its general public advocacy of a counterforce strategy might have a pervasive, if subtle, tendency to reduce the inhibitions against the use of nuclear weapons—in effect, to lower the "nuclear threshold." New bureaucracies, with vested interests in the hardware and rationales of a counterforce strategy, are created. In trying to gain public approval of new policies and programs, leaders find themselves taking more simplistic positions than the uncertainty of nuclear warfare warrants. In this climate some of the risks of nuclear war are downplayed. Unrealistically precise calculations suggest that limited nuclear war can be kept limited and even result in positive gains.

There are some disturbing parallels here to the vogue of limited conventional

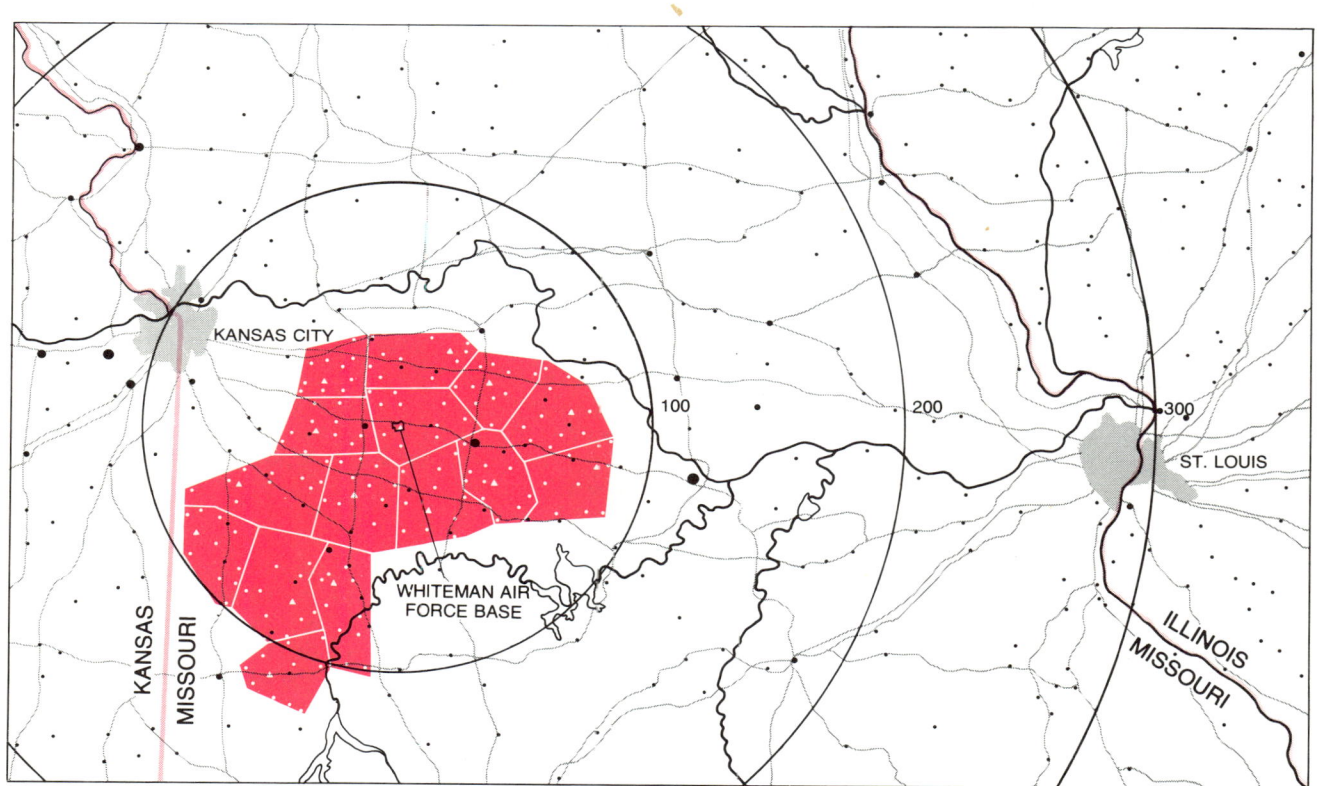

RUSSIAN PLANNERS MUST CONSIDER that a hypothetical "limited counterforce" attack against the U.S. Minuteman ICBM fields (such as the one shown here in the vicinity of Whiteman Air Force Base in Missouri) would create an enormous cloud of lethal radioactive fallout that would presumably extend for hundreds of miles downwind of the target area, killing or injuring millions of exposed civilians in nearby cities and towns and thereby making massive U.S. retaliation seem very likely. (For comparison, a single 15-megaton nuclear explosion at Eniwetok in 1954 contaminated an area of some 7,000 square miles, extending 300 miles downwind and 20 miles upwind; to be at all effective, any contemplated counterforce attack against a Minuteman field would require the ground-level explosion of hundreds of megatons of nuclear warheads and would accordingly produce a much larger area of radioactive contamination.) The Minuteman field at Whiteman, one of six such fields in the north-central U.S., has 150 Minuteman missiles arranged in 15 "flights" of 10 missiles each (*irregular colored shapes*); the missiles are installed in hardened underground "launch facilities," or "silos" (*white dots*), with each flight of missiles having its own "launch control facility" (*white triangles*). The concentric scale rings are centered on the main airfield at Whiteman and are drawn at 100-mile radial intervals. Gray lines are principal roads. Black lines are major rivers. Gray areas are main metropolitan regions. Black dots are smaller cities and towns.

war in the early 1960's. In pushing for changes in conventional strategy and new procurement, advocates of limited conventional war ignored some of the pitfalls and costs of such a strategy. The searing national experience of the war in Vietnam was needed to demonstrate these oversights.

Exactly where the line should be drawn on "selective targeting options" is not at all clear. It seems most inadvisable, however, to take the gamble of developing missiles with improved counterforce capabilities, whether this is to match a specific Russian capability or for any other reason.

Opponents of U.S. counterforce improvements, nonetheless, must recognize certain practical limits to their arguments. Even if Congress declines to fund the new and accelerated development programs Schlesinger is proposing, continued U.S. testing of strategic missiles and various research-and-development efforts already under way inevitably will lead to some improvements in missile accuracy. (As Schlesinger has pointed out, some refinements in existing guidance systems will occur almost as a matter of course—through better software programs, greater purity in rocket fuel, better measurement of the earth's gravitational field and numerous other factors. The development of a terminally guided MARV, something further beyond the state of the art, requires more of a conscious bureaucratic decision to proceed.) Besides U.S. advances, moreover, Russian counterforce improvements are likely to continue, raising serious questions about Russian intentions.

Faced with these likely developments, the solution is still not to follow the Schlesinger approach. Rather, the solution should be to seek actively to negotiate for limits on MIRV's and for the reduction of vulnerable strategic forces.

Limits on MIRV's would be designed to slow the perceived threat to U.S. ICBM's, a Russian threat that many consider destabilizing. In return for the U.S. slowing certain of its strategic programs, for example, the U.S.S.R. might agree to limits on the deployment of the SSX-18, the "follow on" missile to the large SS-9. This would push at least a few years further into the future the time when analysts would estimate that only a particular level of Minuteman could survive a Russian counterforce attack.

Negotiating missile reductions represents another approach: to limit not only the threatening forces but also the threatened ones. This approach would

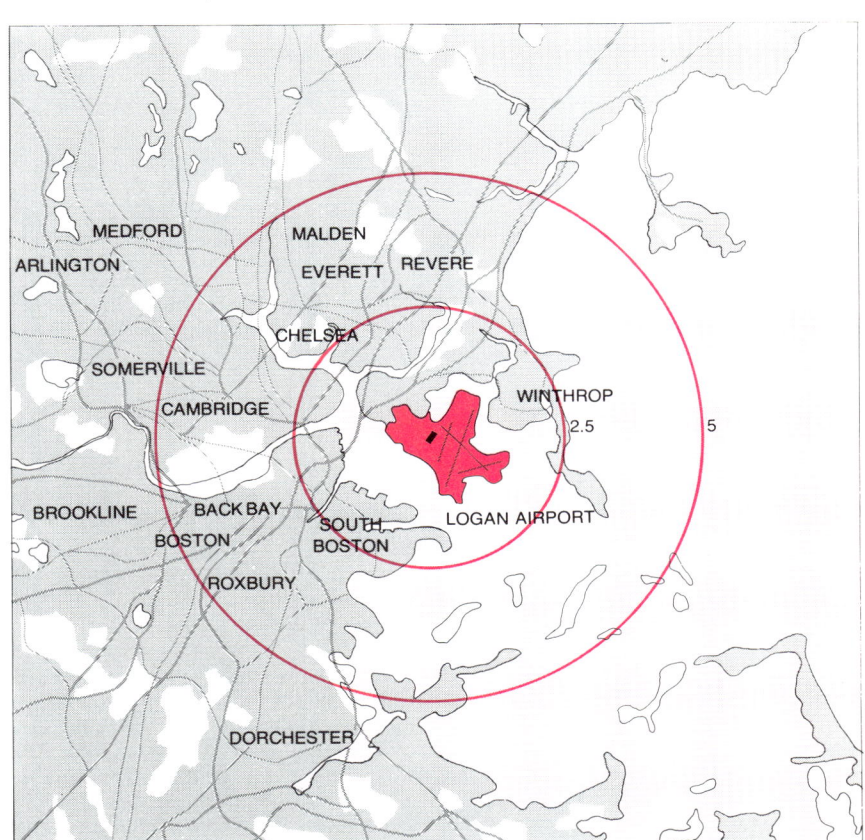

"UNINTENDED COLLATERAL DAMAGE" resulting from a "limited counterforce attack" against a military target such as a large airfield would also be considerable, particularly since many such targets are located near major cities. For example, Logan airport near Boston, shown on this map, must be considered a military target, since strategic bombers are likely to use it in a war. (B-52's were reportedly stationed there during the Cuban missile crisis.) A 100-kiloton nuclear warhead exploding directly over Logan would create an "overpressure" of between three and four pounds per square inch out to a radius of about 2½ miles (*smaller colored circle*); a one-megaton warhead would create the same overpressure out to five miles (*larger colored circle*). This overpressure would kill many people in the area and would cause severe to moderate damage to most structures. (For a surface explosion the damage radius would be about three-quarters of that for an airburst of the same yield, but the fallout would be greater.) An improvement in missile accuracy of a few hundred feet or so would clearly not alter the position of these large circles by much.

essentially mean bilateral reductions in ICBM's, presumably in a way that would retire the more threatening ICBM's, so that the remaining ICBM's would be less vulnerable. Some asymmetrical reductions might also be considered. For instance, the U.S. could reduce its ICBM's, whereas the U.S.S.R. (having less to fear in the short run about the vulnerability of its ICBM's) could reduce some ICBM's plus other forces.

Reductions in the land-based missiles of both sides would reduce the importance of this strategic strike force. It would thereby undercut the rationale for an expensive contest of matching counterforce improvements. More important, it would reduce the greatest potential source of instability in a crisis. Both countries would have less incentive to adopt an unstable, launch-on-warning posture or to launch an attack out of fear of a preemptive strike.

The reductions approach has received support recently from such diverse sources as the Federation of American Scientists and Fred C. Iklé, director of the Arms Control and Disarmament Agency. It was even accorded the status of a possibility in Schlesinger's recent annual report.

Rather than focusing on how to match the U.S.S.R. in a particular capability when such matching does not bode well for either country, the strategic debate in the U.S. in the coming months should focus on MIRV limits, force reductions and other measures designed to minimize the chances of nuclear war and to decelerate the arms race.

12 Limited Nuclear War

by Sidney D. Drell and Frank von Hippel
November 1976

The U.S. may be committing itself to preparing for a war limited to attacks on military bases, with relatively few civilian casualties. Would the casualties really be few, and could the war stay limited?

For more than a decade U.S. strategic policy has been dominated by the recognition and acceptance of a few simple facts: We and the Russians are each other's nuclear hostages; in the event of nuclear war neither this country nor the U.S.S.R. would be able to defend itself against virtual annihilation; even if one side were to initiate the war with a massive preemptive attack, the other would retain an "assured destruction" capability, the ability to devastate the attacker. In one form or another this recognition has underlain most of the past quarter century of mutual deterrence.

It has also been recognized, however, that nuclear weapons might be launched with restraint on both sides, with less than devastating results. President Nixon emphasized in 1970 the importance of having options other than "massive retaliation" for replying to a small (and possibly accidental) attack. That formulation of flexible response was nothing new. U.S. leaders have for many years had the option of launching a limited nuclear attack rather than an all-out one. The requirements of flexible response were expanded, however, by former Secretary of Defense James R. Schlesinger in Congressional testimony on March 4, 1974. According to his formulation, the U.S. should include in its flexible-response repertory the possibility of replying to a limited nuclear attack with selected strikes, notably "counterforce" strikes targeted against enemy military installations. Schlesinger argued that such strikes would be qualitatively different from intentional attacks on population centers, reducing the probability that a limited nuclear war would escalate into a massive exchange resulting in large civilian casualties, and that a flexible capability would make the possibility of a U.S. nuclear attack more credible and would thus increase the leverage provided by U.S. nuclear forces in international confrontations.

Since 1974 Schlesinger and other defense spokesmen have emphasized what they now seem to regard as two necessary new ingredients of a flexible-response strategy. One is the development of intercontinental ballistic missiles (ICBM's) capable of destroying "hardened" Russian military targets, such as missiles emplaced in blast-resistant underground silos. The other is a major expansion of the civil defense program, which has been largely inactive since the early 1960's. The purpose of the civil defense program would be to improve the credibility of the U.S. limited-nuclear-war posture by protecting the civilian population from the effects of limited Russian nuclear attacks. The new emphases give more weight to achieving a capability for fighting and "winning" a limited nuclear war.

This proposed shift in strategy and the weapons-development and civil defense measures being sought to support it have come under attack on two broad grounds. First, detailed calculations based on the properties of nuclear weapons of the coming decade suggest that the casualties from any militarily significant nuclear counterforce strike would be so devastatingly high that this concept of limited nuclear war loses meaning. Second, a counterforce strategy founded on the ability to destroy enemy ICBM's increases the chances of nuclear war.

In his testimony before a subcommittee of the Senate Committee on Foreign Relations in March, 1974, Schlesinger supported his advocacy of such a counterforce capability by suggesting that a counterforce strike against the U.S. might result in "hundreds of thousands" of civilian casualties "as opposed to tens and hundreds of millions," which could result from an all-out nuclear exchange. Several senators were skeptical that a militarily significant strike could cause so few casualties; Senator Clifford P. Case of New Jersey in particular asked that the basis for the casualty calculations be further explained. In September, Schlesinger returned with Department of Defense computer calculations on the consequences of limited nuclear war. The figures indicated that if extensive civil defense protection were available and taken advantage of, a Russian attack on all 1,054 Minuteman and Titan ICBM's, with one one-megaton warhead targeted on each silo, would cause about 800,000 civilian deaths. Schlesinger concluded from this that "the likelihood of limited nuclear attacks cannot be challenged on the assumption that massive civilian fatalities and injuries would result."

Some senators were still skeptical, and the Congressional Office of Technology Assessment (OTA) was asked to review the Defense Department calculations. An expert panel including one of the present authors (Drell) reported back in February, 1975, that "the casualties calculated were substantially too low for the attacks in question as a result of a lack of attention to intermediate and long-term effects" of the nuclear explosions. Pointing out that the Russian strike postulated by the Defense Department was "evidently not designed to maximize destruction of U.S. ICBM's," the panel insisted that a real Russian effort to cause maximum damage to U.S.

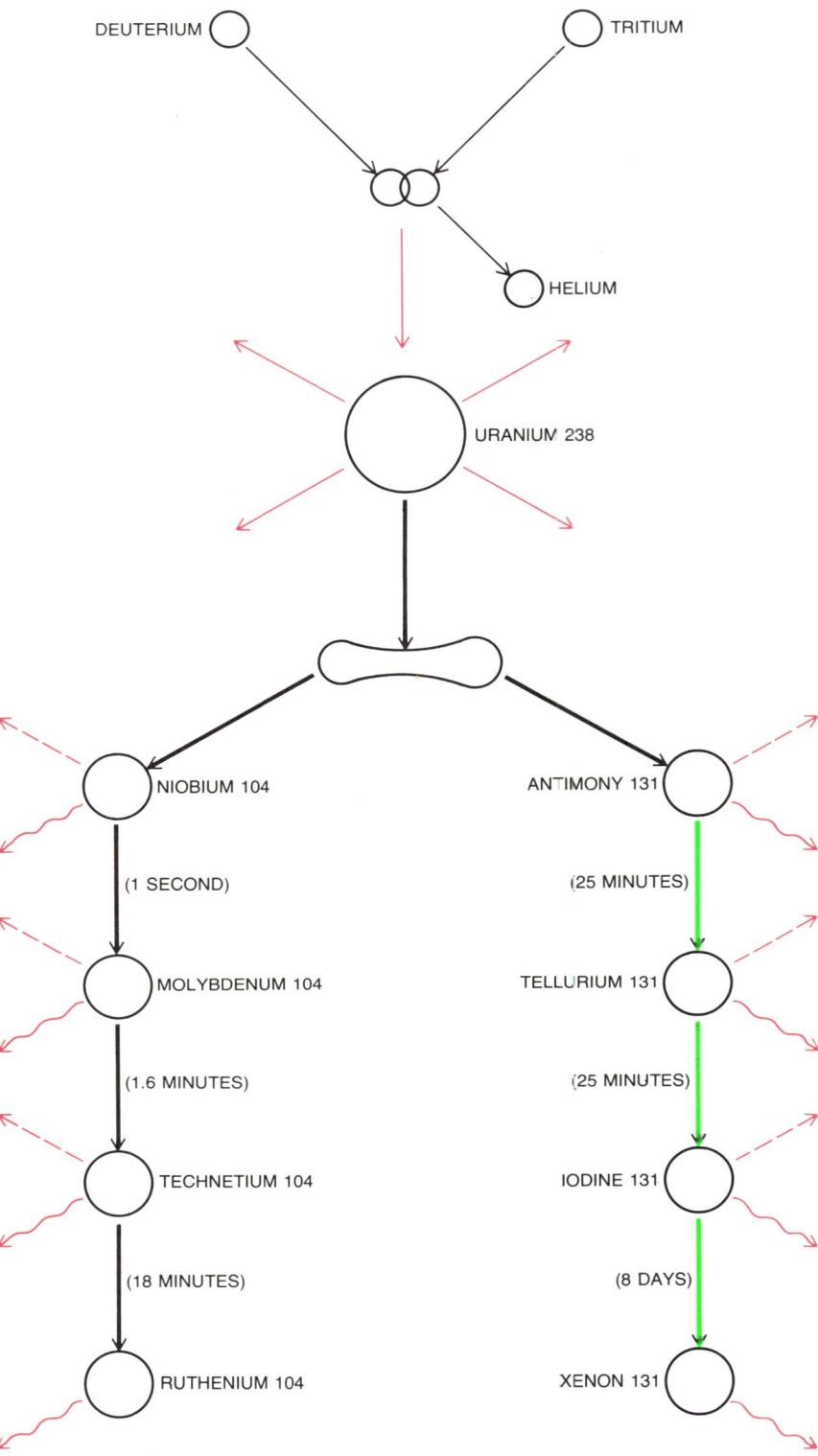

FISSION PRODUCTS, the source of fallout radiation, are produced in the chain of events following a nuclear explosion, in this case a typical fission-fusion-fission explosion. Heated by an initial fission explosion, the hydrogen isotopes deuterium and tritium fuse to form helium, releasing an energetic neutron (*colored arrow*). The neutron enters the nucleus of a uranium-238 atom, making it unstable; it fissions, releasing four neutrons and two radioactive daughter nuclei, or fission products. The fission products emit beta rays, or electrons (*broken arrows*), and gamma rays (*wavy arrows*), thus decaying to form new products. Each decay chain ultimately terminates in a stable isotope. For each transition there is a characteristic half-life, which tends to become longer as the stable stage is approached. Other decay chains, not illustrated here, produce the important long-lived radioisotopes strontium 90 and cesium 137.

to become available in the next decade, such an attack might be delivered by one megaton or two megatons of nuclear explosive fuzed to detonate near the surface at each of the 150 or 200 hardened ICBM silos at the base.

Radioactive fallout originates with the thousands of tons of soil, rock and other material that would be melted or vaporized by the heat of each explosion and mixed with its radioactive by-products. This debris would be carried to a height of some eight miles with the rising fireball. In the stratosphere the fireball would cool and the larger particles would descend to the ground within a day or so, over an area extending some hundreds of miles downwind, as "local" fallout. The smaller particles would drift great distances and eventually descend as global fallout.

The hazards of local fallout were dramatized by the events that followed the first U.S. test of a fission-fusion-fission bomb (with a yield of 15 megatons) at Bikini Atoll on March 1, 1954 [*see illustration on opposite page*]. Fishermen 80 miles downwind received radiation doses that ultimately killed one of them. At the south end of Rongelap Atoll, 100 miles downwind, people suffered severe short-term and long-term radiation effects. If they had been living at the north end of the atoll, the higher radiation levels there would almost surely have killed them.

If people in the local-fallout zone did not (as the residents of Rongelap did) ingest contaminated food and water, the principal hazard would be external radiation from radioactive particles. (Most of the particles in local fallout would be too large for inhalation into the lungs.) If people did not stay outdoors and come into direct contact with fallout, thereby sustaining burns caused by beta particles (the short-range electrons emitted by radioactive nuclei) the major hazard would be the more penetrating gamma radiation.

In order to determine the distribution and consequences of local fallout one needs to know the fission yield and height of burst of each warhead, the biological effects of a given absorbed radiation dose, the dependence of the fallout pattern on weather conditions, the degree to which the population is sheltered and the geographic distribution and total megatonnage of the attack. Predictions of fatalities and injuries are sensitive to the assumptions one makes about each of these factors, which we shall consider in turn.

The radioactivity in the fallout would come mostly from fission. A "thermonuclear" weapon is typically a fission-fusion-fission device. A "small" fission explosive (one of the chain-reacting isotopes uranium 235 or plutonium 239)

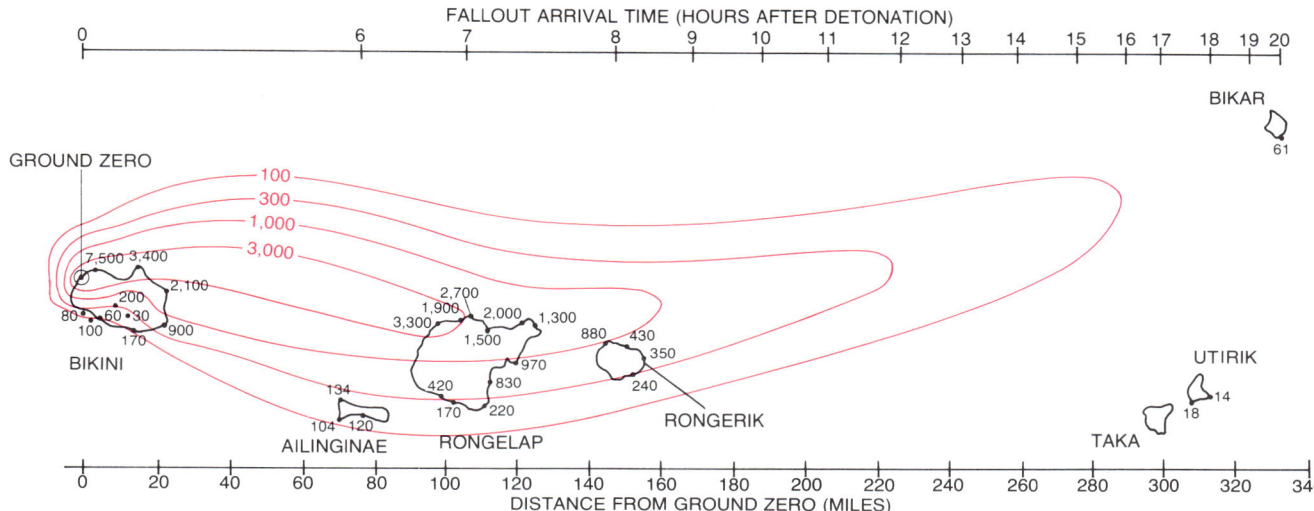

HAZARDS OF LOCAL FALLOUT downwind from a thermonuclear explosion were dramatized by the U.S. test of a 15-megaton fission-fusion-fission bomb on Bikini Atoll on March 1, 1954. The measurements (*black numbers*) give the total dose, in rems, that had accumulated 96 hours after the explosion. Contour lines calculated on the basis of those measurements outline the fallout pattern.

triggers a fusion explosion involving, for example, the hydrogen isotopes deuterium and tritium. The high-energy neutrons emitted by the fusion reactions then fission the nuclei of a large amount of the non-chain-reacting isotope uranium 238, releasing more fission energy [*see illustration on opposite page*]. In the Defense Department calculations 50 percent of the energy release was assumed to be due to fission, and that is a representative fraction.

The biological consequences of gamma radiation depend on the total dose received and the time period over which it is delivered. The median lethal radiation dose was taken by Defense Department analysts to be 450 rems for doses received within a few days. (The rem, standing for "roentgen equivalent man," is a unit of the biological effect of radiation.) For doses delivered over a longer time the lethal dose was taken to be somewhat higher because, given time, a biological system can repair a considerable amount of radiation damage. The effective dose suffered by the exposed population when the rate of repair just balances the rate of damage being done by the decaying ambient field of radiation would be the "maximum biological dose" and would determine the lethality of the exposure.

Death from radiation sickness would be neither quick nor painless. As described in the Glasstone book, "the initial symptoms are...nausea, vomiting, diarrhea, loss of appetite and malaise." Beginning two or three weeks after the exposure "there is a tendency to bleed into various organs, and small hemorrhages under the skin...are observed." Spontaneous bleeding from the mouth and intestinal tract is common. "Loss of hair...also starts after about two weeks.... Ulceration about the lips may...spread from the mouth through the entire gastrointestinal tract." Eventually "the decrease in the white cells of the blood and injury to other immune mechanisms of the body...allow an overwhelming infection to develop." One has only to multiply that description by the millions to get a partial picture of the possible consequences of "limited" nuclear attacks on the U.S. and the U.S.S.R.

If the fresh fission products from one megaton of fission were spread uniformly over a perfectly flat area of 1,000 square miles, the gamma-ray dose rate one meter above the ground would be about 250 rems per hour after 10 hours. For human beings the median lethal dose at such a high dose rate is about 450 rems. The gamma-ray dose rate would decrease about sixteenfold for every tenfold increase in time for the first six months after the explosion and more rapidly thereafter. In our example the radiation intensity would be down to about 15 rems per hour after four days and about one rem per hour after 40 days. For a person remaining in the radiation zone, however, the cumulative dose would continue to rise significantly for quite a long time. Consider the local fallout beginning about 10 hours after an explosion, which is a typical time for the fallout to reach ground level. A full 40 percent of the dose accumulating after that time would remain to be delivered after four days, and 25 percent of it would still remain to be delivered after 40 days.

The height of burst of the warheads, which has an important influence on the amount of fallout deposited downwind, would be affected by the choice of target. In the counterforce attacks envisioned by the Defense Department most of the megatonnage would be directed against underground Minuteman silos. The Department reported that the Minuteman-killing effectiveness of surface bursts and of airbursts at the "optimum height of burst" would be about equal. (The optimum height of burst is the height that, for a given yield, provides a blast pressure exceeding a certain value over the largest area; for a one-megaton yield and an overpressure of 1,000 pounds per square inch it would be about 1,000 feet.) The attacker would thus be faced with a trade-off. On the one hand a surface burst does not have to be as precisely placed as an airburst (an important consideration, since attacks on hardened targets put a high priority on accuracy). On the other hand, Defense Department calculations show that, other things being equal, for an attack on the U.S. ICBM's fallout fatalities could be four times higher for surface bursts than for airbursts.

The fireball from a one-megaton nuclear explosion and the fission products it contains rise rapidly until the top of the cooling fireball cloud enters the stratosphere, about six miles above sea level at middle latitudes. At a height of about eight miles the cloud stabilizes, with its fission products spread over an area about four miles in diameter. An average settling time for the local fallout from a one-megaton explosion might be about eight hours. The settling time and the average speed of the winds between the top of the fireball cloud and the ground determine how far the particles drift downwind. For a typical aver-

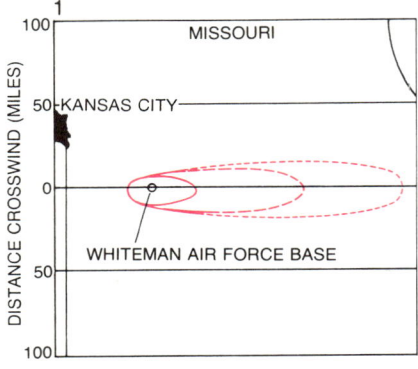

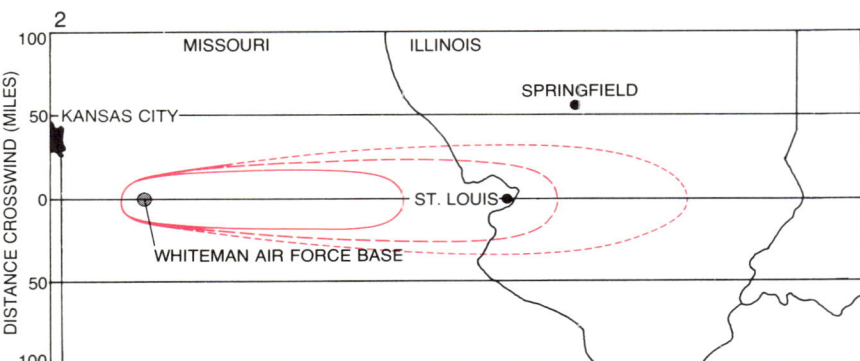

age wind velocity of 20 miles per hour the average drifting distance would be 160 miles. (The settling time also determines the extent to which short-lived radioactive isotopes decay harmlessly before reaching the surface.) The width of the fallout pattern is determined primarily by the differences in the speed and direction of the winds to which particles are subjected at various heights in the cloud. For a typical wind shear of one mile per hour per mile of height and an average wind speed of 20 miles per hour, the pattern of fallout 100 miles downwind from ground zero would be about 25 miles wide.

Clearly the number of casualties depends to a considerable degree on what weather conditions are assumed. In the Defense Department calculations the total casualties from one postulated attack were three times higher with typical March winds blowing than they were with typical June winds. Such variations are largely due to changes in wind direction and wind speed that cause the fallout pattern to cover certain densely populated areas or miss them. Consider the fallout pattern downwind from the Minuteman wing at Whiteman Air Force Base in central Missouri after a Russian attack by two one-megaton surface bursts (with 50 percent of the yield from fission) on each of the base's 150 silos. With an average wind velocity of 20 miles per hour the lethal fallout zone for people indoors would stretch to the Illinois-Indiana border; with an average wind velocity of 60 miles per hour (which is not an unusual speed high in the troposphere, where the fallout would be for most of the time before it

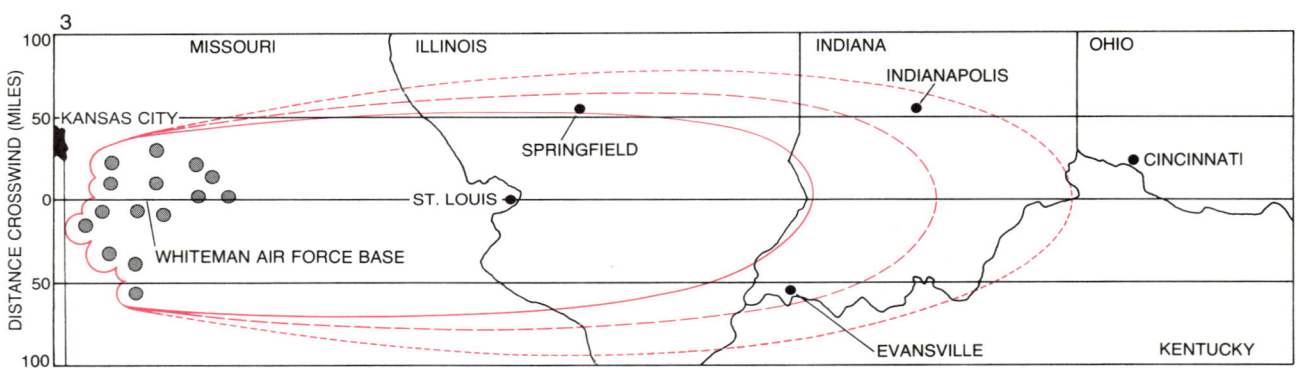

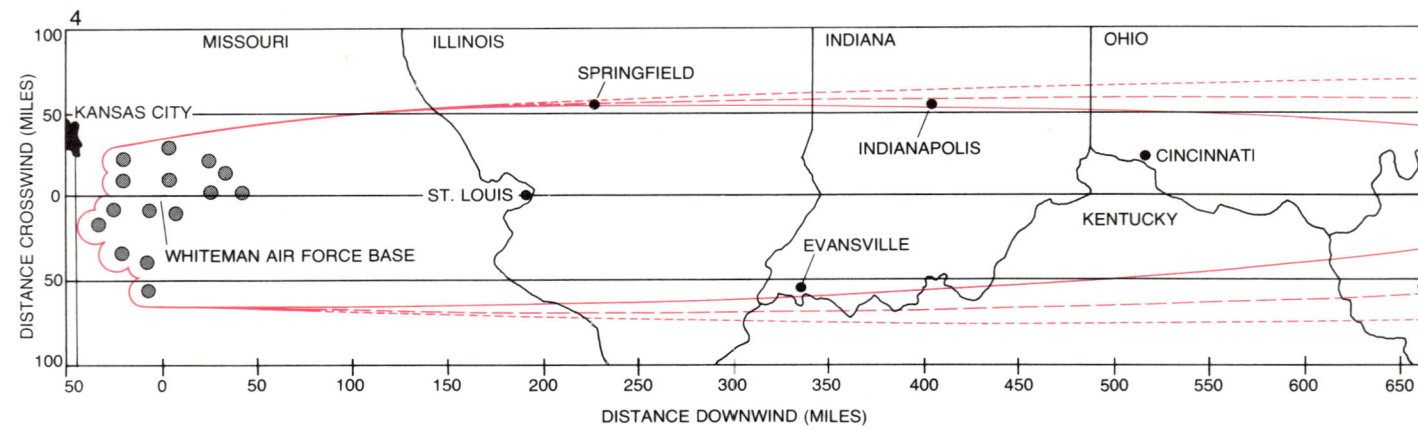

FALLOUT PATTERNS are shown for attacks by one-megaton warheads (with 50 percent of their explosive yield from fission) exploded at the surface on ICBM's at Whiteman Air Force Base in Missouri. The contours correspond to maximum biological doses of 1,350 rems outdoors, or 450 rems (50 percent fatalities) inside an average residence (*solid line*); 450 rems outdoors (*broken line*), and 150 rems outdoors (*dotted line*), the approximate threshold for fatalities. The four patterns are for a single warhead (*1*), for one warhead

settled to the ground) it would stretch all the way to the Virginia border [see illustration on these two pages]. The area within the lethal-dose contour would be very large: about 2 percent of the land area of the continental U.S.

There are six Minuteman bases from which comparably massive fields of lethal radiation would extend, and three 18-missile Titan bases as well. Hence in the event of a counterforce strike against U.S. missiles a substantial portion of the U.S. would be covered by the downwind radiation patterns from the thousands of nuclear explosions. And a significant fraction of the population, including the residents of many major Middle Western cities, would be in the zones of lethal radiation [see illustration on next page]. Presumably a map of the U.S.S.R. would show a similar pattern for a U.S. counterforce attack on that country.

The consequences of being caught in the fallout pattern downwind from a low-altitude or surface fission explosion would depend, of course, not only on the level of ground contamination but also on where one took refuge. Currently the U.S. civil defense program requires that for a shelter space to be identified as such it must shield against all but 1 to 2 percent of the fallout gamma radiation. The degree of protection a given shelter provides is characterized by its "protection factor," which is the reciprocal of the fraction of radiation that penetrates it. The current requirement is therefore a protection factor of 50 to 100. That degree of shielding can be provided by cover of approximately two feet of dirt or 16 inches of concrete. Those parts of a single-story residence that are above ground level have a protection factor of 3. The basement of the residence may have a protection factor of 20 to 40 if it is completely below ground level and therefore receives gamma radiation almost entirely from fallout that lands on the roof of the building.

In the Defense Department calculations the postulated distribution of protection factors corresponds to assuming that about 60 percent of the people in the U.S. would seek and reach the best shelter available in their area [see top illustration on page 152]. The 40 percent who did not seek shelter or for whom shelter was not available were assigned a protection factor of 3, that of an average residence. It was found that halving the protection factors increased the number of deaths by more than 50 percent.

It is important to note that the Defense Department analysts assumed that people would remain sheltered for 30 days. At the current level of civil defense preparation it is highly unlikely that the population could remain so well sheltered for such a length of time. For a limited nuclear war to be taken seriously as a policy option—as a realistic threat in a confrontation with the U.S.S.R.— it would be necessary to make much better shelter arrangements. In other words, the U.S. would have to embark on a greatly enlarged civil defense program.

Indeed, the development of civil defense procedures requiring the massive evacuation and relocation of populations during crises has recently been proposed in the annual U.S. defense budget request as a necessary adjunct to the new strategy. The preparations required for such mass movements and for the support of the population for long periods away from home would have a major impact on U.S. peacetime society. Identified shelter spaces and evacuation plans by themselves would not constitute an effective civil defense program; a total system would have to be organized and woven into civilian life through training programs, rehearsals and volunteer activities.

An idea of the magnitude of a civil defense program that could achieve high shelter occupancy and maintain it for several weeks or longer can be gained from the system envisioned by the 1962 U.S. civil defense guide. The plans, which were never implemented, contemplated that for every shelter accommodating 100 civilians there should be an operating cadre of 25, of whom 10 or 12 would need training. That is, 10 percent of the sheltered population, or 20 percent of the adult population, would have to be trained. To recruit such a large cadre the Government would have to look beyond existing community safety personnel such as policemen, firemen and National Guard units.

One task of these trained people would be to operate communication systems over substantial distances in order to deal with any local shortage of food, water or medical supplies. They would also have to know how to use radiation dosimeters, because in the immediate postattack period the fallout levels could vary greatly from one place to another. (Like snow, radioactive debris accumulates where it is driven, depending on the wind, the weather and the topography, including buildings. There could be pockets of relative safety in the midst of areas with lethal levels of radiation.) The trained cadre would have to provide leadership in the long period of extreme social duress after the attack and reestablish services for a so-

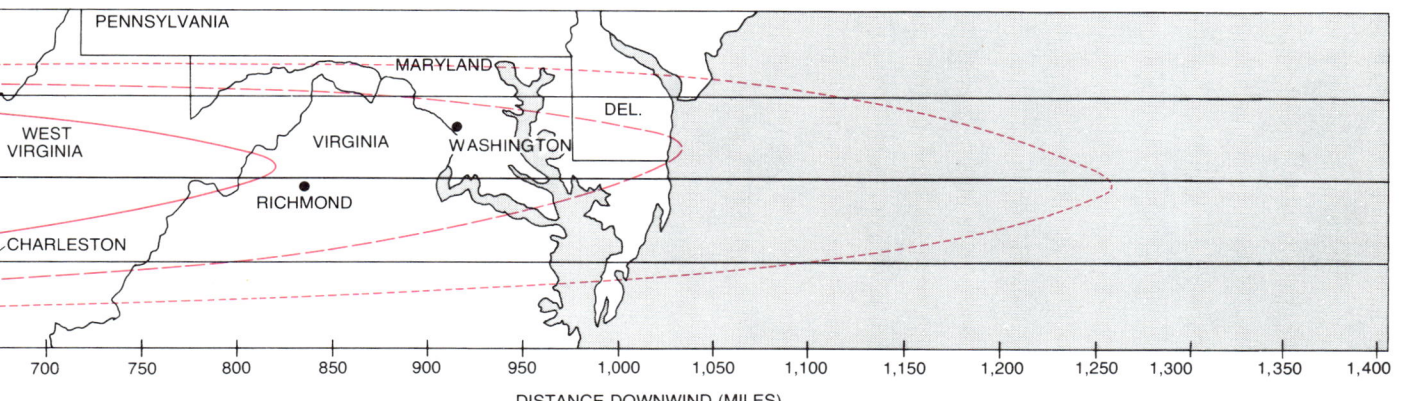

on each of the 10 silos in a flight (gray circle) of Minutemen (2) and for two warheads on each of the 150 silos in Whiteman's 15 flights (3 and 4). The large difference between the bottom two patterns is the result of a change in the assumed wind speed. In all four cases the wind is assumed to blow toward the east. In the first three examples the wind speed is assumed to be constant at 20 miles per hour. In the bottom example the wind speed is assumed to be 60 miles per hour (averaged at altitudes between the surface and the stratosphere).

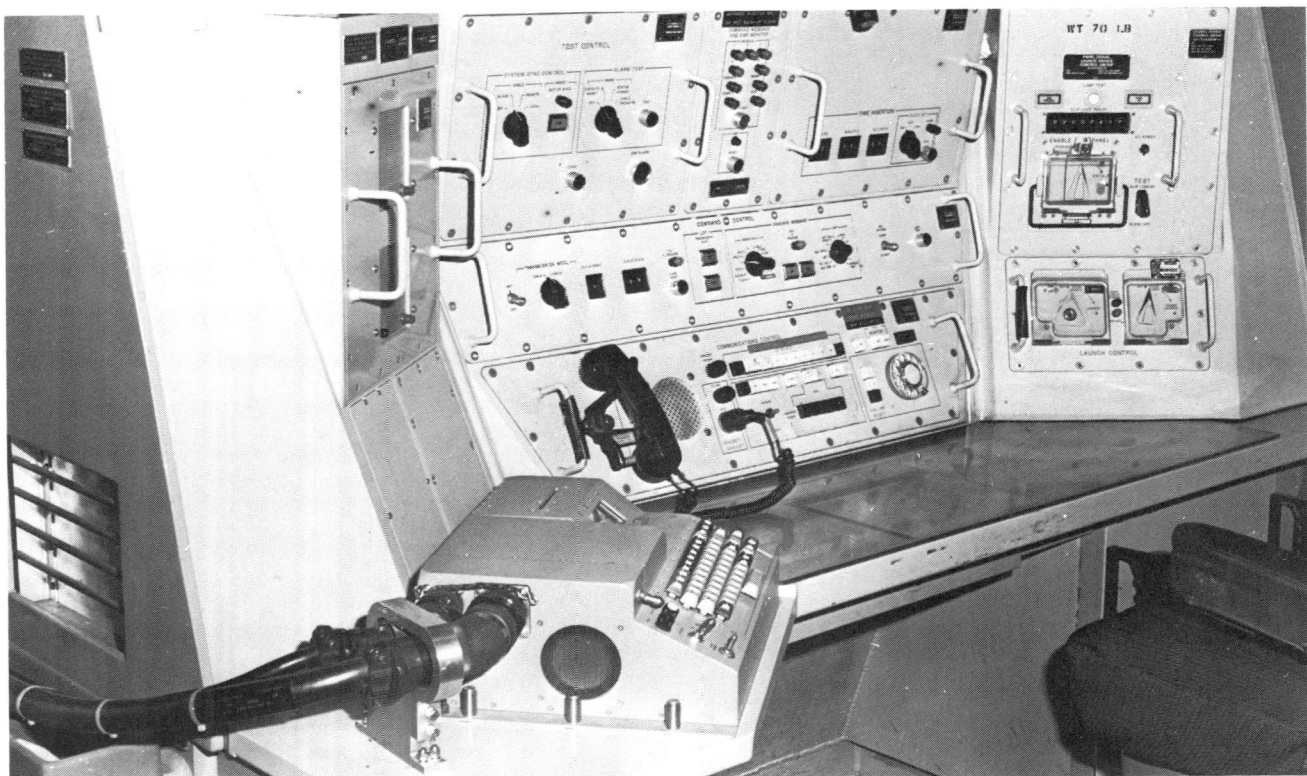

MINUTEMAN III missile combat-crew commander's console controls the launching of a flight of 10 missiles. The keyboard (foreground) is that of the Command Data Buffer system, which makes possible the resetting of targets in on-board computers in 36 minutes.

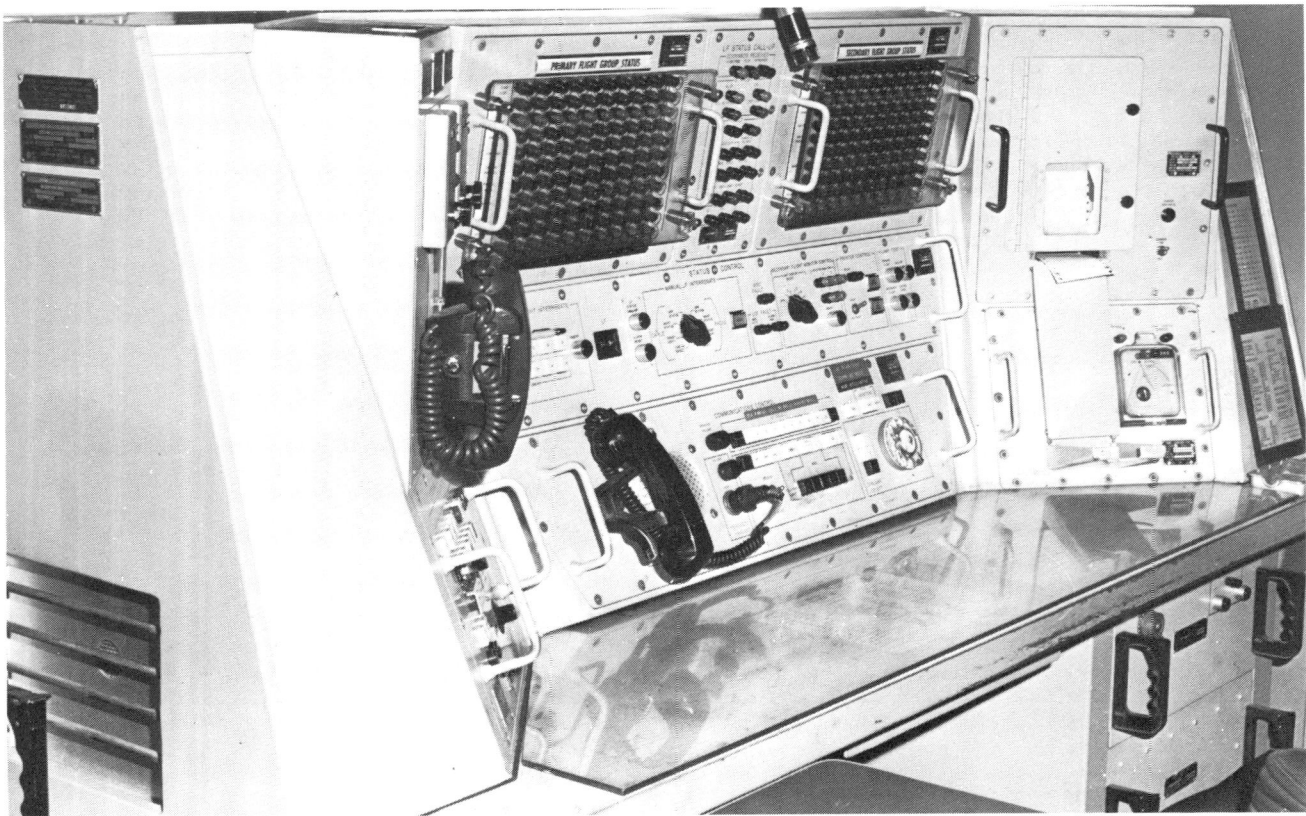

MINUTEMAN II console shown here is that of the deputy combat-crew commander. The consoles are in underground launch-control centers. The U.S. has 450 Minuteman II's and 550 Minuteman III's, the latter with multiple independently targetable reentry vehicles.

ciety with a large population of sick, injured and dying citizens. It should be noted that Defense Department calculations of the consequences of limited nuclear war are almost certainly serious underestimates. For example, the calculations omit any estimate of what may be one of the gravest consequences of all: the disruption of the intensely interdependent components that enable a modern society to function. The difficulties imposed on a society trying to recover with totally unprecedented levels of mortality and morbidity, with insufficient medical care and with profound dislocations in the supply of food and water are simply ignored. Moreover, the calculations omit any consideration of long-term consequences such as the millions of genetic defects and cases of cancer that would occur worldwide in the decades after the postulated nuclear attack.

A higher level of public awareness and concern and a willingness to participate in repeated civil defense exercises would be required if the U.S. intended to develop a viable system for a massive evacuation and shelter. In the absence of sustained preparation chaos and panic would surely ensue at the time of an attack. It is difficult to see how commitment to such plans could be obtained without a deliberate and sustained intensification of public apprehension concerning a nuclear war. One of the lessons of the relatively ineffective civil defense program of 1961 and 1962 was that the large expenditures for civil defense and the inconveniences of a major shelter program could only be made plausible to the American public by exaggerating the probability of nuclear war.

Today we are again hearing allegations that the U.S.S.R. is developing and rehearsing civil defense plans involving the evacuation and relocation of large populations, along with the dispersal and hardening of industry. These programs are cited to indicate that the U.S. may be losing its deterrent and to spur a renewed U.S. civil defense effort. What evidence is there in support of these allegations?

The Russians have written much on the subject and have given their people more intensive exposure to civil defense than Americans have received. Apparently they have also spent much more money on plans and organizations and have involved in exercises small numbers of individuals with key skills. In view of the unprecedentedly large scale of the nationwide disaster being considered, however, an effective civil defense program would surely have to include among its essential components full-scale rehearsals and survival-living exercises involving the population. If there had been any such rehearsals, we would have heard about them. They would be very difficult to conceal, and many people who would have participated in them or would have had knowledge of them have now left the U.S.S.R. and would have called attention to them. Yet no evidence of such exercises has been presented. The editor of the U.S. Government translation of the official Russian civil defense manual for 1974 comments that "the Soviet Union has not conducted mass shelter living experiments or even simulated ones as has been done in the U.S." Plans and manuals are very different from an effective operating system.

The Defense Department's response of July, 1975, presented new casualty figures and also estimates of the military effectiveness of the postulated attacks. According to the new calculations, a strike with two 550-kiloton warheads, one a surface burst and the other an airburst, against each of the 1,054

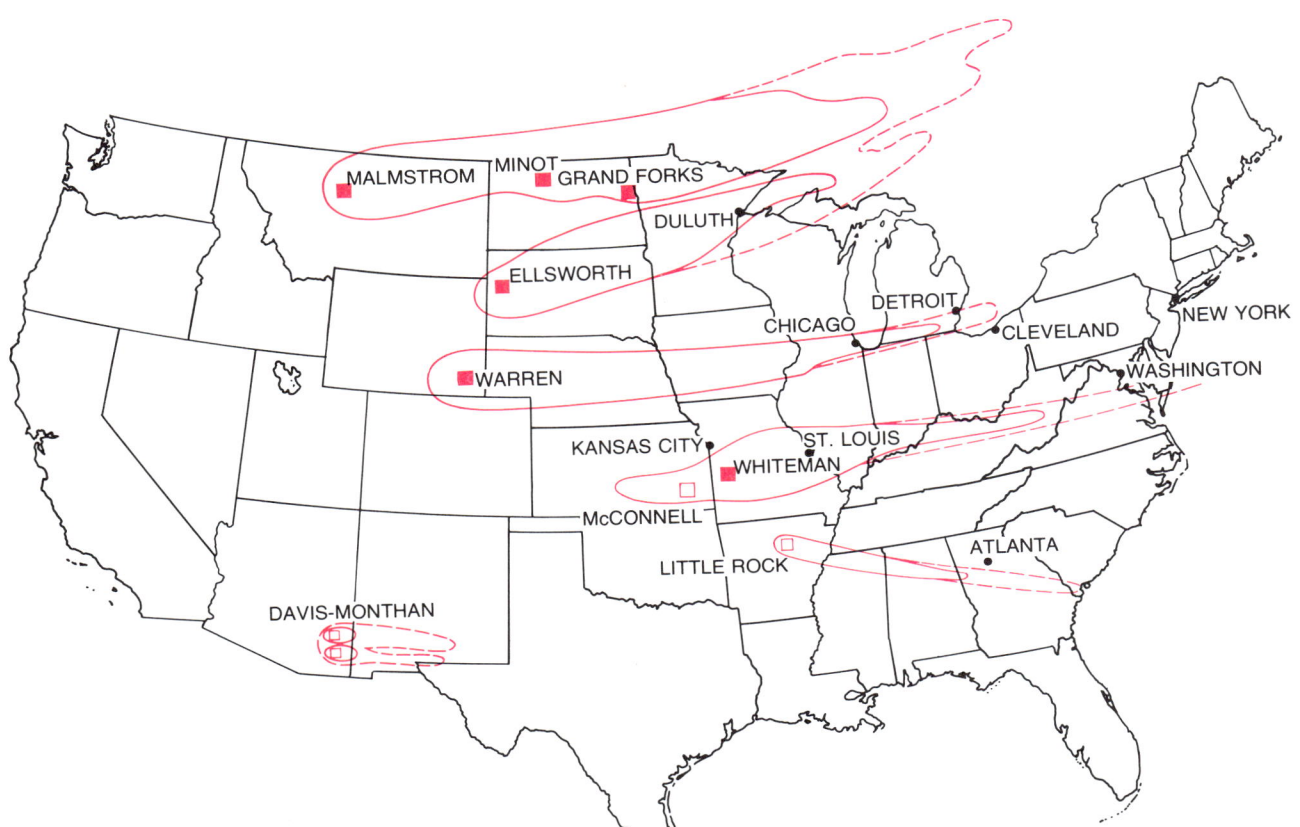

COUNTERFORCE ATTACK on all Titan (*white squares*) and Minuteman (*color squares*) ICBM bases, with two one-megaton surface bursts (50 percent fission yield) per silo, could produce these patterns. Each inner contour delimits a 450-rem dose indoors (50 percent fatalities) and each outer contour a 200-rem dose indoors (50 percent hospitalized). Typical March wind speeds are assumed.

U.S. ICBM silos would cause 5.6 million fatalities (assuming a 25 percent reduction of the population-protection factors given above) and destroy only 42 percent of the silos. A heavier strike with two three-megaton warheads, one a surface burst and the other an airburst, directed at each silo would cause 18.3 million fatalities and destroy 80 percent of the silos. A "comprehensive" attack, with two one-megaton surface bursts on each ICBM silo and strikes against the 46 Strategic Air Command (SAC) bases and the two bases for ballistic-missile submarines, would cause 16.3 million fatalities and destroy 57 percent of the ICBM's, 60 percent of the bombers caught on the ground and 90 percent of the missile submarines in port [see bottom illustration at right].

The effectiveness of all these attacks would be somewhat higher if one assumed that the incoming missiles were more accurate and would be somewhat lower if one assumed that the attacking force was less than 100 percent reliable. An additional factor in a massive attack involving many warheads arriving at about the same time in the same area is "fratricide" among the incoming missiles. In a concentrated attack the atmospheric disturbances created by the first warheads to arrive must necessarily destroy, disable or deflect many of the warheads that arrive later. Only the almost perfect synchronization of the arrival of warheads that are aimed at the same silo or nearby silos can avoid this effect.

In any case it is clear that even with a massive attack resulting in enormous devastation, including the direct death of 20 million Americans, the U.S.S.R. would have accomplished little of strategic military value. After the heaviest of the anti-ICBM strikes considered by the Defense Department, more than 200 ICBM's would survive: an overwhelming retaliatory force even if one ignores the SAC bombers, the missile submarines and the thousands of U.S. tactical nuclear weapons deployed overseas and on aircraft carriers. It is therefore at least misleading to suggest that a successful and strategically effective counterforce attack could be carried out with low civilian casualties.

A major danger associated with a policy reorientation that emphasizes preparations for actually waging a limited counterforce war is that it would tend to undermine the stability of the strategic balance. Flexibility is one thing and an efficient hard-target kill capability is another. Flexibility is inherent in the wide range of U.S. strategic weapons, which are targeted on a variety of urban, industrial and military objectives. Any one or any 100 of these weapons could be launched selectively. Furthermore, each missile or bomber has multiple tar-

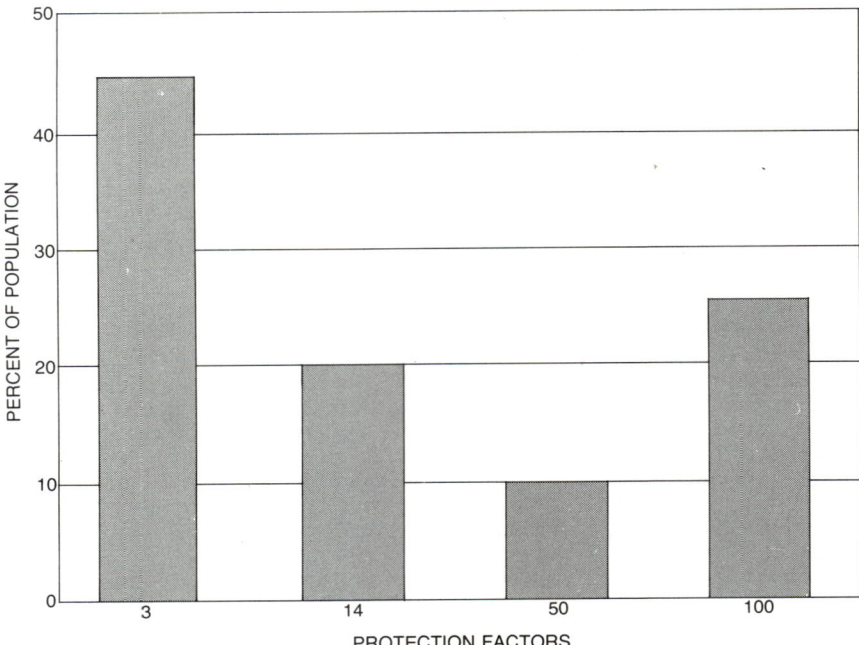

"SHELTER POSTURE" assumed in Department of Defense calculations is given by bars showing what percent of the population is in shelters that have given "protection factors" (the inverse of the proportion of outside gamma radiation penetrating the shelter). A protection factor of 3 is roughly that provided on the ground floor of a one-story residence; the basement of a one-story frame house could provide a factor of 15 to 20, that of a two-story brick house as much as 50. A trench covered by two feet of earth provides a protection factor of about 100.

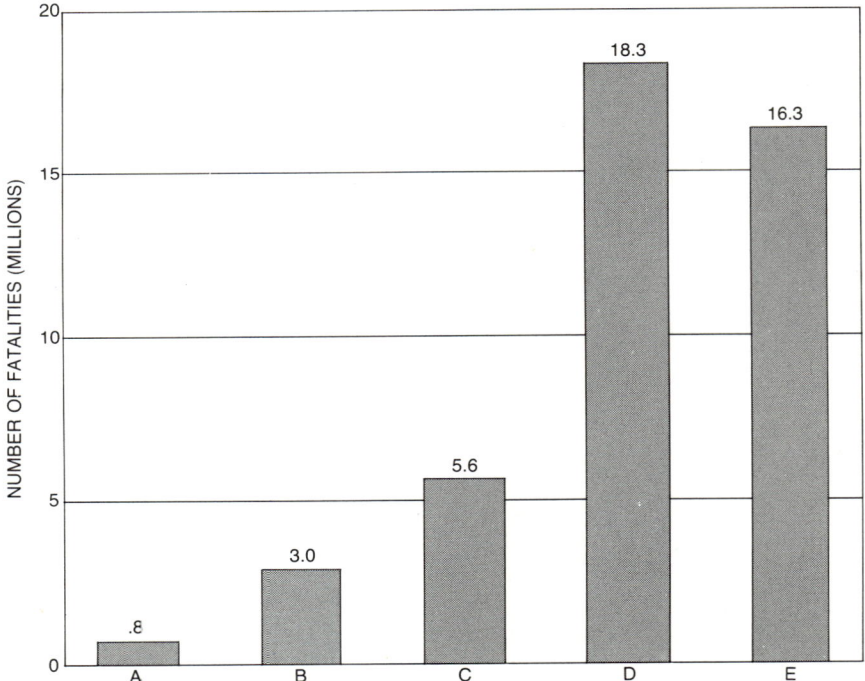

FATALITIES estimated for five postulated Russian counterforce attacks are shown: one one-megaton airburst on each U.S. ICBM silo (A); the same attack with surface bursts (B); two 550-kiloton warheads per silo, one airburst and one surface burst (C); two three-megaton warheads per silo, one airburst and one surface burst (D); a "comprehensive" attack, with two one-megaton surface bursts per silo and with airbursts over all 46 Strategic Air Command bases and the two ballistic-missile submarine bases (E). In the last three cases the shelter posture shown in the illustration at the top of the page is "degraded" by 25 percent and March winds are assumed instead of August winds. Also in the last three cases Defense Department evaluated effectiveness of attack: 42 percent of the ICBM's destroyed (C); 80 percent destroyed (D); 57 percent of the ICBM's destroyed as well as heavy damage to aircraft on ground or flying within eight miles of a base and to submarines in port and base facilities (E).

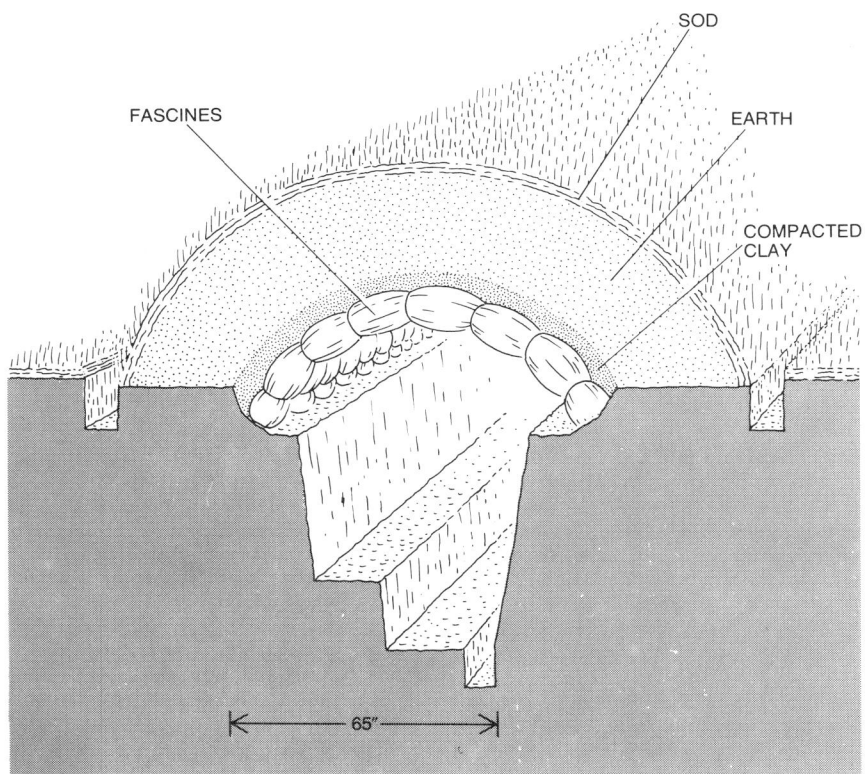

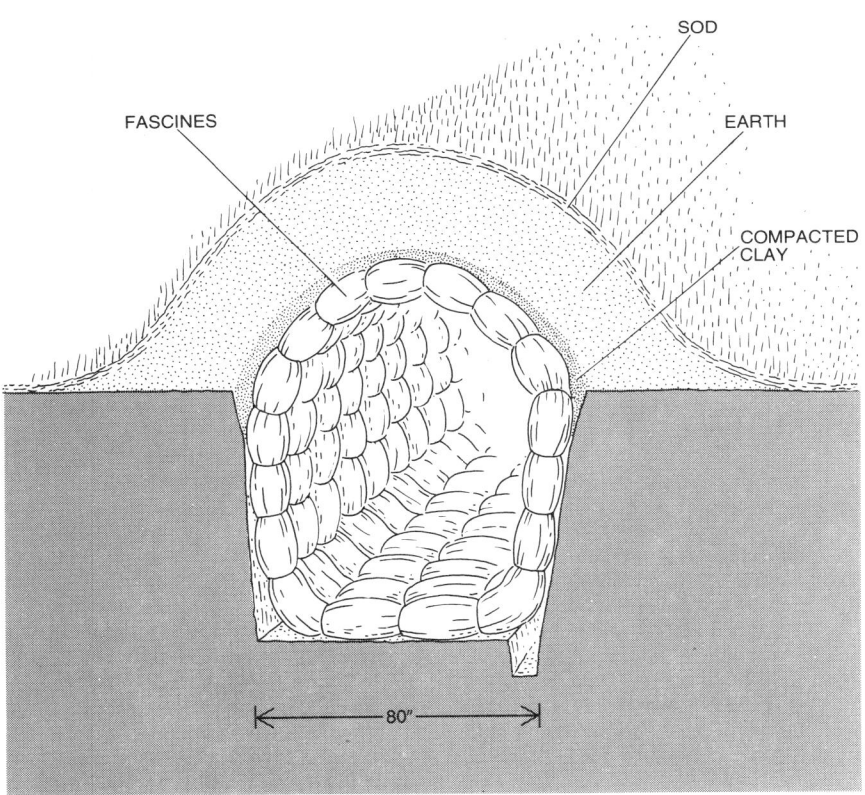

RUSSIAN SHELTER DESIGNS, from a 1970 U.S.S.R. handbook, are for simple structures to be built by people "using available materials and their own labor." A dugout (*top*) in firm clay soil is roofed by rows of fascines (bundles of brushwood, canes or reeds) covered with compacted clay and 30 inches of soil. Rings of fascines are required in looser soil (*bottom*).

get options. The new Command Data Buffer system currently nearing completion makes possible the remote resetting of targets in the on-board computers of Minuteman III missiles from launch-control centers in 36 minutes.

As a result of all this flexibility the U.S. also already has a substantial counterforce capability even without highly accurate warheads. There are, for example, "soft" military targets such as airfields and submarine bases that could be selectively destroyed with a few warheads. Even hard missile silos could be destroyed by hitting each one with a number of Minuteman missiles. The Defense Department nonetheless wants more: the ability to deliver counterforce strikes efficiently and with high confidence against hardened Russian ICBM silos. As Schlesinger put it in his 1976 appropriation request: "I believe we should improve our hard-target kill capability so as to have higher confidence of executing limited hard-target attacks." Indeed, the U.S. is currently progressing toward that goal with funded programs.

These developments clash directly with the need for strategic stability. A U.S. missile force with multiple independently targetable reentry vehicles (MIRV's) or with the maneuverable reentry vehicles (MARV's) now being developed, and with a demonstrated combination of very high reliability, very accurate guidance and high-yield warheads would suggest to Russian leaders the possibility of a U.S. preemptive strike against their ICBM silos. It would further suggest to them that in a time of confrontation they should not be caught with their missiles in their silos, that at such a time they should either strike first or adopt a "hair trigger," or launch-on-warning, policy. The same arguments apply with the U.S. and Russian roles reversed. The current national debate indicates that there is widespread concern, as there should be, about the possibility that the U.S.S.R. might be developing a hard-target counterforce capability, particularly in view of the larger size of the Russian ICBM's.

To be sure, it is impossible to envision a disarming first strike that would really threaten the retaliatory capacity of the U.S.S.R. (or of the U.S.), if only because missile submarines at sea and bombers in the air or on alert are not subject to destruction in a preemptive attack. In order to maintain a stable strategic environment such as the one that now exists for the two superpowers, however, there should be neither a real nor a "perceived" vulnerability of any major component of the strategic deterrent forces on either side. (From the Russian point of view this is true in particular of the land-based ICBM component, since it constitutes a much larger fraction of

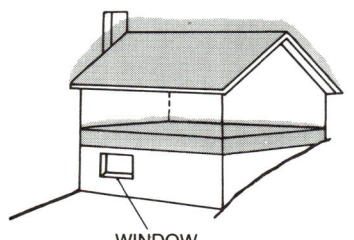 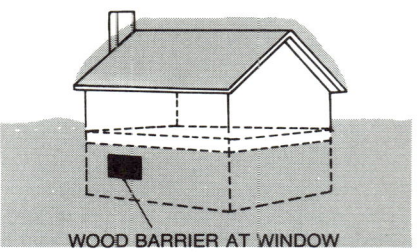 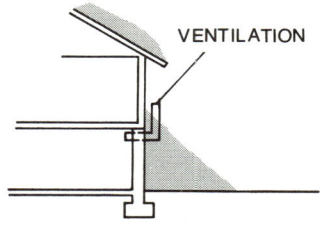

U.S. SHELTER DESIGN, redrawn from an illustration published by the Defense Civil Preparedness Agency, is for an "expedient shelter" intended primarily to accommodate evacuated populations. In order to provide adequate fallout protection in a basement that is only partially below ground level it is necessary to put a 12-inch layer of earth overhead and to pile earth against exposed basement walls.

their deterrent power: roughly 75 percent compared with 25 percent for the U.S.) The deployment of missiles with hard-target capability would therefore create tension, because each side would fear that such deployment might lead to the possibility of an effective first-strike threat against its force of silo-based ICBM's. The fact that formidable technical and operational difficulties, such as the fratricide problem, lead many people to challenge the feasibility of achieving such a capability is almost beside the point; there would still be serious concern about the ability of land-based ICBM's to survive a preemptive first strike.

U.S. officials recognize the danger of seeming to threaten Russian retaliatory capacity, and so they couple proposals for an improved hard-target kill capability with announcements that deployment of new offensive weapons would be limited, at least for the time being. But can one acquire just a little hard-target counterforce without bringing on the ill effects of a lot? After all, it is no more than the fear of a possible future Russian ICBM counterforce threat against U.S. Minutemen that has been cited in support of the ongoing programs for improving U.S. missiles. It has been argued that we must be able to respond in kind against each and every perceived potential threat. Schlesinger said that there should be "no perceived asymmetries in levels or capabilities of force—conventional or nuclear."

The danger in this logic is that we will almost inevitably find our own development program triggering a Russian commitment to the very program we fear (and vice versa, of course). All precedents, including in particular the history of MIRV deployment on both sides, indicate that once the technology has been developed and tested for attacking hardened counterforce targets with high confidence, the dynamics of the nuclear arms race will take over and make it difficult if not impossible for the U.S. to refrain from deploying the new weapons extensively and for the U.S.S.R. to refrain from responding in kind.

Neither side has yet developed weapons designed specifically as hard-target killers: weapons that have a high probability of destroying a hardened military target, such as an underground silo, with a single warhead. Research-and-development programs directed toward that goal are, however, funded in this year's U.S. defense budget. Before both countries are committed further and perhaps irrevocably to reciprocally stimulated and mutually reinforcing programs for developing such weapons, the hard questions should therefore be faced up to. Do we really want or need them? What is the value of being able to destroy an enemy silo (which may be empty by the time our warhead arrives) in response to an attack on our own silo? If a small response is wanted, will not an air base or a naval base or a military storage depot do as a target? Is not our current broad flexibility adequate? Will hard-target counterforce weapons make a compelling military contribution to national security or does their justification rest solely on ephemeral politico-strategic argument?

We have argued that such weapons would complicate the problem of maintaining strategic stability. It would therefore seem that it would serve the security of both the U.S. and the U.S.S.R. to avoid their development and deployment. A significant precedent for restraining new weapons in the interest of stability is the treaty, negotiated in the first round of the strategic-arms limitation talks, stringently limiting antiballistic-missile defenses. Now again the U.S. and the U.S.S.R. each have a critically important opportunity to limit their traditional technological arms competition by restraining the testing and deployment of new weapons designed to destroy hardened ICBM silos.

In the three decades since Hiroshima and Nagasaki there have been many crises involving the two superpowers, and the U.S. has fought two major land wars in Asia. Yet the armed nuclear truce has persisted. Why has neither side launched a single one of the thousands of nuclear warheads that each has had deployed? Surely it is because of the overwhelming fear of political leaders and citizens on both sides that once a nuclear weapon is detonated there will be an answering detonation, with subsequent exchanges escalating until both nations are destroyed and hundreds of millions of people are dead and dying. The issue created by the new emphasis on a selective, hard-target counterforce strategy accompanied by intensive civil defense efforts is whether or not there is any real prospect of escaping this "balance of terror." Should the assumption that a general nuclear war is prevented by the certainty of mutual destruction be abandoned in favor of the objective of fighting, winning and "surviving" a limited nuclear war when the evidence indicates that even a limited war would cause many millions of fatalities?

In the 1960's the U.S. adopted a strategic policy giving top priority to the prevention of nuclear war through deterrence rather than to preparation for fighting nuclear wars if deterrence should fail. Since then weapons technology has progressed, so that new and more sophisticated kinds of limited counterforce strikes, including attacks on hardened military targets, can be seriously considered. The political reality of deterrence, however, remains unchanged. New technology and new strategy do not significantly reduce the risk of all-out nuclear war breaking out once the first nuclear weapon has been fired.

It is important to recognize that once the nuclear firebreak has been crossed the decision to keep a war limited is no longer in the hands of one side alone; it has to be made by both—or all—participants in the conflict. As Secretary of State Henry A. Kissinger wrote in 1965: "No one knows how governments or people will react to a nuclear explosion under conditions where both sides possess vast arsenals."

Enhanced-Radiation Weapons

by Fred M. Kaplan
May 1978

Although President Carter has deferred production of "the neutron bomb," it is still an alternative of U.S. policy. It remains a weapon of doubtful utility that could result in an all-out nuclear exchange

The enhanced-radiation warhead (or, as it is widely and somewhat misleadingly known, the neutron bomb) is the latest development in the U.S. military's search for a "cleaner," more usable nuclear weapon. This new type of warhead, which could be available in some versions by 1979, is designed to kill more enemy soldiers per kiloton of explosive yield detonated over the battlefield than the types of nuclear weapon currently deployed for that purpose, while minimizing collateral, or unintended, damage to buildings, the countryside, friendly soldiers and nearby noncombatants.

Many military officers contend that by using these more precise and refined enhanced-radiation warheads a "limited nuclear war" could be kept limited, its damage virtually confined to the battlefield. The enhanced-radiation warhead, like the generation of tactical nuclear weapons that preceded it, is intended for use in a European ground war between the nations of the North Atlantic Treaty Organization (NATO), including the U.S., and the nations of the Warsaw Pact, including the U.S.S.R. The Carter Administration's military budget for the fiscal year 1979 allocates unprecedentedly high expenditures for U.S. forces committed to the European-war contingency. The new tactical nuclear weapon therefore merits detailed discussion, particularly in view of the extraordinary notice given the weapon and the various misunderstandings that have arisen as a result. How did the weapon come into being? How does it work? What are its effects? What is its military utility? Should it be produced and deployed?

It is important to emphasize at the outset that there is nothing new about the notion of a neutron bomb. The possibility of developing a tactical nuclear weapon of this type was recognized soon after the invention of the hydrogen, or fusion, bomb in the late 1940's. A few scientists engaged in nuclear-weapons development, principally at the Lawrence Livermore Laboratory, worked on the concept of an enhanced-radiation warhead throughout the 1950's and 1960's, and they and others were politically active on behalf of its further development and deployment.

It was not until the early 1960's, however, that Secretary of Defense Robert S. McNamara ordered a general study of the prospects of tactical nuclear weapons. On the basis of that study and various simulated war games he concluded that a European-theater nuclear war would be a losing battle for both sides. Millions of civilians would die, and the use of such weapons would not necessarily turn a European war to NATO's advantage. Far from serving as substitutes for manpower and conventional firepower, tactical nuclear weapons would necessitate higher manpower levels, so that the NATO soldiers who would be killed as a result of the U.S.S.R.'s nuclear retaliation could be readily replaced. In fact, it was decided that since the Warsaw Pact forces plan to reinforce front-line troops in echelon style, whereas the NATO forces plan for individual replacements within existing division structures, a European-theater nuclear war would probably favor the U.S.S.R. and its allies, even if NATO possessed more or "better" nuclear weapons.

Moreover, the risk of escalation to an all-out strategic nuclear war between the U.S. and the U.S.S.R. as a result of such a strategy was held to be too great, primarily for two reasons. First, the "firebreak" between conventional and

SOME EFFECTS of three different types of tactical nuclear weapon are indicated in the idealized scenes on the next page. The setting in all three cases is a semirural area in West Germany, where military officials of the North Atlantic Treaty Organization anticipate an invasion by the forces of the Warsaw Pact nations. Each salient of such an offensive would presumably be led by an attacking force of hundreds of Russian tanks, which in such situations are expected to move in two or three echelons with the tanks in the first echelon spaced approximately 75 to 100 meters apart. An echelon of this kind is shown just to the right of center in each scene; a second echelon follows three kilometers behind the first at the upper right. In all three cases a Lance missile bearing a tactical nuclear warhead has been launched against the first echelon of Russian tanks by NATO forces located some 130 kilometers away. The scene at the top shows the estimated blast and thermal effects (*black*) and prompt-radiation effects (*color*) of a nuclear-fission warhead with a one-kiloton explosive yield detonated on target at an altitude of 500 meters. The middle and bottom scenes respectively show the corresponding effects for a 10-kiloton fission warhead and a one-kiloton enhanced-radiation fission-fusion warhead (the neutron bomb). In all three cases the inner black circle delineates the extent of the blast damage resulting from a shock wave with an overpressure of five pounds per square inch, enough to destroy most buildings. The outer black circle corresponds to a thermal-radiation exposure sufficient to cause second-degree burns to unprotected people in the open. The inner colored circle shows the limit of the area exposed to at least 8,000 rads of prompt radiation (mostly neutrons), enough to cause "immediate permanent incapacitation" of soldiers or, given current tank-protection factors, "immediate transient incapacitation" of tankmen. Outer colored circle corresponds to a prompt-radiation dose of 150 rads, enough to kill about 10 percent of the exposed individuals and cause a high incidence of cancer in survivors. Distance scale is given at top right in first panel. Effects of residual radiation (radioactive fallout) are not shown.

156 III | SALT II: LIMITED NEGOTIATIONS

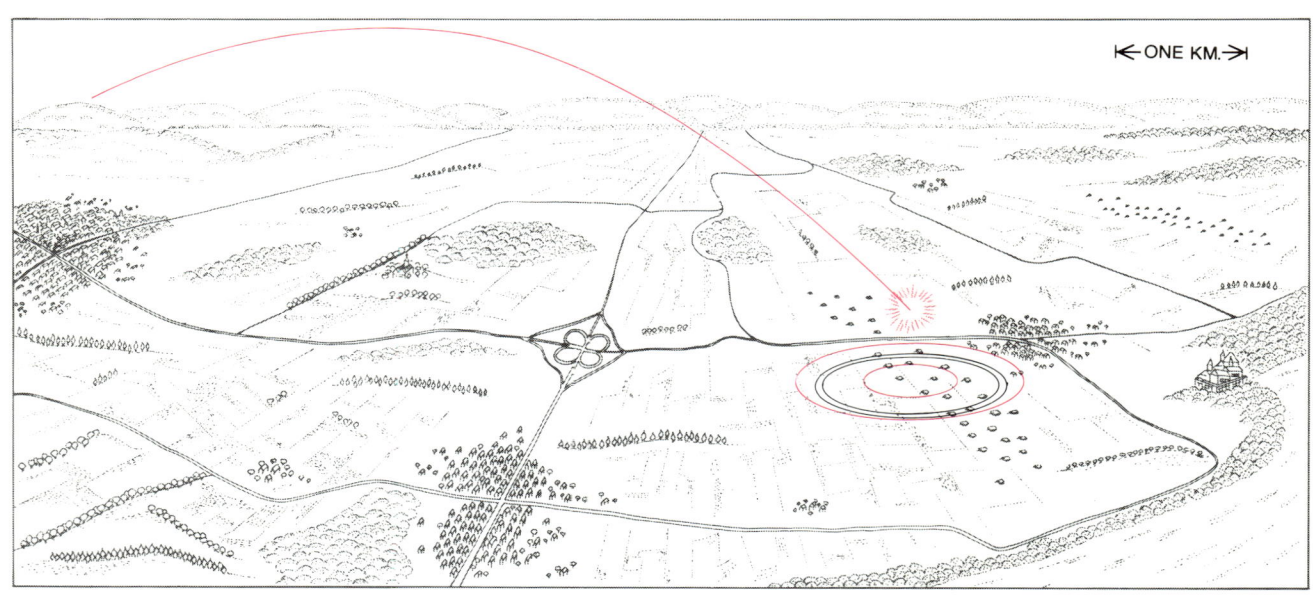

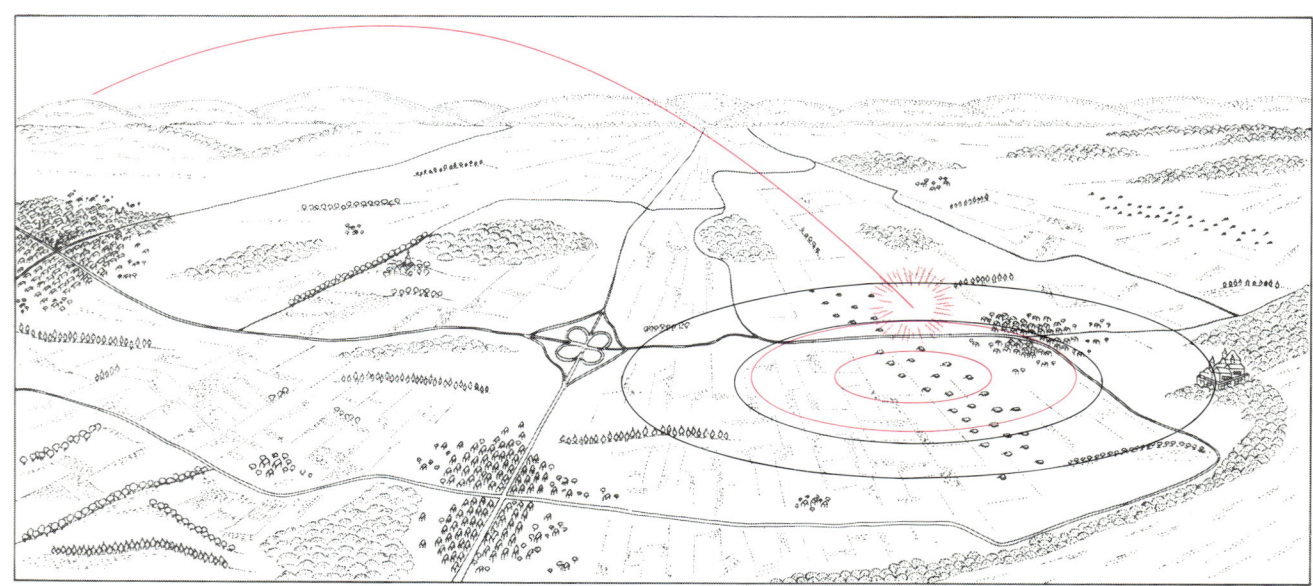

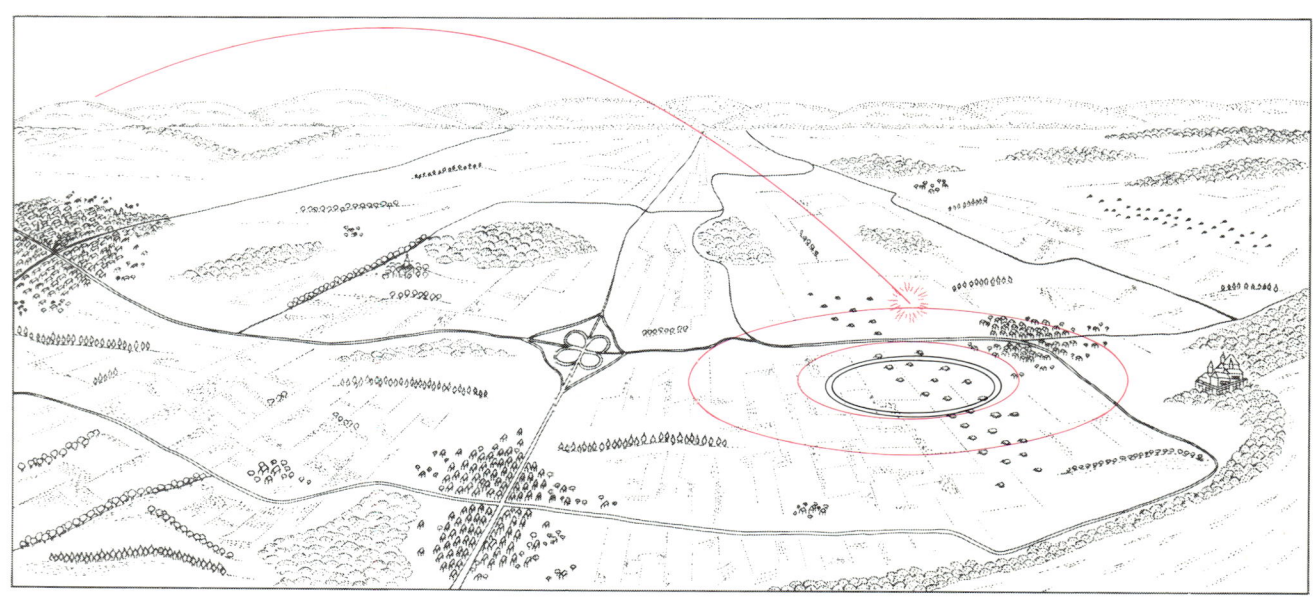

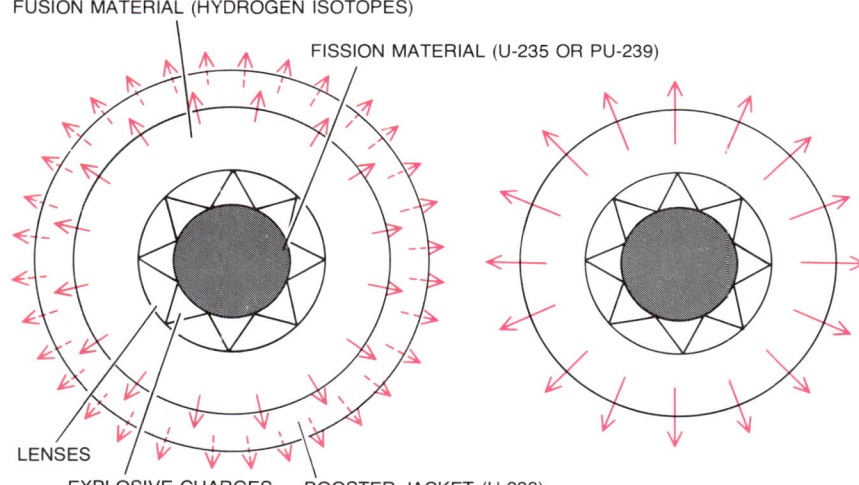

TWO TYPES OF FISSION-FUSION WEAPON are compared in these highly schematic diagrams. In both cases a set of chemical explosive charges detonates the weapon, causing fission reactions in its core that in turn trigger fusion reactions in a surrounding layer. The standard fission-fusion device (*left*) is enclosed in an additional jacket of uranium 238, a nonfissionable isotope that boosts the weapon's explosive yield considerably by capturing many of the fast neutrons (*solid colored arrows*) released by the fusion process. The U-238 nuclei then fission, emitting large numbers of much slower "thermal" neutrons (*broken colored arrows*). Most strategic nuclear weapons are based on this concept. The enhanced-radiation warhead (*right*) omits the U-238 jacket. In effect a greater proportion of fast neutrons are released by the enhanced-radiation weapon at the expense of explosive yield. Slow neutrons are captured by atomic nuclei in the air much more readily than fast neutrons. Hence beyond a short range the enhanced-radiation warhead produces many more neutrons than a standard fission-fusion warhead.

nuclear warfare was at that time clear; trying to blur the distinction between tactical and strategic nuclear war would create considerable ambiguity, leading to mutual suspicion, tension and possibly to preemptive strategic nuclear strikes. Second, the U.S.S.R. had many nuclear-armed intermediate-range ballistic missiles (IRBM's) deployed in its territory, some of them in the same areas occupied by intercontinental ballistic missiles (ICBM's); the temptation would be great in the early stages of such a European-theater nuclear war for NATO to preemptively knock out those IRBM's inside the U.S.S.R., possibly triggering a strategic nuclear exchange between the two superpowers.

After weighing these considerations McNamara turned to a policy of building up conventional, or non-nuclear, war-fighting capabilities, and he put off spending money on a new generation of tactical nuclear weapons. (He did accept the nuclear-armed Lance missile, however, because of its longer range and consequent reduced vulnerability.) During Melvin R. Laird's term as Secretary of Defense more money was allocated to develop a new generation of tactical nuclear weapons, but the negative attitude toward the modernization of tactical nuclear weapons essentially prevailed until James R. Schlesinger became Secretary in 1973.

During Schlesinger's earlier tenure as Chairman of the Atomic Energy Commission he had shown considerable enthusiasm for tactical nuclear weapons. By the time he was appointed Secretary of Defense, however, his interest appeared to have lessened. Still, Schlesinger apparently felt compelled to make some concessions to the advocates of tactical nuclear weapons, an assortment of converging interests that included the Atomic Energy Commission, the Congressional Joint Committee on Atomic Energy, the weapons laboratories, certain military departments and the Atomic Energy Division of the Office of the Secretary of Defense. Schlesinger, who had little bargaining power in the White House during the Nixon and Ford administrations, had to manage his own complex coalition. To gain support from these disparate interests for his plans to further build up conventional forces for NATO, he gave them money for the modernization of tactical nuclear weapons.

The coalition in favor of a modernization program for tactical nuclear weapons was actively aided by Schlesinger's own emphasis on enlarging the range of U.S. "options" in nuclear-force planning. Thanks in part to new technologies, such as highly accurate inertial-guidance systems for missiles, Schlesinger reprogrammed strategic nuclear weapons to have "selective strike" capabilities and greater "flexibility," creating new "target packages" that were far more diversified than those available to the defense planners of the preceding decade. Along with the expansion of strategic options, he ordered an increase in the available options for fighting a European-theater nuclear war. This new emphasis gave what appeared to be official support to those military officers who were beginning to think seriously about the possibility of fighting and winning a limited nuclear war and about the necessity, under such circumstances, of limiting collateral damage.

Meanwhile the development of the Sprint anti-ballistic-missile (ABM) system at the Los Alamos Scientific Laboratory in the mid-1960's and the subsequent ban on further ABM production imposed by the SALT I treaty of 1972 led some weapons-laboratory scientists to think about reducing the yield of the Sprint warheads to adapt them for use as tactical nuclear weapons. (Sprints were short-range nuclear-armed antimissile missiles designed to be detonated in the atmosphere, depending primarily on neutrons rather than X rays for their effectiveness.) All these various interests—of the armed services, the weapons laboratories, the Congressional committees and the Department of Defense—have converged to create the present situation.

Today enhanced-radiation nuclear warheads are being developed for the Lance missile and for the eight-inch artillery shell. An enhanced-radiation warhead for the 155-millimeter artillery shell is also in prospect, although it still appears to be in the early stages of development. (At least one of these warheads, probably the one for the Lance, has already been tested at an underground site near Las Vegas.) Currently deployed Lance warheads have explosive yields ranging from one kiloton to 100 kilotons; the charges of the eight-inch nuclear shells range from five to 10 kilotons. The new enhanced-radiation version of the Lance warhead will have two yields, which can be preset simply by pushing a few buttons; one yield is considerably smaller than a kiloton and the other is slightly larger than a kiloton. The eight-inch enhanced-radiation shell will have three yields, ranging from substantially under a kiloton to roughly two kilotons.

The effects of a nuclear explosion consist of blast (a shock wave of overpressure), thermal radiation (heat), prompt radiation (mostly neutrons and gamma rays) and residual radiation (radioactive fallout resulting from decaying fission products). The energy released from a fission explosion is divided into several fractions: typically 50 percent blast, 35 percent thermal radiation, 5 percent prompt radiation and 10 percent residual radiation. In a hypothetical pure-fusion weapon the effects would be 20 percent blast and thermal radiation, 80 percent prompt radiation (mostly neutrons) and comparatively little residual radiation (the precise amount depending on the characteristics of the soil under the explosion).

The fusion reaction that takes place between ions of deuterium and tritium (two heavy hydrogen isotopes) is accompanied by the liberation of very-high-energy, or fast, neutrons. The energy of these neutrons is about 14 million electron volts (MeV), which is substantially more than the still quite fast 2-MeV neutrons released by a typical fission reaction. Neutrons are slowed down and eventually captured by debris from the weapon itself, by objects in their path and by the air. The faster the neutrons are, the more collisions they experience before being completely captured. Moreover, fusion produces 10 times more neutrons per kiloton of explosive yield than fission does. Thus neutrons released from a fusion weapon are higher in radiation intensity, and penetrate greater distances before being completely absorbed, than those released from a fission weapon.

The present incarnation of the enhanced-radiation warhead is a fission-fusion weapon. The fission-fusion mix differs slightly between the Lance device and the eight-inch device, but the detonating process is the same in both of them. When the weapon is detonated, the fission reaction triggers a fusion reaction, which in turn releases many fast neutrons. That is why the enhanced-radiation warhead is often called a neutron bomb. The term is correct in the sense that the enhanced-radiation warhead releases many more neutrons than other weapons of equivalent yield. It is misleading, however, in that the warhead's detonation also releases a great deal of energy in forms other than neutrons. (In fact, any nuclear weapon smaller than about two kilotons could be called a neutron bomb in the sense that at ranges corresponding to the lethal radius of the weapon, even if it were completely a fission one, the energy released in the form of prompt radiation would be greater than the fraction that goes into blast and thermal radiation, and prompt radiation in the form of neutrons would dominate prompt radiation in the form of gamma rays. If such a weapon were exploded in the air at a height of several hundred meters, it would cause only slight blast and thermal effects on the ground, even though the damage from neutrons would still be substantial.)

The enhanced-radiation warhead is not close to being a pure fusion weapon. In terms of explosive yield the subkiloton and one-kiloton enhanced-radiation warheads for the eight-inch artillery shell are roughly 50–50 fission-fusion devices. The enhanced-radiation version of the Lance warhead is about 60 percent fusion and 40 percent fission. The two-kiloton eight-inch enhanced-radiation shell is between 70 and 75 percent fusion. The energy released from the Lance and the lower-yield eight-inch enhanced-radiation weapons is divided approximately into 40 percent blast, 25 percent thermal radiation, 30 percent prompt radiation and 5 percent fallout. The highest-yield eight-inch enhanced-radiation shell produces about 10 percent more prompt radiation and slightly less blast, thermal radiation and residual radiation. In other words, the enhanced-radiation warhead promises to be neither the collateral-damage-free weapon that its supporters see nor the "ultimate capitalist weapon" (destroying only people, not property) that many people in peace groups fear.

The fundamental distinction between the enhanced-radiation warhead and other, more fission-dominated nuclear weapons of very low yield is that the former releases many more and much faster neutrons. Of the energy released by the Lance and the lower-yield eight-inch enhanced-radiation weapons, six times as much is in the form of prompt radiation than is the case in a fission warhead of equivalent yield; in the highest-yield eight-inch enhanced-radiation shell the energy available for prompt radiation (particularly neutrons) is reported to exceed that of fission weapons by as much as 10 times.

There is also a distinction, apart from the number of kilotons, between the enhanced-radiation warhead and fission-fusion weapons of higher yields. Standard fission-fusion weapons (including most strategic nuclear weapons) are surrounded by a "jacket" of uranium 238 that boosts the weapon's explosive yield; the jacket captures or considerably attenuates the fast neutrons released by the fusion process. Since enhanced-radiation weapons by definition call for very low thermal yields and the release of many fast neutrons, an enhanced-radiation warhead has no U-238 jacket.

What, then, is the military mission of the enhanced-radiation warheads supposed to be? The chief concern among many NATO military officials is the possibility of a Russian-led Warsaw Pact blitzkrieg across the northern plains of West Germany. Russian military doctrine and the deployment of Russian forces suggest that such an attack, if it were launched, would involve the onslaught of thousands of tanks as the prime mover of the offensive. Some military planners believe that an attack of this type, particularly if it were mobilized with little warning time, could not be met by NATO without the use of nuclear weapons. (This contention is vigorously disputed.) For several years some U.S. military officers have criticized the "impracticality" of most of the tactical nuclear weapons currently deployed in Western Europe, drawing attention in particular to their comparatively high yields, some of them much higher than the yield of the 20-kiloton bomb that destroyed much of Nagasaki at the end of World War II. Such

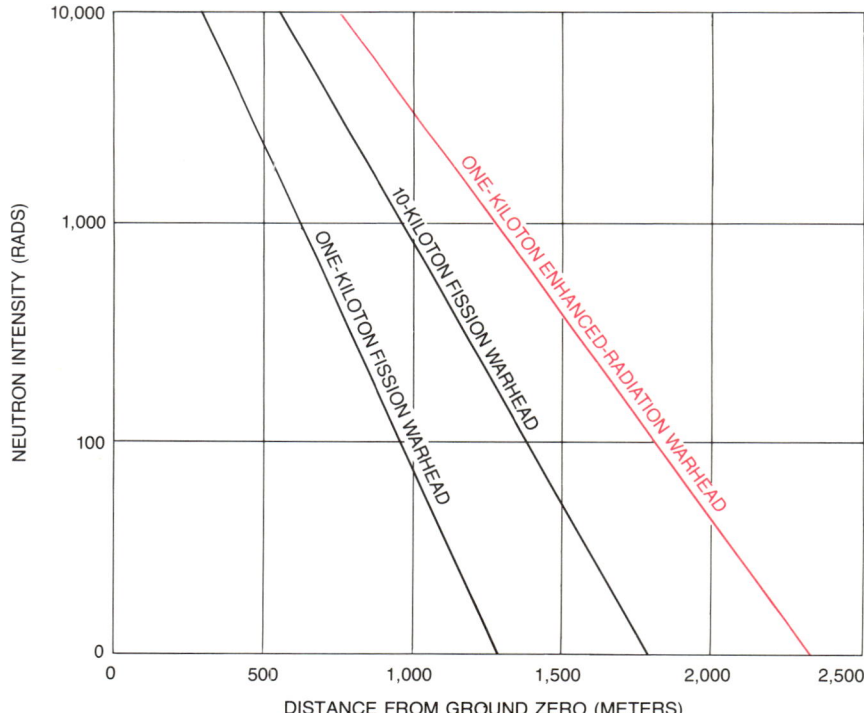

NEUTRONS EMITTED by three different types of tactical nuclear weapon are represented as a function of distance from the point at which the weapon is detonated. Two black curves give the neutron intensity for a one-kiloton fission weapon and a 10-kiloton fission weapon. The colored curve gives intensity for a one-kiloton enhanced-radiation fission-fusion weapon.

high-yield weapons would be effective for stopping Russian tanks, but they would also kill or severely injure many NATO soldiers and German civilians and would devastate much West German territory. Moreover, the effects of induced and residual radiation could make the occupation and recovery of the affected territory a lethal prospect for some time.

With the enhanced-radiation weapon the military has hit on a different tactic: to kill the Warsaw Pact soldiers inside the tanks instead of destroying the tanks themselves. This result, they say, is possible with the high neutron flux generated by the enhanced-radiation weapons.

Radiation doses are measured in rads, one rad being the absorbed dose of any nuclear radiation accompanying the liberation of 100 ergs of energy per gram of irradiated material. If tactical nuclear weapons are to be useful in a war, they must kill their intended victims as quickly as possible. "Immediate permanent incapacitation," according to recent U.S. Government tests conducted with rhesus monkeys, requires 8,000 rads. Since modern tanks have a radiation-protection factor of roughly .5, tanks must be exposed to 16,000 rads instantaneously if NATO's aims are to be optimally achieved. Recently, however, the NATO military doctrine has been revised to read that "immediate transient incapacitation," which requires only 2,500 to 3,500 rads (or, given tank protection, 5,000 to 7,000 rads), may be sufficient to neutralize invaders for military purposes.

Within five minutes a person exposed to 8,000 rads is incapacitated, and he remains incapable of performing physically demanding tasks until his death, which occurs within a day or two. A dose of 3,000 rads also incapacitates within five minutes, but the victim may partially recover within 30 minutes; still he remains a doomed man until his death four to six days later. He may also remain a helpless man, but maybe not. (It turns out that this uncertainty has significant military implications.) Exposure to 650 rads functionally impairs a human being within two hours, and he may respond to medical treatment; more likely a painful, lingering physical deterioration ends in death within a couple of weeks, a gruesome prospect, to be sure, but perhaps enough of a respite for the victim to fight on for some time.

These results are due to the ionizing effects of neutrons colliding with protons inside living cells. Ionization breaks down chromosomes, swells cell nuclei, increases the viscosity of the cell fluid, enhances cell-membrane permeability and destroys cells of all kinds, particularly those of the central nervous system. Moreover, exposure to ionizing radiation delays or destroys the process of mitosis, a long-term genetic effect that inhibits normal cell replacement.

In effect, enhanced-radiation weapons distribute given rad doses over larger areas, compared with fission weapons of an equivalent or even somewhat higher yield. For example, anyone within a 375-meter radius of a one-kiloton fission explosion (and anyone within a 630-meter radius of a 10-kiloton fission explosion) would be exposed to at least 8,000 rads. If a one-kiloton enhanced-radiation warhead were exploded instead, the 8,000-rad circle would widen to a radius of 850 meters. Thus a one-kiloton enhanced-radiation warhead could potentially kill about twice as many tankmen as a 10-kiloton fission weapon, but the blast damage to an area would be only about a fifth as large.

This feature is of course the main selling point for the enhanced-radiation warhead from the perspective of NATO military officers. The key is that the new weapon can substantially reduce the collateral damage of a nuclear explosion, meaning that blast, thermal radiation and fallout effects will be less dominant. This sounds all to the good at first. Nevertheless, it is misleading to assume, as some of the weapon's advocates seem to have done, that with this new generation of tactical nuclear weapons a European-theater nuclear war can now be safer and more easily managed than was once thought possible.

For one thing, it takes two sides to fight a "limited nuclear war," and the Russians seem to have neither the ability nor the disposition to join in. Of the 3,500 tactical nuclear weapons they have deployed to strike targets in the European theater (compared with NATO's 7,000) the majority are thought to have a yield in excess of 20 kilotons, and about 600 of the Russian missiles have a yield of between 500 kilotons and three megatons. The Warsaw Pact nations' tactical nuclear missiles are far less accurate than NATO's, making the selective-strike tactics necessary for effective damage-limiting war-fighting strategies difficult if not impossible for them to accomplish. Russian military doctrine does not seem to recognize any fine distinction between different types of tactical nuclear war, as U.S. military planning often does. Indeed, most of the

	NAME OF DELIVERY SYSTEM	NUMBER OF WARHEADS IN EUROPE	EXPLOSIVE YIELD (KILOTONS)	MAXIMUM RANGE (MILES)
NATO	HONEST JOHN MISSILE	196	20	25
	PERSHING MISSILE	180	60–400	450
	LANCE MISSILE	80	1–100	70
	SERGEANT MISSILE	56	LOW	85
	PLUTON MISSILE	24	15–25	75
	SSBS-2 MISSILE	18	150	1,875
	M-110 EIGHT-INCH HOWITZER SHELL	360	5–10	10
	M-115 EIGHT-INCH HOWITZER SHELL	27	5–10	10
	M-109 155-MILLIMETER HOWITZER SHELL	691	LOW	10
	LANCE MISSILE WITH ERW	?	ABOUT 1	85
	EIGHT-INCH HOWITZER SHELL WITH ERW	?	1–2	>10
	155-MM. HOWITZER SHELL WITH ERW	?	?	?
WARSAW PACT	SS-4 SANDAL MISSILE	500	1,000	1,200
	SS-5 SKEAN MISSILE	100	1,000	2,300
	SS-20 MISSILE	20(X3)	?	3,000
	SS-1b SCUD A MISSILE	} 880	?	50
	SS-1c SCUD B MISSILE		?	180
	SS-12 SCALEBOARD MISSILE		>1,000	500
	FROG 3-7 MISSILE	650	?	45
	M-55 203-MILLIMETER HOWITZER SHELL	?	?	18

TACTICAL NUCLEAR WEAPONS currently deployed in Europe by the NATO countries (including the U.S.) and the Warsaw Pact countries (including the U.S.S.R.) are listed in black type in this table. The new enhanced-radiation weapons proposed by the U.S. for the NATO arsenal are listed in colored type. The enhanced-radiation version of the Lance missile would have two possible yields, one somewhat less than a kiloton and the other slightly more. The enhanced-radiation version of the eight-inch shell would have three yields available, ranging from substantially less than one kiloton to roughly two kilotons. The Russian SS-20 intermediate-range ballistic missile (IRBM) carries three independently targetable nuclear warheads.

RUSSIAN MAIN-BATTLE TANK, designated the T-62, was photographed during a military parade in Red Square in Moscow. The Warsaw Pact forces are estimated to have 20,000 heavy tanks (mostly T-62's but also older models) deployed in the European theater.

Russian writings on the subject assume the inevitability of escalation, drawing no distinction between tactical nuclear war and all-out strategic nuclear war. In discussing a European-theater nuclear war such writings make virtually no mention of pinpoint accuracy and selective targeting except occasionally to hold them up to ridicule. A mass barrage punching wide holes in NATO's defenses, followed by a breakthrough with heavy tanks (whose structure and surface materials provide some protection against nuclear effects), seems to be the kind of mission envisioned for tactical nuclear weapons from the viewpoint of the U.S.S.R.

If NATO were to use enhanced-radiation weapons against Warsaw Pact tanks, the Russians would almost certainly strike back with nuclear weapons of their own. As a U.S. Army intelligence study of Russian military operations notes: "Should the first echelon [of tanks in an offensive] collapse, a series of counterattacks will be instituted, coordinated with all combat units to include... nuclear strikes." The Russians would probably not be very concerned about collateral damage to the West German civilian population; even if they were, the high yield and poor accuracy of their weapons would keep them from doing much about the unavoidable consequences.

Even before the virtually certain Russian nuclear retaliation the damage caused by NATO's use of enhanced-radiation warheads would be substantial, regardless of the presumed limitations of the blast, thermal and fallout effects of individual weapons. The posture statement of the U.S. Department of Defense for the fiscal year 1977 states that if nuclear weapons were used in Europe, such action "should... induce the Soviet Union to terminate the conflict quickly.... It should be done with decisiveness and shock effect to cause the Soviets to reconsider their activities." To achieve such a shock effect NATO would have to do more than stop a small number of tanks; much more damage would certainly be needed to make a dramatic impression on the Russian leaders.

How much more damage might that be? When Russian tanks are beginning an offensive, they move in two echelons (three under some circumstances). Tanks in the first echelon are spaced 75 meters apart in non-nuclear situations and 100 meters apart in nuclear situations. The second echelon moves up about three kilometers behind the first. The Warsaw Pact has some 20,000 tanks deployed for the central region of Europe, where the first battle of a NATO/Warsaw Pact war would probably be fought. Assertions by U.S. Army officers that the enhanced-radiation warhead causes little collateral damage are contingent on the weapon's being used in highly selective, even individual, strikes. Yet if NATO wanted to stop an impressive fraction of the first-echelon tanks, that is, if the enhanced-radiation weapons are to be at all useful militarily, the action would call for a barrage of many hundreds or even thousands of nuclear weapons. They would most likely include not only low-yield enhanced-radiation weapons but also low-yield and medium-yield fission weapons. Under such circumstances much radioactivity could be induced in the soil, particularly if some of the weapons were accidentally to detonate on or near the ground. In any event the number of fatalities and irradiated "walking ghost" casualties would be very high even if the nuclear war could be kept quite limited.

The enhanced-radiation warheads might reduce the collateral damage caused by blast and thermal radiation, but they would increase the damage caused by prompt radiation. Exposure even to comparatively small doses of radiation can have grave consequences for human beings, and enhanced-radiation warheads would extend the distance within which people are exposed to dangerous doses. For example, 10 percent of the people exposed to 150 rads will die from radiation sickness, and Hiroshima and Nagasaki survivors exposed to 150 rads showed a disproportionately high incidence of breast cancer. Exposure to only 30 rads doubles the mutation rate in progeny, and defective genes can be expected to appear for 10 generations. The inhabitants of the Marshall Islands who were exposed to a mere 14 rads as a result of U.S. nuclear testing in 1954 later developed thyroid nodules, cancers and leukemia.

A one-kiloton enhanced-radiation warhead releases 150 rads out to a distance of 1.7 kilometers, 30 rads out to 2.1 kilometers and 14 rads out to 2.3 kilometers. These effects can be compared respectively with 900, 1,170 and 1,300 meters for a one-kiloton fission weapon and 1,285, 1,570 and 1,700 meters for a 10-kiloton fission weapon.

With the enhanced-radiation warhead the collateral damage caused by prompt radiation would be even more extended. For radiation damage caused by gamma rays there is thought to be a threshold rad level below which no biological damage is caused. No such threshold is believed to exist for neutron radiation. Furthermore, in terms of genetic damage, leukemia and cataract of the eye, the biological effects from neutrons are about six times greater than those from gamma rays. Thus as few as one or two rads of neutron radiation could cause leukemia and cancers. Exposure to a mere five rads could double the mutation rate in the progeny of those exposed. If a single neutron collides with a strand of DNA in a sperm or egg cell, the probability of irreparable long-term genetic damage is high.

In other words, the notion that enhanced-radiation weapons are fairly benign to people on "our side" is highly questionable. Both NATO combatants and friendly noncombatants are likely to suffer much harm. The hazard to the noncombatants is increased by the fact that the eastern lands of West Germany have become highly urbanized.

The military utility of the enhanced-radiation warhead is questionable on an even more elementary level. Except for the tankmen who were fairly close to the actual detonation the exposed enemy personnel would remain alive for hours, days or even weeks; many of them could fight on, perhaps even more aggressively than before because of their knowledge that death from radiation was certain. Of course, NATO could accommodate to this problem by setting off a much larger number of enhanced-radiation weapons. Since the alleged virtues of the enhanced-radiation warhead stem mainly from its capability for precise, selective, limited strikes, however, this kind of massive barrage would undercut the entire rationale of the weapon. Besides, armor-penetrating neutrons would not make a tank so radioactive as to exclude the possibility of other tank crews' replacing those exposed to radiation. The tanks could drive on.

The effective use of these weapons also assumes a massive concentration of tanks. Yet it is a safe assumption that the NATO nations would not order the firing of any nuclear weapons unless the Warsaw Pact nations had first exhausted and overrun NATO's non-nuclear defenses. Even if the Russians had concentrated their tanks in the initial phases of the offensive, they would almost certainly disperse their armored forces after breaking through the NATO frontline defenses. (In fact, their writings on tactical operations suggest that this is exactly what they would do.) Under such conditions many thousands of enhanced-radiation warheads would have to be employed to immediately incapacitate the occupants of a significant number of Warsaw Pact tanks, again nullifying the alleged virtues of the enhanced-radiation weapon.

In spite of the apparently minimal military utility of enhanced-radiation weapons, the U.S. Department of Defense justifies them on the grounds that "if NATO arsenals contained the neutron warhead, opposing countries would be aware of NATO's ability to defend itself with less damage; this *could be* a deterrence to attack." Although the Department of Defense does not explicitly state that this weapon would enhance deterrence, the implication is that the Russians might think NATO would be more likely to use the enhanced-radiation weapons than the older, more fission-dominated weapons.

Here three comments should be made. (1) Even without the threat of enhanced-radiation weapons the Russians would be taking a big risk in attacking, since the U.S. has consistently refused to adopt a policy of not being the first to fire nuclear weapons. (2) Enormous damage would result from NATO's use of enhanced-radiation weapons, to say nothing of the damage that would be caused by a virtually certain Russian nuclear retaliation. (3) Although the topic is much too complex to treat in detail here, there is no reason to believe that NATO is incapable of defending Western Europe without resorting to nuclear weapons. Conventional firepower ratios between NATO and the Warsaw Pact nations are virtually even, and it is a well-known maxim that an attacker requires substantial superiority. The often-mentioned superiority of the Warsaw Pact nations in number of tanks is offset by the advantage NATO holds in superior antitank weapons, particularly with the recent advances in precision-guided munitions and remotely piloted vehicles. Weapons of both new types have greater ranges than the guns on Russian tanks, and both can, in the words of a U.S. Army field manual, "hit what they see, kill what they hit."

Military training in the U.S.S.R. and the other countries of Eastern Europe is notoriously poor and extremely rigid. The political reliability of the Czechoslovak and Polish divisions, at least for offensive warfare, is doubtful. Tactics and strategy in the Warsaw Pact armies rely heavily on the tank, which is becoming an increasingly vulnerable and obsolete weapons system. Moreover, the numerous surprise-attack scenarios circulating these days do not take into account the low readiness levels of the Warsaw Pact armies, the hundreds of ways intelligence agencies can observe and track signs of mobilization, the deficient Russian logistics network and many other weaknesses in the Russian war machine.

This is not to say that there is no room for improvement in NATO. Various maldeployments of forces could be corrected; lines of communication could be moved farther back, away from the forward edge of the battle area; more conventional antitank weapons could be deployed; airfields could be more widely dispersed; more aircraft could be deployed at "hardened" sites. The present U.S. Administration appears to be addressing itself to these problems. Since some of these tasks call for very substantial expenditures, it seems wasteful to spend large sums on such weapons as the enhanced-radiation warhead.

The costs of producing enhanced-radiation warheads would be enormous. The eight-inch enhanced-radiation artillery weapon will cost about $900,000 per shell (including the costs of the projectile, the casing and so forth). The enhanced-radiation version of the Lance missile is expected to cost only slightly less. Instead of buying two rounds of eight-inch enhanced-radiation shells the U.S. could obtain, say, three M-60 main-battle tanks, 50 or so advanced non-nuclear antitank weapons or more than 5,500 rounds of conventional artillery shells. In other words, if the U.S. decides to invest in enhanced-radiation devices, NATO will be acquiring an extraordinarily costly weapon that will probably never be used at the expense of comparatively cheap weapons that would markedly improve NATO's defense posture. Assuming that the Russians dispersed their tanks widely and that they adopted certain measures against neutron radiation, then conventional antitank weaponry would probably be both cheaper and militarily more effective.

It remains true that the enhanced-radiation warhead could do as much damage to an attacking force as higher-yield weapons without causing as much collateral damage. Against this clear advantage, however, one must take into account the enormous damage that would ultimately result from any introduction of nuclear weapons into a conventional war. It might also be said in favor of enhanced-radiation devices that, as the systems of this new generation of tactical nuclear weapons are currently planned, they incorporate features other than enhanced radiation. They will have a longer range (about 130 kilometers for the enhanced-radiation version of the Lance), improved command-control communication systems and securer lock mechanisms. These added features would probably have a stabilizing effect in that they would make tactical nuclear weapons less likely to be overrun by a conventional Warsaw Pact attack and less susceptible to accidental firing. Nevertheless, these features could easily be incorporated in the present generation of tactical nuclear weapons; the enhanced-radiation feature is not necessary for such purposes.

The enhanced-radiation warhead is a particularly dangerous weapon insofar as it might mislead anyone into believing that its deployment would make it possible for nuclear warfare to be safely limited and tightly controlled; in this sense its very deployment could lower the threshold separating conventional warfare from nuclear warfare. Enhanced-radiation weapons are no more (and perhaps they are less) "humane" than chemical weapons, whose first use has long been outlawed by international treaty. Moreover, the enhanced-radiation warhead has little more military utility than any other type of low-yield nuclear weapon. Finally, to the extent that the U.S.S.R. believes the U.S. will use enhanced-radiation weapons in a European ground war, their deployment invites a preemptive Russian nuclear attack in any extremely tense situation, perhaps as the first move in a European war. In any event there is no reason to believe the enhanced-radiation warhead would in any way diminish the likelihood that a European-theater nuclear war would escalate to an all-out nuclear war, or that its introduction would somehow moderate the probable response of the U.S.S.R.

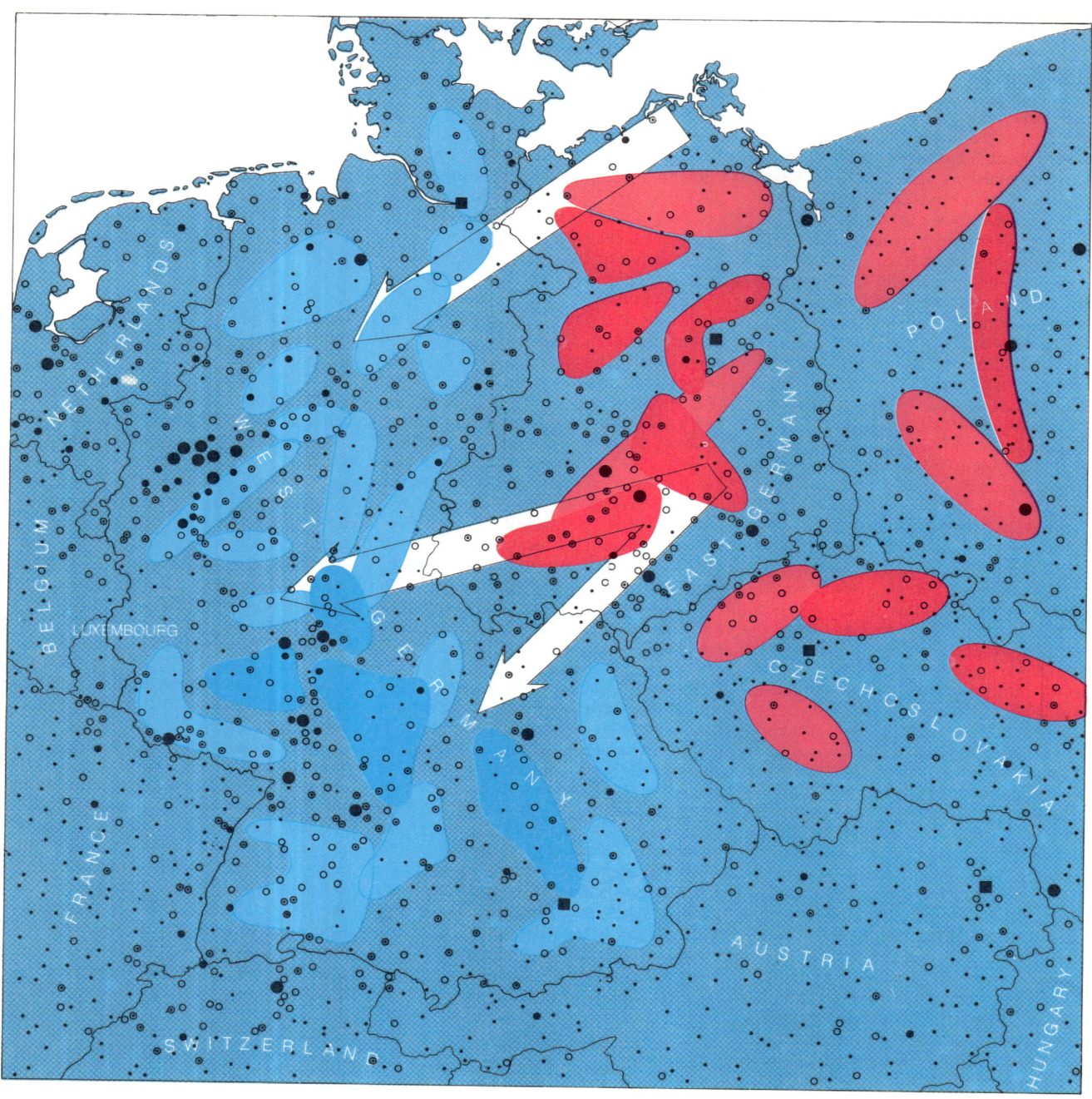

HYPOTHETICAL INVASION of Western Europe by the forces of the Warsaw Pact countries is depicted on this map. Irregularly shaped colored areas show the approximate deployment of NATO and Warsaw Pact forces on mobilization day (see key for color coding of the deployment areas). The forces would be redeployed between mobilization day and D day (the first day of the war). The arrows show what are considered to be the most likely major invasion routes. The three most likely axes of attack are along the main autobahns. An attempt by the NATO forces to stop the Russian armored divisions leading any one of these major attacks by resorting to enhanced-radiation nuclear weapons would require a barrage of hundreds of such warheads well within the borders of West Germany. Because of the growing urbanization of the region a counterattack of this kind could kill several hundred thousand, and conceivably several million, civilians and NATO combatants (not including the deaths that would be caused by probable Russian nuclear retaliation). Population distribution is indicated by keyed symbols.

The SALT Negotiations

by Herbert Scoville, Jr.
August 1977

Current strategic-arms-limitation talks can put a real ceiling on the quantitative arms race and restrain the qualitative race. A failure to do so may destabilize the present strategic balance

The Carter Administration is in the process of reviewing national security policies and assembling its first defense budget. A central question in the deliberations is the part arms control can and should play, and the strategic-arms-limitation talks (SALT) with the U.S.S.R. are the most critical negotiations currently under way. Both the U.S.S.R., with its new family of large-payload intercontinental ballistic missiles (ICBM's) and the U.S., with its programs for replacing Minuteman ICBM's with more accurate ones, are contemplating new deployments that could greatly reduce the stability of the strategic balance and would also cost billions of dollars. The interim agreement on offensive arms that was reached in 1972 expires on October 3, and unless some new agreement is reached by that date the pressures for stepping up the arms race will be very great. Success in this round of SALT is therefore a matter of grave consequence for U.S. security and also for the size of the armament bill Americans have to pay.

The U.S. and the U.S.S.R. achieved their first broad arms-control agreements in 1972, when the anti-ballistic-missile treaty and the interim agreement were signed at the conclusion of the first round of strategic-arms-limitation talks (SALT I). The second phase of the talks (SALT II) has been occupying the two superpowers on and off since then. Now a deadline looms, because the interim agreement ran for only five years. A step toward meeting the October deadline was taken almost three years ago by the Vladivostok accords, a set of guidelines for SALT II that set numerical ceilings on the major strategic weapons: 2,400 strategic delivery vehicles (bombers and missiles), with no more than 1,320 of them to be armed with multiple independently targetable reentry vehicles (MIRV's). The good news then was that the accords for the first time put a ceiling on bombers as well as missiles, and also on the number of missiles that could be fitted with MIRV's (although not on the total number of MIRV's). The bad news was that the agreement established ceilings so high as to be in effect nonlimiting; that it was imprecise about the definition of what types of weapons—in particular cruise missiles and medium-range bombers—should be included under the ceilings, and that by failing to deal with advances in weapons technology it institutionalized a new kind of arms race, a qualitative race instead of a primarily quantitative one. These have since turned out to be significant issues. What is complicating the current phase of the SALT negotiations is that each side is attempting to deal—in different ways—with those shortcomings of the Vladivostok guidelines.

The new Carter Administration took the initiative in March, when Secretary of State Cyrus R. Vance went to Moscow with two alternative proposals. One was "comprehensive." It sought to reverse the quantitative arms race by actually reducing existing arsenals and to curb the qualitative race by restricting the modernization or replacement of existing weapons systems. The other was a fallback "deferral" proposal. It would simply have confirmed the Vladivostok ceilings, leaving for future consideration the two issues that had blocked a final SALT II agreement during the Ford Administration: the control of the American cruise missile and the Russian "Backfire" medium bomber. The Russians turned down both propositions. The deferral proposal's overall ceilings were apparently satisfactory to them, but they could not accept its deferral of the cruise-missile issue. As for the comprehensive proposal, the Russians said its particular limitations and prohibitions were calculated to freeze U.S. strategic superiority.

After that initial rejection the negotiations resumed within a three-part framework established in Geneva in May. There would be, first, a five-year treaty confirming the Vladivostok overall ceiling or a somewhat lower one; second, a protocol, to run for three years, constraining the development or deployment of cruise missiles, mobile missiles, heavy ICBM's and the Backfire, and third, a statement of principles to govern continuing negotiations on long-term, substantial reductions in strategic arms and on controlling the qualitative race. This summer's negotiations have presumably dealt with the details to be fitted into that framework.

Here I shall mainly describe and analyze the various provisions of the original comprehensive proposal put forward by the U.S. in Moscow, attempting thereby to demonstrate the nature of the major current issues in arms control, the complex interrelations of numerical and qualitative controls and the difficulty of establishing meaningful controls in an era when technological advances are becoming far more significant than such conventional measures of strategic supremacy as the number and megatonnage of each side's missiles. I shall try to relate the provisions of the comprehensive proposal to the three-part framework now under discussion.

The American comprehensive proposal went far beyond any controls that had been formally put on the table by either country in eight years of SALT negotiations. It represented in particular an effort to limit those weapons systems most calculated to endanger the stable mutual-deterrence balance between the U.S. and the U.S.S.R., that is, systems that can give either side a "counterforce" capability threatening the land-based intercontinental ballistic missiles of the other side. Any weapon, such as an ICBM with several MIRV's, each having a combination of accuracy and yield that gives it a high probability of destroying a "hardened" intercontinental-missile launcher, is a counterforce weapon. It threatens an important component of the other side's retaliatory arsenal and thus of its deterrent strength.

The nine basic elements of the U.S. proposal (as they have been revealed so far) fell into two categories. The first four provisions imposed limits—lower than those now in effect—on the number of strategic delivery vehicles. The last five provisions addressed the problem of qualitative control by imposing various restrictions on the development, testing and deployment of new weapons.

The quantitative provisions would have reduced the total number of delivery vehicles, or of ICBM's, submarine-launched ballistic missiles (SLBM's) and strategic bombers, from the Vladivostok level of 2,400 to between 1,800 and 2,000. Only 1,100 to 1,200 of the missiles could be MIRVed (compared with 1,320 under the Vladivostok terms), and only 550 of those MIRVed missiles could be land-based ICBM's (a subtotal that was not specified at Vladivostok). Finally, the number of very heavy Russian ICBM's would be reduced from the 308 established by the interim agreement to 150.

By making some assumptions about how each side might decide to allocate its forces among ICBM's, SLBM's and bombers, and also about bomb loads and the number of MIRV's that would be fitted on various missiles, it is possible to assess the impact of the lowered limits on the two sides' arsenals [*see illustration on pages 166 and 167*]. The actual allocations might be different, but that would probably not alter the strategic balance significantly. (The major uncertainties in the allocations have to do with the Russian program for installing MIRV's on their SLBM's, a program that has had low priority until now but that would presumably become more urgent, as I shall explain, if the MIRVing of land-based missiles were to be curtailed.)

The U.S.S.R. has concentrated on larger ICBM's that can carry bigger payloads, which can be translated into either more explosive yield per warhead or more warheads per missile, or some of each. I have assumed on the basis of Russian tests that the heavy Russian ICBM's would carry eight warheads and that the light ICBM's would carry six. The U.S. land-based Minuteman III missiles carry three warheads. As for bombers, I assume that the American B-52 could carry up to 10 weapons, either bombs, long-range cruise missiles or short-range air-to-surface missiles. There is uncertainty about the bomb load of Russian strategic bombers, but the U.S. Department of Defense generally estimates two or three weapons per aircraft; the Russians have a very small strategic bomber force and so the uncertainty is of little consequence. I have excluded the Backfire medium bomber from the strategic-force calculations because there is a real question as to its value for intercontinental missions; it falls in a category similar to that of the U.S. bombers stationed in Europe within range of the U.S.S.R., what is called the forward-based system.

Reaching the lower levels contemplated by the comprehensive proposal would present different kinds of problems, involving both real and perceived inequities, for the U.S. and the U.S.S.R. The proposal would require the Russians to cut back their heavy ICBM's from 308 to 150, all of which could be fitted with multiple warheads. That requirement provoked a strong reaction from the Russians, since the U.S. has no heavy ICBM's and nothing in the comprehensive proposal would require the U.S. to eliminate any specified existing weapons. This particular controversy could have been avoided if the provision had been phrased differently, simply setting a ceiling of 150 on the number of heavy missiles the Russians could MIRV or even on the number of older Russian heavy SS-9 missiles that could be replaced by the newer SS-18. The SS-9 has never been tested with MIRV's, and even most of the SS-18's have only single warheads, so that the Russians now have only a small number of MIRVed heavy ICBM's. A limit on MIRVing, or at least on the number of new SS-18's, would be verifiable by satellite because the SS-18 requires a larger silo than the SS-9. Such a ceiling would have about the same strategic effect as a cutback because the single-warhead SS-9 ICBM's do not pose a significant counterforce threat.

Limiting the total number of MIRVed ICBM's to 550 might be particularly difficult for the U.S.S.R., which relies more than the U.S. on ICBM's. (The limit of 550 also has a "cosmetic" problem, since it was apparently picked to coincide with the present number of MIRVed U.S. Minuteman missiles.) One cannot be sure how many of the

U.S. CRUISE MISSILE is a subsonic, jet-powered drone similar to the World War II "buzz bomb" but with greater range and accuracy. It can be launched from land, from a surface vessel or submarine or from the air—from a B-52 in this photograph. A major SALT issue is Russian insistence that long-range cruise missiles be included under a strategic-weapons ceiling.

RUSSIAN "BACKFIRE" is a supersonic medium bomber able to attain Mach 2 at high altitude. Its combat radius is 3,500 miles, which means it could reach the U.S. only by flying subsonically from arctic bases in the U.S.S.R. on a one-way "suicide" mission, by landing in a "third country" or refueling in flight. One issue is whether or not Backfire is a strategic weapon.

Vladivostok accord's 1,320 MIRVed delivery vehicles the Russians would have allocated to ICBM's, but in view of the low priority given to SLBM's in the past the number might well have been far more than 550. On the other hand, the Russians now have fewer than 200 MIRVed ICBM's, so that they would not be forced to scrap any. And one can argue that if the limit on MIRVed ICBM's were set much above 550, a counterforce capability would be within sight, given reasonable improvements in accuracy.

Merely meeting the ceiling of 1,800 to 2,000 total delivery vehicles would probably force the Russians to scrap ICBM's. They would have the alternative of reducing their SLBM force, but that stood at 840 in the spring and appears to be on the way to the 950 allowed by the 1972 interim agreement. Scrapping ICBM's would presumably be preferable to scrapping expensive submarines, which constitute the more reliable deterrent. If the Russians wanted (as they presumably would) to attain the proposal's ceiling of 1,100 to 1,200 MIRVed missiles, the low limit on multiple warheads for ICBM's would require MIRVing from 550 to 650 SLBM's. The Russians have only recently begun, however, to test a missile with two MIRV warheads for the newest of their two classes of missile-launching nuclear submarines. Such a missile will be very inferior to the 10-warhead U.S. Poseidon, which has been operational for five years, and will be even further behind the Trident I missile scheduled to be deployed in about two years. For various reasons, then, the Russians would almost surely prefer to MIRV a large number of ICBM's. The restrictions on the MIRVing of ICBM's contemplated by the U.S. proposal were therefore understandably viewed as one-sided, in that they curb the weapons the U.S.S.R. values most and the U.S. values least.

The U.S.S.R. is far behind the U.S. in intercontinental bombers, with about 135 aircraft dating from the mid-1950's, and it is apparently making little effort to catch up. The Russians would presumably reduce strategic-force levels, if necessary, by scrapping some old bombers. The U.S., on the other hand, would probably maintain a significant force of B-52's, whose large bomb loads would be a significant element in the total nuclear explosive power that could be unleashed against the U.S.S.R.

The new Russian Backfire, which has attracted so much attention, has very little intercontinental capability. It can reach the U.S. only from bases in the Russian Arctic on a one-way subsonic high-altitude mission. A two-way mission would require in-flight refueling, which has not been given high priority in Russian air tactics. The Backfire's capability as a strategic bomber—defined as a bomber that can reach the other country's territory—is certainly less significant than that of U.S. bombers based in Europe or on aircraft carriers, which can reach strategic targets within the U.S.S.R. The U.S. contends that the primary role of the forward-based aircraft is not strategic but rather to support its NATO allies in the event of a European conflict. Similarly, the Russians maintain that the Backfire is for missions against peripheral targets such as China and Western Europe.

There are, then, various ways the U.S.

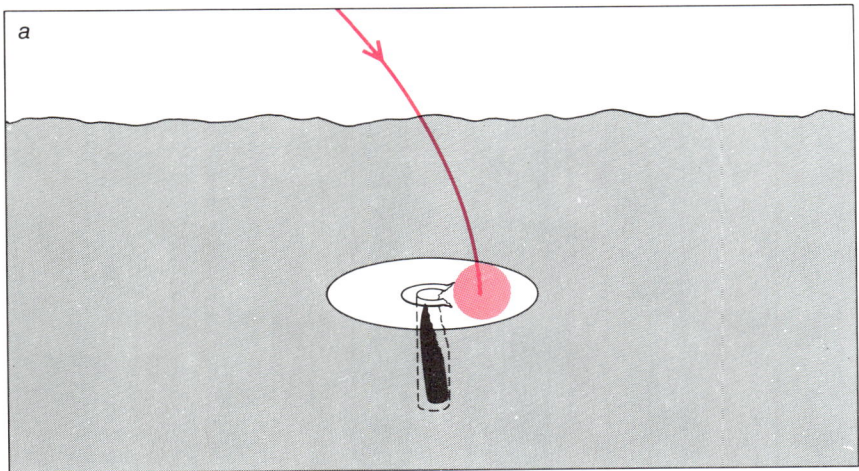

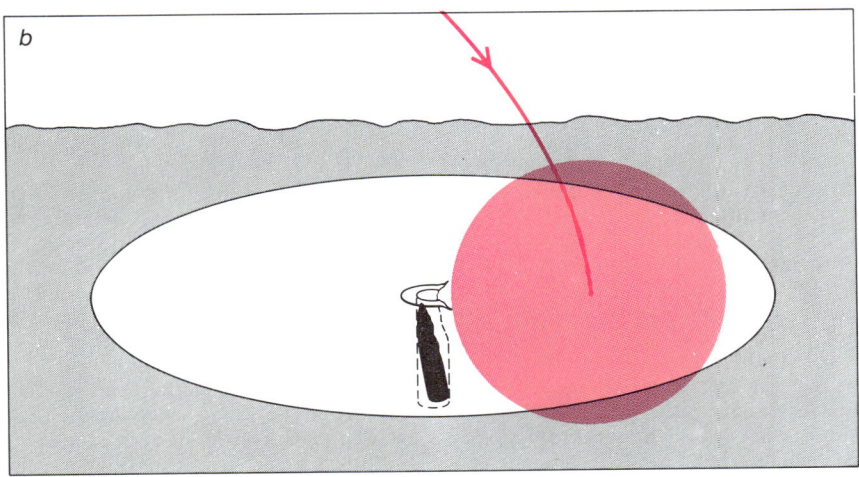

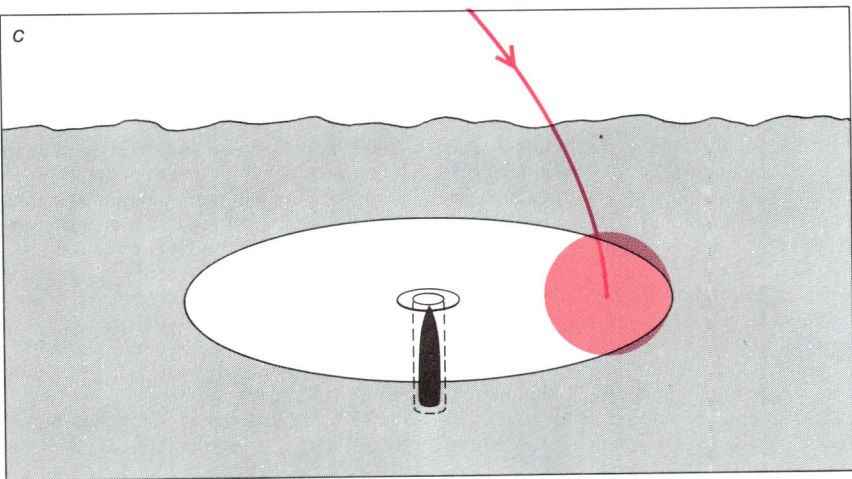

ACCURACY AND EXPLOSIVE YIELD combine to determine the probability of a missile's destroying a "hardened" target. A warhead of modest yield but with a small circular error probability (CEP) can destroy a missile silo (*a*), as can a warhead with a larger yield but a larger CEP, or less accuracy (*b*); either warhead is an effective counterforce weapon. A weapon with insufficient yield or accuracy to knock out a silo is not an effective counterforce weapon (*c*).

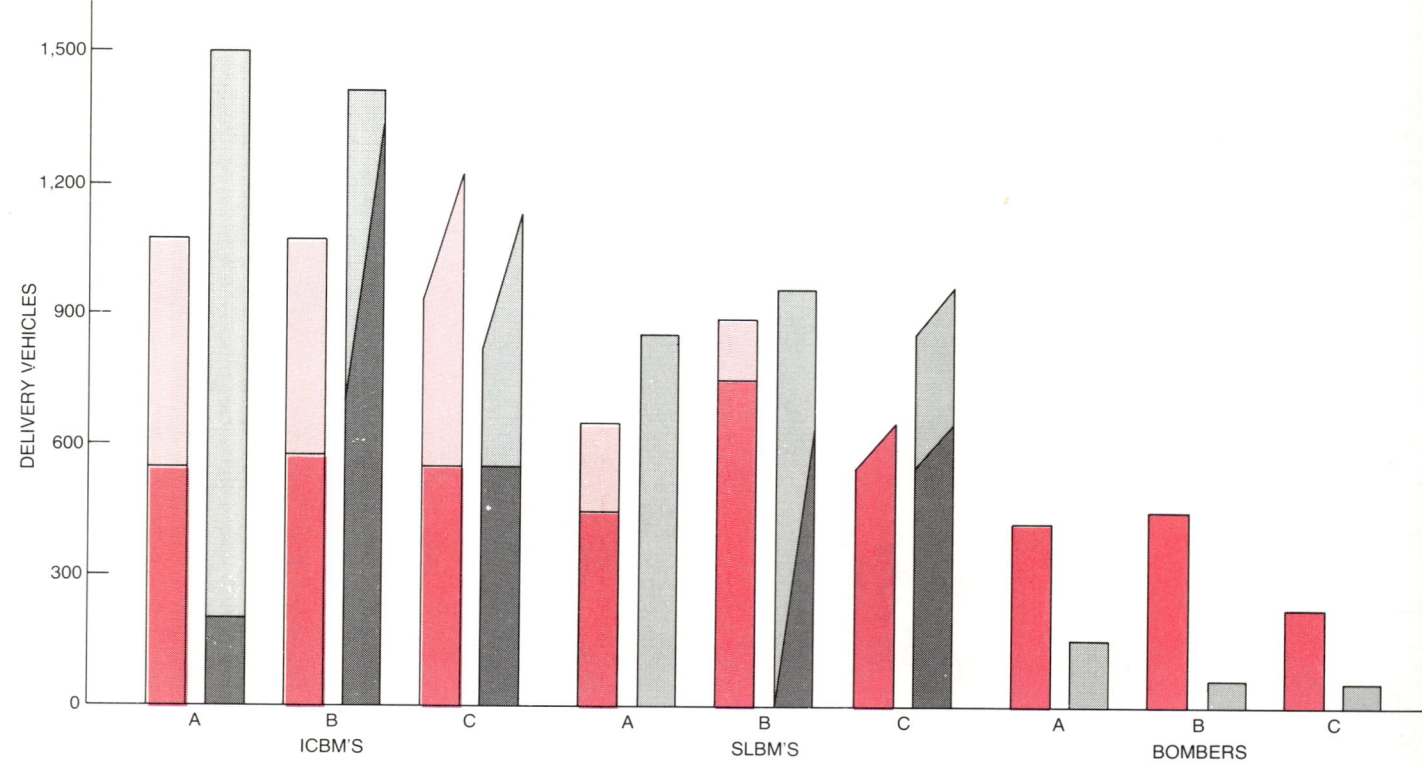

STRATEGIC FORCES of the U.S. (*color*) and the U.S.S.R. (*gray*) are compared as of last spring (*A*) and as they might be in 1985 if the Vladivostok ceilings (*B*) or the lower ceilings set forth in the U.S. comprehensive proposal (*C*) were in force. (Actual numbers might be somewhat different, since assumptions must be made about how the two nations would choose to balance their forces.) The left-hand

and the U.S.S.R. might reduce their strategic forces to reach the ceilings contemplated in the comprehensive proposal, but the options are constrained by existing force structures, by the technology available in each country and by the two countries' respective bureaucracies. To reach the proposed overall ceiling of 2,000 to 1,800 delivery vehicles would be more difficult for the U.S.S.R., for which it would mean a cut of from 500 to 700 from present levels, as opposed to a cut for the U.S. of between 150 and 350. The U.S. could take its reduction easily in bombers or older ICBM's, whereas the U.S.S.R. would have to scrap newer ICBM's or SLBM's as well. The ceiling of 1,100 to 1,200 put on MIRVed delivery vehicles would not in itself require any reduction of existing forces by either country, but the subtotal of 550 ICBM's with multiple warheads would be hard for the Russians to take. The lowered ceiling would force the U.S. to discard some existing MIRVed missiles if it were to go ahead with proposed programs such as the Trident submarine.

Under the comprehensive proposal the Russians might by 1985 have about a two-to-one lead in the number of ICBM warheads; the yield of their warheads would be about one megaton, compared with about 200 kilotons for the American warheads. The Russian numerical advantage in ICBM's would be somewhat smaller than it was under the Vladivostok accords but substantially larger than it is now, since the U.S.S.R. is only beginning its MIRV deployment. The Russian advantage in number and yield would be counterbalanced by U.S. superiority in accuracy and probably in reliability.

In SLBM warheads the U.S. would have a numerical lead of two or three to one. Moreover, the U.S. missiles and submarines are technologically superior, and the U.S. has a significant geographical advantage because of the ease with which its vessels can operate in the Atlantic Ocean. In bombers the U.S. would have an overwhelming lead even if the Backfire were counted as a Russian strategic bomber. The U.S. lead in bombers and SLBM warheads would more than balance the Russian lead in ICBM's. The U.S. would therefore be somewhat ahead in total missile warheads and very far ahead in total "force loadings," or total warheads and bomb loads, although the lead might not be quite as great as it would be under the simple Vladivostok formulas. In truth, however, such leads have no real military meaning and should have no political meaning, since each country has more than enough weapons to destroy the other in any conceivable nuclear conflict.

What counts is that the U.S. and the U.S.S.R. would, on reaching the comprehensive proposal's levels, be in rough equivalence. Each country would have a lead in the weapons it has concentrated on in the past. If technology were frozen (an important "if," which depends on the qualitative limits I shall discuss below), neither side would have a reliable counterforce capability, that is, the ability to destroy most of the other side's ICBM force. Both countries would have a secure deterrent, and the strategic balance would be stable, since there would be little incentive for initiating a nuclear first strike.

The Carter proposals dealing with qualitative advances in weapons were potentially more important than the restrictions on numbers of weapons. It has been clear for some years that the strategic-arms race is driven primarily by the continuous quest for technological improvement and advantage rather than by the mere desire to increase numbers. Yet neither the 1972 interim agreement nor the Vladivostok accords did anything to restrain such improvement; the replacement of existing weapons with new, improved models was either tacitly contemplated or in some cases explicitly allowed.

The comprehensive proposal would forbid the modernization or replacement of ICBM's and the development and deployment of mobile ICBM's. It would limit the flight-testing of ballistic missiles to six tests a year for ICBM's and six for SLBM's. It would ban strategic cruise missiles, defined as missiles

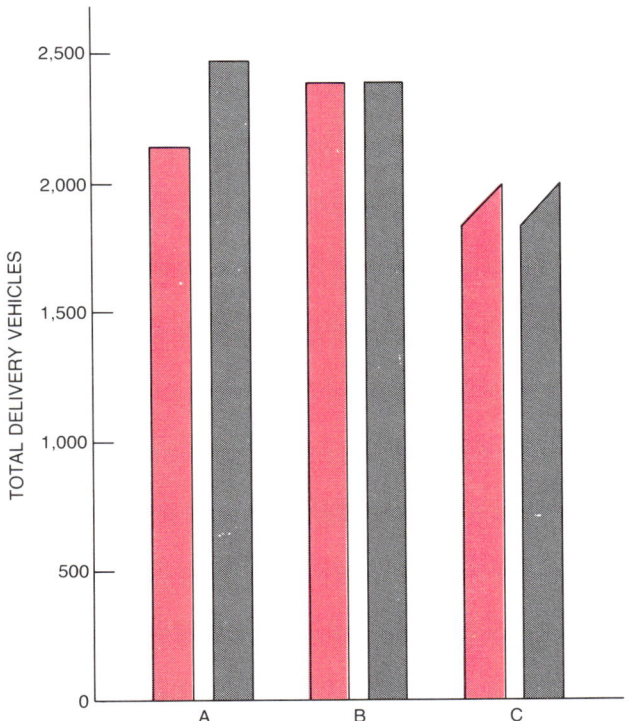
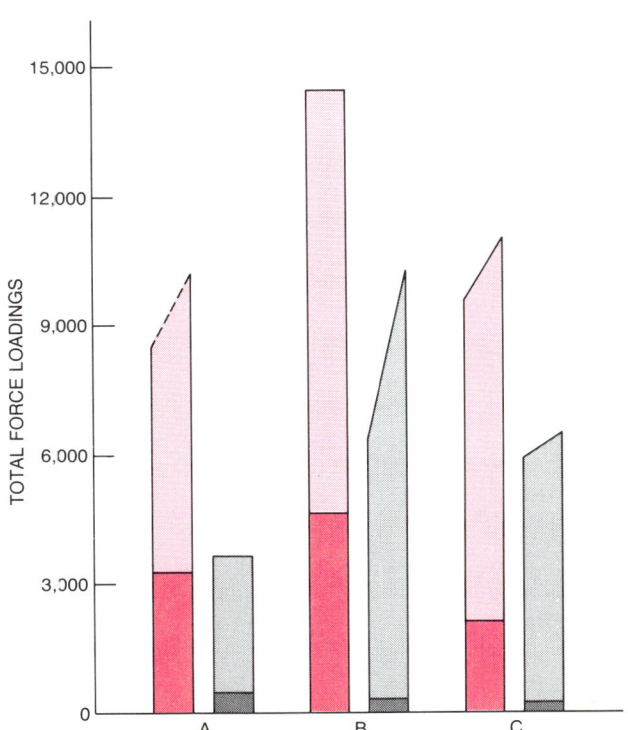

chart shows numbers of ICBM's, SLBM's and strategic bombers and indicates how many of the missiles might be MIRVed (*dark color and dark gray*). Slanted lines are used to indicate a range of possibili-ties. The center chart shows the total number of delivery vehicles. The right-hand chart shows total "force loadings": the sum of strategic-aircraft bomb loads (*dark tones*) and missile warheads (*light tones*).

with a range in excess of 2,500 kilometers (1,550 miles), but shorter-range cruise missiles would be unrestricted. Finally, it would require Russian assurances that the Backfire would not be given intercontinental capability or be deployed as a strategic weapon. The proposed bans on modernization and on mobile ICBM's and the restriction on testing would essentially prevent, or at least delay for a long time, any changes in existing missile forces. The stringent restrictions on ICBM's in particular would keep either nation from acquiring a counterforce capability that could threaten the other side's ICBM force. These provisions would markedly increase the stability of the strategic balance and would actually soon bring the arms race to a halt.

A six-test annual quota would effectively enforce the ban on modernization and replacement because the quotas would have to be used up largely by the "confidence" tests required to make sure weapons already in place are operational. Without additional tests it would become almost impossible to incorporate significant new improvements into existing missile systems; to procure totally new weapons would be out of the question. "National technical means of verification" could ensure that the quotas were honored. Ever since the first Russian ICBM test in 1957 the U.S. has been able to observe missile tests with a high degree of reliability from outside the U.S.S.R. The combination of satellite reconnaissance and electronic or infrared monitoring from the periphery of the U.S.S.R. has provided a wealth of information on both the launch and the reentry phases of the test firings. The ability to monitor could be improved and made more reliable by an agreement that all test firing be done on predesignated test ranges, following a precedent set when the anti-ballistic-missile treaty of 1972 was negotiated.

These qualitative proposals would effectively freeze the two nations at their technological levels as of whatever time the restrictions went into effect. Two American ICBM-development programs would be dramatically affected. The U.S. is now completing the development of the Mk. 12A warhead, with the NS-20 guidance system, to replace the MIRV's on the Minuteman III missile; deployment of the guidance system is scheduled to begin late this year. The new warhead will improve the accuracy of the Minuteman MIRV's and approximately double their explosive yield, giving each of them a high probability (more than 70 percent) of destroying a hardened missile silo. The Minuteman would thus for the first time attain what the Russians could view as a significant counterforce capability. The U.S. has also begun to design a totally new ICBM, the MX missile, as a replacement for the Minuteman. The MX is to have higher-yield warheads that can be terminally guided (steered during the later stages of their trajectory) to zero in on a target. This would be a true counterforce weapon and therefore an extremely destabilizing one. The MX is also to be mobile and hence extremely difficult to knock out; it will be able either to move back and forth in a long, hardened trench or to fire from any one of a number of prepared, hardened launch pads. This will increase its survivability but at the same time will make any ceiling on missiles or launchers virtually unverifiable. If the Russians were to emulate this approach, limits on ICBM's would be forever nonnegotiable. Both of these destabilizing U.S. programs would be halted by acceptance of the U.S. comprehensive proposal.

The U.S.S.R. would be similarly constrained. The new Russian ICBM's, the SS-17, the SS-18, the SS-19 and most likely the SS-16, have probably been tested enough to be deployed in their present configuration, but MIRVed versions of them are not now considered to have the combination of yield and accuracy that can give them a true counterforce capability. Improvements would be foreclosed by the U.S. proposals, thereby preventing the Russians from acquiring a counterforce threat to the U.S. Minuteman force. The ban on mobile ICBM's would keep the Russians from making the SS-16 mobile or making the already mobile intermedi-

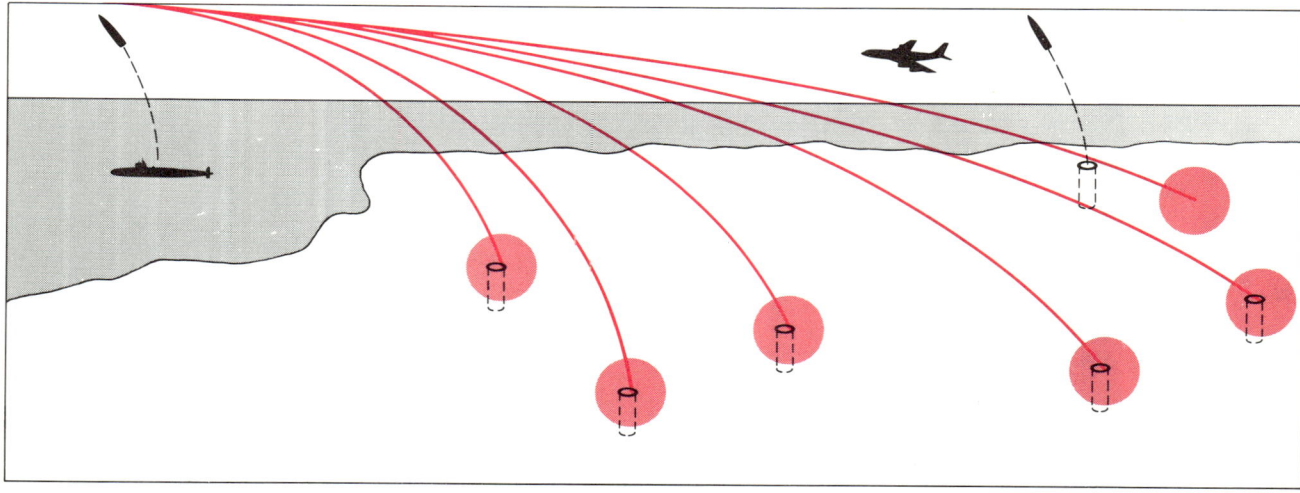

EFFECTIVE COUNTERFORCE ATTACK by missiles with multiple independently targetable reentry vehicles (MIRV's) knocks out most of the targeted intercontinental ballistic missiles (ICBM's). Bombers on alert and missile-launching submarines can still retaliate.

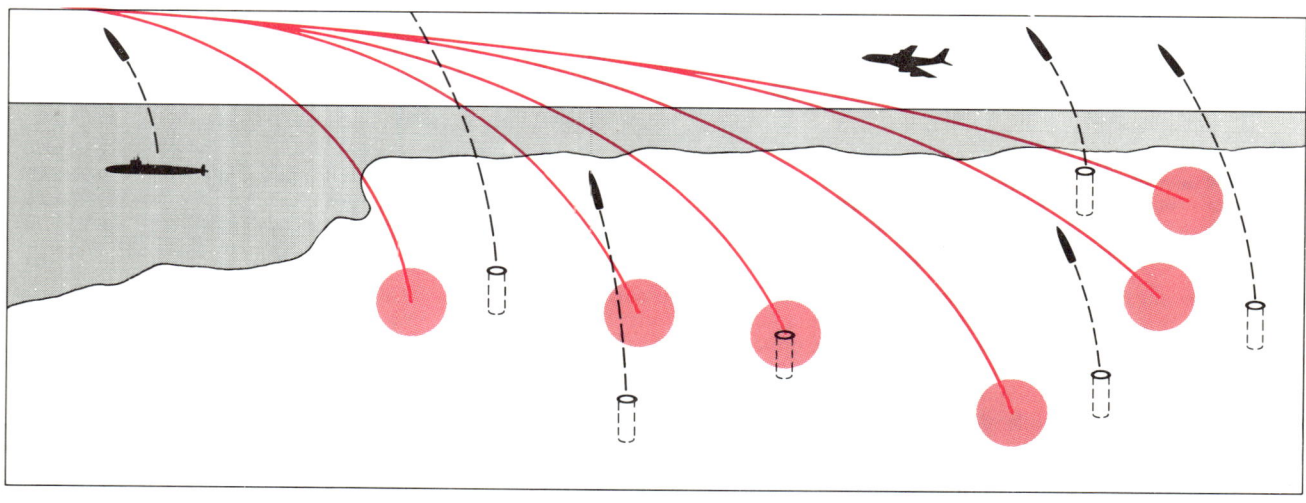

INEFFECTIVE COUNTERFORCE ATTACK is one in which the attacking missiles lack either the accuracy or the explosive yield to destroy many of the targeted ICBM's. Most of the ICBM's survive, and they can be launched to carry out a large-scale retaliatory attack.

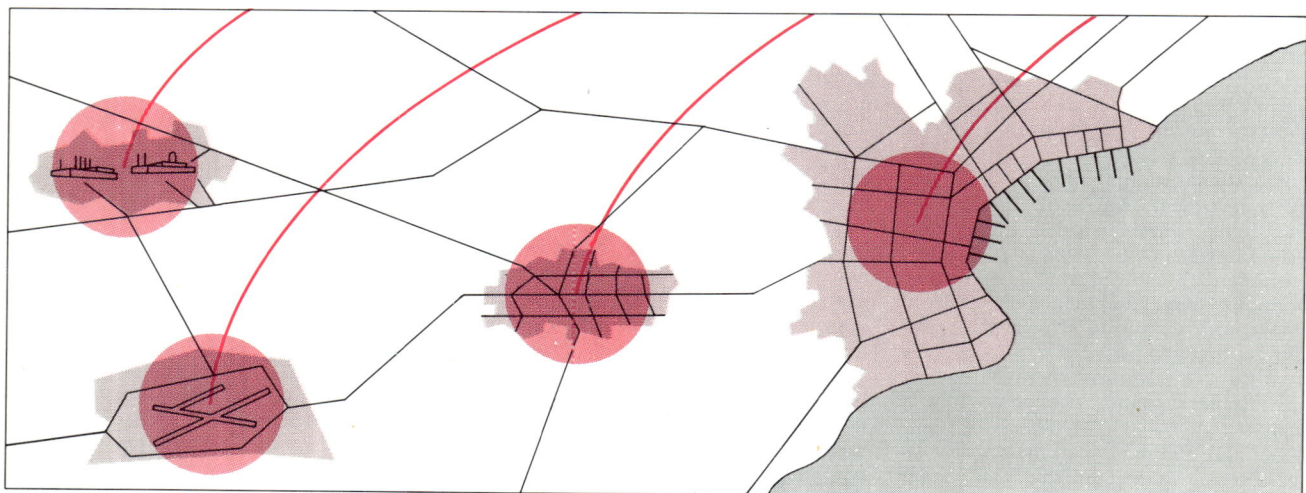

EFFECTIVE RETALIATION by the targeted nation on the nation that launched a first strike is depicted. ICBM's, submarine-launched ballistic missiles (SLBM's) and bombers attack population centers, port facilities, industrial complexes and military targets other than missile silos. Far less accuracy is required for effective retaliation on such targets than is required for a successful counterforce attack.

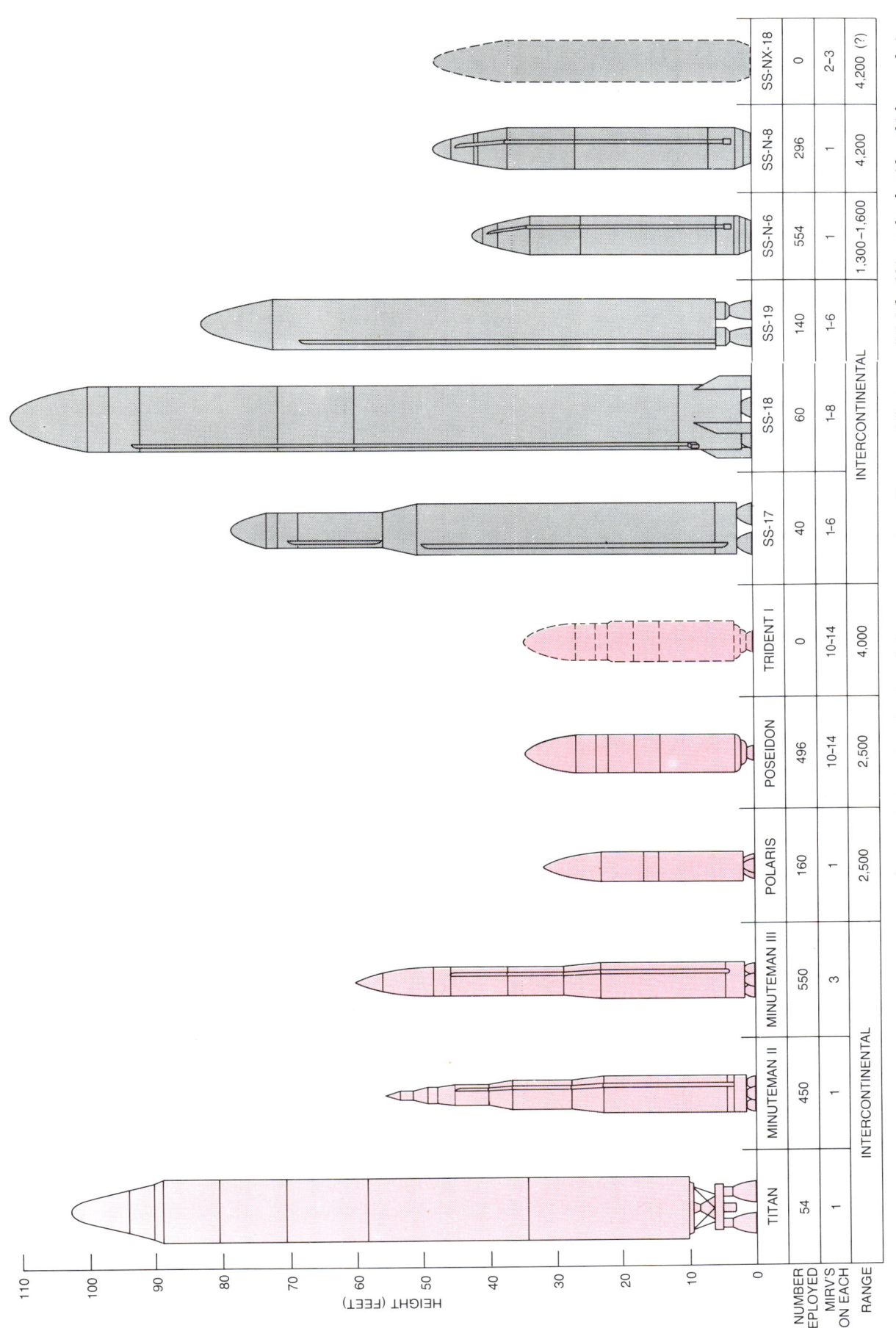

INTERCONTINENTAL BALLISTIC MISSILES of the U.S. (color) and the U.S.S.R. (gray) are depicted. For each missile the number known or estimated to be deployed, the number of MIRVed warheads and the range are given. For each country three ICBM's are shown, followed by three SLBM's. The U.S. has announced it will soon deploy the new Minuteman III Mk. 12A warhead with a higher explosive yield and a more accurate guidance system. The long-range U.S. Trident I is scheduled to be deployed in about two years.

ate-range SS-20 into an intercontinental missile, two possible developments that have caused great concern in Washington. In short, in the ICBM area the U.S. would be left with the higher-technology weapons, but that would be compensated for by the larger payload of existing Russian missiles. Hence there would be an approximate balance of overall capability.

In the SLBM area, however, things would be different. Here, as I have indicated, the U.S. is currently far ahead of the U.S.S.R. Unless some provisions were included allowing the Russians to catch up, or at least to complete the development of a satisfactory long-range MIRV system for their SLBM's, it is unlikely that they would accept a six-tests-per-year quota. If a test limit came into effect fairly soon, the American advantage would be somewhat counterbalanced by the fact that the quota would inhibit the deployment of the Trident I SLBM and prevent the development of the Trident II. The cancellation of the Trident II should indirectly bring the Trident submarine program to a halt, since such a vessel would be almost impossible to justify if it were limited to carrying the Trident I missiles that smaller submarines can launch. (A halt to the Trident submarine program would not be a security loss because smaller submarines would be better in any case.) Since SLBM's are basically deterrent weapons rather than counterforce ones, some arrangement for delaying the SLBM-test limit until the Trident I is developed and until the Russians have a MIRVed SLBM might not undercut arms control too severely, and it might even increase the stability of the deterrent balance.

An important element in the comprehensive proposal was its provision for dealing with the cruise missile, which has been under development in the U.S., but not in the U.S.S.R., since 1972. It is in effect a relatively small and cheap long-range World War II "buzz bomb" plus microelectronics, enabling it to strike a specified small target with remarkable accuracy [see "Cruise Missiles," by Kosta Tsipis: SCIENTIFIC AMERICAN Offprint No. 691]. The Russians have insisted that the Vladivostok accords implied the inclusion of cruise missiles with a range greater than 600 kilometers (375 miles) under the ceiling on strategic delivery vehicles. The U.S. comprehensive proposal, however, defined as strategic only cruise missiles with a range greater than 2,500 kilometers (1,550 miles). That is more than enough to reach strategic targets in the U.S.S.R. west of the Urals from land bases in Europe, from submarines or other vessels or from aircraft flying beyond the Russian border. It was not surprising, therefore, that the Russians questioned the sincerity of the American offer to ban strategic cruise missiles so defined, particularly in view of the fact that the U.S. has itself been designating as strategic cruise missiles several weapons with ranges shorter than 2,500 kilometers.

Spokesmen for the Administration have maintained that cruise missiles with a range up to 2,500 kilometers are no different from other forward-based systems (the U.S. aircraft stationed in Europe) and like them should not be banned by a SALT treaty. The trouble with such an argument is that it reopens the entire question of the exclusion of forward-based systems from the treaty, an important concession the Russians made in the SALT I interim agreement and again at Vladivostok. Since the U.S. has about 500 forward-based aircraft and the U.S.S.R. has none (unless the Backfire is classified as being analogous), it is clearly to the American advantage not to include such aircraft as strategic delivery vehicles. It would be better to exclude the Backfire (unless it is given true intercontinental capability) from SALT and to include in SALT those cruise missiles whose range is not so short as to be demonstrably tactical, in return for continued Russian acquiescence to the exclusion of forward-based aircraft. The Backfire, tactical cruise missiles and forward-based aircraft could be dealt with in the context of the negotiations on "mutual balanced force reduction" that have been under way in Vienna for the past three years between the NATO and the Warsaw Pact countries.

Having been summarily rejected by the Russians in Moscow, the comprehensive proposal was clearly too extensive, and involved too many new and sensitive concepts, to provide a basis for negotiating a SALT agreement before the October deadline. Since the U.S. had put forward the deferral, or Vladivostok, proposal as an alternative, it was logical to end up by combining the two approaches into the three-part framework I described above: a five-year treaty setting limits at the Vladivostok levels or a little lower, a three-year protocol somehow restraining cruise missiles, mobile missiles, heavy MIRVed ICBM's and the Backfire and a statement of principles for negotiating real cutbacks and qualitative restrictions in the future. Exactly how to constrain the cruise missile may be the most important question and the most sensitive issue between the two sides.

A possible approach to such an agreement is suggested by a proposal the Russians made during talks in Moscow in January, 1976. They proposed to ban sea-launched and land-launched cruise missiles with a range greater than 600 kilometers but to leave air-launched cruise missiles with a range of up to 2,500 kilometers unrestricted—provided that the aircraft able to launch those missiles were counted under the Vladivostok ceiling of 1,320 on MIRVed delivery vehicles. There are already 1,046 MIRVed Minuteman III and Poseidon missiles; each of the 10 or more programmed Trident submarines will carry 24 MIRVed missiles, for a total of at least 1,286 MIRVed delivery vehicles. That would leave only 34 U.S. aircraft that could be fitted to launch cruise missiles. Nevertheless, this could be the starting point for a cruise-missile agreement. The concept of counting aircraft equipped to launch cruise missiles as MIRVed delivery vehicles is sound because it inhibits unrestricted procurement of air-launched cruise missiles, makes the rather high ceilings on MIRVed delivery vehicles into a more significant arms-control measure and still allows some aircraft to serve as strategic delivery vehicles without having to penetrate Russian air defenses.

There would be problems of verification. The range of an operational cruise missile cannot be reliably determined by observing tests; it may also be difficult to ensure that a long-range missile announced as intended for air launching is not instead launched from the ground or from a ship, in violation of the shorter-range limit for such weapons. Actually, however, the Russians have never been much concerned about verification, since it is virtually impossible for the U.S. to keep a major weapons program secret. From the U.S. point of view, if the U.S.S.R. does begin to develop modern long-range cruise missiles, and if the missiles exceed the 600-kilometer range, they would still not be a significant strategic threat: even a 2,500-kilometer land-launched cruise missile could not reach the continental U.S. from the U.S.S.R. Putting such missiles on submarines would not be of much military value to the U.S.S.R. or present a security risk to the U.S. because the Russians already have 840 longer-range ballistic missiles against which the U.S. has no defense. Moreover, it would be a poor use of the Russian submarine force and hardly worth the violation of a treaty. If the Russians put air-launched cruise missiles on Backfires to give the bombers an intercontinental capability, those bombers would have to come under the MIRVed delivery-vehicle ceiling.

The Russians have indicated they will not accept the U.S. comprehensive proposal's deep cuts in the Vladivostok ceilings, but a more modest reduction, of perhaps 10 percent instead of 25 percent, might be possible. This would not have much significance for arms control, but it would be important as a signal to the world that the nuclear superpowers were prepared for the first time to slow the arms race. As for qualitative controls, it is probably too much to hope for restrictions on the modernization or replacement of existing weapons by October. Such provisions might be established as goals, however, in the statement of principles to guide future negotiations, which should proceed without delay after a SALT II treaty is signed. It is conceivable that both countries might declare they would independently exercise restraint in their weapons programs during further negotiations, thus establishing a positive climate in which to begin bringing the qualitative arms race under control.

Cruise Missiles

by Kosta Tsipis
February 1977

This new category of inexpensive, highly accurate weapons presents a difficult but not insuperable problem to arms-control negotiators: how to distinguish reliably between strategic and tactical versions

The partial success achieved by negotiators for the U.S. and the U.S.S.R. in the ongoing effort to limit the deployment of strategic nuclear weapons rests on the mutual recognition that each side has at its disposal the "national technical means" (primarily reconnaissance satellites) to distinguish reliably between strategic, or intercontinental-range, weapons and all the other weapons in the other side's arsenal. The long-range cruise missile, a new type of weapon currently under development in the U.S., may prove to be an exception to that rule. The problem is that there appears to be no observable distinction between long-range cruise missiles (that is, those capable of strategic missions) and short-range cruise missiles (those suitable only for tactical missions). In other words, there is no obvious, unambiguous correlation between the physical appearance of a given cruise missile and its intended target.

According to reports in the daily press, the heralded advent of the long-range cruise missile has already created a major obstacle to the successful conclusion of the second round of strategic-arms-limitation talks (SALT II) between the U.S. and the U.S.S.R. The immediate issue is whether or not cruise missiles should be included in the total of 2,400 strategic delivery vehicles that the 1974 Vladivostok understanding between President Ford and Secretary Brezhnev had set as an upper limit for both parties. The basic properties of cruise missiles that have led to the present disagreement threaten to similarly impede future strategic-arms-limitation negotiations.

The arms-control dilemma presented by the cruise missile is compounded by the fact that although cruise missiles appear to be operationally inferior to existing strategic weapons in either a deterrent role or a counterforce role, they have the potential of becoming extremely cost-effective tactical weapons. For example, short-range cruise missiles could eventually replace the manned fighter-bomber in many of its missions, thereby substantially reducing the number of costly facilities such as aircraft carriers and foreign bases that such aircraft require.

Accordingly the U.S. has opposed the inclusion of cruise missiles in the numerical quota for strategic delivery vehicles, because—given the visual indistinguishability of the different types of cruise missile—such a provision would prevent the deployment of tactical cruise missiles as well as strategic ones. The U.S.S.R., on the other hand, insists on including all cruise missiles potentially capable of long-range missions in the quota for strategic weapons, precisely because there would be no way to determine whether a given cruise missile deployed by the U.S. is a tactical weapon or a strategic one. Thus the impasse at SALT II continues.

But what is a cruise missile? How does it work? What can it do, and why is it not possible to tell one that has a range of 5,000 kilometers from one that can fly only a tenth of that distance?

I shall attempt to answer those questions here by describing the various types of cruise missile now under development or planned, by examining the strategic and tactical capabilities of the different versions and by discussing their potential military usefulness and their implications for arms-control efforts. I shall also address the difficult problem of relating the intended mission of a cruise missile to its observable characteristics by offering a suggestion for a possible technical basis on which the problem might be solved.

A cruise missile can be defined as a dispensable, pilotless, self-guided, continuously powered, air-breathing warhead-delivery vehicle that flies just like an airplane, supported by aerodynamic surfaces. Unlike a ballistic missile, which is powered and hence usually guided for only a brief initial part of its flight, after which it follows a free-fall trajectory governed only by the local gravitational field, a cruise missile requires continuous guidance, since both the velocity and the direction of its flight can be unpredictably altered by local weather conditions or changes in the performance of the propulsion system. A ballistic missile is guided for the first five of the 20 minutes or so it takes to travel 5,000 kilometers; a cruise missile, which usually flies at subsonic speed, would require close to six hours of continuously guided flight to cover the same distance. Hence guidance errors that accumulate with time would be almost 100 times larger for a cruise missile than for a ballistic missile with a comparable range. The cumulative deviation from a preassigned track over a trajectory of thousands of kilometers would be very large in the case of the cruise missile, and therefore its accurate arrival on target could be achieved only with continuous guidance that is corrected from time to time by fresh location information. To obtain the necessary location information accurately a long-range cruise missile employs a device that can correlate information obtained by an on-board sensor about the terrain it is flying over with some kind of map stored in the memory of an on-board computer.

Cruise missiles have served as warhead-delivery systems in the past, beginning with the German V-1 "buzz bomb" of World War II and continuing with such weapons as the U.S. Matador, Regulus and Snark missiles and the Russian

Shaddock missile, which is still deployed aboard some Russian submarines and surface warships. None of these earlier versions were capable of obtaining location information to correct their guidance system during flight, and as a result they were not very accurate. Furthermore, they were powered by inefficient jet engines that in general did not allow ranges in excess of a few hundred kilometers.

The main difference between the older versions of the cruise missile and those now under development in the U.S. is that recent advances in technology have made available two important new components: (1) microelectronic devices that can update the location information of a cruise missile while it is in flight and therefore improve its accuracy by three orders of magnitude and (2) small, efficient jet engines that for every hour of flight consume only about a pound of fuel for every pound of thrust they generate. Both of these technological advances affect primarily the performance of strategic cruise missiles, since at tactical ranges the flight time is measured in minutes and therefore even a moderately accurate guidance system needs no mid-flight correction. Moreover, a tactical missile can be fitted with a homing device, such as radar, that detects the target and guides the missile onto it.

A long-range cruise missile employs an inertial-guidance system, consisting essentially of three or more accelerometers mounted on gyroscope-stabilized platforms, to guide it along a preassigned course. A practical inertial-guidance system suitable for a cruise missile could allow the missile to drift about a kilometer or so off course for every hour of flight. The effects of weather and the imperfections of the jet engine that powers the missile increase the drift. After several hours of flight the missile could be 10 or more kilometers away from its intended impact point. If, however, the missile could from time to time "recognize" where it is and compare its actual position with where it should be according to its preassigned trajectory, then the on-board computer could instruct the automatic pilot to make the appropriate maneuvers to bring the missile back to the correct trajectory. Furthermore, the known difference between the actual position and the intended position is used by the computer to calibrate and reset the inertial-guidance system, a process that compensates for and reduces the

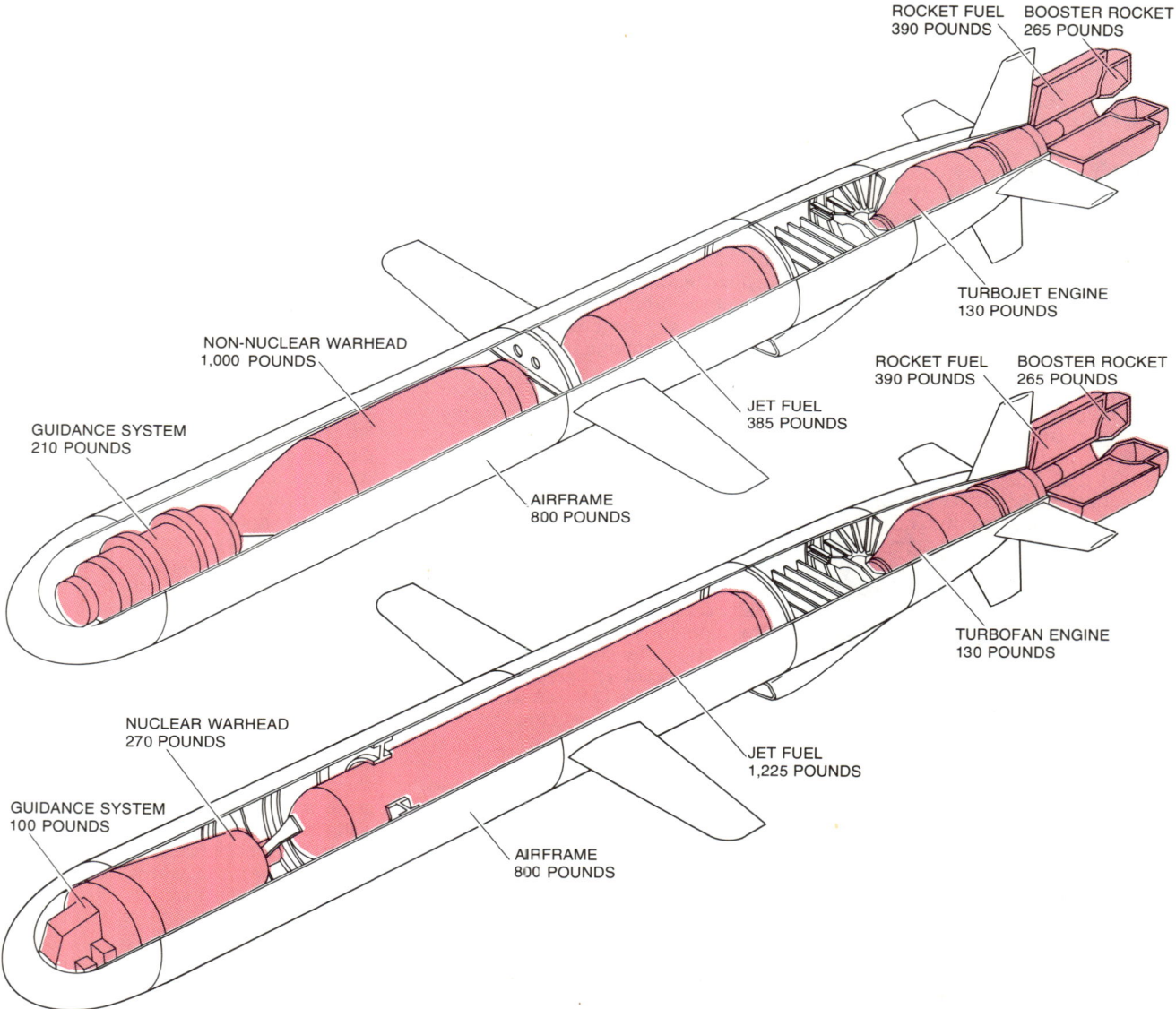

SEA-LAUNCHED CRUISE MISSILE (SLCM), currently under development for the U.S. Navy by the Convair Division of the General Dynamics Corporation, is shown in these cutaway diagrams in both its tactical, or short-range, version (*top*) and its strategic, or long-range, version (*bottom*). Without the booster rocket, needed to launch either weapon from a submarine or a surface vessel, both missiles are 53 centimeters in diameter and 6.24 meters long. Weights of various components are indicated. Externally two versions appear identical.

missile's drift by a factor of two or three.

There are several ways in which a cruise missile can determine its actual location while it is in flight. I shall briefly describe three such systems; they are called the terrain-contour-matching technique (Tercom in current military terminology), the area-correlation technique and the global-positioning-satellite technique.

The terrain-matching technique, first patented in 1958, relies for its operating principle on the simple fact that the altitude of the ground above sea level varies as a function of location. If one were to make a rectangular map of an area two kilometers wide and 10 kilometers long, divide the map into squares perhaps 100 meters on a side and record in each square the average elevation of the ground in it, one would obtain a digital map consisting of 2,000 numbers, each number corresponding to the elevation of a point of known coordinates on the ground. A set of such maps, which can be made much larger and can have squares with smaller sides if required, is stored in the memory of the computer aboard the missile.

The missile is also provided with a downlooking radar altimeter capable of resolving objects on the ground smaller than the map squares from a height of several kilometers. As the missile approaches the region for which the computer memory has a map, the altimeter starts providing a stream of ground-elevation data. The computer, by comparing these data with the elevation data it has in its memory, can determine the actual location of the missile with an accuracy comparable to the size of the map cell. It then instructs the autopilot to take any corrective steps necessary to return the missile to its intended trajectory. As many as 20 such maps can be stored in the memory of the computer to enable the missile to update its location information and correct its trajectory frequently during its overland flight.

FIRST UNDERWATER LAUNCH of the Navy's new SLCM took place on February 13, 1976, at the Naval Undersea Center off San Clemente Island in California. The missile was ejected from a submerged torpedo tube and was propelled to the surface of the water by means of its booster rocket. Once out of the water it automatically jettisoned its protective covers and extended its tail fins as it climbed to an altitude of more than 300 meters, still under booster power; at that stage the wings and the jet-engine inlet scoop were deployed, the spent booster rocket was jettisoned, and the engineless test missile then glided over the range for two miles. (In the operational model the jet engine would take over for the aerodynamic portion of the flight.) The SLCM, which has been designated Tomahawk, is designed to be launched not only from torpedo tubes of a submarine but also from a surface ship, an airplane or the ground.

The area-correlation method, which is still in the research stage, is based on a similar mapping principle. Instead of ground altitude above sea level, however, it measures the microwave reflectivity of the ground as a function of location. Instead of a radar altimeter the missile has a detector that can sense the differences in the microwave reflectivity of the terrain it is flying over. Advanced area-correlation schemes envision missiles with on-board systems that incorporate terrain maps made at one part of the electromagnetic spectrum and detectors that operate at a different wavelength. For example, such a system might be able to match signals from a microwave radiometer or an infrared detector with data from a map made in the visible part of the spectrum. This approach is possible because features such as lakes, rivers, roads, railroads and other man-made structures offer sharp "contrast edges" over a large portion of the spectrum. The area-correlation technique can be applied to determine the location of the missile over all kinds of terrain, whereas the terrain-matching technique works well only over rough, hilly ground. Neither system works over water.

The third way to locate the position of a cruise missile is the global-positioning-satellite system, which is also under development in the U.S. The projected system will consist of 24 satellites in polar orbits positioned in such a manner that any place on the earth's surface will have at least four of the satellites in sight at all times. Every few thousandths of a second the satellites will broadcast exactly synchronous coded signals that can be received by passive equipment on the cruise missile. By determining the difference in the arrival times of four such signals the missile's computer can calculate the distance of the missile from each satellite. In addition the satellites will broadcast information describing their orbits around the earth. With this information and the four different arrival times of the signals the missile's computer can determine the true position of the missile to within 10 meters in three dimensions without any other external data. From that information it can in turn deduce its velocity at any instant.

Of the three techniques I have described only the satellite system promises to be inexpensive enough to be practical for short-range cruise missiles. Because of their brief flight time such missiles do not require position-updating information. Instead they need to recognize and home on their target. For mobile targets radar homing is preferred where it is possible, but for fixed targets beyond the line of sight the global-positioning-satellite system can be used to maneuver the missile onto the known location of the target.

Advances in the technology of small jet engines have been equally important in the development of both tactical and strategic cruise missiles. Small turbofan engines weighing less than 130 pounds and yet capable of generating as much as 600 pounds of thrust are now available. Engines of this type consume less fuel than turbojets of equivalent size; they are more complex systems, however, and hence they cost much more. Accordingly turbofan engines are considered suitable for cruise missiles with a range of more than 500 kilometers that carry expensive payloads such as nuclear warheads, whereas turbojets are cost-effective for cruise missiles with a range of less than 500 kilometers that carry conventional high-explosive warheads.

The difference in the efficiency of the two types of jet engine is related in part to the difference in the temperature of the exhaust gases produced by the engines. Although the turbine-inlet temperature for small engines of both types is limited to about 1,850 degrees Fahrenheit, a turbojet engine exhausts its gases at 1,450 degrees, whereas a turbofan engine, because of turbulent mixing at the outlet, exhausts them at 600 degrees. Obviously the latter engine makes more efficient use of the heat energy of its fuel. The difference between the exhaust temperatures of the two types of engine gives them different infrared "signatures." As a result it should in principle be possible to determine from a distance whether a given missile is powered by a turbofan engine or a turbojet engine.

The rate of progress in microelectronics has been spectacular, but the development of small jet engines is laborious. It takes many years to develop a new engine or to improve the efficiency of an existing one by a few percent. It is therefore reasonable to expect that the power plants for cruise missiles will not change substantially in the next decade or so. Small improvements in efficiency, and hence in range for a fixed volume of fuel, can be expected as new composite materials are adopted for turbine blades, but basically the fuel-consumption rate and the thrust of the small engines are not subject to a technological breakthrough. One can conclude that the aerodynamic performance of cruise missiles will not change greatly in the near future.

The technological advances I have described have been applied in the development of several types of U.S. cruise missile. Of these I shall discuss only two: the Harpoon antishipping missile, which is now entering production and is strictly a tactical cruise missile, and the sea-launched cruise missile (SLCM), which is still under development and which has both a strategic version and a tactical one. These two major types of missile have been chosen because in combination they illustrate the special advantages and disadvantages of cruise missiles.

The Harpoon missile is quite small, measuring 34 centimeters in diameter and 3.84 meters in length. Its total volume is only .3 cubic meter. Without its booster rocket it weighs 1,144 pounds. It can be launched against a ship from a submarine, a surface vessel or an airplane. A ground-based version is also possible. The Harpoon is powered by a turbojet engine that has a thrust of 660 pounds and a fuel-consumption rate of about 1.5 pounds of fuel per pound of thrust per hour of flight. That gives the Harpoon a maximum range of about 100 kilometers at a speed of Mach .85 (85 percent of the speed of sound). Since the engine is expected to work only for a short time it has many cast parts instead of machined ones. Hence it can operate satisfactorily for only a short period but costs substantially less than a turbofan engine of the same size designed to operate for many hours.

The guidance system of the Harpoon missile consists of a radar altimeter that keeps it flying a few meters above the surface of the sea, a mid-course guidance unit that keeps it on a steady course and a sophisticated active radar scanner that can detect a target as small as a patrol boat in all weather conditions at about half its maximum range and a target as large as a destroyer at much greater distances. The missile can distinguish between two targets if they are well separated and will head for the larger one. It carries a 500-pound warhead that penetrates the deck of the target ship and explodes inside by means of a deceleration fuse. In 32 launches from a variety of sea and air platforms the Harpoon has found its target 29 times at operational ranges.

Both the tactical and the strategic versions of the sea-launched cruise missile are 53 centimeters in diameter and 6.24 meters long and have a volume of 1.37 cubic meters without their booster rocket. Without the protective capsule in which they are carried and launched they both weigh about 3,200 pounds. Both versions can be launched from the torpedo tubes of a submarine or from a surface ship, an airplane or a ground platform. The exact ranges of the two versions are classified, but the aerodynamic properties of the missile indicate that the strategic version is capable of a range of 2,000 kilometers at low altitude and perhaps 50 percent more if the first 1,500 kilometers are flown at higher altitude and the rest at treetop level. The strategic version is powered by a turbofan engine with a thrust of 600 pounds and an average fuel-consumption rate at sea level of about a pound of fuel per pound of thrust per hour of flight. At sea level the missile has a cruising speed of Mach .7 and a maximum speed of Mach .85. A much lower fuel-consumption rate is possible at higher altitudes with a lower net thrust. Since the missile cannot fly at speeds lower than Mach .44, a booster rocket is used that ignites on launching and propels the missile for 12 seconds. At a height of 400 meters (assuming an ascent angle of 55 degrees) and a speed of Mach .55 the turbofan engine takes over. The booster is not necessary for missiles launched from aircraft.

The guidance package of the strategic sea-launched cruise missile consists of an inertial-guidance system with an intrinsic drift of about 900 meters per hour of flight, augmented by a terrain-matching system. The radar altimeter of the terrain-matching system enables the missile to fly as low as 20 meters over water, 50 meters over moderately hilly terrain and 100 meters over mountains. This capability makes the missile difficult to detect with ground-based radar. The gyroscopes of the inertial-guidance platform require 25 minutes to align after the missile has been loaded into the torpedo tube of a submarine, a task that in turn requires five minutes. Therefore the strategic SLCM can be launched from a submarine in salvos of two or four (depending on the number of torpedo tubes) at best only once every 30 minutes. The ignition of the booster rocket under water generates a large amount of acoustical energy that can be detected at great distances. In addition the booster creates copious bubbles that are visible on the surface of the water for more than five minutes after the launch, and the exhaust plume of the booster is visible over an area 80 kilometers in radius as the missile climbs to 400 meters. Accordingly the position of the submarine can be determined by a variety of means after it has launched one or more of its missiles under water.

The terrain-matching system of the strategic sea-launched cruise missile is provided with a dozen or more maps, on which the terrain is digitized at intervals of less than 100 meters and the elevations are recorded with an accuracy of better than three meters. Since the missile is expected to fly initially over water, where the updating of location information is impossible, the first land map is made wide enough (perhaps as wide as 10 kilometers) for the missile not to miss the intended landfall. The radar altimeter starts taking readings before the missile is expected to fly over a given map area and stops taking them at an equal distance after it has left that area. The computer uses a simple minimum-absolute-deviance algorithm to match the readings of the altimeter with the points on the map. There is such large redundancy in the altimeter data that synchronization errors or even attempts to jam the altimeter from the ground will not degrade the performance of the system.

The accuracy with which this missile can be guided to its target is at best equal to the size of a map square; in practice it is probably about half that good. Since map squares can be made quite small, say 10 meters on a side, it is possible in principle to have comparable missile accuracy. A number of factors contribute to the degradation of this level of accuracy, however, and so it is expected that the strategic sea-launched cruise missile will have an accuracy of some 100 meters. The biggest errors are expected to come from human errors in mapping, from the injudicious choice of terrain to map and from the absence of suitable terrain for terrain-matching guidance near some targets.

The tactical version of the sea-launched cruise missile is powered by a turbojet engine that gives it a range of about 500 kilometers. It is guided by a system very similar to the one in the Harpoon missile, consisting of a mid-course guidance unit that keeps the missile flying in a straight line but does not adjust for its being blown off course by the wind. In addition the missile has a radar scanner with a comparatively short range, probably no more than 50 kilometers, which is designed to guide it onto the target. The mid-course guidance unit has a drift of about .2 radian per hour of flight. Hence errors as large as 40 kilometers will result at the end of a 500-kilometer flight. Therefore once the missile is in flight it needs some external source of information on the exact position of its intended target.

The line of sight over water does not extend beyond 50 kilometers, so that the necessary information cannot be provided by the launching platform; it has to be obtained by another vehicle, a spotter aircraft or a helicopter, which must be suitably equipped to identify the target and communicate the information to the launching platform or to the cruise missile itself. If the launching platform is a submarine, the tactical version of the sea-launched cruise missile becomes even more troublesome: not only will its launch reveal the position of the submarine but also problems of target acquisition and "friend/foe" identification become extremely complex. The range of the submarine's sonar

OVERLAND FLIGHT of a Tomahawk SLCM was photographed in the course of a recent test of its maneuverability at the White Sands Missile Range in New Mexico. This model is equipped with a turbofan engine and a terrain-contour-matching guidance system.

is considerably shorter than 500 kilometers, and while the vessel is submerged it cannot communicate either with the cruise missile or with an observation platform such as an aircraft. The mismatch of the cruise missile's range to the submarine's target-acquisition range makes the tactical version of the sea-launched cruise missile a weapon of dubious value.

Cruise-missile technology offers such flexibility in range, basing and types of warhead that an almost unlimited variety of alternative designs is possible. Here I have chosen to speculate on the military characteristics and arms-control implications of three possible types of missile because of the particularly challenging policy questions they raise. The first type is a very accurate long-range strategic cruise missile with a conventional high-explosive warhead; the second, which is already under development, is an airborne strategic cruise missile with a nuclear warhead; the third is a short-range land-based or ship-based tactical missile with a conventional warhead.

There is little doubt that guidance techniques either in existence or under development can endow a strategic cruise missile with pinpoint accuracy at the end of a 5,000-kilometer flight. This high degree of accuracy makes it feasible to use conventional warheads instead of nuclear ones against certain strategic targets such as large radar installations, industrial plants, petroleum refineries and so forth. It has been proposed that the U.S. develop a cruise missile that could carry a large conventional high-explosive warhead over intercontinental distances with an accuracy of better than 10 meters. This weapon would have to be about two cubic meters in volume (somewhat larger than the current sea-launched cruise missile), and it would have to be carried by either a surface ship or an aircraft of the cargo type; alternatively it could be land-based. If it were built in sufficiently large numbers, its proponents argue, it could provide the option of a non-nuclear response to some hypothetical coercive actions of an opponent such as the U.S.S.R. Thus it could raise the threshold of nuclear retaliation by enabling the U.S. to destroy specific targets with minimal collateral damage and without the onerous political burdens of a nuclear attack.

The second type of cruise missile that is under serious consideration in the U.S. is the air-launched cruise missile (ALCM). The current version of the air-launched missile is expected to have about half the range of the strategic sea-launched one. It is designed to be carried by either the B-52 intercontinental bomber or the new supersonic B-1 bomber. Armed with such missiles, the bombers would not have to penetrate the terminal air defenses of an opponent; they could merely penetrate to a given point and launch the long-range missiles toward their targets. Proponents of the air-launched cruise missile point out that since such a "standoff" carrier plane would not have to penetrate the air defenses of an opponent, the plane would not have to have supersonic speed, an elaborate system of electronic countermeasures or the capability of flying very low and very fast in order to avoid detection and evade attack; in other words, it would not have to be a combat aircraft at all. As a matter of fact, it is argued, a commercial wide-bodied jet transport such as the Boeing 747 or the McDonnell Douglas DC-10 could serve to carry as many as 100 cruise missiles. Commercial planes of this type have a longer range without refueling than either the B-52 or the B-1 does. If they were armed with air-launched cruise missiles, they would be able to replace the B-52 bomber in the U.S. arsenal at considerably less cost than the proposed B-1 could.

The third possible incarnation of the cruise-missile concept would be a tactical missile with a maximum range of 500 kilometers and a high-explosive warhead of between 400 and 500 pounds. This missile, its advocates say, could be guided exactly to its target either with the aid of the global-positioning-satellite system or by one of the pattern-recognition techniques; it could even be provided with the means to send back by way of a relaying aircraft or satellite a television outline of the terrain it flies over as it approaches its target so that it could be guided remotely by a human operator.

Such a small missile (less than half a cubic meter in volume) could be equipped with an inexpensive turbojet engine and could be programmed to avoid air defenses, fly at a constant altitude and operate in all weather conditions. It could, its proponents maintain, replace the manned fighter-bomber in many of its missions. If it were built in large quantities, it could cost as little as $50,000 per missile. Manned tactical aircraft, in contrast, currently cost more than $10 million and require a large aircraft-carrier task force to be carried within range of their targets. A typical task force can deploy only 36 attack aircraft, each capable of delivering about a ton of bombs per sortie to the target with less accuracy than that possible with cruise missiles. The entire multibillion-dollar task force could be replaced by a naval force capable of launching 180 tactical cruise missiles per day and consisting of a variety of ships less vulnerable and much less expensive than aircraft carriers. Ultimately, the advocates of this version of the cruise missile point out, such a missile could replace all the tactical nuclear weapons stationed by the U.S. in Europe.

In combination with short-range precision-guided missiles on the ground and remotely piloted vehicles carrying out the observation mission of manned aircraft, the tactical cruise missile armed with a chemical-explosive warhead may completely displace manned fighter-bombers and their long and costly logistical "tail" from the U.S. arsenal.

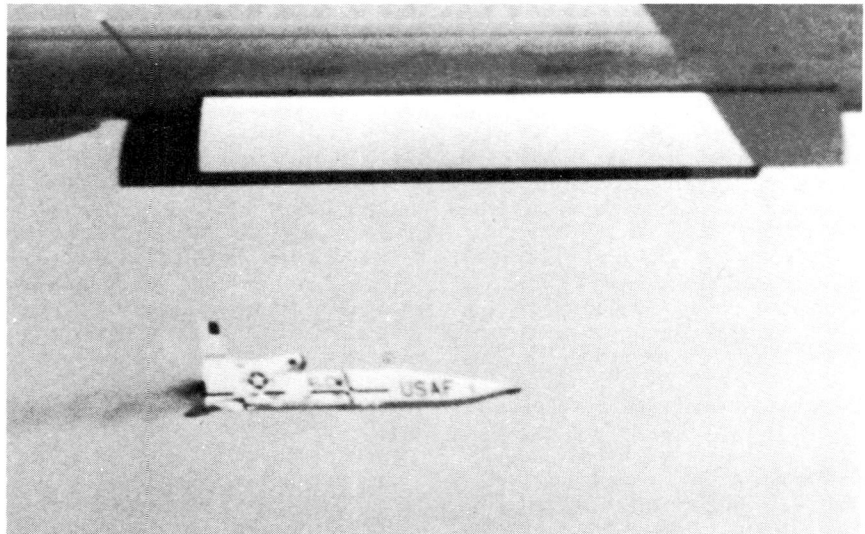

FIRST POWERED FLIGHT of the Air Force's new air-launched cruise missile (ALCM) took place on March 5, 1976, at the White Sands Missile Range. The missile, which is being developed by the Boeing Aerospace Company, was launched from the weapons bay of a B-52 bomber at an altitude of 10,000 feet. The powered portion of the flight lasted approximately 11 minutes. In this photograph the air scoop for the turbofan engine has popped up, the engine has started, the elevons (back wings) are fully extended and the vertical tail fin is unfolding; in a moment the larger forward wings will open. The ALCM can be launched either from the internal rotary weapons rack of the B-52 or from external pylons mounted under the wings.

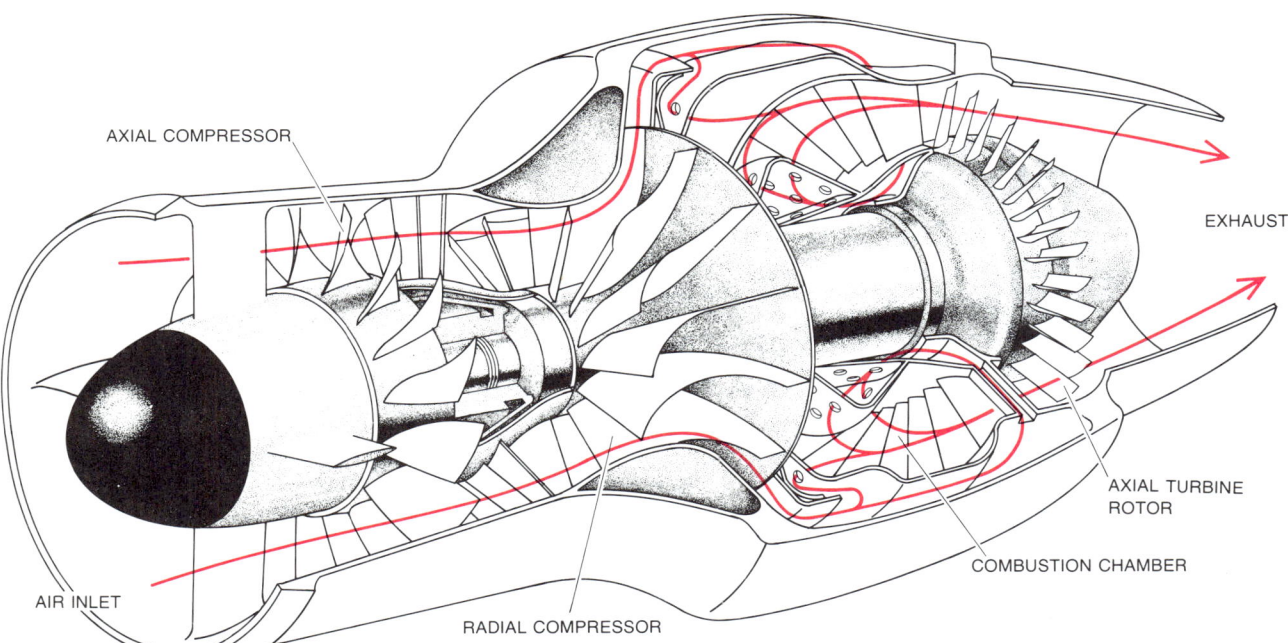

SMALL TURBOJET ENGINE was developed by Teledyne, Inc., for use in the Navy's Harpoon tactical antishipping cruise missile. The expendable engine, which is designed to operate for less than 15 minutes, incorporates mostly inexpensive cast parts and is said to cost about $15,000. Air enters the inlet and passes through an axial compressor and a radial compressor before entering the annular combustion chamber, where it is mixed with fuel and the mixture is ignited. The hot gases then pass through a turbine rotor before being exhausted. The turbine rotor drives the compressors by means of a shaft running down the axis of the engine. Thrust is produced only by the exiting stream of hot combustion products. Engine weighs less than 100 pounds, and yet it is capable of generating a thrust of 660 pounds.

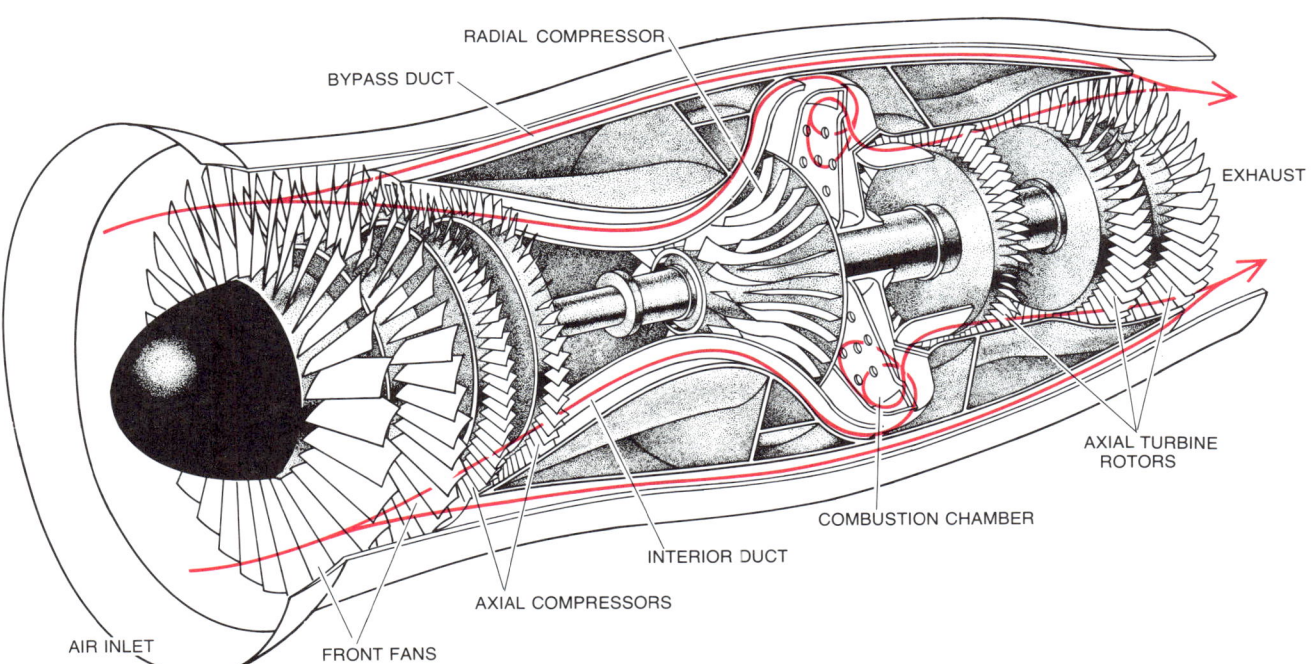

SMALL TURBOFAN ENGINE developed by the Williams Research Corporation for the Air Force's ALCM has also been selected for installation in the strategic version of the Navy's SLCM. A turbofan engine is inherently more efficient than a turbojet engine of comparable size; it is also more complex and contains mostly machined parts and hence costs considerably more. In the turbofan engine the turbines drive not only the compressors for the gas-generator flow path but also a fan system that forces compressed air to flow through an annular bypass duct. As a result the turbofan generates thrust through two separate streams: the fan flow and the gas-generator flow. The ratio of the two flows is termed the engine's bypass ratio. The particular design shown in this diagram is described as a twin-spool turbofan with a low bypass ratio and a mixed exhaust. The low-pressure spool consists of a two-stage axial fan system followed by two axial compressor rotors in the gas-generator flow path, all driven by two axial turbines. The high-pressure spool consists of a single centrifugal compressor driven by an axial turbine. The engine weighs less than 130 pounds and generates more than 600 pounds of thrust.

Such a development would constitute a profound change in the entire military posture of the U.S., since it implies the abandonment of high-cost, low-attrition manned aircraft and their replacement with low-cost, dispensable cruise missiles. This prospect raises a host of technical, military and arms-control questions that have so far remained largely unexamined.

Because of the small size, great accuracy and low cost of cruise missiles, it would seem that they would be inherently superior to ballistic missiles as delivery vehicles for ranges greater than 10 kilometers and less than 5,000 kilometers. The long flight times of strategic cruise missiles and the subsonic speed with which they approach their target, however, make them quite vulnerable to hostile countermeasures. A ballistic missile, in the absence of an anti-ballistic-missile system, cannot be prevented from reaching its target once it is launched. Whereas the outcome of a strategic attack with ballistic missiles is comparatively certain and controlled, the outcome of a cruise-missile attack is uncertain, since it depends largely on the air-defense capabilities of the attacked country. As a result, although the accuracy and range of cruise missiles would suggest that they could serve successfully in a deterrent role, their relatively low speed makes them less suitable than ballistic missiles for that particular strategic mission. In order to be sure that cruise missiles would penetrate to their targets one would have to launch many of them against each target to saturate the air defenses. That would require the deployment of many thousands of cruise missiles, in clear violation of the numerical quota for strategic delivery vehicles established by the Vladivostok agreement.

No matter how many cruise missiles are deployed in a country, however, it would be impossible to verify their number by nonintrusive inspection, since they do not require identifiable launch facilities, such as silos, submarine launch tubes or airfields. Thus it is technically impossible to subject cruise missiles to the kind of numerical limits achieved in SALT II for ballistic missiles. The entire problem of limiting cruise missiles is further complicated by the fact that even during the testing of the weapon it would be possible to deduce from satellite data only the maximum range compatible with the visible characteristics of the missile, not its actual range. Therefore it is not possible at present to tell whether a given sea-launched cruise missile, say, is intended for a strategic mission or a tactical one.

All these considerations may lead one to conclude that the U.S. would have no choice but either to abandon any further efforts at controlling the proliferation of nuclear arms and go ahead with the deployment of cruise missiles or, in order to safeguard the achievements of SALT and the opportunity for further strategic-arms limitation, to forgo the deployment of cruise missiles altogether. Such a conclusion, however, seems unwarranted. A careful examination of the tactical and strategic missions that current and future cruise missiles could perform, and of the required launching platforms in each case, reveals that those applications of this delivery vehicle that make military sense are not incompatible with arms-limitation goals in general and the numerical reduction of strategic delivery vehicles in particular. Furthermore, it appears that the specific cruise missiles that threaten the SALT negotiations are either unnecessary for the security of the U.S. or are hasty and unexamined applications of the new technologies that do not make military sense.

Consider the strategic sea-launched cruise missile now in the advanced-development stage. This system cannot perform any new missions or outperform in any of the existing strategic missions the U.S. "triad" of land-based intercontinental ballistic missiles (ICBM's), submarine-launched ballistic missiles (SLBM's) and intercontinental bombers. Furthermore, launching a cruise missile of this type from ballistic-missile submarines would increase the submarines' vulnerability, first because they would have to abandon their present secure stations and approach the territorial waters of the U.S.S.R. and second because launching a cruise missile would reveal the position of the submarine for hundreds of kilometers. It would be foolhardy to lessen the invulnerability of our securest deterrent weapons system so that it could launch at most four cruise missiles of uncertain fate every 30 minutes, since the same submarine can stay in safe waters and launch 16 Poseidon or Trident I missiles with 10 warheads each in less than five minutes, making much less underwater noise.

The deployment of a limited number of long-range cruise missiles on "hunter-killer" submarines may appear militarily cost-effective, since it would force an opponent to treat every U.S. nuclear submarine as a strategic nuclear delivery system, thereby increasing the opponent's antisubmarine-warfare requirements. Such a policy is not, however, without serious drawbacks. First, to impose a strategic role on hunter-killer submarines would seriously complicate their command-and-control procedures and thereby impair their operational capabilities. Second, and perhaps more significant, the deployment of strategic

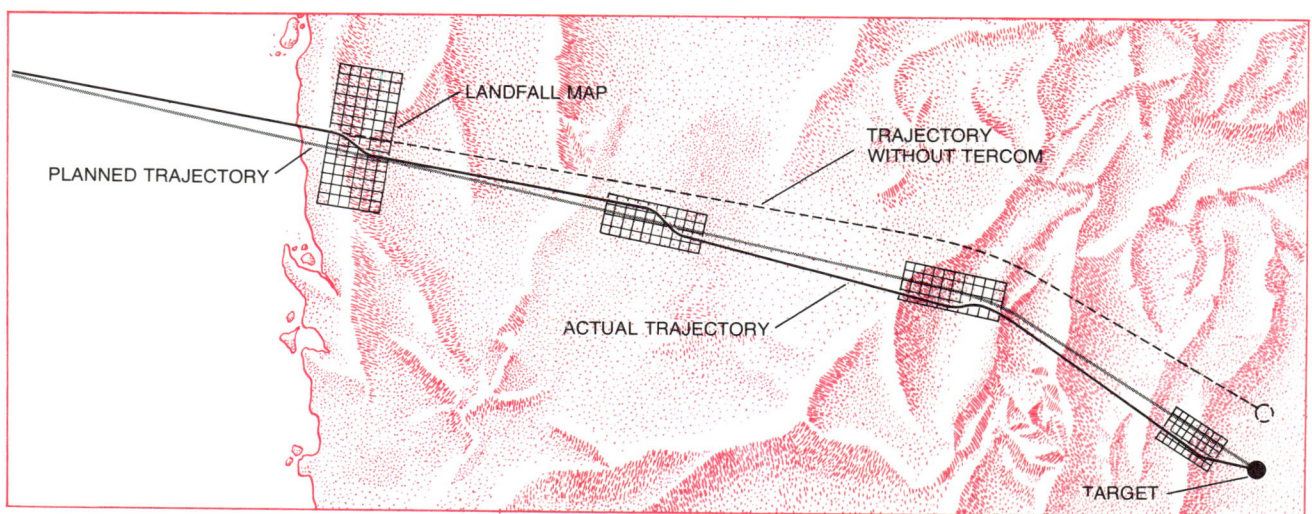

TERRAIN-CONTOUR MATCHING, abbreviated Tercom, is one of the terminal-guidance techniques currently being developed in conjunction with the U.S. cruise-missile program. The system relies on a set of digital maps stored in the memory of the missile's on-board computer; the maps consist of rectangular arrays of numbered squares representing the variation of ground elevation above sea level as a function of location. As the missile approaches an area for which the computer memory has a map, the on-board radar altimeter starts providing a stream of ground-elevation data. The computer, by comparing these data with the information it has in its memory, can accurately determine the actual trajectory of the missile and instruct the autopilot to return the missile to its planned trajectory. Four such nuclear missiles on tactical hunter-killer submarines could reduce the security of the U.S. deterrent fleet of Polaris/Poseidon submarines not only by forcing a rapid growth of Russian antisubmarine-warfare capabilities but also by eliminating the distinction between tactical and strategic submarines and thereby removing the current tacit inhibition against attacks on strategic submarines. In short, the deployment of the strategic sea-launched cruise missile seems on balance to be both unnecessary and unwise.

The hypothetical long-range strategic cruise missile with a chemical-explosive warhead suffers from a different set of fundamental disadvantages. This missile could in principle enlarge the spectrum of strategic options available to the U.S., since it would make possible the precise destruction of selected industrial or military targets without the use of nuclear explosives. Actually, however, such targets in the U.S.S.R. would probably be defended by active or passive air defenses a subsonic cruise missile could not penetrate easily; such terminal defenses would add to the vulnerability of these weapons and therefore make the outcome of an attack with them quite uncertain. Weapons with uncertain results cannot have a deterrent effect against even the mildest provocation, since they are not capable of the assured destruction of their intended targets. Just as the existence of an effective anti-ballistic-missile system could have denied the deterrent role of ballistic missiles, so could a future sophisticated air-defense system deny such a role to cruise missiles, particularly those with chemical-explosive warheads.

Finally, a long-range cruise missile with a chemical-explosive warhead would completely confuse the distinction between strategic weapons, which are now assumed to be nuclear, and tactical weapons, which are usually nonnuclear. Such a development would make strategic-arms-limitation negotiations particularly complex by coupling them to efforts to reduce tactical armaments and by blurring the distinction between nuclear and chemical explosives.

The long-range air-launched cruise missile could in principle have a practical military role. The version of this weapon now under development is burdened with artificial limitations on size and fuel that severely curtail its range to about half that of the sea-launched cruise missile, making it unsuitable as a standoff weapon. A future version capable of longer ranges and carried by large transport planes could, however, replace the B-52 bomber in the 1990's and obviate the deployment of the costly B-1 bomber. The deployment of such a cruise missile would create difficult arms-control problems, since again it would not be possible to ascertain the number of missiles deployed. A possible solution is to agree on the number of deployed carrier aircraft that could transport them and count each aircraft against an agreed number of existing ballistic missiles outfitted with multiple independently targetable reentry vehicles (MIRV's). As a matter of fact, if all land-based MIRVed ballistic missiles were replaced by an equivalent number of transport planes carrying air-launched cruise missiles, the end result could be a more stable strategic balance between the U.S. and the U.S.S.R., for two reasons. First, the long flight time of cruise missiles and their vulnerability to point defenses preclude their use as first-strike weapons; second, their basing, if properly designed, could make them considerably less vulnerable to a surprise attack than land-based ballistic missiles are now.

In spite of the stabilizing effect that such a proposal implies the deployment of the long-range air-launched cruise missile raises some serious verification questions. For example, if cruise missiles were deployed on jumbo jets such as the 747 or the DC-10, how could one determine without intrusive inspection which of these planes is a civilian transport and which carries strategic cruise missiles with nuclear warheads? Moreover, once the development and testing of such missiles is allowed how could another nation ascertain the number of missiles ultimately manufactured in the U.S. or their intended mode of deployment? The U.S.S.R., for example, could fear that in addition to whatever agreed number of air-launched cruise missiles was allowed, the U.S. could secretly deploy large numbers of booster-assisted cruise missiles based on ships or on land in allied countries within easy reach of the Russian interior. Thus it does not seem possible to deploy long-range cruise missiles without upsetting future strategic-arms-limitation efforts.

There are additional disadvantages to such a deployment, even if a formula for the verification of the number of platforms for air-launched cruise missiles and the basing of such missiles could be successfully negotiated. If past experience can be taken as a guide for future behavior, it is almost certain that a U.S. deployment of strategic cruise missiles would induce a Russian counterdeployment. Worse, U.S. development of such a weapons system would serve to validate the cruise-missile concept for other nations desiring a cheap, accurate delivery vehicle and might well convince them to develop a similar missile capable of reaching the U.S. Then it would be necessary for this country to erect a costly air-defense system not

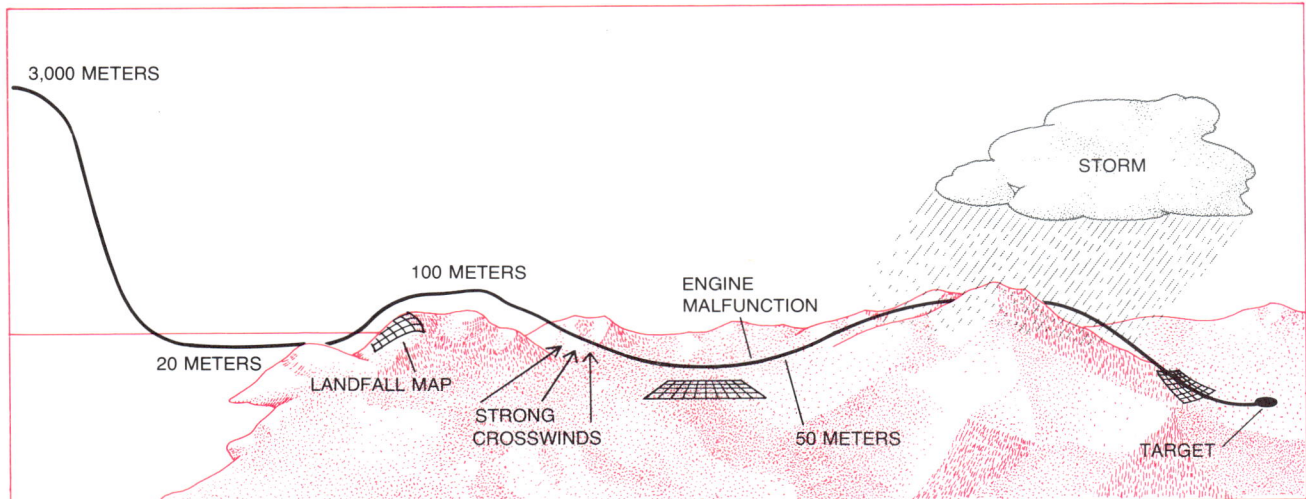

corrective maneuvers are shown in the vertical overhead view at the left. A perspective view of the missile's terminal flight path is depicted at the right. For the sake of fuel economy the early portion of the missile's flight would probably be at a high altitude. In the low-altitude penetration phase of the flight the missile would be able to fly as low as 20 meters over water, 50 meters over moderately hilly terrain and 100 meters over mountains, making the missile difficult to detect by ground-based radar. Unpredictable changes in local weather conditions and in the missile's airspeed due to a malfunction in the propulsion system are among the factors that can cause the missile to deviate from its planned trajectory. A terminal accuracy on the order of 100 meters is considered feasible for the Tercom system.

only against Russian cruise missiles but also against the cruise missiles of other countries. Such a system has been considered unnecessary until now because of the absence of a credible threat from the U.S.S.R. or any other country. It should not be forgotten that the deployment of an anti-ballistic-missile system in this country was justified on similar grounds: as a defense against Chinese ballistic missiles rather than Russian ones.

Tactical cruise missiles, unlike their strategic counterparts, offer considerable military advantages without creating such serious arms-control problems. As the Harpoon missile has demonstrated, it is possible to develop a small cruise missile powered by an inexpensive turbojet engine that has both the range and the accuracy needed for practical battlefield situations. On the other hand, the tactical sea-launched cruise missile is mismatched to the operational conditions of a naval encounter and appears to be grossly inaccurate; moreover, its conspicuous launching jeopardizes the safety of the launching submarine by revealing its position. The tactical SLCM is the perfect example of the misapplication of cruise-missile technology: it creates serious arms-control problems, since it is externally indistinguishable from the strategic SLCM, without incorporating any substantive military advantages.

The proposed tactical cruise missile with a chemical-explosive warhead is perhaps the most sensible current application of the new technological advances that have made cruise missiles feasible. With a volume of half a cubic meter and a turbojet engine, it can be identified by satellite as an unambiguously tactical missile. Although such identification may not be possible with current systems except over water, the technology exists to support the development of a reconnaissance satellite that could be programmed to detect, track and identify infrared signatures in the atmosphere and thereby distinguish a strategic cruise missile from a tactical one during testing.

The operation of such a monitoring system could be impeded by cloud cover, and therefore it could not verify with absolute certainty another country's faithful adherence to a treaty forbidding the development of long-range cruise missiles. Since no country would have any reason to take advantage of cloud cover to hide the development of a short-range cruise missile, however, it would be possible to develop and deploy those tactical weapons that seem capable of replacing the manned fighter-bomber, without fear of their being mistaken for long-range missiles by the U.S.S.R. and therefore without threatening the efforts to limit strategic nuclear weapons.

Two central conclusions can be drawn from the foregoing analysis of the technology and the performance characteristics of existing and contemplated cruise missiles. The first is that with one possible exception the development and deployment of strategic cruise missiles at this time is counterproductive for three reasons: they are unnecessary, their deployment would nullify the existing strategic-arms-limitation agreements and obstruct similar future efforts, and their deployment on nuclear submarines would increase the vulnerability and probably reduce the operational efficiency of that important deterrent force. The one possible exception is a future version of an air-launched cruise missile that could be deployed on transport planes in place of long-range bombers. The price of such a system, however, must be measured not only in dollars but also in terms of lost arms-control opportunities, the creation of new threats against this country and the abandonment of any numerical ceilings for strategic weapons.

The second conclusion is that negotiable criteria for differentiating between tactical and strategic versions of cruise missiles can and should be devised and incorporated into the design of future cruise missiles. The limiting criteria must be based on observable physical variables such as the volume of a cruise missile or the type of engine it is equipped with rather than on unverifiable variables such as the missile's range or the type of warhead it carries. For example, it is possible to differentiate between tactical and strategic cruise missiles by defining as tactical any missile that (1) has a volume of less than half a cubic meter, (2) is powered by a turbojet engine and (3) has a thrust of less than 600 pounds. A strategic missile, on the other hand, would be one that has a volume exceeding half a cubic meter and a turbofan engine.

The physical characteristics outlined above can be detected from orbiting reconnaissance satellites, and they do not impose (for the U.S. at least) any practical restrictions on the design of a cruise missile, since in each case the values of the relevant physical variables would be chosen within the proposed limiting criteria for economic and technical reasons. Reconnaissance satellites can provide the U.S. with information that something may be taking place in the U.S.S.R., but they cannot ensure that something is not taking place. Therefore although the U.S. can rely on such monitoring systems for early intelligence about cruise-missile developments in the U.S.S.R., the systems do not offer the unambiguous verification capability the U.S. Senate would need in order to ratify a treaty with the U.S.S.R. banning the development of strategic cruise missiles. What such monitoring systems do allow the U.S. to do is to exercise unilateral restraint in the development and deployment of long-range cruise missiles while inviting the U.S.S.R. to agree to a similar restraint. The U.S. can be certain that monitoring systems with the capabilities outlined here can detect the development of long-range cruise missiles at an early stage and so enable this country to abandon the unilateral restraint in plenty of time, if it chooses to do so.

The position of unilateral restraint is feasible for two reasons. First, no urgent response is necessary in case the U.S.S.R. is found to be developing long-range cruise missiles, because according to official accounts the U.S. is at least 10 years ahead in the technologies relevant to cruise-missile development. Second, the stability of the strategic balance between the two countries, in view of the many thousands of deliverable nuclear warheads available to both, cannot be upset unless one of the two deploys many thousands of long-range cruise missiles armed with nuclear warheads. Such a deployment, however, would take several years to complete and would be detected at a very early stage by the other side's monitoring satellites. A policy of unilateral restraint in the development and deployment of long-range cruise missiles by the U.S. not only is safe and desirable on economic grounds but also would allow for the orderly development of an effective tactical cruise missile.

Such a policy would of course impose stringent demands on the reconnaissance capabilities of both sides. It is essential for the success of present and future strategic-arms-limitation efforts to look ahead and define what reconnaissance capabilities will be necessary in order to bring these new weapons under control. The new technology that has made cruise missiles possible can also be applied to the development of monitoring systems with the resolution necessary to ensure compliance with the terms of agreements based on the criteria I have outlined. What has been lacking so far is political leadership with the will and the wisdom to exploit technology for the control of nuclear weapons rather than for their proliferation.

IV

The Global Politics of Arms Control

IV The Global Politics of Arms Control

INTRODUCTION

By some standards there has been progress in arms control. At least the world has not blown up; no nuclear weapon has been exploded in anger since 1945. Despite common fears in the 1950s, the number of states with nuclear weapons in 1978 may not have exceeded seven. (Israel is generally acknowledged to have had untested nuclear weapons for years and is counted as one of the seven. South Africa and possibly one or two other states may also have built but not tested weapons.) U.S. military spending declined in real terms for almost a decade. There have been international agreements to bar nuclear weapons from many environments (Antarctica, outer space, the seabed) as well as to prohibit atmospheric testing and proliferation (not accepted, however, by all the relevant states). Various U.S.-Soviet agreements, as part of the SALT process, have established procedures for consultation and some quite high limits on weapons deployment.

Nevertheless, this progress is extremely limited when compared with the dangers that nuclear weapons pose to humanity. Proliferation of nuclear weapons now appears much more likely during the next few years. U.S. military spending is increasing again, and Soviet military spending increased throughout most of the period when American spending declined. The very limited value of the SALT agreements was discussed in the preceeding section. If anything, the dangers of an upward spiral in the arms race seem greater now than at any time since détente began after the 1962 Cuban missile crisis. Why?

We earlier identified explanations that blame the malignity of one side or the other, focus on action-reaction dynamics, blame bureaucratic momentum, employ military-industrial complex arguments, or fault the negotiating process itself. All of these probably do affect the arms race to different degrees and at different moments. In the middle and late 1970s there was certainly widespread alarm at the continued expansion of Soviet military capability, which was manifested not only in the realm of strategic arms but also in greater capabilities for tactical war on land and at sea. Tables 1.1, 1.2, 1.3, 3.2, and 3.3 indicate some dimensions of that increase. While the Soviet increase was in part a growth toward parity (which was not attained in every instance) from a position of marked inferiority, the Soviet Union did appear to be gaining a clear upper hand in some dimensions. Increased strength for ground warfare in Europe raised special fears, especially if Sino-Soviet relations should ever improve enough to permit the U.S.S.R. to withdraw some of the troops now guarding the Chinese border. The appearance of a new Soviet capability for air transport and sea-based military intervention in the Third World—a capability previously limited largely to the United States—also caused much worry in America. Soviet-Cuban interventions in Angola and Ethiopia were interpreted as portents of wider action. Before the mid-1970s, America's strategic nuclear superiority, as well as its conventional mobile general-purpose forces and global presence, served essentially to maintain a worldwide political status quo and to deter local Soviet military interventions. By 1977 both elements of American dominance had deteriorated.

The response of the American public to the relative shift in world military power can be seen in Figure 4.1. Graphed over a 40-year period is the readiness of Americans to spend less or more for defense as measured by national public opinion polls. The question used varied somewhat in different surveys, especially in the early years, but generally was as follows: "There is much discussion as to the amount of money the government in Washington should spend for national defense and military purposes. How do you feel about this: do you think we are spending too little, too much, or about the right amount?" During the cold war years there was some fluctuation in response to international events such as the coup in Czechoslovakia (1948) and the Korean war (1950). But generally the percentage of the population who wanted to spend less on defense stabilized at around 20 percent and was significantly less than the percentage who wished to spend more. By 1968, however, in the midst of the Vietnam war, the situation was quite the reverse. About half the population wanted to reduce military spending, and only around 10 percent wanted to increase it. This situation remained fairly stable for the duration of the war and then changed again. In 1976, for the first time since 1964, more people wanted to increase defense expenditures. By July 1977

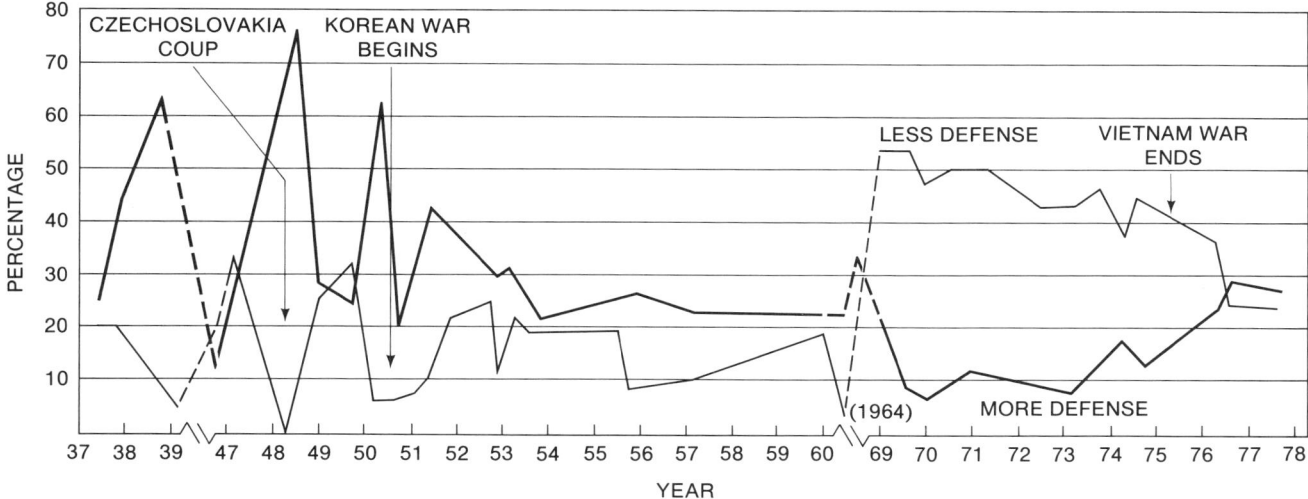

Figure 4.1 Percentage of Americans favoring less or more defense spending, 1937–1977. (Data from Bruce M. Russett, "The Revolt of the Masses: Public Opinion on Military Expenditures," in B. M. Russett, ed., *Peace, War, and Numbers,* Beverly Hills, Calif.: Sage, 1972, pp. 302–306. Material for years after 1971 from surveys by American Institute for Public Opinion and Potomac Associates.)

only 23 percent wanted to reduce defense spending. Domestic opinion in the United States complicated the search for arms control in a new way.

Part of the reason for alarm in the United States is that the superpowers' weapons are designed not only to deter each other but to maintain overpowering superiority over all other countries. The fact that this superiority exists is well documented by Tables 1.1, 1.2, and 1.3. Soviet and American military expenditures exceed by at least seven times those of any other country. The number of American deliverable strategic warheads in 1977 exceeded 10,000; that for the Soviets was nearly 4,000. For the third-ranking country, the United Kingdom, the number was not greater than 250 (allowing for the MRVed Polaris A3 missiles).

One of the selections in this part is by Alva Myrdal. In 1976 she published a book entitled *The Game of Disarmament: How the United States and Russia Run the Arms Race.* The title of the book is its message. She charged, "Behind their outwardly often fierce disagreements . . . there has always been a secret and undeclared collusion between the superpowers. Neither of them has wanted to be restrained by effective disarmament measures." For her, the reason is rooted in international politics: "Military competition results in an ever-increasing superiority—militarily and technologically—of the already overstrong superpowers, thus sharpening the discrimination against all lesser powers." To her, the game is duopoly, with the superpowers not merely stimulating each other to acquire ever more expensive and sophisticated weapons, but also, in so doing, continually outpacing any military force available to any other state or combination of states by an enormous margin.

Among the evidence she marshals to support the argument in her book are the following:

1. The failure of the SALT agreements to produce any disarmament by the superpowers, or even to limit effectively the acquisition of qualitatively more horrendous weapons systems. According to her, "Only when the arms race has reached a point where some type of bomb or delivery vehicle is obsolete or further weapons development has lost any military usefulness to the superpowers will a gesture of 'disarmament' be made."

2. The superpowers' resistance to effective prohibition of biological and chemical warfare, especially the latter. There seems little prospect that existing stocks of chemical weapons will be destroyed.

3. The superpowers' sponsorship of the Non-Proliferation Treaty to prevent the rise of new nuclear powers, while themselves resisting nuclear disarmament and not, for a decade and a half, moving beyond the Partial Test Ban Treaty.

4. The superpowers' retention, as key elements of both doctrine and preparation, of the option of "first use" of nuclear weapons in response to even conventional (nonnuclear) attacks by each other or each other's allies anywhere in the world (for example, Europe, the Middle East, and Korea).

Whether Myrdal's argument is basically correct, much of the world agrees with it. William Epstein, in the first piece in this part, "The Proliferation of Nuclear Weapons," discusses some of these perceptions. Elsewhere Epstein remarked, "It seems that the agreements already concluded, indeed those being negotiated, are designed not to halt or reverse the arms race but rather to institutionalize it and regulate it." The smaller states have consistently argued that the Non-Proliferation Treaty grossly discriminated against them; that while they are supposed to forego the acquisition of nuclear weapons, the superpowers increasingly rely on them. The smaller states refer to the superpower arms race as "vertical proliferation," in contrast with the "horizontal proliferation" involved in the spread of nuclear weapons to new countries. K. Subrahmanyam, former director of the Institute for Defense Studies and Analyses in New Delhi, India, wrote that the price of the superpowers' strategy "is to convert the nuclear issue into a confrontation between North and South, and make the development of nuclear techology a symbol of declaration of autonomy from neo-colonialist dependence."

Epstein discusses the state of nonproliferation efforts at the time his article was written (1975). Since then a few states have ratified the Non-Proliferation Treaty—notably Italy and Japan—but important states remain outside, and the status even of some of the signatories is far from certain.°

The proliferation problem has two distinct dimensions. One is the acquisition of material and know-how for governments to make bombs. New nuclear powers will lack the experience of current nuclear powers in controlling the use of such weapons and will lack resources for the elaborate command and control capabilities required (this is especially true of the less developed countries). Also, many of these governments are involved in serious local conflicts, which would increase pressures to use such weapons in warfare.

The second dimension of the proliferation problem is the opportunity for nongovernmental actors, that is, terrorists, to gain control of nuclear material or finished weapons. Such terrorists may be based within the countries in question or may, while based far away, simply respond to targets of opportunity for acquiring nuclear materials from governments who are unable to take sufficient security precautions. The Epstein article and the second selection by Rose and Lester discuss various facets of this problem and some of the unilateral and international steps that have been or might be taken to deal with it.

In meeting the threat of proliferation by governments, several different kinds of incentives for proliferation must be recognized; different incentives are important for different countries. For some, the problem of security vis-à-vis present nuclear powers may be paramount (for example, the case of Taiwan with regard to China, or Pakistan with regard to India). More often security is sought against local powers that are not yet avowedly nuclear (for example, Israel and South Korea). For still other states, military security is not a primary concern; rather they may wish to obtain the prestige of a big power or the technological information that can come from the development of peaceful and military nuclear capabilities (as in the case of Brazil). And for still others, perhaps all three kinds of incentives are involved (for example, Iran).

While some further proliferation is inevitable, there is nothing inevitable—in speed, extent, or form—about the process. For example, different policies may affect the following:

1. The number of nuclear reactors in use around the world.
2. The number and kind of facilities for reprocessing nuclear material.
3. The kind and extent of international controls imposed on nuclear materials.
4. The incentives to governments to produce nuclear weapons from the material in their reactors.

Two decades from now we could see one thousand, or many thousand, nuclear power reactors in the world in countries not now possessing nuclear weapons—reactors with little international control or with reasonably effective international control over their use. We could see 8 or 9 or 30 governments with nuclear weapons in their arsenals. Because there are so many facets to the problem, control must proceed along several fronts. Measures directed primarily at dissuading governments from acquiring nuclear weapons would include the following:

1. A pledge by the superpowers, backed by appropriate contingency planning, to *avoid "first use"* of nuclear weapons. This would help to diminish the allure of nuclear weapons to governments that have yet to decide whether to go nuclear. A pledge specifically prohibiting the use of nuclear weapons against nonnuclear states is particularly relevant. That may be easier to obtain than an absolute no-first-use pledge, which might apply to American actions in response to a massive Soviet conventional invasion of Western Europe.

2. *Security guarantees*, individually or jointly, by the superpowers to those nonnuclear states that may be tempted to acquire nuclear weapons for deterrence against local powers. The guarantees would contain a promise to defend such states against nuclear attacks or possibly against any kind of attack. It should nevertheless be recognized that such agreements will conflict with any efforts to reduce American alliance commitments and troops abroad (as in South Korea and Taiwan).

3. The establishment, by the states concerned, of *nuclear-free zones* in various parts of the world, where states would agree not to manufacture or possess nuclear weapons. Such a zone has been attempted in Latin America by the Treaty of Tlatelolco, signed in 1967. However, it is not yet in force for the major states at issue—Argentina, Brazil, and Chile—nor have the United States and France ratified the protocol pledging them to apply the treaty to their territories in the zone (although Argentina and the United States in 1977 indicated their intent to ratify.) Efforts to develop such zones in other parts of the world have met with still less success.

4. Unilateral and bilateral moves by the superpowers to show that their nuclear nonproliferation efforts are part of a program of *restraint by the superpowers*, not just part of a U.S.-Soviet condominium to retain their own domination and freeze new powers out. Serious nuclear arms reduction in SALT and a unilateral or joint U.S.-Soviet cutoff of production of fissionable material for weapons use (the United States has no apparent use for more such material) are two such measures.

5. Achievement of a *comprehensive test ban* by the principal nuclear powers (at least the United States, the U.S.S.R., and the United Kingdom). Such a ban, including provisions foregoing "peaceful" nuclear explosions,

---

°The map on pages 188–189 is accurate as of 1975 and is identical to the one on pages 226–227 in the subsequent article, except that the latter contains two small errors.

would also help slow those forms of nuclear development that were not immediately directed toward weapons production but could be diverted to weapons use by governments or by nongovernmental actors.

Other steps directed against both government decisions to acquire nuclear weapons and the worldwide spread of nuclear facilities that might tempt nongovernmental actors include the following:

6. *Strengthening the International Atomic Energy Agency* (IAEA) and its program of inspection and safeguards. During recent years less than one-third of IAEA's budget has been devoted to inspection and regulatory efforts; two-thirds was devoted to promoting the use of nuclear energy. Funds for expanding inspection and regulation will have to come primarily from the developed countries that export nuclear technology, not from the less developed countries.

7. Some *institutional innovations* in the U.S. government. At present no government agency has jurisdiction over the entire spectrum of *foreign and domestic* issues (energy plans, export policy and control, arms control issues, etc.) involved in nuclear proliferation. While some steps to coordinate these policies have been taken, further effort is required to avoid contradictory long-term policies among the agencies involved.

8. More critical *attention to the interaction of economic interests* that support the global trade in nuclear technology as well as in armaments. Sales of nuclear technology are important sources of export earnings for a number of industrial countries. Control of this trade requires attention both to economic interests within the United States and to international agreements among the principal arms and nuclear exporting countries that might compete for these markets. New legislation in the United States and the 1978 agreement among the 15 nations exporting nuclear technology (Supplier Group) for a code of safeguards against military use and theft in purchasing countries are important although still insufficient steps.

9. Assurance to other countries that *supplies of fissionable material for their nuclear power plants will be assured* so long as they observe safeguards. Concern about the reliability of such supplies can exacerbate other countries' desires to have their own reprocessing facilities. Access to an international nuclear-fuel bank (rather than dependence solely on U.S. exports) might help, as might the creation of an international reprocessing facility. In the second article of this section, "Nuclear Power, Nuclear Weapons and International Stability," David Rose and Richard Lester argue that the United States should permit the export of nuclear reprocessing facilities (to be operated under strict safeguards) as the best means of assuring other countries that they will not need to depend on American supplies of enriched uranium.

10. Finally, rapid and effective promotion of *research on fusion, solar energy, and other alternatives* to nuclear fission and petroleum as energy sources. Following the OPEC price rises, nuclear fission now seems to be a cost-efficient source of energy to many oil importers. Japan, some Western European countries, and some less developed countries have been especially interested in the fast breeder reactor so that they can avoid dependence on foreign sources for virtually all their energy supplies. (Such countries have little oil, coal, or uranium.) The sooner new energy sources can be made attractive, the fewer nuclear power reactors and processing plants there will be around the world.

Beyond the nuclear proliferation problem remain all the concerns that have been the subject of negotiation and intensive consideration among arms control and security analysts for the past few decades. Some of these have been discussed, however ineffectively, in the SALT discussions. They include not only questions of nuclear arms in the hands of the superpowers, but biological, chemical, and exotic conventional technology as well. Other such concerns are the sale of conventional weapons to other states, a business that amounted to over $13 billion in FY 1978 for the United States alone, with about as much again for all other arms-exporting states. Most of this trade is now concentrated on the Third World, where the waste of human resources is most acute and where the risks that these arms will be used in warfare, perhaps engulfing states far beyond local areas, are most threatening.

In the final selection of this book, "The International Control of Disarmament," Alva Myrdal discusses some far-reaching plans to redress the failures of the past decades. She is especially forceful about the possibilities for monitoring adherence to international arms control and for disarmament agreement, and about the absence of need for detailed, comprehensive inspection by governments. Indeed, in her book she characterized Soviet-American dialogues on controls and inspection as merely a charade: "The Soviet government has often felt free to launch broad proposals for disarmament . . . [but] it can safely rely on the United States to raise demands for controls, which the Soviet Union can then decline." While this is an extreme view, her article nevertheless is a good statement about other ways to enforce international agreements and about the need to stimulate new intellectual and institutional creativity by a variety of governments and peoples. She proposes the creation of a new UN agency responsible for verifying and controlling disarmament agreements. Perhaps that is too visionary. In any case, the concerns to be addressed for human survival include not just arms control but also true disarmament.

The Proliferation of Nuclear Weapons

by William Epstein
April 1975

Unless the major nuclear powers begin to live up to their obligations under the Nonproliferation Treaty, it seems likely that a large number of near-nuclear countries will emulate India and join the "nuclear club"

Next month, five years after the entry into force of the Treaty on the Nonproliferation of Nuclear Weapons, the representatives of the 84 nations that are party to the agreement will meet in Geneva in fulfillment of a pledge "to review the operation of this Treaty with a view to assuring that the purposes of the Preamble and the provisions of the Treaty are being realized." How well has the Nonproliferation Treaty worked toward the accomplishment of its stated goals? It is hard to escape the conclusion that it has failed in almost every important respect.

The magnitude of this failure was emphasized last May by India's successful underground test explosion of a "peaceful" nuclear device. Now that India, a poor, underdeveloped country, has joined the other five nuclear powers in demonstrating its potential for making nuclear weapons, one can hardly expect that membership in what once seemed to be an exclusive "nuclear club" can be held to six.

The roots of the failure of this arms-control effort, however, go deeper. The preamble and the provisions of the Nonproliferation Treaty call for, among other things, the discontinuance of all nuclear-weapons tests, the cessation of the nuclear-arms race, the enactment of effective measures in the direction of nuclear disarmament and the commitment of the nuclear powers to make available the benefits of the peaceful applications of nuclear technology (including non-military nuclear explosives) to all parties to the treaty. Nothing seems clearer than that the major nuclear powers—in particular the U.S. and the U.S.S.R., both of whom (unlike India) signed and ratified the treaty—have failed to live up to those obligations. How has this situation come about? And what can be done at this late stage to prevent things from getting even worse?

Let us begin by considering what the Indian nuclear explosion means, both in terms of the proliferation of nuclear weapons and in terms of the structure of international relations. First of all, it is important to realize that there is no essential technological difference between a nuclear explosive intended for peaceful purposes and one intended for waging war. The same device that blew a hole in the earth under the Rajasthan desert and left a large crater on the surface could just as well wipe out a city and its inhabitants. Indeed, the explosive yield of the Indian device, estimated to be equivalent to from 15 to 20 kilotons of TNT, was of the same order as the yield of the bombs that destroyed Hiroshima and Nagasaki. The main difference was in the ostensible purpose of the explosion. Indian government officials have repeatedly declared that their explosion was for peaceful purposes only and that India has no intention of developing nuclear weapons. Intention is a subjective matter based on a unilateral decision, however, and as such it can be changed at will, with or without notice. Thus in the absence of any binding legal commitment there is nothing to prevent the Indian government from changing its mind whenever it wants to. Even if one fully accepts the Indian declaration of intention to use nuclear explosions exclusively for peaceful purposes, the plain fact is that India's nuclear devices can also be used as nuclear weapons whenever India so decides. Other powers can only regard India's peaceful nuclear devices as nuclear weapons. Henceforth, in spite of repeated protestations by the Indian government, India must be regarded by other powers as being not only a nuclear power but also a nuclear-weapons power. This perception will be regarded as all the more valid in view of the fact that a public-opinion poll taken in India soon after the explosion showed that two-thirds of the Indian people favored India's making nuclear weapons.

The Indian test explosion has also shown the way for other nations to "go nuclear" under the guise of testing devices for peaceful purposes. Any one of the potential nuclear powers that has not become a party to the Nonproliferation Treaty can emulate India's example. Even countries that are party to the treaty retain this option, since the text of the treaty provides that any party can withdraw on three months' notice.

It is much easier for a government to assuage both domestic and international opinion by proclaiming its intention to conduct nuclear explosions solely for peaceful purposes than to say outright that it intends to make nuclear weapons. Nuclear weapons are, after all, still regarded with abhorrence as weapons of mass destruction. All the first five nuclear-weapons states have declared that they produced nuclear weapons solely for defense and not for aggression. One can now look forward to a new chapter in the nuclear story, where countries that want to become nuclear-weapons states, for whatever reason, would first go through the stage of producing nuclear devices for "peaceful" purposes. This cosmetic façade would be sufficient to enable a moderately advanced nation over a period of time to produce a wide range of nuclear warheads.

The Indian leaders insist that they broke no law, treaty or agreement in conducting the Rajasthan test, and they are right. The Partial Test-Ban Treaty of 1963, to which India is a party, bans tests in the atmosphere, in outer space and underwater, but it does not ban them underground. The only restriction on underground tests is against those that vent and carry radioactive debris beyond the territory of the country where the test is held. Several tests conducted by both the U.S. and the U.S.S.R. have vented and carried radioactive debris beyond their borders, but these were regarded as mere "technical violations" of the treaty since they were accidental in the sense that no violation was intended or expected. It would appear, however, that there was no violation, technical or otherwise, as a result of the Indian test.

The Nonproliferation Treaty is the only international instrument that bans the explosion of nuclear devices for peaceful purposes by states that do not have nuclear weapons. The transfer or acquisition of "nuclear weapons or other nuclear explosive devices" is specifically banned for non-nuclear-weapons states by Article II of the treaty. Peaceful nuclear explosions, however, to be conducted only by nuclear-weapons states under an appropriate international regime for the benefit of non-nuclear-weapons states, are expressly envisioned by both the preamble and Article V of the treaty. India is in any case not a party to the Nonproliferation Treaty. In fact, both during and after the negotiation and conclusion of the treaty, India publicly announced its opposition to the accord as discriminatory and unfair, and declared that it reserved the right to conduct its own nuclear explosions for peaceful purposes. Hence India cannot be accused of any breach of either the letter or the spirit of the Nonproliferation Treaty.

On the other hand, India is a party to and an active participant in the work of the International Atomic Energy Agency (IAEA) in Vienna. The statute of that agency, which went into force in 1957, specifically bans the use of atomic energy "in such a way as to further any military purpose" but positively encourages "the development and practical application of atomic energy for peaceful purposes." A number of United Nations and IAEA conferences from 1958 to 1971 held out high hopes for the potential benefits that would be obtained from nonmilitary nuclear explosions. These benefits may be largely illusory or downright mythical, but there can be no doubt that over the years nuclear and non-nuclear powers alike were dazzled by the glittering prize that could be theirs when nonmilitary nuclear explosions became

CRATER formed by India's underground nuclear explosion on May 18, 1974, appears in this aerial photograph released by the Indian Department of Atomic Energy. The test was conducted "for peaceful purposes" at a site in the Rajasthan desert east of New Delhi. The yield of the device was between 15 and 20 kilotons, approximately the same as the yield of the Hiroshima bomb.

feasible. Although the nuclear-weapons states are apparently becoming increasingly disenchanted by their failure to achieve any important technical or economic objectives after investing years of effort and hundreds of millions of dollars in testing nonmilitary nuclear explosives, the poorer nations of the world seem to regard such devices as the key that could help them to unlock the door to great industrial and engineering undertakings at little cost. As recently as July, 1974, in the Threshold Test-Ban Treaty signed by Secretary Brezhnev and President Nixon in Moscow, specific provision is made for entering into a new bilateral agreement for the exchange of data about nonmilitary nuclear explosions at the earliest possible time. Thus India can hardly be criticized for wanting to achieve what was not prohibited for it by any international treaty or agreement and what was given the specific blessing of a number of international treaties and studies.

Regardless of what one may think of India's tactics and behavior, and convinced as one may be that India will eventually turn its peaceful nuclear devices into nuclear weapons, its declared intention to use these devices exclusively for peaceful purposes cannot be disproved. One can only regret that the nation of Gandhi and Nehru (who first proposed the end of nuclear testing in 1954) may be responsible for undermining efforts to prevent the proliferation of nuclear weapons. One might also be allowed to doubt the wisdom—in terms of India's own ultimate political, economic and military interests—of its having decided to go nuclear.

Public reactions to the Indian explosion have been rather few and mixed. Not a word of criticism has been heard from the two Asian nuclear powers, China and the U.S.S.R. China has attacked the Nonproliferation Treaty from its inception as a device by the two superpowers to maintain their nuclear hegemony and to dominate the non-nuclear states. The Chinese have for many years in effect advocated the proliferation of nuclear weapons as a means whereby the underdeveloped countries of the "Third World" could protect themselves from nuclear threats and blackmail by the nuclear superpowers. In any event it is unlikely that India can become a threat to China in the foreseeable future, even if India decides to become a nuclear-weapons power. Nevertheless, in view of India's close relations with the U.S.S.R. and the fact that India was clearly the strongest military power in southern Asia even before last May, China can hardly regard India's growing nuclear power with equanimity. In the context of Chi-

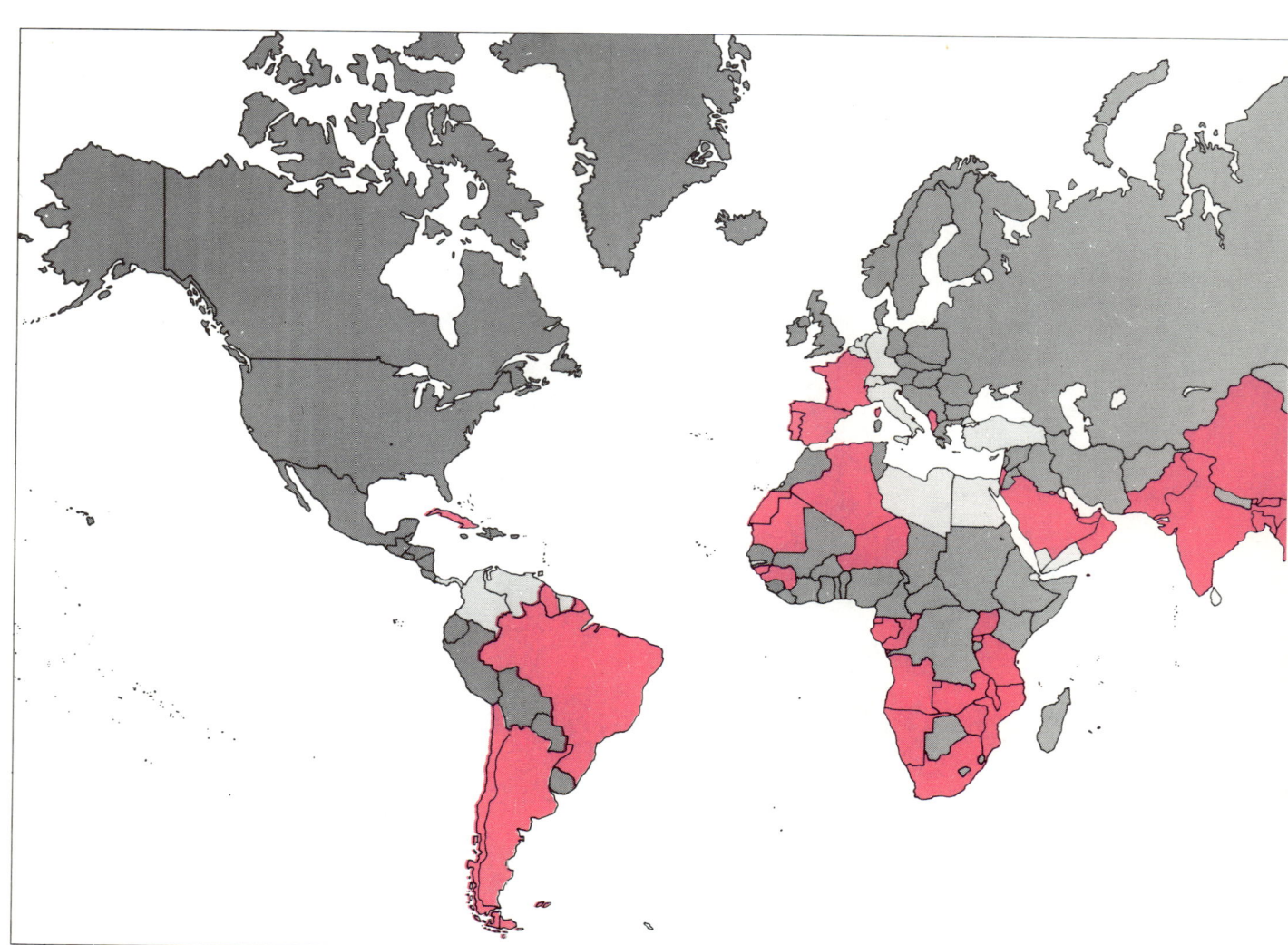

CURRENT STATUS OF NONPROLIFERATION TREATY is depicted on this world map. The 84 nations that are full parties to the agreement are shown in dark gray. The 22 nations that have signed the treaty but have not yet ratified it, and hence are not bound by

nese and Indian relations with other Asian countries and the Third World, and in particular with Pakistan, with whom China has close and friendly relations, the political implications of the Indian explosion are of greater importance than the military ones. Moreover, if Taiwan, which is a party to the Nonproliferation Treaty, should be encouraged by the Indian example to withdraw from the treaty and go nuclear, this would pose some new and difficult problems for China. It is also difficult to believe that China would be completely unconcerned if South Korea, Indonesia, Iran or Australia were also to go nuclear. The official silence from Peking, which is itself conducting tests in the atmosphere, may therefore mean only that China has not yet worked out its final position with respect to the Indian explosion or is biding its time pending a clarification of Third World opinion.

On the other hand, the U.S.S.R., which together with the U.S. was the chief protagonist of the Nonproliferation Treaty, must surely find the Indian action disquieting. Although the U.S.S.R. too has not uttered a single official word of complaint, Russian diplomats and arms-control experts have privately indicated their unhappiness. It could hardly be otherwise. It may be that a nuclear India that continues to be friendly to the U.S.S.R. provides some benefits or leverage for the U.S.S.R. with respect to China, but any such possible advantage would be far outweighed if India's action should lead to the further erosion of the Nonproliferation Treaty and to the spread of nuclear-weapons capability to other states, particularly those around the periphery of the U.S.S.R.

France, which is also conducting tests in the atmosphere, has made no official statement, although the chairman of the French Atomic Energy Commission sent a congratulatory message to the chairman of the Indian Atomic Energy Commission. The French position is anomalous. France is not a party to the Nonproliferation Treaty, but it has announced from the start that it will behave exactly as if it were a party. Nevertheless, France is busy selling nuclear reactors to a number of countries, and although these deals are subject to IAEA safeguards, as far as is known they do not bar peaceful nuclear explosions.

Great Britain, which has also been a strong supporter of the Nonproliferation Treaty, was at first strongly critical of the Indian explosion. After the initial criticism, however, little has been heard from the British, who have themselves been criticized for resuming underground testing in June, 1974, when they set off an explosion (in the U.S.) for the first time since 1965.

The U.S. was at first rather cautious in its official reaction to the Indian explosion. It did reiterate its views to the Indian government that peaceful and military nuclear explosive devices are indistinguishable, but it seems to wish to avoid any public dispute with India. Privately it has sought a commitment that plutonium produced from nuclear fuel supplied by the U.S. would not be used for any kind of explosion. Failing to receive adequate assurances, the U.S. delayed the delivery of enriched uranium to fuel the Tarapur reactor, which was built with American technical and financial assistance. At the moment it appears that India will give the necessary assurances and that the U.S. will continue supplying uranium to India.

As was to be expected, Pakistan, which signed but never ratified the 1963 Partial Test-Ban Treaty and which has not signed the Nonproliferation Treaty, immediately protested in every possible forum against the Indian explosion and called for a halt to further tests. Pakistan also announced that it would acquire a similar nuclear capability. It has proposed that the UN General Assembly discuss the creation of a nuclear-free zone in South Asia; the proposal (which India rejected) must be regarded as a tactical political move intended to make clear to the world where the blame lies.

Apart from Pakistan, only Canada, Japan and Sweden, all of which have the capability of undertaking nuclear explosions, have taken a strong public stand against the Indian test. Canada cut off all further nuclear cooperation with India almost immediately, and all three countries in statements in their capitals, in the Geneva disarmament conference, in messages transmitted to the Indian government and in the UN General Assembly deplored the Indian explosion and its possible adverse effects on international efforts to prevent the proliferation of nuclear weapons. Australia and the Netherlands have also criticized the Indian test.

As for the nonaligned and underdeveloped countries, while saying little in public, they have in large part welcomed the Indian test as a technological achievement demonstrating that even a poor country can accomplish the sophisticated task of successfully exploding an underground nuclear device, which had for a decade been the exclusive preserve of the five great powers. Yugoslavia, one of the leaders of the nonaligned countries, congratulated India on its technological achievement. Nigeria said that the Indian action was not surprising in view of the lack of progress by the nuclear powers in stopping underground nuclear tests and the nuclear-arms race.

Without the wide support of the non-nuclear-weapons states of the Third World, the Nonproliferation Treaty would never have received the overwhelming commendation of the UN General Assembly. Most of them have no significant nuclear programs and are in no position to go nuclear for several decades to come. In 1968 these countries entered into a tacit alliance with the nuclear powers, because it seemed clear that the further "horizontal" spread of nuclear weapons to the near-nuclear countries, nearly all of which were developed countries, was not in the interest of either group. The Third World coun-

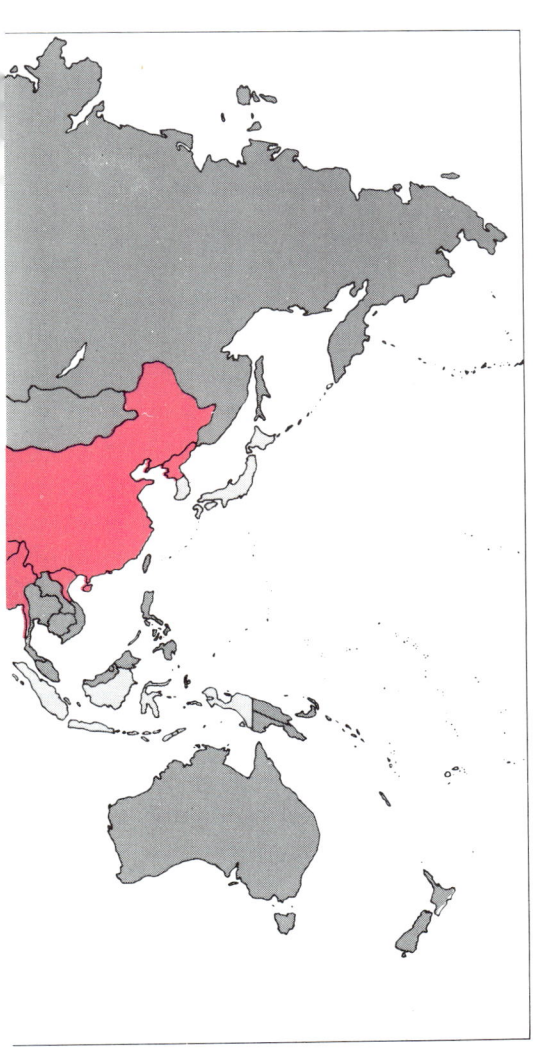

its provisions, are in light gray. The 38 nonsignatories (among them India) are in color.

tries as a group, however, were never greatly impressed by the Nonproliferation Treaty.

Many of those who decided to support the treaty did so in the dual expectation that the nuclear-weapons powers would halt the "vertical" proliferation of nuclear weapons (their further sophistication, development and deployment) and would also make available to the underdeveloped countries the benefits of the peaceful uses of nuclear energy, including nonmilitary nuclear explosions. These countries have become disillusioned by the failure of the nuclear powers to halt the nuclear-arms race and by the paucity of the benefits received from the peaceful applications of nuclear energy. They are impressed by the achievements of China and India, and some of the more advanced among them are much more receptive now to the argument, illusory though it is, that nuclear weapons are "equalizers" that would better enable them to withstand the unspoken threats of the nuclear-weapons states and promote their own security and economic development. In fact, some of the Third World countries seem to be increasingly inclined to accept the idea that the acquisition of nuclear-weapons capability by some of the near-nuclear powers would place greater restraints on the monopoly position and freedom of action of the nuclear-weapons states, and that this could bring some advantages to the Third World as a whole. At the UN General Assembly in the fall of 1974 apart from the six countries mentioned above there was practically no criticism of the Indian explosion (and none from any Third World country except Pakistan). In short, India has apparently succeeded in becoming a nuclear power with remarkably little adverse reaction.

Why did India go nuclear? To be sure, India had throughout the negotiation of the Nonproliferation Treaty and after its conclusion denounced the treaty as a discriminatory instrument and had repeatedly announced that it reserved the right to conduct its own nuclear explosions for peaceful purposes. That, however, is not the whole story.

India was obviously greatly concerned by the Chinese nuclear explosion of October 16, 1964. On December 4 of that year Prime Minister Lal Bahadur Shastri, discussing the Chinese nuclear bomb, stated that all non-nuclear countries needed a guarantee by the existing nuclear powers against nuclear attack. He added that it would be "very wise" for the nuclear powers "to give serious thought to this aspect of the problem."

In May, 1965, the Indian ambassador to the UN, Birendra Narayan Chakravarty, told the Disarmament Commission that an "integrated solution" was required to solve the problem of the spread of nuclear weapons. He said: "It is no use telling countries, some of which may be even more advanced in nuclear technology than China, that they should enter into a treaty which would stipulate only that they must not acquire or produce these weapons. Again it is no use telling them that their security will be safeguarded by one or another of the existing nuclear powers. Such an assurance has to be really dependable. Unless the nuclear powers... undertake from now on not to produce any nuclear weapons or vehicles for weapons delivery and, in addition, agree to reduce their existing stockpile of nuclear weapons, there is no way of doing away with proliferation."

In July of the same year the Indian ambassador to the Geneva disarmament conference, Vishnuprasad Chunilal Trivedi, said that the "essential" requirement for a "rational and acceptable" treaty on nonproliferation was "tangible progress toward disarmament, including a comprehensive test-ban treaty, a complete freeze on production of nuclear weapons and means of delivery as well as a substantial reduction in the existing stocks." He added that the institution of international controls on peaceful nuclear reactors and nuclear power stations, while leaving free the vast weapon-producing facilities of the nuclear powers, was "like an attempt to maintain law and order in a society by placing all its law-abiding citizens in custody while leaving its law-breaking elements free to roam the streets."

On April 27, 1967, the Indian External Affairs Minister, Mahomedali Currim Chagla, criticized the draft nonproliferation treaty as "discriminatory" because, among other things, it sought to

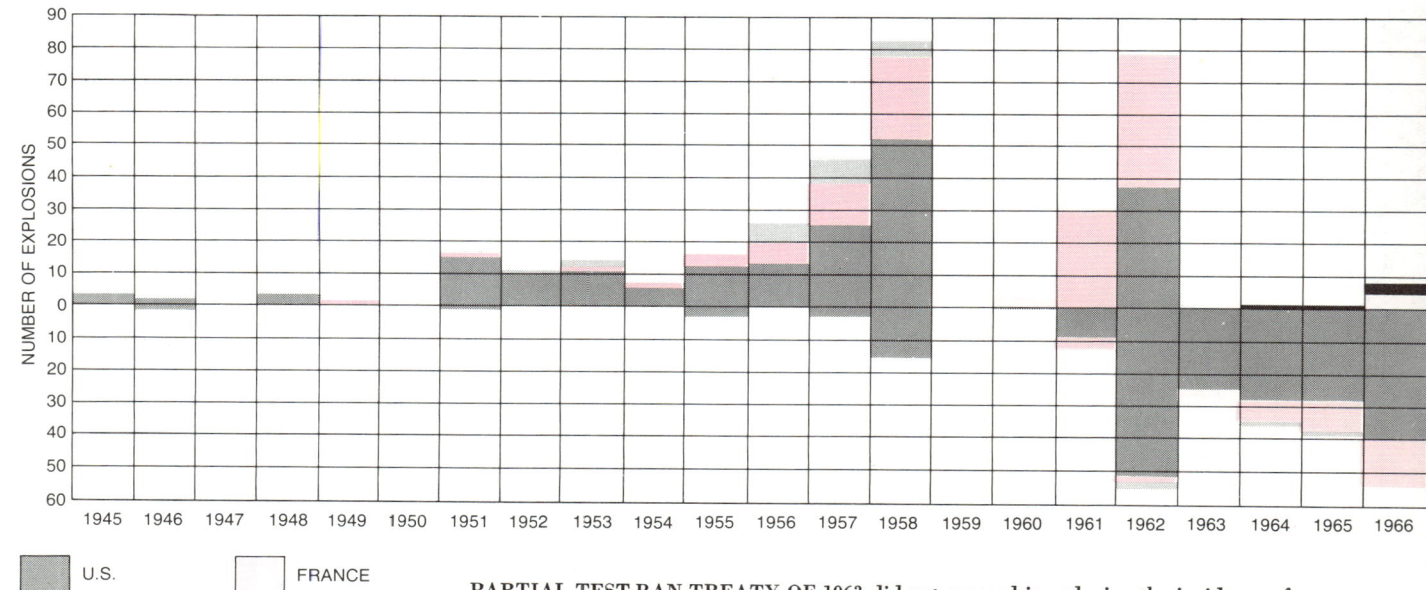

PARTIAL TEST-BAN TREATY OF 1963 did not succeed in reducing the incidence of nuclear-test explosions; it merely drove most tests underground, as is shown in this chart. The bars indicate the total number of known nuclear explosions conducted each year from 1945 through 1974. Bars above the baseline represent explosions in the atmosphere; bars below the baseline count underground (and a few underwater) tests. The data were compiled mostly by the Stockholm International Peace Research Institute (SIPRI) on the basis of of-

maintain the monopoly of the nuclear powers. Only the non-nuclear powers would be prevented from conducting underground explosions for peaceful nuclear research. He added that India was in a "peculiar position" because it was a nonaligned country not under the "nuclear umbrella" of any nuclear country, because it was far advanced in nuclear research and because it was under the "continuing threat and menace" of China, which had become a nuclear power. If India was not to explode a bomb, it must have a "credible guarantee" of its security.

For several years India sought effective guarantees of its security by the nuclear powers, but its efforts were in vain. Failing to obtain any adequate direct security assurances, India shifted its emphasis to the indirect approach by insisting that all the nuclear powers stop testing and manufacturing nuclear weapons and start reducing their nuclear arsenals. When this approach also seemed likely to fail, India began stressing its right and need to conduct its own peaceful nuclear explosions for economic development.

At this late stage one can only speculate that India might not have gone ahead so soon, if at all, with the explosion of its own nuclear device if it had been offered adequate guarantees of its security, and that it might have been willing to accept the protection of a joint American-Russian nuclear umbrella, as Japan seemed content to accept an American one. Unfortunately that possibility was never put to any real test. In fact, none of the main demands in India's "integrated" approach were met.

Are there any benefits to be gained from peaceful nuclear explosions? Ever since the discovery of nuclear fission high hopes have been held out for the potential blessings that would be conferred on mankind by the peaceful uses of nuclear energy and technology. At first attention was devoted to the benefits from power reactors and from the use of radioactive isotopes in science, medicine, industry and agriculture. It was only after the U.S. Atomic Energy Commission launched its "Plowshare" program in the late 1950's that interest developed in peaceful nuclear explosions. At that time great engineering projects were visualized: the digging of canals, harbors and so forth. Those ideas were soon discarded by the U.S. when the dangers of radioactivity from cratering explosions became apparent. Interest then turned to the idea of fracturing oil-bearing or gas-bearing rock by underground nuclear explosions in order to stimulate the flow of oil and gas; the idea of blasting underground cavities for their storage was also promoted, as was the idea of leaching minerals, such as copper ore, by such means. None of the American underground explosions has been successful in achieving any of these goals. It has become apparent that to succeed in fracturing rock to produce substantial quantities of oil and gas not one explosion or two but hundreds or even thousands would be required. Such operations would be extremely costly as well as hazardous, and no practical way of dealing with the radioactive by-products has yet been discovered.

Curiously enough, as American nuclear experts began to lose interest in the peaceful uses of underground explosions and to doubt whether they had any practical end that could not be achieved as well or better by ordinary high explosives or by other conventional means, their Russian counterparts began to show greater interest in them. They spoke of achieving the same goals as the Americans had at an earlier stage and added some new ideas of their own. In the past few years they have suggested diverting water flowing to the Arctic Ocean by means of a canal to the Volga River and thence to the Caspian Sea. This would require from 250 to 400 cratering explosions, with all the hazards attending the release of huge amounts of radioactivity. The U.S.S.R. was successful in throwing up a dam to create a lake and in putting out, by means of underground explosions, two runaway gas-well fires that had been out of control for more than a year, but here too it is not clear that the jobs could not have been done better with high explosives. Apparently the U.S.S.R. has been no more successful than the U.S. in increasing the flow of oil and gas or in the extraction of minerals by means of nuclear explosions.

Within the past year there has been increasing evidence that the U.S.S.R. is also becoming disillusioned by its inability to fulfill the expectations it once had for the benefits from peaceful nuclear explosions. Although it was the U.S.S.R. that insisted on the inclusion in last year's Threshold Test-Ban Treaty of the article providing for an agreement governing such tests, in private Russian scientists have been stating quite freely their opposition to nonmilitary nuclear explosions because of their harmful rather than beneficial potential.

Some American experts hold the view that there never was a good case for peaceful nuclear explosions, and that the idea was fostered and publicized in the U.S. by the very scientists who wished to promote the military rather than the peaceful applications of nuclear energy; in other words, that the campaign on behalf of peaceful nuclear explosions was conducted as a stratagem, somewhat similar to the campaign for "clean" nuclear weapons, to prevent or circumvent any agreement to ban or halt underground nuclear-weapons tests.

Be that as it may, those who were promoting the potential benefits of nuclear explosions were most successful in promoting their ideas. Three international conferences on the Peaceful Uses of Atomic Energy sponsored by the UN and the IAEA in 1958, 1964 and 1971 stressed the importance of nonmilitary nuclear explosions and the encouraging prospects for them. The same conclusions were drawn by an international group of experts convened by the UN Secretary-General in 1969 at the request of the non-nuclear-weapons states that were interested in an impartial report on the possible peaceful uses of nuclear energy. These conclusions and results were again confirmed by three international panels of experts (mostly American and Russian) convened by the IAEA in 1969, 1970 and 1971. Thus it is not surprising that the underdeveloped countries hold out such high hopes for the potential benefits they will receive from nonmilitary nuclear explosions, or that India has now revived the old arguments.

Nevertheless, in the past two years the evidence from the tests conducted by both the U.S. and the U.S.S.R. leads to

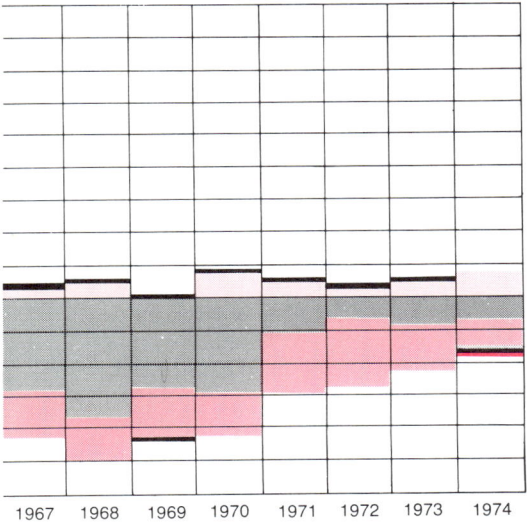

ficial announcements and other sources. The figures do not include several dozen secret tests conducted by the U.S. and the U.S.S.R. France and China are not party to the Partial Test-Ban Treaty and hence are not legally prohibited from testing in the atmosphere.

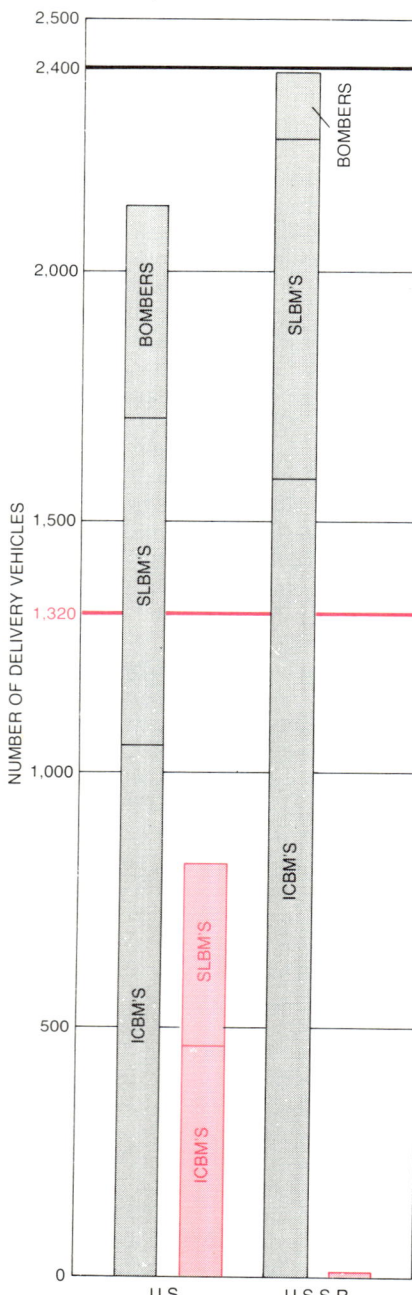

CEILINGS imposed on the numbers of the strategic nuclear weapons of the two superpowers as a result of their Vladivostok "understanding" of November, 1974, are clearly higher than either country's present strength. Gray bars indicate the total number of strategic delivery vehicles deployed at present by each side; the bars are broken down into land-based intercontinental ballistic missiles (ICBM's), submarine-launched ballistic missiles (SLBM's) and heavy bombers. Colored bars indicate number of missiles equipped with multiple independently targetable reentry vehicles (MIRV's). The Russians have just begun to install MIRV's on some of their land-based missiles. By the terms of the Vladivostok agreement, which runs until 1985, each side is allowed to have no more than 2,400 strategic delivery vehicles, of which 1,320 can be armed with MIRV's.

more doubts than answers, from both the technical point of view and the economic. If the potential benefits elude the highly industrialized and technically sophisticated nuclear-weapons powers, they would seem to be even more remote and more questionable for a country that is still in the developing stage with respect to both industry and nuclear technology. This is an additional reason why many experts look with suspicion on the Indian test as a public peaceful cloak for a private military purpose.

No other question in the field of arms control and disarmament has been the subject of so much study and discussion as the question of stopping nuclear-weapons tests. Ever since Prime Minister Nehru called for a halt to such tests in 1954 the subject has been at or near the top of the disarmament agenda.

By the Partial Test-Ban Treaty of 1963 the nuclear powers undertook to seek "to achieve the discontinuance of all test explosions of nuclear weapons for all time" and expressed their determination "to continue negotiations to this end." That commitment was repeated in the Nonproliferation Treaty. One measure of its implementation can be found in a comparison of nuclear-weapons tests before and after the signing of the Partial Test-Ban Treaty [see illustration on preceding two pages].

After the signing of the Partial Test-Ban Treaty there were in fact no serious discussions between the two main nuclear powers on an underground-test ban for more than a decade, in spite of many resolutions adopted by the UN General Assembly every year calling for a comprehensive test ban. The non-nuclear powers appear to regard an underground-test ban as a litmus test of the seriousness of the intentions of the two superpowers to stop the nuclear-arms race. Although such a halt would not by itself end the further technological improvement of nuclear weapons, it would be an important step in that direction. There is an increasing conviction among the nations of the world that a ban on underground tests is the single most important measure, and certainly the most feasible one in the near future, toward halting the nuclear-arms race. They also seem to regard an underground-test ban by the U.S. and the U.S.S.R. as possibly having a beneficial effect on persuading China and France to curb and ultimately halt their testing. It would certainly put the superpowers in a better moral position to urge the non-nuclear countries that are capable of going nuclear to resist the temptation to do so.

The Threshold Test-Ban Treaty agreed to by the U.S. and the U.S.S.R. in Moscow last year allows the parties to continue unrestricted underground tests of whatever size they wish until March 31, 1976; thereafter they will limit weapon tests to 150 kilotons each, which is about 10 times larger than the yield of the bomb that was dropped on Hiroshima and which exceeds in size all but a few of the tests conducted in recent years [see illustration on pages 194 and 195]. No limitation whatsoever was put on underground explosions for peaceful purposes. This is not just a cosmetic agreement; it is a mockery of a test-ban treaty. Indeed, it may be harmful to the cause of nuclear nonproliferation. It will not help to curb the qualitative improvement, testing and development of new nuclear weapons. Therefore it will not serve to halt the nuclear-arms race. And it will not alleviate the concerns or satisfy the demands of the non-nuclear powers or provide any cogent reason for them to forbear from testing.

The delayed threshold ban has led some interested non-nuclear powers to conclude that once again they were being misled by the nuclear superpowers and that there was no early prospect of any real action to stop the nuclear-arms race. The same can be said of the strategic-arms-limitation talks (SALT). On the day of the signing of the Nonproliferation Treaty (July 1, 1968) it was announced that the U.S. and the U.S.S.R. would begin bilateral discussions on the "limitation and reduction of both offensive and defensive strategic-nuclear-weapon delivery systems." The SALT meetings did not begin until November, 1969. In May, 1972, the U.S. and the U.S.S.R. at the summit meeting in Moscow signed the Treaty on the Limitation of Anti-Ballistic-Missile Systems and also an Interim Agreement on Certain Measures with Respect to the Limitation of Strategic Offensive Arms. Under the ABM treaty each of the parties agreed to deploy no more than 100 ABM launchers and 100 missiles at each of two launch sites in both countries. They also agreed to certain limitations on their ABM radars, but modernization and replacement of ABM systems was allowed. Under the Interim Agreement on Offensive Arms, which has a duration of five years, the U.S. is entitled to increase the number of its nuclear submarines from 41 to 44 with 710 nuclear missiles, and the U.S.S.R. is entitled to build up to 62 submarines carrying 950 nuclear missiles; the U.S. can also retain 1,000 land-based intercontinental missiles and the U.S.S.R. can retain 1,410. No limitation was placed on installing multiple independently targetable reentry vehicles (MIRV's) on either sea-based or land-based missiles.

Last year's Summit III meeting in Moscow also did little to halt or reverse the nuclear-arms race. The two parties agreed to restrict their ABM's to only one site each instead of the two allowed under the 1972 agreement. (The new agreement is practically without significance, since neither party intended to build a second site anyway.) There was complete failure to reach any agreement to limit offensive strategic weapons.

The Vladivostok understanding of November, 1974, was hailed as a "breakthrough" that put a "cap" on the strategic-arms race. It incorporated the interim agreement and fixed a ceiling on the number of all strategic nuclear weapons until December 31, 1985, on the basis of equality between the two superpowers. Each side is allowed to have 2,400 strategic delivery vehicles, including land-based intercontinental ballistic missiles (ICBM's), submarine-launched ballistic missiles (SLBM's) and heavy bombers. Of that number 1,320 may be armed with MIRV's. The agreement was said to establish ceilings well below the levels that otherwise could be expected in 10 years. The ceilings established, however, are clearly higher than the levels each side has at the present time, and even higher than those envisioned for 1977 under the interim agreement.

The ceiling of 1,320 MIRV's is also much higher than either country's present strength. The U.S., for example, has announced that it intends to fit 550 land-based Minutemen with three warheads and 496 Poseidon missiles with from 10 to 14 warheads, for a total of 1,046 missiles with multiple warheads. At present it has about 800 multiple-warhead missiles. The ceiling of 1,320 therefore represents not only a higher level than the U.S. now has but also a higher level than it apparently had ever planned to have.

Meanwhile the U.S.S.R. has tested and is beginning to deploy its MIRV's. It has also developed several new missiles with multiple warheads. It has not announced how many of its land-based or sea-based missiles it intends to equip with multiple warheads, but 1,320 obviously represents a high and costly ceiling that will take several years to reach.

The Vladivostok agreement put no limit on either the number of warheads that can be carried by each missile or on the size of the warheads. Since it is generally believed the Russian warheads are bigger than the American ones, there will be pressures for the U.S. to increase the size or number of its warheads. The agreement also puts no limitation on the modernization of missiles by improving their accuracy and maneuverability.

In December of last year Secretary of Defense Schlesinger said that he foresaw a need for larger and restructured strategic forces for the U.S. as a result of the Vladivostok agreement, including 12 instead of 10 of the giant Trident submarines (which together would carry 288 missiles, each with 14 warheads, for a total of 4,032 warheads), larger intercontinental missiles with MIRV's and the new B-1 bomber. This program, he said, would call for "some upward adjustment" in the strategic-arms budget.

It is clear that the "limitation" envisioned by the Vladivostok agreement,

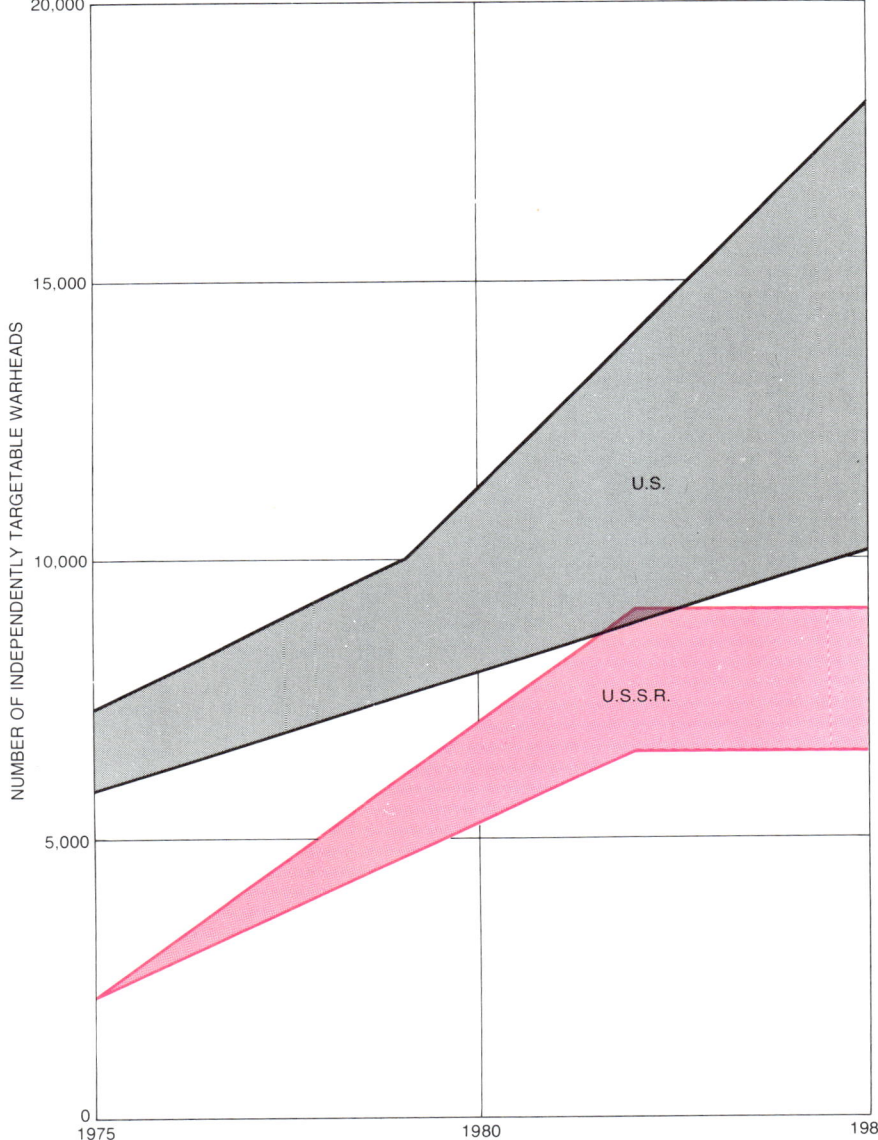

POSSIBLE FUTURE LEVELS of independently targetable strategic nuclear warheads allowed under the Vladivostok accords are estimated conservatively in this graph, which is based on material that appeared originally in *Arms Control Today*, a publication of the Arms Control Association. U.S. warheads are represented in gray, Russian warheads in color. The graph reflects the results of current strategic-weapons programs and projects these programs through 1985 on the assumption that they will be revised in order to build force levels up to the Vladivostok ceilings. Shaded areas suggest range of options. Not included in the projections are future U.S. bomber levels, the possible deployment on both sides of strategic cruise missiles, possible increases in the number of MIRVed warheads per missile or changes in present Defense Department estimates of the likely MIRV capabilities of the new Russian ICBM's. Multiple warheads that are not independently targetable are counted on the basis of one warhead per missile. The graph does not take into account the thousands of medium-range nuclear weapons deployed by both sides in Europe.

although it will put an eventual cap on the number of strategic nuclear weapons, allows an expansion in both the quantitative nuclear-arms race and the qualitative one. Since no limit is fixed for the number and size of warheads on the 1,320 missiles with multiple warheads or of nuclear arms carried in bombers, each of the two superpowers can emplace 20,000 or more strategic nuclear warheads under the agreement. This immense "overkill" capacity can be measured by the estimate made about a year ago that the U.S. at that time had enough strategic weapons to destroy 36 times all 218 Russian cities with a population of more than 100,000.

One of the reasons given for maintaining such an unconscionably high overkill capacity is the "counterforce" argument. According to that argument, strategic nuclear arms should not be programmed primarily for the task of knocking out cities and their populations but rather should be aimed at military targets such as missile silos, ammunition dumps, nuclear bases and so on. For that purpose two or more warheads are needed for each target; in addition enough arms must be kept in reserve for a second strike against the other side's cities in case it launches a large-scale first strike. What this argument conveniently overlooks is that a nuclear exchange of such magnitude would poison most of the inhabitants of the Northern Hemisphere with radioactive fallout. In either case, whether a nuclear exchange involved cities or nuclear targets, it would constitute a form of international suicide.

In addition to MIRV's the U.S. is currently developing a new maneuverable missile called MARV, and there is talk in both the U.S. and the U.S.S.R. of building mobile intercontinental missiles, even though the U.S. announced at the time of SALT I that it would regard the building of such weapons as being contrary to the spirit of the SALT I agreements. The U.S. is also proceeding to develop a shorter-range (1,500-mile) cruise missile that could be launched from aircraft, submarines or surface vessels. Further international negotiation may be needed to decide whether or not these missiles will be considered strategic weapons.

The SALT agreements, in short, may have been a diplomatic success in that they tend to stabilize mutual deterrence between the two superpowers, at least for the present, on the basis of each side's retaining a second-strike capability, but they have not served to achieve a cessation or any real limitation of the nuclear-arms race. In fact, many critics of SALT's lack of achievement say that these negotiations have only served to replace the quantitative arms race with an even more dangerous qualitative one. It seems that the agreements already concluded, and indeed those now being negotiated, are designed not to halt or reverse the arms race but rather to institutionalize and regulate it. They can, in fact, be regarded as blueprints for the continuation of the nuclear-arms race by the two superpowers.

The picture that emerges from these agreements is hardly likely to reassure the other nations of the world, nuclear as well as non-nuclear, that the arms race is being brought under control or that their security is being enhanced. The failure of the SALT negotiations to produce any real limitation or reduction of offensive strategic nuclear weapons, and the expansion of the arms race that will result from the Vladivostok agreement, will only serve to confirm the fears of the non-nuclear states that the nuclear powers are unwilling or unable to halt the nuclear-arms race.

The continuing credibility and viability of the Nonproliferation Treaty was in question even before India exploded its nuclear device. The failure of the nuclear superpowers to live up to their commitments under that treaty is likely to give added force to the arguments of those in the near-nuclear countries who, for a variety of reasons, also want to go nuclear. Some of the criticisms voiced by India were echoed by Japan when the text of the Nonproliferation Treaty was approved in 1968. The Japanese ambassador to the nonproliferation talks, Senjin Tsuruoka, warned: "Unless the nuclear-weapons states keep their part of the bargain... the treaty will lose its moral basis." And when the treaty went into force in 1970 Prime Minister Wilson of Great Britain said: "We know that

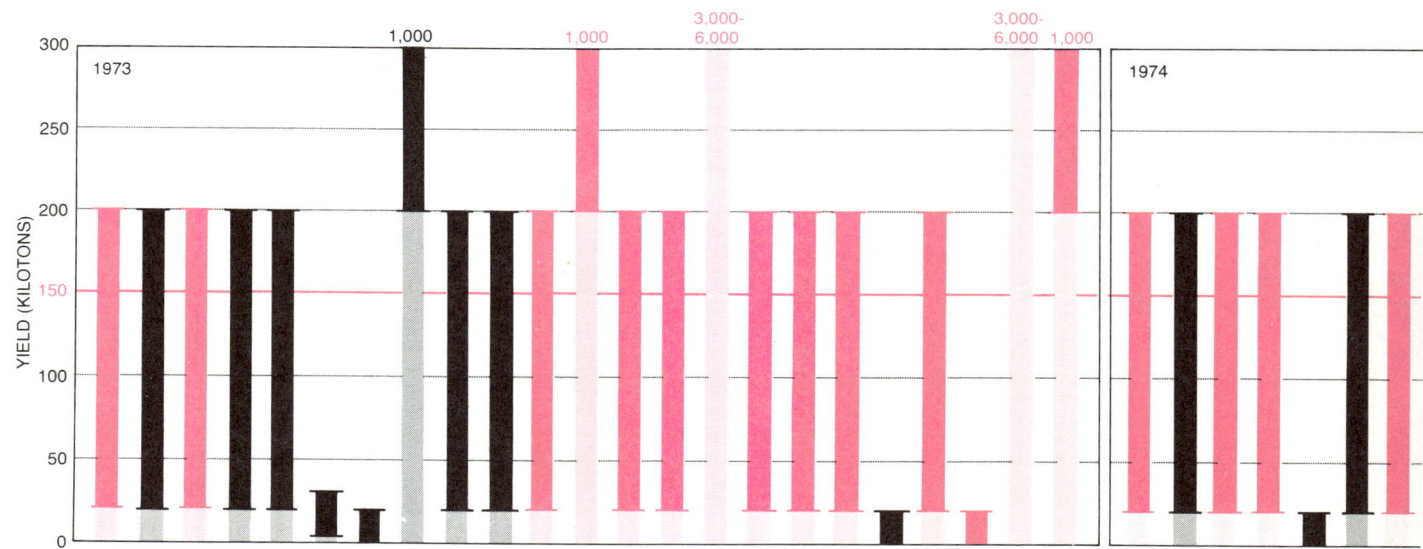

MOST UNDERGROUND NUCLEAR TESTS conducted by the U.S. and the U.S.S.R. in recent years have had yields well within the limit of 150 kilotons set in last June's Threshold Test-Ban Agreement. These bars, black for U.S. explosions and solid color for Russian ones, are based on data released by the U.S. Energy, Resources and Development Agency (formerly the Atomic Energy Commission), which announces yields only in terms of very broad ranges. Independent seismic evidence, obtained by the Research Institute of the Swedish National Defense, suggests that the yields of the great majority of tests in the announced range of 20

there are two forms of proliferation, vertical as well as horizontal. The countries...which are now undertaking never to possess [nuclear weapons] have the right to expect that the nuclear-weapons states will fulfill their part of the bargain."

Talk of the "nth-country problem" had gone out of fashion during the decade that had passed since China exploded its first nuclear device in 1964. After all, it was argued, France (which went nuclear in 1960) and China were great powers, if not as great as the two superpowers, then at least in a class with Great Britain. In any case, all five—and only these five—were permanent members of the Security Council and, as such, were given a special status under the UN Charter. Japan and West Germany were also great powers, but they were special cases as defeated enemy powers in World War II. Canada, Italy and Sweden were highly developed near-nuclear countries that could easily go nuclear, but they had no desire to do so if the nuclear club was confined to five members, and no need to do so since, with the exception of Sweden, they were protected by the American "nuclear umbrella." As for the rest of the world, although there were several countries with the potential of going nuclear, such as India and Israel, it was asserted that they were either too poor or too small and that they faced no serious immediate threat from their neighbors, such as might impel them to undertake an intensive program to become a nuclear-weapons state.

Surprisingly, it was the nonaligned non-nuclear states that had first proposed the nonproliferation of nuclear weapons: Ireland in 1958, followed by Sweden in 1961 and India in 1962. The U.S. and the U.S.S.R. were at first reluctant but finally came to see that it was even more in the interests of the nuclear powers to prevent the spread of nuclear weapons to additional countries. The idea took hold in the 1960's and finally culminated in the compact between the nuclear and the non-nuclear powers that was formalized in the Nonproliferation Treaty. The non-nuclear-weapons states agreed not to acquire or manufacture nuclear weapons or other nuclear explosive devices in exchange for the promise on the part of the nuclear-weapons powers to assist them in exploiting the peaceful uses of nuclear energy and to end the nuclear-arms race. A number of potential nuclear powers did not sign the treaty, including India, Pakistan, Israel, Spain, South Africa, Argentina and Brazil. Among the stated reasons for their not signing were considerations of security, the discriminatory nature of the treaty and the desire or need to develop their own capability in the field of peaceful uses of nuclear technology, including nonmilitary nuclear explosions.

Nevertheless, in the heady atmosphere of 1968, when because of the tacit alliance between the nuclear-weapons states and the least developed of the non-nuclear-weapons states the treaty was commended by the UN General Assembly by an overwhelming vote, it was felt that the danger of proliferation had been put to rest. It appeared that the momentum of a tidal wave of signatures would carry along some of the reluctant non-nuclear-weapons states and that the others would not dare to flout the opinion of the vast majority of the nations of the world. France announced that although it would not sign the treaty, it would behave exactly as though it had done so, and China was considered as comparatively unimportant and isolated. (China, although publicly supporting the idea of proliferation to Third World countries, is in fact the only nuclear power that has not provided any kind of nuclear assistance, military or peaceful, to other countries.) The U.S.S.R. was pleased that West Germany and all the North Atlantic Treaty Organization countries had agreed to sign the treaty. With the announcement, when the treaty was opened for signature on July 1, 1968, that the U.S.S.R. and the U.S. had agreed to begin the SALT negotiations, it was felt that the world was finally on the right road toward control of the nuclear-arms race.

Within four years of the entry into force of the Nonproliferation Treaty those high hopes had all but vanished. Moreover, they had vanished in spite of the settlement of the Berlin problem, the admission of China and the two Germanys to the UN, the withdrawal of American forces from Vietnam, the 1972 SALT agreements and the beginnings of a détente between the U.S. and the U.S.S.R.

The developing non-nuclear-weapons states on the whole felt that they had been cheated. They had received little in the way of assistance in exploiting the peaceful uses of nuclear energy, particularly in the area they were most interested in: nuclear reactors for the production of power. On the other hand, some of the more advanced countries (such as Italy, Japan and West Germany) that were not parties to the agreement seemed to have been treated better by the nuclear powers in this respect even though it was contrary to the terms of the Nonproliferation Treaty. Moreover, no negotiation had been started to set up an international regime to make peaceful nuclear explosions available to non-nuclear-weapons states, as was pledged by the treaty. Most disappointing of all, the nuclear-arms race was going full speed ahead. France and China continued to test in the atmosphere; the U.S. and the U.S.S.R. had not halted underground tests (on the contrary, they were conducting them at a greater rate than ever before); the Sea-Bed Treaty and the SALT agreements seemed to have been arranged more for cosmetic purposes than as real arms-control measures. On any showing, in spite of the pledges in the Nonproliferation Treaty, the arms race was proceeding apace, particularly in its technological and qualitative aspects, and the gap between the nuclear and the non-nuclear powers was steadily widening.

In addition the so-called security assurances to the non-nuclear-weapons states in the declarations of the nuclear-weapons states in the Security Council in June, 1968, had lost what little meaning they had ever had. With China having the power of veto, action by the Security Council to implement the assurances seemed at best doubtful.

Under the circumstances it was not surprising that even before the Indian nuclear explosion the Nonproliferation Treaty had lost a great deal of its force. The pent-up frustrations of a number of

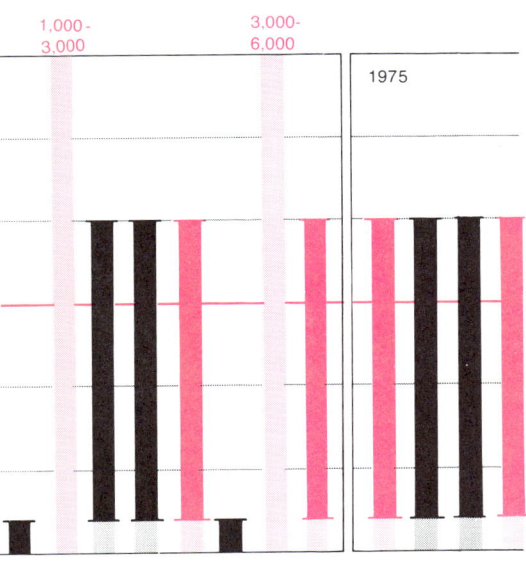

to 200 kilotons are toward the lower end of that range. The 150-kiloton restriction is not scheduled to go into effect until next year. Moreover, "peaceful" explosions may be excluded altogether from the final agreement.

non-nuclear-weapons powers may have found a psychological release in India's having breached the walls of the exclusive big-power club.

The Indian explosion also came at a time when there had been a sudden upsurge of interest in nuclear power as a source of energy. The energy crisis and the quadrupling of the price of oil have stimulated the search for alternative sources of energy and have made nuclear power much more economically attractive than it was before. There now appears to be a kind of commercial competition among a number of countries in the Western world to sell reactors, fissionable material and nuclear equipment. Sales to Argentina, Egypt, India, Indonesia, Iran, Israel and South Korea are merely the most publicized ones.

It may take a year or two for another country to explode a nuclear device, and several years for some of the other potential nuclear powers to do so, but there are about a dozen countries that can, if they choose, go nuclear over the next five years, and another dozen can do so over the following five years. Although few of these countries have their own chemical-separation plants for reprocessing the spent fuel from reactors into fissionable plutonium, such plants can be built without much difficulty. It has been estimated that a reprocessing plant capable of producing enough plutonium for two or three explosive devices a year could be built in a year by any reasonably advanced country at a cost of a few million dollars. Even if the cost has been grossly underestimated, it is clear that the amount of money involved is not large. Moreover, a French company stands ready to sell complete plutonium-reprocessing plants.

There would seem to be a kind of "domino theory" that is more applicable to countries going nuclear than to countries falling prey to a foreign ideology. Whether it is regarded as the nth-country problem or as a kind of chain reaction, each time a country goes nuclear it increases the incentives or pressures for its neighbors and other similarly situated countries to do so. Few doubted that once the U.S.S.R. had joined the U.S. as a member of the nuclear club all the other great powers would follow suit. As long as there was a "firebreak" between the big powers, which are permanent members of the Security

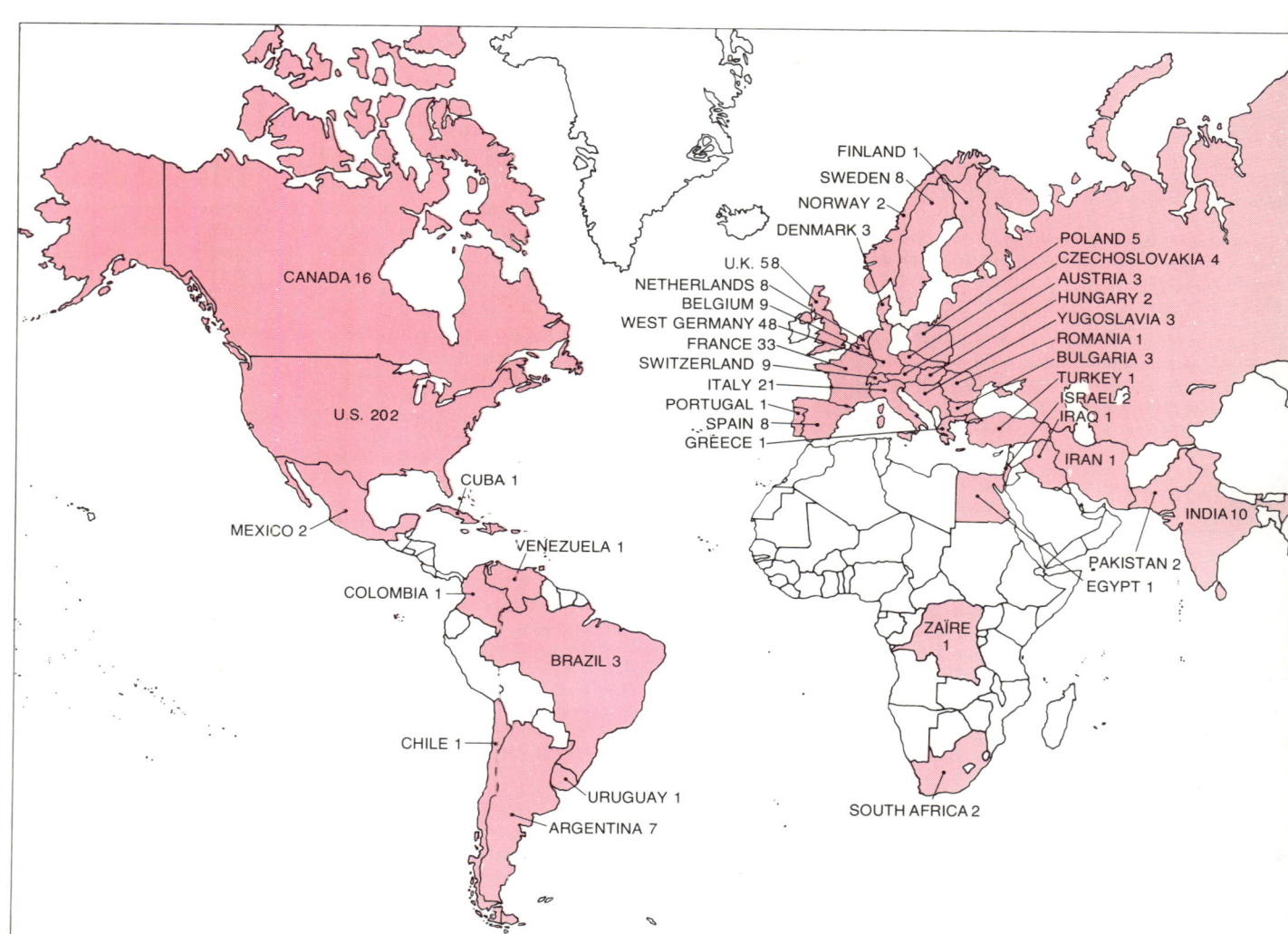

NUCLEAR REACTORS currently in operation or under construction in 48 of the 106 member states of the International Atomic Energy Agency (IAEA) are indicated on this world map. The numbers shown include both power reactors and research reactors; they are derived from the 1974 edition of *Power and Research Reactors in Member States*, published by the IAEA. In principle weapons-grade material (either plutonium or uranium) can be diverted from the fuel cycle of any fission reactor. The Nonproliferation Treaty provides that the parties agree to accept the safeguard procedures set up by the IAEA to prevent the "diversion of

Council, and all other powers there was a chance of holding the line against the further horizontal proliferation of nuclear weapons. Once a middle-sized or smaller power joins the nuclear club, however, there is little reason for other middle-sized or smaller powers to refrain from joining.

The countries that have not signed the Nonproliferation Treaty are the most likely candidates to go nuclear. They refrained from signing the treaty precisely because for one reason or another they wanted to keep their options open. The fact that India has now dared to go nuclear, with overwhelming domestic approval and comparatively little international criticism, may well encourage other countries to do so, or at the very least weaken those elements in such countries that oppose their going nuclear. The delays in ratification by countries that have signed the treaty but have not yet become parties to it is an indication of their desire to move slowly in this field. Each of these countries has its eye on the others, and what any one will do may depend on what others do. No country wants to be placed in a position of perceived inferiority to others. If one other country should go nuclear, it would be difficult to keep the dam from bursting. Even those countries that had ratified the Nonproliferation Treaty could withdraw on three months' notice. As one country after another went nuclear, it would not take long for some parties to give notice of their withdrawal. That would mark the inglorious end of the attempt to prevent the spread of nuclear weapons.

If this rather gloomy scenario is acted out, the prospect for world survival itself becomes rather gloomy. A serious problem arises from the fact that at least some of the new nuclear powers may not have the resources or the time to build sophisticated second-strike deterrent forces. They may opt for a small nuclear striking force that would provide them with local military superiority or with a deterrent against attack by a neighbor. The ultimate result will probably reduce rather than increase their security, as may well turn out to be the case with India if Pakistan, Indonesia or Iran should go nuclear.

The danger is that a small or middle-sized nuclear power involved in an acute crisis might fear that a nuclear neighbor might launch a first strike against it and in order to prevent such an attack might decide to launch a preemptive strike. Since the advantage would lie with whichever country struck first, that would create almost intolerable pressures to be the first to take action and could set off a nuclear war no one wants. Apart from the danger of the outbreak of such nuclear war by design, there is the more likely possibility of its happening as the result of accident, miscalculation, misinterpretation of orders, blackmail or sheer madness.

There are real dangers of such an "accidental" war even between the great nuclear powers, but the dangers are becoming less because of "hot line" communication links, better command and control, and the evolution of détente. In a world of nuclear first-strike powers the dangers become infinitely greater. If one could work out all the permutations and combinations of the possible ways in which such a war could begin, the probability of its beginning sooner or later would become almost a certainty. That a local or regional war could take place without involving the great nuclear powers is quite doubtful.

Prime Minister Gandhi has assured Pakistan and the world of "the peaceful nature and the economic purposes of this experiment" and has stated that "India is willing to share her nuclear technology with Pakistan in the same way that she is willing to share it with other countries, provided proper conditions for understanding and trust are created." One can only speculate whether or not such sharing would extend to the design of nuclear explosive devices either by agreement with Pakistan or by participation in a regional or a global international regime for the conduct of peaceful nuclear explosions under safeguarded conditions.

If India is sincere in its intention to use nuclear explosive devices solely for nonmilitary purposes, it should be prepared to convert this unilateral statement of intention into a binding legal commitment by treaty or otherwise on a bilateral, regional or global basis. It is likely that India would insist that any commitment it undertakes be universal and not selective or discriminatory.

One can certainly conceive of an international regime for the conduct of nonmilitary nuclear explosions, whereby all parties, including nuclear-weapons powers, would agree not to conduct such explosions themselves; they would instead be undertaken either by some international authority composed of nuclear powers or by some designated nuclear powers, and only after the project in question had been examined and approved by some international body. The parties would all have to pledge never to use such explosives for military purposes. It might well be in the interest of all the nuclear powers to agree to undertake any approved project free of charge; the costs are in any event quite small (from $150,000 to $600,000 per explosion). If they were free, it might provide some inducement to underdeveloped countries not to seek to acquire their own capability.

The Nonproliferation Treaty already commits the parties to create such an international regime and provides that the potential benefits of such explosives "will be made available to non-nuclear-weapons states party to the Treaty on a nondiscriminatory basis and that the charge to such parties for the explosive devices used will be as low as possible

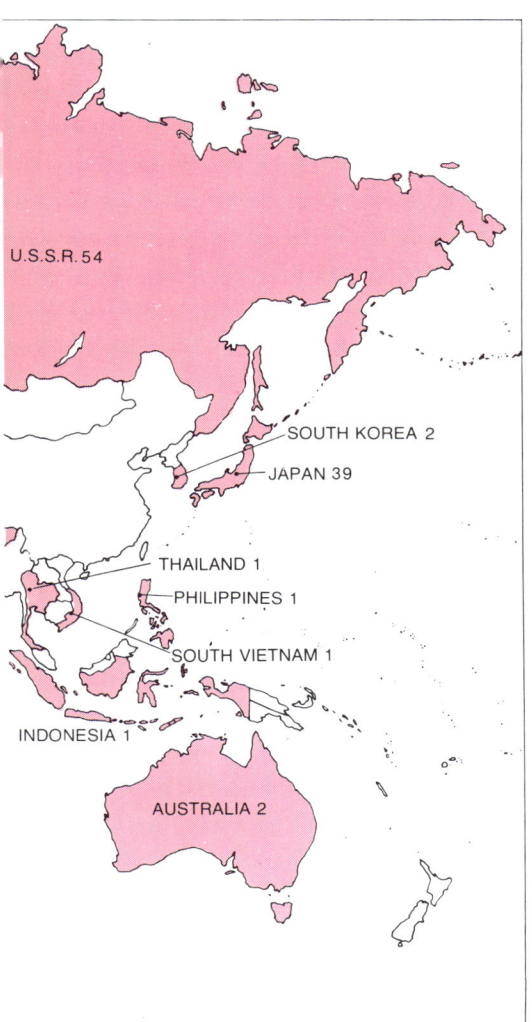

nuclear energy from peaceful uses to nuclear weapons or other explosive devices." The IAEA safeguards apply to all fissionable materials and all peaceful nuclear activities. China does not participate in the IAEA.

and exclude any charge for research and development." Because of opposition to the Nonproliferation Treaty, it might be better if the international regime were set up by the UN outside the framework of the treaty.

Although such an international regime would appear to be technically and legally feasible, it is far from clear that it would be politically acceptable either to the nuclear powers or to those nonnuclear states that might want to acquire their own explosive capability. Nevertheless, the idea is worth exploring.

An immediate step that might be undertaken would be to have a moratorium on all nonmilitary explosions by all powers, pending the examination of the idea of an international regime for such explosions. If the nuclear-weapons states would agree to such a moratorium, even if only for a fixed period of time, it might be possible to obtain the agreement of India and of all the other potential nu-

CANDIDATES FOR THE NUCLEAR CLUB

Of the countries that have not signed the Nonproliferation Treaty the most obvious candidate to join the second-rank club of nuclear powers is **Pakistan,** which has announced its intention to keep abreast of India. Pakistan, like India, has a nuclear power reactor supplied by Canada, fueled by enriched uranium. Unless Pakistan is helped by China or some other power, however, it may take several years before it acquires a plutonium-reprocessing plant and is ready to undertake testing. It is noteworthy that Pakistan is not a party to either the 1963 Partial Test-Ban Treaty or the Nonproliferation Treaty and therefore need have no legal inhibitions about testing in the atmosphere.

Argentina, like Pakistan, is not a party to the Partial Test-Ban Treaty or the Nonproliferation Treaty. In addition to having several nuclear reactors (under IAEA safeguards) Argentina is one of the few countries that have a plutonium-reprocessing plant. Thus Argentina is in a position to produce its own plutonium and to explode a nuclear device whenever it so decides. Argentina has also recently entered into a nuclear-cooperation agreement with India. If Argentina goes nuclear, **Brazil,** which has always upheld its right to conduct peaceful nuclear explosions and which regards itself as an emerging great power, will not be far behind. **Chile** also might decide that it too has to go nuclear.

South Africa, in addition to having several nuclear reactors (under IAEA safeguards), is one of the largest uranium-producing countries. Moreover, South Africa has announced that it has a new secret process for enriching uranium, in which case it can explode a uranium device without waiting to acquire a plutonium device. The vice-president of the South African Atomic Energy Board stated after the Indian explosion that South Africa has the capability of making a bomb and is more advanced in nuclear technology than India. He stressed that South Africa would use its available uranium and nuclear technology only for peaceful purposes (whatever that may now mean). Apart from military reasons, South Africa may have an additional incentive to go nuclear. If it has in fact invented a new process for enriching uranium, it will want to find markets for the sale of its enriched material. It has recently entered into an agreement providing for the sale of uranium to France, and it may want to explode a peaceful uranium device of its own to demonstrate the effectiveness of its enrichment process and the quality of its product.

Israel has repeatedly stated that it "will not be the first country to introduce nuclear weapons into the Middle East," a rather cryptic statement. Most experts believe that all that Israel needs to make an atomic bomb is to turn the last screw. The French-supplied reactor at Dimona, which is not subject to IAEA safeguards, has since 1964 had the capacity to produce enough plutonium to manufacture one bomb a year. It is not known, however, whether Israel has a plutonium-reprocessing plant. Although Israel does have a grave security problem, many observers believe that it has a tacit agreement with the U.S. not to go nuclear, in exchange for an American commitment to provide all the conventional armaments that Israel may need to defend itself against Arab attack. Nevertheless, it is generally believed that Israel may have several untested nuclear weapons that it might use in an extreme situation if the survival of its cities and people were in serious jeopardy. In December, 1974, President Katzir stated concerning nuclear weapons: "If we need them, we will have them." As long as the present uneasy truce continues, there is no reason for Israel to go nuclear, but if the negotiations should break down or an acute threat should suddenly arise, it is possible that Israel might wish to demonstrate its nuclear capability by exploding a nuclear device for peaceful purposes. The Indian test explosion will certainly make it easier for those in Israel who support such action to argue in favor of such a test.

Egypt has signed the Nonproliferation Treaty but has not ratified it and has announced that it will not do so unless Israel does. Egypt is far behind Israel in nuclear technology, and stories have circulated in the diplomatic world for some years that Egypt has asked India and other countries to help it acquire nuclear weapons or nuclear-weapons capability (without success). The agreement last June by President Nixon to provide two 600-megawatt nuclear power reactors, one to Egypt and one to Israel, has raised serious questions. Such a reactor could produce enough plutonium to make more than 10 medium-sized nuclear bombs a year. No matter what safeguards are written into the agreement, including placing the reactor under IAEA safeguards and returning the spent fuel to the U.S. for reprocessing, it is always possible for a country wanting to do so to evade its commitments or abrogate the agreement. In answer to those who oppose the supply or sale of nuclear reactors to Egypt and Israel, American officials say that if the U.S. does not go ahead, then France or some other country will do so and will probably not insist on safeguards as strict as those the U.S. would require. Because of Israel's opposition to placing all its fissionable material under international or American safeguards and inspection, the future of the agreement to supply reactors to Egypt and Israel is unclear. In any case Egypt is arranging to obtain a large power reactor from France.

Spain has not signed the Nonproliferation Treaty and has drawn attention to its discriminatory character and to Spain's security situation. Spain is the only large country in western Europe that is not a member of the North Atlantic Treaty Organization, although it does have various defense agreements with the U.S. It also has uranium re-

clear powers while the question was being studied. India cannot be too comfortable at the thought of her neighbors going nuclear, and the other potential nuclear powers would have little to lose by agreeing to the delay. Once again, however, as in all nuclear matters, the nuclear-weapons states would have to lead the way. It would clearly be in their interest to do so.

During the moratorium, or independently of it, it might be useful if another international group of experts were convened by the UN to consider all aspects of nonmilitary nuclear explosives. It is becoming clear that such devices are unlikely to bring the benefits that were hoped for. The first underground explosion was not detonated until 1957, and it is barely a decade since the exploration of the practical possibilities was undertaken. Here again nothing would be lost by allowing a year's delay for a more thorough study of the entire question.

---

sources, several nuclear reactors and a pilot plutonium-reprocessing plant, which would enable it to acquire a nuclear capability if it so chooses.

In the category of countries that have signed the Nonproliferation Treaty but not ratified it, the main countries are all potential nuclear powers. They include the technologically advanced Euratom countries: **West Germany**, **Italy**, **the Netherlands** and **Belgium**, all of which have several nuclear reactors. In addition there are plutonium-reprocessing plants in West Germany, Italy and Belgium. West Germany and the Netherlands are also partners with Great Britain in centrifuge plants for enriching uranium. West Germany is bound by a 1954 treaty not to manufacture nuclear weapons on its territory. All the Euratom countries have signed safeguard agreements with the IAEA, and West Germany, the Netherlands and Belgium have obtained approval from their parliaments to ratify the Nonproliferation Treaty. Italy, however, is reluctant to complete the process of ratification, and the entire matter is therefore in abeyance. Italy's reluctance seems to be linked to fears that other less advanced Mediterranean countries, such as Israel, Egypt or Spain, may go nuclear. It is questionable whether the other Euratom countries could or would go ahead with ratification without Italy. **Switzerland**, which is also advanced in nuclear technology, appears to be holding up its ratification of the treaty until the Euratom countries ratify it.

Japan not only has a highly developed nuclear technology but also has a plutonium-reprocessing plant. It can thus go nuclear whenever it chooses. Public opinion in Japan is overwhelmingly opposed to all forms of nuclear tests and weaponry, and Foreign Minister Toshio Kimura announced in September, 1974, at the UN General Assembly that Japan was preparing to ratify the Nonproliferation Treaty. Nevertheless, there is a small but growing tendency in Japan to delay ratification until the future of the Nonproliferation Treaty is clarified, and this tendency seems to have been strengthened by the Indian explosion. It is unlikely that Japan will deposit its instrument of ratification until it is satisfied that the Euratom countries will also do so. Rather surprisingly, some Chinese nuclear experts have privately urged Japan to go nuclear.

South Korea, although not as advanced technologically as Japan and the Euratom countries, does have two research reactors in operation and two power reactors under construction. Security problems are a major consideration for South Korea, but its ultimate decision whether or not to go nuclear will probably depend on what other countries do, particularly in that part of the world.

Indonesia also has a research reactor and appears to be in the process of acquiring some power reactors, which should not be difficult in the light of that nation's rapidly growing oil revenues. Following the Indian explosion there were public statements predicting that Indonesia would go nuclear or calling for it to go nuclear. It is not likely to do so, however, for several years.

Among the potential nuclear powers that are party to the Nonproliferation Treaty, **Canada** and **Sweden** are examples of countries that have had the capability for a number of years to go nuclear but have unilaterally decided that it is not in their interest to do so. Other countries with a highly developed nuclear technology are **Taiwan**, **Australia** and **Norway**, probably in that order. Taiwan also has a pilot plutonium-reprocessing plant and thus can quite easily exercise the nuclear option if it chooses, particularly if it regards its security as being in jeopardy. **Iran**, which now has a research reactor, is somewhat farther down the line, but it has recently embarked on a program to acquire 12 large power reactors and has entered into agreements with France, West Germany and the U.S. to obtain several power reactors. In addition Iran has an agreement with the U.S. whereby the U.S. will undertake enrichment work with Iranian uranium. Iran is also participating in the construction of a large uranium-enrichment plant in France. With its rapidly increasing wealth from oil, Iran can readily acquire a potential nuclear capability, and there are some elements in the country that are urging it to do so.

Apart from Israel, Egypt and Iran no other Middle East country has any potential nuclear capability at present. Nevertheless, the combination of the unstable political situation in that part of the world, the Arab-Israeli conflict and the vast wealth that is being accumulated by the oil-rich countries of the area would seem to make the Middle East an area of particular concern. There have already been press reports of countries in the region being interested in buying or otherwise acquiring nuclear weapons or nuclear-weapons capability. The Indian explosion will certainly not damp any such ideas; it might even tend to encourage them. Apart from action by governments of states in the region there is a growing danger that terrorists will try to steal a nuclear weapon or fissionable material for either blackmail or ransom. That danger will, of course, increase over the years as nuclear power reactors, fissionable materials and nuclear technology proliferate in the area and in the world at large. The world has not been conspicuously successful up to now in dealing with Arab hijacking and blackmail involving less dangerous weapons.

All the Warsaw Pact allies of the U.S.S.R. have been assisted by the Russians in the building of research reactors, and nearly all of them have power reactors in operation or under construction. **East Germany** and **Czechoslovakia** are the most advanced technologically. All of them are party to the Nonproliferation Treaty. It is clearly in the interest of the U.S.S.R. that none of them should acquire any nuclear explosive capability, and they are not likely to do so as long as the Nonproliferation Treaty remains an effective treaty and retains any legal or moral force.

Another idea that merits careful consideration is the possibility of establishing nuclear-free zones in different regions of the world. Among the lessons to be drawn from the creation of a nuclear-free zone in Latin America (by the Treaty of Tlatelolco, signed in 1967) is that the idea must have the sympathetic general support of all the important countries in the area. It is useless to think that a country can be maneuvered by political gamesmanship into agreeing to a treaty unless that country perceives the treaty as being in its own interest. It is also axiomatic that even if a country is a party to a treaty, it will not remain a party if it considers that events have caused the treaty to be contrary to its most important interests.

Finally, it has been suggested that the countries that export fissionable materials should form a "suppliers' club" and agree to supply nuclear materials and equipment only to those countries that would agree not to undertake nuclear explosions of any kind, to place all their nuclear facilities under IAEA safeguards and to return all spent fuel to the supplier countries for reprocessing. Such measures would, of course, be useful, but like any embargo they would be fully effective only if all supplier countries agreed to abide strictly by the rules.

In August, 1974, the U.S. joined other important supplier nations in a public undertaking contained in letters to the IAEA stating that it would not provide fissionable material or nuclear equipment to any non-nuclear-weapons state unless the material and equipment were subject to safeguards under an agreement with the IAEA. Some important supplier states, such as France and South Africa, have not, however, joined in the undertaking. Moreover, the agreement applies only to future supplies and does not affect previously supplied material. Even the regulations promulgated by Canada last December, which provide the strictest safeguards imposed by any supplier country, can be evaded by countries that build their own small reactors and plutonium-reprocessing plants, since most countries have at least low-grade uranium resources.

Unless the safeguards govern all nuclear activities (as is required by the Nonproliferation Treaty) and not merely current and future transfers of material and equipment, opportunities for evasion will remain. Moreover, it would seem to be highly discriminatory if any non-nuclear powers that are not party to the treaty could acquire nuclear materials, equipment or technology under less stringent conditions than parties to the treaty. In fact, if the non-nuclear powers that are not parties are subject to safeguards less strict than those required

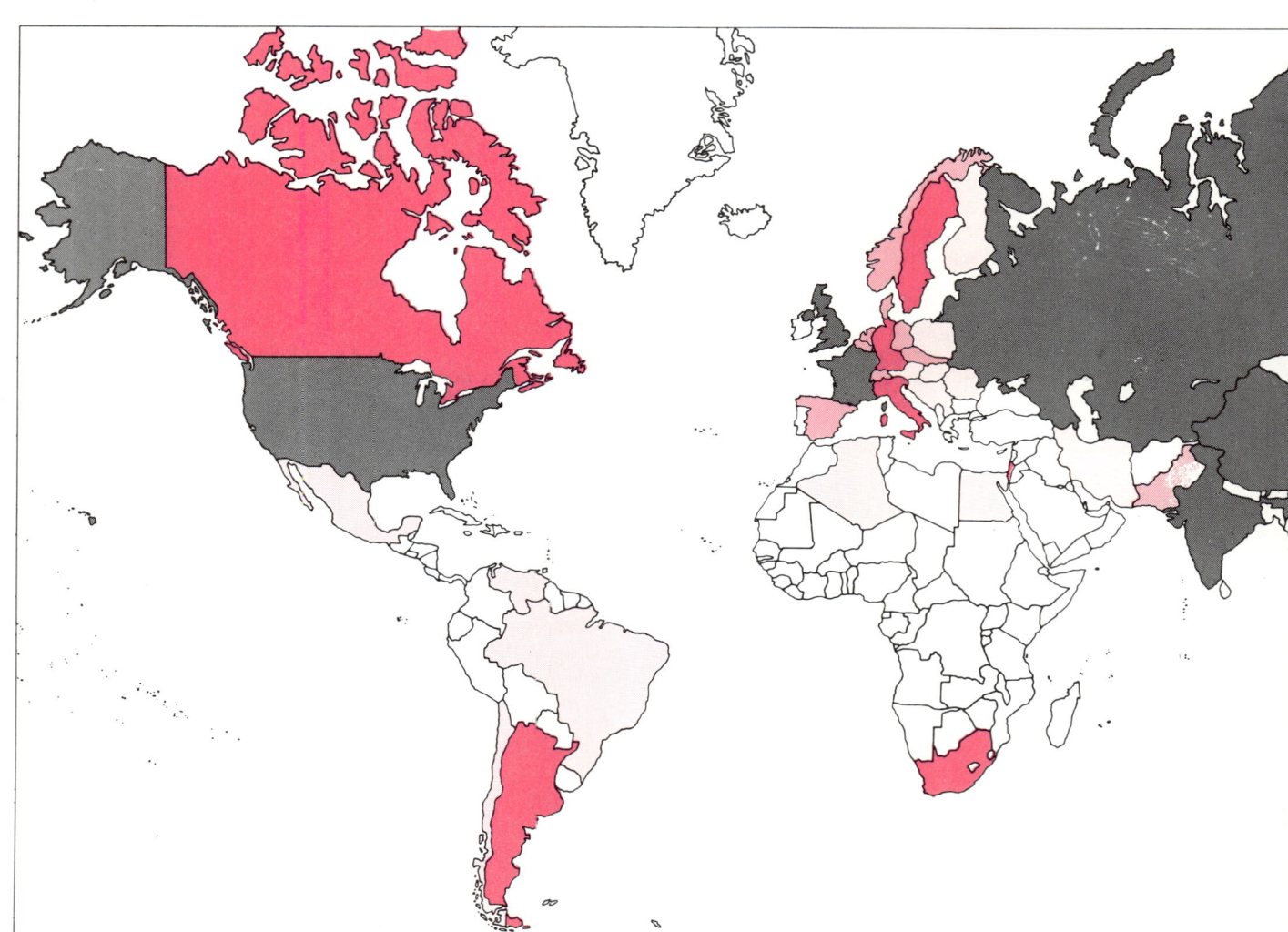

POTENTIAL FOR NUCLEAR PROLIFERATION is represented graphically on this world map. The six current members of the nuclear club are shown in gray. The eight near-nuclear countries (that is, those with the capability of making nuclear weapons in a comparatively short time, given the political decision to do so) are in the darkest color. The countries that would require a somewhat

of the powers that are parties, that would provide an inducement to avoid becoming a party.

One would have thought that, given the prospect of the further proliferation of nuclear weapons, the nuclear powers, which have the most to lose, would be galvanized into some kind of action in an attempt to prevent the emergence of a world of nuclear powers, but such is not the case. There is no evidence that the nuclear powers have any understanding of the seriousness of the situation. If they do have any such understanding, they have shown no urgency in attempting to cope with the situation.

There have been three sessions during the past year of a preparatory committee for the holding of next month's review conference in Geneva. In the course of these preparations the nuclear-weapons powers have given no indication that they have learned any lessons from the Indian explosion or that they have any intention of abiding by their commitments under the treaty. They of course want to see as many nations as possible become parties to the Nonproliferation Treaty, and they have attempted to put pressure on the Euratom countries and Japan to ratify the treaty before the review conference. It seems that the only other measures contemplated by them are to tighten the safeguard provisions of the treaty in order to ensure that in the future no fissionable material can be diverted to nuclear explosions of any kind, whether peaceful or military, by a non-nuclear state.

These objectives are commendable in themselves, but they hardly approach the requirements of the situation in the world today. The situation is that more and more countries will go nuclear unless it can be clearly demonstrated to them that it is in their interest not to do so. Sanctions in the way of withholding nuclear assistance are hardly likely to be effective against the newly rich oil-exporting countries in a situation where the nuclear powers and other supplier states are competing to sell nuclear reactors, materials and equipment to them. Nor are they likely to be more effective against the poor countries that are determined to close the gap between themselves and the rich countries and that see nuclear technology as one of the ways of closing it. Countries that are determined to evade controls will find ways to evade them. With China encouraging them to be more activist, and with the example of India as evidence that the wishes of the big powers can be flouted with impunity, they may attempt to exploit their sheer numerical majorities to engage in confrontations with the rich countries in order to extract concessions from them.

The longer-term goal of the underdeveloped countries is to readjust the balance between themselves and the developed countries, which means a more equitable sharing of the world's wealth. A shorter-term goal is to acquire nuclear capability either as a step toward attaining their longer-term goal or as a means of their using nuclear threats or blackmail to achieve political and economic gains, somewhat in the way that the oil-producing countries have used oil as a weapon.

Both the longer-term and shorter-term goals are still distant. The immediate preoccupations of the non-nuclear countries are their security and their economic and political situation. A decisive role with respect to the future of the concept of nonproliferation of nuclear weapons will be played by a handful of near-nuclear powers that have not signed the Nonproliferation Treaty. Whether or not these countries proceed to exercise the nuclear option within the next few years will depend in large part on the international climate of opinion. The Indian test explosion has undoubtedly weakened the entire principle of nonproliferation, but the situation may not be entirely hopeless. Domestic considerations and a country's perception of its security requirements, its role and status in the world and its aspirations for future economic development through the application of nuclear energy (whether rightly or wrongly held) will determine whether or not it decides to go nuclear. A most important element in these considerations will be the actions of the great powers, in particular the two superpowers. The standard of international behavior they set, particularly in the field of nuclear-arms control, is bound to have a great and perhaps decisive influence on the actions of the non-nuclear powers. The two superpowers must take the lead. They are the ones that must replace the ethic of the arms race by the ethic of arms control.

The U.S. and the U.S.S.R. must accept the burden of changing the world attitude toward nuclear weapons. Only they can halt and reverse the vertical proliferation of nuclear weapons, which is a necessary condition to preventing their horizontal proliferation. If they continue to militarize the world with both nuclear and conventional weapons, they can hardly expect that other countries will refrain from acquiring such weapons. They have the responsibility of establishing the illegitimacy of the nuclear-arms race and the legitimacy of nuclear restraint and arms control.

If it becomes clear at next month's review conference that the nuclear-weapons states are prepared to live up to the obligations they undertook in the Nonproliferation Treaty, then there is a chance that the treaty can be strengthened and reviewed. This is probably the last chance for the prevention of an uncontrolled nuclear-arms race. There is no guarantee, even if the nuclear-weapons states avail themselves of this last chance, that they would be successful in halting the trend toward proliferation. If they do not make a credible attempt to do so now, however, it would seem to be inevitable that other non-nuclear countries will follow the lead of India. We shall then all have to learn to live as best we can in a world full of nuclear powers.

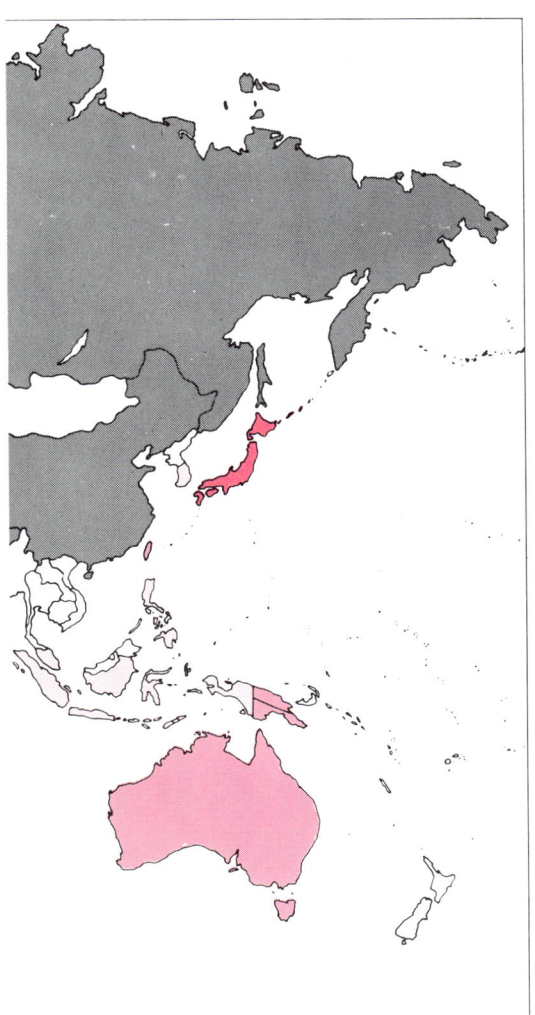

longer time to acquire a nuclear-weapons capability are represented in lighter shades of color: the lighter, the longer the time.

Nuclear Power, Nuclear Weapons and International Stability

by David J. Rose and Richard K. Lester
April 1978

Irresolution over domestic energy policy and the role of nuclear power may act to undermine current U.S. efforts to control the proliferation of nuclear weapons

A year ago this month the Carter Administration put before Congress a comprehensive national energy plan that included as one of its key components a revision of this country's long-standing policy on the development of civilian nuclear power. The proposed change, which would have the effect of curtailing certain aspects of the U.S. nuclear-power program and of placing new restrictions on the export of nuclear materials, equipment and services, was based explicitly on the assumption that there is a positive correlation between the worldwide spread of nuclear-power plants and their associated technology on the one hand, and the proliferation of nuclear weapons and the risk of nuclear war on the other. This point of view has become the topic of a lively debate; at the periphery of opinion some see nuclear war lurking behind every reactor on foreign soil, whereas others argue that the connection between civilian nuclear power and nuclear-weapons proliferation is vanishingly small.

We shall advance here the heretical proposition that the supposed correlation may go the other way, and that the recent actions and statements of the U.S. Government have taken little account of this possibility. In brief, it seems to us that if the U.S. were to forgo the option of expanding its nuclear-energy supply, the global scarcity of usable energy resources would force other countries to opt even more vigorously for nuclear power, and moreover to do so in ways that would tend to be internationally destabilizing. Thus actions taken with the earnest intent of strengthening world security would ultimately weaken it. We believe further that any policy that seeks to divide the world into nuclear "have" and "have not" nations by attempting to lock up the assets of nuclear technology will lead to neither a just nor a sustainable world society but to the inverse. In any event the technology itself probably cannot be effectively contained. We believe that the dangers of nuclear proliferation can be eliminated only by building a society that sees no advantage in having nuclear weapons in the first place. Accordingly we view the problem of the proliferation of nuclear weapons as an important issue not just in the context of nuclear power but in a larger context.

Fundamental tensions exist between the energy objectives and the nonproliferation objectives of U.S. policy, and on a different plane between the respective consequences of measures designed to achieve their primary effect either domestically or internationally. In what follows we shall analyze the complex set of interrelated issues that bear on the entire question of nuclear power and world security.

The most important of the new nuclear measures announced by the Administration last April were that the U.S. would defer indefinitely the reprocessing of spent nuclear fuel from domestic nuclear-power plants to recover and recycle plutonium and unused fissionable uranium, and that it would try to persuade other nations to follow its lead. Legislation submitted to Congress demonstrated the Administration's intention to restrict exports related to the nuclear-fuel cycle and to prevent the retransfer of exported U.S. nuclear technology to third parties. (A modified version of the Adminstration's nonproliferation bill has since then been approved by Congress.) Along with these restrictions the U.S. capacity to enrich uranium to standards suitable for use in conventional light-water (as opposed to heavy-water) reactors was to be increased to help meet the growing world demand for this service.

On the domestic front the regulatory requirements for installing light-water reactors were to be streamlined. The Administration also proposed a substantial slowdown of the U.S. program to develop a liquid-metal-cooled fast breeder reactor, a type of nuclear-power plant designed to create and consume fissionable plutonium out of the vast store of ordinary, nonfissionable uranium in the earth's crust. Specifically, the Clinch River breeder reactor, which was to have been built in Tennessee at a cost of some $2 billion, was scheduled for cancellation. The operation of breeder reactors requires reprocessing the nuclear fuel periodically, so that the retreat from fuel reprocessing and the deemphasis of breeder-reactor development complement each other. (Unfortunately the Clinch River reactor has become a focal point of the debate for both the critics and the proponents of nuclear power. The situation is doubly unfortunate because on the one hand that particular program was technologically and institutionally vulnerable and on the other the stopping of it has not helped resolve the deeper issues we discuss.)

The U.S. was also to redirect its nuclear research and development programs to place more emphasis on alternative fuel cycles and reactor designs that might offer reduced access to material suitable for use in nuclear weapons. This initiative has been carried into the world arena with the establishment of an international program to evaluate alternative technical and institutional strategies for the nuclear-fuel cycle.

In the months since the Administration's program was announced it has provoked much discussion within the U.S. and throughout the world. It has dissatisfied both critics and supporters of the U.S. nuclear-power program, and (partly because of the way it was presented) it has generated concern in many foreign capitals. Some of this country's partners in the development of nuclear power feel that they were not consulted adequately during the genesis of the new policy, and that policy communications, at least initially, have been clumsy and insensitive. Deeper-rooted anxieties underlie this irritation, however, since fuel enriched in the U.S. and reactors manufactured by U.S. companies still play significant roles in many national nuclear-power programs, and the effects of U.S. nuclear policies are widely felt.

What was the motivation behind the Administration's new nuclear policy and the related Congressional actions? Several possibilities come to mind. The first is simply that the Administration means what it says, namely that its goal is to increase international stability by taking actions thought to inhibit the proliferation of nuclear weapons. It would do so by reducing the availability of nuclear materials and technology helpful to a weapons program, even though the same materials and technology had hitherto been commonly assumed to be a part of civilian power programs.

Another possibility is that both the Administration and Congress are undecided as to whether the collapse of the U.S. nuclear industry is desirable. This indecision contributes to the Government's apparent inability to formulate a coherent nuclear-energy strategy.

It is also possible that the Administration announced its policy in sympathetic response to the critics of nuclear power but expects that the policy will not work, and that after this demonstration of good faith a new, more pragmatic program will be unveiled at an appropriate time. One danger in such a tactic is that the Administration might delay its denouement too long. The reaction to an Administration generally perceived to be resigned to the demise of nuclear power in the U.S., or even actively to desire it, might develop its own irreversible momentum.

It may also be that the Administration, frustrated by the diplomatic rigidity of world discussions about international security and arms limitation, is casting about for some new approaches. Such approaches are to be found; we hope that this article is an example. These four general motivations are not mutually inconsistent, and the Government could shift its priorities among them as the consequences of its actions unfold.

Various circumstances created the context in which the Administration formulated its national energy program and in which its set of nuclear-energy and nuclear-nonproliferation goals were to be pursued. The first circumstance was the urgent need to reduce the growing outflow of U.S. funds, currently running at more than $40 billion per year, to pay for imported petroleum. Such an expenditure, although not liable to bankrupt the country, was inconceivable as recently as 1973. Furthermore, the situation suggested excessive dependence on the policies of the principal oil-supplying nations. The increasing dependence on oil imports was (and is) seen as probably the major contributor to the U.S. energy problem.

The second circumstance was the presence of vast coal deposits in the U.S., amounting to perhaps 10 times the entire domestic oil and gas resource. Only 19 percent of the U.S. energy supply comes from the 650 million tons of coal currently mined each year. Estimates of the amount of coal recoverable at current prices with current technology range from 200 to 600 billion tons; thus even if coal production were to be tripled, the minimum estimate amounts to a 100-year supply. Moreover, the total amount of coal in the U.S. might be as much as 3,000 billion tons recoverable eventually at increased cost—a quarter of the earth's known reserves. Besides coal, an energy resource equivalent to perhaps 1,000 billion tons of coal resides in the oil-shale deposits in the vicinity of northwestern Colorado. Technological advances would surely make many of these resources available later, it was thought. In no absolute sense is the U.S. "running out of energy." Thus arose the goal of increasing coal production rapidly, to several times the present rate by the year 2000. In this

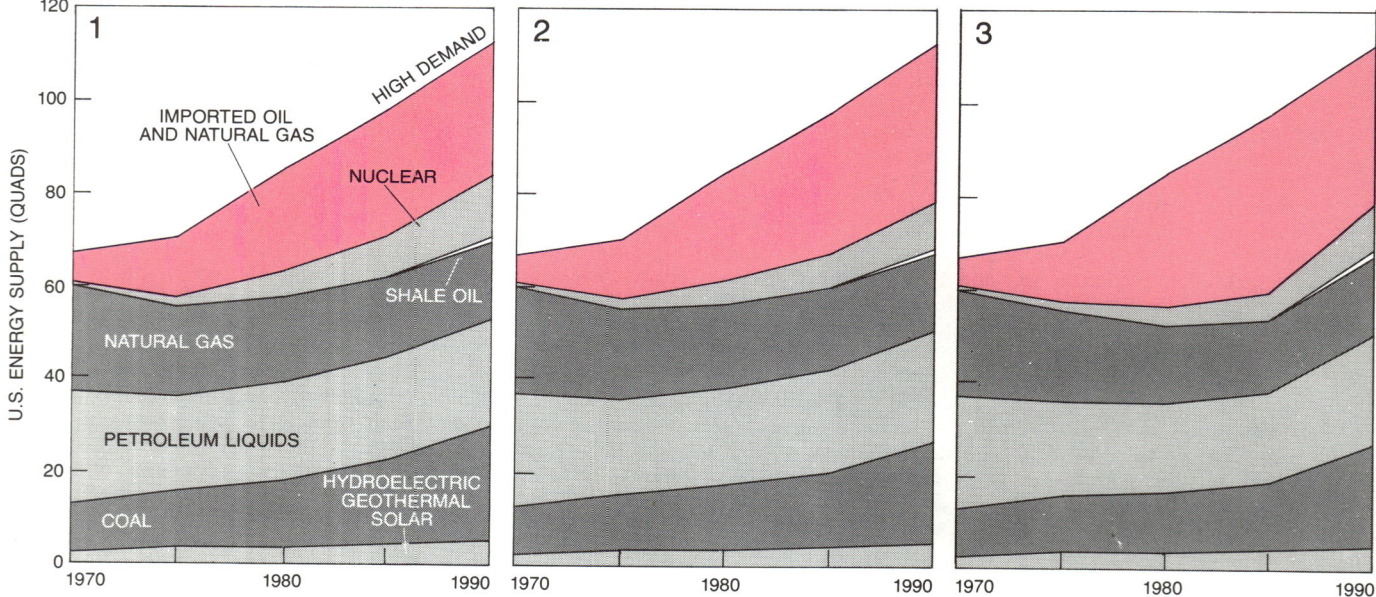

ALTERNATIVE U.S. ENERGY PROJECTIONS through 1990 are outlined in the set of graphs beginning on these two pages. The graphs represent 12 possible demand-and-supply scenarios constructed by the staff of the Congressional Research Service on the basis of different assumptions about economic growth rates, energy prices, the elasticity of energy demand and the constraints on various energy supplies. The tables from which the graphs were drawn were compiled in the course of a two-year study conducted at the request of several committees of Congress responsible for dealing with energy-related issues; the data appeared originally in *Project Interdependence: U.S.*

way the U.S. could reduce its dependence on imported petroleum, and perhaps also afford a more leisurely nuclear program.

The third circumstance was that energy conservation began to be taken seriously. Many studies under way between 1975 and 1977 showed not only that substantial increases in energy efficiency were possible but also that much energy was being wasted. Energy conservation had received significant recognition but little actual support during the previous Administrations, and Congress had not been overactive compared with what could have been done.

Several arguments had been marshaled against conservation, the main one being that economic activity and energy use were closely bound; hence restricting energy use would probably exacerbate a recession or cause one. In the short term energy and economic activity are indeed closely bound, because machines use energy, and they cannot be replaced overnight. By replacing more energy-intensive machines at the end of their life span with more energy-frugal ones, however, the energy demand could be cut in a matter of decades by 1 or 2 percent per year from what would have been otherwise forecast. With an economic growth rate of 3 or 4 percent per year, energy use might then grow at only half that rate; by the year 2000 the gross national product would have almost tripled, and the energy used per unit of economic output would decline to about 60 percent of its present value. Even so, domestic energy use would have increased by a factor of approximately 1.6, through the diligent exploitation of coal, solar power, light-water reactors and perhaps other technologies. (These numbers are meant only to indicate what many energy planners thought would be possible.)

The fourth major circumstance relates to several aspects of nuclear power itself. First, the U.S. industrial capacity to make light-water reactors is large—perhaps too large. A substantial part of this capacity would be needed to produce some of the base-load electric-generating plants, leaving coal for other electric plants and many other uses. Second, the nuclear-power industry, beleaguered by critics of many persuasions and by a Nuclear Regulatory Commission that it had come to regard as increasingly demanding, also needed some organizational relief. Thus arose the goal of simplifying procedures for fulfilling siting and other licensing requirements. The light-water-reactor industry was to be encouraged by these activities, and electric utilities would be encouraged to "go nuclear" by building light-water reactors wherever such plants were economically attractive.

The fifth circumstance relates to the uranium resources, particularly in the U.S., with which to fuel all those light-water reactors. Each reactor that produces 1,000 megawatts of electric power requires about 5,500 tons of uranium (in the form of uranium oxide) to operate during an expected 30-year life span. The Administration knew that the equivalent of about 680,000 tons of uranium oxide had been located in deposits in the U.S. with characteristics that would make economic recovery possible with current technology, together with an additional 140,000 tons that will be available between now and the end of the century as a by-product of other mineral-extraction operations. It also estimated that roughly another three million tons would be found when it was necessary and that this amount could be produced at a cost of $50 per pound or less. All this uranium would fuel about 700 reactors for their full life span or an even larger number if a full lifetime commitment of fuel were not made for each plant when it began operation.

Considering also that nuclear-power stations take 10 years or more to build and that orders would increase gradually, the Administration judged that adequate nuclear fuel would be available to last several decades into the next century. All this could be done without reprocessing spent fuel from the reactors. Besides, a number of studies had shown that the recycling of uranium and plutonium in the current generation of light-water reactors would at best be only marginally attractive economically and could in fact result in higher fuel-cycle costs than a "once through" fuel cycle.

This brings us to the sixth circumstance: the Administration's concern about the connection between the technology of nuclear-fuel reprocessing and the development of a nuclear-weapons capability. The past few years have brought increasing doubt about the ability of international safeguards to function satisfactorily in a "plutonium economy," that is, one in which large amounts of plutonium would be present at various stages of the fuel cycle in comparatively extractable form. The objective of international safeguards is

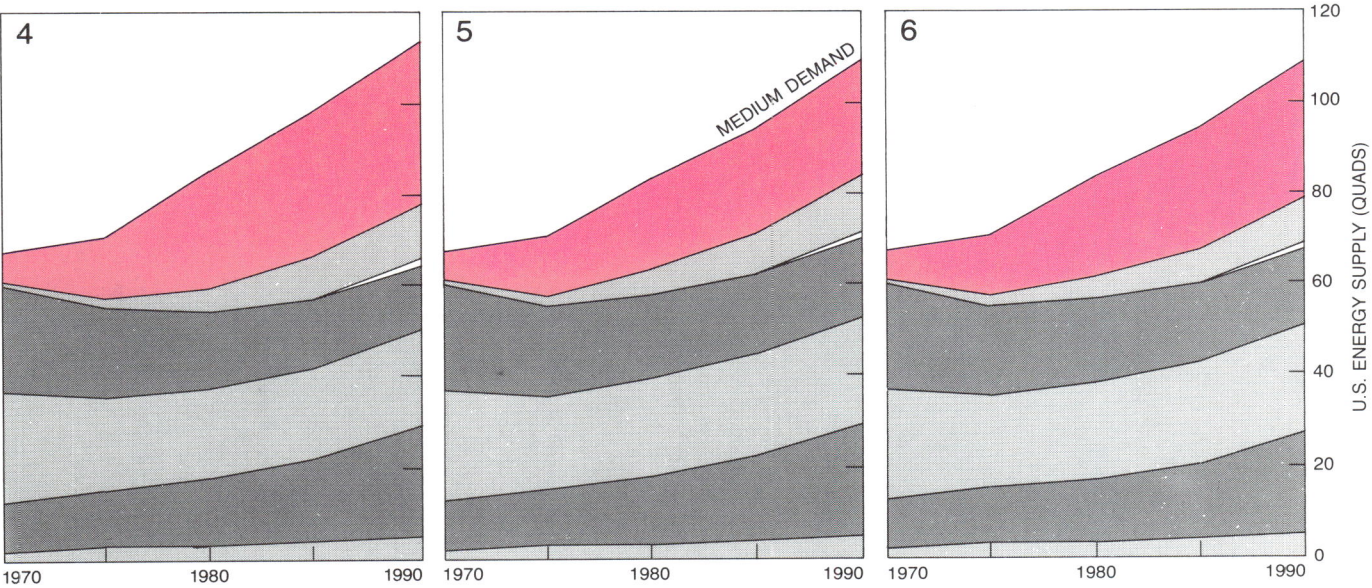

and *World Energy Outlook Through 1990*, a 939-page report published in November by the U.S. Government Printing Office. The first six scenarios in the set, depicted in the graphs on these two pages, are characterized as follows: high demand, high coal and nuclear supply (*1*); high demand, medium supply (*2*); high demand, low supply (*3*); high demand, low oil and gas supply, high coal and nuclear supply (*4*); medium demand, high coal and nuclear supply (*5*); medium demand, medium supply, also referred to in the study as the "base case" (*6*). All figures are given in "quads": quadrillions (10^{15}) of British thermal units. The graphs are continued on the next two pages.

to detect the theft or diversion of nuclear material by nations early enough for diplomatic or other international countermeasures to achieve their objective before the material can be made into an explosive. It was argued, however, that plutonium that had been recovered by spent-fuel reprocessing and then recycled could be turned into an explosive so rapidly after national diversion of the recycled fuel that the ability of the safeguards system to work adequately would be fatally undermined, even if the loss of material were detected. International safeguards do not prevent diversion; they deter it through the threat of timely detection. If plutonium were adopted as a commercial fuel, the deterrence effect of safeguards would be lost. In addition, the presence of plutonium would increase the risks of nuclear terrorism, and there were unresolved questions about the effectiveness of the predominantly national safeguards that would be introduced to deal with this threat.

If, on the other hand, there were no reprocessing, there would be no plutonium either to fuel breeder reactors or to make plutonium-based nuclear weapons; a nation that did not reprocess the fuel from its nuclear-power reactors could not then imperceptibly slip into the position of having a nuclear-weapons capability, and it could not in some temporary passion easily pervert a civilian nuclear-power program. Either it would have to extract almost pure fissionable uranium 235 from natural uranium, an activity that is associated with nuclear weapons and not at all with conventional light-water or heavy-water reactors, or it would have to flagrantly set about reprocessing used reactor fuel to extract plutonium. Furthermore, both of these activities are widely thought to be beyond the present capability of any subnational group acting clandestinely.

If the U.S. was mainly worried about the international proliferation of nuclear weapons, why then did it stop the domestic reprocessing of nuclear fuel? The best answer seems to be that in order to argue its case persuasively, it would have, so to speak, to come to court with clean hands.

To be sure, breeder reactors would be delayed, perhaps indefinitely if some better prospect such as economic central-station solar power or controlled fusion came along. Clearly the latter options were to be encouraged. Meanwhile even the U.S. breeder program was to benefit because there would be time to explore a more varied set of technological options, both conceptually and through experiments on a modest scale. Far from being canceled, the breeder program would take on a needed diversity; perhaps more nearly proliferation-proof fuel cycles could be found.

Many doubts about the public acceptability of nuclear power had built up, and the new goals would surely be seen as being responsive to those doubts: no plutonium, no reprocessing, no breeder reactor in this century and so forth. Meanwhile little public concern had yet arisen over the social, environmental or health hazards of coal, the energy-supply option the Administration planned to promote most vigorously.

The Administration's perception of this complex issue can be analyzed with the aid of a sequential logic diagram, which is useful in clarifying some of the main proliferation-related trains of thought and their impact on international security [see illustration on pages 212 and 213]. Two main paths appear in the diagram. First, there is a horizontal decision path that could be followed by a nation (let us call it Y) that does not now possess the nuclear technologies in question. The central questions affecting international stability are whether or not nation Y decides to develop a general capability with respect to nuclear weapons and, once it has decided to do so, how long it would take to acquire that capability. The second path consists of several vertically arranged inputs to Y's decisions. The U.S. sees the capability to reprocess nuclear fuel as a stimulant to weapons proliferation because Y would then have a source of weapons-grade fissionable material; such accessibility might be instrumental in a decision by Y to acquire nuclear weapons, and in any case once the decision had been made the reprocessing capability would help Y to move toward the right in the diagram: toward the weapons themselves.

The sequential arrangement of events depicted here is too simple. A decision to acquire nuclear weapons might be a prolonged process, and it could be made in parallel with (or could even follow) the acquisition of some of the technological components of a civilian nuclear-power program, which would also be useful for the development of a weapons system. For example, that would be the case with a commercial reprocessing

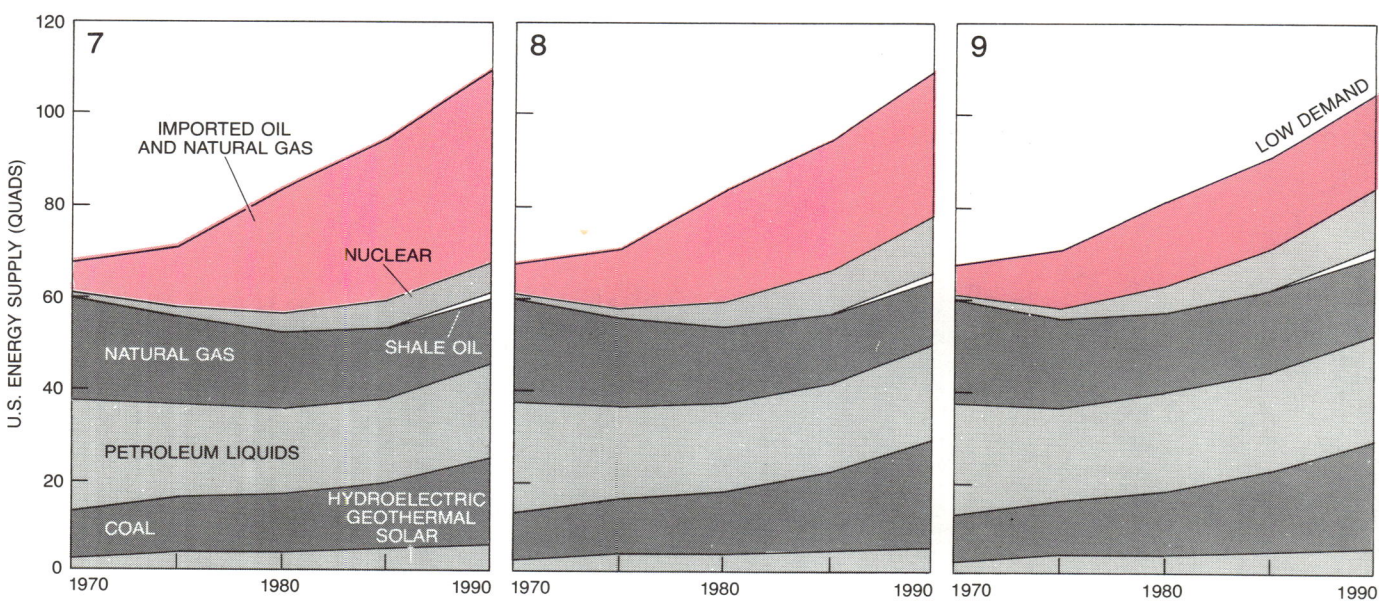

U.S. ENERGY ALTERNATIVES are continued on these two pages. The characterizations of the six remaining scenarios in the Congressional Research Service study are as follows: medium demand, low supply (7); medium demand, low oil and gas supply, high coal and nuclear supply (8); low demand, high coal and nuclear supply (9); low demand, medium supply (10); low demand, low supply (11); low demand, low oil and gas supply, high coal and nuclear supply (12). The authors of the *Project Interdependence* report point out that even with a low energy-demand projection coupled with high coal use, an expanded nuclear-power capacity, an increase of about 50

plant, assuming that in its normal operating procedure it produces plutonium separated partially or completely from the other constituents of irradiated fuel. Such a reprocessing plant would therefore be ambiguously perceived by observers, even if that were not the intention of a peaceful nation Y. The Administration saw that by blocking the connection at the top of the figure a substantial barrier would be erected against Y's either sidling consciously or sliding unconsciously into a technological competence applicable to the manufacture of weapons.

Of course, the Administration realized that other routes exist whereby Y could obtain fissionable material suitable for weapons. First, it might import the necessary technology from elsewhere, but for some time the U.S. has been actively attempting to close those routes by seeking to persuade the other major suppliers of nuclear materials and equipment (through bilateral channels and in the multilateral forum of the London Suppliers Group of nuclear exporting nations) to exercise restraint in the transfer of "sensitive" items that might offer increased access to weapons-grade material.

All the other routes involve a conscious decision by nation Y and a substantial effort on its part. It could develop its own civilian fuel-reprocessing technology, fully intending peaceful uses only, then have it subverted later after a change of attitude on the part of its government. Alternatively, it could attempt the production of weapons-grade plutonium in research reactors (as India did for its 1974 nuclear explosion) or in a small clandestine reactor, in either case recovering the plutonium from the irradiated fuel in a small reprocessing plant built expressly for the purpose, a task much easier (and cheaper) than the development of the technology and the construction of the plants for commercial reprocessing. Still another alternative could involve diverting irradiated commercial fuel to a clandestine reprocessing plant from a temporary storage facility, where it might have been awaiting either commercial reprocessing or, in the case of a once-through fuel cycle, ultimate disposal.

Rather than work with plutonium from spent fuel Y might attempt to extract the fissionable isotope uranium 235 either from natural uranium (which contains less than 1 percent U-235) or from the low-enriched uranium used for power-reactor fuel (about 3 percent U-235), concentrating it to, say, 90 percent. For this approach there are several candidate technologies at various stages of development. For the past 25 years practically all enrichment, either for power-reactor purposes or for the production of weapons-grade uranium, has been carried out in the huge gaseous-diffusion plants of the U.S. and the U.S.S.R. Gaseous-diffusion plants do not need to be built on such a heroic scale, however; furthermore, other enrichment technologies now challenge the dominant position of gaseous diffusion. Ultracentrifuge enrichment is being actively developed in several countries and is on the verge of commercialization in some of them. It requires less power than gaseous diffusion and has other advantages as well. These factors, together with the greater operational flexibility of centrifuge plants, suggest that this technology would offer a smoother path to weapons material, either with a plant built specifically for that purpose or through a facility built initially to fulfill civilian nuclear-power needs. It would be much easier to carry out the adjustments necessary to convert a gas-centrifuge plant from a low-enriched product to a high-enriched military-grade one than it would to similarly convert a gaseous-diffusion plant; alternatively a small string of centrifuges can be used over and over again progressively to enrich single batches of uranium.

Other enrichment technologies that are gaining in importance include the aerodynamic, or nozzle, approach, variations of which are being developed concurrently in West Germany and South Africa, and the laser technique for isotope separation, which is also being pursued in several countries. A pilot aerodynamic-enrichment plant in South Africa may have already been used to produce enough weapons-grade uranium for one or more explosive devices. Furthermore, although work on laser enrichment has so far been limited to laboratory research, enough information has been made available to suggest that the technique might ultimately provide a cheaper and more flexible route than any other enrichment process. All the known methods, at whatever stage of development, require sophisticated technology but nothing that is beyond the capability of many of the more advanced developing nations.

Turning to seemingly more bizarre ac-

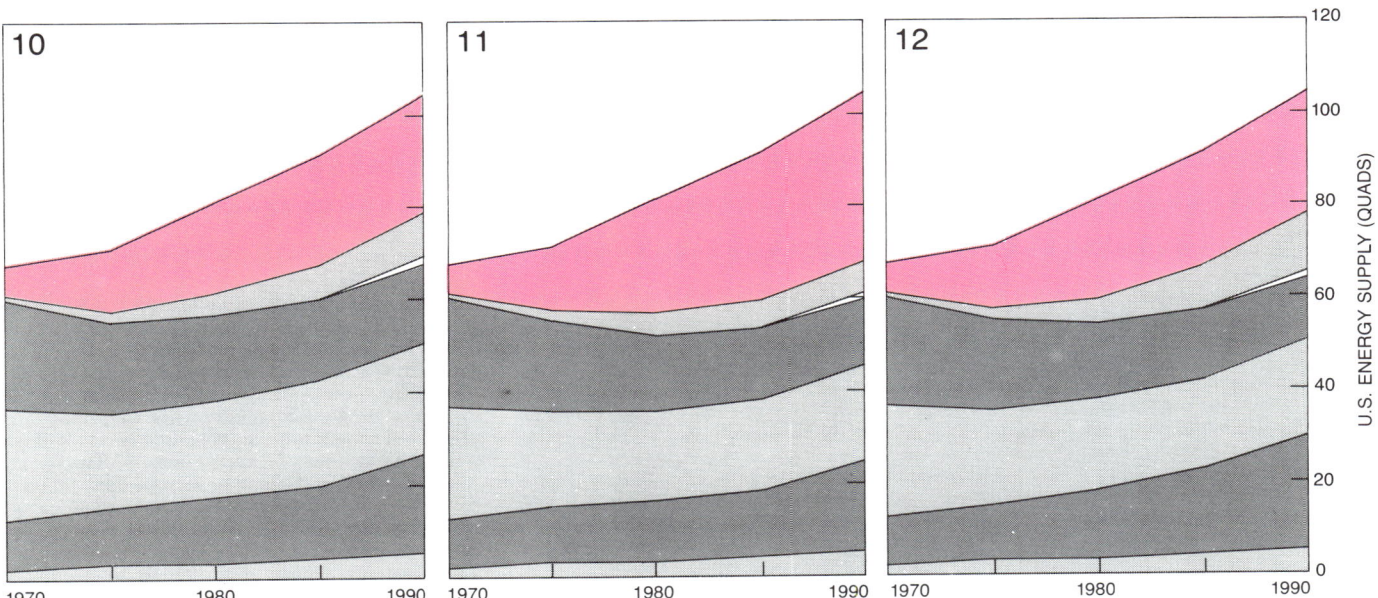

percent in additions to domestic natural-gas reserves and a 100 percent increase in additions to domestic oil reserves compared with the preceding decade (*scenario No. 9*) the U.S. would still have to import close to 20 quads of energy by 1985, equivalent to almost nine million barrels of crude oil per day. On the other hand, if the rate of economic growth is greater than the 3.5 annual increase in gross national product projected in the base case and all areas of domestic energy supply turn out to be less productive than expected (*scenario No. 3*), the U.S. could be importing 17.7 million barrels of crude oil per day in 1985. The role of imported oil as a "swing" fuel (*color*) is evident.

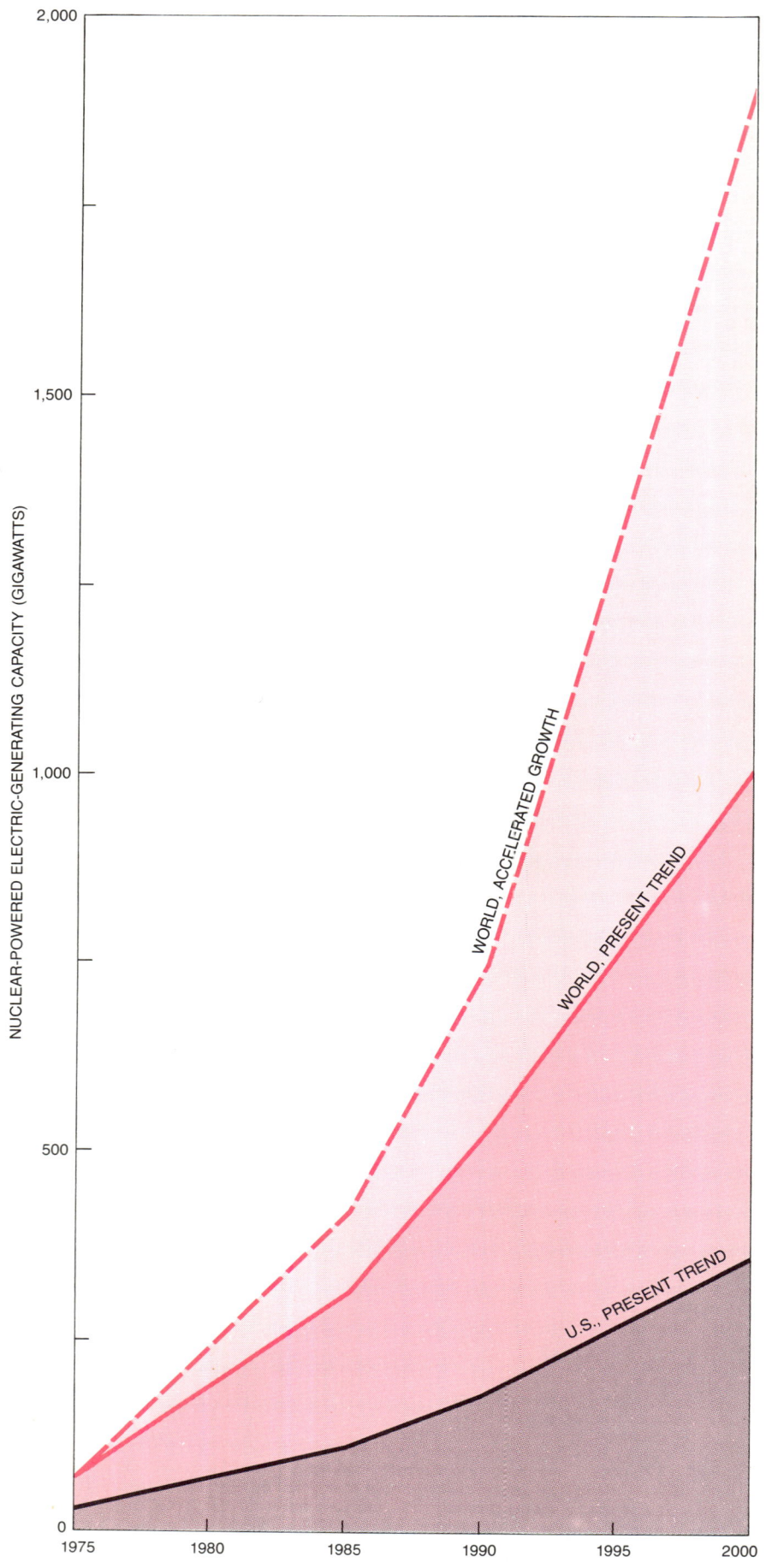

tivities, country *Y* might employ agents to steal material from abroad or buy it in a black market, an open market or an intermediate "gray" market. It could receive such material as a gift or a loan from another government. It might steal an assembled weapon or even be given one. None of these activities can be excluded, and some may be more likely to occur than those we described above.

A really effective barrier to weapons proliferation would involve blocking all the lines marked with a black bar in the diagram. That is impossible, but the U.S. is only trying to make weapons proliferation substantially more difficult. Combining technological denial with an assortment of incentives related to the supply of enrichment services for light-water-reactor fuel (to be used by *Y* under tightly specified conditions) would, the Administration thought, significantly increase international stability.

Several other decision paths of a different nature exist, on which the U.S. Government has only an indirect influence; the principal ones are marked with gray bars. Why does *Y* decide to acquire a weapons capability in the first place? Why does it actually build nuclear bombs? Why might it use them? The answers to such questions depend on many things, and a long-term policy not to proceed at any one of these decision points makes all the technological elaborations irrelevant. The converse, however, is not necessarily true. As we implied when we were discussing reprocessing plants, a decision to proceed might be heavily influenced by the technological capability in place at that time.

When the U.S. policy described here is viewed from other countries or other domestic vantage points, it looks quite different. The main line of devel-

POTENTIAL TRENDS in the growth of nuclear power are shown through the end of the century for both the U.S. and the world (excluding China, the U.S.S.R. and the other countries of Eastern Europe). For the world the lower estimate is based on present trends in energy utilization and supply, including delays in the construction of new nuclear reactors, and assumes a continuation of these trends. The "accelerated growth" estimate assumes that the goals of ambitious nuclear programs will be met and that the world will return to higher rates of energy growth. The "present trend" estimate must be regarded as the more realistic of the two and may itself be too high. The data for these curves were obtained from a recent joint report by the nuclear-energy agency of the Organization for Economic Cooperation and Development (OECD) and the International Atomic Energy Agency (IAEA). U.S. projection is based on recent estimates by the Department of Energy. All such estimates must be viewed with caution, the authors point out, in view of the many uncertainties discussed in their article.

opment—in particular decisions by nation Y—can best be discussed in relation to a second diagram, which is similar to the first but starts with a U.S. decision to act restrictively and includes several additional logic paths. To understand its full significance we must start farther back, with the electric-power sector.

The U.S. electric-power industry abhors uncertainty about the future, for several reasons. One is the long time needed to construct new facilities (10 years is typical) and long expected life of these facilities (40 years, say). The industry also needs a stable fuel supply and is required by law to provide reliable service. In this regulated industry justifiable costs can be charged to the consumer. The present program of the Administration increases uncertainty about the future of nuclear power for several reasons. First, the decision against reprocessing spent fuel has raised fears, not yet completely alleviated by the Federal Government, that the electric utilities may in practice be left holding the spent fuel for a long time (for example by long-drawn-out court challenges to the Environmental Impact Statement for a Federal spent-fuel storage facility), a very unappealing prospect to them.

In addition, conflicting Federal opinions about the acceptability of nuclear power make the electric utilities both suspicious of Government motivations and better targets for anti-nuclear-power groups. Many electric utilities also fear that the Nuclear Regulatory Commission will order expensive, and in their view capricious, retroactive modifications to existing nuclear plants, in spite of current efforts to modify the Commission's legislative foundation. Many experts, concerned at the inherent uncertainty associated with the four-million-ton estimate for U.S. uranium resources that could ultimately be made available, feel that a "prudent planning estimate" for the purpose of setting nuclear-power policy should be appreciably lower. A National Academy of Sciences resource-evaluation group recently estimated that 1.8 million tons is all that is likely to be mined in the U.S. by the year 2010 at a cost of $30 per pound or less, even with a Government policy of maximum stimulation.

Furthermore, doubts have been expressed as to whether the U.S. uranium-supply industry, itself troubled by uncertainty about the size of the market for its product, will be prepared to invest in exploration, mining and ore-processing-plant construction at levels that will be sufficient to fuel a growing number of nuclear-power plants. Part of the uncertainty permeating the electric-utility sector stems from concern over the availability of nuclear-fuel supplies, so that the problem exhibits circular characteristics; it is also aggravated by the fact that the strength of the uranium supply industry's commitment to keeping power reactors adequately fueled is less than the utilities might find desirable. For example, it has been estimated that within a few years petroleum companies will own about 40 percent of all U.S. ore-processing capacity and as much as 50 percent of low-cost U.S. uranium resources. In short, the uranium suppliers do not constitute an industry "captive" to the electric-power sector. (Indeed, increasing corporate diversification in the various energy supply industries has led to the suggestion that the reverse might be true.) As a result uncertainty arising from the Administration's program may be compounded, unwittingly or otherwise. Similarly, each U.S. manufacturer of nuclear reactors has 75 percent or more of its business elsewhere (for example in other power systems), and the nuclear business is not essential to it. In a period of rising costs, large-scale cancellations of orders and excess production capacity, the business appears less than inviting.

The last point is worth further comment. The U.S. manufacturers of light-water reactors could turn out between 20 and 30 nuclear-power systems a year. The Administration has estimated that full implementation of its national energy policy would lead to an installed nuclear electric capacity of more than 300,000 megawatts by the year 2000. With 50,000 megawatts already installed, and a further 25,000 megawatts scheduled for completion by 1980, there would be, on the average, a dozen or so reactor systems completed each year for the last 20 years of the century, a situation that implies a large-scale restructuring of the reactor-manufacturing industry sooner or later.

Compounding these difficulties, the electric-utility sector suffers the additional one of raising enough capital. One cause is the host of uncertainties we have described. Another involves the general flight during recent inflationary times from long-term investment; the rate of economic return from the regulated utility industry has become unattractive, a circumstance that also affects other generating plants, particularly those that burn coal.

The upshot of all this is the paradoxical situation that although the existing nuclear reactors run pretty well and deliver economical electric power in many parts of the country, the nuclear industry in the U.S. may nonetheless be close to collapse. The proximate cause is a movement by the electric-utility industry and manufacturers away from nuclear power as they attempt to reduce their own institutional uncertainty, but deeper causes drive these changes and are coupled with the Administration's attitude toward nuclear power. This train of thought points toward the second possible motivation mentioned above: that the Administration, through internal indecision, is incapable of acting to prevent the nuclear industry from collapsing. The indications, however, are ambiguous.

What then is the U.S. electric-utility sector likely to do? The conventional option is coal, with the Administration's apparently enthusiastic backing. Oil and natural gas are expensive and in such uncertain supply that the Administration has submitted legislation prohibiting all new power plants from burning them, with only limited environmental and economic exceptions. Other legislative provisions would, through taxation and prohibitive clauses, encourage utilities not to burn oil and gas in existing facilities and to convert them to coal.

But what if the coal cannot be mined, transported and burned in time, and in socially accepted ways? Even before the Administration announced its national energy policy widespread doubts had grown about the wisdom, or even the possibility, of increasing coal production very quickly. In particular, can a goal of increasing coal production from its current level of 650 million tons per year to a projected total of 1.25 billion tons per year by 1985 actually be achieved? Industrial problems associated with such an expansion, land-use problems, states' policies and obstacles created by the Administration's environmental policy for coal have all been repeatedly raised as evidence to suggest that there will be hesitation on both the supply and demand sides of the coal industry. Even coal transportation, which currently accounts for about 30 percent of the U.S. rail tonnage, will be difficult for the disheveled railroad industry.

The environmental problems with coal appear to grow with time and increased understanding. The comparatively large amounts of disturbed land, the chemically and biologically active complex molecules present in coal and produced by the burning of it, and the ubiquitous nature of these effects create difficulties at local and national levels. On a global scale potentially the most serious long-range environmental impacts resulting from the large-scale burning of coal (or indeed of any fossil fuel) may arise from the effects of the increased concentration of carbon dioxide in the atmosphere. At this stage the problem is not well understood, and the potential contribution of planned U.S. coal-burning activities is therefore also shrouded with uncertainty. Nevertheless, in this problem area and others the prognosis looks more serious as more information accumulates. The U.S. electric-utility sector, generally aware of these difficulties, looks on coal with increasing anxiety.

Irresolution about nuclear power, increasingly apparent difficulty with coal, a partial ban against oil and a half-hearted attitude toward energy conservation make an impossible combination; something has to give. If the electric-utility industry waits a few years for public debate to resolve these issues, the concomitant pressure for rapid and comparatively pollution-free installations will drive it toward oil-burning plants. That would be doubly disastrous, because the conversion of some transportation, industrial, commercial and domestic systems from oil to efficiently used electric power, based on coal or nuclear fuels, is seen as a way of reducing oil imports. If the electric utilities are unable or unwilling to provide the means for this substitution, oil consumption will continue to exceed Administration targets.

Thus imported oil may once again fill the role the Administration has sought to prevent it from playing: the "swing" fuel that satisfies increased energy demands. Reinforcing this trend is the present concentration on increasing domestic production, which will have the effect of keeping up oil-based activities that must surely in the next decade or two be fed by imports.

The international importance of President Carter's attempts to reduce oil imports, and the dangers implicit in failing to do so, cannot be overemphasized. Today the U.S. imports nearly half of its immense consumption of 17 million barrels a day, an amount equal to almost a quarter of all internationally traded oil. A reduction to the Administration's stated import target of less than seven million barrels a day by 1985 from levels that would otherwise be reached if present trends are allowed to continue unabated would save annually an amount of crude greater than the current oil imports of Japan or half those of Western Europe. If the target is not met and the U.S. imports increase, the competitive pressures for oil, particularly Middle East oil, may reach dangerous proportions even without another politically motivated interruption in supplies. No other nation in the world (with the possible exception of Saudi Arabia, with its vast potential production capacity and its role of "swing" producer) can exert such an influence on the world's energy outlook through its domestic policies.

After this analysis, we can now enter the logic diagram on pages 56 and 57 at the point where the U.S. states its nuclear-policy position and then explore the international consequences.

All the foregoing trains of thought have been quite apparent to both developed and developing nations. Japan and most of the advanced industrial nations of Europe have meager coal or oil supplies themselves, relatively speaking; even North Sea oil harvested at the maximum planned capacity will supply only about 20 percent of Western Europe's needs. Thus all those countries, facing their own difficulties and the distinct possibility of a continuingly gluttonous U.S., see an increased incentive to push ahead with their own nuclear programs, including reprocessing and breeder reactors. Further encouragement to do so seems to be arising from an unintended source. Along with the U.S., Australia (currently not a uranium producer but potentially one of the world's two or three major exporters of uranium within the next few years) and Canada (the world's biggest uranium exporter) have also recently imposed stringent proliferation-related controls on their exports. In all three cases these controls include the requirement that consent must be obtained from the exporting nation before any of the fuel can be reprocessed. In at least one case deliveries of fuel have been delayed pending agreement to these and other conditions by importing nations. Although the controls have been implemented with the intention of creating a more rigorous nonproliferation regime, for the uranium-deficient, fuel-supply-sensitive Japanese and Europeans such manifestations of external political involvement in their domestic fuel-cycle operations, together with the unsettling prospect of further mercurial behavior by their suppliers in the future, may ultimately act to increase the vigor with which these nations set about reducing their dependence on fuel imports by the use of plutonium and breeder reactors. According to statements of intent from many of them, that is already happening.

What will leaders in developing countries see? They will see a rich U.S. liable to forgo nuclear power, in spite of what it might say about preserving light-water reactors. They will see increased short-term pressure on the world's supply of oil, inevitably resulting in shortages and still higher prices. They will see pessimistic projections for world petroleum and gas resources that will allow neither continued profligate use by the industrialized nations nor any chance for their own countries to follow a development path anything like that followed by their predecessors. They will see an offer of nuclear-fuel supplies that binds them to the goodwill of the U.S. and other developed countries for even limited nuclear assistance. (The recent suggestion of an international nuclear-fuel bank is a partial response to this point.) They will see the growing appearance of a world divided into an oligopoly of developed states that turns into an oligarchy as nuclear power becomes more important throughout the world, and a coterie of less developed nations that must fall farther and farther behind. (This latter impression becomes reinforced by U.S. actions that treat certain of its industrialized trading partners as "exceptions" in view of their continued insistence on the need for reprocessing and breeder reactors in their countries without delay.) And they will see little promise of help from the U.S. to become truly independent in terms of nuclear power.

The inevitable result will be increasing distrust of the U.S. and a growing sensation of unwanted dependence. Both developed and developing nations share these feelings of insecurity. Considering only uranium enrichment as an example, would a U.S. offer of more enrichment services suggest an extension of U.S. market control of enrichment supply, which in turn would suggest increased dependence on U.S. whims? Troubled in large part by the somewhat fickle nature of the decision-making process governing U.S. exports, the out-

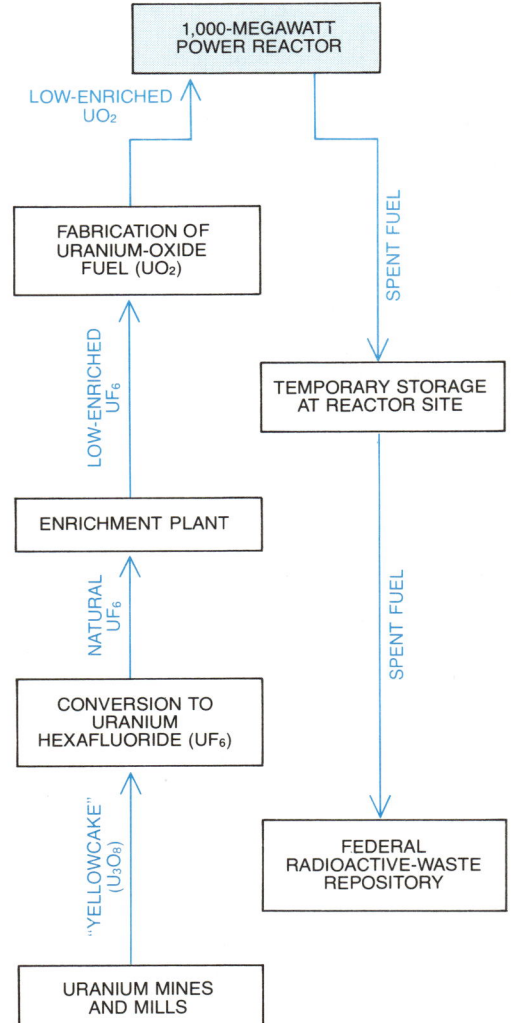

THREE NUCLEAR-FUEL CYCLES suitable with conventional light-water reactors are shown in these simplified diagrams, adapted from a recent report to the American Physical Society by its study group on nuclear-fuel cycles and waste management. In the prevailing "once through" approach (*left*) the spent-fuel rods, which still contain an appreciable amount of fissionable isotopes (principally "unburned" uranium 235 and plutonium 239 produced by the transmutation of the urani-

side world, including the less developed countries, sees more incentive to set up its own enrichment programs and to go nuclear with or without U.S. assistance.

Both developed and developing countries also share other reactions. Among both groups, for example, there are suspicions that the U.S. program is really designed to improve the sagging fortunes of U.S. nuclear exports: either to increase the attractiveness of U.S. light-water reactors or to curb the global movement toward plutonium and the breeder reactor until U.S. technology in these areas has caught up with capabilities in Western Europe. It has also been pointed out that the exemplary nature of the U.S. decision to defer indefinitely the reprocessing of its own commercial power-reactor fuel was compromised from the outset by the fact that fuel reprocessing in connection with the U.S. weapons program would continue as before. Related comments address the entire network of U.S. weapons-manufacturing activities and deployed weapons, suggesting that the scale and wide distribution of this system presents a more attractive target to would-be proliferators than a commercial plutonium fuel cycle would. Furthermore, some observers have speculated that the subsequent decision to use gas-centrifuge technology for the next increment of U.S. enrichment capacity rather than a more proliferation-resistant gaseous-diffusion plant compounds the already present inconsistencies.

To be sure, some of these reactions are mere rhetorical flourishes; nevertheless, they may still have wide-ranging international reverberations. Moreover, many of the reactions are contradictory. How can a rich U.S. liable to forgo nuclear power also be attempting to increase its share of nuclear exports? How can one explain the fact that some of the nations where complaints about the in-

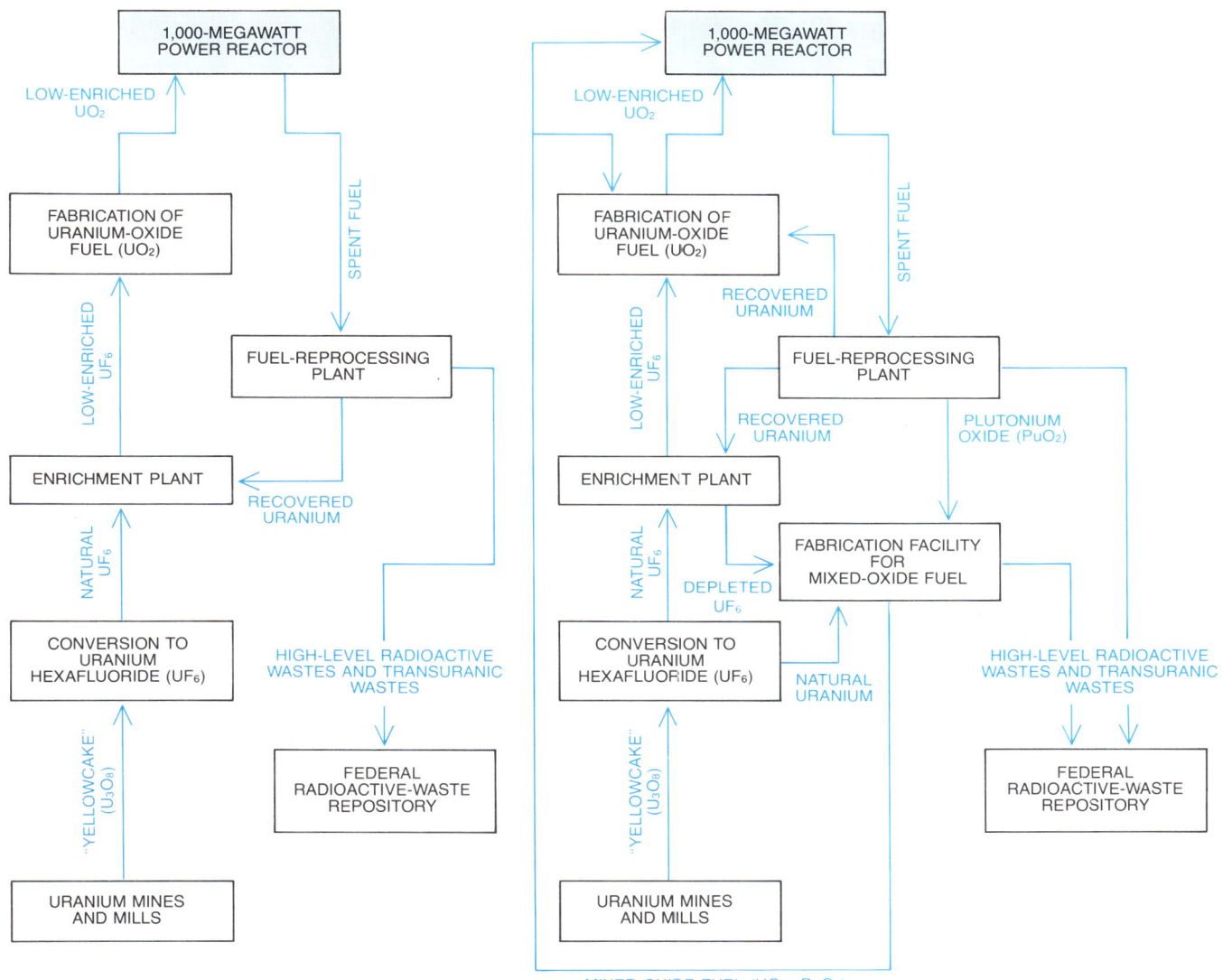

um-238 nuclei in the fuel are disposed of without reprocessing; disposition of the spent fuel can in principle be either temporary or permanent. In the uranium-recycle option (*center*) the spent fuel is reprocessed to recover only the residual uranium, which can then be enriched in the fissionable isotope U-235 or used as it is to replace some of the virgin natural uranium in the fabrication of new fuel assemblies. In the uranium-and-plutonium-recycle option (*right*) the spent fuel is reprocessed to separate both uranium and plutonium from the wastes. The recovered plutonium can then be combined with uranium having a very low concentration of U-235, in effect substituting the plutonium for some of the U-235 in the normally low-enriched fuel. Useful mixed-oxide fuels can be made by combining plutonium with uranium derived from a number of different sources, including the normal low-enriched uranium product from an isotope-separation plant, the uranium recovered from spent fuel or the depleted "tails" from a uranium-enrichment plant. It has been estimated that with both uranium and plutonium recycling the industrial operations required to supply enriched uranium could be reduced by about 20 percent in the year 2000 compared with what they would be for either the uranium-recycle or no-recycle options. This saving would of course require the introduction of the costly and complicated fuel-reprocessing and mixed-oxide fuel-fabrication operations.

consistency of U.S. policies toward domestic and military reprocessing have been heard are also those that rely most heavily on the presence of the U.S. nuclear deterrent for their defense? Such contradictions, however, do no more than mirror the ambiguities and contradictions we have recognized in the U.S. policy, as it attempts to strengthen the barriers between peaceful and violent uses of nuclear energy and simultaneously wrestles with an immense and growing demand for energy, both domestic and international.

The Nonproliferation Treaty, to which more than 100 nations are now parties, embodies an internationally negotiated agreement on the framework in which the energy v. proliferation enigma should be resolved. In it the non-nuclear-weapons states party to the treaty undertake not to develop or otherwise acquire any form of nuclear explosive and to accept international safeguards on all peaceful nuclear activities. In return for this commitment the right of all parties to the treaty to develop and use nuclear energy for peaceful purposes is affirmed, as is the right to participate in exchanges of equipment, materials and technology for the peaceful use of nuclear energy.

The restrictive export policies of the U.S. (and of other major nuclear suppliers) are viewed in many parts of the world as extending the inequalities that have always been inherent in the Nonproliferation Treaty between nuclear-weapons states and non-nuclear-weapons states. The new expression of these inequalities is the attempt to influence criteria for the international distribution of certain "sensitive" peaceful technologies, particularly reprocessing. Implied in this policy is a redrawing of the line separating peaceful uses of nuclear energy from violent ones, and therefore a redefinition of proliferation. Traditionally the latter had been defined as the acquisition of nuclear weapons. Now, however, the new U.S. position is being interpreted as an attempt to redefine proliferation as the capability of acquiring nuclear weapons. Had this always been the case, it is argued, negotiating the Nonproliferation Treaty would have been impossible in the first place.

We make no attempt to determine whether in fact the U.S. would be failing to comply with its international legal

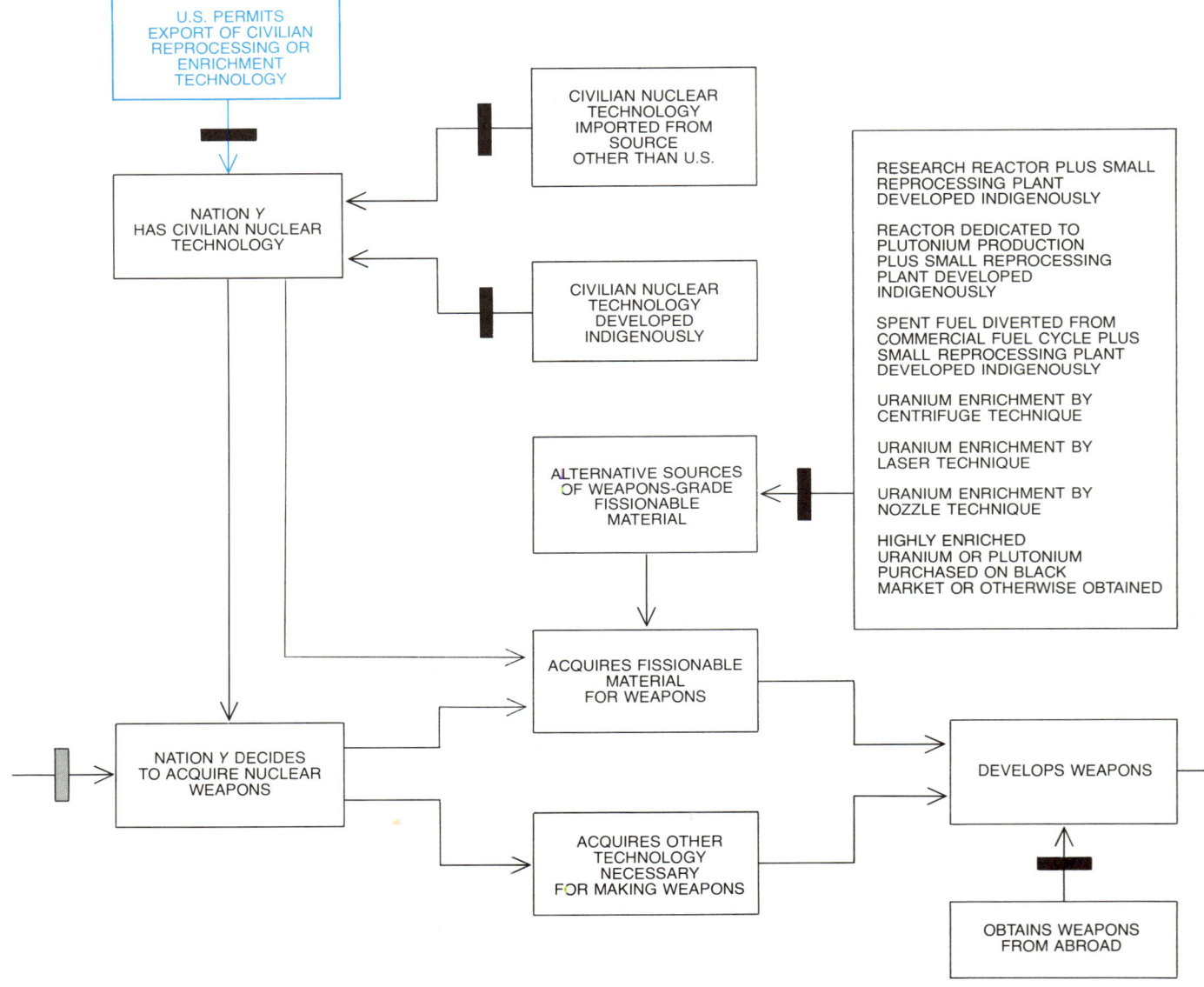

NUCLEAR-PROLIFERATION SCENARIO currently perceived as being worrisome by the U.S. Government is illustrated in the form of this sequential logic diagram. The main horizontal decision path shows the series of steps that could be followed by a non-nuclear-weapons nation, designated *Y*, to acquire nuclear weapons and to use them. The vertical paths show several possible inputs to *Y*'s decision. For example, the U.S. sees the acquisition of a nuclear-fuel-reprocessing capability as a stimulant to weapons proliferation. Accordingly

obligations as a party to the Nonproliferation Treaty by implementing its proposed export criteria. We do observe, however, that the loss of confidence in the effectiveness of international safeguards that has taken place in the U.S. is reflected in many non-nuclear states by a corresponding loss of confidence in the ability of the Nonproliferation Treaty to provide an acceptable legal framework for the international distribution of peaceful and military applications of nuclear energy. In such circumstances the fabric of the global nonproliferation regime is inevitably weakened.

All the considerations we have discussed here show up as destabilizing routes in our second proliferation scenario. Not only does country Y find logical incentives to install domestic nuclear-fuel facilities, but also it perceives a world more fragmented and less secure. Feeling less secure itself, it naturally imagines others feeling the same way and hence it must increase its own security unilaterally. Escalation of uncertainty leads to escalation of international instability; a program originally intended by the U.S. to decrease the dangers of nuclear proliferation inadvertently has the opposite effect. Meanwhile the U.S. isolates itself from the mainstream of world nuclear policy, and its ability to favorably affect that policy diminishes.

More caveats and auxiliary views remain to be displayed. None of this analysis is meant to overstate the role of nuclear power in solving the world's energy problems. That mistake has been made too many times before. Some of the problems currently facing the nuclear-power industry in non-Communist developed countries can probably best be understood in terms of a backlash against earlier technological overoptimism. For the majority of the less developed countries nuclear-generated electricity cannot play a significant part in meeting energy requirements for a long time. Costs have risen alarmingly, and besides, the type and scale of the energy supplied by currently available nuclear-power stations seem less compatible with the energy-demand structure in many of these countries than the output of other energy-supply systems.

Moreover, in some developing countries where nuclear power is intended to play a major role the overall development targets frequently appear overambitious and unlikely to be realized. Fears have been expressed that nuclear-power technology could critically exacerbate rivalries among the various political, industrial and technocratic elites and increase the gap between such elites and the remainder of the population. Until now suppliers have not discernibly modified any "hard sell" policies because they might ultimately contribute to domestic political instabilities with unpredictable international consequences, and it is unlikely that such self-restraint will be shown in the future. The point here is not, of course, that the industrialized supplier nations should decide what is good for the development of the poorer countries and impose export restrictions accordingly but that nuclear technology may be "sensitive" for many reasons other than the increased access to weapons-grade material it may provide.

We conclude, therefore, that the conventionally defended analyses have been inadequate. The various original motivations virtually disappeared from our discussion, and rightly so; they were more nearly goals than real policies. Both are necessary; to neglect the hard work of developing policy causes much trouble because then the original vision, however high-minded, is washed away by a sea of events, and only consequences remain.

What to do? In answering this question we have had to assume that many other issues related to nuclear power can be resolved. To us the three largest of those issues seem to be reactor safety, the management of nuclear wastes and the prevention of subnational nuclear felonies. Although we have not dealt with these matters, we realize their gravity. Our analysis and recommendations would be irrelevant, however, only if both the U.S. and almost all other countries opted out of nuclear power. Nuclear power might disappear in the U.S., but neither present reactors nor breeders will go away in many other places. If the activities of Western Europe and Japan are unconvincing, one need only consider the U.S.S.R. and its Eastern European allies; they also develop nuclear power, with the most sensitive activities being reserved to the U.S.S.R. The U.S. must stop acting from time to time as though nuclear power was about to go away, or as though its disappearance would have little consequence.

The Administration has begun to discuss some of the necessary changes: for example a gradual shift to a more flexible policy, more emphasis on providing an assured nuclear-fuel supply and a suggestion to set up an international storage facility for spent fuel. Owing to significant reductions in projected overall energy demand and particularly in forecasts of installed nuclear capacity, the next few years seem to us a period of grace, perhaps overperceived in the U.S. and underperceived abroad, during which fundamental repairs can be made to the fabric of nuclear goals and policies. The period may be a decade, but it can hardly be much longer, being limited by the consequences of the inexorable pressure on other energy resources. The time is technically long enough to develop variations in the current fuel cycle, perhaps long enough to devise a brand-new one and even reactors and other facilities to use the fuel, but such activity would require far firmer decisions and much prompter (and more expensive) implementation than we have seen. Both the preparation of fissionable fuel from new or reprocessed material (the "front end" of the fuel cycle) and the reprocessing of spent fuel must be carefully considered, not just the latter. As we have said, we consider the front end of the fuel cycle, the enrichment of natural uranium for example, to be a sensitive proliferation issue. The exis-

the Administration has sought to restrict the export of commercial reprocessing technology as a way of blocking this access route to the acquisition of nuclear weapons. Other routes exist, however, whereby Y could gain access to weapons-grade material; some of these possible routes are listed in the large box. In order to erect a really effective barrier to weapons proliferation, the U.S. would have to block all the lines marked with a black bar. Decision paths on which the U.S. can have only an indirect influence are marked with gray bars.

tence of about 200 power reactors around the world working on the present fuel cycle must also be considered, and the opportunities for technological innovation that might be applied to them are limited.

All these things make large demands on one decade or a little more. So do institutional accommodations among nations, not only with respect to the currently developed nuclear-fuel cycles but also to many other things. Time is short, whether for technological modification or for international institution-building. Whatever the outcome of the former, the latter is an indispensable part of efforts to deal with the problems of nuclear-weapons proliferation and energy scarcity. Although the Administration's proposals have created many problems, they have succeeded in injecting a new sense of urgency into the situation. It is essential that this asset not be allowed to evaporate.

Regarding present fuel cycles and other matters directly related to nuclear power in the next decade or two we have five main recommendations to offer:

1. Nuclear power should be kept alive in the U.S. at least as a long-term "insurance" option, and that means not only the continued development of light-water reactors but also progress toward de-

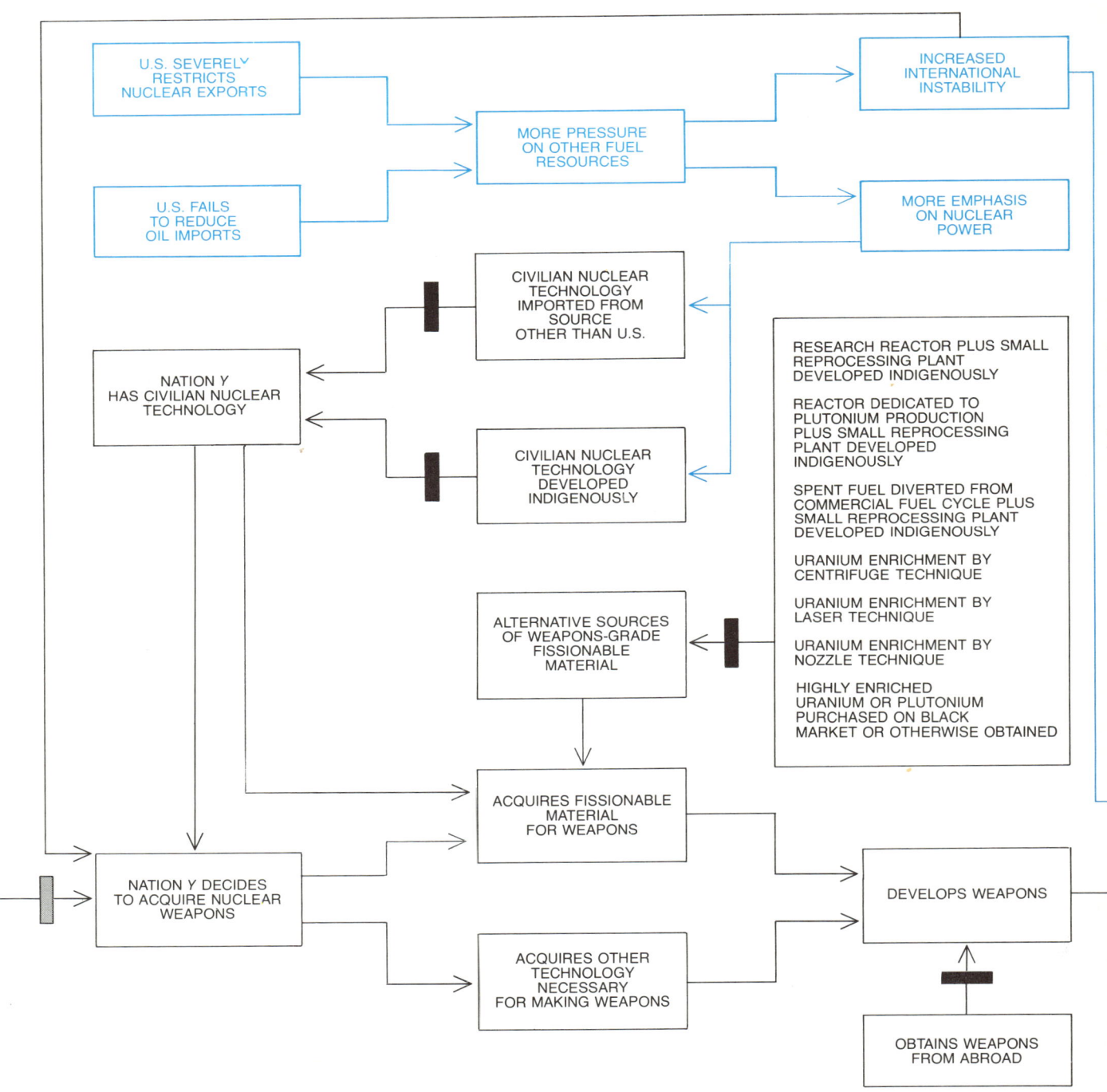

MORE COMPLEX SCENARIO is needed to portray more realistically the likely effects of an overly restrictive U.S. nuclear-export policy on the entire problem of international stability and the proliferation of nuclear weapons. The main decision path followed by nation Y toward the acquisition of a nuclear-weapons capability is the same as it is in the preceding diagram, as are a number of other elements in the diagram. In this case, however, the vertical inputs to Y's decisions start with the new U.S. restrictions on nuclear exports,

veloping a viable breeder reactor. Central-station solar power and controlled fusion are only long-term possibilities, oil is only a short-term source of energy and we have little faith in coal for the long term.

2. To reduce uncertainty for the U.S. electric-utility industry and others the Federal Government should take several steps. First, it should reaffirm that the reprocessing of spent nuclear fuel is being delayed but not abandoned. Second, the Federal Government should assure the electric utilities of a review of national policy on reprocessing as the debate about it matures, and certainly within five years; that would include an assessment of the projected uranium supply, which would draw on the current national uranium-resource evaluation and other programs. Third, the complexity and prolixity of the licensing process for nuclear-power plants should be eased by making it more difficult for license applications to be recycled again and again to the Nuclear Regulatory Commission. The nuclear licensing bill currently under consideration appears to be facing formidable obstacles at several stages of the legislative process, and in any case it seems to address these issues only partially in its present form. Finally, the Federal Government should take on the entire burden of managing spent fuel, and guarantee to take responsibility for the fuel reasonably soon after its discharge from power reactors. That includes spent-fuel reprocessing, if and when a decision comes to do it. No other sector has an adequately long time perspective to plan and operate the appropriate facilities. In particular, the chemical industry, on which the task might otherwise be expected to fall, traditionally expects a payback on investment in a very few years, and therefore discounts far-future profits too much to match the long-term nature of the tasks, particularly waste handling and storage.

3. The U.S. should offer to explore with other nations the costs and benefits to the international community of completing the reprocessing plant now sitting idle at Barnwell, S.C., and operating it as an international facility. The principal objectives of such a project would be to gain experience with commercial reprocessing technology, to assess the effectiveness of international safeguards and to demonstrate the institutional viability of international cooperation in the provision of fuel-cycle services.

4. Efforts to increase the security of the international supply of uranium and enrichment services should be intensified. Domestically, differences among the various branches of the Government should not be allowed to interfere with the pivotal task of reestablishing the U.S. as a reliable supplier of enriched uranium fuel.

5. In all these activities we note the need for an international agency. We see none better prepared than the International Atomic Energy Agency (IAEA), and we believe it should be greatly strengthened so that it can continuously inspect sensitive facilities. The answer does not, however, lie in the mere strengthening or even proliferation of agencies. For example, restrictions on the export of appropriate nuclear systems may undermine the Nonproliferation Treaty, and the IAEA can do nothing about it.

Beyond all these issues we see others seeming to stand out in the distance. First, it is noteworthy that the diagrams we have drawn differ from the conventionally discussed diagrams of causes and effects. Our discussion has been almost entirely international, as befits the problem. The U.S. approach has been too self-centered, insufficiently sensitive to the problems of other nations and lacking in awareness of its own potentially disruptive character.

Near the beginning of this discussion we mentioned that the Administration has attempted to breathe new life into the larger issues presented by nuclear weapons. If governments and people are so concerned with the risks of future proliferation, how much more should they worry about the huge numbers of nuclear weapons already deployed? One who lives on the edge of an abyss should not squander his effort avoiding small ditches. The real threat of nuclear weapons is seen once again, more clearly than before, in the illuminating perspective provided by the juxtaposition of thousands of existing megatons on the one hand and a few hypothetical kilotons on the other.

This brings us to the more general question of international peace and stability. In the worldwide search for routes to a juster and more sustainable society it has become clear to many observers that a peace in which the world is divided ever more rigorously into haves and have-nots is neither just nor likely to be very sustainable, whether the basis for division is social, economic or (as here) seemingly technological. Such a division not only defeats itself in the long run; even worse, it is wrong.

We propose that the real long-term solution both to the nuclear-power problem and to the larger problems of international instability lies not in fostering division but in its opposite: mutually cooperative international interdependence. Since nations must depend on one another, they lose more by going separately than by staying in partnership. Our analysis shows that this partnership must include the developing countries, since many of them, if they are excluded, are capable of upsetting the international order through the acquisition of nuclear weapons and other acts.

All of this will not be easy, but other approaches have yielded nothing but unstable arms escalation. The partnership should logically involve food, health care and many other sectors where the U.S. can make valuable contributions. Only in that way will we have a chance of answering constructively the question that can no longer be put aside: Why do people want to make nuclear weapons in the first place?

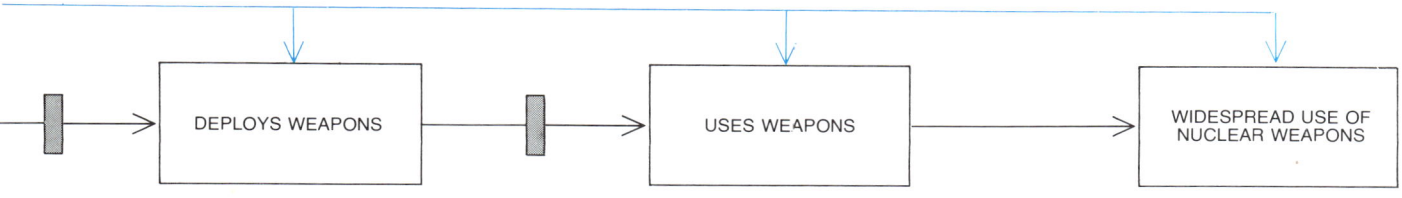

coupled with the failure of the U.S. to reduce significantly its imports of crude oil. Several additional logic paths, shown in color, represent the possible sequence of events that could result in added incentives for nation Y not only to push ahead with its own civilian nuclear-power program, including uranium-enrichment technology, spent-fuel reprocessing plants and breeder reactors, but also perhaps to respond to increased international instability arising out of growing competition for energy resources by joining the nuclear-weapons "club."

The International Control of Disarmament

by Alva Myrdal
October 1974

The widely acknowledged need for a separate United Nations agency responsible for verifying and controlling disarmament agreements is intensified by the current impasse in bilateral "summit" talks

Two recent developments—the failure of the latest round of bilateral "summit" meetings between the U.S. and the U.S.S.R. to make any significant progress toward the immediate goal of strategic-arms limitation (let alone toward the ultimate goal of nuclear disarmament) and the announcement by India that it had become the sixth nation to successfully test a nuclear explosive—serve to emphasize the urgent need for renewed international efforts to end the continuing waste and insecurity of the arms race. As Sweden's delegate to the Political Committee of the United Nations and to the ongoing UN disarmament conference at Geneva from its beginning in 1962 until my retirement last year, I have been in a position to witness the ebb and flow of the arms-regulation proposals that have been put forward at various times by various nations. Out of this experience I have distilled a few general observations about how (and how not) to negotiate an effective arms agreement.

First and foremost it should not be tolerated that the two superpowers exercise a world hegemony based largely on their incessant arms race and at the same time play an insincere game of disarmament at the negotiating tables. Moreover, in view of the fact that objections have so often been raised against agreements on arms limitation or genuine disarmament on grounds of the difficulty or the alleged impossibility of controlling their implementation, the problem of control and verification must be tackled in a new and dynamic way.

I have therefore come to the conclusion that there is one practical measure that could serve to bind together and facilitate all disarmament efforts. That is to create a new UN agency charged with the collection and dissemination of information regarding the fulfillment by the nations of the obligations they incur under disarmament agreements and regarding ongoing changes in national armaments. Such an agency would begin its work modestly, depending on information available from national sources, but ultimately it would stand ready to accept control functions. It might even become a repository and publisher of pertinent satellite-surveillance data. I am convinced that this approach to the internationalization of knowledge about arms and disarmament would secure the foundations for the mutual confidence among nations on which the negotiation and observance of significant disarmament agreements must in the first and last instance rest. Here I shall set forth some of the reasoning behind this proposal.

The value of any agreement on disarmament or the regulation of armaments depends not only on how large a part of the community of nations subscribes to it but also on mutual confidence that it will be duly upheld. Ultimately such confidence depends on the trustworthiness of the nations that are parties to the agreement. All properly share in the concern that they should be able to rely on the other parties to fulfill their obligations. The overriding assumption must be that any government that has negotiated a disarmament (or nonarmament) agreement, and that during the preparatory period has worked to get the agreement tailored as much to its wishes as mutuality allows, will enter as a party to the agreement with no intention of breaking it or of cheating.

The historical record speaks for the validity of this assumption. It is doubtful, in fact, that there has ever been an instance of a clandestine violation in the arms field. Some Americans have charged that the U.S.S.R. violated the nuclear-test moratorium that prevailed at the end of the 1950's. In the first place there could not have been any such violation because there had been no formal agreement; moreover, the U.S. had already indicated its intention of resuming testing. In the second place the Russian test explosion was not secret. Even less was India's recent nuclear explosion a violation, inasmuch as India had for 20 years worked assiduously for a ban on all nuclear-weapons testing, and when it did not sign the Non-Proliferation Treaty, it led those nations that openly expressed reservations about the treaty's discriminatory character.

In fact, open abrogations of treaties are rather more likely than clandestine ones. It is of course true, as some commentators have pointed out, that certain ultramodern weapons (for example binary chemical weapons) might be easier to conceal than nuclear weapons. Nonetheless, the main assumption retains its strength, namely that the political commitment made when entering an arms agreement is the most reliable guarantee, whether or not it is supported by technical devices for detection.

If willful violations of an arms agreement should occur, they would raise problems that would be essentially political and not technical. Collective sanctions could not be enforced against such breaches; penalties could not be meted out by an international organization, nor could punitive expeditions be put into the field. The risk is the political one that other parties will find reasons to abrogate the treaty. In arms-regulation treaties there are often provisions for such withdrawal, according to the formula that a party may decide "that extraordinary events...have jeopardized the supreme interests of its country."

Concern about loyal adherence to agreements has been surprisingly and, in my view, irrationally vociferous during disarmament negotiations. It has caused considerable attention to be paid to questions of control and verification. The fact that the matter of control is held to be important, however, sets out the practical limits of the area of agreement. There is a plethora of differing demands for control and even different interpretations of

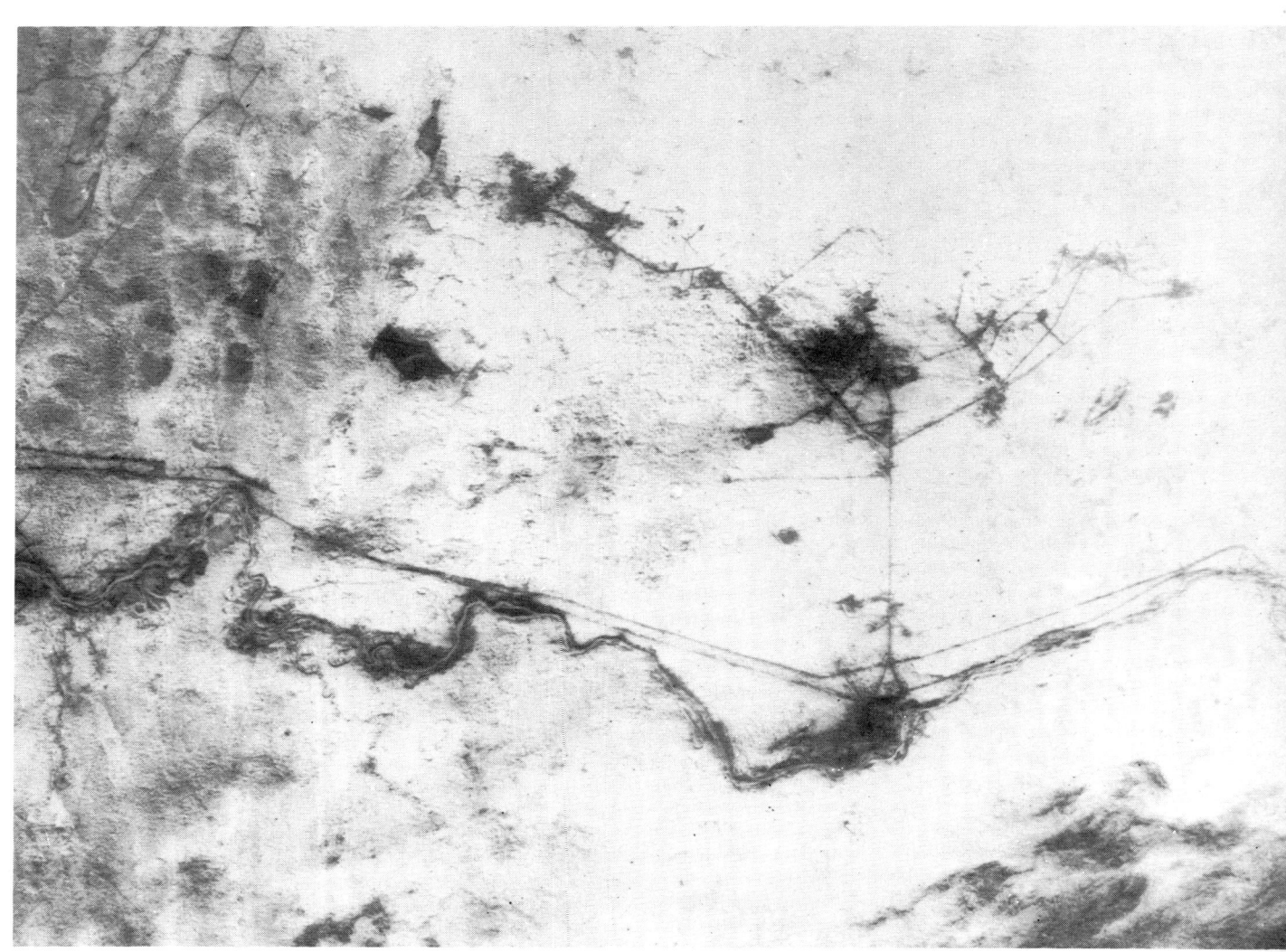

RUSSIAN SPACE CENTER near Tyuratam in southern Kazakhstan appears in this U.S. satellite photograph. The photograph, which was made from an altitude of about 570 miles by a camera aboard the first Earth Resources Technology Satellite (ERTS 1), was released by the National Aeronautics and Space Administration in 1972 following a decision to make all such nonmilitary-satellite photographs available to the public on request, regardless of the possible strategic significance of the area photographed. The author argues that the same policy of openness should be extended to include the currently secret military-satellite programs of both sides, on the grounds that such an approach would encourage the mutual confidence among nations on which the verification and control of disarmament agreements depend. The ultimate repository for all such arms-surveillance data would be a new United Nations agency to be called the International Disarmament Control Organization. The military satellites of both the U.S. and the U.S.S.R. are of course capable of obtaining photographs with much greater resolution. The comparatively poor resolution of this

what control clauses in already signed and ratified treaties really mean.

I believe two major unresolved issues are at the bottom of the confusion. One is the remaining uncertainty about what the real purpose of a control system is to be in relation to an arms-regulation agreement. I shall return to this issue. The other issue is the continued dominance of a long-standing tendency to view the problem in terms of the control deemed to be both necessary and acceptable in a totally disarmed world. It was in this context that the control problem was originally raised and discussed. Questions about what control measures are necessary and applicable to partial or collateral measures should be related to the specific conditions, which differ from case to case, if they are to be relevant to the pragmatic attitude that is now the prevailing approach to disarmament negotiations and debates.

It was on the submerged reef of obfuscations concerning the scope of control that the first major postwar arms-limitation effort on the part of the U.S. and the U.S.S.R. foundered. Since the debate over the Baruch Plan right after World War II the accusations have become stereotyped: the U.S.S.R. wants to confine control to what is being disarmed, whereas the U.S. wants to control what exists of armaments.

Although this is a rather quixotic feud, it regrettably still turns up and causes vexations at point after point. I am convinced, however, that a meeting of minds must and will occur. In their abstract form both positions are impossible. In concrete cases both positions may well be abandoned, as they were in the first strategic-arms-limitation talks (SALT I), or considerably modified, as they were in the nuclear-test-ban negotiations.

In a strict sense "control of disarmament" could be interpreted as being limited to monitoring the destruction of armaments. Indeed, in the early days of the Geneva disarmament conference there was often talk of such "bonfires" of bombers and other weapons. In the convention prohibiting the production of biological weapons the destruction of the existing stock is explicitly required. President Nixon in 1969 made the magnanimous gesture of promising such destruction of U.S. stockpiles. The fact remains that international observation teams have never been invited to witness the destruction of any weapons. The logical flaw in the demand that control be limited to the implementation of disarmament is, of course, that in order to appreciate how much has been destroyed or eliminated one has to know what share of the total it represents.

"Control of armaments retained," on the other hand, is a logically more defensible proposition. In its most literal sense—corresponding to the "bonfire" in the preceding category—it would require proof in the form of physical inspection of all facilities of any party to a treaty in order to ascertain that elimination or reduction of armaments has been effected so as to correspond to the levels agreed on. So far the Russians have been categorically opposed to incorporating the right to obligatory inspections in any of the treaties that have been negotiated. Objections might well be raised by other countries with regard to possible future arms agreements.

What is confusing the issue is to a large extent the fact that the postures taken by various nations are not clearly addressed either to a situation of general and complete disarmament or to one where disarmament is less perfect. One reason is probably, as I have mentioned, the lingering dominance of the idea of a foolproof control system. This criterion has always been associated with a state of world affairs where nations were totally disarmed and the UN had the duty of policing the world society. Such an ambitious scheme was embedded, for example, in the basic guidelines for disarmament negotiations that were submitted to the UN General Assembly in 1961 and go under the name of the McCloy-Zorin Agreed Principles. The agreement states as the sixth principle:

"All disarmament measures should be implemented from beginning to end under such strict and effective international control as would provide firm assurance that all parties are honoring their obligations. During and after the implementation of general and complete disarmament, the most thorough control should be exercised, the nature and extent of such control depending on the requirements for verification of the disarmament measures being carried out in each stage. To implement control over the inspection of disarmament, an international disarmament organization including all parties to the agreement should be created within the framework of the United Nations. This international disarmament organization and its inspectors should be assured unrestricted access without veto to all places as necessary for the purpose of effective verification."

The two contrary positions held by the superpowers can, I surmise, be disregarded in their extreme form, when (as is now the rule) all relevant negotiations have moved on to the practical consideration of varied and limited disarmament measures. Problems of verification and control are considerably easier to solve in practice than in theory—either on the political ground that enough confidence prevails or on the technological ground that sufficiently reliable means of monitoring events in the field of interest are becoming available. Even so there will often remain margins of uncertainty that may require a mustering of political will to compromise if they are not to be used as excuses for disagreement.

The futility of demanding control pro-

ERTS photograph is enhanced somewhat by the fact that it was made in winter; roads, railroads and other installations show up clearly as black lines and spots against the light-colored background of the surrounding snow-covered desert. The main "cosmodrome," or rocket-launching complex (*top center*), is approximately 15 miles north of the railway town Tyuratam (*bottom center*).

visions that would give 100 percent assurance that no violation of an arms regulation agreement would ever go undetected becomes much more indisputable when one considers the other continuing source of confusion, namely that there has not as yet been any clear analysis and unambiguous acceptance of what is to be the function of control and verification. In general, interest has been focused on only one function: the ability to check whether or not a violation of treaty obligations has occurred. I would call this an after-the-fact approach. The main interest here has been the legalistic one of keeping the parties accountable. The evidence sought should be so strong that it would hold up before a judiciary authority. Thus the accused party should preferably have been caught red-handed in the act of violation or should have left indisputable material proof—hence the insistence on obligatory inspections. Only if guarantees were given that such a practically foolproof system for after-the-fact verification existed, the reasoning goes, would enough trust be engendered to allow an agreement to be signed. That is still the U.S. position in regard to some important treaties, including a total ban on nuclear-weapons tests. As a result negotiations on this issue have for decades just been treading water.

Control can be regarded from a theoretically different angle, however, insofar as it has another important function, namely to prevent violations. This might be called the before-the-fact approach. The role of control and verification would then be to establish sufficient risks of disclosure that the risks as such act as a deterrent against any nation's attempting to violate a treaty obligation.

In relation to a treaty banning nuclear tests, for example, the before-the-fact approach could be effective if the parties were willing to accept the now very low margin of uncertainty that some of the lowest-yield tests might go undetected and to apply to those uncertainties a strategy of nonresponse. The risk would

SIGNED	IN FORCE			NUMBER OF PARTIES
1959	1961	ANTARCTIC TREATY	PROHIBITS ALL MILITARY ACTIVITY IN ANTARCTIC AREA	17
1963	1963	PARTIAL-NUCLEAR-TEST-BAN TREATY	PROHIBITS NUCLEAR EXPLOSIONS IN THE ATMOSPHERE, IN OUTER SPACE AND UNDER WATER	106
1967	1967	OUTER-SPACE TREATY	PROHIBITS ALL MILITARY ACTIVITY IN OUTER SPACE, INCLUDING THE MOON AND OTHER CELESTIAL BODIES	71
1967	1967	TREATY OF TLATELOLCO	PROHIBITS NUCLEAR WEAPONS IN LATIN AMERICA	18
1968	1970	NON-PROLIFERATION TREATY	PROHIBITS ACQUISITION OF NUCLEAR WEAPONS BY NON-NUCLEAR NATIONS	82
1971	1972	SEA-BED TREATY	PROHIBITS EMPLACEMENT OF NUCLEAR WEAPONS AND OTHER WEAPONS OF MASS DESTRUCTION ON OCEAN FLOOR OR SUBSOIL THEREOF	52
1972		BIOLOGICAL-WEAPONS CONVENTION	PROHIBITS DEVELOPMENT, PRODUCTION AND STOCKPILING OF BACTERIOLOGICAL AND TOXIN WEAPONS AND REQUIRES DESTRUCTION OF EXISTING BIOLOGICAL WEAPONS.	31

MULTILATERAL ARMS AGREEMENTS negotiated in recent years are listed here in chronological order, together with short statements of their major provisions. The column at extreme right gives the total number of parties to each treaty as of December 31, 1973. The convention on biological weapons had been ratified by 31 nations but was still not in force at the beginning of this year.

strategy of nonresponse. The risk would be minimized by the factor of deterrence: the calculable probability that violations will be detected. That is obviously a far more effective method than to search for 100-percent-positive proof in every single suspected event whether or not the event is a violation.

In practical terms solutions to these theoretical riddles do not present great difficulties. The degree of trust is always of the essence when an agreement is contemplated. The before-the-fact deterrence approach presupposes a climate of confidence, but it has the comparative merit of motivating a willingness to take a first step on somewhat shakier ground, since it then allows confidence to grow gradually as it is tested by experience. To demand foolproof methods for after-the-fact verification is to impose an impossible requirement.

It can be safely stated that for both after-the-fact verification and before-the-fact deterrence a main interest is to increase the scope of knowledge about what happens to armaments as well as disarmament. It would be particularly true, however, that the more pertinent knowledge was available, the more reliance could be placed on the before-the-fact approach.

Speaking generally, the imperative task for practical policy should be to reduce the margins of uncertainty in order to change the demand for control from an impossible absolute requirement to a manageable relative requirement. Increased knowledge is really the link between the two extreme requirements concerning what to control: armaments sacrificed or armaments retained. In addition increased knowledge serves the purpose both of deterrence (the before-the-fact risk of disclosure) and of monitoring (the after-the-fact search for evidence of violations).

In this light the prospects for progress should become brighter. Where a fair degree of knowledge prevails, even without any specific verification apparatus, the margin of uncertainty correspondingly decreases, making it less likely that a would-be violator might be tempted to play a hazardous game.

How to expand the store of knowledge in fields that become sensitive when disarmament measures are being negotiated is a practical question having to do with the availability of techniques. Nonetheless, even this technological problem has a political aspect. It involves the question of what kind of world society one wants to foster for the future: one based on openness or one based on secretiveness. With respect to disarmament there is much to be said for the view that maximizing the common fund of knowledge through a total abandonment of secrecy would best serve all interests. Confidence would be encouraged and deterrence would become particularly strong if all the nuclear powers were to participate. Niels Bohr suggested toward the end of World War II that the only way to deal with the problem of nuclear arms was to totally abandon the secrecy surrounding nuclear explosions.

Even Edward Teller, a man not given to accepting such a thorough change of the ways of the world, has said that a possible path is "a gradual and well-planned abandonment of all secrecy concerning technical and scientific facts." The spread of knowledge is unavoidable anyway, and the lack of knowledge is not the main factor limiting nuclear-weapons production. The policy of openness must be actively pursued. As Teller argues: "We should at the same time exert as much pressure as we possibly can on every nation in the world that they likewise permit complete freedom for the flow of information. At the present time technical facts are subject to secrecy in many nations. We should try by every means to reverse this trend toward secrecy. Every additional secret is an obstacle to the free collaboration and the eventual union of nations. A strong and widespread condemnation of all practices of secrecy may in the long run have a strong effect even on those countries which value this form of security most."

Secrecy has many negative ramifications. It cannot long preserve a purely technical military monopoly. On the other hand, spreading exaggerated notions about an adversary's superiority or one's own insufficiency tends to cause overreaction. The notorious "missile gap" of the early 1960's was a case in point, but the phenomenon has a timeless ability to open up terrifying perspectives.

Among the important positive aspects of openness is that it both increases knowledge about ongoing developments that might threaten to step up the arms race and multiplies opportunities for verification. The most advanced means of observation have been by-products of the arms race (satellites, sonar and so forth). Regrettably these devices are now monopolized by a few nations. Ideally they belong to mankind's accumulated fund of knowledge and should be allowed to serve the interests of everyone's security.

The one dictum that is generally valid is that openness promotes all knowledge. Knowledge does not thrive in the dark. This wider aspect of the ethics of access to knowledge is beyond the scope of this article. Here I wish only to emphasize that military secrecy is the most obnoxious of all attempts to conceal truth.

Verification is no substitute for trust. The question of trust in a disarmament agreement remains preeminently a political problem, but verification can obviously contribute to trust and thus to a buttressing of international agreements. Technical means can facilitate trust even outside the domain of verification, as is evidenced by the "hot line" set up between the U.S. and the U.S.S.R. in 1963.

It would nonetheless be a mistake to rely too much on technical controls. In the early days of disarmament negotiations great store was set by "strict and effective international control" (as had been stated in the McCloy-Zorin principles), undoubtedly because it was then hoped that general and complete disarmament would emerge out of one set of decisions, in spite of the fact that the political realities were far from ripe for it. Particularly as new methods of verification with technical aids emerged, "control" sometimes was in danger of becoming a technical pipe dream. An example was the plan to build hundreds of seismological stations around the world for monitoring a test ban.

Overreliance on the inspection approach was pervasive throughout the period from 1958 to 1965, even in academic studies of arms control and disarmament. The search went on for perfect methods of control, until it looked as though what disarmament would lead to was a world police state. The consoling thought is that this approach is now virtually a thing of the past. It was based on a mixing of mental images: a scheme for general and complete disarmament introduced into a political situation that was totally inhospitable to such brave idealism.

The task as seen from the perspective of today is rather how to obtain increasingly wide and reliable knowledge of armaments and potential changes in their quantity and quality throughout the world. A reassuring openness, I would hold, is the avenue to disarmament control. Even if the goal of total openness is distant, to take steps in that direction is clearly in line with the trend of our time, which is toward increasing communication of all kinds.

In the field of interest to arms-limitation endeavors, however, the problems of verification and control have also suffered from being treated too much as generalities. The search for verification methods must span a great diversity of problems. The choice of method must be specific, depending on the type of armament proscribed and the developmental stage to be verified, as well as on the technical means at one's disposal.

This requirement for deciding on specific verification methods should not exclude the usefulness of cross-checking events by employing several different approaches. Hence efforts to observe changes in hardware can be augmented not only by the examination of budget figures but also by the analysis of trade statistics. For example, trade in phosphorus can be analyzed for the purpose of monitoring the possibility of chemical-weapons production.

To date no systematic analysis has been attempted to determine what different disarmament measures would optimally require of verification methods and whether some measures might not make use of a common operative handling. Instead disparate approaches to control have been taken in an unsystematic way in the treaties and recommendations negotiated so far. The picture of

SIGNED	IN FORCE		
1963	1963	"HOT LINE" AGREEMENT	ESTABLISHES DIRECT RADIO AND TELEGRAPH COMMUNICATIONS BETWEEN U.S. AND U.S.S.R. FOR USE IN EMERGENCY
1971	1971	"HOT LINE" MODERNIZATION AGREEMENT	INCREASES RELIABILITY OF ORIGINAL "HOT LINE" SYSTEM BY ADDING TWO SATELLITE-COMMUNICATIONS CIRCUITS
1971	1971	NUCLEAR-ACCIDENTS AGREEMENT	INSTITUTES VARIOUS MEASURES TO REDUCE RISK OF ACCIDENTAL NUCLEAR WAR BETWEEN U.S. AND U.S.S.R.
1972	1972	HIGH-SEAS AGREEMENT	PROVIDES FOR MEASURES TO HELP PREVENT DANGEROUS INCIDENTS ON OR OVER THE HIGH SEAS INVOLVING SHIPS AND AIRCRAFT OF BOTH PARTIES
1972	1972	SALT I ABM TREATY	LIMITS DEPLOYMENT OF ANTI-BALLISTIC-MISSILE SYSTEMS TO TWO SITES IN EACH COUNTRY
1972	1972	SALT I INTERIM OFFENSIVE-ARMS AGREEMENT	PROVIDES FOR FIVE-YEAR FREEZE ON AGGREGATE NUMBER OF FIXED LAND-BASED INTERCONTINENTAL BALLISTIC MISSILES (ICBM'S) AND SUBMARINE-LAUNCHED BALLISTIC MISSILES (SLBM'S) ON EACH SIDE
1973	1973	PROTOCOL TO HIGH-SEAS AGREEMENT	PROHIBITS SIMULATED ATTACKS BY SHIPS AND AIRCRAFT OF EACH PARTY AIMED AT NONMILITARY SHIPS OF OTHER PARTY
1973	1973	NUCLEAR-WAR-PREVENTION AGREEMENT	INSTITUTES VARIOUS MEASURES TO HELP AVERT OUTBREAK OF NUCLEAR WAR IN CRISIS SITUATIONS
1974		SALT II ABM TREATY	LIMITS DEPLOYMENT OF ANTI-BALLISTIC-MISSILE SYSTEMS TO ONE SITE IN EACH COUNTRY
1974		SALT II THRESHOLD NUCLEAR-TEST-BAN TREATY	PROHIBITS UNDERGROUND TESTS OF NUCLEAR WEAPONS WITH EXPLOSIVE YIELDS GREATER THAN 150 KILOTONS
1974		SALT II INTERIM OFFENSIVE-ARMS AGREEMENT	COMMITS BOTH PARTIES TO NEGOTIATE EXTENSION OF SALT I INTERIM OFFENSIVE-ARMS AGREEMENT THROUGH 1985

BILATERAL ARMS AGREEMENTS between the U.S. and the U.S.S.R. cover mostly peripheral matters of immediate concern only to the two "superpowers." Critics of the agreements reached in the strategic-arms-limitation talks (SALT I and II) contend that the bilateral approach has succeeded only in outlawing weapons systems that neither side wanted anyway, with the net result that the arms race has merely been redirected. The SALT II treaties, which were signed in Moscow on July 3, have not yet been ratified by the U.S. Congress and hence are not yet in force; the SALT II "threshold" nuclear-test ban is not intended to go into effect until 1976.

the controls attempted is therefore one of great disarray.

Thus the problems of verification are to a large extent concerned with the right choice of techniques and procedures. Such choices should, however, be guided by the overarching aims of maximizing trust and minimizing policing on the one hand and gradually widening the appropriate knowledge through international cooperation on the other.

It is of prime importance to resort as little as possible to intrusive methods of investigation, be they conducted by spies or through on-site inspections. Modern technology is very helpful in this regard, since it provides ever more efficient means for unobtrusively checking events from a distance. Radar and sonar, the analysis of radioactive emissions and the monitoring of telecommunication frequency patterns are just a few of the less intrusive methods of surveillance made available by modern technology. One such method has had special prominence in the recently concluded agreements, namely observations from satellites. The satellite surveillance of launchers for land-based strategic missiles, for example, made it unnecessary for the parties in the SALT I agreement to seek the right of direct observation of the missiles.

The use of sensors on satellites for making observations raises in the most acute form problems of ethics that are inherent in all attempts at control and verification. Control by whom? Because satellite observations are now virtually the monopoly of the superpowers, there must be an international demand that the observations of military satellites be made openly available, at least to the countries being observed. Only a certain sharing of data of relevance to environmental matters is in the offing so far. At a recent meeting of the UN Working Group on Remote Sensing of the Earth by Satellites the representative of the U.S. promised that data from his country's satellites would be released regularly for international use. The same demand for the internationalization of knowledge must be made in regard to observations of relevance to armaments and disarmament. The most desirable development would be direct international management of a satellite system.

Internationalization of at least the pertinent data is a *sine qua non*. It must be realized how great the inequality between nations is with respect to information that may be highly relevant for fostering mutual trust. Satellites are the most prominent example of the advanced techniques for observation that only certain nations possess. More generally, international equity demands that information should not be secretly held by the strongest powers but should be placed under international control. Great emphasis must be put on both increasing and internationalizing knowledge.

To cement the basis for mutual trust, cooperation should be directed to a gradual increase of knowledge. A wide, nonpolitical dissemination of information will serve this purpose in a general way, but there would also be occasion to build up a body of reliable knowledge in specific cases where doubt has arisen about the fulfillment of pledges.

Even in these specific cases the type of verification and control that relies on police surveillance and aims at a verdict by judicial authority is as far as possible to be avoided. Instead a gradual process of mutual contributions by the parties concerned to clarify matters should be tried. The Swedish delegation on international disarmament negotiations has sketched such a system of a largely voluntary control procedure, called "verification by challenge." The official presentation of it in brief form stipulates that under the proposed arrangement "a party suspected of having conducted an underground test, in violation of the treaty, would be expected voluntarily to offer clarifying information to allay suspicion, the assumption being that the suspected party would itself be vitally interested in establishing its innocence. An 'invitation to inspection' might be forthcoming spontaneously in some instance and under pressure in more severe cases of doubt. If such a challenge went unheeded on several occasions, other parties to the treaty would acquire the right to withdraw from it.... The threat of withdrawal might induce the accused party to offer clarification of the suspected event, or if the accusation persisted, to invite inspection. The system of 'verification by challenge' would be useful whether or not obligatory inspections were envisaged in the treaty. If obligatory inspections were envisaged, 'verification by challenge' would help reduce the size of the unresolved problem, and if inspection were not envisaged, it would help resolve suspicions."

In more concrete terms it can be said that in this scheme of verification by challenge the sanction of publicity in effect replaces the sanction of on-site inspection. Thus the method of deterrence is expected to be effective. The key to the entire problem of disarmament control is not reliance on specific formulas in a treaty but the construction of a firm basis of universal confidence through a cumulative process of fully shared factual information.

All the arguments advanced in the foregoing point to the need for some international agency to which the functions of verification and control can be entrusted. That some such body is necessary has also been acknowledged in all the more general plans for disarmament.

Sometimes these plans have been ambitious enough to aim at a kind of "managing agency for disarmament." That was the idea indicated in the McCloy-Zorin Agreed Principles, which called for an international disarmament organization within the UN. No date was set for its creation, but the demand that "the most thorough control should be exercised... during and after the implementation of General and Complete Disarmament" suggests an early inception of the control machinery.

The two draft treaties on general and complete disarmament submitted in 1962 by the U.S. and the U.S.S.R. respectively differed on several points having to do with inspection and control but not with respect to the establishing of an international disarmament organization, which both regarded in principle as being fundamental. They did not differ much on the timetable either. The U.S.S.R. wanted such an organization to begin operating "as soon as disarmament measures are initiated," which is not much different from the U.S. formulation to establish it "upon the entry into force of the Treaty." In the painfully protracted but unproductive negotiations that have followed, not much attention has been given to this organization, which in its draft shape was quite a full-fledged one with a complex organizational pattern.

Several tentative proposals along less ambitious lines have been made, however. Thus an early initiative was taken in 1962 by the nonaligned delegations to the Geneva Disarmament Committee to set up an international commission of scientists for the specific purpose of verifying a test-ban agreement. Soon thereafter the Swedish delegation pleaded that such a scientific commission be set up on an interim basis even before an agreement was reached. In 1972 the delegations of the Netherlands, Sweden and Yugoslavia made separate proposals for a similar institution, this time in relation to the verification of a prohibition on the production of chemical weapons.

In 1973 I widened the suggestion to

	ANTARCTIC TREATY	PARTIAL-TEST-BAN TREATY	OUTER-SPACE TREATY	TREATY OF TLATELOLCO	NON-PROLIFERATION TREATY	SEA-BED TREATY	BIOLOGICAL-WEAPONS CONVENTION
COLLECTION OF INFORMATION							
OBLIGATORY DECLARATION AND NOTIFICATION	■	■	■	■			
GROUND, NAVAL AND AIR OBSERVATION	■					■	
SPECIAL DETECTION AND IDENTIFICATION TECHNIQUES							
INTERNATIONAL EXCHANGE OF REPORTS OR DATA				■			
INQUIRY	■			■		■	
ON-SITE INSPECTION BY PARTIES							
OBLIGATORY AND CONTINUING, PERIODIC OR IN A LIMITED NUMBER							
ON THE BASIS OF FREE ACCESS	■		■	■			
ON THE BASIS OF CONSULTATION, COOPERATION OR INVITATION	■		■	■		■	
INTERNATIONAL SUPERVISION AND INSPECTION							
SPECIALLY ESTABLISHED CONTROL ORGANIZATION				■			
EXISTING ORGANIZATION				■	■		
INVESTIGATION BY UN SECRETARY GENERAL							
NATIONAL SELF-SUPERVISION AND SELF-INSPECTION	■	■	■		■		
COMPLAINT PROCEDURE							
CONSULTATION AND COOPERATION	■		■			■	■
REFERENCE TO CONFERENCE OF PARTIES	■			■			
REFERENCE TO INTERNATIONAL COURT OF JUSTICE	■			■			
RECOURSE TO UN SECURITY COUNCIL				■		■	■
REVIEW OF VERIFICATION SYSTEM				■		■	■

encompass all aspects of disarmament control and monitoring. A similar position was endorsed in a statement by P. H. Kooijmans of the Netherlands. My proposal that a central disarmament-control organization be set up immediately was motivated by two main concerns. The primary justification for the establishment of some organizational framework on a preparatory basis was that we risk, through *ad hoc* methods of work, heaping on one another control arrangements that remain unintegrated and even unrelated to one another. The second thesis was that we need such an organ as soon as possible because, in addition to following the implementation of control arrangements that are already presumed in various treaties, a constant watch should be kept on progress in the general direction of disarmament.

In the wake of the laborious search for some international agreement incorporating at least a semblance of disarmament, signs have become visible that international cooperation on control issues might become feasible. The nonaligned nations, supported in general terms but not strongly by the Western side, have struggled in vain to get such operational cooperation under the aegis of the UN Secretary General incorporated in some treaties. In the current discussions of a comprehensive test-ban agreement the socialist countries also seem to have moved somewhat closer to acceptance of organized international cooperation with respect to the exchange of data. An interesting signal was detected in relation to a prospective treaty on chemical weapons in a working paper by seven socialist states. That side has always been the one upholding the view that "national means" were sufficient for verification. In this paper a quite comprehensive system of internal control was outlined, based on national committees of control, but also

VERIFICATION PROCEDURES relied on to ensure compliance with the recent multilateral arms agreements have varied widely, as can be seen in this tabular presentation prepared as part of a working paper submitted last year by the Swedish delegation to the UN disarmament conference in Geneva. In the author's view the task of negotiating specific verification and control measures for specific disarmament agreements is much easier in practice than in theory, "either on the political ground that enough confidence prevails, or on the technological ground that sufficiently reliable means of monitoring events...are becoming available."

with a "possibility for publication of reports for general information," the system also in certain cases to be accompanied by the voluntary exchange of information among states.

A significantly more active role for this international data-exchange system, presupposing also an international committee to furnish guidelines for making such reporting comparable and standardized, was indicated by a group of Russian scientists in a paper on chemical disarmament published by the Stockholm International Peace Research Institute (SIPRI) in 1973.

My proposal is nominally attached to the idea of an international disarmament organization, since such an organization was in principle accepted by the UN as early as 1961, but the plan as I now want to present it envisions a system much more than an agency. Such a comprehensive system must be organically and hierarchically built up from the national level to various international levels, of which the one with judiciary functions should be not only the highest but also the last one resorted to. The design of the proposed system corresponds to a structure with four levels.

The broad base of such a structure must be the national means of detection and verification that are organized within countries not only for internal purposes (for the control of poisonous chemical agents, weapons production and the like) but also for monitoring events abroad by remote observation (by means of seismological stations, analysis of radioactive particles in the air and so forth). All such data should be published.

Questions referring to the machinery needed for control at the national level will obviously be handled by each state according to its own traditions. In all countries with aspirations to democratic government there is already one parliamentary standing committee or more scrutinizing the activities of the military, with decision-making power closely tied to the sanctioning of allocations.

Parliamentary action, however, is rarely enough to keep an issue under vital civic control. Thus in the working paper I have mentioned the seven socialist states call for the establishment of national committees comprised of "representatives of governmental and public organizations" including "specialists in chemistry and economics" with broad responsibilities in relation to the production of chemical means of warfare. In Sweden a citizens' committee has been appointed to scrutinize the acquisition of weapons from the viewpoint of compliance with the international humanitarian rules of war.

The ideal of openness should be pursued first and foremost at the national level. Citizens should be counted on to serve as the watchdogs ensuring that disarmament agreements are respected and that any moves in the direction of militarization are pushed back. When information on all matters relating to arms and arms limitation is spread openly within a nation, the information usually becomes available to other nations as well. It would obviously be more of a building block for a world system of verification if such nationally assembled information could be regularly, systematically and as a matter of routine addressed to an international center for further dissemination instead of finding its way sporadically to more than 100 countries. A broad flow of information would enhance everyone's sense of security—and security, after all, is the main objective of all verification.

The most general feature of such an approach would include greater publicity about arms production, arms deployment and arms trade. A kind of unobtrusive, broadside monitoring of disarmament dynamics would be gained by the more detailed publication of defense budgets. More specific information can be requested by separate agreements, including information obtained by methods of distant detection.

The crucial question then arises of whether this requirement calls for the creation of an international disarmament organization for centralizing all pertinent information emanating from national sources, or whether it is sufficient that such information be relayed to one of the likewise international but delimited organs in the appropriate specialized field. There are, however, few such bodies already in existence that have been given the function of monitoring matters of relevance to disarmament. Only the International Atomic Energy Agency has a surveillance function so far, and that is limited to surveillance of the production of nuclear weapons. For chemical weapons, where the need for an international control body is currently being discussed, no suitable existing agency has been indicated. Other agencies that exist or might be created are likely to have constitutions and constituencies of their own, often outside the framework of the UN, and they might not want to add the monitoring of disarmament to their functions.

Moreover, the areas to be covered for civilian benefits and for arms control are often not at all congruent. This would be the case with an International Ocean Regime, if it is established after the Law of the Sea Conference concludes its work. It might, of course, be of assistance in monitoring the deployment of unwanted marine installations (for example platforms for military refueling that may be forbidden). Such a regime, however, must be limited to surveillance in its own environment; it cannot serve as a guard against the land-based production and development of vessels or devices that may have to be ruled out for the sake of disarmament. Marine development, environmental protection and disarmament nonetheless have a joint stake in the internationalization of knowledge.

There are large areas of interest to disarmers that would remain outside the purview of even the most ambitious scheme for a world system of transnational agencies. Here a two-pronged approach is imperative. On the one hand, the access to technologies, particularly advanced ones requiring instrumentation beyond the national means of every country, must be internationalized together with the institutionalizing of sectorial networks for the wide dissemination of scientific and technical data. This would greatly benefit the accumulation of knowledge on developments related to armaments and disarmament. On the other hand, the specialized need for keeping disarmament matters in focus makes it inescapable that an international disarmament control organization must be established, possessing from the outset enough independent status and access to scientific expertise to command respect for objectivity and impartiality.

My proposal is therefore that a new body should be set up to receive such notifications and to perform all kinds of services for the cause of disarmament. It would be the second level in a control system, but it would be the first international level. I suggest that it be called the International Disarmament Control Organization. Its immediate function should be to act as an intermediary, or a clearinghouse, for providing knowledge about the implementation of disarmament agreements and also about spontaneous developments in the direction of disarmament. Such knowledge could be provided by member states using their national means of detection, verification and control.

As a supplemental activity the center should collate knowledge derived from various open sources: from scientific publications and statistics on production, trade and the transfer of arms and sensitive raw materials or commodities. It should profit by close cooperation with international agencies established for specialized purposes. It could also provide guidelines and even establish a more systematic international program for collecting national information, including the setting of rules and procedures for making the data of verification comparable. The process of verification itself, however, is conceived of as being conducted by national authorities within individual states.

An International Disarmament Control Organization might, particularly at the start, function as an open clearinghouse at the service of all nations by relaying information on disarmament matters to them in the form of bulletins. If its competence were broad enough to include its serving as a channel for an obligatory input of data from member states, it would have considerably more impact than the few existing international institutions, such as SIPRI, that have been set up independently to serve a similar purpose.

So far no mandatory verification by special investigations has been made a part of the proposal for an International Disarmament Control Organization. There will, however, be a need for extending the function of the organization to take on the responsibility as coordinator and referee for collecting evidence of a more active, investigatory character. Even for the future, with the possibility of enhanced world cooperation, it would seem necessary to have an International Disarmament Control Organization functioning for the purpose of directing specific inquiries to existing specialized bodies in cases of disagreement on questions of compliance with disarmament treaties.

The most critical question is how such a disarmament monitoring service could move toward a more inquisitive process of verification in cases where doubts have been expressed. Such activity would correspond to a third level in the control system. A difficulty is introduced by the fact that different disarmament treaties have, and will continue to have, quite differently composed constituencies or parties. Here the solution must be that the same secretariat serve a circle of "collateral constituencies," consisting of the full membership of parties concerned in each treaty. Their constituencies would assemble in regular review conferences, which several treaties already prescribe but which have so far not been given any organizational basis.

Such a separation of constituencies becomes particularly necessary when there is dispute about whether or not a specific treaty has been violated. The "verification by challenge" procedure would then begin by the complaining party's directing a query to another party (or other parties) through the good offices of the International Disarmament Control Organization. If the series of challenges and responses does not lead to satisfactory results, an investigation might be appropriate. If it were, the international control body would be the correct organ for handling it. For the actual "field investigations," if such a procedure is in order, it may well be that the international body should entrust them to various existing expert bodies or to *ad hoc* expert groups. The material collated and

SIGNERS AND NONSIGNERS of the Non-Proliferation Treaty are identified on this world map, the signers in gray and the nonsigners in color. The principal nonsigners are China,

accumulated by the international organization could then, if one of the parties wanted to lodge a complaint about treaty violation, accompany such an accusation to the appropriate judiciary organ. Presumably that would be the UN Security Council, which can thus be conceived of as being the fourth tier in the control system. It would be important, however, to maintain a strict separation of powers: the International Disarmament Control Organization should never itself pronounce verdicts. It should only assemble, collate, coordinate and transmit data.

The separation of the investigative and jurisdictional functions, referring them to different organs, must be made clear and explicit. The Security Council should not be asked to take on this dual responsibility. Only the creation of an International Disarmament Control Organization, independent of the Security Council with its veto powers, can guarantee a fair, equitable and expert collation of evidence. The lack of such an institution is a fundamental deficiency at this time, giving arguments to those who are reluctant to enter disarmament agreements. During the debate in the

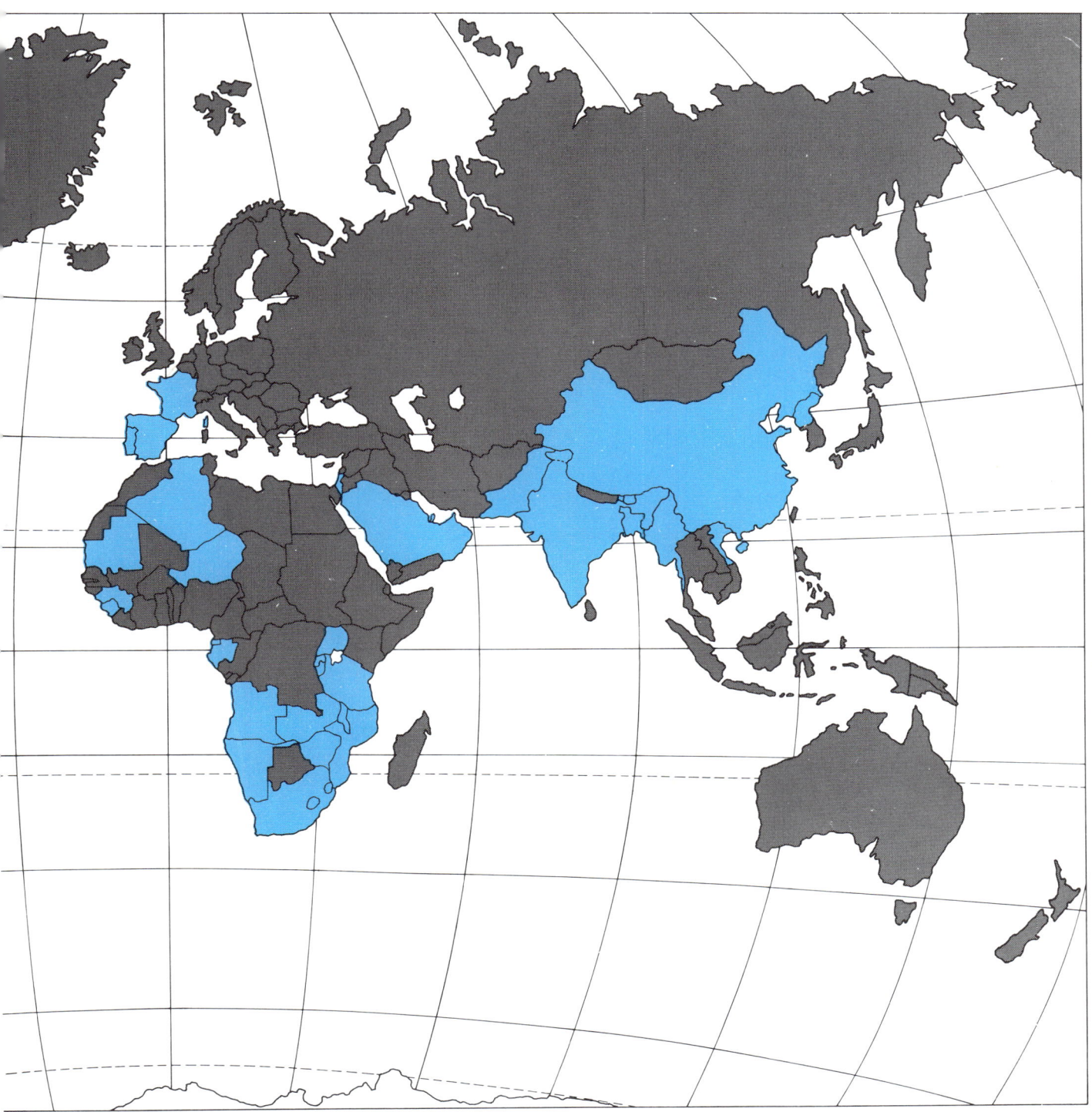

France, India, Israel and South Africa. Several of the signers have delayed ratification, and some (for example Egypt) may not at present have any intention of ratifying. There are now 84 full parties to the treaty together with 22 signers that have not (yet) ratified.

228　IV | THE GLOBAL POLITICS OF ARMS CONTROL

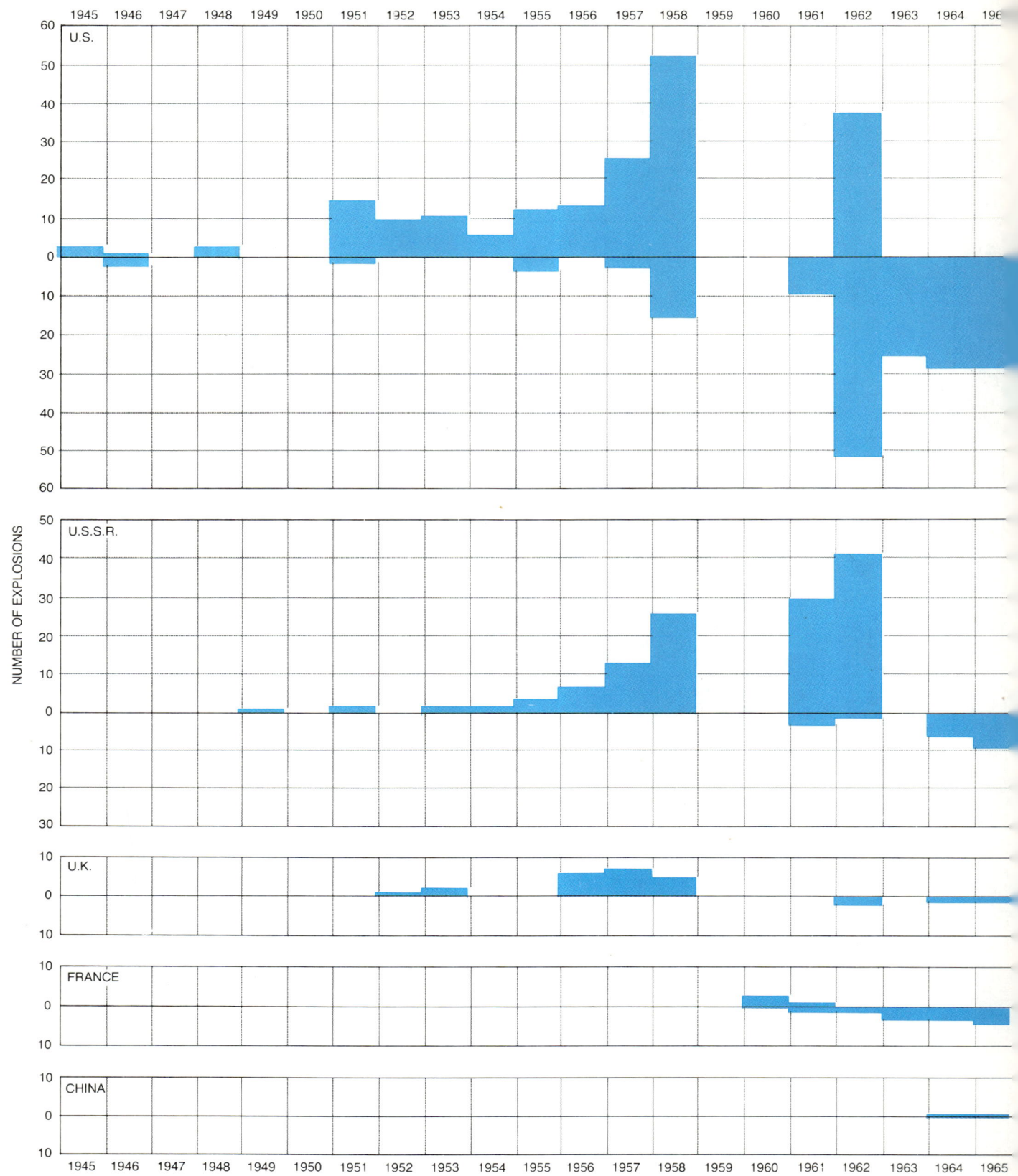

KNOWN NUCLEAR EXPLOSIONS from 1945 through 1973 are tallied by nation in this bar chart according to whether they took place in the atmosphere (*bars above base lines*) or underground (*bars below base lines*); the latter category includes a few cases of underwater explosions. The totals, which were compiled by the Stockholm International Peace Research Institute, are based not only on official announcements by the nations responsible but also on seismic monitoring and other data-gathering techniques employed by various nations, including Sweden. The totals do not include 33 nuclear tests known to have been conducted by the U.S.S.R. before 1958, for which exact dates are unavailable, nor do they include 23 unspecified U.S. explosions that are known to have

occurred between 1961 and 1963. The abrupt change from atmospheric testing to underground testing by the U.S., the U.S.S.R. and the U.K. coincides with their signing of the Partial-Nuclear-Test-Ban Treaty in 1963. The 1974 totals would of course include India.

UN on the convention prohibiting the production of biological weapons strong objections were raised against the handing over of decisions concerning investigations directly to the Security Council, with its veto power to protect allies and friends.

There are convincing arguments for not postponing action on establishing such an organizational nucleus. There is, in fact, no reason to wait for agreements in treaty form before starting to monitor what happens in one field or another of interest with regard to disarmament. The sequence can just as well start with the monitoring. Indeed, monitoring activities for the verification and control of arms-regulation measures might well stimulate the emergence of formal agreements. If a target date should be set for launching such an organizational innovation for the sake of disarmament, I would suggest the Review Conference for Non-Proliferation of Nuclear Weapons in May, 1975, when the need will make itself felt strongly and urgently.

In regard to the form of organizational structure, it would be of value to examine whether one might follow fairly closely the pattern set for continuous international work on problems of the environment. The general constituency must be the same worldwide one in both cases, encompassing the full range of the UN membership.

An interim International Disarmament Control Organization need not be large. Costs should be kept to the minimum of administrative necessities. Unlike the UN Environment Program, the International Disarmament Control Organization would hardly need a fund for operations. Like the Environment Program, however, it should have a semi-independent status within the UN, its budget allocation being underwritten by the UN. Such a relative degree of independence is particularly needed for an agency whose entire usefulness hinges on its objectivity and freedom from political shackles.

In sum, it appears highly desirable that a new international body should be set up for detecting possible transgressions of international rules in the field of arms and for following changes in the quality and quantity of armaments in various parts of the world. Such a body would be responsible for collating the relevant data, initiating specific inquiries, disseminating its findings and acting as a referee for those who are parties to various treaties. Such a body might also have to order the installation of specific equipment as well as produce manuals and guidelines for the art of monitoring. An agency of this type can be expected to grow on the basis of its own merits as a service organ.

As for deterrence—the threat of disclosure that would discourage clandestine violations—the process could take a more general, "passive" course. The new agency could then link up with existing or prospective sectorial international agencies, collating and distributing data from many sources. The main requirement for deterrence is that knowledge be widened and internationalized; the more information that is amassed and the more transparent all fields of human activity become, the more repellent becomes the risk of disclosure of any activities that are formally forbidden or even those that just go against the sense of what is commonly accepted as being internationally right—of being in the true interests of mankind. The denser the data exchange in a field is, the more it can serve as an alarm system, awakening some nation, some organization, some individuals to take action to get more of the unwanted developments prohibited.

Here is a promising connection between the suggested more informal approach to the control problem and the formalization of prohibitions by treaties with their specific control obligations. My contention is that such formalization will be eased when knowledge becomes more reliable, and when a consensus on desirable disarmament measures becomes firmer. These trends grow together, mutually reinforcing each other.

Moreover, it should be emphasized that any treaty prohibition extends beyond the parties who have gone through the formal process of ratification; the treaty tends to take on a character of customary law and can often be argued to be binding on all. At least the psychological and "ethical" impact is not to be minimized. There is a true bond of universal interest in the verifiability of how loyal and widespread is compliance not only with prohibitions but also with rules for good conduct among nations.

Initiatives allowing the UN to study the most appropriate forms and functions for fulfilling the dual task of spreading knowledge about armaments and of verifying disarmaments are the most urgent ones that I should have wanted to press if I were still a disarmament delegate. A proposal for an International Disarmament Control Organization ought to be forthcoming from some farsighted member nation, such as the nonaligned countries have often proved to be.

Major Provisions of the Treaty on the Non-Proliferation of Nuclear Weapons*

Article I

Each nuclear-weapon State Party to the Treaty undertakes not to transfer to any recipient whatsoever nuclear weapons or other nuclear explosive devices or control over such weapons or explosive devices directly, or indirectly; and not in any way to assist, encourage, or induce any non-nuclear-weapon State to manufacture or otherwise acquire nuclear weapons or other nuclear explosive devices, or control over such weapons or explosive devices.

Article II

Each non-nuclear-weapon State Party to the Treaty undertakes not to receive the transfer from any transferor whatsoever of nuclear weapons or other nuclear explosive devices or of control over such weapons or explosive devices directly, or indirectly; not to manufacture or otherwise acquire nuclear weapons or other nuclear explosive devices; and not to seek or receive any assistance in the manufacture of nuclear weapons or other nuclear explosive devices.

Article III

1. Each non-nuclear-weapon State Party to the Treaty undertakes to accept safeguards, as set forth in an agreement to be negotiated and concluded with the International Atomic Energy Agency in accordance with the Statute of the International Atomic Energy Agency and the Agency's safeguards system, for the exclusive purpose of verification of the fulfillment of its obligations assumed under this Treaty with a view to preventing diversion of nuclear energy from peaceful uses to nuclear weapons or other nuclear explosive devices. Procedures for the safeguards required by this article shall be followed with respect to source or special fissionable material whether it is being produced, processed or used in any principal nuclear facility or is outside any such facility. The safeguards required by this article shall be applied on all source or special fissionable material in all peaceful nuclear activities within the territory of such State, under its jurisdiction, or carried out under its control anywhere.

2. Each State Party to the Treaty undertakes not to provide: (a) source or special fissionable material, or (b) equipment or material especially designed or prepared for the processing, use or production of special fissionable material, to any non-nuclear-weapon State for peaceful purposes, unless the source or special fissionable material shall be subject to the safeguards required by this article.

3. The safeguards required by this article shall be implemented in a manner designed to comply with article IV of this Treaty, and to avoid hampering the economic or technological development of the Parties or international cooperation in the field of peaceful nuclear activities, including the international exchange of nuclear material and equipment for the processing, use or production of nuclear material for peaceful purposes in accordance with the provisions of this article and the principle of safeguarding set forth in the Preamble of the Treaty.

4. Non-nuclear-weapon States Party to the Treaty shall conclude agreements with the International Atomic Energy Agency to meet the requirements of this article either individually or together with other States in accordance with the Statute of the International Atomic Energy Agency. Negotiation of such agreements shall commence within 180 days from the original entry into force of this Treaty. For States depositing their instruments of ratification or accession after the 180-day period, negotiation of such agreements shall enter into force not later than eighteen months after the date of initiation of negotiations.

Article IV

1. Nothing in this Treaty shall be interpreted as affecting the inalienable right of all the Parties to the Treaty to develop research, production and use of nuclear energy for peaceful purposes without discrimination and in conformity with articles I and II of this Treaty.

2. All the Parties to the Treaty undertake to facilitate, and have the right to participate in, the fullest possible exchange of equipment, materials and scientific and technological information for the peaceful uses of nuclear energy. Parties to the Treaty in a position to do so shall also cooperate in contributing alone or together with other States or international organizations to the further development of the applications of nuclear energy for peaceful purposes, especially in the territories of non-nuclear-weapon States Party to the Treaty, with due consideration for the needs of the developing areas of the world.

Article V

Each Party to the Treaty undertakes to take appropriate measures to ensure that, in accordance with this Treaty, under appropriate international observation and through appropriate international procedures, potential benefits from any peaceful applications of nuclear explosions will be made available to non-nuclear-weapon States Party to the Treaty on a non-discriminatory basis and that the charge to such Parties for the explosive devices used will be as low as possible and exclude any charge for research and development. Non-nuclear weapon States Party to the Treaty shall be able to obtain such benefits, pursuant to a special international agreement or agreements, through an appropriate international body with adequate representation of non-nuclear-weapon States. Negotiations on this subject shall commence as soon as possible after the Treaty enters into force. Non-nuclear-weapon States Party to the Treaty so desiring may also obtain such benefits pursuant to bilateral agreements.

Article VI

Each of the Parties to the Treaty undertakes to pursue negotiations in good faith on effective measures relating to cessation of the nuclear arms race at an early date and to nuclear disarmament, and on a treaty on general and complete disarmament under strict and effective international control.

---

*Selections from text of treaty signed at Washington, London, and Moscow on 1 July 1968. U.S. ratification deposited 5 March 1970. Entered into force 5 March 1970. Not published in *Scientific American*.

BIBLIOGRAPHY

Basic Sources of Current Material

Arms Control Today.
Bulletin of the Atomic Scientists.
Defense Monitor. Published by Center for Defense Information, Washington, D.C.
F.A.S. (Federation of American Scientists). *Public Interest Report.*
International Institute for Strategic Studies (IISS). *The Military Balance, 1978–1979.* London: IISS, 1978. Annual publication.
International Institute for Strategic Studies (IISS). *Strategic Survey 1978.* London: IISS, 1978. Annual publication.
International Security.
Orbis.
Sivard, R. L. *World Military and Social Expenditures, 1977.* New York: Rockefeller Foundation, 1977. Annual publication.
Stockholm International Peace Research Institute (SIPRI). *World Armaments and Disarmament: SIPRI Yearbook, 1978.* Stockholm: Almqvist & Wiksell, 1978. Annual publication.
U.S. Department of Defense. *Annual Report, FY 79.* Washington, D.C.: Government Printing Office, 1978. Annual publication.
U.S. House Committee on Appropriations. *Department of Defense Appropriations.* Annual hearings. Washington, D.C.: Government Printing Office.
U.S. House Committee on Armed Services. *Military Posture.* Annual hearings. Washington, D.C.: Government Printing Office.
U.S. Senate Committee on Appropriations. *Defense Appropriations.* Annual hearings. Washington, D.C.: Government Printing office.
U.S. Senate Committee on Armed Services. *Department of Defense Authorization for Appropriations.* Annual hearings. Washington, D.C.: Government Printing Office.
Washington Review.

I Arms Acquisition and the Threat of Armageddon

Barnard, C. I., J. R. Oppenheimer, C. A. Thomas, H. A. Winne, and D. E. Lilienthal. *A Report on the International Control of Atomic Energy.* Prepared for the Secretary of State's Committee on Atomic Energy. Garden City, N.Y.: Doubleday, 1946.
Barton, J. H., and L. D. Weiler, eds. *International Arms Control: Issues and Agreements.* Stanford, Calif.: Stanford University Press, 1976.
Bechhoefer, B. G. *Postwar Negotiations for Arms Control.* Washington, D.C.: Brookings Institution, 1961.
Bethe, H. A. "The Hydrogen Bomb: II." *Scientific American,* 1950, **182**(4), 13–17.
Brennan, D. G. "A Comprehensive Test Ban: Everybody or Nobody." *International Security,* 1976, **1**, 92–117.
Bullard, Sir E. "The Detection of Underground Explosions." *Scientific American,* 1966, **215**(1), 19–29.
Burns, R. D. *Arms Control and Disarmament: A Bibliography.* Santa Barbara, Calif.: ABC-Clio, 1977.
Glasstone, S., and P. J. Dolan. *The Effects of Nuclear Weapons.* 3rd ed. Washington, D.C.: Government Printing Office, 1977.
Hewlett, R. G., and F. Duncan. *A History of the United States Atomic Energy Commission.* Vol. 2. *Atomic Shield, 1974/1952.* University Park: Pennsylvania State University Press, 1969.
Lilienthal, D. E. *The Journals of David E. Lilienthal.* Vol. 2. *The Atomic Energy Years, 1945–1950.* New York: Harper & Row, 1964.
Myers, H. R. "Extending the Nuclear-Test Ban." *Scientific American,* 1972, **226**(1), 13–23.
Ridenour, L. N. "The Hydrogen Bomb." *Scientific American,* 1950, **182**(3), 11–15.
Stockholm International Peace Research Institute (SIPRI). *Armaments and Disarmament in the Nuclear Age.* Stockholm: Almqvist & Wiksell, 1976.
U.S. Arms Control and Disarmament Agency (ACDA). *Arms Control and Disarmament Agreements: Texts and History of Negotiations.* Washington, D.C.: ACDA, 1977.

U.S. Atomic Energy Commission. *In the Matter of J. Robert Oppenheimer: Transcript of Hearing before Personnel Security Board.* Cambridge, Mass.: MIT Press, 1971.

Wiesner, J. B., and H. York. "National Security and the Nuclear Test Ban." *Scientific American,* 1964, **211**(4), 27–35.

York, H. *The Advisors: Oppenheimer, Teller, and the Superbomb.* San Francisco: W. H. Freeman and Company, 1976.

York, H., ed. *Arms Control: Readings from* SCIENTIFIC AMERICAN, San Francisco: W. H. Freeman and Company, 1973.

II SALT I and Its Background

Berman, R. P., and J. C. Baker. *Soviet Strategic Forces and Soviet Security.* Washington, D.C.: Brookings Institution, forthcoming.

Blair, B. "Arms Control Implications of Strategic Monitoring Programs." In *Analysis of Arms Control Impact Statements Submitted in Connection with the Fiscal Year 1979 Budget Request.* Washington, D.C.: Government Printing Office, 1978.

Brown, H. "Security through Limitations." *Foreign Affairs,* 1969, **47**, 422–432.

Chayes, A. "An Inquiry into the Workings of Arms Control Agreements." *Harvard Law Review,* 1972, **85**, 905–969.

Chayes, A., and J. B. Wiesner, eds. *ABM: An Evaluation of the Decision to Deploy an Antiballistic Missile System.* New York: Harper & Row, 1969.

Davis, L. E., and W. R. Schilling. "All You Ever Wanted To Know about MIRV and ICBM Calculations But Were Not Cleared To Ask." *Journal of Conflict Resolution,* 1973, **17**, 207–242.

English, R. C., and D. I. Bolef. "Defense against Bomber Attack." *Scientific American,* 1973, **229**(2), 11–19.

Freedman, L. *U.S. Intelligence and the Soviet Strategic Threat.* Boulder, Colo.: Westview Press, 1977.

Garwin, R. L., and H. A. Bethe. "Anti-Ballistic-Missile Systems." *Scientific American,* 1968, **218**(3), 21–31.

Greenwood, T. "Reconnaissance, Surveillance and Arms Control." Adelphi Papers No. 88. London: International Institute of Strategic Studies, 1972.

Halperin, M. H. *Bureaucratic Politics and Foreign Policy.* Washington, D.C.: Brookings Institution, 1974.

Kaplan, M. A., ed. *SALT: Problems and Prospects.* Morristown, N.J.: General Learning Press, 1973.

Lodal, J. M. "Verifying SALT." *Foreign Policy,* 1976, **24**, 40–64.

Lucas, H. "ASW: Threat and Counterthreat." *Sea Power,* 1977, **20**, 9–15.

McNamara, R. S. *The Essence of Security.* New York: Harper & Row, 1968.

Newhouse, John. *Cold Dawn—The Story of SALT.* New York: Holt, Rinehart and Winston, 1973.

Russett, B. *What Price Vigilance? The Burdens of National Defense.* New Haven: Yale University Press, 1970.

Scoville, H., Jr. "The Limitation of Offensive Weapons." *Scientific American,* 1971, **224**(1), 15–25.

Smith, R. H. "ASW—The Crucial Naval Challenge." *U.S. Naval Institute Proceedings,* 1972, **98**, 126–141.

Steinbruner, J., and T. Garwin. "Strategic Vulnerability: The Balance between Prudence and Paranoia." *International Security,* 1976, **1**, 138–181.

Stockholm International Peace Research Institute (SIPRI). "Antisubmarine Warfare." In *World Armaments and Disarmament: SIPRI Yearbook 1974.* Stockholm: Almqvist & Wiksell, 1974.

Stockholm International Peace Research Institute (SIPRI). "Reconnaissance Satellites." In *World Armaments and Disarmament: SIPRI Yearbook 1975.* Stockholm: Almqvist & Wiksell, 1975.

Stockholm International Peace Research Institute (SIPRI). "Reconnaissance Satellites." In *World Armaments and Disarmament: SIPRI Yearbook 1976.* Stockholm: Almqvist & Wiksell, 1976.

Stockholm International Peace Research Institute (SIPRI). "Military Satellites." In *World Armaments and Disarmament: SIPRI Yearbook 1977.* Stockholm: Almqvist & Wiksell, 1977.

Tsipis, K., A. H. Cahn, and B. T. Feld, eds. *The Future of the Sea-Based Deterrent.* Cambridge, Mass.: MIT Press, 1973.

U.S. Congress, House Committee on Foreign Affairs, Subcommittee on National Security Policy. *Diplomatic and Strategic Impact of Multiple Warhead Missiles.* Hearings. Washington, D.C.: Government Printing Office, 1969.

U.S. Congress, House Committee on International Relations, Subcommittee on International Security and Scientific Affairs. *First Use of Nuclear Weapons: Preserving Responsible Control.* Hearings. Washington, D.C.: Government Printing Office, 1976.

U.S. Congress, Senate Committee on Aeronautical and Space Sciences. *Soviet Space Programs, 1971–1975.* 2 vols. Staff report. Washington, D.C.: Government Printing Office, 1976.

U.S. Congress, Senate Committee on Armed Services. "Antisubmarine Warfare Programs." In *FY 1977 Authorization for Military Procurement.* Hearings. Washington, D.C.: Government Printing Office, 1976.

U.S. Congress, Senate Committee on Foreign Relations. *Strategic Arms Limitation Agreements.* Washington, D.C.: Government Printing office, 1972.

U.S. Congress, Senate Committee on Foreign Relations, Subcommittee on Arms Control, International Law and Organization. *AMB, MIRV, SALT, and the Nuclear Arms Race.* Washington, D.C.: Government Printing office, 1970.

U.S. Congress, Senate Committee on Foreign Relations, Subcommittee on International Organization and Disarmament Affairs. *Strategic and Foreign Policy Implications of ABM Systems.* Washington, D.C.: Government Printing Office, 1969.

Willrich, M., and J. B. Rhinelander, eds. *SALT: The Moscow Agreements and Beyond.* New York: Free Press, 1974.

Wohlstetter, A. "Is There a Strategic Arms Race?" *Foreign Policy,* 1974, **15**, 3–20.

Wohlstetter, A. "Rivals, But No 'Race.'" *Foreign Policy,* 1974, **16**, 48–81.

York, H. *Race to Oblivion: A Participant's View of the Arms Race.* New York: Simon & Schuster, 1970.

III SALT II: Limited Negotiations

Bertram, C. "Beyond SALT II: The Future of Arms Control (Part I)." *Adelphi Papers* No. 141. London: International Institute for Strategic Studies, 1978.

Blechman, B., R. P. Berman, M. Binkin, S. E. Johnson, R. G. Weinland, and F. W. Young. *The Soviet Military Buildup and U.S. Defense Spending*. Washington, D.C.: Brookings Institution, 1977.

Brewer, G. D., and M. Shubik. *The War Game: A Critique of Military Problem Solving*. Cambridge, Mass.: Harvard University Press, 1978.

Brown, H. Speech at Thirty-fourth Annual Dinner of National Security Industrial Association. Department of Defense News Release #430-77, 1977.

Brown, H. *Department of Defense Annual Report, FY 1979*. Washington, D.C.: Government Printing Office, 1978.

Burt, R. "The Cruise Missile and Arms Control." *Survival*, 1976, **18**, 10–17.

Burt, R. "Arms Control and Soviet Strategic Forces: The Risks of Asking SALT To Do Too Much." *Washington Review*, 1978, **1**, 19–33.

Davis, L. E. "Limited Nuclear Options: Deterrence and the New American Doctrine." *Adelphi Papers* No. 121. London: International Institute for Strategic Studies, 1976.

Donnelly, C. N. "Civil Defense in the Soviet Union." *International Defense Review*, 1977, **10**, 635–643.

Doty, P., A. Carnesale, and M. Nacht. "The Race To Control Nuclear Arms." *Foreign Affairs*, 1976, **60**, 119–132.

Enthoven, A., and K. W. Smith. *How Much Is Enough? Shaping the Defense Program, 1961–1969*. New York: Harper & Row, 1971.

Fiscal Year 1979 Arms Control Impact Statements. Statements submitted to the Congress by the President pursuant to Section 36 of the Arms Control and Disarmament Act. Washington, D.C.: Government Printing Office, 1978.

Ford, H. P., and F. X. Winters, eds. *Ethics and Nuclear Strategy?* Maryknoll, N.Y.: Orbis, 1977.

Foster, J. L., and G. A. Brewer. "And the Clocks Were Striking Thirteen: The Termination of War." *Policy Sciences*, 1976, **7**, 225–243.

Frye, A. "Strategic Restraint, Mutual and Assured." *Foreign Policy*, 1977, **27**, 3–24.

Garwin, R. L. "Effective Military Technology for the 1980s." *International Security*, 1976, **1**, 50–78.

Gompert, D. C., M. Mandelbaum, R. L. Garwin, and J. H. Barton. *Nuclear Weapons and World Politics*. New York: McGraw-Hill, 1977.

Greenwood, T. *Making the MIRV*. Cambridge, Mass.: Ballinger, 1975.

Ikle, F. C. "Can Nuclear Deterrence Last Out the Century?" *Foreign Affairs*, 1973, **51**, 267–285.

Long, F., and G. Rathjens, eds. *Arms, Defense Polciy, and Arms Control*. New York: Norton, 1976.

National Academy of Sciences. *Long-Term World-Wide Effects of Multiple-Nuclear Weapons Detonations*. Washington, D.C.: National Academy of Sciences, 1975.

Nitze, P. "Assuring Strategic Stability in an Era of Detente." *Foreign Affairs*, 1976, **54**, 207–232.

Nuclear Energy Policy Study Group. *Nuclear Power Issues and Choices*. Cambridge, Mass.: Ballinger, 1977.

Panofsky, K. H. "The Mutual-Hostage Relationship between America and Russia." *Foreign Affairs*, 1973, **52**, 109–118.

Pfaltzgraff, R. L., and J. K. Davis. *The Cruise Missile: Bargaining Chip or Defense Bargain*. Cambridge, Mass.: Institute for Foreign Policy Analysis, 1977.

Quanbeck, A. H., and A. L. Wood. *Modernizing the Strategic Bomber Force: Why and How*. Washington, D.C.: Brookings Institution, 1976.

Rathjens, G. W. "Future Limitations of Strategic Arms." In M. Willrich and J. B. Rhinelander, eds., *SALT: The Moscow Agreements and Beyond*. New York: Free Press, 1974.

Record, J. *U.S. Nuclear Weapons in Europe*. Washington, D.C.: Brookings Institution, 1974.

Shreffler, R. G. "The Neutron Bomb for NATO Defense: An Alternative." *Orbis*, 1978, **21**, 959–973.

Smith, G. "Negotiating with the Soviets." *Survival*, 1977, **20**, 117–120. Originally appeared in *New York Times Magazine*.

Steinbruner, J. "National Security and the Concept of Strategic Stability." *Journal of Conflict Resolution*, 1978, **22**, 411–428.

Trofimenko, H. "The 'Theology' of Strategy." *Orbis*, 1977, **21**, 497–515.

Tsipis, K. "The Accuracy of Strategic Missiles." *Scientific American*, 1975, **233**(1), 14–23.

U.S. Congress. *Analysis of Arms Control Impact Statements FY 1978*. Washington, D.C.: Government Printing Office, 1977.

U.S. Congress, House Committee on Armed Services. *Review of the State of U.S. Strategic Forces*. Hearings. Washington, D.C.: Government Printing Office, 1977.

U.S. Congress, House Committee on International Relations, Subcommittee on International Security and Scientific Affairs. *The Vladivostok Accord: Implications to U.S. Security, Arms Control and World Peace*. Hearings. Washington, D.C.: Government Printing Office, 1975.

U.S. Congress, Joint Committee on Defense Production. *Civil Preparedness Review*. Washington, D.C.: Government Printing Office, 1977.

U.S. Congress, Senate. *United States and Soviet City Defense*. Document #94-268. Washington, D.C.: Government Printing Office, 1976.

U.S. Congress, Senate Committee on Foreign Relations. *Briefings on SALT Negotiations*. Hearings. Washington, D.C.: Government Printing Office, 1978.

U.S. Congress, Senate Committee on Foreign Relations. *Detente*. Hearings. Washington, D.C.: Government Printing Office, 1975.

U.S. Congress, Senate Committee on Foreign Relations, Subcommittee on Arms Control, International Law and Organization. *Briefing on Counterforce Attacks*. Hearings. Washington, D.C.: Government Printing Office, 1975.

U.S. Congress, Senate Committee on Foreign Relations, Subcommittee on Arms Control, International Law and Organization. *U.S.-U.S.S.R. Strategic Policies*. Washington, D.C.: Government Printing Office, 1974.

U.S. Congress, Senate Committee on Foreign Relations, Subcommittee on Arms Control, International Organizations and Security Agreements. *Effects of Limited Nuclear Warfare.* Hearings. Washington, D.C.: Government Printing Office, 1976.

U.S. Congress, Senate Committee on Foreign Relations, Subcommittee on Arms Control, Oceans and International Environment. *United States/Soviet Strategic Options.* Washington, D.C.: Government Printing Office, 1977.

Vershbow, A. R. "The Cruise Missile: The End of Arms Control?" *Foreign Affairs*, 1976, **54**, 133–146.

Warnke, P. C. "Apes on a Treadmill." *Foreign Policy*, 1975, **16**, 12–29.

IV The Global Politics of Arms Control

Arms Control Association. *NPT: Paradoxes and Problems.* Washington, D.C.: Arms Control Association, 1975.

"The Arms Race and Nuclear Proliferation." *Bulletin of Peace Proposals*, 1977, **8**(1), entire issue.

Betts, R. K. "Paranoids, Pygmies, Pariahs, and Nonproliferation." *Foreign Policy*, **26**, 157–183.

Blair, B. G., and G. D. Brewer. "The Terrorist Threat to World Nuclear Programs." *Journal of Conflict Resolution*, 1977, **21**, 379–404.

Epstein, W. "Nuclear-free Zones." *Scientific American*, 1975, **233**(5), 25–35.

Epstein, W. *The Last Chance: Nuclear Proliferation and Arms Control.* New York: Free Press, 1976.

Executive Office of the President, Energy Policy and Planning. *The National Energy Plan.* Washington, D.C.: Government Printing Office, 1977.

Flowers, B. "Nuclear Power: A Perspective of the Risks, Benefits and Options." *Bulletin of the Atomic Scientists.* 1978, **34**, 21.

'Myrdal, A. *The Game of Disarmament: How the Superpowers Run the Arms Race.* New York: Pantheon, 1976.

Quester, G. H. *The Politics of Nuclear Proliferation.* Baltimore: Johns Hopkins University Press, 1973.

Schelling, T. C. "Who Will Have the Bomb?" *International Security*, 1976, **1**, 77–91.

Stockholm International Peace Research Institute (SIPRI). *Nuclear Proliferation Problems.* Cambridge, Mass.: MIT Press, 1974.

U.S. Congress, House Committee on International Relations and Senate Committee on Governmental Affairs. *Nuclear Proliferation Factbook.* Washington, D.C.: Government Printing Office, 1977.

U.S. Congress, House Committee on International Relations and Senate Committee on Governmental Affairs. *Bibliography: Nuclear Proliferation.* Washington, D.C.: Government Printing Office, 1978.

U.S. Congress, Office of Technology Assessment. *Nuclear Proliferation and Safeguards.* Washington, D.C.: Government Printing Office, 1977.

Weiss, L. "Nuclear Safeguards: A Congressional Perspective." *Bulletin of the Atomic Scientists*, 1978, **34**, 27–33.

Willrich, M., and T. Taylor. *Nuclear Theft: Risks and Safeguards.* Cambridge, Mass.: Ballinger, 1974.

Wohlstetter, A., et al. *Moving toward Life in a Nuclear Armed Crowd?* Los Angeles: Pan Heuristics, 1976.

INDEX

Able-Star, 127, 128
ABMs. *See* Antiballistic missiles
ABM Treaty, 82, 114, 118, 130, 154, 163, 192–193
   and Sprints, 157
   text of, 106–111
   and verification, 31–32, 94, 103, 104, 105
Accident Measures Agreement, 31
Accuracy, 104, 140, 141, 143
   of cruise missiles, 172, 175
   of Minutemen, 134, 137, 139, 167
   MIRVs and, 129, 134, 138–139
   of SLBMs, 71, 73–74, 137
ACHESON, DEAN, 16
Acoustics in ASW, 84–87
Action-reaction phenomenon, 28, 37–43, 63, 119, 140
Advanced Research Projects Agency (ARPA), 44, 127
AEC. *See* Atomic Energy Commission
Aerospace Corporation, 127–128
Agena, 97, 98, 99, 127
Aircraft carriers in ASW, 91
Air-launched cruise vehicles (ALCMs), 115, 120, 176, 179, 180
ALVAREZ, LUIS W., 10
Antiballistic missiles (ABMs), 8, 18–20, 29, 37, 38, 44–56, 119
   and MIRVs, 20, 28, 30, 33–67, 114, 118, 122, 127–131, 133
   radars for, 103, 108, 110–111
   and SLBMs, 70, 76, 77, 81
   Soviet, 18–19, 37–38, 41, 46, 48, 53–54, 100, 121, 134
   Vladivostok Accords and, 118, 193
   See also ABM Treaty; Safeguard; Sprints
Antisubmarine warfare (ASW), 31, 67, 70–71, 76–93, 139, 178–179
Area-correlation method, 174
Argentina, 184, 198
Arms Control and Disarmament Agency, 22, 28, 131
Assured destruction, 3, 16, 29, 46–47, 64
   and counterforce, 63, 114, 118, 132–136, 144
   vs. damage limitation, 60, 62–63

ASW. *See* Antisubmarine warfare
Atlas, 28, 44, 98, 99, 127
Atomic bomb, 3, 9
Atomic Energy Act, 10
Atomic Energy Commission (AEC), 9, 10–13, 14, 16, 22, 145, 191
Australia, 189, 199, 210
Autism, national, 4

B-1 bombers, 115, 119, 138, 176, 179, 193
B-52 bombers, 116, 134, 135, 165, 176, 179
B-70 bombers, 37, 38, 119
Backfire bombers, 115, 116, 120, 163, 164, 166, 170
   capability of, 139, 165, 167
BAKER, J. C., 121
Balance of terror, 2, 14, 33, 40, 60, 131, 154
Ballistic antimissile boost interceptor (BAMBI), 127
Ballistic missiles defense (BMD), 32
Bargaining chips, 118, 141
Baruch Plan, 3, 11
Belgium, 199
BERMAN, R. P., 121
BETHE, H. A., 11, 14, 35, 51
Big Bird, 99–100
Blackout phenomenon, 19
Blast overpressure, 123–124
BOHR, NIELS, 3, 221
Bombers, 28, 48–49, 55, 70, 133, 134, 165
   and cruise missiles, 115, 178, 179
   Vladivostok Accords and, 163, 164, 166, 193
   See also B-1 bombers; B-52 bombers; B-70 bombers; Backfire bombers
Bombs, 146
   atomic, 3, 9
   hydrogen, 3, 9–16
   neutron, 8, 21–22, 119, 155–162
Boosters, 105
   for satellites, 98, 99, 127
   and SLCMs, 175
   tests of, 10, 11, 14, 15

BORDEN, WILLIAM L., 10
BRADBURY, NORRIS E., 9
BRADLEY, OMAR, 11
Bravo, 14, 16
Brazil, 184, 198
BREZHNEV, L., 8, 32, 121, 171, 188
BROOKE, EDWARD W., 131
BROWN, GEORGE S., 138
BROWN, HAROLD, 19, 28, 45, 114, 116, 119, 129
BUCKLEY, OLIVER E., 11, 12
Bulletin of the Atomic Scientists, 3
Bus, 36, 76, 122–123, 130, 137

Canada, 189, 195, 199, 200, 210
CARTER, BARRY, 119, 120, 132–143
CARTER, JAMES EARL, 2, 8, 115, 116, 119, 121, 210
CASE, CLIFFORD P., 144
Casualties, human, 3, 114, 119, 144–152, 159, 160–161
Cavitation, 86
Central Intelligence Agency, 97
CEP. *See* Circular error probable
CHAGLA, MAHOMEDALI CURRIM, 190
CHAKRAVARTY, BIRENDRA NARAYAN, 190
CHAYES, ABRAM, 50
Chile, 184, 198
China, 7, 8, 9, 43, 59, 121, 135
   nuclear explosions by, 25, 33, 38, 58, 190, 191, 195
   and proliferation, 188–189, 192, 195, 201
   reconnaissance over, 98
   Safeguard and, 64
   Sentinel and, 20, 33, 35, 38, 45, 50–51
   and SLBMs, 70
CHURCHILL, WINSTON, 3
Circular error probable (CEP), 47, 115, 129, 134
Civil defense, 144, 149–151
CLIFFORD, CLARK, 133
Clinch River breeder reactor, 203
Cloud cover and monitoring, 97, 101, 180
Coal, 204, 209
Cold war, 3–5, 7, 9

Command and Control System, 52, 55
Command Data Buffer system, 153
Communications systems, 29–30, 31, 71, 74–76
Computers, 15
CONANT, JAMES B., 11, 12, 16
Convergence zones, 84
Cost:
  of antisubmarine mines, 90
  of counterforce, 139
  of cruise missiles, 176, 180
  of hydrogen bomb, 12
  of neutron bomb, 161
  of Safeguard, 53
  of submarines, 76, 90
  See also Expenditures
Counterforce, 118, 120, 132–143, 194
  casualties during, 144–152, 159, 160–161
  and MIRVs, 37–40, 63–67, 77, 114, 122, 128–131, 143, 153–154, 164–167
  Schlesinger and, 119, 131–144 *passim*, 153, 154
  SLBMs and, 69, 77, 79, 132, 133, 134, 137, 139, 141
Cruise missiles, 116, 119–120, 163, 166–167, 170, 171–180, 194
  air-launched, 115, 120, 170, 176, 179, 180
  sea-launched, 29, 83, 170, 174, 175, 178–179, 180
Czechoslovakia, 9, 28, 57, 182, 199

Damage limitation, 41, 60, 62–63, 67, 119
Deaths, human, 3, 114, 119, 144–152, 159, 160–161
Decoys, 125–126
Defender Program, 44
Department of Defense, 22, 44
  on bomb loads, 164
  on casualties, 114, 119, 144–152
  and counterforce, 144–153
  and MIRVs, 48, 76–77, 122, 123, 124–125
  and neutron bomb, 160, 161
  radars of, 103
  on Russian arms, 45, 100, 122
Destruction:
  in ASW, 87–90
  and yield, 123–124
  See also Assured destruction
Detection in ASW, 83–86
Détente, 118
Deterrence, 29, 48–49, 142, 154, 164, 229
  and ABMs, 82
  submarines and, 69–81, 82–83, 91–93
Deuterium, liquid, 14
Discoverer satellites, 97–98, 99
Discrimination techniques, 51
Displacement effect, 115, 117
DRELL, SIDNEY, 119, 120, 144–154
DUBRIDGE, LEE A., 11, 12

E-6, 99
Eastman Kodak Company, 100

Economics, 2, 4, 121, 185, 205
  See also Expenditures
Effects of Nuclear Weapons (Glasstone), 145
Egypt, 198
EISENHOWER, DWIGHT D., 14, 54, 65
Electric-power industry, 209–210, 215
Electromagnetic pulse (EMP), 20
Energy sources, 185, 204–205, 209–210, 213, 214–215
Enhanced-radiation weapons, 8, 21–22, 119, 155–162
Eniwetok, 11, 13, 14
EPSTEIN, WILLIAM, 183, 184, 186–201
Essential equivalence, 119, 136, 137, 138, 139
European theater, 141, 155–162
Exchange ratio, 50, 70, 90
Expenditures, 2, 5, 28, 64, 65, 67, 182–183
  for ASW, 139
  for bombers, 134
  for European theater, 155
  of IAEA, 185
  SALT and, 121, 163, 182–183
  for ULMS, 80, 81
  See also Cost
Extremely-low-frequency (ELF) waves, 31, 75

FB 111 bombers, 134
Federation of American Scientists, 3, 143
FERMI, ENRICO, 11, 12, 16
Fission, 146–147
Flexibility, 132, 136, 144, 152–153
FOBS. *See* Fractional orbital bombardment system
FORD, GERALD, 171
Forward-based systems, 30, 120, 164, 165, 170
FOSTER, JOHN STUART, JR., 24, 45, 78, 127
FOSTER, WILLIAM C., 22, 24, 25
Fractional orbital bombardment system (FOBS), 46, 70
France, 7, 8, 25, 184, 189, 192, 195
FY 1979 *Annual Report*, 114, 117
FY 1979 *Arms Control Impact Statement*, 115

Game of Disarmament (Myrdal), 183
GANDHI, INDIRA, 197
GANDHI, MAHATMA, 188
GARWIN, RICHARD L., 31, 32, 35, 51, 82–93, 145
General Advisory Committee, 10–13, 14, 16
George, 13, 14, 16
George Washington, 71
Germany:
  East, 199
  West, 195, 199, 207
GLASSTONE, SAMUEL, 145
Great Britain, 7, 183, 189, 194–195
GREENWOOD, TED, 31–32, 94–105
Ground resolution in photoreconnaissance, 94–95

Hair-trigger response, 52, 139, 153
HALPERIN, MORTON, 141
Hardening, 54, 63, 64, 69, 135, 144, 154
Harpoon missile, 174, 180
Helicopters in ASW, 86, 91
HEWLETT, RICHARD G., 12
HOFFMAN, FRED, 54
HOLADAY, WILLIAM M., 124–125
HOLIFIELD, CHET, 24
HORNIG, DONALD F., 45
Hot line, 25, 29–30, 221
Human casualties, 3, 114, 119, 144–152, 159, 160–161
Hydrogen bomb, 3, 9–16

IAEA. *See* International Atomic Energy Agency
ICBMs. *See* Intercontinental ballistic missiles
IKLÉ, FRED C., 143
Incidents-at-sea agreement, 31
India, 7, 186–191, 195–201, 217, 218
Indonesia, 199
Initial defense communication satellite program (IDCSP), 127
Instability, arms-race and crisis, 28, 40
Institutional innovations, 185
Intelligence in ASW, 83
Intelsat, 30
Intercontinental ballistic missiles (ICBMs), 3, 19, 44, 48, 114–120, 122, 167–170
  and counterforce, 37, 39–40, 63–67, 77, 132–143, 144, 152, 153–154, 164–167
  vs. cruise missiles, 178
  in European theater, 157
  forecasts on, 28
  and hair-trigger response, 52, 139, 153
  Interim Agreement on, 30, 107, 109, 110, 163
  and launch on warning, 29, 118, 139, 153
  vs. submarines, 70, 77
  verification of, 69, 94, 97, 98, 100, 102–105, 167
  Vladivostok Accords and, 163, 193
  See also Minutemen
Interim Agreement, 30, 32, 107–111, 114–117, 139, 163–170, 192–193
Intermediate-range ballistic missiles (IRBMs), 46, 63, 115, 157
International Atomic Energy Agency (IAEA), 185, 200, 215, 225
  and nonmilitary nuclear energy, 187, 189, 191, 230
Iran, 199
Ireland, 195
Israel, 182, 198
Italy, 184, 195, 199
Itek Corporation, 95
Item, 13

JACKSON, HENRY M., 53
Jackson amendment, 30, 118
James Madison, 129
Japan, 184, 185, 189, 191, 194, 195, 199
Joe bombs, 13, 14

INDEX

Johnson, Louis A., 16
Johnson, Lyndon B., 28, 45, 48, 100
Joint Chiefs of Staff, 19, 45
Jupiter, 44

Kaplan, Fred M., 119, 120, 155–162
Kelly, Henry C., 145
Kennan, George F., 11
Kennedy, John F., 7, 25
Khrushchev, Nikita S., 7, 14, 18, 129
Kill, 47
Killian, James R., Jr., 45
King, 14, 16
Kissinger, Henry A., 154
Kistiakowsky, George B., 30, 45, 57–67
Kooijmans, P. H., 224
Korea, South, 199
Korean war, 3, 182
Kosygin, A., 53, 130

Laird, Melvin R., 48, 49, 63, 135, 157
Lance missile, 157, 158, 161
Latimer, Wendell M., 10
Launch on warning, 29, 55, 56, 118, 139, 153
Lawrence Livermore Laboratory, 155
LeBaron, Robert, 10
LeMay, Curtis E., 24
Lester, Richard, 184, 185, 203–215
Lethality, 115
Lilienthal, David E., 12, 14, 16
Limited Test Ban Treaty, 17, 24–25, 29, 127
Localization in ASW, 86–87
Lockheed Aircraft Corporation, 97, 127
Los Alamos Scientific Laboratory, 9, 10, 157

McCarthy, Eugene, 131
McCloy-Zorin Agreed Principles, 219, 223
McCormack, James, Jr., 10
McMahon, Brien, 10
McNamara, Robert S., 40, 98, 132, 133, 155–157
    and ABMs, 18, 33, 34, 45
    and MIRVs, 128, 130, 131
Magnetic-anomaly detector (MAD), 86
Maneuvering reentry vehicles (MaRVs), 81, 118, 119, 143, 153, 194
    for ICBMs, 137, 139
Mao Tse-tung, 16
Mark torpedoes, 89
Marshall Islands, 16, 160
MaRVs. See Maneuvering reentry vehicles
Middle East, 2, 121
Mike, 14, 15, 16
Military-industrial complex, 4, 65
Mines, antisubmarine, 89–90, 92
Minutemen, 28, 37, 38, 44, 45, 82, 163
    and counterforce, 133–135, 137–141, 149, 153
    and MIRVs, 36, 54–56, 81, 115–116, 122, 128–130, 134, 167, 193
    Safeguard and, 48–56, 64
    yield of, 123, 134, 137, 139, 167

MIRVs. See Multiple independently targeted reentry vehicles
Missile gap, 37, 54, 98, 138, 221
Missile-site radar (MSR), 48
MK-12A, 115, 167
Molniya II, 30
Monitoring systems. See Verification
Moorer, Thomas H., 81
MRVs. See Multiple reentry vehicles
Multiple-aim-point (MAP) system, 32
Multiple independently targeted reentry vehicles (MIRVs), 8, 82, 118–119, 122–131, 179
    and ABMs, 20, 28, 30, 33–67, 114, 118, 122, 127–131, 133
    and counterforce, 37–40, 63–67, 77, 114, 122–128–131, 143, 153–154, 164–167
    and exchange ratio, 50, 69–70
    and Minutemen, 36, 54–56, 81, 115–116, 122, 128–130, 134, 167, 193
    for SLBMs, 23, 36, 76, 81, 115, 127, 134, 139, 170
    on Soviet missiles, 49, 116, 117, 120, 138, 139
    in ULMS, 80
    verification of, 31–32, 104
    Vladivostok Accords and, 163, 164, 193
Multiple reentry vehicles (MRVs), 104, 126–127, 129
Mustin, Lloyd M., 21
MX, 3, 115, 118, 119, 167
Myrdal, Alva, 183, 185, 217–229

National Academy of Sciences, 114, 209
National Aeronautics and Space Administration (NASA), 128
National Intelligence Estimates (NIEs), 28, 29, 113
National security, 44, 55, 56, 120, 122
National Security Council, 16
NATO. See North Atlantic Treaty Organization
Nautilus, 71
Naval Research Laboratory, 127
Nehru, J., 188, 192
Netherlands, 189, 199
Neutron bomb, 8, 21–22, 119, 155–162
NIEs. See National Intelligence Estimates
Nigeria, 189
Nike-X, 19, 33, 34, 45, 51
Nike Zeus, 44, 51
Nitze, Paul, 28
Nixon, Richard M., 119, 132, 134, 135, 144, 219
    and ABMs, 36, 48
    on submarines, 78
    and treaties, 8, 28, 32, 59, 188
Noel-Baker, Philip J., 25
Nonproliferation Treaty, 17, 25, 183, 184, 186–201, 212–213, 218
    text of, 230
North Atlantic Treaty Organization (NATO), 8, 111, 155–162, 165, 170, 195

Norway, 199
Nuclear-free zones, 184, 200
Nuclear-powered ballistic-missile-launching submarine (SSBN), 31, 83, 115

Office of Technology Assessment (OTA), 144
Operation Castle, 14
Operation Greenhouse, 13
Operation Ivy, 14
Oppenheimer, J. Robert, 3, 10–12, 14, 15–16
Overkill, 47, 57, 60, 63, 67, 194
Over-the-horizon (OTH) radar, 102–103

Packard, David, 45, 47–48
Pakistan, 189, 197, 198
Panofsky, Wolfgang K. H., 48
Parity, 46–47, 56, 57, 78, 118
Partial Test-Ban Treaty, 16, 183, 187, 189, 192
Peaceful nuclear explosions (PNEs), 8
Penetration aids, 45, 51, 125, 127, 130
Perimeter acquisition radars (PARs), 35, 48
Perkin-Elmer Corporation, 100
Permissive action link (PAL), 31
Petroleum, 204, 210
Photoreconnaissance, 94–105, 116
Plowshare, 191
Plutonium, 205–207
Polaris, 28, 30, 44, 45, 48, 55, 71–81
    and hair-trigger response, 52
    with MRV, 126–127, 129
    yield of, 123
Politics, 64–65, 67, 131, 183
Poseidon, 30–31, 37–38, 77, 129, 138, 141, 165
    MIRVs on, 23, 36, 76, 81, 115, 123, 127, 134, 193
Post-boost control system (PBCS), 122, 130
Posture statement, 38, 40
Powers, Francis Gary, 97
Preemptive attack, 37, 39, 40, 63, 69, 144
Proliferation, 59, 130, 182, 183–184, 186–201, 203–215
    See also Nonproliferation Treaty
Protection factor, 149
Pugwash conferences, 4

Rabi, I. I., 11, 12, 16
Radars, 35, 48, 102–104, 108, 110–111
Radioactive fallout, 5–7, 16, 25, 34, 140, 145–149
Rand Corporation, 127
Random-barrage system, 127
Rathjens, George W., 28, 30, 33–43, 49, 57–67, 115, 131
Reactors, 203, 205, 206, 209, 214–215
Reconnaissance, 31, 94–105, 116, 167, 180, 223
Reentry Body Identification Group, 125
Rickover, Hyman G., 77
Roosevelt, Franklin D., 3
Rose, David, 184, 185, 203–215

Rowe, Hartley, 11, 12
Rusk, Dean, 25

Safeguard, 20, 48–56, 59, 60, 64, 135
SAGE, 50
Sakharov, Andrei D., 51, 56
SALT. *See* Strategic-arms-limitation talks
Samos II, 98
Sanguine, 31, 75
Satellites, 29–30, 75, 127
   with cruise missiles, 120, 174
   early warning, 29, 102, 139
   global positioning, 115, 174
   reconnaissance, 31, 69, 94–105, 116, 167, 180, 223
Schlesinger, James R., 122, 157, 193
   and counterforce, 119, 131–144 *passim*, 153, 154
"Science and the Citizen," 7, 8
Scoville, Herbert, Jr, 30–31, 69–81, 115, 119, 131, 163–170
Sea-Bed Treaty, 25, 195
Seaborg, Glenn T., 11, 12
Sea-launched cruise missile (SLCM), 174, 175, 178–179, 180
Secrecy, 3, 32, 221
Security guarantees, 184, 191
Semenov, Vladimir, 28, 29, 109, 111
Sentinel, 28, 34–36, 43, 48, 52
   and China, 20, 33, 35, 38, 45, 50–51
Sequential payload delivery (SPD), 128
Serber, Robert, 11
Shastri, Lal Bahadur, 190
Shell game, 54, 55
Shell-and-pea concept, 32
Shipping, surface, and ASW, 90–91, 93
Shotgun technique, 45
SIPRI. *See* Stockholm International Peace Research Institute
SLBMs. *See* Submarine-launched ballistic missiles
SLCM. *See* Sea-launched cruise missile
Smart, Ian, 141
Smith, Cyril S., 11, 12
Smith, Gerard C., 28, 29, 109, 110, 111
Smith, Levering, 81
Sonar systems for ASW, 84–87
Sonobuoys, 84, 86
South Africa, 182, 198, 207
Space Detection and Tracking System, 104
Space patrol air defense (SPAD), 127
Space Technology Laboratory, 128
Spain, 198–199
Spartans, 33, 35, 48, 49
Sprints, 33–34, 35, 48, 49, 157
Sputnik I, 102
SR-71 aircraft, 37
SS-9s, 45, 48, 49, 63, 117, 164
SS-11s, 45, 49–50, 54, 117
SS-16s, 114, 167
SS-17s, 114, 167
SS-18s, 114, 117, 143, 164, 167
SS-19s, 114, 116, 167
SS-20s, 115, 170

SSBN. *See* Nuclear-powered ballistic-missile-launching submarine
Stalin, Joseph, 16
Standing Consultative Commission (SCC), 101, 109
Stand-off bombers, 115
Stockholm International Peace Research Institute (SIPRI), 2, 122, 123, 225
Strategic Air Command (SAC), 152
Strategic-arms-limitation talks (SALT), 28–32, 57–67, 70, 77–81, 131, 135, 140–142
   and expenditures, 121, 163, 182–183
   See also ABM Treaty; Interim Agreement; Nonproliferation Treaty; Verification; Vladivostok Accords
Strauss, Lewis L., 10
Submarine-launched ballistic missiles (SLBMs), 48, 69–81, 115, 164–166, 170, 178
   and ASW, 70–71, 77, 78, 81, 82, 91–92
   and counterforce, 69, 77, 79, 132, 133, 134, 137, 139, 141
   Interim Agreement and, 30, 107, 108, 109, 111, 165
   verification of, 94, 100
   Vladivostok Accords and, 164–165, 193
   See also Polaris; Poseidon; Trident
Submarines:
   for cruise missiles, 29, 83, 175–176, 178–179
   hunter-killer, 84, 87, 178–179
   See also Antisubmarine warfare; Nuclear-powered ballistic-missile-launching submarine; Submarine-launched ballistic missiles
Subrahmanyam, K., 183
Sufficiency, 41, 119, 135–136
Suppliers' club, 200
Surface-to-air missiles (SAMs), 50
Sweden, 189, 195, 199, 217, 223, 225
Switzerland, 199
Symmetry, 118

Taiwan, 199
Tallinn, 37, 38, 76
Teller, Edward, 18, 24, 221
   and hydrogen bomb, 9, 10, 13, 14
   and neutron bomb, 8, 22
Terrain-matching system, 173, 175
Terrorists, 184
Third World, 2, 182, 185, 188–191, 195–201
Thompson Ramo Wooldridge Corporation, 128
Thor, 44, 98, 99, 127
Threshold Test Ban Treaty, 8, 188, 191, 192
Thurmond, Strom, 18–19
Titan, 28, 44, 46, 99, 127, 134, 149
Torpedoes, 89, 91

Tracking in ASW, 87–89, 93
Transient radiation effects on electronics (TREE), 20
Transit II-A satellite, 127
Transtage, 127
Treaty of Tlatelolco, 25, 184, 200
Treaty on Underground Nuclear Explosions, 8
Trident, 31, 115, 129, 138, 165, 170
   and accuracy, 137, 141
   and Vladivostok Accords, 193
   See also Undersea long-range missile system
Trivedi, Vishnuprasad Chunilal, 190
Truman, Harry S., 3, 13, 15, 16
Tsipis, Kosta, 120, 171–180
Tsuruoka, Senjin, 194
Turbofan engines, 174
Typhoon, 115

U-2 reconnaissance aircraft, 97
Ulam, Stanislaw, 14
Undersea long-range missile system (ULMS), 31, 79, 80–81
   See also Trident
United Nations (UN), 2, 217
   and proliferation, 187, 189, 190, 191, 192, 195, 198, 199
   and verification, 185, 219, 223–229
Uranium, 16, 189, 203, 205, 209, 215

Vance, Cyrus R., 163
Vela, 127, 128
Verification, 31–32, 57, 93, 185, 217–229
   of cruise missiles, 120, 170, 178, 179, 180
   by reconnaissance, 31, 69, 94–105, 167, 180, 223
Very-low-frequency (VLF) radio waves, 31, 75
Vietnam, 57, 182
Vladivostok Accords, 116–120, 163–166, 170, 171, 178, 193–194
von Hippel, Frank, 119, 120, 144–154

Walske, M. Carl, Jr., 23
Warnke, Paul, 8, 117, 136
Warsaw Pact nations, 155–162, 170
Wheeler, John A., 22
Wiesner, Jerome B., 3, 17, 45, 50
Wilson, Harold, 194–195
Wohlstetter, Albert, 54
Worst-case analysis, 28, 54, 58, 76, 133

Y-class submarines, 77–78
Yield, 123–124, 141
   of Lance missiles, 157
   of Minuteman III, 123, 134, 137, 139, 167
   of SLBMs, 123
York, Herbert F., 3, 17–25, 29, 31, 32
   and hydrogen bomb, 4, 9–16
   and MIRVs, 7–8, 20, 23, 44–56, 118–119, 122–131
Yugoslavia, 189